Patriot Above Profit

Patriot Above Profit

A Portrait of Thomas Nelson, Jr.,
Who Supported the American
Revolution With His
Purse and Sword

NELL MOORE LEE

Rutledge Hill Press
Nashville, Tennessee

Published in Nashville, Tennessee, by Rutledge Hill Press, Inc., 513 Third Avenue South, Nashville, Tennessee 37210

Typography by ProtoType Graphics, Inc., Nashville, Tennessee.

Library of Congress Cataloging-in-Publication Data

Lee, Nell Moore
    Patriot above profit : a portrait of Thomas Nelson, Jr., who supported the American revolution with his purse and sword / Nell Moore Lee.
        p.   cm.
    Bibliography: p.
    Includes index.
    ISBN 0-934395-68-3
    1. Nelson, Thomas, 1738–1789.   2. Virginia—History—Revolution, 1775–1783.
3. Generals—Virginia—Biography.   4. United States. Declaration of Independence—
Signers—Biography.   5. Virginia—Governors—Biography   I. Title.
E263.V8N435   1988
973.3'13'0924—dc19
    [B]   88-12032
                                                                              CIP

Manufactured in the United States of America
1 2 3 4 5 6 7 8 9 10 — 94 93 92 91 90 89 88

DEDICATION

To the men and women who have answered the call of our country in the fight for freedom from the American Revolution to the present time. And with an especial remembrance to our soldiers who made the supreme sacrifice to preserve the principles of our republic, this book is affectionately dedicated.

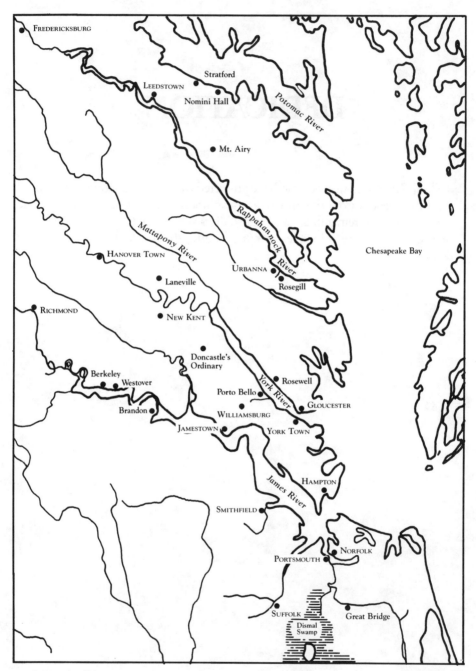

Area map of Virginia.

TABLE OF CONTENTS

PREFACE

Thomas Nelson, Jr., of Yorktown, Virginia, deserves being recognized for his vital role in the American Revolution with the other leaders of his state.

The names of Patrick Henry, Thomas Jefferson, Richard Henry Lee, Edmund Pendleton, and George Washington are well known not only for their part in breaking the bonds with Britain but also for feats beyond this eventful era.

Nelson's fifty years on earth could have been spent as a country gentleman of Virginia—enjoying the entertainments of the socially elite, riding to hounds, attending the assembly, and serving his church, if the cause of the colonies had not arisen. This dramatic circumstance revealed Thomas Nelson, Jr., as an ardent patriot whose altruism and commitment led him to sacrifice his financial and physical security in the war for independence.

Nelson, born to an affluent family December 26, 1738, belonged to the Tidewater aristocracy. His father, William Nelson, was the foremost merchant in the thriving town of York. His mother was Elizabeth Burwell whose connections included Grandfather "King" Carter. Young Nelson was educated in England, but his character was influenced by his social class and the events which developed from opposition to the Stamp Act in 1765 against British tyranny through the conflict.

Family influence and friends' support easily elected him to his first term in the House of Burgesses in 1761. He fulfilled the faith of all freeholders since his constituents re-elected him over a score of years and, in addition, made him a delegate to the Continental Congress, representative to the House of Delegates, Brigadier General of the Virginia militia, and wartime governor.

When the colonists' petitions and protests concerning Great Britain's arbitrary acts failed to move the monarch and his ministers, Nelson urged separation from the English empire.

His congressional contemporaries characterized Thomas Nelson, Jr., as active, alert, a speaker, and a man of excellent disposition. He demonstrated generosity to a marked degree assisting the distressed folk of Boston as well as victims of the Richmond fire. Thomas continued his father's custom of feeding the poor who attended Sunday services at York-Hampton Parish. When, as a general, he organized and rode with cavalry corps in 1778 to Philadelphia only to be dismissed hastily by Congress, much expense came from his own pocket. Nelson is also credited with raising a large portion of the state's $2,000,000 loan in 1780 by the security of his own funds. Opposing the Sequestration Acts to dispense debts Virginians owed the British, General Nelson declared he would pay *his* obligations.

He assumed the affairs of a wartime administration in June 1781 after Thomas Jefferson quit his post. In the dual role of governor and general, Nelson, with indefatigable energy, impressed men and materiel to assist the French force in beating the British.

Although generosity and integrity permeated his philosophy, he was not a paragon of perfection. He was impatient, often to the point of testiness, although his temper was short lived. He could become discouraged by deficiencies and disgusted with the indifference of people. Nelson despised the war profiteers, and toward the end of his life he was depressed by his debts. Overall, however, he was an optimistic person, preferring action to profound analysis, not given to deep philosophical contemplation.

Much of the material for this manuscript has been secured through secondary sources. Primary sources like assembly accounts, official letters, and scattered correspondence substantiated Nelson's service to the state. It is unfortunate that one of his descendants destroyed personal family letters which would have shed light on more intimate details. In consequence, as other biographers have done, conjecture has been employed for some daily occurrences.

This portrait of Thomas Nelson, Jr., reveals a gentleman devoted to family, a man dedicated to duty, a lover of liberty so profound that he belongs among the ranks of the illustrious leaders of the American Revolution.

ACKNOWLEDGMENTS

The extensive research for this book encompassed years of securing references on a wide range of topics to present a broad scope of life in the eighteenth century.

Credit is cited in the chapter notations to the American Philosophical Society and the Pennsylvania Historical Society, the Library of Congress, and the Clements Library at the University of Michigan for special letters.

I am also indebted to the staffs of the College of William and Mary, the Virginia State Library, the University of Virginia, and the Colonial National Park Service at Yorktown, Virginia, for specific collections.

My appreciation to many individuals who have assisted me in securing source materials among whom are the late Dr. G. MacLaren Brydon, Richmond, a direct descendant of General Nelson; the late Mr. Charles E. Hatch, Yorktown; Mr. Waverly K. Winfree, Virginia Historical Society; my cousin Sarah Moore, former cataloger at Middle Tennessee State University; the late Bettye Bell, Nashville Public Library and Dorothy Dale and Mary Glenn Hearn of the present staff; Catherine Prince, Tennessee State Library; Lois Griest, Vanderbilt University Library, and Ethel Rea, Williamsburg, Virginia.

My special thanks to the staff of Colonial Williamsburg Foundation where much of my research was obtained through the years and the editorial staff of Rutledge Hill Press.

Nell Moore Lee
March 10, 1988

Patriot
Above
Profit

Painted by Mason Chamberlain, this portrait of Thomas Nelson, Jr., at sixteen was done while he was a schoolboy in England. Courtesy of the Virginia Museum of Fine Arts.

CHAPTER ONE

Return: 1761–1762

Young Tom's Return ✦ *The World He Entered* ✦ *Tom's Social Position, Its Power and Privileges* ✦ *Parties and Pleasures, Maids and Matrimony* ✦ *Marriage to Lucy Grymes* ✦ *York Town Views* ✦ *Early Assembly Accounts* ✦ *Capitol and Council*

It was the year 1761, and Tom Nelson, Jr., was returning from England after eight years of the best education Virginia aristocracy could buy: Hackney Preparatory, Trinity, Christ College, and Cambridge. Since the fourteenth century English kings had bestowed land upon the Nelson family—principally for military service. Two centuries later, the colonial Nelsons owned thousands of acres of rich Virginia soil, a thriving mercantile business, and a tavern where gentlemen gathered for news and repast. At twenty-two, Tom's prospects for a more than comfortable life were indisputable; he would be a welcome member in enchanted circles of prestige and power.[1]

In 1753 his father had shipped him off to England rather unceremoniously with hardly more than a day's notice. The Honorable William Nelson had been strolling along York Town's river front when he saw Tom seated on a sandy beach surrounded by a group of young black boys.[2] Perhaps Tom's transgression of seeking amusement on the Sabbath had spurred the senior Nelson to action. Perhaps the tableau seared into William Nelson's consciousness the fact that it was time for his son to proceed to England for a proper education. Many sons of the gentry spent their formative years in England; learning English manners, mores and approaches to life served them well in later years.

Indeed, Tom was the perfected product of several generations of prosperous Nelsons in Virginia. His great grandfather, "King" Carter had accumulated vast acreages and lived like royalty. Grandfather "Scotch" Tom controlled thousands of acres and owned a thriving mercantile business. His father, William Nelson, would count five colonial governors among his friends; while his uncle, Thomas Nelson, was the Secretary of the House of Burgesses, and Tom was looking forward to his own term as a Burgess.[3]

Half a century before Thomas Nelson, Jr., had arrived on this earth, France and England had been struggling for control of North America. The conflict and its roots would inevitably shape Tom's life more than most colonial Virginians could ever have imagined.

◆   ◆   ◆

In 1688, William, Prince of Orange, was thrust on the throne of England replacing the refractory James II, who fled to France after failing to reconcile the old Cavaliers of England to the Roman Catholic Church. For a few years after that, Anne, sister-in-law of William III, occupied the throne; during that time the people of the colonies called the contest Queen Anne's War. Under the Hanoverian Georges, I and II, the conflict was known as King George's War. When revived between 1756 and 1763, Europeans called it the Seven Years' War, but Americans knew it as the French and Indian War.[4]

A fresh outbreak a few years later over boundary claims had frontiersmen in the New World answering the muster call of rival nations, rarely knowing the progress of their allies in the Old, enduring the fight after a temporary truce, unmindful of, or perhaps ignoring, the change of incidents. Some men converted the issues to private quarrels and fought on.

In 1756, the continental stage was set for the final act. European monarchs plotted a political drama, shifting and dangling kingdoms in their greed for world rule. Russia, Austria, Poland, and France united against the designs of Prussia's Frederick the Great. England, standing in the wings, cast her strength to Frederick. By this indirect method of opposing France, she expected to retain her American colonies.

In 1763 the Peace of Paris gave Great Britain almost all of the immense territory east of the Mississippi River, although the previous year Louis XV of France had given Louisiana to his cousin, Charles III of Spain. It was a transitory conquest for the English Empire, lasting scarcely more than a decade.

Both George I and II crowded the English court with German attendants. Not so with George III, however, for he had been born in England although his use of the English language was never fluent and his total education was little more than elementary schooling. Later, in his determined effort to be King in deed as well as designation, he became aware of his lack of knowledge, for no one had trained him for the tasks.[5]

In June 1738, just six months before Thomas Nelson was born in December, George III had made *his* entry into the world. He was to reign over England for sixty years—decades filled with domestic and foreign difficulties. His mother's admonition, "Be King, George, Be King!" rang in his ears; he was firm in his policy of maintaining "royal authority" and reaffirming the long-practiced principle of "governing for, but never by, the people."[6]

George III's tribulations—personal, political, and physical—were sufficient to tax a lesser intellect; five times the fatuous George lapsed into insanity. He ascended the throne October 25, 1760, a few months before Thomas Nelson, Jr., embarked from England for his Virginia homeland.

◆   ◆   ◆

The English education of Thomas Nelson, Jr., had begun in 1753 when he was fourteen. His father, William Nelson, had engaged the Reverend William Yates of Gloucester, just across the York River, to teach Tom fundamental subjects to prepare him for an English university. Yates was minister of Abingdon Parish Church while serving as president of the College of William and Mary years later.[7]

Letters from William Nelson to Beilby Porteus, a fellow at Cambridge, as Tom had embarked upon his English education, informed Porteus to stress religion and morals; he depended on Porteus and Edward Hunt to convey desirable traits to Tom. Porteus had a close connection with the Nelson family, for his father had lived in Virginia many years and Elizabeth Jennings, the first wife of the elder Porteus, was a distant cousin of the Nelsons. During his son's vacations, Nelson requested that Porteus place young Thomas with an agricultural scientist so he might learn about soils. Since Tom would someday manage vast plantations, his summer study would be profitable; his father also felt a well-planned schedule was the best antidote for mischief.[8]

Tom's father was a "visitor" for the College of William and Mary at Williamsburg, an office possessing a great deal of power. In an incident of November 1757, the visitors intervened and reversed a decision of the president and masters who had ousted James Hubard, usher of the grammar school. William Nelson, John Blair, Philip Grymes (Tom's future father-in-law), Tom's uncle, "the Secretary," and others were appointed to question the authorities on the action as it was alleged he had been dismissed "without any Equitable Cause," although Hubard "was justly esteemed by his capacity and Diligence . . . ."[9] The inquirers interrogated President John Camm, who refused to answer. On November 11, the visitors acted thus:

> Resolved Mr. Camm. Mr. Graham, Mr. Jones removed Wednesday 14 December for refusal of masters to give reason to visitors and Council.[10]

Though Mr. Blair, Mr. Grymes, and the two Nelsons were visitors for the local College, all four sent their sons to England to be educated. Doubtless such disturbances affected their decisions. As wealthy planters of the Colony, they wished to imitate the English way of life in the New World. They revered the time-honored traditions of the Established Church, expansive estates, and venerable institutions. These four friends were typical of the aristocratic planter group and true to its goals. They had remained firm in the faith of the Established Church, had acquired large acres of land, and were intent on improving intellectual opportunities for their sons. No doubt they discussed the advantages of an English education with its emphases on classical languages and mathematics. They thought an institution should offer intellectual stimulus to a student, but the gentry were interested in liberal learning rather than serious scholarship. Learning was for leadership. The church chose its vestrymen from the powerful planter class and the Colony elected its representatives from its ranks. The essentials of education incorporated an elegant culture. The gentry had established a code of conduct for a gentleman requiring that he be constant to the church, faithful to his family, responsible in his duties to the Colony. He should be free from artifice, fair, and generous to the less fortunate. He must act with affable courtesy, dance gracefully, and be skilled in sports. These desirable attributes could be learned best in the ancient colleges of England.[11]

John Blair, Jr., had started his study of the law in London at the Middle Temple in 1755 and James Blair enrolled at the University of Edinburgh—already illustrious for its instruction in medicine—in 1761. Dr. James Blair returned to his native town of Williamsburg to practice his profession in a big frame house on Nicholson Street.[12]

Ralph Wormely, Jr., enrolled at the ancient college of Eton in 1757. Philip Ludwell Grymes and John Randolph Grymes, sons of the Honorable Philip Grymes of Brandon in Middlesex County, entered Eton in 1760. Stemming from the mid-fifteenth century, the royal rulers had liberally bequeathed lands to support the school. A succession of reigning kings could stroll to the terrace of Windsor Castle and peer across the Thames River to Eton's handsome stone chapel. The Grymes boys were Tom's future brothers-in-law, their paths would cross many times but divide on the question of political independence, for when the crisis came with England, Philip and John cast their lot with England.[13]

Alexander and John Spotswood, who attended Eton from 1760 to 1764, were Tom's associates at London. They were grandsons of Sir Alexander Spotswood, Soldier-Governor of Virginia in the early part of the century, who established the writ of habeas corpus when he arrived in 1710 and thereby endeared himself to the colonists. Arthur Lee of Westmoreland County, two years younger than Tom, was educated at Eton and Edinburgh. He later studied law at the Middle Temple. Like his brothers, he would become a lover of liberty. England's most patrician boys attended the ancient colleges. Charles James Fox, who later became a famous English statesman, sat beside Tom in the classroom.[14]

Thomas was advanced to Christ College in May 1758 under the meticulous private tutelage of Dr. Beilby Porteus, who was to become Bishop of London and chaplain to George III. (In later years Porteus would send his first book of sermons to the Thomas Nelson family.)

Other contemporaries with Tom in the classroom were John Ambler of

York and James Burwell, a cousin, who entered Eton a year before Tom left England. William Nelson, the Secretary's son, about eight years younger than his cousin, and Tom represented the second generation of Nelsons to enroll in the great universities of Britain.[15]

Tom's grandfather, "Scotch" Tom, had believed that his boys would benefit from studies offered in the schools overseas. He sent Tom's father at eleven years of age to England and, evidently, the lad learned easily by his exposure to the courses in the classics as he developed effective expression in speaking and writing. Later in life William recalled his school years as time spent profitably and pleasurably.[16]

Thomas Nelson, "the Secretary," was five years younger than his brother William, Tom's father. In addition to a comprehensive curriculum at the old English universities, he had studied law at the Inner Temple. Hours spent poring over fine print and struggling with legal technicalities were fine preparation, for when he was only twenty-seven years old in 1743, he was appointed to the influential post of Deputy-Secretary for the Colony of Virginia.[17] The Secretary started to build an impressive library of law books. Property owners often ordered legal texts and treatises for their personal use, because an understanding of legal transactions was indispensable for the holder of vast plantations. A year earlier, William Nelson had been elected to the House of Burgesses, so the Nelsons began their long careers of service to the Colony under the Crown.[18]

Tom Nelson, Jr.'s, close contact with British minds gave him an insight that later proved of inestimable value to the colonial cause. When others hesitated in their courses and puzzled over their opponents' aims, Thomas Nelson knew there were only two choices: sink in subjection or stand in opposition to the British lion.

Tom would have been home several months sooner except for a singular notion maintained by William Nelson who had heard rumors that several native sons had succumbed to the temptations of immoderate eating, drinking, and smoking tobacco. Gawin Corbin, the Spotswood boys, and even Thomas had indulged themselves in these excesses. Since Mr. Nelson understood that two boys "whose habits he feared were not good" might sail on the same ship, Tom was not allowed to leave England in the spring but had to wait until August. He arrived in York Town in the company of Samuel Athawes, son of the merchant Edward Athawes, in the autumn.[19]

✦   ✦   ✦

For a few months Tom enjoyed a little leisure, and this pleasure-filled period was the most carefree time he would ever experience. William Nelson told his friends in England that he was pleased to see Tom's "good principles" and "general advancement."[20] All comments were not on the credit side, however, for the father deplored his son's indulgence in "juvenile diversions," probably referring to his card playing. He also regretted that Tom was following the fashion of the English in smoking "filty tobacco."[21]

As a producer, seller, and trader in this commodity, William Nelson profited from the tobacco industry, but none of these facts apparently obliged him to tolerate the taste or promote the product. On the other hand, William Byrd, II, always dabbling in medicine and a fanatic on physic, had plugged the product enthusiastically in his pamphlet, "A Discourse Concerning the Plague with Some Preservation Against It." The diarist declared partaking of several species of tobacco in abundant amounts would prevent smallpox.[22]

Mr. Nelson further observed concerning his son's drinking habits: "though not to inebrity, [were] more than was conducive to good health and long life."[23]

Tom was plump, contoured like many of his contemporaries, for eighteenth-century folk did not diet. Loaded tables were the keynote of hospitality and good hostesses vied with one another in heaping victuals on their tables. The reddish-blonde hair, ready smile, and blue eyes of Thomas gave him a personable appearance, but it was family and fortune that paved the way for young Tom.[24]

He was fortunate to live just a few miles from Williamsburg, the capital of the Colony. While some travelers wrote that it should be called a "town rather than a city,"[25] and that it was a "pleasant little town with wooden houses and unpaved streets,"[26] nevertheless, it was the center of Virginia's social life.

As an eligible bachelor and a popular gentleman with an extensive education, Tom was present at many gatherings of the Tidewater grandees, aristocrats still basking in the radiant bloom of the tobacco leaf. He could be found carrying on spirited colloquies or pacing a quadrille on the wide-planked, unpolished ballroom floors. After Tom met Lucy Grymes in Williamsburg, however, his pleasure in the Williamsburg social scene increased even more. Some of their happiest moments were spent stepping off the graceful movements of a minuet.[27] No doubt Lucy had been among the young ladies who had filled the classes of Chevalier Peyronney, a French dance instructor. Peter Pelham had taught Lucy to hold the quill point properly in playing the harpsichord to achieve the instrument's full resonant tone. The versatile Mr. Pelham's lifelong occupation was organist for Bruton Parish Church at a salary of twenty-five pounds per year, but to support his big family, he did a little printing, operated a shop, and in 1771 became keeper of the gaol. Residents on Nicholson Street, like Peyton Randolph, often saw Pelham escort his charges to church on Sunday, then hurriedly don his robe, seat himself ceremoniously at the fine English organ, and give the signal for one of his prisoners to start pumping.[28]

Tom's Lucy and most women in the eighteenth century believed they were born to be brides. Almost as soon as they began to toddle around their nurseries, they learned about the homemaking arts. Just as they looked like miniature models of their mothers, so were their activities. Four- and five-year olds started simple sewing, learned their letters by stitching samplers, and understood that knitting involved interlacing the yarn through the loops repeatedly. Younger girls stretched threads across their tiny fingers to make cat's cradles. Rows of real cradles usually lined their homes, and as the girls grew older, they became baby sitters for their brothers and sisters, further supporting the belief that their roles in life meant marriage and motherhood. Young ladies showing especial skill in sewing could fill their hope chests with artistic needlework, muslin sheets, and pillow slips embroidered in delicate designs.[29]

Acquaintance with cookery would come earlier to children of humble homes than to those born in a manor, for the kitchen was the hub of modest households. Big forty-pound pots that would hold fifteen gallons of nourishment filled fireplaces, and children were constantly cautioned not to venture too close. The savory smell of beef simmering in the stewpot, fresh baked bread, and the aroma of apple cider was too often offset by stale meat slabs, musty meal, and the souring malt of the beer barrel. The privileged young woman might need permission from the mansion cook to mix up a fresh fruit flip or bake a cream flummery.[30]

Customs and courts attempted to protect inexperienced girls from undesirable alliances. Laws enforced rigorously brought swift punishment to culprits who lured the innocent into clandestine marriages: death for grasping fortune hunters. If very young widows were not wiser, they were at least wealthier as their riches were regained. Despite loss of love and property, some daughters defied their parents to follow the dictates of their hearts. John Thompson disinherited his daughter after her elopement and would not even see her, then married his housekeeper so that their progeny would receive his property.[31]

Romance was ruined for Evelyn Byrd by her domineering father. On occasion, the colonel was known to hobnob with the impecunious peerage in England, but it was unthinkable that his daughter marry a ne'er-do-well nobleman. William Byrd, II, strengthened his oral reproaches with written warnings:

> Tis high time for me to reproach you with breech of duty. . . . repeat to you my strict & positive Commands, never more to meet, speak, or write to that Gentleman, or to give him opportunity to see, speak, or write to You. . . . deluded afterwards with Vain hopes of forgiveness . . . I never will. And as to any Expectation, you may fondly entertain of a Fortune from me, you are not to look for one brass farthing, if you provoke me by this fatal instance of disobedience.[32]

21

Laws aided the loveless for they charged bachelors an additional tax; a fellow without a family was evading his civic obligations.[33]

Newspapers were used to assist courtships. One woman petitioned the press to help her in urging a bashful suitor to action:

> Whereas the gentleman who towards the latter end of the summer usually wore a blue camlet coat lined with red and trimmed with silver, a silver laced hat, and a Turpee wig [no wonder this dandy dazzled the lass] has been observed by his Amoret [it was fashionable to use fictitious names suggesting feeling] to look very languishingly at her, the said Amoret, desires the Gentleman to present himself.[34]

Another requested the *Gazette* to become a go-between in her goal to get a husband:

> Sir: I am just nineteen, and, without vanity believe as well qualified for a husband as any of my neighbors. I will not say that I am handsome, though I am persuaded I am not the only one who thinks so. . . . believe men stupid. . . . women should do the courting. . . . A Gentleman of good family . . . neither very dark or fair, good nature, common sense.[35]

"Diana Languish" desired that he have some fortune; however, she had a fortune herself of five thousand pounds. She implored the printer to take letters for her.[36]

✦   ✦   ✦

Balls sometimes lasted far past midnight. Tom and Lucy could be the last to leave the Governor's Palace since her father's house nestled in its shadow. No doubt Tom thought the stroll far too short, and longed for more privacy while lingering over a farewell. Then spurring his horse and feeling light-hearted, Tom would gallop down the tree-lined main road from Williamsburg to York Town—just over a dozen miles—his hat and wig on the pommel of the saddle. A wondering smile deepened on his clean, young face as he thought of lovely Lucy Grymes who had promised to become his bride in the summer.

Whether Lucy was the typical eighteenth-century maiden who put up a little pretense of protest before accepting Tom's proposal is not known, but genteel girls were sometimes stellar actresses in affecting aloofness. "Heart breaker" curls and fans were useful props in coquetry, but young women knew when to shift from caprice to seriousness.

Since the Grymes and Nelson families were faithful followers of the Colony's Established Church, much of the young people's courting centered around the church, and Tom's proposal probably occurred in the most conventional and formal fashion. Marriage was not only the concern of the couple but also that of the family. Mothers as well as fathers aided the cause of Cupid. Matchmaking was considered an appropriate pursuit by the gentry, and they ardently practiced it to maintain a self-perpetuating aristocracy. The influence of the first families was felt in social, political, and religious realms, but the dominance of the dynasty achieved its culmination in the Governor's Council. It became a closed corporation. Just over fifty names connected by consanguinity, led the list of lawmakers for nearly a century. The intermarriage of relatives resulted in close, complicated kinships and many double cousins. "Scotch" Tom Nelson was the grandfather of both Thomas Nelson, Jr., and Mrs. John Page. Only the immediate members of the family could straighten out the relationship. Tom's mother, Elizabeth Burwell Nelson, was a sister to Robert Burwell, father of Frances, who would marry John Page. William Nelson and Sarah Nelson Burwell, mother of Frances, were stepbrother and sister.[37]

After the initial proprieties of courtship, parents evaluated the two significant considerations according to the aristocrats: social suitability and a satisfactory settlement. The family trees of Tom and Lucy were bountiful indeed with bloodlines that sprang from the best seed; consequently, their heritage was socially strong and financially stable.

Britons didn't believe in bestowing high honors on the colonials. The rank of peer was always reserved for men of the home realm. As an exceptional envoy between the Colony and the Crown on sundry missions, however, Lucy's maternal grandfather, Sir John Randolph, had received rewards from grateful governments on each side of the Atlantic. The English kingdom made him a knight, and the Virginia Assembly paid him thousands of pounds for his service.[38]

A regal title, if not a royal one, was conferred upon Tom's great grandfather by his contemporaries. He was called "King" Carter, an appropriate connotation implying his imperial mien and immense influence. As Lord Fairfax's factor for an approximate five-million-acre area between Chesapeake Bay and the Shenandoah River, he had acquired three hundred thousand acres for himself and his heirs. He lived in luxury on the beautiful Corotoman River. No one looked more like a monarch than "King" Carter, dressed in scarlet and gold braid, stepping into his carriage to ride across the Rappahannock and to ferry the York for Council meetings in Williamsburg.[39]

For more than a decade Tom and Lucy's fathers, William Nelson and Philip Grymes, had sat side by side in the coveted seats of the Council chambers. Their positions allowed them the privilege of "Esquire" after their signatures, a title that signified top social and political stations. Both men had served apprenticeships in the House of Burgesses, receiving ten shillings a day but saving their counties the extra cost of ferriage. Philip Grymes moved from his home, Brandon, in Middlesex County to his town house in Williamsburg when the Assembly met, and William Nelson trav-

eled from York Town in less than two hours for the session, or he and the
Secretary stayed at their dwelling on Francis Street in the capital.[40]

John Blair's diary often reported his meetings with these influential men
to facilitate the affairs of the Council. Typical entries included the following:

> Attend president in council at his home. Mr. Nelson, Mr. Commissioner,
> Mr. Grymes and myself only attended. . . . June 1 Consult Mr. Nelson,
> Grymes, and Ludwell and gave Mr. Nelson 6 papers. . . . March 28 Dined at
> Mr. Nelson's charming day. . . . August 2 Do communicate the whole to Mr.
> Grymes and desired him to speak to the two Mr. Nelsons.[41]

Devotion to duty was also demonstrated in the Nelsons' concern for the
church, a common bond. Present on Wednesday, April 22, 1752, at a meeting of the Hanover presbytery were Governor William Fairfax, John Blair,
Philip Grymes, William Nelson, Thomas Nelson, William Dawson, John
Lewis, Peyton Randolph (Philip's brother-in-law) and Philip Ludwell, all distinguished gentlemen as well as dutiful churchmen.[42] Perhaps the future in-
laws and their compeers traveled together from Williamsburg to Hanover
after the spring session of the Assembly.

✦   ✦   ✦

Wedding announcements in the *Virginia Gazette* left little to the imagination as the who, when, what, and where were summed up succinctly. A
compliment for the bride and disclosure of the dowry stifled reader speculation.

The announcement of the wedding of Tom's parents in the *Virginia Gazette* of February 10, 1737, was an example:

> . . . Mr. William Nelson, eldest son of Mr. Thomas Nelson, an eminent
> merchant in York, was married at Mrs. Page's in Gloucester County, to Miss
> Elizabeth Burwell, a very genteel accomplished young lady of great merit
> and considerable fortune.

When their wedding took place in 1738, Rosewell had been under construction for twelve years. It soared into the sky majestically on its promontory between the York River and Carter's Creek.[43] The marriage of Elizabeth
Burwell and William Nelson was only one occasion for gathering the elite at
this castle in the countryside. In its great days of glory and grandeur, Rosewell had been a house of hospitality for the cream of the Colony. Weeks
before the wedding it was astir again with activity as the bride's aunt, Judith
Carter Page, who was mistress of the mansion, set the servants to scrubbing
marble mantels and straightening luxurious English tapestries in the entrance hall. The expansive paneling, wainscoted walls of several lovely
shades in the reception rooms, and the lofty Ionic pilasters must glow. Newcomers entering the east room would admire the broad stairway rising

straight upwards lighted by tall, eleven-paned arched windows. Spiraled bal-
usters hand carved with clusters of blossoms, tendrils and acanthus supported the stair rail.

Betty Burwell had presented a picture of grace and poise with her even
features, fine eyes, and handsome figure. After the ceremony, perhaps William led her to the deck-on-hip roof where, from the rounded cupola, they
could gaze eastward fifteen miles toward the site of the two Nelson houses—
the buttress-type one soon to be their home.

Like his father, Tom was marrying a woman of manners and money. Manners were important. Even though the age had its affectations, aristocrats
understood that a gentleman was polite, honest, honorable, faithful, prudent, and fearless. He displayed skill in sports, cleverness in conversation,
and generosity to family, friends, and lesser folk. The gentlewoman was modest, patient, complaisant, pious, and compliant. She was accomplished in
the arts, domestic and artistic, and discharged her household duties faithfully.[44]

Lucy Grymes measured up as a good match. She was a graceful, genteel
girl well educated for the era, having acquired academic as well as artistic

*Children of Philip Grymes (left to right): Lucy, who married Thomas Nelson, Jr., Philip Ludwell
Grymes, John Randolph Grymes, and Charles.* Courtesy of the Virginia Historical Society,
Richmond.

accomplishments. The Reverend Mr. Yates, Tom's former teacher, had taught Lucy reading, writing, and cyphering.

In the summer of 1762, parishoners of Bruton Parish Church presumably heard the marriage banns for Tom and Lucy proclaimed three times, as the colonials continued this English custom. Each announcement cost fifteen shillings. Well-to-do couples also had to secure a special license from the county court clerk. If the clerk dawdled in this duty, Tom might urge his uncle, Secretary Nelson, to expedite the process. The preacher might prefer to be paid the usual twenty shillings or he could take two hundred pounds of tobacco for his service. Unlike their English cousins who clung to the church ceremony, colonials were married at home, but they used the same solemn wedding service from the Book of Common Prayer of the Established Church.

For the wealthy, nuptial rites were performed before noon. On the sultry twenty-ninth day of July 1762, Lucy Grymes and Thomas Nelson, Jr., were wed at her mother's house in Williamsburg, the Reverend Mr. Yates, rector of Bruton Parish Church and president of the College of William and Mary,[45] officiated.

Though there is no record of a guest register, the social standing of the two families would guarantee a gathering of the gentry. One can imagine Governor Fauquier, attired in gold-braided velvet moving gracefully among the crowd to congratulate the couple. Their fathers had been close colleagues in the Council, and the death of Philip Grymes a few months before cast the only shadow on the scene for Mary Randolph Grymes, Lucy's mother. She knew her husband would have felt a parent's pleasure and pride in their lovely Lucy, whose beauty now matched the promise that portrait painter Charles Bridges had captured in his 1750 canvas of the four Grymes children. In the painting, Lucy stands at the left, head held high, her apron filled with red, ripe cherries. Her brothers, Philip Ludwell, John Randolph, and Charles Grymes, complete the quartet.

A little fancy and a few fragments weave Lucy's wedding dress from three time-honored sources: the Bridges portrait, a well-preserved brocade ball gown that she wore several years later, and a later list of her daughter's trousseau. These suggest the bride wore a fashionable Flemish lace sacque, perhaps with three-quartered sleeves finished in falling cascades of ruffles, fitted over a satin skirt with folds gracefully gathered into a billowing back row and flowing train.[46]

As an heiress in her own right, Lucy's portmanteaus were probably filled with stylish sacques, lustrous gowns, Mechlin lace, quilted petticoats, sprigged lawn aprons, a fashionable stomacher and knot, a warm Capuchin, a dozen pairs of French gloves, everyday mitts, white woolen hose and silk stockings, various yards of colored cambric, dark brown cotton cloth, corded dimity, and fine purple and white linen. A suitable supply of bonnets in their own hat boxes and at least a dozen pairs of pumps in colorful green and purple leather, black Calamanca, pink satin, and embroidered white satin crowded her trunks.

Thomas Nelson, Jr., stood beside his bride, doubtless in brocade and broadcloth, a picture of contentment. Wedding guests could enjoy the success of this "merger" without a trace of envy since they were all part of the same social fabric.

Tom watched his father greeting guests, clasping the hands of his Council colleagues, as well as those of heavy-set Peyton and handsome John Randolph, Lucy's uncles. Old John Blair and Robert Carter Nicholas, half brother to Elizabeth Nelson, were surely in the crowd. William Nelson, no doubt, sensing a slight undercurrent beneath the surface amenities, would try to shield his wife from the talk about her brother, Robert Burwell. Despite the protest of Governor Fauquier, the resistance of the Council, and also the bitter opposition of Secretary Nelson, Burwell had been awarded an appointment to the coveted Council seat.[47]

Thomas Nelson, Jr., took his bride home to his father's house as was the custom in colonial days. Lack of finances was not the reason; it was simply the accepted practice for families to reside under one roof—ofttimes three generations the rule rather than the exception.

William Nelson's spacious H-shaped brick residence above the bluff on the York River was roomy enough to spare a bedroom for some seclusion; but otherwise, all activities were shared en masse. Privacy was as unknown as the atom. From birth to death, families dined, entertained and attended church as a unit. Even in writing to friends abroad, William Nelson often mentioned that his wife was beside him and wished to join him in his compliments.

The Nelson household was predominantly male, headed by William for over twenty-five years. Typical of the patriarchal prerogative of the times, he would say, "my" sons, not "ours," in speaking of the boys ranging from twenty-three-year-old Thomas, through Hugh, Lewis, Robert, Nathaniel and two-year-old Billy.

In colonial days parents interpreted literally and personally the biblical admonition, "Multiply and replenish the earth." Mothers who had the most children were highly commended. Elizabeth had borne many daughters, but none lived longer than a dozen years. Calamity also struck the sons. One boy had burned to death and now Lewis had lost his mind as a result of a fall from an upper story window of the house. Thereafter, he experienced convulsions and loss of consciousness with increased frequency.[48]

Patsy Custis, George Washington's stepdaughter and a cousin to the Nelsons, also suffered from seizures; her malady baffled the doctors. It is not known whether the Nelsons permitted doctors to place a ring around the waist of Lewis to prevent recurrence of the attacks, but on one occasion the master of Mount Vernon yielded to desperate pleading and allowed the treatment to be tried on Patsy.[49]

Though York Town had more distinguished doctors than other towns, they could not diagnose intricate illnesses at a time when physicians were puzzled by the simplest ailments. They knew little of anatomy, chemistry, or even ordinary hygiene. Hypnosis sometimes substituted for unknown anesthetics. The maxims of medicine were bleed and blister, plunge and purge—the more serious the illness, the stronger the treatment. Patients were administered medicines odious in smell and taste; the surgeon's unsterilized tools were saws, knives, and two-edged lancets. Only the stalwart survived.[50]

Over the door of Dr. Benjamin Catton's shop hung a colorful sign of the mortar and pestle, ointment bottle, and a golden bowl. He advertised a fine array of drugs; most folk were familiar with the anchovies, capers, olives, sugar, and tea on the list, but they might be curiously charmed by the pungent gum mastic and vitriol Roman. Dr. Catton possessed an impressive library, but few physicians of the period had a collection comparable to William Byrd's one hundred books on medicine.[51]

Dr. George Riddell rented Lots 12 and 18 from William Nelson for thirty-two pounds a year. In 1751, he had opened his apothecary shop diagonally across the street from the Swan Tavern and parallel to the Court House, a conspicuous spot to ply his trade. On his shelves stood scales, spatulas, tinctures of terebinth, dried leaves and roots, bitter myrrh, and, no doubt, the popular Hungary water with its fragrant rosemary ingredient.[52]

◆　　◆　　◆

Lucy looked forward to the late afternoon when she would walk the length of the lawn to the edge of the bluff and wait for Tom to come up from the wharf. From this vantage point, they had a panoramic view of York Town. Glancing eastward, they could see the long sweep of sandy shore and the river running into the sea. Across the broad stream lay Gloucester where clusters of thick green shrubs and trees lined the low bank. Looking back, they could locate the York-Hampton church, the Court House, and the square Custom House. The scene looked like a compact, cozy community, but its people were as far apart as the poles. The chasm between the top of the hill and below the bluff was insurmountable.[53]

Swan Tavern, still catering to its select clientele after forty years of service, stood across the street from the Court House. "Scotch" Tom Nelson and his partner, J. Walker, had opened the ordinary nearly a score of years before the famous Raleigh Tavern in Williamsburg had begun bestowing "Jollity, the Offspring of Wisdom and Good Living." In front swung the large-lettered sign with its picture of a graceful swan, big enough for the tired traveler to see from a distance. The long white planks of the building contrasted pleasantly with the tawny bricks of the Court House. Six dormer windows were spaced between the snubbed gables on the arched roof and patrons often peered at passersby or crowds gathering on the Court House Green.[54]

A wide entry hall invited one into the ordinary, but loafers would not find it a haven of hospitality. Loungers who begged cold water in the summer and hovered near the heat in the winter were asked to leave or else to pay for these privileges. A sign in the taproom counseled visitors:

> My Liquor's good, My Measure's just,
> But Honest Sirs, I will not trust.[55]

Paying customers could quench their thirst in the taproom from an array of assorted containers: six-quart decanters of rum, peach or apple brandy, sherry, port, Madeira, and tall pewter tankards of ale.

The tavern keeper sold his liquors straight from cask, jug, or rundlet. Colonial gentlemen bought a "tickler" in a half pint, a quart, or as much as a gallon in quantity. To "share the tickler" with a friend was typical hospitality. If the supply of spirits ran low, a bartender would resort to adding a little water, calling the result "grog" derived from a nickname given an English admiral who ordered his sailors' rum diluted; thereafter, they referred to him with disdain as "Old Grog" because of his wearing a cloak of grogram.

The liquid refreshment induced conviviality among gentlemen, travelers, ships' captains, and sailors—who sat at the same table—thus making the tavern a social melting pot where gentry broke bread with ordinary men whom they would not have considered inviting into their parlors. The daily menu consisted of crabs, clams, oysters, bear, venison, and wild turkey, served with hot batter bread, corn pone, and hoe cake. Berries, nuts, and fruits were passed. A dozen leather chairs were scattered around the rooms. Several sturdy walnut and mahogany tables established suitable arenas for backgammon and chess players. Long billiard tables lined the wall.[56]

The Swan provided a free press for its patrons. The *Virginia Gazette* had been published in nearby Williamsburg since 1736, and regular postriders brought the popular newspaper to the ordinary every week. Since the courier had access to correspondence as well as newspapers, he felt no qualms in reading the one as well as the other. His common custom passed the time for him and the relaying of the news made him seen important. Some clever correspondents thwarted his perusal by devising codes; later, during the Revolution, a code system became indispensable.[57]

In newspaper columns, the curious could check up on the latest crimes of felons, robbers, or runaways; this type of notice occurred frequently:

> Whereas my wife Mary refuses to live with me and cohabit as a wife, this is to forewarn all persons from crediting her on my account.[58]

In the February 12, 1762, issue an irate husband published this ultimatum:

> Whereas my wife Elizabeth has eloped from me, without any reasonable cause, I do therefore forewarn all Persons from harboring her, on any pretense whatsoever, under Pain of incurring the Rigours of the Law. I do likewise give notice that I will not pay any Debts she may contract.[59]

The press felt its civic responsibility and aided the lawful authorities to apprehend the guilty:

> On Friday night last, about 9 o'clock, the Post Office here was broken open and robbed of a sum of money . . . consisting of milled dollars, paper currency, crown and half-crown bills. Not contented with the robbery, the villains took a shovelful of red hot coals and threw them on the bed which burnt through the clothes, but stopped at the feathers.[60]

The paper cautioned that houses on the street could have been consumed by the fire and stated:

> Such alarming villainy calls for the assistance of the Publick to detect it, and we make no doubt of the readiness.[61]

Conservative citizens shook their heads with amazement as they read on the front page of the paper:

> The Religion of Free Thinkers, which makes so much Noise in the World, and is every Day increasing, is a Production of our Age . . . good cheer, good wine, fine Women, music, Dance, Public Diversion, gaming, in fine Every Thing that conveys pleasure to the Senses.[62]

Masters of runaway slaves avidly scanned the paper and often noticed that Peter Pelham, keeper of the gaol in Williamsburg, also used the services of the press to notify the owners:

> Committed to the public jail . . . Molly . . . has a prominent nose, and by her complexion would pass for one of the Indian race. Her owner is desired to apply for her, prove his property and pay charges.[63]

Wedding announcements and obituaries reported not only essential facts but also revealed personal characteristics in the flamboyant, flowery style of the period. The ages of the parties involved in this May-December alliance set tongues wagging.

> Yesterday was married in Henrico, Mr. William Carter, the son of John Carter, aged twenty-three, to Mrs. Sarah Ellyson, relict of Mr. Gerald Ellyson, deceased, aged eighty-five; a sprightly old Tit, with Three Thousand Pounds fortune.[64]

Old men often assuaged their sorrow by re-embarking on the sea of matrimony.

About a fortnight ago the wife of an old Gentlemen of this city, who is now upwards of 84 years of age, took her flight from the world to the spirits, and her husband affectionately followed her to the grave on crutches; since which he has had the resolution to take into his arms by marriage, a young vigorous nymph of twenty-five, who kindly consented to supply the place of the deceased matron. May they enjoy all possible nuptial felicities.[65]

The socially elite found their names in accounts of birthday balls at the capital and other entertainments they had attended.

After catching up on the local news, learned gentlemen might peruse the London papers, since the Swan Tavern subscribed for its select clients. William Nelson read them regularly and often sent for books that he had seen advertised in the English publications. One order listed three Dodsey poems, one Gordon's *Young Man's Treatise Companion*, one Boyers' *New Pantheon*, and Blackstone's *Commentaries on English Laws*.[66] Few men and women of the era were as well educated as the Nelsons. A sign in the Swan warned, "Gentlemen Learning to Spell Are Requested to Use Last Week's Newsletter."[67]

Below the bluff lay the notorious York-under-the-hill, where prostitutes lured men into their hovels and crowded taverns served ruffians, sailors, and thugs an abundance of ale, grog, and liquor—triggering ready brawls.

From his lawn, Tom could point out to Lucy the Nelson warehouse still standing on the waterfront site "Scotch" Tom had selected. Like his grandfather, Tom always loved the sea and the sight of ships. He and Lucy might sit in the shade of the tulip trees and gaze toward the harbor feeling the caress of the soft river breeze and September sun.

Since York Town was a port of entry, Tom had seen many grand ships. He remembered the great three-decked galleons filled with rum, molasses, and sweet Madeira; the swift-moving schooners that transported sugar, salt, and spices. He could distinguish between the two-masted brigantine and the three-masted bark, its balanced square sails cupped to catch the wind. Atop each ship flew a colorful standard.

Though Tom basked in his domesticity, no young man in York Town had more interests—in politics, plantation tasks, commercial, and church concerns.

Early in the morning William Nelson and his eldest son would go down the hill to the warehouse. For over three decades the enterprise had stood in this lucrative location, a symbol of "Scotch" Tom's shrewdness in founding the establishment, for in 1728 the record reads:

Petition land between appointed said Town and River lyes Beach sand high tide overflow—nevertheless may be made convenient for building warehouse—said Thomas Nelson have leave to survey 80 square feet of said beach adjoining to landing but now useth in Yorktown and that a patent be granted him for the same with power to extend a wharf into river so as not to encroach on public landings on those streets leading to town or river side.[68]

William Nelson's acumen had enabled him to expand the enterprise; he believed, "Industry and integrity seldom fail of Success in Business."[69]

Now Thomas Nelson, Jr., as the third generation, was ready to try his hand in the trade.

Tom was also enmeshed in the political net. When he returned home from England in 1761, the voters of York County had elected him to the House of Burgesses.[70] Though he was fourteen when he left Virginia and had been gone over seven years, the freeholders felt no apprehensions concerning his character or capability. In February 1762, he was appointed a member of the York County Court, and not long afterward he became colonel of the county militia. He was following in his father's footsteps. William Nelson had already served a score of years in government, beginning in 1742 in the House of Burgesses; then scarcely a week after "Scotch" Tom's death in October 1745, he was chosen a member of the coveted Council.[71]

William's younger brother, Thomas, had already preceded him in this august assemblage and had been appointed Deputy Secretary of the Colony in April 1743. In this position, he had the authority to issue his own certificates, to assign clerks to the county courts, to assist the judgments of the general court, and to keep records.[72]

It was undoubtedly a post of patronage, and many a colonial governor fretted over the privileges of a position that could bestow so many favors.

William Nelson believed that politics was a reputable profession, as did other powerful planters, that it was not only the right of property owners to enter politics but also an obligation to become an officeholder. As representative of the gentleman's rank, duty, honor, and generosity governed his conduct; he exhibited disgust at the penny-pinching, power-hungry officials of Great Britain who used the poor as pawns in their lobbying. On August 14, 1767, he wrote his friends Capel and Osgood Hansbury:

> You talk of great disagreement among the Ministry—I am almost sick with thinking of a set of men who contend for Power to do I know not what. I hoped it was for Honour they did acquire by relieving the Distress of the poor labourer and Industrious Manufacturer.[73]

By this time a reciprocal obligation existed between the gentry and ordinary men and seemed to operate to the mutual satisfaction of both; the planter aristocracy furnished candidates and the freeholders voted for the approved slate.[74]

CHAPTER TWO

Retrospect

Capitol Construction ✦ *Governor Nicholson and Rejected Romance* ✦ *"Scotch" Tom Nelson's Arrival Establishes the Family Name in the Colony* ✦ *Governor Spotswood* ✦ *Industry and Improvements* ✦ *Transmontane Trek* ✦ *"Knights of the Golden Horseshoe"* ✦ *William Byrd, II, and the Nelsons* ✦ *"Scotch" Tom Dies in 1745*

The moving of the colonial capital from Jamestown to Williamsburg near the beginning of the eighteenth century presaged a period of social as well as political significance for the Colony. By 1705, Virginia had a new Capitol, and credit must be accorded the man who was ousted the same year. Governor Francis Nicholson, the colorful castoff from New York, changed the capital's site and called it Williamsburg after his King, but his impractical plan to shape streets in the form of a W and M for William and Mary failed.[1]

Nicholson became noted for his arbitrary manner with the Assembly. His boast to "beat them into better manners" and "bring them to reason with halters around their necks" naturally met with resistance.[2]

Robert ("King") Carter, young Tom Nelson's great-grandfather, with other Council members, often opposed the Crown's official. Rejection by the representatives *and* by *romance* caused the Governor to brush Blair's hat off and grab the Attorney General by the collar. Lucy Burwell was engaged when Nicholson declared his devotion. Middle-aged Nicholson's ardor for the girl resulted in a plea to her father, Lewis Burwell, to make his daughter betray her betrothal. Burwell demurred. In a rage, Nicholson shouted his revenge, threatening a triple throat-cutting for the groom, the justice, and the minister.[3]

Colonel Lewis Burwell and the Reverend James Blair called Nicholson's bluff. The clergyman and the Council brought charges against Nicholson for his conduct, and he was transported to England for trial.[4]

The Capitol was a handsome H-shaped brick structure with corresponding wings fashioned in a balanced arrangement. The Burgesses met on the lower floor while the Royal Governor and the Councilors convened in elegantly furnished chambers above.

Because the first state house had burned at Jamestown, the Williamsburg Capitol was constructed without chimneys. Burning candles and smoking tobacco were forbidden. For eighteen years, representatives were deprived of these comforts. Later, when the Secretary complained that dampness was destroying records, the statesmen ordered the installation of two chimneys and permitted the use of candles. More comfort and cheer mollified the lawmakers when the ban on pipe smoking was removed.[5]

"Scotch" Tom Nelson had made three voyages to Virginia before settling on the shores of the York River in York Town after 1700. He first came to the Colony in 1696 at age nineteen, then again in 1698 on his prospective tours, probably as a merchant. York Town was already an established village having been made a town by the Assembly in 1660. In 1634, Virginia had been divided into eight shires or counties to be governed as those in the old country, and York was one of the original group. It was a propitious time for a young man to come to the Colony, for Virginia was embarking on that elegant era known as the Golden Age.[6]

By the beginning of the eighteenth century York Town was booming. The 1691 Act for Ports created a town on paper. Following a court ordinance, the commissioners met on Mr. Reade's land (he was to be "Scotch" Tom's father-in-law) to lay out eighty-five lots from fifty acres and to plan for public buildings. The sites sold fast. In 1707 "Scotch" Tom bought Lot 47, then Lot 52, and acquired others across the street. Gradually, he bought Lots 46, 84, and 85 to complete a rectangle which ran to the edge of the river. Later, he purchased other plots until by 1738, the year Thomas Nelson, Jr., was born, the name of "Scotch" Tom Nelson led the list of lot owners in the town.[7]

Though Governor Nicholson had "swaggered and swashbuckled," he had been serious about civic concerns and contributed toward the construction of a court house and church for the town of York before his removal to England. He had pledged "five pound sterling towards building the cott. house at York Town, and twenty pound sterl'g if within two years they build a brick church att the same towne. As witness my hand ye day and year above written."[8]

To expedite building, the legislators had set a deadline date and a penalty of fifty pounds sterling. The sum was not forfeited, for when "Scotch" Tom made his second trip to the Virginia shores in 1698, many meetings had convened in both the civil and church structures.

Whenever "Scotch" Tom went to Williamsburg, he was no doubt impressed with the Capitol's ornamented hexagonal cupola, Queen Anne's coat of arms emblazoned in bright colors, its unusual clock, and the English flag flying high.

In England, Queen Anne ushered in the century, ascending the throne in 1702, but her twelve years' reign experienced political complications the vacillating Anne could not control. In Virginia, however, the loyal subjects proudly displayed their comely queen's portrait in the Capitol and commemorated her name in Princess Anne County, and the North and South Anna, Rapidan, and Rivanna rivers.[9]

But politics did not intrigue "Scotch" Tom much—that would be the role for his progeny—although in 1712 he was selected as a justice for York County and served in this post for twelve years. His forte was trade, and his mind focused on making money. As a former sea captain he had accumulated some capital, and an adequate purse opened many doors. In the summer of 1711, he furnished sundry supplies for the fortifications of York Town. Batteries had been erected at Point Comfort, Tindell's Point, Jamestown, and York Town to guard against French attack. After the guard ships were removed, "Scotch" Tom petitioned the Council to be paid in money, for he said, "He might have had the price in ready money if he had sold those goods to private persons."[10]

The House of Burgesses, however, did not agree with the Council; he was paid in tobacco for the supplies.

In fashion, it was an age of affectation reviving the Restoration's exaggerated styles. The extreme farthingale was in favor and its diameter—sometimes extending six feet—forced women to step sideways through doorways. Coiffures were elaborately curled, powdered and adorned with ribbons and jewels. Tight-fitting bodices laced over ornate stomachers with parallel stays on the outside; plunging necklines bared bosoms halfway. (It is strange how the styles of one generation flaunt a physiological feature that shocks the next. The eighteenth-century lady would have felt disgraced to display her legs or even an ankle, but she frankly revealed her bosom; nineteenth century women were clothed from head to toe, and the twentieth-century miss casually exhibits all parts of her anatomy.)

Too much covering placed the eighteenth-century girl in an unpopular minority, for even the decorous Fithian petulantly wrote in his journal concerning Miss Betsy Lee:

> She was pinched up rather too near in a long pair of new fashioned Stays, which, I think, are a Nusance both to us & themselves. . . . are produced upwards too high that we can have scarce any view at all of the Ladies Snowy Bosoms.[11]

The tutor thought this style not only thwarted the prerogative of man but was uncomfortable for the woman as he asserted, "The Stays which is hard & unyielding—I imputed the Flush which was visible in her Face being swathed up Body & Soul & limbs together."[12]

A building boom began in the Colony in the new century. In October 1705, the Burgesses passed an act recommending the construction of a residence for their Governor and appropriated three thousand pounds sterling to start the project.[13] The specifications stated:

The said house be built of brick fifty four feet in length, and forty eight foot in breadth, from inside to inside, two stories high, with convenient cellars underneath, and one vault, sash windows, of sash, glass, and a covering of stone slate.[14]

By the time Alexander Spotswood arrived in 1710, the appropriation had been spent and construction checked. The large, thirty-four-year-old leader made an instant impression on the Virginians. When he handed them the writ of habeas corpus, they responded by voting twelve thousand pounds sterling to continue the construction of the residence. Later, when they felt the iron grip in his gauntlet, their gratitude faded. Spotswood's bright, bushy-browed eyes belied the stubborn strength of a decisive character.[15]

The following year when representatives failed to furnish moneys to fight the French, an angry Spotswood prorogued the Assembly; but Governor Spotswood's positive side was evident in improvements in the capital. The imposing plans for the Palace, in the style and symmetry of the Court House, the octagonal arsenal, and Bruton Parish Church are proof of his interest in architecture and artistry.[16]

Parsimony never figured in the Governor's plans. When he drew up a draft for the church, he dipped into his own pocket to build part of it. Then the Assembly graciously reciprocated by providing a pew for their Governor and his twelve Councilors. What a splendid scene the Crown's officials set, adorned in velvet and gold, sitting in canopied chairs surrounded by the cream of the Colony in silks and satin. (Spotswood's managerial success with servants was evident in 1711 when he insured a smoothly run birthday ball in honor of Queen Anne by promising the servants enough spirits for a drunken spree the *following* day.)[17]

The energetic Governor turned his attention to industrial enterprises, repeating the pattern of one hundred years before when English explorers had been spurred by the spread of the Spanish net of commerce. They had publicized the "soyle & clymate" of the virgin wilderness suited to growing sugar cane, almonds, lemons, oranges, and olives. Eventually, time exposed the truth; the newcomers realized that much of the lavish abundance flourished in the minds of the tellers. Colonists struggling to survive in the new continent had to combat the threefold specter of sickness, starvation, and the savage.[18]

In 1608 the adventurers had attempted to establish glassworks and ship out gold dirt from Jamestown. The gold dirt proved worthless, but twenty turkeys—the first known on the continent—transported from Virginia to the homeland proved their value. Crude iron was also shipped to the furnaces of England, but the factory was not a thriving enterprise. Glassworks had been started in the spring of 1608 at Jamestown. Pure white sand was imported from England and German glass blowers were brought over. Red men came with fur skins and cereal grass to trade for the shiny ornaments. Powhatan gave John Smith more than two hundred bushels of corn for some glass trinkets. Very soon the craftsmen went to live with the Indians where their cleverness won them tawny brides for companions.[19]

A century later, about 1713, Governor Spotswood had acquired nearly sixty thousand acres around the Rapidan and Rappahannock rivers. Whether special persuasions and promises of an inexhaustible supply of spirits to his slaves was necessary to spur them into exploring his uninhabited region is not known, but they did discover iron deposits on his acres. Spotswood found forty-two German miners in the newly-named Spotsylvania County and started them digging the iron ore. The Governor informed the Assembly that the men at Germanna Ford would be a bulwark against Indian invasions. Eventually, four furnaces were in operation producing metal bars, nails, and wire.

Spotswood explained his preparations in his correspondence:

> I have placed here a number of Protestant Germans, built them a Fort, and finish'd it with 2 pieces of Cannon and some Ammunition, which will awe the stragling partys of Northern Indians. . . . I have obtain'd for them from the Assembly an Exemption of all Taxes for seven years, which may be an encouragement to others of the same Country to come over, but I hope their passage will be at their own charges.[20]

His handsome French friend, John H. Fontaine, reported realistically . . . "could not see that there was any gold mine. We took some ore and endeavored to run it, but could get nothing from it, and I am of the opinion it will not come to any thing. No, not as much as lead."[21] (Fontaine's judgment was correct. Although the operation produced enough ore for exportation, excessive English duties and mismanagement forced the closing of the iron forge.)

As the father of the iron foundry, Governor Spotswood was called the "Tubal Cain of Virginia," a title of which he was particularly proud.[22] Another crowning achievement that added a feather to his cap, literally and figuratively, was the triumphant transmontane trek.

Since he was already becoming a confidant of the Governor, "Scotch" Tom was no doubt invited to join the jaunt but declined. He had married into the first family of York about 1710 when Margaret Reade, daughter of Elizabeth Martiau and Colonel George Reade, became his bride. The Reades had vast landholdings and the town site of York was purchased from the 850-acre tract they had willed to their son Benjamin. The court was ordered to meet on July 29, 1691, on this desirable river frontage,[23] "beginning at the lower side of Smyth's Creek and so running downward by the river towards the ferry being ye land appointed by Law for a port in order to laying out of the same for a town."[24] Benjamin had received ten thousand pounds of tobacco for fifty acres.

The founder of the Nelson name in Virginia also engaged in another enterprise with the royal executive. The administrator appealed to outstanding citizens to invest in the Virginia Indian Company. A share cost fifty pounds for charter membership and by the spring of 1715 prominent planters like Richard Bland, Cole Digges, Nathaniel Harrison, Mann Page, and "Scotch" Tom had become stockholders in the shipping firm. In a few months, London merchants began to bombard the Board of Trade with violent protests against the Virginia-based business. Claiming that the company was a monopoly, they were backed by William Byrd, II, as a ringleader in the proceedings. The independent Virginian had found a reason to voice his objections against the vigorous Spotswood. The company was forced to dissolve, and the subscribers were only partially repaid for their investment.[25]

By the time of Spotswood's grand adventure, however, "Scotch" Tom had put down his roots. His three children had been born: William, in 1711; Mary, in 1713; Thomas, in 1716. His brother, Hugh Nelson of Penrith County, Scotland, had made his will in December 1708, leaving his shops and warehouses to be sold and conveyed to "My brother, Th. Nelson, of York Town, Virginia, America." The enterprising immigrant tried out his versatile talents and became a merchant, operator of a ferry and a mill, a farmer, gentleman jurist, and trustee of the port landing.[26] A journey across the mountains did not appeal to hard-working "Scotch" Tom.

A commonplace comment appearing in John Fontaine's diary on August 20, 1716—"Waited on the Governor, who was in readiness for an expedition over the Appalachian mountains"—hardly conveyed Spotswood's enthusiasm for the excursion. He imbued others with his excitement, for the entourage included exuberant Cavaliers from the Carter, Harrison, Lee, Moore, Page, Pendleton, Randolph, and Wormeley families. The men wore broadcloth and fine leather boots, the Governor a green cape and a hat adorned with peacock plumes.[27]

Pushing off at five in the evening on August 29, the adventurers pitched camp near Germanna. A moving bar with champagne, barrels of brandy, Burgundy, canary, and claret wines was carefully attended. Minor mishaps of cuts and stings were treated with spirits. All fifty men were assigned different duties, and even the Cavaliers cooked for themselves. John Washington, accustomed to the wilderness, advised the men on the perils of a region Fontaine reported as "thickets so tightly-laced together." It was not a common practice to protect horses' hoofs, but for this expedition every horse had been shod for rough terrain. Five axemen cleared a path to the mountaintop from which on September 7, the group peered down into the crest of a blue ridge at a shining stream winding through the valley like a silver ribbon; the Indians had called the river Shenandoah, "Daughter of the Stars."[28]

Spotswood claimed the property for the Crown; the Cavaliers toasted all the royal family with champagne and fired volleys in salute. If spirits and sound could convey the country into the British lap, the task was certainly accomplished.

Fond memories of this remarkable exploration inspired Governor Spotswood later to order from London sentimental horseshoe-shaped souvenirs studded with red garnets and brilliant diamonds for which he, himself, paid. He presented one to each proud explorer who became known thereafter as the "Knights of the Golden Horseshoe."[29]

✦ ✦ ✦

Though only a lad of nine when the first Capitol had burned in 1747 on the thirtieth day of January, Tom remembered the catastrophe vividly. He had heard his father and uncle considering the cause of the fire as others had done. Some immediately guessed that improvements to the fireplace and the use of candles had caused the blaze; others cited arson. Early expansionists seized the moment to urge once again the moving of the capital out of Williamsburg to a more accessible location for trade. New settlements were springing up along the broad James River and adjoining streams. Colonel William Byrd, one of the expansionists, had laid the foundations for his "not castles only, but also cities in the air" and called them Richmond and Petersburg.[30]

In 1748 the act authorizing the construction of the second colonial capitol in Williamsburg was passed by only a two-vote majority, with John Blair and John Robinson tying the vote. William Nelson was appointed to the committee to handle details of rebuilding the structure.[31]

✦ ✦ ✦

The Nelsons were prominent enough to appear on the pages of the diary of William Byrd, II. In 1741 from February to May, the master of Westover mentioned the family members many times. The colonel had studied a system of shorthand (now fortunately deciphered) taught by Mason and kept a charmingly frank diary. On February 23, 1741, Colonel Byrd related:

> I rose about five and prepared for my journey. I drank three dishes of chocolate and recommended my family to the Almighty. The weather cold and cloudy, the wind north. About 8 we got into the chariot and got to . . . where we got without anything remarkable about 3 and found young Nelson and his family and Betty . . . there. I ate dry beef. We talked and were courteously entertained. I prayed.[32]

His diary does not record that he played with two-year-old Thomas, Jr. The eighteenth century was an adult-centered world, wherein fathers like William Nelson, had absolute authority over family affairs.

A month later the young William Nelsons from York Town returned

Byrd's visit on a "cold but clear day." Byrd had "read Hebrew & Greek," then "Danced" for exercise, then "read news till one when Mr. Nelson and wife and sister with two Miss Harrisons arrived. . . . I ate pigeon pie."[33]

On May 2 court was convening. Colonel Byrd recorded: "I prayed and had tea at Colonel Grymes's. . . . I sat in court till 11 and then my daughters and I went to York in Mrs. Needler's chariot to young Mr. Nelson's."[34] After dining on roast fowl, they visited Colonel Lightfoot and had tea. This Saturday was cold with a blustery north wind, but the company walked about the town and the colonel spent the night with the Nelsons.

On Sunday, May 3, the colonel did not rise until eight, prayed, and had the customary chocolate. At eleven o'clock, the company walked to church, and the colonel commented, "had a good sermon." This was high praise since the candid Mr. Byrd often criticized preachers. Then after dinner, he mentioned that he "had tea with old Nelson ["Scotch" Tom who was sixty-four, Byrd being sixty-seven] . . . & in the evening we supped . . . [at] Mr. Ambler's with Col. Fairfax & his lady, went home about 9 and prayed."[35]

Four years later, "Scotch" Tom was gone, his passing noted in the *Virginia Gazette* of October 10, 1745:

> Early Monday morning last, died at his home in York Town, in a good old age, Mr. Thomas Nelson, an eminent Merchant, and 40 years an inhabitant of that place.

For colonial times, sixty-eight years was indeed a good old age, beyond the mortality norm for the eighteenth century; and as the passing of years would show, his life span far exceeded that of his son William and his grandson Thomas Nelson, Jr.

Death was always close to the colonials, expected and accepted as an act of Providence; consequently, they were not disconcerted by a candid discussion of the deceased. The Armisteads, Digges, Berkeleys, Burwells, Jamesons, Carters and Nortons who gathered certainly agreed with the announcement.

> As he lived just, so was he blessed, not only with the increase of wealth, but also in the comfort of his children, whom he lived to see (following his good example), all happily married and settled, and enjoying the greatest honours and Preferments.[36]

The people present had played a part in heaping "honours" and promoting "preferments" on "Scotch" Tom's two sons, William and Thomas. The limited electorate was composed of gentlemen freeholders, white, and over twenty-one. (Voting was denied the dissenter, but many unbelievers manipulated to cast their ballots.)[37] Family, fortune, and friends were necessary rungs for the latter of success; and the Nelsons were blessed with all three.

The yeomen in the yard, dressed in dark gray kersey, mingled with the humble folk in blue duffel, while the servants and slaves in loose-fitting shalloon and thin faded fustian attested that "Scotch" Tom was a good neighbor, charitable to the poor, and benevolent to all; they had been recipients of his generosity.

Young Thomas was awed by the black-broadclothed-robed figures hovering around the draped casket. Black velvet was often used by the gentry to cover a coffin, and dark mourning urns were the usual funeral pieces placed in parlors. Young Tom's father and his uncle might even have blacked their silver shoe buckles for this grave occasion. Black crepe bands were tied around their arms. Tom's mother, his Aunt Mary Berkeley, and Aunt Sarah Burwell were swathed in somber silk, black fringed linen, and dark muslin. His grandfather's second wife, Frances Tucker Nelson, wore the dark widow's "weeds" she would affect for the rest of her natural life. Some wives smarted under this tribute to the bereaved, yet mourning garb was donned by women into the twentieth century.[38]

Unlike the English people, the colonials conducted their funerals at home, but every parish had an established burying plot. Proximity to the parish afforded at least two advantages; it provided a minister and burial in the church cemetery. Under certain circumstances, the lawmakers confirmed that the clerk might "be allowed to bury when a minister cannot possibly be had before the corpse would corrupt in hot weather, or if the minister be sick or infirm, if the clerk can read tolerably well."[39] Many people removed from the periphery of their parish set aside a plot of ground for a graveyard in their gardens, as did William Byrd of Westover.

The potter's field was unknown. Final rites at forty shillings cost twice as much as the marriage ceremony. In the eighteenth century, even middle-class folk strained for an impressive burial, a sumptuous funeral table and mementoes for distribution in memory of the deceased. Many wills allocated amounts for these expenditures: sermon, 200 pounds of tobacco; coffin, 150 pounds; turkey, geese, hogs, and fowls, about 400 pounds; butter, 100; sugar and spice, 50; cider and rum, 300. Other wills, however, stipulated that expenses were not to exceed three hundred pounds.[40]

Often mentioned in the wills were bequests to purchase expensive emblems; the favored mourning ring inscribed with the initials of the deceased, watch papers, gloves, or gold and silver brooches filled with the pressed locks of the lamented. "Rings to all my brothers and sisters—deathhead gold, which I desire they will wear and keep in remembrance of me." These ornaments and obligations became cherished keepsakes."[41]

Although "Scotch" Tom's will did not stipulate a specific sum to be spent toward these mourning emblems, it would not have strained the family purse to provide such adornments.

Almost a quarter of a century later, William Nelson would write to John Norton of the widow Donaldson's grief:

> She seems to be in great Distress, & real object of Compassion. Mrs. Nelson, I believe has shown her some Kindness; but I fear it will be difficult to get her into any Way of providing for herself and her little Family . . . delivered 47 Mourning Rings she bought from you.[42]

Ignoring practicality in her plight and continuing the age-old custom, the widow proudly distributed outward symbols of sorrow though she was a welfare case.

Many made explicit requests to curb the practice. Charles Carter deplored the action:

> The ridiculous custom of involving familys by pompous funeral & mourning which serve only to enrich men who watch for these occasions to impoverish their neighbors. . . . If any of my [good] Children or other relations purpose to attend my Corpse, I desire it may be in Common clothes, the men wear black Crape on their left arm and the women with a black Knot on their left side.[43]

His will stated that the minister was to preach an annual sermon on the day of his death for a payment of ten barrels of corn.

Philip Grymes, later to be Thomas Nelson, Jr.'s, father-in-law, also felt that common clothes were appropriate for mourning; he stated in his will "no one was to go in mourning except his wife, if she chose."[44]

Some seventeenth century records reveal that after mourners had rowed down the rivers or traveled many miles over rutty roads for the final rites, gravity often gave way to levity. Free-flowing spirits prompted toasts to the deceased as well as fusilade blasts that caused needless accidents.[45]

From "Scotch" Tom's house on the top of the hill to the parish churchyard was not much more than a couple of blocks as we measure distance today, but to little Thomas the time seemed endless as he watched the hearse move slowly down the street. Costly coaches and light chaises crowded with family and friends formed an imposing cortege.

Now little Thomas began to realize that never again could he slip across the street to tag along after his grandfather to the dock. The thudding sound of dampish sod thrown into the grave brought the little boy back to reality. Perhaps the minister read an oft-quoted passage from Saint Paul: "To him who by patient contination in well doing seek for glory, and honour, and immortality, eternal life . . . glory, honour and peace to every man who worketh good."[46] As his father's arm fell across his shoulder, Tom left the cemetery content that his grandfather had gained the promised repose.

CHAPTER THREE

Rights, Romance, and Restraints: 1763

French and Indian War Ends ✦ *Nelsons and Their Cousin George Washington* ✦ *Credit Conditions of the Colony* ✦ *Rebecca Burwell and Thomas Jefferson* ✦ *Ohio and Loyal Companies* ✦ *William Born* ✦ *James Otis and Patrick Henry* ✦ *Expansion and Enterprises* ✦ *Parsons' Cause*

In 1763, Thomas Nelson, Jr., his father, William, and his uncle, Secretary Nelson, joined in the general rejoicing when Governor Fauquier announced the end of the French and Indian War.

The war-weary militiamen wandered into Williamsburg wanting to hang up their flintlock muskets, hoping time would blur memories of men left behind on the frontier. Some soldiers, tossing up their coonskin caps in cheer, revealed prematurely gray hair "turned overnight," they said, from seeing the red man's atrocities, yet preferable to a scalped skull. A few confessed they had run from the bloodcurdling screams and tomahawks, but not Colonel George Washington, who had spent the first five years fighting in the conflict. Though bullets had pierced his hat and uniform and struck his mounts, he had continued to fight. Any acclaim was no more than he merited, the Nelsons told fellow Assemblymen, for the Nelsons had always known that Washington was a man of extraordinary calm and courage. Captain Nicholas Martiau, the first settler of York County, was a progenitor of both the Nelson and Washington families.[1]

The discreet colonel, however, brushed aside compliments, recalling that his renown sprang from the disastrous defeat at Fort Duquesne. It was best to forget the disdain of the British toward the colonials, their camp consorts, the cowardly shirkers, and only remember the valor of the Virginia militiamen. How ironic and untimely was the boast General Braddock had made to Benjamin Franklin: "These savages may, indeed, be a formidable enemy to your raw American militia; but upon the King's regular and disciplined troops, Sir, it is impossible they should make an impression."[2] As though on parade, Braddock had led his well-trained troops in precise military formation and the French, aided by their Indian allies, had attacked from ambush routing the redcoats. Washington had rallied his "raw" militia and pro-

43

ceeded from a rear-guard position to rescue the remnants of the English army. Washington wrote:

> The Virginia troops showed a good deal of bravery, and were nearly all killed. . . . the dastardly behaviour of those they called regulars exposed all others, that were inclined to do their duty to almost certain death.[3]

Braddock had lost his life in the battle and the conflict had claimed as casualties three-fourths of the officers and eight hundred men.

In order to hear timely news of an English conquest, Governor Dinwiddie had organized relays of horsemen along all roads leading out of the capital. How stunned the old Scotsman must have been to hear that the British army was vanquished. Despair and distrust followed.[4]

Precarious credit conditions prompted Governor Fauquier to summon the Council to Williamsburg April 28, 1763.[5] Since 1758, he had called together eleven sessions. Assemblymen living at a distance were at a disadvantage, but the Nelsons were lucky to live nearby and could ride from York Town to the capital in two hours. Further, in 1749, they had purchased a modest one and one-half story house on Francis Street convenient to the Capitol so William, the Secretary, and Thomas could step around the corner when public affairs demanded several days of attendance.[6]

The Board of Trade in Britain had exhorted Fauquier to bear down on the financial situation. Consequently, when the Burgesses convened with the Council on May 19, Tom Nelson heard Fauquier's imperative plea for payment to the merchants. The Governor admonished the Assembly: "I should recommend to your Consideration in what Manner you could better provide for their Security in recovering Sterling Debts due from the Colony to them. . . . It is absolutely necessary that something should be done to give the Merchants satisfaction for which they called upon you."[7]

The proud representatives around the great oval table felt like schoolboys reprimanded by their headmaster, and Fauquier continued, "As the support of Public Credit is of the most urgent Importance to a trading Country, I must press you to take care that the Paper Money now in Currency may be effectually redeemed."[8]

Tom Nelson watched the powdered-bewigged heads turn and wondered if heavily-jowled Treasurer John Robinson had a solution. He knew the feelings of his father about cheap money, for William Nelson had often observed, "when we have a large Quantity of Money in Circulation it is easily obtained, it serves only to promote and cherish that spirit of extravagance which hath been our Ruin."[9]

Many planters probably agreed with his philosophy but didn't curtail their expenses. They lived lavishly on unlimited lands in mansions. They bought luxuries from abroad, ornamented carriages, silver-engraved with their coats of arms. Despite debt, the gentry gathered in the capital that warm May day were still buying slaves and attempting to secure more land. Penny pinching was not part of their pattern.

William Nelson had confidence in coin and mistrust of paper money as his correspondence revealed:

> You mistake me to think I was one of those clamoring for paper money. I perfectly agree with you in your notions of paper Money; that no man, Merchant or other should be forced to take on payment anything called Money, that of doubtful or uncertain Value.[10]

Overextension and extravagance were not the only causes of trouble. Tobacco crops had been bad. In 1765, William Nelson was to produce only seventeen hogsheads from his Hanover plantation.[11] In a good year the tract yielded 150 casks. A drought had damaged the crop throughout the dominion, but Hanover County was hardest hit. The parched plants looked so dull and dry they didn't even seem alive. Since tobacco was currency, finances fluctuated. In 1755 the Assembly had been forced to issue paper money for the first time to finance troops to fight the French. The lawmakers had planned to plug the leaks with taxes on tithables (slaves) and tobacco.

In years when crops were poor, Page's and Crutchfield's warehouse contained only 1,500 hogsheads as opposed to the usual 4,000. The few planters who produced tobacco commanded fifty shillings for their crop.[12] The shortest tobacco crop that he had grown in thirty years was that of 1758, William Nelson wrote to his friend James Gildart.[13]

Short supply should spur a demand for the staple next year, optimistic growers told one another, but in 1759, instead of prices rising, they dropped. Despite the drop and dwindling profits, William Nelson did not consider recalling Tom from his education in England.

William Nelson was as good an accountant as one might find among the Assemblymen, but his books were not in exact balance. Planters and yeomen, sailors and tradesmen were all engaged in a complicated circle of exchange. Without hard cash, turkeys might be traded for tools, wheat for wine, salt for seed, and pitch for a pig. An inventory of items trafficked in might be laughable if it were not so lamentable in revealing the lack of capital.

Governor Fauquier declared, "I shall quit this unpleasant subject, to enter upon one which must communicate Joy to all true Lovers of their Country, I mean the Conclusion of the most glorious and Honourable Peace between his Majesty and all his Enemies, of which Happy Event I take this Opportunity to congratulate you."[14]

Englishmen were reeling with intoxication at their rise to the first-ranking power in the world when France signed away her empire in the

Treaty of Paris, February 10, 1763, giving Great Britain control of Canada and the immense Mississippi territory.

Nevertheless, the toasts of victory soon turned sour when Fauquier had to explain the treaty's terms. The two chief proclamations prohibited further settlements of the frontier and trade with the Indians. The Nelsons and other land speculators were stunned.

◆　　◆　　◆

While Nelson men talked of a troubled economy, declining tobacco trade, and an uncertain frontier situation, Nelson women discussed the romance of Rebecca Burwell and Tom Jefferson. Theirs was not idle curiosity but an intense interest, since the teenagers were cousins. Tom Nelson was "Becky's" first cousin as her deceased father, Lewis Burwell, was his mother's brother; after Burwell's death, William Nelson had become the girl's guardian. Lucy's relationship also came through the maternal line. Her mother, Mary Randolph Grymes, was a first cousin to Thomas Jefferson's mother, Jane Randolph Jefferson.[15]

In letters to his friend John Page, the young Jefferson mixed logic with love—indecisively. Could he survive Rebecca's rejection if he declared his love? Perhaps, he told John Page, he might escape to Europe; John recommended that he pursue his suit. The young law student turned twenty in April 1763, but he was reluctant to speak to Mr. Nelson regarding Rebecca. Both youngsters survived the romance, however, and Rebecca soon gave her heart to Jacquelin Ambler.[16] Evidently, the Ambler brothers had great appeal, for they wooed and won the two belles who had refused Washington and Jefferson. Mary Cary, who had dazzled young Washington, married Edward Ambler; Rebecca wed Jacquelin.

◆　　◆　　◆

After the colonists had crossed the coastal fringe and pushed up to the Piedmont, they found the Indians at the foot of the mountains checking their approach. Adventurers brushed aside caution and took their chances. For the flesh and furs of wild game, many French hunters tracked through the entangled forests. The Indians didn't fear the French as they did the English. The former seemed on a transitory conquest, securing only cessions to the tributaries of the Ohio River to build their forts, but the latter made lasting claims for colonization. Englishmen put down their roots and built homes, however rough hewn and ephemeral at first.

As the rivers ran from the upper regions eastward to the sea, the Tidewater planters gazed westward and pressed their patents and petitions to spread the settlements between the streams. The majestic Allegheny mountains pulled the pioneers to an apparently limitless land beyond.

If Governor Fauquier could momentarily have forgotten the Indians terrorizing the frontier and Pontiac's conspiracy to capture the English forts, he might have detected consternation on the faces of the commercial competitors of the Ohio and Loyal land companies who sat before him. For a score of years, Council members and their influential parents before them had petitioned to acquire the abundant land; land to them meant affluence.

Secretary Nelson had about 1,700 land patents lying in his office awaiting the official seal. Edmund Pendleton was trying to be patient about the delay.[17]

As far back as the fourteenth century records reveal that many Nelsons had received large land tracts for military service in England. In the eighteenth century, the Nelson clan, like its contemporaries, were intrigued with the western wilderness. Their friend, popular Treasurer John Robinson, had interested them in the gigantic Greenbrier grant of one hundred thousand acres as early as 1745 and helped to project them further along the road to prosperity. At that time William Nelson was thirty-four years old; his brother, twenty-nine. His key position as the Colony's Deputy Secretary enabled him to know of enormous land areas and empowered him to attain vast acres.[18]

While Tom had been away at school in England, his father had obtained about one thousand acres on the frontier in Albemarle County in 1755. Three years later, he purchased a more than two-thousand-acre tract in Louisa County near the parish of Fredericksville from James Power, paying him £625 for the property.[19]

Prominent planters of the Colony became petitioners seeking patents for large land areas across the Allegheny mountains. Before the middle of the century two enterprising companies engaged in fierce competition for claims to the western wilderness.

Thomas Lee, a noted name of the Northern Neck and father of six famous sons, organized the Ohio Company. Secretary Nelson was the second signer on the original petition applying first for two hundred thousand acres and then asking for three hundred thousand additional acres when conditions of the royal grant were fulfilled. The roster contained other Lees, as well as Council colleagues and Burgesses interested in the plan. Robert Carter, Gawin Corbin, George Fairfax, George Mason, George Mercer, James Mercer, John Mercer, John Tayloe, Francis Thornton, Lawrence Washington, and George Washington were patentees of the project.[20] Young Lieutenant Colonel Washington was sent by the organization to survey some of the vast stretches of territory and to consider the feasibility of ousting the French from the region. The gentlemen agreed to send one hundred families to settle on the land and to build a fort within seven years. Before the commission could be granted, Thomas Lee died in 1750. The company also had to contend with powerful competition, for Governor Gooch and the Council had also granted a charter to land speculators called the Loyal Company on July 12, 1749—the same time that the Ohio Company was issued its official charter. It was an odd coincidence that the contracts were signed the same day. Rivalry between the two companies for land claims on the frontier inevitably caused friction among the ruling clique of the Old Dominion. Two years later, the Ohio Company had an influential sponsor in Governor Robert Dinwiddie, who arrived in the autumn of 1751. When Dinwiddie demanded that a pistole fee be paid him for signing the documents, however, the Burgesses balked.[21]

Secretary Nelson and other petitioners of the Ohio grant withdrew from the organization to cast their lot with the Loyal Company. This enterprising project encompassed eight hundred thousand acres extending past the southwest section of Virginia into the Kentucky territory. Politically powerful John Robinson initiated the venture and interested several prominent Tidewater planters in the property. William Nelson became a stockholder in the scheme as did Colonel William Byrd. Colonel Joshua Fry, scholar, soldier, and surveyor, supported the undertaking. John Lewis, the Pages, Edmund Pendleton, Dr. Thomas Walker, and Thomas Jefferson's father, Peter Jefferson, also became shareholders in the huge operation.[22]

When Governor Fauquier came to the Colony in 1758, he favored the Loyal Company yet shunned land speculation since he had lost his entire estate in England one evening at the card table.[23]

Gambling also proved detrimental to George Mercer. When the Loyal Company sent the young man to London in 1763 to act as its agent, he became enamored with a young noblewoman and eloped with her. Lacking sufficient money to live lavishly, he gambled but lost more than he won and was imprisoned for debt.[24]

In 1763, William and Thomas Nelson, John Robinson, Robert Burwell, and George Washington with other ambitious investors applied to the Council for a patent to a large land area in Norfolk and Nansemond counties known as the Great Dismal Swamp.[25]

✦ ✦ ✦

When Tom talked with Lucy, he knew she would listen with comprehension, and her companionship made him realize that his wife was like the worthy woman of the Scriptures whose price was above rubies.[26] He could confide in her his impatience over tedious debates in the sessions or the tactics used by Indian chiefs in securing treaty terms, but he did not talk of money matters, because he couldn't really explain the mechanics of complicated credits and tardy collections.

Since Tom had been elected commander of the York County militia in the spring he was called "Colonel" Nelson. He was intensely interested in this new task and mustered the men regularly for drill. His brother Hugh, at thirteen, was not eligible to join, but with Robert and Nathaniel enjoyed watching.[27] When the citizen force formed on the Court House Green, a crowd quickly gathered. The gentlemen at Swan Tavern watched from the windows and thought William Nelson's boy did a creditable job with the drill. The sun highlighted his tawny hair and Tom grew accustomed to hearing youngsters call out "Carrot-top, Carrot-top!" as they pranced along imitating the marchers.

To escape the hot stillness of a summer night, Lucy and Tom would walk to the edge of the bluff at dusk as the gold roundness of the sun melted into pink ribbon splashes across the horizon. As Lucy grew heavy with child, she marveled with Tom at the miracles of nature and the omnipotence of the Lord recalling the passage: "In His hands are all the corners of the earth; and the strength of the hills is His also, the sea is His, and He made it; and His hands prepared the dry land."[28] As she viewed the sweeping vista, she thought truly God was mighty to call the earth from the rising sun and to gather the waters of the sea into a perfection of beauty. The rising moon cast a row of diamond dots on the river like scattered silver coins. Tree boughs bent with a gentle breeze and shadows stretched across the lawn from the tulip poplar trees creating a mosaic of jagged grays and greens. Above the sibilant sound of the chirping crickets, raucous laughter rang out from the taverns below the embankment. Sailors straggled along the beach ready to board ship.

Tom shared his reflections about the York River, with his wife, imagining aloud the parade of fleets that had sailed into the seaport. In the sixteenth century the conquistadores of Spain had glided smoothly into the harbor. Roanoke Colony emigrants had come up the inlet before settling along the sandy shore. The weary voyagers found their haven in the level land beyond the banks of the river, land entangled with cypress, evergreens, hickory, and pine. They were delighted with the ivory blossom of the dogwood and the rosey buds of trailing sweet myrtle.

Pirates' ships had sought escape in the estuary, their captains trading iron from Spain for the tobacco of Virginia, brushing aside impeding restrictions. For over two centuries, Yankee slavers had used the river. (Twenty Negroes had been sold at Jamestown in 1619, the slavery stranglehold was rooted to cast its shadow up to Appomattox.)[29]

On August 9, 1763, the Nelson household was astir; Lucy had embarked on a maternal voyage that would span almost a score of years and produce thirteen children.[30] As her lying-in began, the scurrying started, Sukey supervised the kitchen chores, baking cakes for the company that would be coming soon. Elizabeth Nelson sent her younger sons across the street. Though Frances Tucker Nelson was an old lady and need not look after Hugh, Robert, and Nathaniel at thirteen, eleven, and eight, they were not needed at home. Lewis, with his affliction, was always watched and three-year-old Billy must be kept in tow.

No doubt Lucy had stacks of child-bed linen and a layette of woolen bootees, cotton hose, diapers, long slips with lace inserts, dainty embroidered Irish linen dresses, and ruffled caps. Probably a quilted satin blanket lined the cradle.

Tom dispatched a message to his mother-in-law at Williamsburg. She could arrive in her carriage from the capital within two hours. Whether Lucy's first-born son was delivered by a doctor or the hovering midwife is not known, though the reputable Dr. George Riddell was residing at York Town and practiced physic and surgery. Midwives were united in their efforts to discredit doctors. These women deplored administrations by men in an "Art so eminently necessary to the Good of Mankind," and they clinched their arguments with the conclusion that "True Modesty is incompatible with the idea of employing a Man-Midwife." To them labor was the work of nature, and they stated that only male mid-wives would resort to force.[31]

The family smiled when Tom Nelson lifted his baby boy toward the window to see if the fringe of hair might be burnished like his. The new baby was heavier than his mother at birth, for she had been tiny enough to be placed in a quart pot![32]

The next day Lucy was propped against pillow bolsters in a new sprigged muslin gown to receive congratulations. Besides the Nelson clan, her mother, and three young sisters, the Norton neighbors, the Jameson, Lightfoot, Jerdone, and Digges families might drop in. They were plied with cakes and fruit shrub and on the next day attended the ceremony at York-Hampton Church, when Tom Nelson took his son to the church for his christening. According to family custom for the first grandson, the newborn was named William after his grandfather. Now there were three Williams in the household. With a proud, firm hand, Thomas Nelson duly noted the name and birth date in his family Bible.[33]

For Tom the year 1763 ended pleasantly, but the political skies were overcast with clouds of discontent.

In 1761, when Tom was still at school in England, he had heard of the writs King George III was enforcing in British America. Earlier laws had been passed by Parliament, but distance and indifference had made it difficult to clamp down on colonial shippers. Smuggling and bribing customs officials were commonly practiced. The Crown was now determined to stop these tricks. In reality, the Writs of Assistance were search warrants. James Otis of Massachusetts, urged by the Boston merchants, delivered an outspoken four-hour address in the State House against the writs declaring that Parliament had no power to pass the law, that when the King's men invaded a man's house, they violated the English tradition that "Every man's home is his castle." Though Otis lost the case, his repeated questioning started the men of Massachusetts thinking of independence.[34]

In December 1763, at Hanover Court House, Virginia, Patrick Henry questioned the right of Parliament to veto a law of the local Assembly.[35]

In lean tobacco years the House of Burgesses had passed a law declaring all debts payable in money at two pence a pound of tobacco. The clergy felt this was a blow, for instead of receiving their usual sixteen thousand pounds of tobacco annually, their salary would be about one third of the value in tobacco. The indignant ministers appealed to the Crown by sending the Reverend John Camm to England to intercede for them. The colonial law was discredited. Then the clergymen began to demand their back pay. Settling the arrearage of salary would be decided by a jury.[36]

Camm had attacked the Two-Penny Act through a pamphlet and championed the claims of the clergymen. People throughout the Colony read of the controversy as Colonel Richard Bland and Colonel Landon Carter filled newspaper columns with answers to Camm. The *Gazette* refused to publish the impassioned rejoiner of the parson.[37]

The Reverend James Maury of Hanover County sued for his salary of sixteen thousand pounds of tobacco, and the relatively unknown Patrick Henry became the spokesman against the clergy. The atmosphere was tense that December day when a large crowd assembled to hear the case. Colonel John Henry, Patrick's father, presided. At the suggestion of the young lawyer, his preacher uncle did not attend the proceedings. The angular young man rose to make his first great speech. It was faltering at first and hesitant, much to the chagrin of his parent, but then became forceful and positive as his voice rang out with indignation. His terse criticism of the ministers drove many clergymen from the courtroom; his vigorous denunciation of the King for disavowing a colonial law brought cries of "Treason!" from the conservative group, yet many gathered there were influenced by the orator's persuasion. In five minutes the jury decided to award the plaintiff only one penny for his back pay and the crowd shouted its approval of this defiance of royal authority.[38]

A routine test case had made history, and a young man had found his niche. A failure at business and farming, Henry would use his talents for the next dozen years as the "Tongue of the Revolution." Virginia had produced her eloquent trumpeter of independence.

Thus James Otis of Massachusetts challenged the power of Parliament to pass certain acts, and Patrick Henry of Virginia questioned the right of the royal government to veto a local law of the General Assembly.

◆　　◆　　◆

In addition to their avid interest in acquiring land, the Nelsons advocated advancement of the arts and the establishment of enterprises.

Although William Nelson, a merchant, imported articles from England to retail to the colonists, his philosophy was one of self-reliance. Tom also realized that dependence on the merchandise of the mother country defeated the development of manufacturing. He thought many worthwhile products could be made from the native raw materials.

Early expansionists had visualized thriving industries in the virgin land.[39] Since clothing was a necessary commodity, the raising of silkworms was advanced by the Assembly. In 1619, Assemblymen passed an act requiring colonists to plant one mulberry tree for every ten acres, but the changing of the caterpillar in its chrysalis state is a delicate process and many worms died. Although the survivors could have spun hundreds of feet of fiber, 1,600 worms were required to raise a pound of silk. Experienced dyers and weavers were imported from England to assist in this intricate industry, but disease and climate defeated the project.[40] Gnarled mulberry tree trunks still stand as testimony to the unsuitable undertaking.

The legislature had passed laws as well to stimulate the growing of flax. Two houses were constructed at Jamestown for the spinning wheels and two children were to come from each county to learn the art of twisting linen threads from the flax fiber. Every tithable person was to produce two pounds and public premiums would pay for every ell of the fine fabric. Even up to 1666 the Assembly was still trying artificial stimulation.[41]

Tobacco, however, became entrenched very early in the economy of the Colony when the founding fathers realized it was more profitable to produce the leaf and purchase the linen.[42] By the middle of the seventeenth century, tobacco had become so popular that according to one account, it had no peer as a panacea since it was "a bachelor's friend, a hungry man's food, a sad man's cordial, a wakeful man's sleep, and a chilly man's fire."[43]

A French traveler testified that tobacco smoking had become such a fad in England that the students took along their pipes to school and the master proceeded to show them the proper manner of puffing.[44]

The seventeenth century continued with its tribute to tobacco claiming that it "cureth griefs, fumes good against rumen, catarrh, hoarseness, ache in the head, stomach, lungs, and breast."[45]

The Englishmen found wild grapes growing in the New World and gave little attention to their cultivation. French wine experts brought in slips from Europe to plant vineyards in Virginia. As early as 1620 some economic isolationists encouraged the enterprise by expressing that no gold or silver coins should be conveyed from the Colony to purchase port or canary wine, however, lack of care for the vines, animals, blackrot, and mildew took their toll. Grape growing soon ceased.[46]

Virginia was a territory with valuable timber tracts. Although trees were still sawed by hand in England, sawmills were set up in the Colony by 1620 and experienced millwrights from Hamburg and two dozen carpenters from Holland were brought to the new land to launch the lumber enterprise.[47] To maintain supremacy of the seas, Britain needed naval stores of black tar pitch and gray potash ashes that could be produced from the Colony's conifer trees. The Nelsons and their partners in the Dismal Swamp scheme proposed tapping the trees to produce pitch and potash.

The problem of manufactured products had become more perplexing during the seven-year struggle of the French and Indian War when shipping was stymied. English goods had always been the epitome of elegance for well-to-do colonists, even when the same article might be obtained at home. The conflict stopped such imports.

For over half a century, aristocrats had enjoyed a lavish lifestyle emulating the English gentry on their estates. Each proprietor was ruler of his realm and had developed an independent and self-contained complex. Surrounding the mansion were different dependencies, and in these buildings the business of the plantation was performed. The owner and the overseer occupied offices often connected to the manor house by colonnades, as at Washington's Mount Vernon.

A large slave force tended the fields of tobacco and cereal crops raised for food. Some owners operated their own mills as the Nelsons did in York and Hanover counties. Big families and a large labor force consumed hundreds of pounds of flour and meal slowly ground by the grist mills. Some slaves became carpenters and coopers. A few were trained as tanners and shoemakers.

Household arts were handled by the women servants. Kitchens were removed from the main house because of fire hazard and uncomfortable heat. Even an adroit cook found baking, boiling, and roasting food a painstaking task in the open fireplace. Different dishes were prepared simultaneously by hanging the pots in the crane and trammel attachment. A wash house was provided on the premises. Spinning wheels and looms were set up in special places, the wool or flax from the distaff twisted into thread and later interwoven into fabric on the loom.

Foreigners visiting Virginia plantations thought of them as villages with their varied industries producing necessities for the household.

As the French and Indian War had worn on, the Assembly had once again attempted to spur production and passed "an Act For Encouraging Art and Manufactures" in 1759.[48] John Blair, William Nelson, and Thomas Nelson headed a committee to award twenty pounds to anybody who perfected an article that would be of service to the public. Evidently, this reward was not sufficient recompense to stimulate production so the next year it was increased to one hundred pounds. After 1760, the producer of the finest ten hogsheads of wine would receive five hundred pounds. Private pledges were to pay for the prizes. Following Governor Fauquier's contribution of ten pounds was the generous gift of five pounds William Nelson donated, and two others of the same amount from other sources. The Secretary put up four pounds for the project. One hundred subscribers sponsored the undertaking.[49]

Many factors discouraged the development of industries in the Colony. Tobacco still ranked first in the interest of Virginians and was too strong a rival for most other ventures. Because the plantation was a self-sufficient unit and the Colony had no cities, there was no home market for merchandise. The English economy was predicated on the mercantilist theory that a colony existed to enhance the mother country. Ingenuity and inventiveness by "the children" were discouraged. A monopoly market and a tight rein on trade through numerous navigation laws choked the commercial endeavors of the colonists.

CHAPTER FOUR

Past and Present, Petitions and Protests: 1764–1765

Old Traditions Treasured ✦ *New Spirit Stirring* ✦ *The Monarch and the Minister* ✦ *Remonstrances and Memorials* ✦ *Thomas Is Born* ✦ *Stormy Session in the House of Burgesses* ✦ *Money Matters* ✦ *Patrick Henry and the Stamp Act Resolutions* ✦ *Drought and Debts* ✦ *Mob Meets Mercer* ✦ *Stamps, Ships, and the Nelson Store*

Tom Nelson, as well as other Virginians, had an ambivalent attitude—a curious mixture of reverence and independence—toward the homeland, as British Americans still thought of England. They treasured the traditions of England; Governor Fauquier continued certain ceremonies, presiding over the Council in velvet and ermine looking as regal as any ruler.

When Fauquier entertained at the Palace, Tom and Lucy joined other colonial elite in a properly measured gavotte or minuet. No doubt the Governor concurred with the assessment of his predecessor, Governor Gooch, who had declared three decades before that "the gentlemen and ladies are perfectly well bred, not an ill dancer in my government."[1]

A new spirit, however, was stirring in the land. Tom sensed the self-sufficiency in the veterans of the French and Indian War and noticed a strong confidence among the York Town men in his own militia. Ambitious postwar planners had developed ideas, which, Tom reflected, had been evident at the establishment of the Colony.

As early as 1625, the Virginia Assembly had affirmed "That the Government shall not lay Taxes or Ymposition upon the Colony, their lands or commodities, other than by the authority of the General Assembly . . . levyed and ymployed as the said Assembly shall appoynt."[2]

In 1718, when "Scotch" Tom Nelson had been living at York Town less than a score of years, Virginians refused to pay a penny postage on letters from England, reaffirming their assertion that only their own Assembly had the authority to tax[3] and they were just as sure that freedom of trade was "the blood and life of a community."[4]

The Crown under James I and Charles I had recognized these rights. Charles I did not execute his tobacco monopoly and neither did Cromwell compel his Navigation Acts of 1651 prohibiting free trade, although these laws had been passed as a retaliation to the Virginians in their preference to the King over Parliament. In 1660, the cheers of the Cavaliers had rung out for the Restoration. From then on the name "Old Dominion" was given to the Colony, for when Charles II was in exile, only Virginia had remained faithful to the monarchy. His accession became an empty gain for them, though, as the old ordinances of shipping only in English vessels and trading with English merchants was re-established and enforced. Thus, double duties were paid on all exports at home and in England, and excise taxes were placed on all commodities exchanged with other countries. Like sheep quickly sheared of their wool, the Virginians found themselves stripped of foreign trade.[5]

A score of years before, Prime Minister Robert Walpole had declined to enact a doctrine of direct taxation. He tolerated goodnaturedly widespread smuggling in the colonies, for he knew that a high percentage of the colonists' products would always be sent to the mother country.[6]

Not so with George Grenville who succeeded him in 1763, the year that the French and Indian War ended. He would not coddle the colonists as the Crown and his predecessors had done for over a century. Britain's treasury was empty, her commercial equilibrium upset. Ten thousand troops remained in America after the war, and the national debt rose to £130,000,000 sterling. Being Chancellor and Treasurer of the Exchequer did not enlighten Grenville's political acumen; he repeated the old monopoly pattern, the shortsighted policy of obstructing free production.[7]

Probably neither Grenville nor Tom Nelson knew of the discerning observation that the Reverend Andrew Burnaby had made while traveling through the Colony in 1759 when he remarked:

> The public or political character of the Virginian corresponds with their private one: they are haughty and jealous of their liberties, impatient of restraint, and can scarcely bear the thought of being controlled by any superior person. Many of them consider the colonies as independent states not connected with Great Britain, otherwise than by having the same common king and being bound to her with natural affection.[8]

The postwar period was an unsettled time. Tobacco crops, the staple for currency, had been bad for seven years; adding to the discontent, the Crown had closed the frontier to further settlement thinking that would check border clashes.[9] Colonel Andrew Lewis led a volunteer force to western Virginia to dispel Pontiac's Indian conspiracy. Yet on June 4, 1765, the Assembly, probably under political pressure, offered a reward of one thousand pounds for the arrest of Lewis claiming that he had incited the conflict.[10]

Disappointed soldiers and homesteaders added to the unrest. Large land speculators were disturbed, and Tom listened as his father and uncle discussed their doubts over the imposed restraint. All men had anticipated land grants in the acquired territory as just prizes for their victory in the French and Indian War.

The monarch and the prime minister were in agreement in their foreign policies, yet could not foresee that their unpopular restrictions would pave the way for an American revolution as Parliament made a determined bid for the total trade of colonial merchants and shippers. New England traders decried the Sugar Act of 1764. Everyone suffered from the non-importation of salt. Still Britain was determined that goods must be bought from the homeland and all shipping cleared through British ports.

Grenville's most galling measure was the Stamp Act, which placed a direct tax on almost everything printed on paper, ranging from legal documents to playing cards. Silver coin might be required immediately. Collectors would be stationed throughout the colonies to sell the specially stamped paper.[11] Since the minister suspected that this bill would not be accepted passively, the assemblies were given an alternative of proposing a substitute law. Throughout 1764 colonial lawmakers could whip up no interest in this internal tax; the people distrusted it. Distrust developed into opposition when lawyers, editors, and landholders transferring property realized that although the tax affected everyone, it weighed most heavily on their dealings.

All duties affected the Nelsons except the tax on playing cards, as they did not indulge in this diversion. They would be hardest hit by the tax on land deeds. But the fact was that the Assembly was satisfied with the old requisition system, since its members considered a voted contribution was a gift granted to the home government, not a charge levied against them.

Many members besides Tom Nelson missed the January 1764 starting session of the Assembly. The Governor mentioned the inclement weather, and the absence of the irascible clergymen for the Burgesses had banned the preachers for their part in the Parsons' Cause.

Williamsburg was astir over taxes, troops, and the Stamp Act. Since the British government had also forbidden the colonists to use colonial currency for payment of debts after September 1, 1764, lawmakers Bland, Lee, Pendleton, and Randolph had prepared a report that boiled down to no more money, no more troops. Governor Fauquier thought his position was stronger on paper than in actual practice.[12]

William and Thomas Nelson were in Williamsburg January 18, 1765, as members of the important Committee of Correspondence, no doubt staying in the Francis Street house to avoid uncomfortable trips back and forth to York Town. Influential members from the Council and House of Burgesses serving with them included John Blair, Richard Bland, Lewis Burwell, Dudley Digges, Robert Carter Nicholas, Peter Randolph, Peyton Randolph, John Robinson, and George Wythe.[13]

The committee had already communicated with the colonial agent, Edward Montague in London, concerning the currency situation. On the twentieth and twenty-sixth of January 1764, the committee sent two letters to Montague detailing its thoughts on taxation, followed by others dated February 11 and March 10. The dates of the latter two letters would almost parallel significant communiqués of the succeeding year, for on February 17, 1765, George III would give his consent to the Stamp Act, and on March 10, Grenville would prevail on the House of Lords to approve it unanimously. There would be one dissenting vote in the House of Commons. (Later, it would be discovered that members had given little thought to its purpose and import.) During the discussion George III would succumb to another derangement. English lawmakers hadn't really listened to the colonists' protests or studied the communications from Virginia. Nelson's committee was more particular in its proceedings, even instructing Montague to address his communications to Chairman William Nelson, but not as a member of the committee as some curious persons might be tempted to confiscate the correspondence.[14]

For the Virginians, the year 1765 might be known as the one of remonstrances and memorials, petitions and protests. Ships leaving York Town port always carried condemning messages to colonial agents abroad sometimes threefold, for William Nelson believed in sending his communiqués in three different ships to insure that at least one reached its destination.[15]

From January to July 1765, the Nelsons spent much time in Williamsburg and Tom joined the group. He agreed with the concepts that free born subjects still had affection for the mother country, but Virginians simply wanted their just liberties and privileges. Tom would also approve of the June 15 missive when the committee gave specific instructions to Mr. Montague to "oppose with all his influence, and as far as he may venture insist on the Injustice of laying any Duties on us and particularly taxing internal Trade of the colonies without their consent."[16]

About this time the agent's April 11 communication arrived that gave "fresh apprehension of fatal consequences that may arise to posterity." Mutterings of discontent spread like a swollen stream from a raging storm. Did Parliament recognize the difference between "power and right"?[17]

✦　　✦　　✦

During the summer the Nelsons were saddened that their Norton neighbors were leaving York Town to live in London. Although both Courtenay and John Norton regretted their departure from kith and kin, their expanding business required the move; a sign to show that expansion (John Norton & Sons, Merchants of London and Virginia) would soon be proudly posted.[18]

Tom recognized all the well wishers at the wharf. In the group were the Burwells and Digges, Jamesons and Reynolds. Chatty Martha Goosley was there with one of her medicinal potions. In the center of the crowd the Nortons accepted gifts and letters to carry abroad the *Hatley* for delivery to English families and friends.

Almost before John Norton had settled his family in London's fine Gould's Square, a letter from John Baylor, his brother-in-law, explained Baylor's financial plight and then, commented on the economic pinch:

> Poor Virginia what art thou reduced to, held in scorn and derision by the merchants of Great Britain & torn to pieces by theirs & our Country law suits.[19]

On July 28, 1764, William and Thomas Nelson forwarded another communication to Mr. Montague:

> The proposal to lay a Stamp Duty upon Paper & Lether is truly alarming; Should it take place the immed. Effects of an additional burthen imposed upon a people already laden with Debts contracted chiefly in Defence of the Common Cause . . . will be severely felt by our Children.[20]

Their real resentment, however, stemmed from the ministry's failure to recognize both colonial service in the war and the domestic difficulties that resulted from their participation.

Autumn slipped into winter, but its cool winds did not calm the colonials' fiery feelings. The Assembly passed resolutions at the November 14 meeting to send three forceful remonstrances: one to the King, one to the House of Lords, a third to the House of Commons. Just before Christmas, the special committee climaxed its labors with one final appeal instructing Montague to place it before the King and Parliament and have it published in the newspapers so the people of England would know of colonial problems.[21]

Richard Henry Lee, realizing his lack of foresight when he had asked for the post of tax collector, withdrew and turned his talents to voicing objections to the hated stamps.[22]

Thus the year closed and the evaluation that the Reverend Mr. Burnaby had made of the Virginians seemed true indeed, for they were still "jealous of their liberties & consider (themselves) as independent states."[23]

As Tom rode along the familiar route to York Town, the road was ridged with ruts caused by autumn rains. On these dark December days all color seemed drained away. Even the York River glided along in a cold gray lethargy. Reaching town, he could see smoke curling from the sturdy brick chimney of his home. Soon, he was seated with Lucy and young William in front of a crackling fire, ready to enjoy a hot drink, home-baked bread, and rich roast beef.

The year 1764 ended happily for the Thomas Nelson, Jr., family. A second child made his entry into the world just two days after Christmas. As was the custom, the first boy had been named William for his grandfather. Following family procedure, the second lad was called Thomas for his father.[24]

On Wednesday, May 1, 1765, the *Journal of the House of Burgesses* opened with the mild order that the "Chaplain of the House resolves to attend to read Prayers every morning at nine o'clock."[25] From this simple pronouncement, Tom supposed that the regular procedures of the Burgesses would progress at the usual pace, principally concerned with the revision of the tobacco law. The warm winds of spring made him hope the representatives could discharge their duties directly so that they could spend time out of doors. The Nelsons often joined their colleagues on the Capitol lawn. These planters presented a kaleidoscope of color from their shiny shoe buckles to the tops of their powdered wigs. Some wore glossy gray, while others chose blue, brown, bottle green, or black broadcloth. Representatives from the Piedmont were recognized by less elaborate garments of homespun unbleached shirts and leather knee breeches above coarse hose. There was a difference between the rustic inland Cohees and the aristocratic Tuckahoes of the Tidewater lowlands.[26]

Tobacco talk dominated their discourse. British merchants were paying only about one-fourth remittances for the product compared to previous years. The price had dropped to an all-time low of eighteen shillings per pound.[27]

Planters continued to spend in spite of their debts, ordering fine furnishings, elegant china, silk fabrics, and sweet wines. Even George Washington was typical in this behavior. Although he owed Cary & Company a large bill, he was astounded when Cary wrote that Washington should reduce the obligation and pay interest on the debt.[28] William Byrd, III, was not the only gentleman planter who gambled in grand style. All the plantation operators counted on crops that might not materialize; not only the squanderers but also the savers were squeezed in the situation. Relatives of the Nelsons were so involved with indebtedness that their bills were protested. Lewis Burwell had a fifty-pound bill refused as was Benjamin Grymes's for ten pounds.[29]

Wealthy Richard Corbin, receiver general of the Colony and in the best position to know, felt that "General circumstances of Virginia were such that no man's promise of payment could be depended upon and that there was no knowing who to trust."[30]

Of the five standing committees in the House of Burgesses, one of the most influential was that of the Committee of Propositions and Grievances.[31] Tom had been elected a member in October 1764. Peyton Randolph, trained in the law, was chairman. No matter how capable and conscientious Tom might be, no doubt his appointment came through family connections. His father and uncle were members of the influential Council; Peyton Randolph was a cousin and Lucy's uncle. No young man had a firmer base for political progress.[32]

Since this committee handled all general civic cases, its agenda was usually crowded. As bills were always read twice, Tom was learning patience in the art of listening. He noticed that his Carter cousins showed more restiveness at the long list than his thirty-three-year-old kinsman, George Washington, who had been a member of the committee since 1759. He gave equal attention to the necessary but tedious matters of establishing ferries and clearing roads as he did to the complaints of the merchants or the prevention of "raising and suffering hogs to run at large in Richmond."[33]

Tom sympathized with the petitions of Peter Pelham, Lucy's former musical instructor, who stated that the church organ was "much out of Order almost unfit for Use with great labor and expense repaired, and tuned same." Eventually Mr. Pelham was reimbursed for his time and toil.[34]

Since young Tom Nelson was no prophet, he could not predict the significance of the stormy session that was to ensue. A champion of causes would soon appear in the Assembly who would shake the stronghold of conservative oligarchy and upset the urbane Fauquier with forensics.

Nor could Tom foresee that this gathering was a galaxy of greats. To him, at twenty-six, the youngest of the group, these fellows were just family and friends, dependable men dedicated to their duties. Only in retrospect would he and others realize this May meeting was the prelude for those who would break the bonds with Britain ten years later. Fate would thrust the torch of liberty into their hands.

Conservative Peyton Randolph, conciliatory to the Crown, would change his convictions and become the first president of the Continental Congress.[35] George Wythe and Tom's moderate cousins, Benjamin Harrison and Carter Braxton, staunch advocates of the aristocracy, would all later align themselves with the cause of the American Revolution. Persuasive Richard Henry Lee and his brother Francis Lightfoot Lee had strong feelings from the beginning and would join forces with the young red-haired Thomas Jefferson who had left his college classroom to visit the Assembly. Jefferson would one day capture on vellum their broadening belief in human rights and declare decisively their reasons for political independence.

Tom's English education had lessened rather than strengthened his ideas about royal prerogatives. By background he was an aristocrat. Family and fortune had placed him at the top rung of the social and political ladder, but liberty inflamed his heart with an idealistic dream. To triumph over tyranny, he would renounce security, spend his funds, and shatter his strength in the struggle. At the end of the Revolution, Thomas Nelson, Jr., would have a new freedom but less material fortune, more criticism and more creditors for his courage, as well as impaired health; he would leave, however, a heritage of illustrious heroism and honor for his descendants.

◆　　◆　　◆

A lone horseman from Hanover County rode into Williamsburg on his bay Shandy in May 1765. Patrick Henry was a new member of the House of Burgesses elected by the residents of Louisa County to be their representative although he owned no property there.[36] Many folk along Duke of Gloucester Street recognized the fledgling lawmaker whose fame had spread since his scathing attack on the clergymen in the Parsons' Cause tried in Hanover County just eighteen months earlier. The name of Patrick Henry was still anathema to many ministers, but others praised him for taking a stand against the ministry. Most people stared at the slightly stooped posture of this recruit and thought he looked older than his nearly twenty-nine years. Though an indifferent storekeeper, he had the reputation of being a spell-binding storyteller. He also had self-confidence since he was trying cases after reading law for only six weeks.

Tom Nelson noticed their stares as Henry took his place among the peers on Thursday, May 24, 1765.[37] George Wythe, an able attorney, had dismissed Henry's petition to practice at first but later signed it. Robert Carter Nicholas looked kindly toward the newcomer; he had signed the certificate after advising Henry to continue reading law. Peyton Randolph and Edmund Pendleton peered at him obliquely; both Burgesses were forty-eight years old, serious and stable. Peyton and his brother John had affixed their signatures to Henry's petition but doubted his ability. Richard Bland gave him a more sympathetic glance. Many associates in the Assembly might look askance at him, for his homespun suit contrasted sharply with the silks and satins of the blue-blooded Burgesses. It soon became apparent that there were other differences.

As Tom looked at the long-faced lawyer, he recalled that the Nelsons, the Burwells and the Carters, Robert Carter Nicholas, the Randolphs, and other devoted members of the Established Church, had discussed Henry's impassioned defense of an itinerant Baptist minister who would not apply for a license to preach. Attorney General Peyton Randolph had declared that the British Toleration Act, which permitted dissenters to preach, was void in Virginia.[38] Henry's indignant defense of the preachers of dissenting congregations and his defiance of the clergy of the Established Church had naturally disconcerted this cohesive elite. Some suspected Henry's own religious convictions were not very deep.

But the Burgesses had more on their minds than Patrick Henry. All wanted to increase their incomes. William Nelson advocated converting some tobacco land to corn and wheat. Robert Beverley of Blandfield was cultivating hemp. Washington had planted some wheat and, in the first days of May before he left to attend the Assembly, his hands had sowed hemp, oats, and lucerne. Most growers, however, continued with the one-crop system, and the one-market plan imposed by England was choking the Colony's commerce.[39]

Tom assumed that the Assemblymen were acquainted with the account presently published in the newspaper of the seventeenth proposing that Virginians obtain loans in England to ease their economic obligations. Though immature in financial matters, he thought how curious it was to expect Englishmen to issue funds to people who could not pay their English debts. Though Tom's father was caught in the controversy, William Nelson did not approve of the advances. He desired a stable system based on hard coin and felt people should practice frugality.

In these opinions he took an opposite stand from his old friend Speaker John Robinson and his protegé Pendleton, for they were the leaders in favor of paper money.[40] From this large loan, funds would be lent to the landowners on the security of their property. John Robinson, sixty, who already had served as Speaker for thirty years, had instigated the idea.[41] As Treasurer, too, he was a mainstay of power politics. Surreptitiously, for several months he had been supplying specie to the hard-pressed planters through the treasury notes received for taxes; he had not burned the old bills. People had talked. In December 1764, Richard Henry Lee, overriding opposition, had insisted on an investigation. Edmund Pendleton was appointed chairman of a committee to check into the matter and Richard Bland, Lewis Burwell, Archibald Cary, Dudley Digges, Benjamin Harrison, Richard Henry Lee, and John Page served with him.[42]

Speaker Robinson resented the situation. No figurehead, he was highly respected for his ability and attention to duty. He studied the bills and resolutions, reducing them to understandable terms for the representatives. Mindful of the gentlemen who had been recipients of his generosity, he was confident of their loyal support. He was right; no irregularities were reported.[43]

Six months later, Tom's uncles, Secretary Nelson and Robert Burwell of the Council, also reported that the accounts had been examined and "found truly stated."[44]

The bluish-gray eyes of Patrick Henry surveyed the impressive scene of the House of Burgesses when he entered. A Britisher might feel that he was in his own House of Commons, for the colonists of Virginia had emulated their English counterparts in the appointments of the chamber.

At one end of the room Speaker John Robinson sat in his chair on a dais surmounted with a canopy drawn over a gilded rod. While the Speaker was in his chair, no member was to chew tobacco. Clerk John Randolph glanced at the heavy mace, symbol of authority, that lay on the long oval table covered with a rich green cloth. The Burgesses sat on long, straight benches facing one another from both sides of the House. Despite the impressive room with its complement of Assemblymen or the fact that he had just arrived, Patrick Henry arose to speak. He suspected the loan plan Robinson favored was a dodge for the debt-ridden planters, and he reduced the resolves to simple terms that back countrymen could comprehend. Scornfully he questioned, "What, sir, is it proposed then to reclaim the spendthrift from his dissipation and extravagance, by filling his pockets with money?"[45] This outcry enraged the obligarchy. Who was Henry to threaten the Tidewater patricians? John Robinson and Peyton Randolph, recognized leaders, were startled and shocked. Pendleton stared unbelievingly at the bold Burgess who dared challenge the old guard.

Since the leaders had already lined up the votes, the House passed the resolution; but before sending it to the Council for approval, a special conference committee was appointed. Tom knew this was an unusual occurrence. When Peyton Randolph returned from the upper chamber, he made an effort to control his expression as he announced that the Council had taken no action and had returned the resolution. This procedure was rare.[46]

By May 26, 1765, most of the members of the House of Burgesses had left Williamsburg in carriages raising clouds of dust along Duke of Gloucester Street or on horseback. A roll call count revealed only 39 out of 116 elected legislators remained; however, if Tom Nelson had assumed the rest of the session would be uneventful, he would have been mistaken.[47]

When a copy of the Stamp Act Resolutions arrived, a bomb had been handed the Burgesses. Grenville's program had grown more unpopular day by day. Correspondence up and down the Atlantic coast divulged a concerted grumbling of the colonists against forced contributions. The document disclosed fifty-five detailed demands listing a direct tax on claims, deeds, contracts, declarations, grants, licenses, mortgages, pleas, surveys, and wills costing a few shillings; almanacs, calendars, pamphlets, and papers would require a charge from one-half penny to two shillings. For the privilege of selling spirits, the retailer must pay twenty shillings to four pounds for a license; a college graduate would be charged one pound for his diploma. In short, "for every skin or piece of vellum or parchment, or sheet of paper, on which shall be engrossed, written, or printed," charges were laid, and sometimes the stamped paper required hard coin on the spot.[48] Since sterling was scarce in the Colony, this severe stipulation promised to work a hardship on many citizens.

Speaker Robinson relinquished the chair to head the officials convening into a committee as a whole.[49] All thirty-nine Assemblymen were alert as Patrick Henry stood to speak again just five days after his scornful statements on the loan scheme. He read his resolves from the flyleaf of an old law book where he had written them without advice from anyone.[50]

The first and second resolutions restated the privileges of free born subjects. In the third resolve, Henry spoke of a people's taxing themselves. Tom, as well as the other members, knew these sentiments were substantially the same statements lawyers had prepared in previous remonstrances and petitions, but on his fourth resolution the orator raised his voice to attack the authority of the Crown. Counselors who understood the British Constitution, and they thought Henry did not, shook their heads in disapproval, as Henry said, "A King by disallowing acts of so salutary a nature, from being the father of his people has degenerated into a Tyrant, and forfeits all rights to his subjects' obedience."[51]

Henry's flexible voice rose to a climactic crescendo on his fifth point:

> Resolved—therefore, that the General Assembly of this Colony have the only and exclusive right and Power to lay Taxes and Impositions upon the Inhabitants of this Colony, and that every Attempt to rest Power in any Person or Persons, whatsoever, other than the General Assembly aforesaid has a manifest tendency to destroy British as well as American freedom.[52]

Before Henry was seated, the older leaders leaped to their feet. Tom was amazed at the confusion these conservatives created, but he noticed that his younger associates were impressed by Henry's short, simple statements and delivery. Probably, they felt just as relieved as he to be spared the prolonged speeches studded with classical quotations that they sometimes endured. Henry's straightforward statements also stirred a young student standing in the doorway. Tom Jefferson might forget the classes he had cut at the College that day,[53] but he would always remember the ringing words of Patrick Henry.

The old-line legislators moved to consider the sections separately. Though the first three resolutions were a paraphrase of the same principles formerly expressed, they passed by only a slender majority. The old guard gathered its forces to fight the fourth and fifth resolutions.[54] Robinson thought them inflammatory. Richard Bland, though not graceful in debate, was tenacious in argument. Conscientious Robert Carter Nicholas spoke as did Peyton Randolph whose prestige was at its peak. Attorney George Wythe acutely analyzed the points. Henry's inexperience was no match for their capabilities and comprehensions of English constitutional law; but, incited by their censure, he was inflamed with eloquence to exclaim, "Caesar had his Brutus, Charles the First his Cromwell, and George the Third. . . ." "Treason!"[55] shouted the indignant Speaker Robinson, surprised that the members seemed so mesmerized they hadn't stopped the speech. Henry, of course, neatly making use of the interruption concluded that George III and those present might profit from history's lessons. The old guard arose to abolish the fifth resolution, but their nineteen votes against the measure were surpassed by Henry's supporters who tallied twenty ayes.[56] Governor Fauquier, as shocked as the conservative faction, wrote the Lord of Trade that the advocates of authority had been overpowered by "young and giddy members."[57]

Peyton Randolph lost his aplomb and rushed past young Tom Jefferson in a rage uttering, "By God, I would have given 500 guineas for a single vote."[58]

Young Tom Nelson had thrown his support with the "young and giddy members" who shocked the Governor.[59]

Four days later, Patrick Henry was riding back to Hanover County. With many other lawmakers already at home, Randolph and the old-line leaders tried to expunge the resolutions, but the supporters held firm, and the first four measures passed. The controversial fifth was erased from the record.[60]

Royalist Joseph Royle, editor of the *Virginia Gazette*, was as astounded over the resolutions as the aristocrats, so he did not print them in his paper; however, other editors throughout the colonies, either lacking in such loyalty or believing more in a free press, published them all. The resolves spread up and down the Atlantic seaboard like the waves that sweep its shores.

Richard Corbin's statements reflected many other opinions that appeared continually in newspapers and conversations, "The opposition to the Stamp Act is not the least abated, the infatuation is spread quite through the Continent, and the people seem ripe for mischief."[61]

A disastrous summer drought caused crop failures intensifying the planters' aggravations.

Resistance to the stamps ripened. Customers told the Nelsons they must curtail their orders. As proprietor of the Swan Tavern, Tom had to pay four pounds for his license to sell wine. Travelers stopping at the inn told of the rumors that men in the upper regions were ready to march on Williamsburg to seize the stamps. Some disgruntled gentlemen united in groups and called themselves "Sons of Liberty." William Nelson, writing to his commercial associates in Britain, predicted a revolt.

America had its defenders abroad where Benjamin Franklin appeared before Parliament.[62] In its April 11, 1766, issue the *Virginia Gazette* attested that "the assiduity of Dr. Franklin, in assisting to obtain a repeal of the Stamp Act, is really astonishing. He is forever with one member of Parliament or another."[63]

Capel Hansbury, with whom the Nelsons traded, explained the economic hazards to the English officials and was adamant in his arguments regarding repeal.[64] As British manufacturers began to feel the effects of Americans' refusal to order articles, the colonists read this announcement about the stalemate: "We are told that one considerable stocking manufacturer near the city has discharged no less than 40 workmen within these few days."[65]

Merchants wrote Parliament about the unemployment problem and Virginia's tobacco planters read the news: "Petitions have been presented from the principal merchants, & c. of Bristol, York, Liverpool, and other trading places, complaining of the hardships they labour under by the great decay of trade to the American colonies."[66]

George Mercer in London had also testified before Parliament that the duty demanded by the stamps would ruin commerce and work an imposition on the poor.[67] This disillusioned young man left England but, ironically, had to bring a considerable supply of the detested stamps for Virginia, North Carolina, and Maryland. He had been adrift in Britain since 1763 hoping for an official position and Grenville, seizing the opportunity, offered Mercer the post of distributor of stamps. When Mercer became acquainted with the Virginia Resolves, his aversion to the appointment increased.[68]

By September 14, the Nelsons were back in Williamsburg to meet again with the Committee of Correspondence. These gentlemen were greatly distressed over the Stamp Act situation and also over a "spurious Copy of the Resolves . . . being dispersed and printed in the newspapers . . ." so they sent their agent, Mr. Montague, "a true copy of votes on the occasion."[69]

Mercer arrived at York Town on October 30.[70] Whether he was warned to leave the stamps aboard the vessel or caution prompted him, Colonel Mercer made a discreet decision and persuaded Captain Stirling of the *Rainbow* to store the stamps on the British warship for safety.

On the two-hour trip from York Town to Williamsburg, Mercer's preoccupation with his problem made him oblivious to the cool autumn air and the changing colors of the seasons. Almost before Mercer could greet his father and brother, John and James, news spread of his arrival and a hostile group began to gather. If the young man had read the October 25 issue of the *Virginia Gazette*, his uneasiness would have increased. Joseph Royle had devoted his front page to the Boston riots. There, in the sweltering heat of August, an uncontrollable mob of thousands had expressed their vengeance, looting and plundering property. Hanging the stamp collector in effigy was a mild caper compared to demolishing Governor Hutchinson's house.

Virginians shuddered to read of such destruction. Indignant men of the Northern Neck, however, egged on by Richard Henry Lee (the Mercers were already planning revenge) had burned Colonel Mercer's image in effigy.[71]

Mercer had descended from hero to heel. As soon as he stepped out on the street, an angry crowd converged on him in front of the Capitol demanding to know if he would distribute the stamps or resign. Cool under fire in the French and Indian War, Mercer assumed control although calmly replying that he needed time to think and would answer their questions at ten o'clock Friday morning—two days hence. "Too late," and "Tomorrow" were the loud rejoiners. The men muttered discontentedly and seemed ready to grab the offender.

Governor Fauquier's summation later stated, "The vast concourse I should call a mob, did I not know it was chiefly, if not altogether composed of gentlemen of property, some of them at the head of their respective counties."[72]

When Colonel Mercer reached Mrs. Campbell's tavern, he must have been relieved to see the Governor seated on the porch surrounded by the

Council, old John Blair, William Nelson, Secretary Thomas Nelson, and the other symbols of authority. Speaker Robinson of the Burgesses stood firmly against the seething crowd. As the men rushed forward, all the Councilors rose; the men hesitated on the steps, but they did not disperse. Negotiations ensued. Mercer decided to give an answer the next afternoon at five o'clock, yet the throng still tarried. Maintaining their confident mien, Governor Fauquier and Mercer walked through the multitude toward the Palace; no one molested them. Within the protection of the Palace, Fauquier and Mercer, with his brother and father, both attorneys, discussed the legal aspects. Deep shadows enveloped the capital, but one flickering lamp burned far into the night. Colonel Mercer was composing a statement to clarify his position.

On Thursday, October 31, long before the appointed five o'clock, an even larger crowd than the one that had accosted Mercer the day before assembled in the Capitol area. Tom Nelson saw many unknown faces as well as familiar ones. The Governor had remarked it was unfortunate for Mercer to come "at a time the town was fullest of strangers."[73]

George Mercer read his carefully worded statement explaining why he had accepted the commission, candidly admitting that he had heard of the Virginia Resolves against the Stamp Act but not from an authoritative source. Since he now understood that his countrymen found the act disagreeable, he would do nothing until further orders from England. The tide turned. Mercer had taken his stand. Men who had maligned him forty-eight hours before now hoisted him on their shoulders and carried him to the coffee house for food and drink.

Governor Fauquier was still distressed over "the present unhappy state of the Colony," believing that business and shipping would be at a stalemate, and courts closed. The executive expressed his concern to the Board of Trade:

> I must confess that I have never in the course of my life been in a situation which required so much circumspection. . . . if the first Gentlemen of the country refuse to act (as justices) become a fashion for others to follow their example.[74]

◆　　◆　　◆

Back in York Town, Tom dreaded to think that vessels would be stalled at the pier. He had always enjoyed watching a ship from its first appearance on the distant horizon until its arrival in port. Tom could call many captains by name and connect these matters with their craft. He smiled to recall that at the age of thirteen he had eagerly checked the columns of the *Gazette* to note *Nelson* and then had read to his father: 3 July 1752—entered York River—the *Nelson*; 7 August 1752—*Nelson* cleared toward Whitehaven; 3 November 1752—*Nelson* safe in arrival in London.[75]

In addition to the *Nelson*, his father owned half interest in the *Madeira Packet* with Edward and Samuel Athawes of London, an arrangement that displeased him. He wrote the Athawes September 13, 1766, "But why am I kept in the dark about the profit or loss of the *Madeira Packet?* I am quite tired of her; I fear I shall pay £200 a year by my loss while the captain I intend to serve gets only about £100. I wish she were sold."[76] He was considering buying an interest in the *Czar of Muscovy* that had a 600-hogshead capacity.

Tom had always followed with interest Captain Hamlyn's *Nancy* and Captain Hamilton's *Molly*, a sturdy ship that carried the Nelson tobacco to London for several reasons. Tom had often watched Captain Hubbard's *Elizabeth* and Captain Anderson's *Rachel* and *Mary* maneuvered into dock. All the Nelsons felt especial closeness to the Norton commercial company because they were allied by family as well as business. One of their ships, the *Hatley*, a family appellation, was later listed as the *Virginia*.[77]

Aside from his own pleasure in observing the ships, Tom knew Lucy and others would be deprived of laces and cambrick lawn. His mother wanted some India-worked muslin and had already mentioned needing some spectacles since she was forty-seven years old. His father would miss the London *Magazine* and was still waiting for Blackstone's *Laws* to arrive. Mr. Nelson always gave detailed instructions about the garden seeds he ordered annually and once had to remind the shipper that the carrot and parsnip seeds had been omitted from his order.

When the Stamp Act was really enforced, Tom could imagine how bare the shelves in his store would be—stripped of finer fabrics, exquisite china and decanters, beaver hats, and calf shoes. Yet Tom had to agree with his father and said, "Why import Goods wch the people are willing to buy but unable to pay for. Necessity and some Resentment for cruel Impositions and clogs on our Trade oblige people of all Ranks to less their Expenses."[78]

CHAPTER FIVE

Discord, Deaths, and Defection; Repeal, Relief, and Rejoicing: 1766

Townspeople and Tom at Swan Tavern ✦ *Philip Born* ✦ *Family Deaths* ✦ *New Home* ✦ *Repeal of Stamp Act* ✦ *Robinson Defection* ✦ *Crime and Culture in the Capital* ✦ *Colonel Chiswell Kills Routledge* ✦ *Elite Entertainments at the Palace* ✦ *Recreation and Racing*

It seemed to Tom that more men were dropping into the Swan Tavern during the chilling days of January and February in 1766. Tom's brother Hugh had turned sixteen and the Secretary's teenaged sons, William and Thomas, gathered with the older Nelsons as well as neighbors Jacquelin Ambler, Dudley Digges, and David Jameson. Clerk of York County Thomas Everard was concerned over the use of stamps pertaining to court proceedings. The gentlemen's conversations ran the gamut of grievances from the stamp situation to too much rain following a prolonged drought that had ruined tobacco and other crops.

Though Edmund Pendleton continued to preside over his court in Caroline County, the prediction of Governor Fauquier that courts would close had come to pass. The General, Oyer and Terminer as well as the county courts were at a standstill.

> Court was held October 2, 1765, and did much business. The Stamp Act went into effect November 1, 1765. After that the court met January 31, 1766. Laid the levy but did no other business.[1]

Despite the discord of the days, Tom had reason to rejoice, for on March 14, Lucy presented him with their third son whom they named Philip after her deceased father. Fortunately, a sufficient number of servants in the Nelson household helped Lucy with the three toddlers.[2] Jacquelin and Rebecca Ambler had a baby daughter, Mary Willis, a few days after Philip. Their daughter would eventually capture the heart of John Marshall.[3]

Domestic content was almost set aside, however, when both men heard that Archibald Ritchie, a Scottish shipowner and merchant of Hobbs Hole, on Northern Neck, announced he would defy the ban and send out his ships of wheat with the correctly stamped certificates. The news spread rapidly among the planters along the Rappahannock River; they feared if one merchant submitted to the Stamp Act, they would all be forced to succumb. Forgetting that Ritchie was a respected justice and vestryman, the planters viewed him only as a violator of the principle that they had a right to tax themselves.[4]

The Nelsons were not surprised to learn that the Lees were leading angry patriots in their protest to Ritchie. (Lucy was related to the Lee family through her Ludwell kin and Randolph relatives, and her second cousin, also named Lucy Grymes, had married Henry Lee, II.) Thomas Ludwell Lee notified his brother, Richard Henry Lee, that an armed group would gather at Leedstown on February 27, suggesting that his brother consider a plan of action. Richard Henry had already incited the region's planters against the Stamp Act. He was ready for the Leedstown rally and wrote six resolves which protestors adopted.[5] His resolutions reiterated that persons could be taxed only by their direct representatives; that people must have the privilege of trial by their peers. The group strongly affirmed:

> We do determine at every hazard and paying no Regard to Danger or Death, we will exert every Facility to prevent the Execution of the Said Stamp Act in any Instance whatever within this Colony—and every abandon' Wretch . . . so lost to the public good . . . by using Stampt Paper, we will with the utmost Expedition convince all such Profligates that immediate danger and disgrace shall attend their prostitute Purpose.[6]

A committee called on Ritchie demanding that he not send out his ship with the stamped paper. The Sons of Liberty threatened that if the merchant refused to comply he would be seized and "stripped naked to the waist, tied to the tail of a cart, and drawn to the public pillory, where he would be fixed for an hour."[7] Ritchie stared at the stern faces of four hundred Virginians who had turned Hobbs Hole into a hotbed of rebellion. He signed the statement.

The newspaper reported that Norfolk's Sons of Liberty had expressed gratitude to Lucy's relative, Richard Bland, for his treatise on "An Inquiry into the Rights of the British Colonies." On Monday, March 31, at a meeting these indignant men "desirous [that their] sentiments [be] known for posterity . . . openly expres[ed] detestation of the said act, which is pregnant with ruin. . . . Anyone using directly or indirectly within the colony the detestable papers called stamps was deemed an enemy of the country and would be treated accordingly."[8]

Tom often read the counsel of "Honest Buckskin" in the *Gazette* and agreed with his comments that if the colonists would "suffer your private

The Nelson house at Yorktown, Virginia, still standing, was built in the early eighteenth century. Courtesy of Colonial Williamsburg Foundation.

purses, paltry pique, rash resentments or the supercilious sallies of genius to stir up contention among you, your situation as to liberty will then be weak and tottering."[9] The young York Town citizen was overjoyed to realize that colonists up and down the coast were pulling together to resist the Stamp Act.

Despite Prime Minister Grenville's defense of the stamps and his denunciation of the Americans, William Pitt of the House of Commons, though crippled with gout and on crutches, proclaimed in Parliament that he thought the *"tax illegal, unjust, unfair, and impossible."*[10]

Tom read in the March 21, 1766, issue of the Purdie-Dixon *Virginia Gazette*, "Friday the House of Peers sat until ten near night, and the Commons until eleven." British correspondents communicated their impressions of the events, "There is at present a total stagnation in shipping goods to any part of the American colonies, during the investigation of the Stamp Act, which makes all kinds of business dead upon the public quays."[11]

Another writer observed, "For of late there has been a total stagnation of all business; thousands of poor manufacturers at Birmingham, Sheffield, Yorkshire, & c have been turned off, and are now starving for want of employ; and what the consequences will be, unless the Stamp Act is repealed, God only knows."[12]

With his business acumen, William Nelson must have been astonished to read, "An estimate of the value of stamp papers lately destroyed by the

72

populace of North America is preparing to be laid before an August Assembly: the loss is computed to exceed £40,000."[13]

Notwithstanding all this alarming news, Tom was optimistic over the outcome of the controversy. On April 26, Tom and other colonists read the climactic announcement in the *Virginia Gazette:* "Last night our great Assembly voted for the repeal of the Stamp Act. They did not break up until three this morning."[14] The customers at the Swan Tavern now hoisted their tankards with toasts to the cheerful news.

On May 2, the Nelsons and other York Town folk watched the *Lady Baltimore* sail into the river seaport carrying confirmation that the Stamp Act had been repealed. A rider conveyed the joyful news to Williamsburg in well under two hours. The *Virginia Gazette* contained a report on the front page that same day:

> Great and glorious news to America and comfortable news to the printer of the Virginia Gazette. In the Lady Baltimore, Captain Mitchell, arrived in York River from London, who brings certain account of the repeal of the abhorred Stamp Act. Publication of our paper, upon this account will be later than usual, but the occasion ought, we are almost sure will plead our excuse.[15]

When John Robinson died on May 11, just nine days after the repeal of the Stamp Act, rumors that the Treasurer's records were erroneous became a reality.[16] Patrick Henry and the men of the mountains had mistrusted the motives of Robinson and his friends in the loan scheme the year before. Richard Henry Lee had insisted on an investigation in 1764, but it had become a mockery and thus made Lee seem a meddlesome busybody.[17] Tradespeople had gossiped that the accounts were inaccurate. Not only had the hard-pressed planters importuned the tender-hearted Treasurer for money to tide them over, but also some shopkeepers had borrowed from him.

Economic conditions had been uncertain with the collection of obligations indefinite and little coin in circulation. Under these circumstances, Robinson, feeling he could not turn a deaf ear to debt-ridden people, had not burned all the treasury notes received for taxes. Instead, he had become a benevolent banker—lending his friends money from his own funds and dipping into the public purse. He had trusted his planter friends, for he believed they were gentlemen with honor, pride, and property who could be depended upon to repay.[18]

For almost forty years, John Robinson had been the foremost figure in government, diligent in handling the Colony's affairs. He had reached the pinnacle in politics in the dual office of Speaker-Treasurer. Even wealthy Richard Corbin could not unseat the popular Mr. Robinson from the position. Edmund Pendleton, a protegé of the late Speaker-Treasurer and one of the administrators of the estate, explained that Robinson's goodness and

generosity caused him to assist the needy. Pendleton appealed in the newspapers to the creditors for immediate repayment and attested that, if necessary, they should sell their estates to pay their debts. Robert Carter Nicholas,
who became Treasurer, also believed that Robinson's compassion had
prompted his actions.

William Nelson summed up the situation later in a letter to the Athawes:

> . . . your Friend Peyton Randolph is chose speaker by a great majority, but
> was yesterday notified by a vote that the Treasury should be separated from
> the Chair, wch Resolve is occasioned by some misapplications the late trea-
> surer who was thought by some said thereby gaining undue influence, wch
> placed him above their Breach though most Abuses had long been the Sub-
> ject of conversation & private complaints. It hath grieved me to think that
> so good a man as he was in private Life should be prevailed upon by a set of
> men he was connected with and who pretended to be his Friend, to do
> anything to stain a character otherwise so amiable. But the Truth is he had a
> Benevolence for all mankind and so great a Desire to please everybody and
> make them happy that he never could resist an Application to him for
> money, wch he hoped to be able to replace before he should be called upon
> for it.[19]

Many details of the embezzlement were not disclosed and despite the
defense offered by his friends, Robinson's actions caused much criticism to
be cast on the cream of the Colony.

Administrators of the Robinson estate, Peter Randolph, Edmund Pendleton, and Peter Lyons had to untangle the complicated accounts. Ultimately,
they uncovered the astounding amount of £130,000 owed by debtors. The
Nelson name was conspicuously absent from a long list of creditors involved,
but many of their Assembly associates, family, and friends were among the
notable names owing obligations.[20]

William Byrd, III, owed about half the £30,000 that Robinson had provided personally from his own pocket to the planters. For years Byrd's gambling antics had supplied gossip for gabbling tongues.[21]

The Nelson men may have attempted to conceal from their wives that
their kin were indebted to the Robinson estate, but Elizabeth Burwell Nelson knew that her brothers, Lewis and Robert, were borrowers. Lucy had
already learned that her brother, Philip Ludwell Grymes, and her uncle,
Benjamin Grymes, had also been recipients of Robinson's relief. Her uncles,
Peyton and John Randolph, had received credit too; and Tom's cousins,
Carter Braxton and Benjamin Harrison, were liable for large loans. Richard
Bland, Landon Carter, Dudley Digges, and Richard Henry Lee, were on the
list, as well as Richard Corbin. A stranger reading the roll would have sup-
posed it was a social register of the first families of Virginia.[22]

Many planters began to sell property to pay their debts.[23] Mann Page
advertised many times:

Scheme of Lottery for disposing of 146 lots in town of Hanover. The consideration of money will not be required of gentlemen willing to become adventurers and subscribers to the scheme until April next.[24]

Mr. Nelson acquainted the Athawes merchants about a property sale:

I had almost forgot to tell you that Ralph Wormeley hath sold his land in York County for £3600. Money exchanged at 25 per cent out of which I suspect he will pay you as I shall press him rather hard for it.[25]

The womenfolk in the Nelson household wanted matters settled. They did not have to work with their hands as at least ten servants cleaned, cooked, washed, ironed, and tended the babies. Distributing tasks among them often required statesman-like diplomacy. Resentment could flare between indoor and outdoor workers, sickness could be feigned, goods stolen or runaways staged. Capture and severe punishment were the inevitable results of such desperate attempts.

Martha Goosley, the town gossip, still chattered about the crime several years back of William Nelson's Peter. He had slipped up the hill, broken into her home, and stolen sundry articles of clothing. The York Town court considered Peter's plea of benefit of clergy, though, so he had escaped the death penalty. His punishment was burning in the hand and thirty-nine lashes applied to his bare back at the public whipping post.[26]

Not long after Tom had brought Lucy home to York Town as his bride, another similar incident had occurred. A Negro belonging to Tom's step-grandmother had stolen cloth and money from the Nelson storehouse. On that occasion, colonial justice had been swift and severe. Davy was hanged.[27] Lucy still recalled her repugnance at the circumstance and the regret of the family.

◆　　◆　　◆

True to its pledge, the Purdie-Dixon *Virginia Gazette* devoted the front page of its June 13, 1766, issue to the repeal of the Stamp Act. In bold black type the Honorable Francis Fauquier, Governor, announced: "Act to Repeal An Act. . . . Applying to certain Stampt Duties." This published account would probably be the first confirmed news that many of the colonists in remote counties had received.

Williamsburg went wild with joy. Crowds came and the celebration continued for days. At noon a royal salute was sounded and at night torches lit Duke of Gloucester and lanterns lined the driveway leading to the stately Palace. Chownings, Raleigh, and the Kings Arms taverns were crowded with diners consuming dozen-course meals. The same issue of the *Gazette* reported, "The Gentlemen and Ladies made a genteel appearance, and seemed to vie with each other in demonstrations of joy on the occasion. . . .

drank all the loyal and patriotick toasts. . . . spent the evening with much mirth and decorum."

These lusty forefathers lifted their glasses to the health of all the royal family, then to Mr. Pitt and the favored members of Parliament who had fought for the repeal. Norfolk men drank twenty toasts while a specially erected cannon for the celebration boomed.

Governor Fauquier attended a glittering ball given at the Capitol though Lady Fauquier and their son Francis had left the Colony in May 1766.

William Nelson and the Secretary would not have attended this festive affair. Neither would Robert Burwell, for Frances Tucker Nelson, "Scotch" Tom's second wife, had died in the early days of June. People who read the paper carefully would have observed the obituary in the same issue that announced the repeal of the Stamp Act:

> On Monday last died at York in the 84th year of her age, Mrs. Frances Nelson, relict of Thomas Nelson, Esquire of York County. She was a lady endowed with many amicable qualities which makes her death much regretted by all who had the pleasure of her acquaintance; and particularly by the poor and needy, whose wants she often supplied with a liberal hand.[28]

She had outlived "Scotch" Tom by a score of years and "held out till Life became a Burthen to her: or rather till she lost all Sensibility of pleasure or pain," William Nelson wrote to Norton in London.[29]

Though she was not a blood relation, Frances Nelson was the only grandmother Tom had ever known so he accorded her affection. He was the only one of his brothers who could remember their grandfather since Hugh, Robert, Nathaniel, and Billy were all born after "Scotch" Tom's death.

As the eldest of "Scotch" Tom's three children, William had been appointed sole executor of his father's will in 1745. After certain stipulations, which included provision for Frances Nelson, William had inherited all the lands, tenements, slaves, and real estate his father possessed, "subject, nevertheless, to the payment of one hundred and fifty pounds sterling per annum, herein before devised to my wife in lieu in her dower, if she survives me and accepts the same."[30] Consequently, under the terms of his father's will, William Nelson now became the owner of the house across the street from his own dwelling and of its furnishings, chariot, cows, and slaves; Dave was dead, but Grace, Penny, Sukey, Frank, Will Caesar, and Tryal had been listed.[31] In colonial days clothes of the deceased customarily passed to the nearest kin. Frances Nelson's daughter, Sarah Burwell, could choose the articles of clothing, rings, or jewelry that she desired. (Yet three years later, Martha Goosley was writing John Norton, whose wife Courtenay was Frances Nelson's granddaughter, about the disposition of the clothes. They had been divided equally between Sarah Burwell and Mrs. Baylor and sent to Tucker's store at Norfolk "for what purpose can't tell." Though the store was struck by lightning and burned, somehow the trunk of clothes had been saved.)[32]

✦   ✦   ✦

Tom and Lucy examined "Scotch" Tom's handsome house, with interest kindled by ownership. Probably the unusual brown bricks had been imported from Britain as ship's ballast. Its windows were well-balanced with spaced modillions and deep arches, its spacious entry hall interestingly off-centered. Lucy liked the long sweep of the stairway; it was not steep, with but seventeen steps leading to the landing before turning toward the east and the upstairs section. The balustrade and rails were carved with spiral scrollwork. All the rooms on the first floor were paneled to the ceiling. Tom thought the back square room on the west side would make a fine library. They lingered in the ornamented drawing room where elaborate Corinthian columns with curved bases and separated shaft sections rose to the ceiling. The couple was elated about becoming prospective housekeepers in a home of their own.[33]

Many months actually passed before Tom and Lucy moved into the house. Sweltering heat and the summer's intermittent rains sapped their energy. Colonial mothers were concerned over children's surviving their first summers so Lucy was especially attentive to five-month-old Philip. William, not yet three, and Thomas, still a toddler, needed constant care.

William Nelson manifested pride in his masculine domain. He was surrounded by six sons and three grandsons. Sometimes he boasted that "there was not a female among us except our wives." Hugh was nearly six feet tall and thin as his uncle Edmund Berkeley. His father was interested in improving his education as well as that of fourteen-year-old Robert who showed promise of becoming a scholar. Mr. Nelson had ordered books from abroad and globes for Hugh's study of geography with Parson Camm.[34]

William was obliged to his cousin William Cookson for his invitation to send Hugh and Robert to England for their education, but his attitude had altered over the years since 1753 when he had shipped Tom off hurriedly to study in British schools. He explained that "they have a mother so extremely tender of them that she cannot bear the thought of parting with them at the time of life that she can hardly expect to see them again. . . . our estates are not equal to the expense.[35]

Nathaniel at ten and six-year-old Billy tried to tag along after their older brothers. Sometimes the contingent slipped in to Dr. Benjamin Catton's apothecary shop. The boys were spellbound when Catton explained the powers of terebinth and treacle and wondered what crocus of antimony was. Dr. George Riddell, who rented lots from William Nelson, might show the sons how to crush camomile flower heads with a mortar and pestle and how to extract oil from juniper berries.[36]

77

On September 12, 1766, death claimed another Nelson. William wrote his cousin Cookson,

> It hath pleased God to take unto himself our poor unfortunate son Lewis who had been troubled with epileptic Fits for some years, which had impaired the Faculties of his Mind without the hope of Recovery, so that after the first workings of natural Affection we became thankful to the Wise Disposer of all things.[37]

✦   ✦   ✦

While the Nelson family was absorbed in domestic affairs, scandal struck again in the capital. Less than a month before, John Robinson's death had prompted the clarification of his mishandling of treasury funds. Serious as that situation had been, Tom felt that money matters were of far less importance than murder.

Colonel John Chiswell of Williamsburg had killed Robert Routledge in Cumberland County on June 3. At the Nelson's Swan Tavern Tom learned of the drunken dispute. Chiswell and Routledge had hurled drunken insults at one another in Moxby's Tavern. Colonel Chiswell called the Scottish merchant a "fugitive, rebel, and Presbyterian." Routledge threw a glass of wine at Chiswell's face; Chiswell retaliated by tossing a punch bowl toward his assailant. They attacked each other with candlesticks and tongs while onlookers attempted to restrain them. When Routledge snatched a chair to hurl at his assailant, Chiswell seized his sword calling the men to take his opponent out. Routledge broke loose from the men attempting to hold him and rushed back into the room. The candle flames flickered out and in the dark Colonel Chiswell's saber struck the heart of Routledge.[38]

Authorities apprehended Colonel Chiswell and sent him to the capital for trial where he was freed on bail. Routledge's relatives and friends resented the fact that Chiswell could walk about at will in Williamsburg. Common folk grumbled that criminals were not kept in custody if they belonged to the upper crust.

In an attempt to explain the ensuing event, Parson Camm said, "Instead of his being lodged in the jail, three judges of the General Court, lead to it no doubt by Chiswell's connections, out of session have carried their power too high as to stop him on the way to Prison and admitted him to bail, which, like, as well it might, to put the whole country into a ferment."[39]

Many felt that Judges John Blair, Presley Thornton, and William Byrd had been highhanded and too hasty in raising a three-thousand-pounds-sterling bond for Chiswell's release. Through articles in the *Virginia Gazette,* Blair attempted to describe the affair and to defend their conduct in the case.[40]

Mr. Nelson later wrote his friend John Norton in London that "The Secretary sends you the *Virginia Gazette,* which will show you the two Subjects which have engaged the Thought of the People here arising from the Death of the Speaker & poor Chiswell's unfortunate Conduct; perhaps too much hath been said upon both."[41]

Even insensitive folk felt some sympathy for Susanna Chiswell Robinson caught betwixt the scandal-shrouded death of her husband, Speaker-Treasurer John Robinson, and her father's murder of Routledge. She was the innocent victim of the two tragedies.[42]

Colonel Chiswell spent the summer at his mines in Fredericksburg, but he found no solace. In September, he returned to his family and their fine house in Williamsburg on Francis Street, not too far from the one owned by the Nelsons. Family devotion, faithful friends, and a comfortable abode could not lessen his guilt; John Chiswell died in October at age forty. His doctor stated the cause of death was "nervous fits owing to constant uneasiness of mind," but the verdict of most Virginians was suicide.[43]

Had it not been for the "Joyful News" of the repeal of the Stamp Act, it would have been difficult to find good news to write about. William Nelson's letters to his English factors and friends abroad still celebrated the event. Typical was his communiqué to John Norton, July 25, 1766:

> You will easily imagine that the Repeal of the Stamp Act hath put us into a good Humour: it hath taken away the hateful cause of Disgust & ill blood between the Mother Country & the Colonies: which might have brought the Ruin of both . . . We ought not on this side to forget to acknowledge the noble Efforts of the Merchants in London & elsewhere; which were so seasonable & so successfully exerted on this occasion.[44]

Just as Tom was trying to settle down to take care of his different duties, another sensational argument shook the solidarity of the gentry. The Mercers aired their animosity toward Richard Henry Lee in an anonymous article in the Purdie-Dixon *Virginia Gazette* of July 18, 1766. John and James Mercer had vowed revenge, and the newspaper sizzled with their spite. Lucy was shocked to see the accusations heaped on her cousin, but the paper gave coverage to both sides of the controversy.[45] The triple scandals of the Robinson disgrace, Chiswell murder, and Mercer-Lee feud spread through all strata of society; some people even predicted the downfall of the powerful planter class.

The emotional events of the summer did not prevent the Nelsons from attending to their numerous affairs. Tom's tasks often took him around the town in a somewhat triangular route, first to the warehouse on the wharf, next to the Digges's and Ambler's stores, then back up the slope past the Custom House on Main Street, a flourishing commercial center for about four decades; the Amblers had served as Collector of Ports.[46] Here captains obtained sailing orders for their ships, cleared their cargoes, and signed crews.

Sometimes the talk in the Custom House turned from tonnage and poundage to trafficking in faraway ports. Tom would listen to the seafaring adventurers tell of sailing beyond the familiar harbors of Bristol, Liverpool, and London to places like Mozambique or Zanzibar. In China they sought bolts of silk, nankeen, and chests of Bohea tea; in Sumatra they loaded their ships with pepper and spices.

✦   ✦   ✦

William Nelson and the Secretary had been observing the shifting scenes of autumn on the way from York Town to Williamsburg for almost a quarter of a century; Tom had been traveling the route to the Assembly for only five years. He never wearied of watching the rich foliage, the broad York River, and the long stretching slopes. If Lucy and the three young boys accompanied the men to see her mother, Mary Randolph Grymes, who was not well, the coach was crowded.

Only affluent folk like William Nelson could afford carriages and coaches, for luxury taxes were assessed on them: twice as much for four-wheeled carriages as for two-wheeled chaises. William Nelson contemplated sending one of his old coaches abroad for repairs but later changed his mind and gave it to his sister, Mrs. Berkeley, so that she and her daughters would have a conveyance to go to church.[47] Four well-matched horses pulled some of the carriages; others were drawn by six horses with polished leather harness as fine as the maroon livery of the coachman. Often, Mr. Nelson used six glossy black horses; others chose to hitch a gray, sorrel, or roan together.

Though the streets of Williamsburg were unpaved, it was a pleasant town, long and level; Tom thought it looked much like an English village with many wide-planked white houses, green shutters framing their small windows—like the Nelson place on Francis Street.[48] There were some two-story brick dwellings topped by broad gabled roofs of tile, slate, or shingle, clay chimneys at either end of the structure. Downstairs windows were balanced on each side of a centered door with five window openings above. Tax rates were based on the number of stories. Since the buildings were close together, the fire laws required that the compact houses be built not more than six feet from the walks.[49]

On each side of Duke of Gloucester Street were parallel roads, neither so broad as the principal thoroughfare. When foot races were run along the main road, the street was cleared of carriages. In April and December when the agricultural fairs were held in Williamsburg, the fleet of foot competed for the prizes. Awards could also be won in wrestling and chasing the greased pig, fiddling, dancing, and singing. Tom knew that his boys were too young to be entranced very long with the running matches, but he believed that even five-month-old baby Philip might notice the puppet show.[50]

During "Publick Times," October and April, the population of Williamsburg more than doubled its normal two thousand people. Although each county elected only two members to sit in the Assembly, many gentlemen brought families with them and opened town houses when the sessions started. The bi-annual meetings convened in October, when a brisk breeze brought relief from sultry summer and in April, when the warm sunshine chased away the vestiges of winter.[51]

Colonial belles and young gallants making their first visit to the capital could choose from fortune telling, bear baiting or ballroom dancing for entertainment. While men thronged to one of the almost thirty taverns for French wines or the cheapest beer, women sought modish fabrics in the shops and bonnets in the millinery stores. Youngsters devised their own games with balls, hoops, and dolls, or expensive miniature coaches and four—presents from indulgent parents.[52]

Yeomen, peddlers, farmer folk, and others of ordinary means found cockfighting a stimulating sport and ventured brisk bets on the fowls. There was no social conscience about cruelty to animals. Whether the game was bear or bull baiting, cock fighting or goose riding, the loser was maimed or torn to shreds. Laws forbade apprentices, indentured servants, or laborers to gamble, but the old seventeenth-century statutes against cards, dice, and tormenting dumb brutes had been abrogated.[53]

Men who would rather participate than be onlookers played backgammon, billiards, and bowls. Besides the popular taprooms, taverns provided recreation rooms for games, and outside many ordinaries were long stretches of lawn called bowling greens. Games of loo, played with cards and ivory or mother-of-pearl fish, provided another opportunity to gamble. Adventurers lost sizeable amounts in the game room or in lottery. Gambling addicts were not criticized by their contemporaries, but cheaters were ostracized. Gentlemen accepted their losses with good grace.[54]

Williamsburg had a good race course close to the Capitol, and many Burgesses and Councilors attended the track on Waller Street. The Nelsons were among the Assemblymen who enjoyed the "Sport of Kings."[55] Love of horses was endemic, and one observer avowed that nobody walked since the Virginians liked riding so much they would spend hours catching a horse to ride a couple of miles. Horses were of great value, and laws and licenses protected them. A duty of one pound had to be paid on horses imported from Spain to England. Connivers who attempted to bribe officers to make false oaths or who failed to show correct receipts were liable for a hundredpound fine.[56]

A 1748 "Act for Keeping Too Many Horses" stipulated that a man must have over fifty acres of land, an overseer, and servants if he wished to begin the breeding business. *Runaway* in bold print—referring both to horses and to slaves—often crowded the columns of the paper.[57]

Tom announced in the *Virginia Gazette* that he had two horses missing: "Strayed from York Town, a black horse about 15 hands high, with a blaze in her face, some white spots on her back, the inside of one of her hind feet white, and never was dockt. . . . 40 shillings reward."[58]

In 1764, William and Secretary Nelson imported a horse they called Vampire, a name that suggests a spirited creature.[59]

Tom knew Colonel William Byrd's (III) steed was a valuable rival which won £100-purses. A speedy horse with a tenacious rider who could win two four-mile heats out of three for the first day's running won that sizeable sum.[60]

Tom would often hear his father and John Tayloe pay tribute to the great Godolphin—imported from England in 1730—who had sired so many famous horses. About that time, horse enthusiasts began to improve the strain so that some thoroughbreds could run a mile in less than three minutes. Ralph Wormeley of Middlesex County, who associated with William Nelson and John Tayloe in sponsoring subscription races, brought in Jolly Roger in 1750, a stallion who sired several crowd-pleasing racers.[61]

Colonel Tayloe probably treated his long-time friends to a toast with sweet Madeira, when his Hero beat Colonel Byrd's Tryal and Richard Henry Lee's Mark Antony in the October race. Tom was glad that Lewis Burwell also had a winner with his bay horse, Janus.[62]

An English visitor commented that "Very capital horses are started here, such as would make no despicable figure at Newmarket; nor is their speed, bottom or blood inferior to their appearance.[63] In spite of many rivals, Colonel Tayloe's Traveller easily won the meet on April 24, 1766.[64]

These same gentlemen were back at the track in the spring. Tom spotted some horses he thought had the speed and stamina to succeed in securing the one-hundred-pound prize offered for the first run of the day. He was willing to wager that Cousin Lewis Burwell's John Dismal—despite the name—could triumph on the track in two of three four-mile heats to win the money.[65]

William Nelson had indulged his interest in horses all his life. When Tom was not a month old, he and Ralph Wormeley had been partners in promoting races at the Gloucester run. He would ride the ferry across York River with his horses ready for the subscription race. Any horse, mare or gelding, could be entered by the owner for the prize purse of thirty pistoles (approximately one hundred dollars). On January 11, 1739, an advertisement announced the exciting event. If the gentleman was a subscriber, he paid one pistole for an entrance fee, if not a signer, he would pay double the charge.[66]

A special race was arranged for the animals that had never won a prize. The run required five shillings to enter and the sum was given to the second place winner. First-place prizes were fine saddles valued at forty shillings. Bridles, whips, and silver soup ladles were also awarded. Another classification was provided for horses thirteen hands high, considered a good size in colonial days. The lucky riders were given fine hunting saddles.[67]

To capture a prize, William Nelson knew that he needed a light rider. The colonial jockey cut quite a figure from top to toe exhibiting racing colors in a jaunty cap, silk jacket, and polished boots. Prancing steeds were hard to hold until the starting signal was given precisely at twelve o'clock. Sometimes the send-off would be a staccato drumroll, another time a sharp gun blast, or the shrill blare of a trumpet.[68]

Expense, as well as social position, disclosed that only equestrian aristocrats could engage in the "Sport of Kings." James Bullocke, a tailor, attempted to run his mare against the horse of Dr. Matthew Slader, a gentleman, at York Town in an earlier period. This prompted the authorities to punish the presumptuous violator. In its ardor to keep the course "clean," the court fined the offender one-hundred-pounds-sterling worth of tobacco and cask and ordered him to sit in the stocks for an hour, where he could contemplate that it was "contrary to Law for a Labourer to make a race, being a sport only for Gentlemen."[69]

A foreign traveler to York Town, in 1764 had observed that "You perceive a great air of opulence among the inhabitants who have (some of them) built themselves houses equal in magnificence to many of our Superb ones at St. James as those of Mr. Lightfoot, Nelson. . . . Everyone keeps an equipage, not matching horses."[70]

Evidently, all the Nelsons were enthusiastic riders, for even Tom's mother enjoyed the "heathful exercise" that William called "the recreation" until a bad fall from her horse required a long rest. Twice Mr. Nelson mentioned the mishap to Samuel Athawes. On January 10, 1769, he wrote, "Mrs. Nelson not quite recovered from a fall she had three months since."[71]

Six months later he stated that "Mrs. Nelson is obliged to you for the concern you express for the hurt she received by a fall from her horse. She is much better, but fears she will always feel the Effects of it."[72]

To John Norton he explained the accident and condition of his wife:

> Mrs. Nelson, who stands by my side, & wishes all Happiness to you & yours, hath Lately had an ugly Fall from her Horse (for she hath rode for about 2 years for her Health & with some Advantage) which hath confined her for about a Month. She now walks about the House & in the Garden, & I hope to get her on horse back again soon.[73]

While in Williamsburg, after attending to the needs of her mother, Lucy would tuck her three boys in bed to spend some time with her three younger sisters. Betty had made her appearance after their father, Philip Grymes, had made his will; he had added a codicil: "Whereas since the making of this my will it has pleased God to bless me with another Daughter. . . . I do hereby give her the same portions that I have allotted to her sisters Susanna and Mary 800 pounds.[74]

At five, Betty preferred playing with her three young nephews, but Susanna and Mary as growing girls of fourteen and twelve were exhibiting interest in stylish clothes and fancy balls. They peered over Lucy's shoulder as she scanned the *Gazette* for announcements concerning gala affairs, "a ball for the Ladies and Gentlemen in the Apollo Room at the Raleigh Tavern every week during the sitting of the General Assembly. Tickets half a pistole."[75]

Called night gowns, elegant silk evening dresses often had embroidered bodices and were ornamented with Brussels, Mechlin, or Minionet lace costing over six shillings a yard. Single stays, half-bone, were worn in or out for support, some attractively arranged to lace over stomachers.[76]

Colonial courtiers were as elegant in their dress as the girls. The peruke maker styled wigs that precluded the wearing of hats, but gentlemen carried chapeaux under their arms, each hat adorned with gold, silver, or cream lace which matched that at wrists and throat. Silk stockings covered straight, knobby, or thin limbs. If a man desired shaplier legs, he could order special padding, but Tom had no need. Like his father, who had informed his factor not to send the stuffing for the stockings, Tom's legs were full enough to fill the hose.[77]

Lucy and her sisters must have read with avid interest the advertisement of Jane Hunter in the Purdie-Dixon *Virginia Gazette* of October 10, 1766, that noted: "Just imported a genteel assortment of Millinery goods, fashionable caps, egrets & fillets, breast flowers, turbans, tippets. Best French beads, pearls, & jet necklaces, earrings. . . . ribands & trimming—French & glazed kid gloves."

When Tom and Lucy visited the Randolph residence on Nicholson Street, the couple could see a congregation of Grymes, Harrison, and Jenings kin gathered there; visiting was as essential to the Virginians as eating. Peyton Randolph had no children of his own so he lavished affection on his nieces and nephews. With two Susannas, he had to specify whether he meant Lucy's sister or his brother John's daughter. He was attentive to Mary and Betty, Lucy's younger sisters, and Ariana, John's daughter, but the boys were his favorites. Uncle Peyton cared for the four Grymes's sons, Philip Ludwell, John Randolph, Charles, and Benjamin after the death of their father, but Edmund, John's son, received more of his time.[78]

Sometimes in the evening Tom and Lucy strolled down Palace Green to meet George Wythe walking in his long garden parallel to the square brick house on the south side of Bruton Parish Church.

Tom knew well the people who had resided in the residence just west of the Palace. His mother's half-brother, Robert Carter Nicholas, had occupied the house until 1761 when he had sold it to his cousin and Tom's, too, Robert Carter. Lucy and Tom could encounter him on the way to a weekly concert at Governor Fauquier's. Carter was an accomplished musician who played the flute, violin, spinet, harpsichord and a fine organ constructed to his own specifications.[79]

Cantankerous Landon Carter, however, did not appreciate the musical accomplishments of his cousin Robert or others, for when he was in Williamsburg he complained of the "constant tutin'" that to him was an irritating clamor.[80]

Governor Fauquier was a gentlemen of grace who lent sparkle to the Colony's social segment; he had formed a firm friendship with the Nelson family.

Although the construction of a suitable structure for the Governor of Britain's largest Colony had sustained a series of setbacks, it now stood complete, a splendid symbol of prestige and power. Its ballroom had been built a few years earlier in 1752, the site of many grand gatherings for the Colony's patricians.[81] (When Robert Dinwiddie had arrived in York Town October 15, 1751, he was met by William Nelson and William Fairfax and driven over to the capital where work was under way on the Palace.)[82]

The College of William and Mary also contributed to the cultural life of the city; a playhouse had been constructed on Palace Green, but it was now used as a meeting hall for Hustings Court.[83] Tom sometimes wondered whether the actors had created any more drama and sound than the heated shouts of the courtroom. (Before the building's conversion, Governor Dinwiddie in August 1752 had attended the debut performance of Lewis and Sarah Hallam in *The Merchant of Venice*. On the evening *Othello* was performed, the emperor of the Cherokees with his wife and small son were Dinwiddie's guests. Theatergoers had just settled down to the second act when the empress became so terrified at the duel on stage she commanded her attendants to stop the sword play.)[84]

Williamsburg officials were not entirely occupied with entertainment. Although Governor Fauquier enjoyed society, he had plans to improve political conditions and to solve social injustices. He realized that government should shoulder responsibility for the good of mankind. In his messages, he asked the Assemblymen to exercise their powers to provide for the poor. Foremost of his civic concerns was care of the mentally incompetent. Usually families bore the burden of an incompetent member as his good friend William Nelson had done in caring for his unfortunate son Lewis.

In extreme cases, some of the mentally ill were boarded out, sent to the almshouse, or put in prison where bad food, beatings, and derision were their lot. It was commonly believed that the mentally ill were possessed of evil spirits so their unusual actions incurred apprehension, punishment, or retaliation.

Since four persons of disordered minds had been sent to the jail in Williamsburg, Fauquier could reinforce his case. Late in November he recommended that a hospital be provided for persons deprived of their reason. The administrator appealed to the Assemblymen to consider charity and the comfort of the community. In the interim, the four patients were sent to a private asylum in Philadelphia.

The Committee of Propositions and Grievances was to prepare a bill regarding the resolution. As a member of the committee, Tom was interested in the project and worked wholeheartedly for its success. An institution for the insane was to be built within three years. William, the Secretary, and Tom would be involved with its operation all their lives.[85]

CHAPTER SIX

Land, Labor, and the Leaf

Land and River Routes to Plantations ✦ Tom and the Tobacco Trade ✦ Residences of Relatives: Fairfield, Rosewell, Elsing Green, Westover, Sabine Hall, Cleve, Carter's Grove, Berkeley, Shirley ✦ William Nelson at Work

Tom Nelson, Jr., his father and his uncle could take the road or the river route when traveling to their plantations in Hanover County. If they chose the overland course, they viewed some of the most charming countryside in all Virginia.

The terrain was a tapestry of green with thickets of loblolly pines, sand hickories, and sycamores bordered by smaller sweetbays, sweetgums, and flowering dogwood. The rich margin lands of the river had been claimed for over a century and were already settled in the dominant design of the plantation pattern. A few farmers had fields of wheat and corn, and Tom was raising some of these crops to supply his family. The great staple of the Tidewater, however, was still tobacco and long rows of the leafy stalks spread across the region.

Arising before dawn, the Nelsons could travel from York Town about thirteen miles to Williamsburg, arriving at their residence on Francis Street in less than two hours; there they would breakfast and rest the horses. Then the group would ride toward Richmond more than fifty miles beyond the capital. Somewhere they would have to cross the Chickahominy River.

If Tom hurried, he could make the fifty-mile journey from Williamsburg to Richmond in about eight hours. Speed was a habit from the hunt, and he sat in the saddle with style.

No doubt William Nelson, who was also noted for his horsemanship, and the Secretary, who was also a planter to some extent, often accompanied Tom on these excursions. William insisted on some stops because of the heat, dust, and rutted roads.

The trio had made the trip many times and probably knew a trail just east of Richmond to bypass the town and save time. It was necessary to spend the night somewhere before resuming the journey to their plantations the next morning.

As the Nelsons reached the rolling hills of Hanover County, Tom admired the acres of fertile land filled with thousands of tobacco plants turning from green to golden brown. His rambling glance took in the panorama of level grasslands and rounded ridges, a few fallow fields, rock fences, rectangular pastures paralleling dense forests and plots ready for fall planting of tobacco. In the distance the slaves swung their arms in a rhythmic rise and fall as they cast wheat into the soil.

Tobacco wouldn't grow wild, so John Rolfe[1] sowed the first seeds at Jamestown while the Colony was still struggling to survive. Later, the Indian weed shaped the structure of society, creating an aristocracy that had not faded, even in the sixties. Land, labor, and the leaf comprised an indispensable trinity. Tom had often heard his father and uncle discuss the changes brought about in this new land because of that trinity. The large landowner—to become a plutocrat—needed a large labor force.[2]

A Dutch ship carried the first African slaves up the James River in 1619. Half a century elapsed before the English began to compete with the Hollanders in selling the black cargo, but by the eighteenth century the pattern was set.

When colonial assemblies protested and levied taxes to stop the importation of slaves, the British disregarded their remonstrances. Merchants and shippers had discovered that trading in chattels was a lucrative practice; slavery was fastened in the fabric of the economy.[3] The third component of the triad was tobacco. Land, labor, and the leaf formed the elements of the economy. Tobacco was a devouring weed. It had a hold on humans, white and black. The plant used up soil and ruined the good earth in a few years.[4]

An avid craving to acquire land was a characteristic of planters. The Nelsons had accumulated property by various procedures: patent, petition, purchase, grant, or gift. Four centuries earlier Nelsons had fought for the Empire and been compensated for their services by large land grants. Twenty-one years ago the brothers had inherited valuable real estate from "Scotch" Tom Nelson. The Secretary's father had bequeathed to him "houses, lots, and plantations bought for him of Dr. John Dixon" and also an estate in King William County. William Nelson, as the first-born son, gained "all my lands, tenements, slaves, and real estate whatever," as stated in the will.[5]

A passion for property was typical not only of the planter, but also a fever in the small farmer. Land was the steppingstone to success, the magic element that allowed a man to emulate his English ancestors, to rise in wealth and position. Wise parents made it their goal to obtain tracts of land for the prosperity of their children.

William and Thomas Nelson put this philosophy into practice. For a score of years they had expanded their estates, acquiring land in the western wilderness. In April 1745, the Nelsons and ten other adventurers had been granted a one-hundred-thousand-acre area near the Greenbrier River. They secured twenty thousand-acre tracts in the northern tip of the Colony, later to become Frederick and Fauquier counties, where the Shenandoah River runs.[6]

Just four years later in 1749, William and Thomas Nelson became charter members of the Ohio Company. The expansive region across the Alleghenies encompassed the claims of the Old Dominion. Later, they had changed their claims to the Loyal Company among more of their Council colleagues since that organization—with no standard fees and more lenient settlement fees—seemed to serve the interest of the Tidewater better.[7]

One of their latest land ventures was a patent secured in 1763 to the Dismal Swamp. The region ran south of Suffolk in a strip through the eastern section of Nansemond and the western portion of Norfolk counties, dipping down into North Carolina.[8]

Several other speculators were enlisted as shareholders in the enterprise, including William Nelson's brother-in-law, Robert Burwell. George Washington could not resist the lure of the land and threw in his lot. His brother-in-law, Fielding Lewis, also became a subscriber. Washington's experience as a surveyor was useful. He traveled to the territory and reported on the tract to his partners first on May 25, 1763, finding the soil and timber generally favorable.[9]

Despite the difficulties in draining a swamp of such scope, shareholders were anxious to pursue the daring project. They felt the land's advantages—rich earth, timber, proximity to the Norfolk market and the ocean (less than thirty miles)—far outweighed the disadvantages. When the practically unoccupied and totally undeveloped marshy expanse was channeled with canals and cleared, the reclaimed soil would produce tobacco, grain, and more timber.

As members of the powerful Governor's Council, the Nelsons could usually expedite some of the tedious paperwork. They could count on the Council's approval of acquisition since the group had the same goal. Therefore, their patents and petitions for thousands of acres were more readily passed.

Tom had already learned some of the intricacies of tobacco culture. He could appreciate the time and work involved in raising tobacco on the huge acreage of the Hanover plantation.

The cultivation of tobacco evolved in cycles beginning in January and February when slaves burned tree stumps and then raked the residue of ashes into the ground to fertilize the fields. Some growers resorted to cow-penning, using the refuse to renew the soil, but the practice was criticized since it produced a rank taste in tobacco. The sweet-scented Oronoco with its long, pointed leaf had a smooth taste and superlative texture. It grew well in the rich, sandy soil of the James and York river areas.[10]

The planting process began when slaves scattered the seeds into the ground, covering them with light layers of straw or brush. When the seeds began to germinate in the spring, the plants were put in hills about four feet apart, to wait on the weather. Rain was required at the right time for transplanting. If by May there wasn't enough moisture in the soil to move the small stalks into the large fields, the crop might be lost. Replanting was a continual process and sometimes it was necessary to sow the temperamental crop six times.

Work went on through the long summer. Each acre had several hundred plants; each one exacted personal attention. If the plants could withstand the vagaries of weather and attacks by insects one acre could produce a thousand pounds of prime tobacco. Barefoot slaves worked their way through the long stretches of stalks with grubbing hoes, building up some hills, leveling others, worming, weeding, topping, and suckering. To prevent flowering and to perfect the plant, they pinched off the principal stems and pulled the smaller shoots or suckers from the lower part of the stalk. A perfect plant had eight or ten leaves. Insects took their toll. Black children were able to grab a few of the pests, but farmers used tinctures of sulphur and sassafras more effectively to kill the flies, gourd worms, and four-inch caterpillar pests.[11]

When the warm sunshine drove the roots deep into the earth and the days were dry, the leaves were ready for cutting. The crop master watched for these signs and then summoned the crews. By August the golden green leaves were stripped and set in rows to receive the sun's rays for a few hours, then lifted and placed on slender sticks to be hung to dry.

A farmer raising small amounts of the leaf would improvise racks or drape his crop across a fence, but larger growers erected big barns where the plants hung in tiers allowing the air to circulate for the four to six weeks of curing. If fall rains were heavy, there was danger of mold. Smoldering fires could correct the dampness, but too much firing caused blight and affected the taste, although this method was employed by some planters to hasten maturing. When no complications interfered with correct curing, the golden brown leaves had an elastic texture, bending without breaking.

Binding the leaves into bundles or twisting them into rope-like pigtails preceded the laborious operation of filling the hogsheads—usually forty-eight inches in height and thirty inches around—that could hold a thousand pounds of tobacco. These big barrels were placed under an improvised pulley made from a sapling attached to a tree, and a flat lever pressed down the layers of the leaves. Crowding cut freight costs but often aroused complaints about the tobacco's condition on arrival.[12]

William Nelson didn't approve of the practice and wrote John Norton that "I find the complaint of prising stem'd Tobo in too high Condition is become pretty general: and to prevent it for the Future, I have given strict Orders to have mine lightly pressed & dry."[13]

By 1730, a standard inspection system for tobacco had been set up in Virginia. At intervals, the planters had tried crop-curbing and price-fixing to eliminate overproduction and reduced prices. Now an examination of the plant would exclude the inferior product. Public warehouses were placed at strategic points along the rivers. Special tobacco inspectors were designated to determine the good from the bad. These men were bonded by five hundred pounds of tobacco and swore that they would not receive any tobacco that was not "well-conditioned, merchantable, and clear of trash." If the planter agreed with the tester that his tobacco was trashy, it was burned. If the planter did not give his permission, he had the privilege of trying to have it endorsed by another examiner. Sometimes it was worth the extra time and trouble.[14]

In October 1765, Tom had been in the House of Burgesses when another act was passed to improve the tobacco industry, ". . . for more effectual[ly] preventing . . . the exportation of . . . bad, unsound, and unmerchantable tobacco, all tobacco which from and after commencement of this act shall be exported out of colony . . . according to laws brought to public warehouses packed and casks and inspected ship, sloop, boat."[15]

After the hogsheads had been opened, it was appraised and repacked within ten days, with identifying initials stamped on the barrel. The receipt issued the grower was a negotiable certificate, exchangeable for many commodities, and useable as payment for taxes and salaries. The crop had become the currency of the Virginia Colony.

Tom liked to watch the hogsheads roll down the roads. Wooden hoops encircled the big barrels and sturdy hickory split saplings were used for shafts fastened with strong spindles. Sometimes the slaves could move the bulky casks down the rolling roads all the way to the warehouse. In more remote regions horses were hitched to the hogsheads to haul them to their destination. A rough trip over rutty roads damaged the brittle plant. Many planters built piers from their property at the river to slide the cargo onto the ships.

Since ships could sail up the York River to West Point, the Nelsons could transport their hogsheads on sloops or barges down the Pamunkey River where the cargo could then be transferred to the waiting tobacco fleets at West Point.

The 1758 crop had been so short that the Assembly had passed the Two-Penny Act stating that debts would be payable at the rate of two pence a pound for tobacco. Since the ministers were paid in tobacco, they stood to lose money by the measure.[16]

Tom recalled the sensational case of 1763 in Hanover County when the Reverend Mr. Maury brought suit for his salary with Patrick Henry leading the defense. Henry had criticized the clergymen and also rebuked the King for rescinding the local law. After that trial, people took more notice of young Mr. Henry.

William and Secretary Nelson hadn't forgotten the fight that their own minister, the Reverend John Camm, staged in the struggle. Tom had been in school in England when Camm sailed to Britain to present the petition of the preachers to King George III. He persuaded His Majesty to repeal the act, and the minister had sent many missives and copies of the revocation back to his clergymen colleagues in the Colony.[17]

In 1760, with mission accomplished, Camm returned in triumph to Virginia. Facing Governor Fauquier with the facts, Camm received a contemptuous rejection for his impertinence; Fauquier called him "ignorant and impudent" and further instructed his footman not to open the Palace door again to Camm.[18]

While the tongues of Williamsburg were wagging over this incident, the obdurate Camm took his case to court. He sued for his salary in York County Court and lost the suit but, still undaunted, proceeded with his plan to the General Court and was defeated again.[19] William and Thomas Nelson, members of the court, were exempted from expressing their views.

William Nelson had informed his associates on the Committee of Correspondence that the Reverend Mr. Camm had started a suit for his salary. The chairman further stated that he "desired the opinion of the Committee . . . so public a nature as to merit attention proposed for consideration to the House of Burgesses."[20]

Personal relations between the preacher and the Nelson family seemed to continue on a cordial basis.

The clergy was not only criticized by the general public for its grasping attitude but also by a visiting minister in the Colony. The Reverend Andrew Burnaby condemned his colleagues for their incivility and discourteousness to the Governor.[21]

Since all claims, fees, rents, and salaries paid to public officers and landlords would be reduced, the committee analyzed the arguments of the parsons thus:

> The clergy contended the law served the Rich—if they received real value—help poor. . . . The whole of this therefore is but a thin Varnish, and leaves too much Room to suspect, from the very nature of murmuring in such Cases, that they themselves rather wanted on Opportunity of feasting as largely as they could on all both rich and poor.[22]

◆   ◆   ◆

Taking the river route to the Hanover plantations had advantages. A deep tidal channel had been chiseled by the sea and the wide watercourse was navigable for seagoing ships. The York River ran straight and smooth until it reached West Point about thirty-five miles from York Town, where it separated into the Pamunkey to the left and started its slender twisting and turning in a serpentine course.

Innumerable inlets and coves embroidered the Chesapeake's edge and tiny isles dotted the coast near Mobjack Bay. Tom leaned against the rail and peered across the river into the deep recesses. Through the soft, gray mist he could imagine how pirate ships slipped into the estuary for escape, their bowsprits dancing above the blue-green water. Tiny waves, cupped with silver crests made Tom think of shiny Spanish pistoles, gleaming doubloons, and sparkling jewels, the stolen loot smugglers hid on board.

He was roused from reverie by his father's pointing out the homes of two Gloucester County relatives. To an objective observer, both houses were arresting architecturally, but Tom viewed them subjectively with pride, because they were homes of his mother's people. The first was Fairfield on Carter's Creek. It had been built in 1692 by Major Lewis Burwell, who had six sons and nine daughters, including Lucy, the woman to whom Governor Nicholson had lost his heart and head. This romantic intrigue was remembered and retold to succeeding generations of the family. To accommodate the Burwells through the years, additions at Fairfield had run the gamut of three traditional shapes: the *H, L,* and *T.* The seventeenth-century residence had the first hipped roof in the area, a feature later used extensively on eighteenth-century houses. "King" Carter's daughter Elizabeth had married Nathaniel Burwell of Fairfield, and Tom's mother, Elizabeth, born in 1718, was the third child.[23]

As the ship sailed up the York, the passengers glanced at massive Rosewell standing proud on its promontory. William Nelson might point out the elaborate brickwork with its segment and soffit trim, the same as in "Scotch" Tom's house, or its water table, unlike any other except the one at the Nelson house. He reminiscenced about his own 1738 wedding party at the mansion when he and Elizabeth Burwell had been married.[24]

As they sailed up the river about ten miles from the mouth of the stream, the Nelsons viewed the territory once inhabited by the ancient tribes of Virginia. In this wilderness had been located Werowacomoco, the lodge of Emperor Powhatan. His empire extended over eight thousand square miles and included thirty Indian tribes. Secretary Nelson recalled the capture of Captain John Smith. The English adventurer had been brought before the grim old Indian king reclining on his throne in a robe of gray raccoon, a proud possession that he later tendered to the King of England. Powhatan had been encircled by young wives and other Indian women festive in puccoon paint and strings of shells.[25]

Smith was feasted and then dragged to a pile of stones where the braves stepped forward to beat his brains out when Pocohontas, a lovely Indian princess, rushed in and threw herself over the prostrate prisoner.[26] Her action melted the heart of her father and saved the life of the soldier of fortune.

Tom could feel the influence of the sea in the surge of its current and a brisk salty breeze. Along the banks stood trunks of water tupelo, bald cypress, and swamp cottonwood, trees common to the coastal plain. Just past West Point the ship approached the acres surrounding two extensive estates, Eltham and White House, on sites beside the Pamunkey River in New Kent County.[27] George Washington had married Martha Dandridge Custis in January 1759, at the spacious White House. Who could predict then that the young planter bridegroom would lead the land in its fight for freedom, become president of the new republic and designate the executive mansion of the new nation the "White House."

The Nelsons thought their cousin George had made a good match in marrying the widow Custis, not merely for the property she owned, but because she was endowed with prudence and good sense. Washington became the stepfather of Jack Parke Custis and Martha Parke Custis, nicknamed "Jackie" and "Patsy." On this late summer day of 1766, Tom would not have been surprised to see eleven-year-old Jackie dash across the meadow on a fast mount with his white cock feather gaily flying in his silver-laced hat. He would be followed by his special servant outfitted in a livery suit bearing the Custis coat of arms.[28]

Eltham was a spacious house owned by Burwell Bassett, who had married Anna Maria Dandridge, Martha's sister. Mrs. Washington and the children often stayed with the Bassetts while Colonel Washington attended sessions of the House of Burgesses in the capital. Once the master of Mount Vernon rode from Williamsburg to his home on the Potomac in three days, stopping en route one night at Eltham. This was indeed a record-breaking ride; few horsemen could stand the pace Colonel Washington set.[29]

In King William County on the banks of the Pamunkey River was another house Tom recognized, Elsing Green. The brick mansion that Carter Braxton had built in 1758 faced the river from the south front, its sloping terraced lawn leading down to the stream. The floor plan differed from other houses, with a long hall running east and west between two extended rooms balanced by an opposite, off-centered hall running north and south.[30]

Although the York was the shortest of the four streams that flowed into Chesapeake Bay, the same plantation pattern was repeated on all the other rivers, from the early settlements along the shores of the expansive Potomac and the Rappahannock in the Northern Neck to the rich peninsula of the York and rambling James rivers.

Gliding up the York made Tom Nelson dream of the day when he and Lucy might live on an imposing estate with their increasing family. His father was continually expanding their property so there were several possibilities for sites to choose. Of course, their immediate plans were to move into the house "Scotch" Tom had built.

Tom probably did not know the exact extent of the Nelson land holdings, but he was already assisting in the management of the York plantations, Pennys, Terrapin Point, and Dowsings. The previous year, 1765, Francis Willis and his wife, Elizabeth, had deeded 1,756 acres of three tracts in Bruton Parish to his father. In nearby Warwick in James City County, Mr. Nelson possessed a plantation commonly called Cheesecake.[31]

About ten years before, William Nelson had acquired over 1,700 acres in Albemarle County; within the last few months, he had purchased 3,500 acres in St. Anne's Parish from John Syme for £800. Tom also knew that his father had bought over two thousand acres in Louisa County near Fredericksville and had possessions in Frederick and Fauquier counties, but by far the largest land holdings were the Hanover tracts, totaling over thirteen thousand acres and divided into plantations designated as Bridge Quarter, Long Row, Mallorys, Montair, Offley Hoo, and Smiths.[32]

Terms describing an era evolve long afterwards, so Tom did not know he was living in the "Golden Age" of the Colony,[33] although the glitter was fading as the peak of the period had been reached. The symbols of this society were extensive estates, handsome houses, fine furnishings from England, costly chariots, and fashionable apparel.

The plantation owner manifested absolute authority. He made decisions for his family and directed the duties of a large labor force. He set the style of living, was a hospitable host, entertaining even strangers. Plantation diversions included dining and dancing, playing cards, singing, playing the harpsichord and violin, and chasing the fox. Tom liked to follow the hounds in a lively hunt.

Life was not all leisure for the landed aristocrat. A producing plantation required regular administration, constant application to crops, continued attention to accounts, and skillful purchasing of supplies. The complex operation of an estate demanded the attention of an owner and an overseer. Supervising a big labor force, largely ignorant, exacted energy. The gentry also felt an obligation to serve the Established Church and the Colony. William Nelson exemplified the spiritual and civic consciousness of his class. He was a vestryman in York-Hampton Parish and had represented his county and constituents first as a member of the House of Burgesses and in the exclusive Council. Tom would follow in his father's footsteps to serve the state as a representative, delegate to Congress, Governor of the Commonwealth, and Brigadier General of the militia forces of Virginia.

Beyond West Point the Pamunkey River was a contrast to the straight, wide waterway of the York, for the Pamunkey's course was narrow and curving, perhaps requiring oarsmen to manuever through sand banks and shallows. The scenery was the same on either side—tangled green denseness broken by the sudden appearance of cleared fertile fields and a long line of trees leading to a large house.

Tom was still thinking about these grand domains dotting the lands along the four great rivers. Many of these miniature kingdoms were known to young Tom Nelson through kinship or by association with his fellow Assemblymen. Foremost of his family's homes was that of his great-grandfather, "King" Carter, who had set his stamp on the social and political scenes of the period. Capable and cunning, he had acquired over three hundred thousand acres in the beginning of the eighteenth century, owned about one thousand slaves, and was considered the richest man in the Colony. He called his grand house Corotoman after the river that ran into the Rappahannock. The mansion burned in 1729.[34] The able and energetic Carter then turned his attention to architecture and had a dominant hand in the design of many of his descendants' dwellings. He constructed classic Christ Church in Lancaster County with its elaborate brick work and elegant paneling.[35] Since Robert Carter funded much of the church, he reserved one-fourth of the pews for his family.

Tom mentioned his meditations concerning the manor kingdoms and the intricate kinship of the Carter connections to his father. William Nelson could enlighten him on some of the intricate constructions of the clan.

As a young man, William Nelson had known William Byrd, II, and he knew that the master of Westover shared a mutual interest in architecture and family intermarriages with the acquisitive "King" of Corotoman. Early in his career, the ebullient Mr. Byrd had contemplated disposing of his vast domain to clear some of his debts, but instead he built "a very good house" when he was past fifty. Westover had two fine facades of exquisite design and seven bay windows with segmented arches. Tulip poplars lined the lawn down to the James River. On the right was the great garden, a precise parterre that delighted its owner. As unique and unusual as its owner were the grillwork entrance gates like those used on elegant English estates. Brass falcons perched above the brick piers and artfully curved finials of graceful urns; round balls, and pointed pineapple topped the clairvoyee.[36]

When widower Landon Carter visited Westover, he made a quick match with Maria Byrd and asked the fifteen-year-old miss to become his wife and mistress of his mansion. Her father wrote to Daniel Parke Custis, his nephew by marriage, on September 23, 1742, the day after the wedding: "Nothing ever fell out more suddenly than this affair, none of us thought any thing about it at ten in the morning, and by Three the Gordian Knot was tyed."[37]

"King" Carter had constructed Sabine Hall for his son Landon about 1730. Situated far back from the northern side of the Rappahannock River in Richmond County and surrounded by fine fields, it had a huge central hall, about eighteen by thirty-eight feet. Similar in structure to other Carter houses, it contained full paneling, a beautifully finished stairway baluster, and special lintel trim.[38]

Landon Carter had inherited two other plantations on the York River, Ring's Neck and Rippon Hall, and when he was in the vicinity visited his Burwell kin, Elizabeth Burwell Nelson (William Nelson's wife) since "King" Carter was her grandfather.

Charles Carter, like his brother, also courted a Miss Byrd after becoming a widower. He lost his wife in the spring of 1742 and married Anne Byrd at Westover in December. He was thirty-five and she was seventeen. Both Carter brothers were twice as old as their young brides.[39]

About 1750, Charles constructed Cleve on the Rappahannock River in King George County. It is a smaller counterpart of Carter's Grove that Carter Burwell, nephew of Charles and uncle to Tom, built on the James River the next year. Both houses face the river and have symmetrical balance with a spacious entrance salon flanked by two large square rooms on either side. On the land side is a smaller stairway hall with two rooms on either side paralleled by narrow lobbies for the servants. The rich details of gauging, moulding, and jointing on the brickwork, the splendid stairways, and superb paneling all reveal the same dominant hand in design.[40]

Young Carter Burwell began his management of the 1,400-acre Carter's Grove plantation in 1738, the year Tom Nelson was born. Carter had married Lucy Grymes, of Brandon, an aunt of the Lucy whom Tom would marry a quarter of a century later. Six daughters were born to the Burwells before they had a boy, but his father didn't live long enough to see young Nathaniel play on the fine plantation. Mrs. Nelson always took an interest in the children of her deceased brother. William Nelson shipped tobacco consignments for the estate and became the guardian of Nathaniel until he came of age.

Carter's Grove is named for the family and also notes the innumerable trees scattered around the spacious grounds. Tulip poplars grow along the front of the terraced lawn facing the river; four lines of locust trees and double rows of cedars border the lane to the dwelling.

Two other houses on the James River had Carter connections and Nelson association. Both Berkeley and Shirley land grants date back to the early seventeenth century. Benjamin Harrison, IV, built the main house of Berkeley[41] in 1726. He had married Anne, third daughter of "King" Carter and sister to Elizabeth, Tom's maternal grandmother. Benjamin Harrison, V, had inherited Berkeley after his father's death in 1744. He sat in the House of Burgesses with his cousin Tom Nelson.

Berkeley was bigger than "Scotch" Tom's house at York Town, but the handsome houses were counterparts. The former had a pediment roof and the Nelson structure followed the Greek form. Both had ridge chimneys. The unusual window sashes at Berkeley are four lights wide, and the Nelson house has decorative details in the keystone arch, window sills, and corner quoins.

Secretary Nelson would remember that the marriage of Elizabeth Hill of Shirley to John Carter, II, merged two extensive estates. When "King" Carter died in 1732, John, the eldest son, inherited the principal portion of the vast plantations. John served as Secretary of the Colony, a lucrative lifetime post, until his death in 1742. Thomas Nelson, second son of "Scotch" Tom, succeeded in this influential position.

Shirley featured four forecourt brick buildings bordering the north entrance to the estate, with two L-shaped stables, a kitchen, and the dwellings for the overseer in the dependencies. The four large rooms of the first floor in the house counterbalance. The north entrance salon corresponds to the forty-eight-square-foot south drawing room, with the two other rooms in reverse order. The characteristic Carter house paneling is evident, but the most distinct design is the suspended stairway sweeping from the second landing to the fourth flight in superb flyer form. Mary Nelson, seventh child of Tom and Lucy, would one day marry Robert Carter and live at Shirley on the James River.[42]

◆　　◆　　◆

Even a cursory glance at the correspondence of William Nelson reveals many facets of his illustrious character and inimitable charm. Effective expression with meticulous spelling and appropriate punctuation disclose the extent of his education. His dedication to duty was not only divulged in the written word but also demonstrated daily, for he practiced his philosophy that integrity and industry were indispensable factors for success in business. Since conciseness was not the criterion for effective eighteenth century correspondence, sometimes his long letters border on tedium, but the characteristics of acumen, candor, and common sense show through his statements. On occasion his opinions would be candid and critical, or persuasive and politic, and oftentimes rare flashes of humor crept into the communications.

During the two hot days of July 25 and 26 in 1766, Mr. Nelson spent many hours in the store writing replies to several letters he had received from abroad. While tobacco was the chief topic with his long-time friend John Norton, he also mentioned family news, the death of Lewis and the "old Lady," Tom's three sons, his moving plans, dislike of the British ministry, and rejoicing over the Stamp Act repeal. Expressing his thoughts on tobacco, William said, "I am very sorry to learn that the Tobo. I sent you did not appear so good as That w'ch went to Mr. Waterman. . . . I have made a good Crop last year on my Taylors Creek plantation of 22 hhds, half of which goes to Mr. Waterman the other half you'll have by Capt. Anderson on w'ch please to insure for me for £110."[43]

To Samuel Waterman he wrote that eleven hogsheads of his Hanover crop would be sent by Captain Hubbard's ship. It, too, was to be insured for £110, which indicated no convoy would accompany the vessels.[44]

A rainy spring followed by drought had damaged much tobacco and William Nelson summed up the situation to James Buchanan of London, "the truth is very little Tobacco made crop in my neighborhood Hanover hath been up to 25 . . ." He thought that was too high a price and wondered how other merchants afforded to pay it. The merchant promised to send twelve hogsheads and acknowledged agreement of their accounts.[45]

Mr. Rumbold Walker of Tabb had conveyed an account of eighteen hogsheads of tobacco from the 1764 crop; that of 1765 would be readied for shipment in the fall of 1766. Nelson still owed him a small balance and had instructed Mr. Backhouse to pay it for him. The merchants were middlemen acting as agents for the sellers.[46]

Nelson frankly explained to James Gildart of Liverpool, who had expressed disappointment in not receiving consignments, the ship arrived so late "subject to a winter passage and is the Principal Reason you have no Tobacco from me lately."[47]

Tom would lift the heavy ledgers for his father to verify the listings. Checking certificates, consignments, bills of lading, and recording receipts was an indispensable part of a prosperous business operation. Balancing books to make credits and debits correspond baffled Tom, but he could see that debit entries were increasing despite his father's industrious attention.

While his father persevered, Tom stepped outside the store to inhale the salty breeze and listen to the rhythm of the river. He reflected on his five years back in York Town, not quite so long as the years he had spent in England acquiring his education. Sometimes it seemed only yesterday that he had returned. He remembered his eager anticipation of the long-awaited welcome.

The rank and riches of both sides of the family had provided many opportunities for him politically, economically, and socially. When he looked at Lucy and his three boys, he felt that life was full. It was a pleasant and profitable period for him personally; for the tobacco planters, the 1760s had brought seasons of scanty crops and poor prices.

CHAPTER SEVEN

Domestic Duties and Political Plans: 1767

York Town in Winter ✦ *April Assembly* ✦ *Interest in the Insane* ✦ *John Hatley Norton Arrives from England* ✦ *Governor Fauquier at York Town* ✦ *Francis Is Born* ✦ *Events in England* ✦ *Tobacco Shortage* ✦ *Death of Friends and Family Affect Nelsons* ✦ *Tom and Lucy Move to "Scotch" Tom's House*

When snow fell day after day, York Town was turned into a world of white. Fast-falling snowflakes looking like flurries of tiny feathers quickly covered pedestrians' footprints and the wheel tracks of peddlers' carts. Wind whirled drifts down the sloping streets. Through the winter, inclement weather isolated the plantations. Roads became impassable. Zero temperatures stilled the rivers into sheets of ice. Despite the freezing cold, men could move about in a compact town like York. Nevertheless, gentlemen were glad it was only a short distance in any direction to the town's taverns. Each ordinary became an outlet for the male inconvenienced by confinement or annoyed by his crying children.

Tom's footsteps crunched as he walked, bundled from head to toe; a hat and muffler covered his ears. Since scarcely any underwear was worn by colonials, a camelot coat was often topped by a woolen one. Thick trousers and heavy boots completed the outfit. Not many men were stirring and business was almost at a standstill.

Captain Esten had steered the good ship *Hansbury* from London into York Town port January 14, 1767.[1] If the captain complained about the decreasing currency or the difficulty in paying his duties on the shipment, he was not alone.

Just the day before the *Hansbury* had reached harbor, Captain Lilly had left York Town for London in his ship *Sally*.[2] Three weeks before he sailed, William Nelson had informed his friend John Norton, "Tho the Misfortune is that the Tobo. will be generally bad in Quality as well as short in Quantity for my own part I shall make 60 hhds. less than I did last in Hanover."[3]

Since the quantity of tobacco exported had been small and prospects for future shipments seemed to be even smaller, Mr. Nelson hoped that the price set on the product would increase.

The *Sally* was loaded with 394 hogsheads of tobacco. The big ship also had 15,000 staves of lumber, 3,000 plank, nearly 40 tons of pig and bar iron, some deerskins, ginseng, and casks of copper ore.[4]

While a few customers basked in the heat of the fire at the Swan and imbibed a beverage, the servants rushed back and forth filling tankards, mugs, and glasses with apple cider, peach brandy, or a hot rum punch that sizzled from the hot poker plunged into the tankards.

Politics was always an intriguing topic. Tom shared his news about the separation of the Speaker-Treasurer office and the resulting election of Peyton Randolph as Speaker, and Robert Carter Nicholas as Treasurer.[5]

Changes in administration had occurred on both sides of the Atlantic. When William Pitt had been advanced to the House of Lords, some people predicted his promotion would alter his sympathetic attitude toward the colonies.

William Nelson was disgusted with the discord among the English ministry. He felt that the British officials should serve their constituents with "Honour" and he was "sick of a set of men who contend for Power."[6] Furthermore, he was distressed over the "extreme Injustice and injurious Reflections" evinced toward Mr. Pitt and felt that "ingratitude to Injustice" had been added to the insults toward Pitt.[7]

Time did not drag when frigid temperatures forced the Nelson family indoors. They were comfortable in the big, fort-like H-shaped house with its rectangular wings. The closely knit clan found cheer in companionship. Perhaps there was not a more literate group than the grownups with their English educations. Elizabeth had been taught to read by her aunt, Mrs. Page; Lucy had been instructed in reading, writing, and music.[8]

The head of the household set the scale of living. William Nelson liberally fulfilled his obligation to feed, outfit, and supply shelter for his family. The slaves were his property; consequently, he provided them with food, clothing, shelter. Not so impatient as Tom was at times, Mr. Nelson set up a regular routine and expected the residents under his roof to follow the schedule. He encouraged his wife to bear the sorrow of losing their children with sense and reflection. He was grateful for their five living sons, and he relied more and more on Tom to assist him at the store and with the tobacco trade.[9]

Cooking was a chore and a continual activity in the colonial kitchen; colonials didn't count calories or snatch snacks on the run. Mealtime played an important part in plans for the day. Breakfast started the day for the Nelsons at nine o'clock; they ate the midday meal at two o'clock; tea at four in the afternoon, and supper at about eight in the evening.[10]

The head cook possessed more culinary skill than the other servants, and she was accorded some authority over her assistants. She sent them to the smokehouse for ham and into the cellar for butter, eggs, and milk. The smell of ham sizzling in the long-handled spider often enticed Tom in for an early bite. Coffee beans boiled in a big pot. If the women wanted chocolate, one of the servants would crush the beans with a roller and stone device, and the powdered mixture would be stirred into hot milk. Pans of bread were placed in the chimney oven. While the family ate breakfast, the cook kept the kitchen help busy with preparations for the next meal. Pulling out the crane and trammel attachment, a servant adjusted the hooks to hang pots of potatoes and beans to simmer. Just like Master William, the cook would be glad when spring came so she could have a variety of beets, cabbage, carrots, parsnips, and peas.[11]

Daily devotions were as essential as eating in the Nelson household. Grace was offered at all meals; praying and reading in the Bible was a daily practice.[12]

◆　　◆　　◆

When Tom went to Williamsburg to attend the April Assembly,[13] he found his associates more aroused over the economic crisis than even his York Town friends. Debts were driving men to outrageous action. They hurled harsh words at the home government; Tom observed former friends who owed obligations avoiding each other, and he noticed that minor matters often touched off quarrelsome arguments.

British merchants had been putting pressure on Parliament to permit Virginia to print more paper money. Of course, they had emphatically stressed that the issue should not be used to settle indebtedness to them, but they suggested that the currency could be exchanged in the Colony to discharge debts. Tom realized that raising revenue was the most troublesome task for the lawmakers. When the old legislation for the loan office came up again, designated "A Scheme for Emitting Paper Money," the Burgesses debated long but passed the measure.[14] Senior members of the Council, old Mr. Blair, and the two Nelsons opposed the plan with the same results as in 1765. William observed to Capel and Osgood Hansbury:

> The Resolutions on the present subject seem to be too narrow, may I say selfish, and what people in their senses will emit a species for partial eyes, and such as is not to serve this principal Purpose That of paying their Debts which are chiefly to British merchants or their agents or factors.[15]

From March 16 until April 13 the Burgesses read resolutions three times, filled blanks, voted on bills and then carried the acts to the Council for concurrences. The latter duty often devolved on Tom, and he was glad to stretch his legs after sitting in the long sessions.

The young York Town representative approved of reimbursing the Colony's agent £69.9 for the philosophical apparatus purchased for the use of students at William and Mary. Tom reminded himself to tell Hugh that he might have a chance to use the equipment when he enrolled at the College. Tom also favored an enforcement compelling ships importing servants or convicts infected with gaol fever or small-pox to "perform a quarantine" for the disease. He hoped the law regulating the militia and supplies of muskets, bayonets, and belts would strengthen the military system in which he was interested since he drilled the detachment in York Town.[16]

On Wednesday, April 8, Tom was appointed with the two Mr. Digges of York Town, his relatives Carter Braxton and Robert Burwell, and others to serve on the committee to examine enrolled bills.[17] The spring session was in full swing by Saturday, April 11, with the divergent topics of disease and debt claiming the attention of the Assemblymen.

With his usual gravity, Robert Carter Nicholas read a resolution from the committee regarding the petition of one Constant Woodson pertaining to her discovery for a cure for cancer. Naturally impressed by her report, the committee recommended that she be paid one hundred pounds out of the public treasury provided that her experiment with claims for curing be certified by Dr. Theodorick Bland, Dr. James Field, Dr. William Black, and Dr. Robert Brown, or any two of them. If the physicians approved her discovery, the female healer would receive a certificate for the cure.[18]

Governor Fauquier called the Council and House together just before adjournment. He could not refrain from reminding the Burgesses that they had not brought in a bill to erect the hospital for the insane and it was their "peculiar province to provide means" for that purpose. Sharing the censure with his colleagues, Tom was impressed with the Governor's efforts on behalf of the hospital. Tom stood with his associates around the Council chamber facing the Crown Deputy. The Council sat in high-backed chairs ranging in rank, beginning with old John Blair, William Nelson, the Secretary, Peter Randolph, Richard Corbin, William Byrd, III, Philip Ludwell Lee, John Tayloe, Robert Carter, Presley Thornton, and Robert Burwell.[19] Governor Fauquier ended his impassioned address saying, "As I think this is a point of some importance to the ease and comfort of the whole community as well as a point of charity to the unhappy objects, I shall again recommend it to you at your next meeting; when I hope, after mature reflection, it will be found to be more worthy your attention than it has been this time."[20]

As Tom rode along the thoroughfare from Williamsburg to York Town, he enjoyed the lushness of the April season. Even above his horse's hoofs, he could hear the birds; he caught flashes of color from the bright orange orioles, scarlet tanagers, and yellow warblers.

Approaching Black Swamp, he recalled the warning, "Beware of the bog," no doubt brought about by an old misfortune on the site of the swamp years ago. A coach full of young people had been headed for a gala ball when a sudden storm struck. Lightning and thunder must have startled the horses, for according to legend, the coach was dragged from the road and swallowed up in swamp. Some folks claimed each anniversary of the tragedy they could hear the sound of the big coach rolling along the road.[21]

+   +   +

John Hatley Norton arrived in York Town the first week in June of 1767 to act as agent for the family firm with whom the Nelsons dealt. People in the busy port enjoyed watching Captain William Anderson guide the great ship *Rachel and Mary* down the York River into the harbor.[22]

A number of Nelsons was among the group of well-wishers who welcomed the young Norton back after his three-year sojourn in London. He became a frequent visitor to the Nelson family throughout the summer. They cautioned him to be careful of overexertion in the hot climate, as his father had also counseled him. Both William and Tom could remember vividly the vast difference in the damp coolness of the mother country compared to the humid heat of Virginia.

At twenty-one, John Hatley Norton was seven years younger than Tom but four years the senior of seventeen-year-old Hugh Nelson. The Secretary's son William was John Hatley's age; Thomas was nineteen, and John, seventeen. Young Norton found companionship and hospitality in the bulging William Nelson household, and expressed his feelings to his father in the ensuing months.

Mr. Norton wrote William of his gratitude and received a gracious reply from William Nelson.

> The little Civilities he meets with in my Family & which you so kindly take Notice, are but a small Effect of the real Friendship & Affection we have for you & Mrs. Norton pray assure her of this.[23]

When John Hatley had left York Town for London in the summer of 1764, only baby William had been born to the couple. Now three years later three more sons had arrived on an approximate sixteen-month schedule. Lucy was evidently healthy and hardy, for she endured the strain of frequent childbearing with equanimity. Thomas had appeared in December of 1764, Philip, on March 14, 1766. In selecting a suitable name for the fourth son, born June 25, 1767, Grandfather William no doubt suggested that the infant be called Francis in honor of their friend, Governor Fauquier.[24] The relationship between the Governor and the Nelson family had ripened over the years, and ties of friendship were further strengthened in the summer.

To assist the ailing executive in recovering from a recurring complaint, William had extended the hospitality of his home. The Governor could then receive immediate attention and constant care from his personal physician, Dr. Matthew Pope, who lived just across the street. Governor Fauquier was soon relieved of his indisposition by the treatment prescribed. Before leaving York Town, however, he had another sick spell, but Mr. Nelson wrote William Fauquier in London that he would be well "with good management of himself."[25]

In its July 16 issue, the Purdie-Dixon *Virginia Gazette* noted,

> We have the pleasure to inform the public that his Honour the Governor, who for some considerable time past has laboured under a very painful and dangerous disorder, is now quite recovered, *under the care of Dr. Matthew Pope, at York, and it is expected will be in town for a few days.*[26]

The newspaper had another item of interest for the public relating to Peyton Randolph: "And we have likewise the satisfaction to acquaint them that the Honourable Speaker who had lately the misfortune to have his leg much bruised by the oversetting of his carriage up James River, and has been at Wilton some time for his recovery is looked for daily, having got *perfectly* well."[27]

In writing to Governor Fauquier's brother, Mr. Nelson noted that the fine Madeira wine which the "old gentleman" had ordered as a gift had arrived and been accepted as a "Mark of His Honor's Politeness and Civility" but he would not taste the sweet drink until the Governor came back to "sit in judgment" on it with him. William could have no forewarning of the future. In less than four months, Francis Fauquier would die.[28]

◆   ◆   ◆

On April 10, 1767, the day after John Hatley Norton had embarked from England, Mr. Norton wrote his son a long letter, the first sentence of which sent the young man searching among his bags and boxes. His father stated: "I am much at a loss for ye Key of my desk in the Counting house with a little reed tyed to it wch. you had the Night before you left us & can't be found. . . . break open ye desk."[29]

High prices for products and payment of £12.12 for his passage were also mentioned in the letter. It was just as well that young Norton had taken "French leave" since it had "saved a good deal of pain & uneasyness on both sides." His father had been sick with "bilious vomiting" the morning his son sailed but dosing with "Daddy Prowting Rhubarb & Magnetia" had made him "quite well," he added.[30]

◆   ◆   ◆

To relieve tension, sometimes the gentlemen at the Swan relayed tall tales. The story of the staunch servant had happened a few days before and was relayed to Tom. A group of gentlemen and ladies had been sailing down the river when the boat suddenly capsized. A servant sitting on the bank saw his mistress sink so he plunged into the stream. Grasping her long hair between his teeth, he started swimming toward the shore, but since the stylish lass had fastened false curls to her coiffure, they slipped off and she sank into the water again. The determined servant dived in a second time and with firmer grasp rescued the drenched girl.[31] The story had its amusing overtones, yet some masters might wonder if their bondsmen would be so bold in a similar situation.

When talk in the tavern turned to trade, the men questioned why colonial commerce had not revived after the repeal of the Stamp Act. Like his father, Tom believed that Britain could not regain her foremost commercial position because of her shortsighted policies. Prime Minister Grenville had forbidden the colonies to trade with the Dutch, French, and Spaniards. When illness had incapacitated William Pitt, Grenville had grabbed the chance to goad the Chancellor of the Exchequer into action. He had found a ready ally in the ambitious and arrogant Charles Townshend whose temper was aroused when Grenville dared him to demand duties from the colonials. The professional politicians had confided to each other over a glass of Townshend's favorite white wine that they thought it absurd for the colonists to split hairs about an internal or external tax.[32]

Grenville admitted that his project to levy tax on colors, glass, lead, paint, paper, and tea was a mild measure in itself. The imposition, however, would not insult the inhabitants of America since the increase was an external type of tax. With a gleam in his eye, Townshend cunningly revealed his coup d'etat. Colonial courts and custom houses would be cleared of local officials and replaced with Crown officials. Strict warrants would be issued to search ships and stores, warehouses, and even homes. Now the provincials would not find smuggling such a sport. Persons found guilty of political crimes would be transported to England for trial. Townshend was triumphant over this plan for an all-powerful triarchy. Thus, with an indisposed monarch and an incapacitated Prime Minister, the Chancellor was reeling with power. He pushed through Parliament the Declaratory Act in late June 1767.[33]

Astutely, Mr. Nelson summed up the situation in the autumn:

> Resentment perhaps revenge for his late disappointment will set them in no very favourable Point of View before him: but plague on the Great little Fellows, who bellow out their Country supream Authority over the Colonies, & are only all the time jostling, croping, & jockeying, in hopes to unhorse some other jockeys that they themselves may mount into the saddle.[34]

♦　　♦　　♦

Colonial newspapers did not announce the arrival of infants but devoted space to the deceased. The beginning of life was understood, but the majority of men and women still felt that the end of existence was an enigma. Loss of life in strange surroundings never failed to arouse interest even in the indifferent. Accordingly, the arrival of Francis in June was transmitted verbally, but citizens of the Colony were alerted to the death of a Councilman through a newspaper account. The July 16 issue of the *Virginia Gazette* stated, "On Wednesday the 8th Instant died at his seat in Chatsworth, in the County of Henrico, universally lamented, the *Hon. Peter Randolph, Esq;* Surveyor General of his Majesty's Customs and one of the *Council of this Colony*."[35]

The previous year a young man from Gloucester across the York River had died unexpectedly from an unusual disease. Richard Parsons played cards with ruthless abandon, and in a bold boast he vowed his eyes would not close and his flesh would rot if he did not win the game. Going to bed that night he noticed a black spot on his leg, "from which mortification began immediately to spread all over his body, so that he died in a day or two, his flesh being quite rotten; nor could his eyes be shut."[36]

If unbelievers scoffed at the veracity of this story, the *Virginia Gazette* asserted, "The truth of this fact is attested by many of the neighbours who were with him."[37] Tom recalled the case although it had occurred in March when the two big items of interest were the repeal of the Stamp Act and the Robinson defalcation.

Losing life by an odd coincidence or an unfortunate calamity was conveyed in correspondence to family and friends abroad. Three deaths in the summer affected William Nelson from a personal standpoint as well as from a legal position. Letters between Mr. Nelson and Mr. Norton and those sent from the father to his son, John Hatley, revealed the first.

On September 12, 1766, William had written Mr. Norton that he would hear from others about "the great Loss our Friend Colo. Tucker hath had on Thur. 4th instant his six Warehouses and his Wharf were burnt down supposed to be set on Fire by Lightening."[38] (This statement surely brought back to the minds of both men the burning of the Norton house in York Town in the spring of 1759. William had felt fortunate that the fire had not swept across the street to engulf his home.) Mr. Norton was shocked to hear of Colonel Tucker's misfortune and informed John Hatley that British friends were attempting to assist the colonel in his adversity.[39]

As the months passed, the pressure of mounting debts of more than £10,000 and his desperate plight preyed on the mental stability of Colonel Tucker, so on August 14, 1767, Mr. Nelson notified Mr. Norton:

> You will have heard of the Death of poor Colo. Tucker, who never could recover his Spirits after his great Loss by Fire and the Failure of some People on yr Side the Water, yet it may be some Satisfaction to you to know that he was never enough in his Senses to be informed of the Bankruptcy of Criss &

Warren so That had no share in the Cause of his Death. Nobody here will prove the Will till Mr. John Tucker arrives from Barbadoes.[40]

In the same communication he reported the demise of his brother-in-law:

We have lost my dear old Friend Colo. Berkeley too, & from a very odd Cause. He had swallowed a large Fish Bone, no one knows how long before, which was extracted thro natural passage with much Difficulty & wounded the Parts internally so much so to produce a Mortification.

Relating the third death of the summer, William Nelson wrote to English merchants Edward and Samuel Athawes, "Captain Wilkinson arrived in a bad state of health. He died the Fifteenth so that the mate Mr. Ennes take the steerage of the Ship. He seems to be a good sort of man."[41]

Colonel Tucker, Edmund Berkeley, and Captain Wilkinson had all been engaged in different endeavors and died of different causes, yet by family connection and commercial concern, William Nelson was involved in the administration of their business affairs.

The Secretary, William Nelson, and the two boys, Edmund and Nelson Berkeley, were appointed executors of the Berkeley estate. As brothers of Mary Nelson Berkeley, Thomas and William were the logical choices to assist the sons. Handling the business of his late brother-in-law was far easier than settling the affairs of Colonel Tucker or Captain Wilkinson. Edmund Berkeley left a will so the executors simply had to follow the legal proviso.

Tom attempted to help his father in the next few months as he pored over papers to straighten out the obligations. Mr. Nelson understood the uneasiness of the creditors and assured the Hunts he would do everything in his power to collect the debt due them. Later he had to admit there was not much hope and conveyed in his communication that Mr. John Tucker had arrived although "Mr. Tucker hath not paid me a shilling yet & what is worse I doubt his ability to do it."[42]

Tom did not dwell too much on the debt situation. He and Lucy discussed their domestic plans rather than money matters. Yet Tom knew his father's communications repeated the same sentence over and over, "I am involved in the general calamity this side of the water, the Want of Money, to pay our debts."[43]

In reality Mr. Nelson was not in the desperate financial plight that many of his planter associates were, but he was distressed over indebtedness to the Hunts to whom he owed a considerable sum. On November 20, he expressed the feeling that "To remain in Debt I could never bear but with the greatest Pain as the Difficulty of getting in money makes me fearful of accumulating more Debt on your side of the water."[44]

Mr. Nelson curtailed his shipments to the other English merchants so that he could send the bulk of his tobacco to the Hunt firm. He stopped ordering articles for his family and stinted on supplies for the store. William's action would have been applauded by the London writer quoted in the paper who caustically criticized the buying habits of the colonials by saying, "Would you believe it? At this juncture, when people are complaining of the want of cash to pay their old debts, they have sent over for orders . . ."[45]

Tom certainly realized that the Nelson plantations were not producing as much tobacco as formerly. His father estimated the crop yield at one-third to one-half below the previous productions and Mr. Nelson stated several times that "I made in 1766 near 70 hogsheads less than the year before . . . . this year the Crop at Hanover 30 to 40 hogsheads only which is 100 short of my usual crop; yet I believe I am as well off as most people."[46]

In general, though, he thought the quality of the tobacco would be good, but he remarked, "the Crop just made will be the shortest of any since that made in 1758."[47]

When the planters stopped by the Nelson warehouse on the wharf or sat a spell in the store, Tom heard the same comments repeated pertaining to the quantity and quality of the tobacco crop. Dudley Digges might drop in to hear the men agreeing with William Nelson that, "Colonel William Digges is the only man I know that made a good crop this year."[48]

Some of the gentlemen were glad they had sown some wheat in August and September. They agreed that farmers should find a crop more certain than tobacco to solve the money situation. A one-crop system had many hazards.

The *Good Intent* had 103 hogsheads on board from the Nelson plantations consigned to the Hunts. Though it was a considerable shipment, Captain Hubbard had already told the firm that he feared he would fall short of his charter.[49]

After four months in the Colony, probably John Hatley Norton had developed some experience in discussing the intricacies of the tobacco trade. There was no reason to relay pessimistic passages from his father's communications to the planters to dampen their spirits. He surely wouldn't blurt out the candid comments Mr. Norton had written him. One said, "I have seen vile Stuff of Mr. Hansbury's out of Necks 'tis a great doubt with me whether the French will take them at any Price."[50]

Tom joined the gentlemen gathered on the wharf to watch the partially filled ships leave the pier. He had become a shipper, too, and eleven hogsheads of his tobacco were on board Captain Backhouse's ship. Tom was pleased that young Norton had been able to obtain a complete load for the *Rachel and Mary*. The cargo carried 661 hogsheads and 590 were consigned to the Norton company.[51]

Experienced planters knew that only the first step of their venture had been undertaken when the vessels left. If a ship survived the crossing, the grower was then faced with a variety of cargo costs. Unlike his counterpart in the colonies, the British customs collector was brisk and businesslike in demanding required duties.[52]

Standing on shore with his fellow merchants, David Jameson might stare at the seal *Vive ut Vivas* stamped on the side of his seagoing ship. Perhaps he mused on the meaning of the family motto, "Live So That You May Live," and wondered what further relief he might render his clients.[53]

Tom and Lucy were absorbed in their domestic plans that autumn. Their four boys were hearty, inheriting their parents' plumpness. Lucy welcomed the fall after a simmering summer and prepared for the move into the home Tom's grandfather had built. The crispness of autumn inspired the servants to stir with a little more alacrity carrying cradles, chairs, bags, and boxes across the street. Obviously, there were countless baby outfits since grandfather William had often remarked there was not a boy "old enough for breeches."[54]

Tom planned to place his special snuff box on his desk.[55] It seemed a long time since he had been a schoolboy in England and had saved Lord North's son from drowning. In gratitude the politician had presented Tom with the elegantly carved ornament that deserved a particular spot in the study. Books would line the walls of the back room. The counterpart room on the front would become a sitting parlor where Lucy would serve tea in the late afternoon. From there, guests could glance through the windows to the terraced garden sloping toward the street.

The second floor plan resembled the downstairs arrangement. The big bedroom above the parlor had a smaller attached compartment suitable for the nursery where only Philip and Francis would be bedded. The Nelson grandparents felt so alone without their boys that they prevailed upon Lucy and Tom to allow William and Thomas to stay with them. William Nelson's bustling household had been depleted with Tom's departure and Hugh attending the College of William and Mary in nearby Williamsburg. Bob and Nat with their cousin Carter Burwell were at a school in town all day and only little Billy was at home with his parents. He would go to a Latin school the following year and had already told his father he planned to be a parson and a merchant.[56]

Tom, Secretary Nelson, and Colonel Digges set out for their inspection of the Hanover plantations on November 23.[57] The men planned to reach Williamsburg for breakfast at the Nelson house on Francis Street. If fall rains hindered the progress of the party, they could throw oilskin capes over their clothes. Prudent owners also protected their mounts by a partial covering.

Though the inclement weather was the principal cause of a poor tobacco crop, the Hanover plantations had not produced even the expected yield for an unseasonable year. Only fifty-nine hogsheads were grown in 1767. In explanation, Mr. Nelson said that he had hired a young man too inexperienced to handle his acreage and that Colonel William Dabney and his eldest son, George, would become the new supervisors for the 13,000-acre spread. With their judgment and skill, Mr. Nelson anticipated a better harvest.[58]

The day after Tom and the entourage left on the excursion for Hanover County, William Nelson caught up on his correspondence. Still disturbed by his debt to the Hunts, he was hoping to collect eight hundred to one thousand pounds at the Court of Oyer and Terminer in December. William was still administering the affairs of the late Captain Wilkinson, and he had also been asked to intercede for an English factor in the complicated case of a Mr. Pride. Intricate debts were not the only problem Pride had and Mr. Nelson notified his agents that "He was fool enough to marry a girl who despised and hated him, and he knew it too. . . . soon after his passion was gratified, he treated her so ill that a separation was immediate and he hath since acted the part of a Madman, or of one in Despair."[59] The York Town counselor believed that the best course for his creditor was to dismiss the chancery suit and sue in the common law court to obtain satisfaction.

CHAPTER EIGHT

Taxes, Tea, and Tobacco: 1768

Grandmother Grymes ✦ Governor Fauquier's Funeral ✦ April Assembly and Accord ✦ Tom as Head of Household ✦ Smallpox Scare ✦ Drought and Discontent ✦ Hanover Trip ✦ Townshend Tax ✦ Hugh Is Born ✦ Governor Botetourt Arrives ✦ Election

An observer might comment that the Nelsons were wearing out the road between York Town and Williamsburg with their trips.

Because of the illness of Mary Randolph Grymes, the young Mrs. Nelson had traveled the thoroughfare at frequent intervals for several months. Her mother had developed dropsy, and by December 1767, her condition had become so serious that Lucy went to Williamsburg to stay.[1] Baby Francis and Philip were bundled up, hugged tightly by the faithful Hannah, and piled in the coach. William and Thomas remained in York Town with their Nelson grandparents. Francis was really less trouble than his brother who was not quite three, but Lucy's two teenaged sisters, Susanna and Mary, and seven-year-old Elizabeth, could cope with Philip. Eleven-year-old Peyton might play with him, but his three uncles, Philip Ludwell, John Randolph, and Charles, were quite grown up and probably gave the youngster only a quick glance. When portly Peyton Randolph presided over the House of Burgesses, he was the epitome of dignity and decorum. It might have amused some of his Assembly associates to see him bounce Lucy's baby boys on his lap or cuddle them close to his double chin.[2]

Since privacy was an unknown state in the eighteenth century, a sick person was not secluded. Visitors were not screened and no sign was put on the door that the ill person was not to be disturbed. Unless the doctor issued strict instructions, family and friends streamed in and out of the room. Blistering and bleeding were regarded as trusted remedies, but neither treatment could relieve the accumulation of fluid that caused the illness of Lucy's mother. To bear pain with patience and to endure suffering were characteristics of the colonial lady.[3]

As the oldest member of the family, Lucy took the lead in the care of Mary Randolph Grymes. Though only twenty-four years old, Lucy was regarded as a responsible matron since she had been married more than five years and was the mother of four children. It was her duty to make decisions. When Mrs. Grymes called, Lucy hurried to her bedside. She induced the patient to eat the delicacies prepared especially for her and maintained the custom of daily devotions.

January blew in with its stinging wind and dark days. As Mrs. Grymes showed no improvement, Lucy concluded that she could care for her better at York Town now that she and Tom had moved into old "Scotch" Tom's large residence across from the senior Nelsons. Dr. Pope, a next-door neighbor, was gaining a favorable reputation as a skilled physician each day. Later on, though, gossipy Martha Goosley would both pan and praise the good doctor reporting that he had been delighted at the demise of one of his old lady patients he had "treated with arrack Punch." On the other hand, she also stated that he had operated on a man who had suffered with stones for twenty years and Martha pronounced the surgery a success.[4]

The events of January would be etched in Lucy's memory as long as she lived. Her mother had reluctantly yielded to being moved to York Town. No doubt Mrs. Grymes felt some foreboding about her future and would rather have remained in her own residence. Nevertheless, Lucy left the capital and went home to make arrangements to care for the convalescent. She delegated the necessary duties to particular servants. Feeding, changing linens, carrying out chamber pans, and cleaning would comprise a continual cycle for the slaves. Flames sputtered in all the fireplaces to warm the big dwelling. Lucy talked with Tom about the preparations for her mother's arrival on the morrow. Dusk fell and a few faint stars flickered in the sky. Suddenly, a loud pounding on the door summoned her to hurry back to Williamsburg; her mother had suffered a relapse. Tom ordered the servants to hitch up the horses and bring the coach quickly. They drove the thirteen miles back to the capital, but as Lucy reached her destination she sensed she was too late. Relatives filled the dimly lighted residence. Her three younger sisters wept; her four brothers reached out to her in their grief. Mortal life was over for Mrs. Grymes.[5] Her youngest, Betty, had been a baby when Philip Grymes had died and now at seven Betty was motherless. Lucy held the little girl close to comfort her.

Despite their sorrow, grown people accepted death as part of a divine plan; to doubt the Wise Disposer would be irreverent. Who could know at this time that Lucy, although the oldest of the family, would live to be eighty-seven, surviving all her younger brothers and sisters.

Tom observed that all the Nelsons extended sincere sympathy to Lucy, the Grymes family, the Randolphs, and other relatives after the death of Mrs. Grymes, but no one was so gracious in expressing commiseration as his father, William Nelson.

A few weeks later he would write Samuel Athawes of his sadness over the loss of his dear friend and business associate, Edward Athawes. To the younger man he wrote these wise words of comfort, "He hath run his race and finished his course. . . . Honour and Reputation esteemed by all men. . . . when we lament the loss of a Man of Virtue & Merit, we have this Comfort reflect that he is removed to a better place where Troubles & Disappointment cannot enter."[6]

William Nelson's letter continued with the comments that the rings had been received and twice he had traveled to Williamsburg to deliver one to the Governor "but the poor old Gentleman is so bad that he is not expected to live many Days but don't mention it this may alarm his family & I am told Mrs. Fauquier was to sail for Virginia this spring."

Mr. Nelson knew that the voyage would be in vain, and long before the letter could reach its destination, Francis Fauquier died of the disorder that had plagued him for many months.

In a few days people all over the Colony would be acquainted with the news from the newspaper accounts. The Purdie-Dixon *Virginia Gazette* of Thursday, March 3, 1768, edged its obituary announcement in black and explained:

> Early this morning died at the Palace, after a tedious illness, which he bore with the greatest patience and fortitude, Hon. Francis Fauquier, Esq. Lt. Governor & Commander in Chief of this Colony, over which he presided for near ten years, much to his own honour, and the ease and satisfaction of the inhabitants.

Editor Rind in his account noted that Governor Fauquier died at two o'clock in the morning.[7]

Representatives would also read in the same issue that the Assembly would convene the last of March, by proclamation of eighty-one-year-old John Blair, who informed the public that the administration of government had devolved upon him.

On March 8, a crowd convened in the capital, and the Nelsons were among the group of mourners. Francis Fauquier's four friends, now executors of his will,[8] were in the forefront; The Honorable William Nelson led the list of legatees and was also the oldest of the appointees. Peyton Randolph and George Wythe, both attorneys, from the House of Burgesses, with Robert Carter of the Council, were the other members. For the past decade these four men had enjoyed Fauquier's stimulating company.

Because of his interest in social justice, the Governor had directed in his will that his slaves be disposed of in such manner that "they experience as little misery as possible as their unhappy and pitiable condition will allow. . . . liberty to choose their own Master. Women and children are not to be separated."[9]

The administrator also appreciated his cook and willed "To Anne Ayscough 150 pounds Sterling recompense great fidelity attention in all my illness. Great oeconomy with wch she conducted expenses of my kitchen during my residence in Williamsburg when it was in her power to have defrauded me of several hundred pounds." [10]

Governor Fauquier's funeral was a formal, stately rite befitting the regal symbol of the Crown in the oldest Colony of the Empire. People congregated along the streets, and lined the double driveway from the Palace to the church to witness the draped casket slowly drawn by caparisoned horses to its final destination. The breath of spring seemed hushed and still as the cortege came to a solemn stop and pallbearers lifted the bier for burial beneath the chancel of the church. This respectful act was the highest honor that the colonials could bestow upon their late Governor. [11]

Some of the Assemblymen who had arrived to attend the funeral stayed on for the spring session. Tom and Dudley Digges found their friends in the House of Burgesses concerned over another British act attempting to impose a tax on them without their consent. Even members of the conservative Council concurred that England had exceeded her authority this time.

Old John Blair as acting Governor was more lenient toward his associate lawmakers than an appointed representative of the sovereign would have been. Although Council members were still disgruntled over the Robinson debacle and enormous debts, Edmund Pendleton managed to maintain the three-year period of payment. He led the paper money faction and the forces for long-time credit. [12]

Tom had talked with his father many times on the subject and knew that William Nelson stood for a strong currency and had just expressed to merchants Capel and Osgood Hansbury his feelings.

> You mistake me if you thought me one of those who are clamoring for Paper Money. I never liked it in my life: I would rather struggle with our Difficulties than have any emitted. . . . no man, merchant or other, should be forced to take in payment anything called money, that is doubtful or uncertain in value. [13]

All of his associates, however, did not possess his business acumen. His brother-in-law, Robert Burwell, was heavily involved in the indebtedness as were his Council colleagues William Byrd and Richard Corbin. [14] The Council could be as cohesive and strong as hoops of steel when they stood together to oppose a royal representative.

John Blair, William Byrd, and Robert Carter became as angry over the assumption of British authority in 1768 as their ancestors had been in antagonizing Governor Spotswood in the early part of the century. Then, Spotswood endeavoring to restrain colonial prerogatives and power, had remarked that "the haughtiness of a Carter, the hypocrisy of a Blair, and the Malice of a Byrd" had ruined the policies of his royal reign! [15]

One favorable outcome of the general proceedings was the removal of some land and poll taxes for 1768 and 1769. Tom was gratified for he knew that his kinsman Robert Carter Nicholas had worked very hard to collect revenues.[16] With Francis Lightfoot Lee, Tom was appointed to prepare a bill relating to land settlement in York-Hampton Parish and to the selling of some slaves.[17] As Tom associated with the younger Lee, he realized that he was even more fervent in his feelings to resist arbitrary acts of the English than was his brother. Though Francis lacked the ability to express himself as articulately as Richard Henry, he took an unswerving stand on colonial rights.

Tom felt an accord among the members as they discussed their dissatisfactions over duties. The Stamp Act protest had pulled them together. The levy on lead and painters' colors was only two shillings; on glass per hundredweight, just four shillings, eight pence on tea, three pence per hundredweight; nevertheless, the representatives resented the encroachment of their rights rather than the amount.

While Tom listened to their lively discourses, he looked at the familiar faces and noted that many of the associates were absent. He wondered why his cousin George Washington had missed the meeting. His crusty kinsman, Landon Carter from Richmond County, was not in the group. Fiery Patrick Henry was also absent as well as Richard Henry Lee.[18] The legislators would soon learn that Lee had lost all the fingers on his left hand while shooting swans on the Potomac. In a letter about the accident, he wrote, "the unhappy wound, which I have received in my hand, will not yet permit me to travel, and indeed, I am sorry for it, as it would give me great pleasure to add, on this occasion, my poor assistance to the friends of liberty, contending for their country's rights."[19] The Burgess from Westmoreland added in a strong stand against the acts.

> History does not more clearly point out, any fact than this, that nations which have lapsed from liberty, to a state of slavish subjection, have been brought to this unhappy condition, by gradual paces.[20]

In his letters Lee continued to dramatize the approaching danger when he declared that such a despotic policy "hangs like a flaming sword over our heads." He advocated setting up committees of correspondence among the colonies.[21] In Massachusetts, Sam Adams had conceived the idea of circular letters.

Trying once again the methods of petition and protest, the representatives again addressed the Crown asserting that the right of taxation "derived from their own consent." The same sentiments were sent both to the House of Lords and the House of Commons. Remembering the role English merchants had played in securing a repeal of the Stamp Act, the lawmakers threw in an ultimatum about trade, that they could "content themselves with their homespun manufactures."[22]

If the British monarch and his ministers read the messages, they could not fail to grasp the meaning. The colonials reiterated the belief that a people had a right to elect their own representatives, to pass their own laws, and to levy their own taxes.

In Boston the citizens would experience the British bite especially when a customs commissioner was established in their city to enforce the enactments.

Sam Adams was already stirring up the Sons of Liberty.[23]

✦   ✦   ✦

Tom was just as agitated over the Townshend tax as his angry customers who thronged the Swan Tavern. John Hatley Norton could not spend much time there as he was working very hard to secure consignments of tobacco for the family ships. His father no doubt was amused and assured to read Mr. Nelson's letter saying that "with your Interest here, & your Son's Diligence & Application you might safely send a Broomstick to load a Ship to you;

The Swan Tavern in Yorktown, Virginia, was owned and operated by Thomas Nelson, Jr., until 1778. Courtesy of the National Park Service.

whilst my old Friends E. H. & Athawes labour for their 2 or 300 bbs apiece!"[24]

Edward Hunt intended to remedy this situation by sending over his son to compete for tobacco consignments in the Colony, and Rowland Hunt arrived in York Town during the summer of 1768. If he listened, he could learn a trick or two about colonial trade practices from John Hatley Norton. Hunt conveyed the latest news of the riots and confusion in English politics to the interested crowd at the inn. Mr. Norton had sent his son some special wine to share with his friends. If he stepped down the hill with the Secretary's sons, his landlady, Mrs. Goosley, no doubt watched him from the window. She was worried about her boarder for he was "too much hurried and fatigued that he Scarcely takes time to eat or Sleep."[25]

From all his customers Tom could hear the same complaints that William Nelson wrote to many of his merchant friends, "that the Crop now shipped is the shortest we have ever made since you have been in the Trade except that made in 1758 & it is good in Quality."[26]

David Jameson had another problem besides tobacco production. He was in a quandary over Billy Reynolds. Mrs. Reynolds, whose residence was near the tavern, had died in the late spring, and young Billy was loose on the town. Though reluctant about taking responsibility for the lad, Jameson had assumed the task of selling household goods and some slaves. Now he wanted to send Billy to London so Mr. Norton could teach him the shipping business.[27] Although Philadelphia was a good place for such training, the men of York Town decided that the counting house at London was more suitable, as "we are sensible of your care and rather wish to see him uncorrupted with a moderate stock of knowledge in the Trade it is most likely he will follow than to find him an adept in that business with tainted morals."[28]

Tom was not inclined to be pessimistic about the various problems as he was absorbed in his own immediate interests. As head of a bulging household of four sons and Lucy's three sisters, he had to apply himself to the needs of his ever-increasing family. He was growing grain for food on a nearby farm and involved with his father's attempt to raise and improve a special breed of sheep.

Attending the Assembly and operating the ordinary were only two of Tom's occupations. He mustered the militia each month and was becoming accustomed to being called "Colonel." Males from sixteen to sixty were conscripted for the company so several Nelson boys were drilling with the contingent.

The summer seemed longer to Lucy as she waited for the birth of her fifth baby. Since smallpox had swept the surrounding area for months, she and the children stayed close to home. York Town had not experienced the epidemic, and the community tried to avoid the disease. Smallpox was the scourge of the times, and it was not unusual to see many disfigured faces pitted by pockmarks. Newspapers informed the public that precautions were being taken to prevent the spread of the disease. Three persons had been removed from the College.[29]

Lucy and Tom probably read the published remarks of a physician stating that smallpox was "tractable," but the Nelsons did not want their children to contract it. The doctor stressed proper treatment for the patient depended on "diligent and judicious" attention,[30] and he advocated inoculation.[31]

Tom also believed in this method against the infection. John Smith had arrived the year before to set up a hospital and was prepared to protect people from the disease. William Nelson informed John Norton about the doctor's procedures of inserting the pus into the broken skin of a person, thus giving the patient a light case of smallpox that assured immunity thereafter:

> Some people object to his bringing the Infection into a Country of Neighbourhood free from it going to Baltimore to bring matter enough to infect the world, a second Pandora's Box.[32]
> Mr. John Smith [a local physician] hath rendered himself very blamable and suffering some of his patients to go abroad too soon: so that the Distemper hath spread into two or three Parts of the Country.[33]

Another former London doctor had a panacea for all the maladies of man. When the colonists read about his claims to cure agues, blotches, cancer, fever, fistula, jaundice, leprosy, piles, sores, scurvy, ulcers, and worms, they were impressed. He further claimed that he could heal the hard of hearing, straighten crooked limbs, and remedy venereal disease with or without physic. An appealing argument concluded his claims: "No Cure—No Money."[34] Yet by careful searching, York Town citizens could not find the doctor's stated cure for smallpox.

Little William became five years old on August 9, when the drought at the end of the summer season was casting a gloom over the grownups. As the child tagged along, he no doubt wondered why his grandfather kept mumbling about the "dog days."[35] Water could be poured on the parched plants in the garden with his special pump and hose, but the lack of rain would ruin the tobacco crop.

It was time for Tom to take his annual trip to the Hanover plantations, and the imminent arrival of their fifth child did not delay his leaving. Bearing babies was an ordinary occurrence of nature. His wife was strong in spirit and hearty in body. William Nelson evidently enjoyed improved health over the previous year because he also made preparations to undertake the journey.[36]

Rowland Hunt also went with the entourage. He was the second English visitor whom Tom had escorted on a tour. He had introduced John Hatley

Norton to the intricacies of tobacco culture the year before. Unused to the heat of Virginia's September sun, Tom warned Hunt to avoid too much exposure.

In a letter before his arrival, Mr. Nelson had already expressed to Edward Hunt a strong welcome, writing that his "coming to this country furnishes me with an opportunity of making some small Returns for the many instances of friendship & Civility wch my son as well as myself have experienced from you."[37]

With his father accompanying him and with Rowland unaccustomed to summer heat, Tom slowed his pace, and spent a night at a wayside tavern. Doncastle's was about sixteen miles outside Williamsburg. When the group arrived in Hanover County, overseer Dabney confirmed the Nelsons' fears that the tobacco crop would be another short one. While William stayed at the plantation, the two younger men moved on toward the mountains. New land had been purchased in Albemarle County and hope was high that fresh fields would yield high quality tobacco.

✦ ✦ ✦

Speculation had been running high in the Old Dominion regarding the new royal representative. In England, there were numerous seekers after the political plum; and in Virginia, there was excited contemplation about the successor the Crown would choose.

William Nelson had replied to Mr. Norton:

> I do not wonder that there are so many Competitors to succeed the good old Governor; for truly it is a place of great Value; and I know there are many hungry for such Emoluments.[38]

Other correspondents voiced their concern about the reaction of Parliament to the protests on the Townshend tax and about the new royal representative. Thomas Everard, clerk of York County, wrote the London merchant that "we are not a little Anxious to know what the Resolutions of the Parliament may be about American Affairs as also who we are to have for a Governor."[39]

John Page also conveyed his thoughts on the turmoil in Great Britain to Mr. Norton and contended that the dissension across the sea and dissatisfaction within the colonies was caused by "Ministerial Ignorance."[40] Only the aging Mr. Pitt and Lord Camden seemed to possess the sensitivity to perceive the stirrings that were stimulating an independent spirit among the oppressed people of the colonies.

Domestically, the birth of Hugh on September 30 was a most important event for Tom.[41] Politically, the arrival of Lord Botetourt was the most exciting incident. Financially, the end of the year saw the credit side of his father's books growing because of the sale of the *Madeira Packet* and the discharge of the large debt to the Hunts.[42]

The christening of baby Hugh occurred at the end of October when Lucy could attend the ceremony. Since the usual custom was to baptize a baby soon after birth, mothers missed the occasion. This time it was the grandmother, Elizabeth Nelson, who could not attend as she had not recovered from an ugly fall received in riding her horse.[43]

The Secretary, who was suffering from gout, might have been absent, although the disease had not kept him from indulging in his favorite diversion of shooting woodcocks from the back of his house or in nearby hills. The Secretary's aggravating condition continued causing gossipy Martha Goosley later to comment that he was doing "penance for past folly." In a letter to John Norton she complained that "the secretary has quite stoped us up in front we have no view but his Back sd & I was going to say all his out Houses are placed Just before our windows have a great mind to set up a Coffee House before his front Door."[44] Mr. Norton then understood her unkind remark about the gout.

When the Nelson clan congregated in church, the sanctuary was crowded. At the font, placed to the left of the center aisle, Parson Camm was an experienced performer and Tom, too, was accustomed to his part, but nineteen-year-old Hugh felt a new thrill when he held his nephew and namesake for the solemn service. Tom was proud of his quintet of boys and boasted about the male members of his family just as his father did.[45]

Life was made up of a mixture of sunshine and shadow. For every blessed event of birth, there was the counterpart in the closing of mortal life. So it was in York Town. Lucy and Tom had exchanged mutual congratulations with Rebecca and Jacquelin Ambler on the birth of their baby boys. Now the couple extended condolences on the death of Jacquelin's father, Edward.[46]

❖   ❖   ❖

Britain, becoming impatient with her colonial children, felt a show of military might was needed to quell the unruly men of Massachusetts.[47] In September regiments were quartered in Boston, parading and patrolling, their muskets gleaming in the sun. Although the Sons of Liberty held secret meetings, the time was not quite ripe for open resistance; but when the smouldering fires of resentment burst into flame, the patriots would be ready.

The method employed by the mother country to coerce her first-born, Virginia, was more conciliatory. The English had an especial affection for its oldest Colony and a peculiar pride in the expansive domain of the Old Dominion. Instead of sentries, she had sent Lord Botetourt to steer the colonial Virginians back into line. He was the personification of their policy.[48] Able, cultivated, and courtly, this peer of the realm would appeal to Virginians. To impress the provincials, the royal representative had come armed with the outward accouterments of his official status: a superb coach, handsome horses, and a retinue of servants. He was vested with the authority of the Crown and the power of Parliament.

Williamsburg welcomed him with open hearts and handsome hospitality. Though William Nelson worried about the short supply of wine in the Palace cellar, the legislators more than made up for the lack. Virginians perusing the *Gazette* experienced a vicarious pleasure to read that "all ranks of people vied with each other testifying their gratitude and joy that a Nobleman of such distinguished merits and abilities is appointed to preside over and live among them."[49]

Anticipation concerning the new Governor had animated the conversation of the colonists for many months as English correspondents had commented favorably that the new appointee was "good humored, sensible, and candid."

Mr. Nelson commented to more than one English friend that "We had Time before his coming to receive the most favorable Impressions of his Lordship's amiable Character & good Disposition toward the Colony."[50]

The ladies learned that Norbonne Berkeley, Lord Botetourt, was fifty and a bachelor. Gay laughter accompanied this announcement. The men were more interested in his attitude on taxes. A distinction that further endeared Lord Botetourt was his willingness to appear in the Colony himself although a peer of the realm. Deputies were often sent to the dependencies. By education and experience he was prepared for the post. He had served in the House of Commons and had been elected to the House of Lords in 1764.[51]

The voyage to Virginia had been a most enjoyable excursion for His Excellency. During the eight weeks' passage across the Atlantic, the captain and crew had been so congenial that the administrator arrived in the Colony in a mellow mood. Captain Samuel Thompson had guided the *Rippon* down the Chesapeake Bay and on Wednesday morning, October 26, the seagoing sixty-gun man-of-war docked at Hampton Harbor. His honor was hailed by a salute of cannon as he stepped ashore in the crisp autumn. After partaking of a repast, he rested until noon and then set out for the seat of government.[52]

About four miles outside Williamsburg, William Nelson and the Secretary met the entourage to escort His Excellency into the capital city. They extended to him a warm welcome and gracious greetings on behalf of the Council.[53]

The straightforward William felt that he should acquaint the Governor with the appointments of the Palace. Although some pieces of furniture remained in the residence, many furnishings had been shipped to the Fauquier family in England. As an executor of the estate, Mr. Nelson had notified William Fauquier that "the worked fire screen & stand, the green silk Damask easy chair, the high Bureau with looking glass Doors, the oval looking glass, Trinkets, swords & etc, which as you are desirous of them, shall be sent to you (though not ordered by the will). . . . We have disposed of none of the wine yet: nor shall we, as you chuse to have it all: & I presume you have declined making an offer of it to your successor as we proposed before we knew of your inclination for it."[54]

Lord Botetourt and the Nelson brothers entered Williamsburg as dusk fell and the capital glowed with candlelight. Citizens greeted the new Governor, and Council members received the Crown official with formal ceremony. Speaker Randolph, Treasurer Nicholas, and other members of the House of Burgesses also welcomed him on this occasion.[55]

Outside the courtyard on the Capitol grounds, the crowd watched the dignitaries conduct Governor Botetourt into the Council chamber. His official commission from the Crown was read and John Blair, William Nelson, and the Secretary administered the oath of office. His Excellency replied with grace, "Everything I have seen and heard since I landed in Virginia has been pleasing to the highest degree."[56]

After the formalities, the executive was escorted down the street to the Raleigh, the town's foremost tavern for an elegant supper. There were many first-rate inns, reputable ordinaries, and renowned taverns in Williamsburg, but none rivaled the Raleigh.[57] Its fame stemmed from a number of reasons, none so important as its excellent hosts. Innkeepers, like the Raleigh's Henry Wetherburn, left their reputation of hospitality and tasty cookery for each successor to uphold.

With his appreciation for smooth spirits, Mr. Nelson could relate the tale of William Randolph's selling two hundred acres of land to Peter Jefferson, father of young Thomas, in consideration of "Henry Wetherburn's biggest bowl of Arrack punch."[58]

At this convivial gathering of the political gentry, Governor Botetourt would not perceive some of the inn's distinctive features. Most taverns were built in a long, straight style, but the Raleigh had a front wing like the base of the letter *L*. Most hostelries had huge fireplaces of stone or brick built on the outside almost covering the wall, but the Raleigh had this feature constructed inside. Every tavern had its tap room and this accessible room was to the left of the entrance hall. An assortment of apple, peach, and French brandies, claret, Madeira, port, sherry wine, and Burgundy as well as Virginia beer had been provided the patron.

Governor Botetourt was up early on October 27 as were the Assemblymen. Up and down Duke of Gloucester Street Burdett's Ordinary, Chowning's, and the Red Lion were crowded with bootmakers, shopkeepers, and townfolk; the Burgesses and Councilmen were breakfasting at the Raleigh and King's Arms taverns. Usual talk of debts, taxes, and tobacco turned temporarily to the new administrator who awed and impressed them.

On this ceremonious day many flowery speeches were tendered the new Governor as the Assemblymen crowded into the Capitol.[59]

Andrew Sprowle reflected credit on the merchants he represented. The Norfolk businessman was the oldest member among the trade and, according to William Nelson, acquitted himself well as he spoke with simplicity and sense. Nelson wrote that "the old Fellow wears his own Hair, white, with a Pig tail to it, but bald . . . and cuts as droll a Figure as you ever saw in a Silk coat & two or three holes in his stockings."[60]

Observing that Sprowle's remarks surpassed the "Studied Performance" offered by professors, the York Town merchant complimented his friend and the canny old Scotsman retorted, "Aye, Sir, the Parsons do Nothing well, unless they are paid for it."[61]

The royal representative was pleased with the people of the Colony and the spacious Palace. He had met the leading legislators of the vast area of Virginia and found them to be as polished in manner as they were competent in administering the affairs of the Colony. Virginians had vied with one another in inviting him to dine and the official confided, "I have been asked every Day to dinner by the principal Gentlemen, and am at present on the very best terms with all. I like their stile exceedingly."[62]

The Governor was impressed with the imposing entrance to his grand residence, especially the Crown and emblems of England atop brick piers. He would also enjoy the formal gardens, copied from England's elaborate estates. The flower gardens were laid out in geometric shapes; hedges had topiary trimmings. Expressing his pleasure, the Governor said, "My House is admirable, the Ground behind it is much broke well planted and watered by beautiful Rills, and the whole in every Respect just as I could wish."[63]

Tom felt that his father was physically tired, overtaxed by his strenuous trip to the Hanover plantation, the festivities for Botetourt and his struggles to collect accounts due him in order to discharge his debts. As a final recourse to secure remittances, cases were taken to court. This procedure was tedious, time-consuming, and costly since the plaintiff had to publish a notice of the impending suit for two months successively. Parishes also printed copies of the order and signs were posted at the front door of the Capitol.

Cases were brought against John Wormeley, Archer and Lightfoot, and a foreclosure against Samuel Roberts. The conclusion of the court for an adjustment of an account was usually just over half of the indebtedness.[64]

Sales of slaves and property to pay debts continued because of bad economic conditions and the columns of the papers were crowded with the advertisements. Typical of the terse notices that announced a sale was this statement:

> On Thursday the 31st of January will be exposed to sale at Gloucester Court House for ready money A parcel of choice slaves now in possession of

John Rootes, in order to satisfy a judgment obtained in General Court by the Honorable William Nelson, against the Trustees.[65]

The planters constantly protested to the English merchants that they deplored being in debt and offered as explanation deficiencies in coin, climate, poor crops, and mismanagement of an overseer. But an increase in family also became a factor since children were an added obligation. John Page attested that "the necessary Expences of an encreasing Family" had caused his accounts to be in arrears.[66]

Debtors faced their distresses in different ways, some imbibing in drink. Captain Posey sought this route. George Washington had been inordinately patient with this unreliable friend and comrade in arms, and had lent him money as had George Mason. Eventually, Posey, like many others in debt, had to advertise his land for sale.[67]

Reckless gentlemen like William Byrd, III, grasped at the will-o'-the-wisp chance of recovering finances by risking more funds. Frantically gambling at cards, he lost and was forced to sell some of his ancestral acres. A large advertisement in the October 18, 1768, issue of the *Virginia Gazette* attracted attention. The land lying at the falls of the James River would be sold through the lottery scheme.[68]

Mann Page also resorted to this method for the disposal of his Hanover County property. His lottery was drawn at Mr. Anthony Hay's in Williamsburg.[69]

Lucy would still be abed after Hugh's birth when she read in the paper that Dr. George Riddell, as the executor of the estate for his deceased partner, Dr. Benjamin Catton, was pressing all persons to "make immediate provision to pay or give bond before December next as the circumstances of the estate will not admit of any indulgence."[70]

Tom was still away on the plantation trip when the October 19 issue of the newspaper notified the public of the Thompson sale. John Thompson was leaving and advertised that Saturday, November 5, he would sell a dwelling house and lot with convenient outhouses adjoining David Jameson's, one lot and stable near Dr. Riddell's, one warehouse, a new storehouse, two lots across the river in Gloucester, and sloops with a capacity of 800 bushels. Credit would be extended for nine months.[71]

With the depression, prices had dropped. William Nelson wrote his factors, "I am sorry to be forced to direct you to send me no more goods of any kind; till you shall receive further orders."[72]

Hardships were not confined to scarcity of coin, shortage of crops, or poor prices. Calamity befell captains and cargo. When the *Charles* was shipwrecked, William Nelson wrote Samuel Waterman about the mishap and complimented the captain for his "Assiduity and Attention" and "indefatigable" efforts to salvage every particle so that the "loss was made to fall upon those interested in the ship and cargo as lightly as possible. . . . misfortune might have happened to the most careful and circumspect man living."[73]

Tom was becoming more adept at casting sums and adding amounts at the Nelson store as he assisted his father with these duties. Fewer hogsheads of tobacco had been stowed in the holds of the ships sailing from York Town in the summer. Mr. Nelson never failed to notify the English factors that since the crop was scarce the price should rise.

The bulk of the crop being consigned to the Hunts to discharge the debt was sixty-two hogsheads stored in the *Elizabeth* commanded by Captain George Hubbard. Robert Cary received sixteen casks of the leaf loaded on the *Liberty*. To the influential firm of Capel and Osgood Hansbury, fifteen hogsheads were entrusted to Captain Esten; but only three barrels were marked for Bosworth Griffith. From the Taylor's Creek plantation, six hogsheads were sent to Mr. Norton. Captain Lilly had steered the *Burwell* out into the broad York River in the late summer to transfer twenty-nine hogsheads of tobacco to Samuel Athawes. At last Athawes had sold the Nelson's share in the *Madeira Packet*. William was satisfied with the settlement and could write on the books: "Balance of £303:8:11 in my Favor."[74]

Tom took a little respite from checking accounts to glance at the *Gazette*. He could imagine the hilarious guffaws of the gentlemen at the Swan Tavern when they read a tale from Ireland printed in the Purdie-Dixon *Virginia Gazette* of November 20, 1768:

> A maiden lady, who lately died in Ireland, left two guineas each to 4 maidens, aged 25, to be her pall bearers, each of whom must swear she was a Maid before receiving the money; but such is the detestation in which perjury is held in Ireland, that the old Lady was buried without a pall bearer!

Hugh seemed to be wearing out his footgear in Williamsburg as a student at the College of William and Mary since five pairs of strong shoes were requested as well as more leather breeches.[75] Soon the Nelsons would be sporting white hats, with eight-year-old Billy the proudest of his light chapeau. Two sets of cart harness were needed and saddles for Robert and Nathaniel, sixteen and fourteen years old. Cousin Cookson was advised not to send any more "woman's saddles which are not saleable."[76]

Tom had to take time out from his duties to stand for election before December 1. Governor Botetourt had dissolved the Assembly after his arrival in October and announced that an order for electing officials was forthcoming. This process was a prerogative of royal representatives who often employed it with the expectation that new candidates would change conditions; however, since the gentry had a firm grasp on the political system, few new faces ever appeared in the Assembly.[77]

William Nelson and the Secretary could recall the spring of 1756 when

Governor Dinwiddie had used the same device to rid himself of some bothersome Burgesses, but he had been surprised to confront the same group of gentlemen reappearing when the Assembly reconvened.[78]

Tom felt confident that the freeholders of York County would return him as a representative to the House of Burgesses. His friend Dudley Digges could also be assured that his Assembly seat was secure. While both men possessed the indispensable requisites of influential families, their own characters and capacities had been tried and not found wanting. The county court was a steppingstone too for a political aspirant, and Tom had this advantage. York Town was always astir on the regular court days with routine cases, trading in slaves, and a few fist fights among the bully boys. An election provided an added attraction.

Citizens from all parts of the county had come to town, and groups of gentlemen gathered on the Court House Green. William Nelson and Colonel Digges, fathers of the candidates, were recognized. The tradesmen meandered through the throng—merchants and millers, carpenters and coopers—while many farmers roamed around the franchised group.

Secretary Nelson was there with his three sons. Thomas, at twenty, and eighteen-year-old John had not reached the voting age, but William, at twenty-two, could cast his ballot for his cousin Thomas and for Dudley Digges, provided he possessed twenty-five acres with a house on it or fifty acres of unoccupied land.[79] None of Tom's brothers had reached majority although eighteen-year-old Hugh was tall and looked mature.

Thomas Everard, clerk of the county, was on hand. Dr. Pope, constantly being confronted by someone for consultation, probably accompanied Jacquelin Ambler and David Jameson.

According to custom, the men filed in front of the sheriff and justices seated at a long table. Tom and Dudley sat at either end. The sheriff called the name of each voter, who then stated the name of the candidate for whom he wished to vote.[80] As the clerks wrote on the poll sheet, Tom or Dudley might stand to acknowledge the support. Clerks were paid liberally for keeping the list. George Washington paid John Orr £1 on December 1 for assisting him.[81] Colonials, apparently, trusted the system.

Since the Nelsons were noted for hospitality, the voters would not voice the comment that young Tom was treating that day because he was running for re-election. His father was still feeding the folk who came to church on Sunday from the distant parts of the parish.

The law forbade candidates from dispensing drinks, furnishing food, or giving gifts to solicit votes, but loopholes allowed much leeway. Providing refreshments for friends was not forbidden. At election time, everybody became a friend. They expected entertainment. A decade before, twenty-six-year-old George Washington had supplied 160 gallons of spirits to numerous bona fide voters and innumerable loungers when he stood for election.[82]

Since the Swan Tavern was just across the street from the Court House, the men offered toasts to the two winners there. Dusk came early on this winter eve. Tucking her boys in bed in the upstairs room, Lucy could glance toward the tavern, and almost hear the merry laughter of the men as they celebrated her husband's election.

CHAPTER NINE

Routine and Romance, Riots and Regalia, Restrictions and Restraints: 1769

Winter Weeks at Home ✦ *Lucy's Sisters* ✦ *College Disturbances* ✦ *British Riots* ✦ *The Executive Eyes His Council* ✦ *Burgesses* ✦ *Non-Importation Association* ✦ *Lucy Ludwell and John Paradise* ✦ *John Hatley Norton and Sarah Nicholas* ✦ *The Reverend John Camm and Betsey Hansford* ✦ *Hurricane* ✦ *Royal Ball*

The winter with its unpredictable weather sometimes made Tom impatient when severe cold confined him at home. Upon reflection, though, he realized that these were his happiest times—enjoying the company of his family.

As mistress of the household, Lucy's duties required diplomatic management of her help. Choosing and guiding the work of a cook with skills enough to keep a large family happily fed was a considerable undertaking. After the nine o'clock breakfast, the young Mrs. Nelson and the cook conferred about the menu for the two o'clock midday meal.[1] Lucy might read aloud certain recipes and repeat the instructions again and again as the servants could not read.

Tom and Lucy's table was loaded with roast beef, pickled pork, bacon, ham, chicken, or turkey. Markets on the wharf provided varieties of fresh fish. Their own lands supplied apples and potatoes year-round. In spring and summer a variety of fresh vegetables filled the big bowls. Desserts to top off the main meal included peach and apple pies, cherry cobblers, tansy puddings, cakes, cookies, and gingerbread. Tom's mill ground corn meal, but most white flour and boxes of biscuit were imported from abroad.

As Tom sat at his walnut secretary in the southwest room catching up on correspondence,[2] he could hear the whirr of spinning wheels mingling with the sounds of rattling pots and pans and the voices of his young boys.

At four the family met for tea time in the cozy west front room with Lucy and Tom. While Susanna cuddled Francis, Mary clutched Philip, and little Elizabeth kept lively Thomas in tow, William sat like a gentlemen on the window seat. Tom relaxed in an easy chair but was ready to restrain any unseemly antics. Upstairs, a watchful mammy tended the infant Hugh. Lucy poured the steaming liquid, the china and silver sparkling in the winter sun. Susanna studied Lucy to learn the tea-time arts. If Philip and Francis misbehaved and crammed their mouths too full, a waiting servant whisked them out of the room. Afterwards, William and Thomas would return to their grandparents' home across the street.

The girls teased Tom about taking a family trip to Williamsburg in May, for Susanna, Mary, and Betty wanted to be eye witnesses to Governor Botetourt's ceremonial opening of the spring session. Lucy urged Tom's acquiescence. It had been more than a year since their mother's death, and they had dutifully complied with the customs of mourning. She realized the girls were growing, filling out clothes too tight for their changing shapes. Susanna would be seventeen in March.

They could stay at the Nelson's home on Francis Street or accept the hospitality of Peyton Randolph in his rambling home on South England Street.[3] Uncle John and Aunt Ariana were master and mistress of their own manor, Tazewell Hall. Edmund, Susanna, and Ariana were always glad to see their cousins.

From Uncle Peyton's home visitors could clearly view activities at Market Square Green, the hub of the town. Lucy's sisters knew if they arrived in the capital before April 23, they could enjoy the town fair held on Saint George's Day. Booths and tents would dot the area with an amazing array of articles.

In Williamsburg every Wednesday and Saturday, farmers came in from the country with their carts loaded with baskets of apples, chicken coops, eggs, and good grain. While they sold their produce, auctioneers chanted the values of their wares.[4]

Young Tom Jefferson was among the group in April gaping at a hog estimated to weigh over one thousand pounds.[5]

Susanna and Ariana Randolph could tattle to the Grymes's girls about the antics of their college-aged cousins. Although Nathaniel Burwell was making progress in his studies and had been promoted to the Moral and Mathematics School at William and Mary, he had also been called before the masters at their meeting in March for a misdemeanor—reprimanded for his rudeness to Mrs. Garrett, a College housekeeper. The Reverend Mr. Camm had been appointed to admonish the boy and "recommend him to better behaviour in the future." No doubt the parson reported the matter to Mr. Nelson who was Nat's guardian until the boy came of age.[6]

Perhaps the close-knit Nelson clan was somewhat comforted when they compared Nat's misdemeanor with that of Thomas Byrd[7] whom College authorities were convinced was the ringleader of student vandals who had broken windows, smashed plates and destroyed furnishings at the College.

When several of Byrd's peers indicted him, Byrd threatened to beat the tattlers. Outraged officials resolved to keep the names of those who supplied evidence an "inviolable secret"[8] and gave Byrd an alternative: whipping or expulsion.

The Honorable William Byrd as well as William Nelson aided the boy, but the president and masters concluded, "If Thomas Byrd should be readmitted, it would be attended with no benefit to himself but a great injury to the rest of the young Gentlemen."[9]

Mann and John Page had also been reprimanded for breaking the College rules. The boys had gone off bounds, were found "frequently in Public House in Town," and the authorities affirmed "if they do not behave better," punishment would result in sending them to their parents for one month. The officials were ready to proceed with "greater Rigour and rusticate them," but Mann Page appeared in the common room and asked pardon for his conduct.[10]

The College powers also had problems with collections. They were pressing Benjamin Harrison to pay his account and alleged, "If he refused, suit be immediately commenced."[11]

The trip to Williamsburg was no light undertaking. Tom's brood filled one coach. Tom's mother and father with their three sons, Robert, Nat, and Billy, required another conveyance. Because he lived in York County, Tom was allowed by law one day for the trip to Williamsburg and one day for the return; he received ten shillings per day while he served as a legislator. Representatives from remoter regions were paid the same amount per day plus ferriage.[12]

When George Washington went to the capital, he had to ford several streams, as well as the Rappahannock and Mattapony rivers. On May 3, the master of Mount Vernon rolled into the capital in his "chair" having taken four days for this trip down the Potomac country.[13]

Tom and his legislator colleagues talked about the riots and confusion at home and abroad. The Sons of Liberty were storming in Boston; in England John Wilkes had rallied public opinion in defense of liberty in the House of Commons. Parliament had expelled the agitator three times, but the aroused people continued to elect this popular champion to represent them. Denouncing the ministry and defending liberty to crowds on London's streets won him support in the colonies.[14]

Dr. Arthur Lee, Richard Henry Lee's brother, became intrigued with the political haranguer.[15] He sent accounts of the riots to Editor Rind who published them in his *Virginia Gazette*.[16] Alerting Americans was Lee's express purpose. Englishmen also read his statements—signed "Junius Americanus"—supporting the cause of the colonies and wondered if they were the work of William Pitt because of their forcefulness.

John Norton and other British merchants were not pleased with the riots led by Wilkes as labor troubles resulted. From Virginia, William Nelson wrote John Norton

> Hang Wilkes & all Rioters among you Say I but we must not call them Rebels tho the Mob at Boston have been honoured with the Name.[17]

The astute Mr. Nelson probably realized that Wilkes was a scoundrel, and he would have no patience with licentiousness.

❖   ❖   ❖

When Tom took his seat in the House of Burgesses on Saturday, May 6, he found many of the same familiar faces, as well as a new representative in young Tom Jefferson, who had arrived from Albemarle County. Jefferson had often slipped away from his classes at William and Mary to hear the debates firsthand. Tom Nelson knew the twenty-six-year-old man, for he was Lucy's cousin. As a suitor of Tom's first cousin Rebecca Burwell, twelve years earlier, Jefferson had been indecisive in speaking to William Nelson, the girl's guardian.[18]

On Monday, May 8, a mass of citizens crowded into the capital to catch a glimpse of their new Governor.[19] Although some Williamsburg residents could watch from their windows, the occasion called for companionship, so the ladies and gentlemen gathered on Duke of Gloucester Street or lined the lanes of Palace Green. Their clothes were as bright as the blossoms in their garden plots.

Tom, his father, and the Secretary assembled with their associates at the Capitol to await the aristocratic Governor's arrival. Lucy and her sisters selected a spot along the thoroughfare.

The crowd surged forward to see the Governor riding in a carriage presented him by the Duke of Cumberland, uncle to George III. A clever artist had changed the heraldic emblems of the Empire so that the arms of the Old Dominion adorned the doors. Six white Hanoverian horses bedecked with silver harness pulled the elegant equipage along the avenue. Dressed in a scarlet coat trimmed in gold braid, His Excellency sat erect, evoking an aura of tradition and sovereign strength designed to convince Virginians that the prosperity and interest of the Crown and the Colony were reciprocal and inseparable.[20]

The Assemblymen greeted him with a gravity and dignity that matched his.

> Your Lordship's Administration will be distinguished by the love of order, the steady and impartial distribution of justice, and the constitution will be fixed on the solid basis of publick liberty.[21]

About ten o'clock, George Wythe, clerk of the House of Burgesses, administered the oaths of Council membership to the Honorable William Nelson, Thomas Nelson, Richard Corbin, John Tayloe, William Byrd, Robert Carter, Robert Burwell, and George William Fairfax, Esquires.[22]

Appointing members to the Council, a position of patronage and privilege, was the prerogative of the Crown. As a coterie of first families, the Council had become a self-perpetuating group. In nearly a hundred years, the same names had occurred over and over again. Early enactments had decreed that only Councilmen could adorn their attire with gold thread; another distinctive cachet was the appearance of "Esquire" after their names. These men gloried in the greatness of the English Empire yet realized they were leaders in a new land owing their loyalty and allegiance to their own fellowmen. They believed that the rich should rule, yet they had a strong sense of service to their own constituents.[23]

His Lordship had already learned that the associates were related either by blood or by ties of marriage. As the chief executive surveyed the men surrounding him in the Council chamber, he could already evaluate them to some extent.

John Blair had served the Colony for over a half-century. As president of the Council, he had served as interim Governor after the departure of Dinwiddie in 1758 until Fauquier came, and after the death of Governor Fauquier until Governor Botetourt arrived.[24]

William Nelson followed John Blair in seniority, both men having become members of the Council in 1745. Thomas Nelson, William's younger brother, had served as Secretary of the Colony since 1743. Lord Botetourt had been impressed with the Nelsons at their initial encounter. He knew they were sound, sensible, English-educated men, that the Nelson name had become synonymous with service. They were, however, not so wealthy as Richard Corbin whom Botetourt studied next. Corbin's abundant property and possessions prompted colonists to coin the phrase "rich as Corbin" rather than "Croesus" when comparing worldly wealth. As Receiver-General for the Colony, Corbin could understand the planters' difficulties. He too had experienced the economic pinch and been involved in the Robinson indebtedness. (Corbin's original manor, Laneville, had burned and been replaced with what he called "a rather big brick building," with wings nearly 100 feet long.)[25]

Colonel John Tayloe was an English-educated aristocrat who operated on a grand scale. Even in progeny he excelled, with a bevy of nine daughters. Whether his endeavors involved land, shipments, houses or horses, size was an impressive element in his enterprises. He and several of his Assembly associates helped to organize the Ohio Company to acquire vast tracts of western territory.[26] His daughter, Rebecca, had married Francis Lightfoot Lee[27]. (The March 16, 1769, issue of the Purdie-Dixon *Virginia Gazette* had announced the nuptials: "On Thursday last Francis Lightfoot Lee, Esq., was married to Miss Rebecca Tayloe, a daughter of the Honorable John Tayloe's." Robert Wormeley Carter had also recorded the event in his diary with the comment, "I received a very slight invitation, but went that I might give no offense to the Bride and Bridegroom. Drank no wine: Because I was expressly within the statute made by Mrs. Tayloe, who said at her Table that she wondered how Persons who were paying interest for Money & kept no wine of their Own; could come to her House and tope in such a manner as they did; that for the future it should not be so."[28])

As Botetourt's eye encountered William Byrd, III, perhaps an interchange of understanding passed between the two men. Both men were heirs to political eminence, social elegance, and enormous estates. The new Governor had been born into a family of position and property. Patronage and prestige had surrounded his youth. He liked fine fruits and had erected an orangery on his English estate to grow citrus in the cool climate. The titled nobleman had been a conscientious colonel when he commanded the Gloucestershire militia but an overindulgent uncle showering nieces and nephews with expensive gifts, a habit which contributed to his indebtedness. When unfortunate business ventures brought him bankruptcy, his connection with the Crown had procured him the governorship of Virginia. He faced a heavy task placating restless colonists, recovering his solvency, and regaining personal as well as British prestige.[29]

William Byrd, III, was descended from ancestors who accumulated nearly 180,000 acres of land in Virginia. He had inherited vast property and political prestige. His erudite father had been elected to the House of Burgesses and then appointed to the Council. Both he and William Byrd, I, had served as Receiver-General for the Colony. When young Byrd brought Elizabeth Hill Carter of Shirley home to Westover as his bride in 1748, his future seemed filled with promise, but Byrd seemed marked for misfortune. His first wife, Elizabeth Carter Byrd, was crushed to death when a tall chest fell on her in 1760. During the French and Indian War he had outfitted the Second Virginia Regiment with French uniforms captured from a ship at sea but generously paid all other expenses. Now he was engulfed with debt. He had squandered £10,000 gambling in London to the Duke of Cumberland and lost Blue Stone Castle on its ten-mile Roanoke River tract during a three-day gambling marathon with William Skipworth at Westover. Indeed, he and Botetourt understood life's adversities.[30]

Governor Botetourt next studied Robert Carter, whose grandfather Robert, "King" Carter, had acquired over three hundred thousand acres of rich land lying between the Potomac and Rappahannock rivers and immense tracts beyond the Blue Ridge Mountains. Lord Fairfax had appointed "King" Carter to act as his agent for the Northern Neck district; "King" had grasped the advantage. He patented grants for five sons—John, Robert, Charles, George, and Landon Carter—and five grandsons—Lewis Burwell,

Carter Page, Robert Carter Nicholas, Benjamin Harrison, and Robert Carter, III.

The progenitor of the famous family became a Burgess, then progressed to Speaker, Chairman of the influential Committee of Propositions and Grievances, and Treasurer, continuing in that post even after he was appointed to the Council. Robert Carter, III, became a candidate for the House of Burgesses just before his twenty-fourth birthday, but he was defeated. The Lees were so entrenched in Westmoreland County that they could not be ousted and continued to be elected until the Revolution. Despite the defeat, Carter was appointed to the Council six years later, no doubt causing comment since he had not served as a Burgess, but the young gentleman possessed the indispensable requisites of fortune and family. He had strengthened his status by marrying Maryland heiress Frances Ann Tasker. Her uncle, Thomas Bladen, was a member of the English Parliament whose prestige and connection with court circles clinched the Council post for Robert Carter, III. Young Carter had taken his bride home to Nomini Hall, the home his father had built. (It differed from the other majestic mansions designed for "King" Carter's descendants in that its rosy red bricks had been painted white.) Councillor Carter possessed some seventy thousand acres scattered through six counties in the Northern Neck region.[31]

Botetourt next observed Robert Carter Burwell sitting in the high-backed chair behind the big oval table. He was a typical example of the tangled alliances that existed among the associates. Colonel Burwell was doubly related to the Nelsons since his sister, Elizabeth, had married William Nelson and was closely connected with the Carter clan through his mother, Elizabeth, who had married Nathaniel Burwell. After the death of Colonel Burwell's father, his mother had married George Nicholas and had two children, Robert Carter Nicholas, and a second Elizabeth. Colonel Burwell's daughter had married John Page in 1765, acquiring another illustrious link through the Page name. Governor Fauquier had not favored Burwell's appointment to the Council. Secretary Nelson had also disapproved. In spite of such powerful opponents, the confirmation had come from the Crown in 1762. Apparently, William Nelson helped to bridge the gap or Burwell did not bear a grudge, for Burwell served with the Secretary to study the state of Robinson's accounts and joined the Nelsons in the Dismal Swamp land speculation.[32]

George William Fairfax was the latest addition to the aristocratic oligarchy. In a letter to Athawes in London, Mr. Nelson had appraised the 1767 appointment:

> I was pleased to hear that George William Fairfax, Esquire, was appointed to the Council in the Room of Colonel Ludwell, deceased, as his family Fortune and good Sense entitled him to a place there. Tho' if I were

> Colonel Fairfax living at such a Distance with his infirmities of body about
> me with I make my most Dutiful and respectful compliments for the Honour
> done me but should beg leave to resign it.[33]

A rich planter from Belvoir in Fairfax County, George Fairfax was endowed
with both land and social status. His ancestor, Thomas, the sixth Lord Fairfax, had become the sole proprietor of the vast Northern Neck territory in
the early eighteenth century. The previous peer had carved out a regal duchy
for the family and Thomas, VI, continued the process until approximately
five million acres were patented embracing an area from the Chesapeake Bay
on the east to the Shenandoah River in the west.[34]

The Fairfaxes had befriended young Washington, teaching him about
maps and mathematics so that he could survey the Virginia frontier. From
this early experience as an explorer, George Washington emerged as a man
of daring and determination, stamina and self-reliance that stamped his
character. The two families became fast friends. Belvoir had been built in
1741 below Mount Vernon on a promontory above the banks of the Potomac
River. Colonel Fairfax inherited the home in 1757, and he and his wife,
Sally Cary, gave grand garden parties there. A range of brick walls surrounded the residence with two 200-foot-long parallel structures which provided exceptional privacy for the guests.[35]

Governor Botetourt must have approved of the patricians in the House
that day. At the May meeting, the Burgesses elected Peyton Randolph
Speaker; he declared he would perform his duties with "fidelity, Diligence,
and Impartiality." When the Burgesses convened with the Council and His
Excellency in the upper chamber, Speaker Randolph departed from the
usual formal petition of Ancient Rights and Privileges and expounded on
the right of "Freedom of speech and Debate."[36]

The Crown official was not oblivious to the obstacles that confronted
him. As Governor Botetourt eyed these determined men, he wondered if
diplomacy could turn the tide. He spoke slowly and sincerely:[37]

> You, Gentlemen, who know immediately the true interest of the Colony,
> are the Best Judges of the Measures necessary to be pursued for the Advan-
> tage and Prosperity. . . . purpose to promote and render permanent Happi-
> ness of Virginia. . . . merit your Confidence and Affection.[38]

Tom thought no one could take issue with these well-meaning words. He
was assigned again to the Committee of Propositions and Grievances[39] to
serve with the stalwarts of the House: Richard Bland, Edmund Pendleton,
Archibald Cary, and Richard Henry Lee. In addition, he became a member
of the Committee of Religion with kinsmen Lewis Burwell, Benjamin Harrison, and George Washington.[40]

As always, the legislators spoke of taxes and trials and summed up their stand on the "late unconstitutional act imposing Duties on Tea, Paper, Glass, etc. for the purpose of raising Revenue. . . . Trade of the Colony and American Commerce in general . . . was in a ruinous condition."[41]

Tom reiterated the remarks of his father who said, "imposing duties for the regulation of trade" had caused these hardships.[42]

Now the hated Townshend tax with its additional threat of transporting colonists charged with treason to Great Britain for trial raised feelings to a fiery pitch.[43]

Richard Bland was too busy on May 6 thinking about the tax troubles to remember that it was his birthday. He had turned fifty-nine though he looked older. His associates readily acknowledged that he was the authority on the British constitution because of his long years of study on the subject.[44] Peyton Randolph and Edmund Pendleton were also well versed in legal procedures. Both were forty-eight years old and used reason in speaking and writing—presenting their views with force, if not fluency. The tall, blue-eyed Pendleton, though naturally cautious and conservative, could refine the aspects of a case to confuse and disconcert an opponent.[45]

George Wythe and Robert Carter Nicholas, barristers in their early forties, were men of import and influence who commanded the confidence of their constituents. Wythe, a serious scholar of Roman and English laws, had been elected mayor of Williamsburg and appointed clerk of the House in March 1768. He replaced John Randolph who had moved up to the position of Attorney General. Robert Carter Nicholas, reliable, religious, and highly respected, had sacrificed a successful law practice to serve as Treasurer of the Colony.[46]

Glancing around the governing body, Tom glimpsed several Carter cousins in attendance: Charles of Ludlow, son of the late Charles of Cleve, and Charles of Corotoman, both nephews of Landon Carter, who had been nearly forty when he first entered the House of Burgesses in 1748. Now at sixty, he was becoming well-known for his contentious character, which Tom and the other young men half his age attributed to his advanced years, rather than to an independent manner.[47]

Ben Harrison, another cousin of Tom's, had served in the body since he was twenty-three. Twelve years older than young Nelson, he was handsome, if overweight, and humorous. Hounded by creditors and juggling finances, he sometimes relieved the strain of an awkward situation with a joke.[48]

Patrick Henry and Richard Henry Lee, the two liberals of the House, aligned themselves against the conservative oligarchy. Henry was two years older than Tom, while Lee was six years his senior. The two orators differed somewhat in their defiance to British policies, but both men were aggressive in argument. Ever since the Parsons' Cause, Henry had continued to voice his opinion that the Crown encroached on the rights of the Colony. By background, Richard Henry Lee belonged to the aristocracy, but his bold beliefs and philosophy placed him with the progressives. Even the more moderate members, although exasperated by his ideas, appreciated the forceful eloquence and graceful gestures of the slender patrician.[49]

Thomas Nelson, Jr., and his taciturn cousin George Washington, a ten-year member of the House of Burgesses, had not taken a prominent part in floor debate, but both delegates had labored patiently on committee assignments and sat dutifully through some dull days of routine business. Washington had given thought to the oppressive Townshend taxes and agreed with his friend and neighbor George Mason that a Non-Importation Association should be formed. Colonel Washington took the plan to Williamsburg that Mason had already drawn.[50]

On Wednesday, May 17, the record reads, "About twelve o'clock his Excellency the Governor pleased by his Messenger to command the attendance of the House of Burgesses in the Council Chamber."[51]

In the chamber Governor Botetourt summed up his reaction tersely:

> Mr. Speaker, and Gentlemen of the House of Burgesses, I have heard of your Resolves and augur Ill of their Effect: You have made it my Duty to dissolve you; and you are dissolved accordingly.[52]

The Burgesses, not too shocked at Governor Botetourt's statement strode down the stairs moving from the Capitol toward the Raleigh Tavern. They gathered in the Apollo Room and appointed Peyton Randolph moderator by unanimous consent. Conservatives emphasized the sad state of the Colony. The men voiced old arguments and searched for new solutions in the charged atmosphere. What about an embargo on English goods? Why not prohibit the purchase of articles through an association? They had tried petitions and protests; it was time to turn the tide. A boycott on British goods would impel Parliament to repeal the Townshend tax. A committee appointed to draft details discussed the plan of operation, the list of prohibited articles, and the pledge to make the association practicable. The men worked far into the night to have their report ready by ten o'clock the next morning. On May 18, the Burgesses gathered once again in the Raleigh's Apollo Room to hear the terms. A preface stated that all people must use "legal Ways and Means in their Power to promote and encourage Industry and Frugality. . . . Discourage all Manner of Luxury and Extravagance."[53]

The Assemblymen approved the agreement. Affixing their signatures to the compact, conservatives and liberals joined in a common cause.[54]

Peyton Randolph signed the non-importation instrument first followed by Robert Carter Nicholas, Richard Bland, and Archibald Cary—conservatives of the House. Liberal Richard Henry Lee was next on the list. Moderate George Washington signed as did conservative Carter Braxton and Lucy's brother, Philip Ludwell Grymes. Patrick Henry's scrawl appeared first in the second column, the progressive opposite the old-line conservative. Thomas Jefferson signed and Thomas Nelson, Jr., took the pen to place his legible signature on the seventh line. In all eighty-eight members approved of the association, a three-fourths majority of the total House membership.[55] All the delegates did not sign for some had returned home and others were more guarded. Benjamin Harrison, Francis Lightfoot Lee, and John Randolph disapproved. Edmund Pendleton's name did not appear, because he had secured a leave of absence.

Burgesses who abided by their bargain would forego cheese, confections, fish, fruit, pickles, port, sugar, and tea, as well as ale, beer, cider, spirits, and wine. A long list of luxuries was to be excluded, including cabinet work, carriages, chairs, clocks, looking glasses, gold, jewelry, and trinkets. Colonists would need to husband their clothing since lace, millinery, muslin, silks, boots, leather, saddles, and shoes were not to be bought from Britain. (They were encouraged to raise lambs for the wool.) Paints, paper, and pigment were prohibited except cheap paper not exceeding eight shillings per ream. No taxed items for raising revenue in the Colony could be ordered. Other provisions forbade the importation of slaves after November 1.[56]

Tom thought the representatives seemed relieved that the deed was done. Hospitable Mr. Hay sent the servants in the Raleigh for tall glasses filled with spirits. Ten times the gentlemen toasted the health of the royal family and Governor Botetourt. An eleventh saluted "all true patriots" who were lovers of liberty.[57]

The next night the Assemblymen and their wives rode to the Palace in their imported English coaches, bedecked in British broadcloth, wondering how long such luxuries would last. Governor Botetourt had planned a ball on the anniversary of the Queen's birthday.[58]

Mr. and Mrs. Robert Carter could walk the short distance from their residence as could the George Wythes. Although the Peyton Randolphs lived just around the corner, their corpulence required a carriage. Like most women, Elizabeth Harrison Randolph left politics to the men; it was their prerogative. If her husband and so many Burgesses believed that a boycott of British goods would be beneficial, why hadn't Benjamin Harrison been convinced? Peyton was provoked with his brother for not having signed the pact, although he knew John had idealistic illusions about the English Empire.

George Washington arrived at the palace alone because his wife had not accompanied him to Williamsburg. Those assembled regarded the Colonel with new respect since his speech on the non-importation plan; colonial belles eyed him because he made a grand partner for the lively reels.[59]

Back in York Town after the Assembly session, Tom acquainted his tavern customers with the Non-Importation Association. He explained the articles that all should omit from their orders to bring Britain to her senses. By practicing frugality and promoting industry, Virginians could make the plan work. Although the list of restrictions had been printed in the paper, Tom promised to post a copy for reference since the record read the "Association was binding on all."

Despite her numerous daily duties, Lucy continued the custom of serving tea at four each afternoon. Visitors called at this social hour to sip their favorite bohea. They wondered when they might be forced to substitute another drink, like perry, made from pear juice, or a honey and water mixture. Roasted rye substituted for coffee, but most doubted the claim that it was more wholesome than the genuine beverage. They chatted, too, about their children. Lucy and Rebecca Ambler compared their offspring, while Elizabeth Nelson and Lucy Armistead Nelson, mothers of grown sons, offered sage advice on when to wean babies and how to remedy fevers and flux.

An announcement of the London marriage of Lucy Ludwell and John Paradise in a May 25 newspaper especially interested Lucy.[60] Her sisters were too young to remember their cousins since Philip Ludwell had embarked for England in 1760 with his two young daughters, Hannah and Lucy. Philip Ludwell, III, was an uncle of Philip Grymes, the girls' father. Philip Ludwell, II, of Green Spring had built a handsome brick house in Williamsburg on Duke of Gloucester Street, and from this forebear the Grymes girls were related to the Lee family since Hannah Ludwell, aunt to their father, had married Thomas Lee of Stratford. (Eventually rumors would reach Virginia of Lucy Paradise's eccentric exploits and long after the Revolution, when she had moved to Williamsburg, the unstable Lucy would demand that a coach be set up in the hall of the grand residence and insist that her guests sit beside her as a servant moved the carriage back and forth. The hapless Lucy Paradise would finally be sent to the institution for the insane.)[61]

Politics interested the men but romance intrigued the women. Martha Goosley could enlighten the ladies on the latest development of the Norton-Nicholas courtship. When he was in town, John Hatley Norton boarded at her house, "commonly Dineing upon two Dishes,"[62] she had informed his father. Across the table the young man had confided his cherished desires. His father had no personal objection to Sarah, daughter of Robert Carter Nicholas; indeed, a young lady of such a fine family would be a most suitable match if she would consent to leave the Colony to live in London. His father's opposition stemmed from fear that the romance would prevent his son from returning to England. Being a partner in the family firm entailed great responsibility and Mr. Norton reminded his son of this fact:

> This Lady is full young to enter into the cares of Life, she has been bred in a genteel way & has a right to expect to live so. . . . one sixth part of the profits of the trade is all in my power to allow you & what will that do to

maintain a family without other assistance which can't be much look'd for in America at present.[63]

To reinforce his arguments, Mr. Norton reproved his son by reminding him of a former romantic attachment, "which I never knew of till you had met with a Repulse."[64]

To young Norton, who was almost twenty-four years old, this thrust cut deep. It was embarrassing that his father had failed to follow through with his approval since he had already spoken to Mr. Nicholas and had secured his consent for the marriage. (They were to marry eventually.)[65]

York Town folk quickly forgot this romantic involvement when they read the following nuptial notice in the Rind *Virginia Gazette*, July 13, 1769:

> Married—Last on Saturday the Reverend John Camm, Treasurer of William and Mary College and rector of Yorkhampton Parish, was married to Miss Betsey Hansford, an agreeable young lady.

This announcement set tongues wagging. Even the men marveled volubly at the minister. Imagine the old parson breaking the precedent that professors must not marry! It took courage to defy convention. Tavern customers concluded that even an old man could become enchanted by a chaste young lass. Why had Betsey Hansford chosen Camm and rejected her young suitor? Girls often married men old enough to be their fathers but in this instance the groom was more than three times the age of the bride.

A young man, enamoured of Betsey, but rebuffed by her, had implored the preacher to intercede for him. When the Reverend Mr. Camm pleaded the deserving young gentleman's cause, Betsey was adamant. (Perhaps remembering the courage of her rebel ancestor spurred her to speak. Thomas Hansford had been an officer under the bold, hot-headed Nathaniel Bacon. When the imperious Sir William Berkeley recaptured Jamestown, he was ready for his revenge. Hansford requested that he be "shot like a soldier and not hanged like a dog," but the rebel was hanged on the gibbet. As the first native Virginian to die on the gallows, he became a martyr for a revolt with no tangible triumphs.) Betsey remained firm. She suggested the clergyman would understand the cause of her rebuff by reading II Samuel 12:7. When the parson did so, he was surprised to see, "Thou art the man." Astonishment yielded to action. The preacher proposed and led Miss Hansford to the altar.[66]

Martha Goosley assessed the situation in a letter to Mr. Norton:

> Mr. Camms Marriage has made a great noise here but Pray why may not an old Man afflicted with the Gout have the Pleasure of a fine hand to rub his feet and warm his flannels comfomtable amusement you will say for a Girl of fifteen but She is to have a Chariot and there is to be no Padlock but upon her mind.[67]

✦   ✦   ✦

Tom's father informed many merchant factors abroad about the antipathy of the colonists toward the restrictions placed on colonial trade. Samuel Athawes, Robert Cary, William Cookson, Osgood Hansbury, Edward Hunt, Thomas Lamar, George Maynard, and John Norton had received communications that aroused their concern. In a long letter to Mr. Athawes, William had written that "Lord Botetourt's HoneyMoon, as twas called, had a severe Checque soon after the assembly met; who resented much the Address of the House of Parliament to his Ministry and the answer."[68]

To William Cookson he wrote:

> I am sorry to be forced to direct you to send me no more goods of any Kind . . . for the people of America have been so extremely ill treated by the Parliament in imposing heavy Duties . . . that we are determined to try to obtain relief by forbearing to import goods from Great Britain till Justice is done to us on this Point.

His letter continued expressing pride in the family:

> My family consists of five sons and the eldest is the father of as many of the same sex; my brother hath three, and not a girl among us all. You see by this that the name is not likely to be extinct soon on this side of the water though we have quitted the ancient seat of the family.[69].

Being fond of Madeira wine, Nelson lamented its proscription, but announced his intention to abide by the agreement:

> Exorbitant Duty of £7 Sterling—Ton on Madeira Wines affects us more immediately than any others. . . . But such strong objections occurred to them all that unless all are repealed, the Harmony and Reciprocal Advantage of Commerce which have so long subsisted between Great Britain and her Colonies will receive a fatal wound.[70]

Although the York Town businessman had been testy with the Hunts for the low price paid for his tobacco, in September fifty hogsheads were rolled down to the river to be put aboard the *Thomas,* with Captain Hubbard on hand to check the consignment.

A beginner in the tobacco trade would have been discouraged by the disbursements and detailed duties demanded to handle the commodity. The innumerable expenses of insurance, interest, and imposts added to charges, commissions, and costs seemed endless.

On September 8 a terrible hurricane hit York Town harbor about one o'clock in the morning from the northeast. Torrential rains poured for ten hours and the wind violently tossed ships waiting to be loaded. The storm swept across the countryside tearing up trees, shattering houses, and destroying corn and tobacco crops.[71]

The *Betsey*, of Liverpool, was driven ashore, smashed, with ten feet of water in her hold soaking the tobacco. The deluge drove the *Nancy* to the bank below the wharf. Since William Nelson had not insured his interest in this ship, his loss was total. A schooner loaded with rum and one with tobacco were tossed into Colonel Digges's marsh, craft and casks broken to bits. (Fortunately for the Nelsons, the *Thomas* sustained little injury and Captain Hubbard soon sailed from the harbor.) The *Friendship* and *Latham* were hardest hit by the hurricane, striking the shore near the ferry landing. Tom, his father, and York Town folk joined Captains Lilly and Waterman to inspect the damage. The commanders set their crews to unloading the cargoes stacking casks, kegs, and hogsheads along the beach.[72]

Captain Lilly guided the *Friendship* up a creek to have her rudder repaired, sheathing plank mended, and a gallery replaced. Athawes was advised by William Nelson that the accident would create a six-week delay. By November 7, the ship set sail with eighty-five hogsheads of tobacco the Nelson firm had consigned from customers. Parcels of letters from the colonists were also on board the ship which arrived safely in London on December 20.[73] By October 30 William was writing Samuel Waterman that six hogsheads of his crop were on board, "which I hope you will receive in good Order notwithstanding the ship's having been in shore."[74]

◆ ◆ ◆

That fall, as chairman of a committee to erect a new jail and the man in charge of building a new warehouse, Tom walked the waterfront talking with other interested citizens about improvements for growing York Town.[75] The people of the county had voted funds, and the cost of the construction would be defrayed by public expense. Tom was busy securing supplies and recruiting slave labor for the projects.

Some days, six-year-old William accompanied Tom to the family business to watch the slaves haul big slabs of stones, unload logs and hewn beams, and mix mortar.

The lad enjoyed being in the midst of another round of repairs at his grandfather's house on the hill with carpenters inside and out. All the casks of nails William Nelson had ordered before non-importation were pounded into two new porches being added to the dwelling. The grandchildren watched from the stairs as workmen installed paneling and wainscoting in the attic and laid a floor. Their grandmother resorted to musk medicine for her nerves or visited with Lucy across the street to get away from the stir.[76]

Through the fall, painters touched up the trim, fitted the windows with glass, and repaired the roof of the residence. Tom and his father adhered strictly to the terms of the Non-Importation Act, for Tom had signed it and his father was an associator in principle. No items prohibited by the pact were ordered, and they instructed their overseers to save the lambs and cull the sheep for wool to be woven into cloth. They were learning how to do for themselves, and in November William Nelson informed the Hunts, "My Son and I dress in Virginia made cloth manufactured at the North Garden equal in Quality to a Yorkshire of 6 or 7 yards. The two suits cost but £5:13 for weaving, filling & dyeing. . . . our shirts of Virginia linnen equal to Irish." [77]

On November 7, the Nelsons were back in Williamsburg to attend the autumn Assembly. Tom concurred with the complimentary expressions of his father concerning Governor Botetourt's clever diplomacy on November 9 in his remarks to the representatives:

> I have again received the King's Commands to meet you in General Assembly for the dispatch of the public business of this dominion, and I hope I need not observe to you that these will best be done by temper and moderation. . . . I think myself peculiarly fortunate to be able to inform you that in a letter dated May the 13th, I have been assured by the Earl of Hillsborough that his Majesty's present administration have at no time tended a design to propose to Parliament to lay any further taxes upon America for the purpose of raising a revenue, and that it is their intention to propose in the next session of Parliament to take off the duties upon glass, paper, and colours, upon consideration of such duties having been laid contrary to the true principles of commerce. [78]

The colonists, who had proffered their opinions on the subject for months, were not oblivious of the fact that the tax on tea still remained.

The Nelsons and Colonel Washington were immediately interested in a petition made by investors in the Dismal Swamp grant for an extension of time to complete draining the vast area. Since William Nelson was second in seniority to President Blair, and the Secretary and Robert Burwell were members of the Council as well as partners, the group quite easily obtained another grant of seven years past the 1770 expiration date to pursue the project.

As an influential man in many ways, William Nelson's example in wearing homemade suits had its effect. On January 29, 1770, he notified Mr. Norton, "I wear a good suit of Cloth of my Son's wool, manufactured, as well as my shirts in Albemarle and Augusta Counties; my Shoes, Hose, Buckles, Wigg & Hat of our own Country, and in these We improve every year, in Quantity and Quality." [79]

Women emulated the men's frugal example. When Speaker Randolph and the House of Burgesses gave a grand ball for the Governor in December, the ladies decided to forsake their imported fabrics. They appeared in somber gray and brown homespun rather than bright brocades, silks, or satins trimmed with beads, lace, and ribbons.

A newspaper notice of December 14 described the "elegant entertainment" in an illuminated Capitol noting that the gentlemen and ladies made "a genteel appearance" dressed chiefly in "Virginia cloth."[80]

CHAPTER TEN

Crises in the Colony, Church, and Court: 1770–1771

York Town Church ✦ *Corrupt Clergymen* ✦ *Established Church Challenged* ✦ *Leading Dissenters* ✦ *Hannah Lee and Liberation* ✦ *President Nelson Confronts the Problems of the Preachers* ✦ *Dunbar-Custis-Washington Case*

On Sundays the Nelsons and their kin composed a sizeable segment of the congregation at York-Hampton Parish Church (now Grace Church). Tom and Lucy's children were increasing the Nelson numbers on the church roll. Tom's ancestors had been Anglicans and Lucy's family were members of the Church of England. Their religious beliefs were firmly entrenched.[1]

"King" Carter, Tom's great-grandfather, had constructed Christ Church in Lancaster County in 1732. The English-style brick building still stands, its vaulted walls topped by a concave roof, its lofty arched windows balanced with three detailed doorways. A curving stair leads to the elevated pulpit with domed sounding board.

No one entered the elaborately arched center portal of the parish, not even the preacher, until "King" Carter. He had constructed an avenue lined with cedar trees between his manor house, Corotoman, and the church. After the lordly owner rolled down the driveway in his coach drawn by six horses, then the clergymen and congregation would follow him into the Church. The "King" would lead his family up the stone aisle to the one-quarter section of the sanctuary reserved for the Carter clan.[2]

John Grymes, Lucy's paternal grandfather, led the list in length of service in the Middlesex Parish as a vestryman.[3] The Wormeleys were also strong supporters for they were rich not only in land—possessing several plantations—but also in learning, with a library of several hundred volumes.

The Grymes's family also had vast property holdings. Their residence, Brandon, was a spacious dwelling suitable for a large family. Lucy's father, Philip Grymes, following in the footsteps of *his* father, served as a church-warden.

Christ Church in Middlesex County was constructed halfway between the Wormeley's Rosegill on the Rappahannock River and the Grymes's Brandon.

The English had emphasized the ideal of establishing a Christian commonwealth in their initial expansion of Virginia.[4] Preachers claimed that God had saved the soil for them and had protected their leaders to found a Colony in the new land. Britain was indeed blessed with the bountiful goodness of divine guidance. Acts passed by the Assembly in the early seventeenth century stated that the Colony should conform by canon and constitution to the Church of England.

When "Scotch" Tom Nelson made his first voyage to Virginia, the church at York Town had been built on the bluff above the river. Though not so spacious as the T-cross churches he had seen in the old country, it was comfortable and compact sitting at an angle, rather than facing the street. The walls were made of rock marl instead of massive stone or brick and at some places "Scotch" Tom could see the countless tiny shells in the slab.[5]

In 1700 just before "Scotch" Tom came to live in the Colony, the Council had ordered that the church at York and the one at Hampton were to be combined into one diocese. York-Hampton Parish stretched twenty miles long from York Town Creek to Queen's Creek, but it was only about four miles wide. One pastor was appointed to serve the two hundred families.

A reward of twenty pounds had been advanced to anyone who procurred a suitable preacher. As a further inducement for the clergyman to come to York Town, he was to be exempt from taxes, given tobacco tithes, and allowed six servants. The vestry and members were required to contribute every twentieth pig, goat, and calf to the maintenance of the minister.[6]

Stephen Fouace had become the first parson of the parish serving from the last decade of the seventeenth century into the next. (He had been threatened by Governor Nicholson when the tempermental executive had tried to win Lucy Burwell's hand.) William Nelson could not remember the second minister, Benjamin Goodwin, but he had been a lad of eleven when Francis Fontaine came to the church in 1722. The Reverend Mr. Fontaine reported to the officials:

> I read prayers and preach twice every Sunday. . . . my living is worth about £150 arising from 20,000 sweet scented tobacco, 5 shillings for every marriage and banns published, 20 shillings for marriage by license, 40 shillings for sermon.[7]

While he had been minister, the members had secured in 1725 the metal bell that hung in the steeple.

Though early regulations of compulsory church attendance had been relaxed, sitting in the Assembly and daily chores on Sunday were not acceptable. A general respect for religious practices existed among the people and

Grace Church, Yorktown, Virginia, was known as York Hampton Parish when the Nelsons attended service. "Scotch" Tom Nelson, William Nelson, and General Thomas Nelson, Jr., are buried in the cemetery yard. Courtesy of the National Park Service.

the church fulfilled divine yearnings and satisfied the colonists' social cravings.

Clergymen were counseled to conduct themselves as gentlemen. Their code set forth that they "Should be persons that have read and seen something more of the world than what is requisite for an English parson. . . . Studied men in business in some measure as well as books; they may act like gentlemen, and be facetious and good humoured without too much freedom and licentiousness."[8]

Some preachers did not measure up to the first requisite and a few had become profligate. Isolation and remoteness of the parishes played a role in the indifference of some parsons; incompetence and unfitness to discharge their clerical duties with dignity and correctness affected others. The organization of the colonial church could not conform to the ritual prescribed by its English parent. Since the parishes were separate and scattered over an extensive area, they often lacked a parson. The rectors began to rely more and more on the laymen for leadership. A "sober and reputable" man was appointed as a reader to assist the congregation with the responsive reading and singing of songs.[9] Lack of an orthodox order in the religious service

148

often shocked Englishmen when they visited Virginia. Clergymen of the Colony were not comparable to their counterparts back home, and this fact evoked criticism from visitors and Virginians alike.[10]

William and Tom Nelson were aware of the failure of many rectors to maintain the revered practices of the Established Church. Once a cleric had shouted to his church wardens while they were serving communion, "This bread is not fit for a dog."[11] Such conduct in the ritual was regrettable.

When pastor Anthony Panton abandoned convention and called the Secretary a "jackanapes," retribution was rigorous and severe. The rector was required to make public admission in all parishes of his indecorous outburst, pay £500, and leave the Colony.[12]

Although William Byrd, II, imbibed, he was impatient with a drinking man who did not discharge his duty. Once after a night of merry carousing in the capital, Colonel Byrd had arisen after five hours' rest and continued his routine activities; however, after a meeting of the College board members, he stated, "it was agreed to turn Mr. Blackamore out from being master of the school for being so great a sot."[13] The measure comprised another black mark on the clergy indirectly, for schoolmasters were well trained in theology.

Corrupt customs, both spiritual and secular, continued to cause criticism of the clergymen. Some ministers were not immune to the frailities of the flesh. Assemblymen often mentioned these matters when they came to the capital from all over the Colony.

Waywardness in Williamsburg was not confined to the plantation gentry though travelers told of all-night carousings with drinking in one chamber, gambling in another. Instead of correcting student indulgences, some of the professors at William and Mary joined the prodigal sons in their indiscretions.

The Reverend Gronow Owen and the Reverend Jacob Rowe were two new professors at the College in 1760 who imbibed too freely in spirits. They became so "merry with the wine cup" that they led the College boys in a row against the lads of the town. Owen was dismissed.[14]

Commissary Dawson appeared in the pulpit in an inebriated condition and was indicted for drunkenness. He had many denouncers but at least one influential defender. Governor Fauquier said it was no surprise that Dawson drank since the clergymen at the College had driven the man to desperation! Before Governor Dinwiddie had sailed from the Colony, Dinwiddie had complimented the clergyman;[15] yet two years later Dawson's successor the Reverend William Robinson wrote of his predecessor:

> I'll tell you my Lord, he is a very immoral man. At a late visitation of the College, he was accused by two of the Visitors of being a Drunkard, of going to his parish church in Williamsburg drunk. I have seen him so intoxicated

by nine o'clock in the morning as to be incapable of doing business; he was likewise accused of seldom if ever attending College Prayers, of being much addicted to playing at cards, and that in public houses. All these accusations he was obliged to acknowledge to be true.[16]

Men gathering in small groups in the capital, criticized the clergy and tried to top one another's tales. Had they heard about the unrighteous reverend who, at the turn of the century, had become so absorbed with horse racing that he served as chairman of the Jockey Club?[17] This disgraceful antic was followed by an account of the enraged cleric who dishonored his church by staging a duel in the shadow of his sanctuary. They repeated the story of a preacher so provoked with his vestrymen that he fought with them, rushing the ringleader, and snatching off the wig of a warden. The triumphant theologian had then selected a special text from Nehemiah to vindicate the scuffle. The following Sunday his startled parishioners heard the pastor shout, "and he contended with them and cursed them, and smote certain of them, and plucked off their hair."[18]

The scandalous conduct of churchmen reached an unprecedented climax of improprieties with one hypocritical parson. He pretended to be a model of piety and virtue but in reality was a person of profanity and vice. Four times a year the pastor traveled to his outlying parish to preach. A handsome sum was contributed by the conscientious Christians for his salary. In his discourses the deceiver counseled his congregation to shun atheism and abstain from swearing. He warned the worshipers to spurn gambling or horse racing. Later, the congregation learned that their minister had indulged in all these iniquities, but the ultimate ignominy occurred on his deathbed when instead of praying for his imperfections, he was heard "hallooing the hounds."[19]

During the Parsons' Cause episode in the 1760s, the Reverend Jacob Rowe, professor of philosophy at the College, visited a friend and gave vent to his feelings, saying, "How many of the House of Burgesses were to be hanged? They were scoundrels wanting to settle the salaries in money. . . . if any Member wanted to receive the Sacrament from him, he would refuse to administer it."[20]

These wrathful remarks were written in the record and the representatives acted as they resolved: "That the said words were scandalous and malicious, highly reflecting on the Honor and Dignity of the House of Burgesses."[21]

The Reverend Mr. Rowe retracted his statements with a humble petition "that he hath unhappily offended and incurred the Censure of this House by uttering Contumelious words."[22]

His apology did not appease the authorities. Jacob Rowe was ordered to pay fees and was discharged from his post.

By the middle of the century, the dissenters had attracted some of the dissatisfied folk albeit for different reasons. Indifferent pastors influenced some to seek other sanctuaries; some felt the Established Church had fallen into meaningless ceremony. Resentment of control in the parish by the privileged motivated a few, but the majority of men who changed churches were seeking a spiritual rejuvenation.[23]

Aggressive Baptists asserted that the Virginia church was contradictory to the beliefs on which the Colony had been founded. Militant Baptists stormed through the Tidewater region and swept up the mountainous ranges, hurling accusations, singing, and preaching from prison. Lack of a license put them behind bars because they refused to pledge allegiance to the Established Church. They had appeared first in 1756 and, notwithstanding attacks, increased in numbers; by 1770 they had started ten churches in seven counties. They resented and continually questioned the tax for the support of the Established Church.[24]

As acting Deputy after the death of Governor Fauquier, John Blair had some sympathy toward the sect. He advised the authorities in Spotsylvania County that conscientious Christians should not be chastised for assembling and observed to the officials that Baptist preachers had saved many sinners. Wiser statesmen realized that penalizing the groups would only cause their congregations to increase.

The Reverend Andrew Moreton, pastor of Drysdale Parish in Caroline County, was so angry when a Baptist pastor appeared that he rushed toward the minister pushing his whip down his throat so that he could not pray. The tables were turned on Moreton a few years later when Edmund Pendleton brought charges against the rector for immorality and misconduct forcing Moreton to answer the complaints before the Governor and Council.[25]

Most of the influential members of the Tidewater gentry fought the Baptist movement. Before the Revolution, converts to the Baptist Church usually came from the commonfolk. The uneducated enthusiastically embraced the tenets of personal regeneration and divine disclosure.

An exception was the aristocratic Hannah Lee Corbin whose independent spirit led her to embrace the Baptist doctrine, defying the laws of the Anglican Church, the regulations of the Colony, and the rules of social convention. She ignored a court summons and subsequent fines for her beliefs. When her parish church petitioned the grand jury saying Hannah had not attended services for six months, the adamant lady still did not appear. The thirty-two-year-old widow also let brothers Richard Henry, Thomas Ludwell, and Francis Lightfoot Lee cool their heels in court awaiting her appearance for the reading of the Corbin will (which decreed that Hannah would lose two-thirds of the property if she remarried). Hannah also resented paying taxes since she could not vote and had often taken Richard Henry Lee to task over women's rights. The independent lady invited Dr. Richard Lingan Hall to reside with her at Peckatone on the Potomac River. Since

Hannah had become a Baptist and by the law of the Colony only rectors of the Established Church could sanction a marriage, the couple lived as man and wife without ceremony. Two children born to the union were called Corbin until their mother's death after the Revolution when her will recognized the name of Hall for the children.[26]

During the Revolutionary period another aristocrat abandoned the Anglican Church; Robert Carter, a representative of the ruling oligarchy who had served church and Colony in the capacities of vestryman and Councilor, became a Baptist.[27]

In 1738, George Whitefield came to the American colonies for the first time; but the renowned reformer would set sail from England seven times more over a thirty-year period. This crusading missionary traveled up and down the Atlantic seacoast shouting his outdoor sermons to thousands of people. After meeting John and Charles Wesley at Oxford, he united with Methodism. This movement of method and order in observance proposed to restore vitality to the Established Church. Its doctrine called for devotion to charity and the uniting of all Christians.[28]

Whitefield arrived in Williamsburg in 1740 to stimulate a revival in religion. Commissary Blair, who represented the Bishop of London, invited Whitefield to preach in Bruton Parish Church. Though the twenty-six-year-old evangelist was not impressive in appearance, his expressive voice electrified audiences. Sometimes he spoke sixty hours a week convincing the curious, inspiring the indifferent, and startling the sinners. Emotional converts often gave way to convulsions, jerking and shaking.

The Presbyterians had pushed into Virginia from Pennsylvania in the 1730s and were reaching out into other regions by mid-century. The frontier was fertile ground for nonconformists, for it fostered tolerance in religion as well as politics. Because of a belief in education, Presbyterian pastors were better trained than their Baptist and Methodist brethren. They established schools and set up printing presses that poured forth religious tracts, essays on moral matters, and articles on social topics. They founded Augusta Academy at Lexington, the forerunner of Washington and Lee University. The group obeyed the laws and were diplomatic in addressing the authorities.[29]

Samuel Davies, however, founder of the Presbyterian church, agitated Attorney General Peyton Randolph. The evangelist had secured a decree from the English ecclesiastic executive that the Act of Toleration was the law in effect in Virginia. The legislation authorized the licensing of the clergymen in the Nonconformist churches.[30]

While in London soliciting funds for Presbyterianism, Davies also emphasized educating clerics in the classics. The pastor preached so persistently on this trip that his Majesty, George III, overwhelmed with the minister's forceful eloquence exclaimed out loud in astonishment. Not intimidated by a commoner or overawed by the Crown, Davies replied,

"When the lion roareth, let the beasts of the forest tremble; and when the Lord speaketh, let the Kings of the earth keep silence." The sovereign sat back in silence but not pique. He summoned the forthright clergyman to his chambers the next day and contributed fifty guineas to Princeton College. To his courtiers the King commented about Samuel Davies, "He is an honest man, an honest man." Davies's work culminated in the establishment of Princeton College, which he served as president from 1759 until his death in 1761.[31]

About mid-century Samuel Davies founded the first Presbyterian church in Virginia's Hanover County. Soon congregations sprang up in Caroline, Goochland, and Louisa counties. The Calvinist converts met together in homes at first. They placed ecclesiastical power in their elected presbyters or elders. Their preachers expounded on the revival of a sustaining religion, reform in Christian conduct, and the impious pastors of the Established Church.

When Patrick Henry was a lad, Davies's oratorical persuasiveness and forceful gestures made a deep impression on the boy. His mother took her children to hear the clergyman as she was a daughter of a Scotch immigrant and often attended the Presbyterian church.[32]

Davies is also remembered for his foresighted remark about George Washington after the defeat of Braddock, "that Providence has raised up the heroic Colonel Washington, whom hitherto Providence has preserved in so signal a manner, for some important service to his Country."[33]

While most men conformed to the church creed, there were a few free-thinkers and a sprinkling of skeptics among the people. Deists declared that God existed but exerted no influence on the individual or the universe. Since deism contended that church and state should be separated, some men joined the deists because of a growing discontent with the government.

John Randolph had the reputation of believing in this principle. Thomas Jefferson, his cousin, was already investigating various doctrines. His extraordinary scope of study encompassed not only Greek and Roman classics but also the emerging British and French philosophers.[34]

John Locke appealed to independent thinkers because he tolerated civil and religious liberty. George Wythe had read Locke and recommended that his law student, Jefferson, study his principles. Both professor and pupil began to evolve enlightened opinions.

Montesquieu spent twenty years compiling the *Esprit des Lois* in which he compared the laws of various countries and their connection with social circumstances. The political treatise became more popular in England and British America than in his native France. The colonials cited his theories as a fundamental basis in their fight for civil freedom.

Rousseau and Voltaire, philosophers of the Enlightenment, also intrigued the Virginia intellectuals. Rousseau was a wandering vagabond who never found refuge. Penniless and unsettled, he poured out his heart in poetic phrases against the inequality and injustice of the age. Voltaire, most famous of the *philosophers*, was strongly anticlerical. He found favor with influential French society and gained entry into English circles. He wrote voluminously in many media: drama; poetry; and historical, philosophical, and political essays. His polished prose proclaimed man's capacity to control his course and pictured a world where justice, equality, and fraternity would exist for mankind as a result of reform and reason.

Conservative leaders of Virginia like Richard Bland, Robert Carter Nicholas, Peyton Randolph, and William Nelson, who were devoted to the Established Church and traditional customs, thought that these "liberal" conceptions were corrupting and detrimental to the minds of men. Tom and Lucy must have remembered the Reverend Mr. Yates with fondness and respect. The rector had instructed both of them in their early schooling and had performed their wedding ceremony. To the young Nelsons, Yates was proof that some ministers were men of merit.[35]

William Nelson, as acting president of the Colony, was confronted with the problem of the preachers.[36] English laws were as strict in relation to the trials of the rectors as they were in restraint on trade. Some parishes really needed protection from their profligate parsons, yet congregations had no recourse for their complaints. No matter what offenses the ministers had committed, they could not be brought to trial before a colonial court.

Because Preacher Camm had earlier incurred the fury of Governor Fauquier, he had been passed over for the post of commissary that represented the Bishop of London in the diocese of Virginia.[37] Commissary William Robinson died in 1768. Governor Fauquier, just two months before he died, replaced Robinson with young James Horrocks.[38] His youth and inexperience contributed to the decline of discipline in the Established Church. In 1760 Fauquier had been determined to assign the Reverend Patrick Lunan to the upper parish of Nansemond County.[39] The vestry refused to accept the appointment so the administrator bided his time for twelve months by the law and then sent Lunan. The minister could not measure up. Incompetence and unfitness for clerical tasks were inexcusable, but immorality would corrupt the churches, the vestrymen argued. Rumors of his scandalous conduct spread. The worshipers of the Suffolk congregation whispered to the members of Notoway who spread the stories to the Cypress congregation and then passed on the tales to the parishoners at Holy Neck.

Finally in 1766, a petition that Lunan must leave was signed by the people of the fourteen charges. The next year further allegations were listed against him, yet they could not shake the transgressor. The desperate parishoners in a few months applied to John Randolph, the attorney general, and to the prominent lawyer, George Wythe, for advice.

Advocates for an American episcopate emerged about this time. They argued that sectarianism was spreading because there was no bishop in British America. They spoke of the time and expense involved for the young men who had to travel to England to be ordained. The reputable clergy were aware of offenses of a few of their colleagues and knew only a superior could get rid of the offenders.[40]

The viewpoint of the majority of Virginia laymen differed. Eventually, the colonists discovered that the English ministry was opposed to the idea of an American episcopate as the goal of the government was conformity and dependency. To divide its power with an ecclesiastic executive in the colonies was not part of its plan.[41]

President Nelson replied to communications from England regarding the proposal "that the Idea of an American Episcopate is very alarming."[42]

> We do not want Bishops; yet from our Principles I heartily think we should oppose such an Establishment; nor will the Laity apply for them; Col. Corbin having assured me that he hath received no petition to get signed or anything else about it from Dr. Porteus, but Mr. Horrocks, the Bishop of London's Commissary here hath invited all the Clergy of the Colony to meet soon in order to consider an application for this Purpose; which he tells me that he hath done in compliance with the pressing Instances of some of the Episcopal Clergy to the Northward.[43]

With his usual discernment, Mr. Nelson predicted the outcome:

> When the Convocation is over, I fancy I can find out what they have done and will let you know, . . . for Parsons are not, like Free Maisons, sworn to Secrecy; . . . so that I should not wonder if we should hear of the Virginia Schism, when the Matter comes to be considered and debated by them; especially as many of our clergy were bred up Dissenters whose Eyes have been opened by the glare of 16,000 lb. Tob. Annum.[44]

The Reverend Jonathan Boucher stated, from his pulpit in Caroline County: "I might almost as well pretend to count the gnats that buzz around us in the summer evening as to count the dissenters."[45]

A general indifference on the part of the parsons caused the collapse of the plan for an American bishop. In the House of Burgesses, Richard Bland and Richard Henry Lee gave the final deathblow declaring that the church office would not be compatible with the civil authority. The House voted its thanks to the four preacher protesters, the Reverends Henley, Gwathkin, Hewitt, and Bland, for "wise and well timed Opposition they had made to the pernicious Project of a few mistaken clergymen for introducing an American Bishop."[46]

President Nelson still had his troubles with the local theologians even if the question of a bishop for the colonies had been settled. Nelson felt he must consider those cases of congregations' starting suits against their clergymen for misconduct. He conveyed to Lord Hillsborough that charges were pending against two unworthy pastors whom he did not name and attested, "We have a few but very few Yet some who come under this description . . . do his duty in relation to the unworthy clergymen, of whom there were some needing discipline, and ask full and undoubted authority for doing so."[47]

Commissary Horrocks left Virginia after losing the battle for an American bishop. Consequently, the problem of the preachers devolved on President Nelson. He wanted the English authorities, civil and church, to decide the correct course for the Colony, but Lord Hillsborough and the bishop of London evaded the issue.

At the October court in 1771, the local officials came to grips with the complaints against the Reverend Patrick Lunan, who was "charged with drunkenness, immorality and neglect of duty."[48]

Court days were usually crowded as groups congregated on the Capitol grounds. The usual talk of tobacco and taxes subsided as the gentlemen speculated on the sensational trial. In all probability, the parishoners of upper Nansemond County wore smug smiles as they thought the dissolute preacher with whom they had dealt for a decade would at last get his just deserts.

Attorney General John Randolph acted as counsel for the clergyman.[49] He was a handsome man in his forties whose commanding air supported his assertion that the General Court had no legal authority to try the defendant.[50]

Arrayed against him in argument were Richard Bland and George Wythe as well as twenty-eight-year-old Thomas Jefferson, whose legal abilities were already admired.

Bland was a veteran of the bar noted for thoroughness and toughness. His pen had already exposed some defects of the clerics in two relevant pamphlets. Seeming older than his sixty years, Bland slightly bent, stood, and contended that the local court could prosecute and pass sentence reiterating that the "right of visitation rested with the vestries under the peculiar setup of the Virginia church."[51]

Jefferson disagreed. He advocated that individual members would have the authority to become a court of visitation to try a minister.

Despite the discussion the case was not closed. Somehow, the Reverend Mr. Lunan kept his post, though his parishoners failed to levy tobacco for his salary "on account of his ill behaviour and neglect of Duty in the church."[52]

In desperation, the vestrymen took matters into their own hands. They barred the church doors, but discovered that only money moved the minister. The congregation bought him off with three hundred pounds.[53]

✦   ✦   ✦

It seemed incredible to Tom that a court case could become so snarled in legal complexities that it had not been settled in almost sixty years, yet such was the suit concerning Colonel Daniel Parke and his heirs; before it was over, it would entangle the Nelsons and a number of the Colony's leading families.[54]

Colonel Parke, the story's central figure, was an adventuresome Virginian, with a roving eye and a restless foot. While in London he enticed Mrs. Berry to leave her husband and sail with him to Virginia. There he introduced her as his cousin Brown, but the inhabitants of the capital were not deluded. The Reverend James Blair and his wife, Elizabeth Harrison Blair, commented caustically about temptations of the flesh. Since Mrs. Blair's fondness for liquid refreshment was well-known, according to Parke's brother-in-law, Colonel William Byrd, II, Parke grew so annoyed with Blair's sermons on adultery that he rushed to Mrs. Blair's pew one Sunday and rudely pulled her from her seat.[55]

Though Daniel Parke was infuriated over talk of his indiscretions, he was also gallant and gracious. He had previously volunteered to serve under the Duke of Marlborough and after the French were beaten at the Battle of Blenheim in 1704, Marlborough had chosen Parke as envoy to convey the news to England. Parke graciously refused the five-hundred-pound gratuity and asked only for a picture of his queen. He received a jeweled miniature of Queen Anne set with diamonds, a splendid set of silverplate, and one thousand guineas.[56] Colonel Parke was proud of his memento and pinned the picture of the Queen to his right breast when he had his portrait painted.[57]

Later, Daniel Parke was appointed Governor of the Leeward Islands where he became enamored with Catherine Chester and illegitimate children were born to the couple. Daniel Parke, in trying to correct lawlessness on the islands, proposed unpopular governmental reforms. Recalled from his post, Parke refused to leave and open rebellion resulted. In December 1710, several hundred natives met in Antigua determined to expel their Governor. The rioters shot him, broke his back with their guns, and dragged his body to the street. The complicated lawsuit that followed his violent death was to last through four generations.

Parke bequeathed all his estates in the Leeward Islands to his illegitimate daughter, Lucy Chester, if she would take his name and coat-of-arms. He left all his property in England and Virginia to his legitimate daughter, Frances Parke Custis, and bequeathed one thousand pounds to his second daughter, Lucy Parke Byrd. Lucy's husband, Colonel Byrd, made a bad bargain when he bought the English estates from the Custises, agreeing to assume the debts. He had been informed that the indebtedness was approximately nine thousand pounds but discovered it far exceeded that figure. Byrd's wife, one of the principals in the case died of smallpox in 1716 after she had joined him in London.[58]

Frances Parke Custis and her husband, John Custis, were required to pay off obligations from the Virginia property. This distribution began the extended inheritance litigation and aggravated the discord in the Custis household. When fiery Frances and the eccentric Colonel Custis decided to speak to each other, they only added fuel to their flaming dissension.[59]

The contentious pair drew up a detailed agreement to settle their arguments. Frances was to return money, plate, and other valuables taken from her husband and never take any item or dispose of any article without his consent. She was also directed by the document to "forbear to call him vile names." Colonel Custis was commanded to pay the expenses and debts of the plantations "freely without grudge" and allow half of the clear products to Frances annually. She could have three servants and one to run errands. If cloth was left over from the flax and wool allowed her for the servants, she could give twenty yards to charity if she chose.[60]

With her marital unhappiness, Frances must have pondered sometimes on the remarks of her wayward parent when he wrote her just before joining Marlborough to fight the French, "God knows if I may ever see you again. . . . therefore do not throw yourself away on the first idle young man that offers, if you have a mind to marry. I know it is the desire of all young people to be married and though few are so happy after marriage as before, yet every one is willing to make the experiment at their own expense."[61]

Once on a drive beside the bay the choleric Colonel Custis guided his horses into the stream along the shore.

"Where are you going," his spouse queried.

"To Hell, Madam!" he raved in reply.

"Drive on," countered the adamant Mrs. Custis. "Any place is better than Arlington."[62]

Colonel Custis saved himself and his wife from drowning that time, but after her demise the testy husband had the last word with the message he forced his son to have carved on his tombstone: "Under this marble tomb lies the Honourable John Custis, Esquire, Aged 71 years, and yet lived but seven which was the space of time he kept Batchelor's house at Arlington on the Eastern Shoar of Virginia."[63]

The Custises had departed their unhappy earthly existence but the Parke problem devolved on their son, Daniel Parke Custis, Daniel Parke's grandson. Now he had to face the perlexities of the case and the postponements of the court. In the intervening seven years between the death of his mother and father, Daniel Parke Custis learned that the illegitimate daughter of his grandfather, Lucy Chester Parke, had married Thomas Dunbar, a captain of Antigua. Her husband started suit for settlement on the Leeward Island property but complications again stopped the proceedings. Even after Daniel Parke Custis married Martha Dandridge, and John Parke and Martha Parke Custis were born, the unpleasant specter was still hanging like a shadow over his shoulders. He endeavored to protect his children's property.[64]

"Scotch" Tom Nelson had been drawn into the dilemma to act as agent for the plaintiff Thomas Dunbar. Although death had removed the principals, another generation pursued the prosecution. After Thomas Dunbar died, his brother continued the case; then his son Charles resumed the suit. Daniel Parke Custis died in 1757 and two years later his widow married Colonel George Washington. "Scotch" Tom had been resting in his grave a dozen years, so William Nelson became the colonial agent for the Dunbar brothers, John and Joseph, who desired that the settlement of the case should be accomplished.[65]

Tom and his father discussed the delays and legal intricacies of the lengthy affair. Tom was as sure as Cousin George Washington was that the Dunbar brothers had the most able agent and competent counsel in William Nelson and Robert Carter Nicholas.[66]

In the fall of 1766, Mr. Nelson had informed John Dunbar that it had been nearly a year since he had heard from him concerning the "defense of the late Colonel Custis's suits but I expect to see Mr. Washington next month who married the widow after which I shall be able to give you then his final answer."[67]

Nelson and Nicholas attempted a compromise with Washington, but he refused. Since Athawes and his father had recommended the Nelsons as agents for the plaintiffs, Athawes was an interested party to the proceedings. The Dunbars were slow in forwarding the necessary documents to continue the case and in November 1768, William Nelson wrote to his friend Sam Athawes, "I disdain the thought for I feel Mr. Dunbar will make nought of his suit here for he seems not to have a friend in Antigua that will send us a copy of his Father's will and other necessary papers to carry on the affair."[68]

Mr. Robert Carter Nicholas withdrew from the case since his duties as Treasurer demanded so much of his time; then Mr. William Nelson secured the service of George Wythe. On June 12, 1769, Nelson stated to Dunbar, "Sir, I cannot omit one hour after receiving them to transmit to you the enclosed papers sent to me by Mr. Wythe in answer to your packet with Power of Attorney for your Brother Joseph. If you will expedite the necessary papers from your side, You may depend on all the Dispatch the cause can possibly receive here."[69]

Dunbar arrived in Antigua to obtain the needed papers. Dunbar must have been disappointed when he read William Nelson's reply: "Return of it at our April court, for this letter of yrs I think been fourteen days in coming from Norfolk to me by post. We have a post established on this Continent by Act of Parliament of Queen Anne's Time, but it is so dilatory & uncertain in its stages, that a private conveyance is more to be depended on."[70]

Colonel George Washington almost concluded that the claimants would become so discouraged over the repeated delays that they would drop the suit. He made up his mind to contest the venerable suit to the finish.

CHAPTER ELEVEN

Calamities and Commerce, Courtships and the College: 1770–1771

Sales ✦ Lord North, English Prime Minister ✦ Tea and Tobacco ✦ Burwell Courtships ✦ Governor Botetourt's Illness and Death ✦ President Nelson ✦ Elizabeth Is Born ✦ Young William Nelson Marries Lucy Chiswell ✦ May Flood ✦ Hugh Nelson Marries Judy Page ✦ William Reynolds Returns ✦ John Hatley Norton Marries Sarah Nicholas ✦ President Nelson Welcomes Lord Dunmore ✦ The College of William and Mary

Sometimes it seemed to Tom that Mr. James Mitchell, Tom's tavern proprietor, spent more time in front of the building selling land, goods, and slaves to satisfy obligations of gentlemen than he did inside the Swan operating the ordinary. Yet he didn't begrudge Mitchell the job. Men came over the York Town ferry, another Mitchell enterprise, from Gloucester, King and Queen, and Middlesex counties to attend the auctions. Human passengers traveled in one vessel, horses in another.[1]

Armistead Lightfoot was just one of the many planters affected by economic difficulties. Tom felt a closeness to him as Tom's mother and Armistead's wife were Burwells.[2] Tom watched, troubled, as Lightfoot first advertised twenty negroes for sale, then a year later 230 acres about two miles from York Town with a strong house to be "sold for ready money to satisfy judgments." This sentence, repeated often, now failed to startle readers. Later that same year a newspaper advertised the sale of 2,740 acres of "land belonging to the estate of Armistead Lightfoot, deceased."[3]

The Nelsons and other plantation owners read about a slave insurrection in Hanover County with fear and frustration. Editor Rind reported the incident and alarm was increased by the comment that the "tragical affair" was caused by "Negroes having been treated with too much leniency and indulgence resulted in their becoming insolent and unruly."[4] Resentment against a new steward had brought a dozen black forms rushing with guns and swords. In the rebellion three slaves were killed, five wounded, and the rest fled.

When Lord North became Prime Minister of Britain in 1770,[5] Tom worried that the man, amiable, good-humored, and witty, would submit to the King's wishes at every turn. Townshend had died and Lord Pitt was too ill to make his presence known. Yet Tom's sense of foreboding about a man with so much power and so little concern for the rights of the colonies did not keep him from telling his son the story of an unexpected meeting with Lord North years before in England.

Strolling along the river one day, Tom had witnessed a young boy slip into the water for a swim. Unfamiliar with the power of the river's current, the child had struggled and soon panicked, flailing ineffectively. Tom jumped into the river, grasped the frightened lad and pulled him back to the safety of the bank. As a reward for saving his son, a grateful Lord North had presented Tom with an ornately carved gold snuffbox. Its three-inch lid lifted to reveal the picture of Lord North,[6] a fascinating aspect for Tom's young William, a visage that troubled Tom.

◆   ◆   ◆

February 1770, Lucy was saddened to learn that her cousin Tom Jefferson's Shadwell had burned.[7] His father had constructed the frame house on two hundred acres acquired by a bet on a bowl of arrack punch. Jefferson had been born there. While a student at the College of William and Mary, he had started collecting a large library; Jefferson told John Page the books were worth £200. Tom Nelson had received a somber letter from the young lawyer relaying that a servant had saved his violin, but his library and briefs had been destroyed.[8] He was so lost in his own grief he scarcely perceived that his mother and sister had also lost their treasured possessions. He asked Tom Nelson to order a list of replacement titles from London and Tom countered with books from his own library and that of his uncle. Thinking in terms of rebuilding, Tom sent pulleys, hinges, and locks as well to the downcast young Jefferson.[9]

Tom and his father were so involved with private and public interests that they didn't indulge in much reminiscing or dwell too long on disasters. William chided his friend Samuel Athawes for his gloomy outlook, and remarked about "some timid people who can't enjoy the present sunshine of a Fine day, for fearing a Thunder cloud should arise; Is it not the better Philosophy to contend with Misfortune when they arrive than to anticipate, or take upon Truth things which may never happen to give us uneasiness."[10]

The retention of the tea tax was a triumph for Lord North, who felt that the colonials must not be coddled. The new Prime Minister had the support of the Crown. Retaining the duty on the popular drink had a double purpose: to prove that Parliament had the power to lay imposts and to derive more revenue.

Tom agreed with his father that the conduct of the English ministry was "mean, uncandid, and destructive" of trade; William Nelson thought Virginia would have to work out its own salvation since "petitions and remonstrances mean nothing with those who are determined to push matters to extremity, in order to establish and support their despotic plan of power." [11]

The embargo on English goods had not been effective. Tom and his father were ashamed of their countrymen. In July William Nelson expressed his feelings to John Norton:

> I believe to fear that the Spirit of the Association in America will grow cool in some of the Colonies: especially at N. York; where the Dutch Blood, thirsting for present Gain, seems still to flow in their Veins, & hath raised much Noise to the Northward about it; but I blush on reading what you say about the Virginians and their Invoices rather encrease than diminish." [12]

After much arguing pro and con, the associators came to the conclusion that their non-importation agreement needed some changes.

Edmund Pendleton would have abolished it altogether, but Landon Carter contended there was no halfway course between slavery and freedom. Washington approved of a strict compact but was willing for a compromise that would be more practicable. Cheap cloth, shoes, stockings, and household furnishings were removed from the forbidden list. Expensive items and luxury goods on the list were not to be ordered. [13]

Tom signed the Non-Importation Act *again* in June, one of 164 signatures. Benjamin Harrison approved the agreement this time, as did Francis Lightfoot Lee and Edmund Pendleton. As one of the five commissioners for his county, Tom had to report any York County merchant who refused to return any prohibited goods, but the young legislator anticipated no trouble on that score. Merchant David Jameson and John Hatley Norton had also signed the agreement. [14]

Evidently, everybody in the Nelson family had worn his stockings threadbare and scuffed his shoes, for as soon as those items were lifted from the non-importation list, William Nelson included in his invoices twelve dozen best broad hose, one dozen calf skins (black or grain for shoes), one dozen washed leather, and a half dozen pieces of sole leather for a "Tryal." Irish linen and Kendall cloth were ordered as well as some books. [15]

Although the price of tobacco was higher in 1770, the exchange rate was lower. Again William Nelson tried to stimulate the attitude of Samuel Athawes on the quantity, price, and quality of the product. Athawes's pessimistic position always made William lose patience, so he reminded the merchant, "a large crop is always of good Quality and it will be making its way to new markets . . . and it is worth 25/100. I reckon that greater part of Europe are still strangers to the Virtues of fine Virginia tobacco wch when they have tasted it a moderate price they be ever after coveting it." [16]

Later, he had to encourage Athawes because of damage to the *Friendship* in the hurricane: "You will be better able to judge the Expediency of having a ship in the Trade, and yet I can't see that you can do without one especially in the ensuing year as Tobacco will probably be so plentiful that we shall not be able to get Freight for it." [17] This optimistic view was usual for planters looking toward the future.

Tom assisted his father in the tedious tasks of collecting past payments and overdue debts. William Nelson sent duplicate copies of invoices in case the first had been lost. He dated every letter to his factors and expected them to do the same. The first sentence in his communication of November 26, 1770, to William Cookson stated, "Dear Sir I have lately received a letter from you *without date*." [18] Yet this oversight was an insignificant omission compared to his vexation in trying to obtain total insurance coverage for his damaged tobacco. The factors abroad thought he could receive only part compensation, so William was writing, "Why not wholly?" or "why for a part only?"

Sometimes William predicted that vessels from Virginia would be stopping at Glasgow, for he stated to the English factors that he thought the canny Scots would soon have the tobacco trade since they sailed their ships faster and always made a profit. [19]

Tom's indebtedness to merchant John Norton had already increased to £832. Items for his growing family and household had been filling his invoices for several months. [20]

If Tom grew weary of taxes and the colonists' economic state he could always visit his cousin, Rebecca Burwell Ambler, who lived next door to the tavern where Martha Goosley often visited to babble about people and events. She vowed it was porter that made Mrs. Norton fat, not the plumpness of pregnancy; Martha declared she would drink some porter herself if she could get it to fill out her thin "carcase" and face which is "sharp as a Hatchet." [21] Since the spring had been as "fatal to old women as old Cows" she was being especially careful of her health. Her eyes continued good and she retained a "passion for reading," (Probably Tom thought she retained a passion for talking, too!) . . . William Reynolds was still in London learning the trade with Mr. Norton. In April, his sister Susan had married a twenty-two-year-old man who was about six feet tall and weighed around 240 pounds. After spouting these statistics Mrs. Goosley stated there was a "great Disparity of age and size" [22] indicating that Susan was the senior of the bridegroom and apparently quite thin. . . . After Colonel Burwell had lost his wife in the spring, he started looking around for a suitable companion. [23] York Town folk had been chatting all summer about his courtship of the comely Mrs. Lightfoot. Probably the Nelsons and the Burwells felt that there was no reason for their kinsman to be so persistent in his pursuit, but the colonel was only continuing an accepted custom. Sometimes as a widower received condolence on the loss of his wife, well wishers congratulated him on his choice of a successor! This was not to be the lot of Mr. Burwell. The young widow Lightfoot rejected his proposal and the repulse stunned the suitor so that his spirits suffered from a slow nervous fever, according to Mrs. Goosley.[24]

Young Nathaniel Burwell's eyes had lighted on his cousin Susanna Grymes two years before when she came to York Town to live with her sister Lucy Grymes Nelson. With the impetuousness of youth, the suitor schemed to see Susanna alone, but privacy seemed impossible in the Nelson household.[25] If Nat escorted Sukey to church, the entire clan accompanied them. If Nat and Susanna stepped out into the garden to stroll up and down the path, little William and Thomas peered over the hedges. By now the boys had discovered the secret stairway that spiraled from the cellar to the top of the house. When the couple decided to sit on the deep window seats in the drawing room, they were surprised by the boys popping from behind the paneled door of the hideaway laughing at them with impish glee.

Tom was more indulgent with the couple than his father who wrote his opinion to Athawes at the end of the year:

> This young Gentlemen though very clever and intent upon the whole hath in my opinion too soon determined to enter into the Married state with the next sister of my Daughter. She is a very good girl but I fear that he as well as most other people in such cases, hath not considered Fortune much.[26]

Nathaniel Burwell had six sisters all older than he. Lucy, the eldest, born in 1740, was after her marriage to Captain Thomas Lilly a close neighbor to the Nelson kin. When Mary, or Molly as she was often called, married Edmund Berkeley who was a widower and twice her nineteen years, family and friends thought nothing of the fact that he was old enough to be her father but felt she had made quite a good match. Romance was a race for the ladies and matrimony was their mark. His sisters set their sights on settled men. Judith, the third girl, had married Dr. Samuel Griffin of Lancaster County and was only twenty-five years old when she had died the year before.[27] The press had notified the public:

> On Monday 20 November Mrs. Judith Griffin, daughter of Carter Burwell, was snatched away by a sudden and violent illness. She was the most affectionate and dutiful wife that ever blessed a marriage state, pious and devout.[28]

In September Tom learned that Governor Botetourt lay gravely ill. Tom and his father had a high regard for the Governor and recalled incidents when the affable executive had endeared himself to the people. He had refused to issue the Writs of Assistance. By his "own Disposition and Intentions" William Nelson noted that Lord Botetourt had endeavored to establish harmony and to effect the colonists' happiness. A cordial relationship had ripened between the Crown official and local legislators because he "wishes and labors for the Happiness of the public and every individual."[29] William had written to Francis Farley on February 20, 1770, "I have often pictured his real character in my own Mind in the few following words vizt that his chief happiness arose from making other Men happy: need I say more: I cannot."[30]

Robert Carter Nicholas had spent some time with Governor Botetourt, talking with him about an afterlife. Nicholas assumed Botetourt would be reluctant to die.

"Why?" queried the Governor.

"Because you are so social in your nature and so much beloved, and you have so many good things about you that you must loath to leave them," Nicholas had replied.[31]

Botetourt smiled but made no response. When the final fever gripped his body, the Governor summoned Nicholas and said, "I have sent for you merely to let you see that I resign those good things of which you formerly spoke with as much composure as I enjoyed them."[32]

His Excellency died the following Monday, October 15. The church bell tolled and couriers conveyed the news to the colonists in neighboring counties before they read the obituary in the newspapers. Both the Purdie-Dixon press and Rind's *Virginia Gazette* paid tribute to the public and private character of the official and the "amiable qualities and great virtues which adorned the noble Lord":[33]

> October 18, 1770—Williamsburg. On Monday the 15th about one o'clock in the morning departed this life universally lamented throughout thie Colony, his Excellency the Right Honorable Norbonne Baron de Botetourt, his Majesty's Lieutenant, Governor General and Commander in Chief of the Colony of the Dominion of Virginia and Vice admiral of the same.[34]

William Nelson and the Secretary hurried from the house on Francis Street to the Capitol where the Council convened on the day Governor Botetourt died. These men fulfilled their two-fold responsibility: to continue the government of the Colony and to conduct the funeral arrangements.

President John Blair faced the group. At eighty-three years, Blair did not feel equal to act as executive again. William Nelson summed up the situation:

> By the Resignation of Mr. Blair, on account of his great age and Infirmities the Government hath devolved upon your humble serv'nt who doth not feel himself much Capacity for so arduous a Situation.[35]

But his heart was disposed to do right and Nelson believed it would not let him stray from his duty.

By education and experience, William Nelson was qualified for the position of President that paid two thousand pounds in salary. Step by step he had climbed to the top of the political ladder. He had served in the county court, been a Burgess, and a member of the Council for twenty-five years. He was also well-to-do and lived about a dozen miles from the capital—all important considerations.

The *Virginia Gazette* of October 18, 1770, contained the following announcement:

VIRGINIA BY THE HONORABLE WILLIAM NELSON, ESQUIRE, PRESIDENT OF HIS MAJESTY'S COUNCIL AND COMMANDER IN CHIEF OF THIS DOMINION A PROCLAMATION WHEREAS BY THE DEATH OF HIS EXCELLENCY BOTETOURT AND BY THE RESIGNATION OF JOHN BLAIR, ESQUIRE, THE ADMINISTRATION OF THE GOVERNMENT IS DEVOLVED UPON ME NOW TO THE END THAT THE PEACE OF THIS HIS MAJESTY'S SAID DOMINION MAY BE BETTER SECURED, AND ALL PROCEEDINGS AT LAW CONTINUED, AND THAT AT THE ORDINARY COURT OF JUSTICE MAY NOT BE INTERRUPTED, I HAVE THOUGHT FIT, BY AND WITH THE ADVICE OF HIS MAJESTY'S COUNCIL OF THIS COLONY IN HIS MAJESTY'S NAME, TO PUBLISH AND DECLARE ALL OFFICERS REMAIN IN OFFICE PROCEED WITH DUTY GIVEN AT THE COUNCIL CHAMBER, IN WILLIAMSBURG, THIS FIFTEENTH DAY OF OCTOBER, 1770 IN THE TENTH YEAR OF HIS MAJESTY'S REIGN

WILLIAM NELSON

GOD SAVE THE KING

So that Virginians all through the Colony would notice the change in government, the newspaper repeated the announcement on October 19.

> By the Resignation of Hon. John Blair, Esq., the Government Devolved on the Hon. William Nelson, Esq., who, we hear, Intends to Give Such Attendance in this City As to Carry on the Public business with the Usual Dispatch.

A supplementary newspaper October 19 printed plans made by President Nelson and the Council for Botetourt's last rites. Persons attending the funeral were to be at the Palace by two o'clock. Long before that time, people took positions along Duke of Gloucester Street. At one o'clock the Bruton Parish Church bell tolled; three militia companies from Williamsburg, James City County, and York Town lined the parallel lanes to the Governor's residence. Thomas Nelson, Jr., commanded the latter militia unit patiently awaiting the signal to fire its salute.

The body of Governor Botetourt was encased in three coffins. A special lead casket, covered with a crimson velvet cloth, had eight silver handles. Six Councilmen served as pallbearers and placed the coffin in the hearse drawn by caparisoned horses. Special staffs were draped in black. (His servants were in mourning twice over, because a venerable servant who had been with the Botetourt family over a quarter century died the same day as the Governor.) At three o'clock the cortege started its slow procession to the church where Burgess Richard Bland expressed the esteem of the Assembly.

President Nelson then led the legislators in the procession to the College of William and Mary where the Governor had requested that his remains be placed underneath the chapel floor. His interest in the College had caused William Nelson to write, "The success in his Endeavours to repress some Neglects and Irregularities in our College hath dome him much Honour with us, and I think gained him the Love and Admiration of every Man."[36]

Governor Botetourt had provided two gold medals to be awarded to the students who attained excellence in classical learning and philosophy. The circular gold medallions, one inch in diameter, depicted King William and Queen Mary in royal robes and crown extending the College charter to the Reverend James Blair kneeling before the sovereigns.[37]

✦　　✦　　✦

President Nelson began to attend to the public affairs of the Colony as assiduously as he pursued his private business. An immediate duty involved assembling a group of discreet men to help in the distribution of Botetourt's effects since the former Governor had left no instructions concerning his considerable private property. John Blair agreed to assist Nelson together with attorneys John Randolph, Robert Carter Nicholas, and George Wythe.[38]

For months the committee exchanged correspondence, including a careful inventory of all items, with the former Governor's heir, Henry, fifth Duke of Beaufort, son of Lord Botetourt's sister. A portion of the correspondence reveals the men's careful approach to their task: "Thinking it rather indelicate to particularize his Lordship's wearing apparel in the Inventory . . . we have there omitted it," yet they informed the Duke that a distinct account of every article would be sent separately to him.[39]

The furnishings were in fine taste, "liquors are good," and while Governor Botetourt had brought white servants with him, he had found it necessary to buy slaves to do "Drudgery out of doors." The blacks would be sold and a gentleman agreed to take the horses at the same price they cost his Lordship.[40] Mr. Nelson gave an account of the animals to Samuel Athawes:

> As a Compliment and to accommodate him, I have bought Lord Botetourt's fine set of horses with the offer to successor same price. I use them to

run between York and Williamsburg and give my own Blacks a Winter's run in Hanover. I have also kept in my Service the Coachman, an excellent Servant to take care of the horses, and in hopes that he may be employed by the next Governor. The gardener is also continued.[41]

Some of the handsome white horses were sold to Colonel Byrd, who in turn transferred them to Colonel Washington. By the spring Nelson noted:

By the Duke of Beaufort's order we have nearly finished the sale of Lord Botetourt's Effects except such things as his Grace hath ordered to be sent to him in the State Coach, the King and Queen's pictures are presented to the Council for the succeeding Governor.[42]

Public and private papers, books, a gold watch, walking cane, silver tea-spoons, gold buttons and seals, diamond buckles, seal skin cases of surveyor instruments, and a handsome toothpick case were packed together with the mahogany desk and library table. The gentlemen recommended that the Duke insure the china and costly articles at nine thousand pounds.

Commissary Horrocks who embarked for England in June 1771 would convey the respects of the committee to the Duke of Beaufort.

As autumn's breezes blew golden leaves across the lawn, the Nelson youngsters rushed into the yard. Ten-year-old Billy led his nephews, seven-year-old William and six-year-old Thomas, in a romp through the swirls of leaves.

Tom appeared to take the boys to the stable to see the Botetourt coach—shiny, with bright upholstery, "hardly the worse for wear," their grandfather had said.[43] Billy climbed up on the front seat where Mr. Marshman, the English coachman, showed him how to hold the reins.

While Virginians mourned the Governor, William Nelson corresponded with Lord Hillsborough, the Colony's English Secretary concerning various land claims, charges, and company operations for the widespread western country.[44]

Twenty years before, young George Washington had traversed some of the west Virginia territory. Before he was twenty-one, at a salary of one hundred pounds a year, he had been appointed adjutant of the Southern District, one of four divisions of defense for the Colony. Because he lived in the Northern Neck, Major Washington desired that post. He achieved it with the aid of William Nelson.[45]

When the French had encroached on the environs of Lake Erie, Governor Dinwiddie had selected young Washington as the emissary to notify the French they were trespassing on English territory. An observant envoy, Governor Dinwiddie was impressed with the young major's report on French preparations, but the Assemblymen demurred. Finally, seventy-five men were recruited by Major Washington to protect the frontier. A tempting consideration for their service was the compensation of two hundred thousand acres of land set aside for the volunteers.[46]

In 1770, President Nelson endeavored to explain to Lord Hillsborough about the operation of the land companies and the settlement situation, as Washington was still striving to secure the rightful claims of his comrades in arms to the vast acres.

The Crown had been petitioned by a third organization for permission to open a Colony in the extensive area of British America. Thomas Walpole, a prominent London banker, headed the company of English, French, and American patentees. This complicated land question reached a climax when Walpole charged the Virginia Council with certain violations.[47]

President Nelson wrote Lord Hillsborough that the accusations were "indecent, illiberal, and unwarrantable."

> As to grantees making large profits by the sale . . . I am confident the fact is otherwise, since the stated price for such lands (except in a very few cases), I think has been £3 Virginia currency per 100 acres. Fortunate for me I do not find my name in any of the grants.[48]

William Nelson was particularly anxious to see that the people's prior rights were protected. James Patton's family received some advantage for his grant and the acting Governor said, "truly I think they might since the old man paid his scalp as the price of it being murdered by the Indians . . ."[49]

Washington was worried that the Walpole claims would usurp four-fifths of the land set aside as security for the soldiers. On the day he wrote Governor Botetourt, Washington visited the Ohio region; not until later would the master of Mount Vernon recall that on October 15, when he was surveying the rich land selected for him, Governor Botetourt had died.[50]

✦   ✦   ✦

Baby Elizabeth was born the day after Christmas and changed the masculine model of the Nelson clan, yet Grandfather William said he believed they were all better off to be blessed by a granddaughter.[51] Secretary Thomas Nelson's family grew too, when their oldest son William married Lucy Chiswell of Caroline County the last of November. At twenty-four, William had a profitable position as clerk of the county, an appointment arranged by the Secretary.[52]

The bride and groom became the center of attention when they appeared in church for the first time after their marriage. The Reverend Mr. Dunlap, rector of Stratton Major Church in King and Queen County, decided it was an appropriate occasion to deliver a sermon on the marital state. Basing his text on the Bible story of Jacob, husband of Rachel, who reckoned seven years with her as "but a few days, for the love he had for her." Marriage lectures often gave the minister a chance to admonish members of the congregation as well as to advise married couples.

The newspaper praised the sermon:

> The preacher in his usual Manner, touched upon the tender Passion of Love, as a necessary Requisite in Courtship and Marriage . . . . The whole Discourse was handled in a new and striking Manner.[53]

Proximity to the parish was important to the Nelson family, and it was a short distance from either residence to York-Hampton Church. If they had lived in an outlying district of the diocese, however, distance would not have kept the family from attending services. William Nelson, concerned for people who came to church from remoter regions of the long parish, ordered food prepared for them every Sunday. If some folk came for the food or just as a mechanical function, the Nelsons did not begrudge them this treat. Later, Thomas Nelson, Jr., continued this custom.[54]

On the other hand, Landon Carter thought people ate too much, and the Colonel observed on one occasion:

> This is our third Barbecue day. I think it is an expensive thing. I confess I like to meet my friends now and then, but certainly the old plan of every family carrying its own dish was both cheaper and better, because then nobody intruded, but now everyone comes in and raises the club, and really many do so only for the sake of getting a good dinner and a belly full of drink.[55]

The twelve vestrymen elected by parishes of the Established Church in Virginia wielded singular power. They were entrusted with the ecclesiastical obligation of obtaining two hundred acres of ground for the preacher, stipulating his salary, and collecting tithes. They set up a system of education and care for orphaned children.[56]

William Nelson served as a vestryman in the York Town church and performed his religious duties with dignity. He not only loathed laxness in church leaders but also laymen's idleness. Once, when the conversation became too clamorous before the regular service, Nelson rose and simply stated, "The Lord is in His Holy temple, Let all the earth keep silence before Him." Chatter ceased.[57]

Elizabeth Burwell Nelson found peace in the church sanctuary. If she glanced out the window, she could see the graves of her girls who had never grown up, her boy who had burned to death, and that of Lewis, who had lingered so long in the shadows before his life was over.[58]

In addition to attending to private and public affairs, Tom and his father had a strong sense of obligation toward their friends and often assumed the burden of a needy neighbor. Mr. Moir was a ne'er-do-well who neglected his children and worried Mrs. Matthews, his mother-in-law, who had reared Moir's two boys and little Nancy after the children's mother had died. When one son went to sea and the other was set up in trade, Moir and his new wife were to embark for England but young Nancy did not wish to go although her grandmother wrote Mr. Norton to locate an aunt in London.[59] William Nelson was cheated by Moir who begged him to cash some certificates. On January 30, 1771, William wrote Samuel Athawes to prevail on a brother-in-law in London to pay Moir's two bills and admitted to his friend, "I own to you I thot I ran some Risque, when I pd. . . . however he was very necessitous & almost naked that I judged there might be some little merit in relieving him though not so honest as he should be."[60]

Doubts also made the seventy-year-old grandmother decide to keep her fifteen-year-old granddaughter in York Town even though she was destitute. The discerning William was not misled by Moir, and he informed John Norton, "Moir proved a Rascal; as I expected when I supplyed him but he was so shabby & necessitous, that I could not send him away naked & empty so I have No great Disappointment, & the Loss but £25."[61]

✦ ✦ ✦

Tom now spent some time at the store and the waterfront warehouse as William had to be in Williamsburg to discharge his duties as the Governor pro tempore, although both men as well as the Secretary took a leading role in planning the construction of a hospital for the insane in Williamsburg. Governor Fauquier had first advocated an asylum for the afflicted in 1766, graphically picturing the plight of those with unsound minds confined with criminals. A separate shelter for culprits and for the mentally incompetent was an advanced idea for the age. Mad folk were feared, shamed, and often tied up but little thought had been given to any special care and treatment. The Nelsons had agreed with Fauquier's arguments and they lent their time and talents to establish the enterprise.

As a member of the Committee on Propositions and Grievances in the House of Burgesses and a trustee for the institution, Tom had met for months with the other trustees trying to get the structure started. Beside his father and uncle, other trustees included Lewis Burwell; Robert Carter; Robert Carter Nicholas; Peyton and John Randolph; John Blair, Sr.; and John, Junior; Dudley Digges, Jr.; and Thomas Everard; John Tazewell; and George Wythe.[62]

These men selected four acres on Francis Street toward the western end of town for the site of the structure. William Nelson was elected President of the Eastern State Hospital. After his death Secretary Nelson served in the post. Tom was a director of the hospital and later became President. The trustees estimated that 200,000 bricks would be required for the building; 16,000 feet of plank for doors and floors about one and one-half inches

172

thick; 2000 feet of plank for good sashes; and 5,000 inch of board for cornices.

The Building Act of 1770 stated that the cost of the construction for the hospital should not exceed twelve hundred pounds, and specified that the 132-foot-long brick structure should have twelve rooms below and above.[63] The directors decided "well-burnt" bricks could be made on the spot but ordered stone steps and window bar grates from England.

As president of the hospital board, William Nelson wrote Robert Cary:

> The Legislature of this Colony having voted Money to erect a Hospital for the reception and Maintenance of Ideots and Lunaticks, I have promised to secure materials . . . desire that you will send the several Articles mentioned in the enclosed Invoice, by the first ship.[64]

In a few months, William wrote Cary again complimenting him on the promptness in shipping the materials that were "all received except the Cross," which he expected later.[65]

◆　　◆　　◆

While Tom and his father were pleased with the progress of the hospital at home, they were concerned about England's enemies abroad forming an alliance. When France had captured Corsica from the Genoese, Britain had objected to this confiscation by her old rival. Then with the support of France, Spain seized one of the British claimed-and-colonized Falkland Islands. England was edgy; her colonies were in confusion and her neighbors were encroaching on the Empire. She prepared to fight the Spanish, but tensions abated after France failed to endorse Spanish efforts, and Spain withdrew from the Falklands.[66]

In May, William Nelson relayed his relief to Edward Hunt in England:

> I am glad that we are not to have a War about the islands. . . . It had been happy for us if Falkland Island had been sunk to the bottom of the Sea before the English had made so futile a settlement on it.[67]

By late May all thoughts focused on the churning rivers at home. For more than ten days, a torrential downpour pounded the land and filled the rivers to a raging crest swamping crops and sweeping away the topsoil. The Potomac, Rappahannock, James, York, and Roanoke rivers were all swollen by the violent showers, but the James and Rappahannock rose to unbelievable heights. In sixty hours the James reached an incredible crest of forty feet.[68]

Houses spun in the stream and submerged with scores of lives lost. Wine casks, broken barrels, and uprooted trees floated down the swirling rivers with cattle, sheep, horse and hog carcasses. The tide soaked tobacco stored in the warehouses. Captain Clarke's yawl was overturned and five men drowned.

In his communication to Lord Hillsborough, President Nelson stated the calamity was "by far the most dreadful catastrophe that hath happened to Virginia since its first settlement by the English. . . . the disaster will greatly affect if not wholly ruin the Credit of many merchants here. . . . if a speedy remedy is not applied, for the Relief of the Sufferers." [69]

The Council concurred with him that the necessity of this case justified calling the representatives to convene in a special session. Accordingly, the announcement appeared in the Purdie-Dixon *Virginia Gazette* that the Assembly would meet, Thursday, July 11, "to take under consideration the distressing situation of the sufferers by the late most extraordinary Fresh."

Tom and his father naturally discussed the disaster and expected to hear the extent of the havoc from their relatives on the James when they went over to Williamsburg. Since the deluge had devastated the land for more than a hundred miles on either side of the river, the Nelsons knew that their kin had not been spared. The public loss of approximately 40,000 to 50,000 pounds of tobacco was trifling, President Nelson stated compared to the personal suffering of the people. Whole families had been washed away in the storm; eventually it was estimated that at least 150 lives had been lost. [70]

Tom marveled that his cousin Ben Harrison, who resided at Berkeley, a handsome house on the James River could turn off misfortune by his humor. (Nathaniel, Ben's brother, had been building Brandon down the river in Prince George County after his marriage to Mary Digges in 1765. When completed, the grand structure would consist of five sections, the centered main house and connecting wings.) [71]

Cousin Charles Carter also had a new house called Shirley that he had constructed on property once owned by his mother, Elizabeth Hill Carter. Finally finished in 1770 after more than four decades of building, the fine brick building had unusually wide windows requiring twenty-four panes of glass. The grand "flying" walnut stairway attracted especial attention. (A score of years later Robert Carter would bring his bride, Mary Nelson, Tom and Lucy's seventh child and second daughter, to live at Shirley. [72] Elizabeth Nelson, the eldest daughter, would be the first of the family to marry, though she had five older brothers. In 1788 when she wed Mann Page, eldest son of Governor-to-be John Page, she started a marital trend, for four of her brothers and her sister Susanna all chose Page cousins for their mates.) [73]

Down river from Berkeley, Shirley, and Brandon was another manor house owned by kin of Thomas. Carter Burwell, his mother's brother, had built Carter's Grove near the capital twenty years before, while he was in his mid-thirties, but he hadn't lived long enough to enjoy it. [74]

As guardian of the Burwell children, Mr. Nelson had attended to their plantation affairs. When Nathaniel had reached his majority in April, he had assumed shipment of his own tobacco and had a private account with the London merchants. He had asked his Uncle Nelson to enclose in his order to Samuel Athawes a long list of household furnishings, and Mr. Nelson had commented in a letter to bachelor Sam, "but his Constitution is so very different from yours; that I expect he will be married soon after he comes of age."[75]

Nat was still considering marrying his cousin Susanna Grymes, and his remarks on romance found an eager ear in Hugh, who was already in love. The close cousins and roommates at the College of William and Mary confided their dreams for the future to each other. Through the early spring, the boys made their plans for a promising life. In fact Hugh felt he had finished his studies and was ready to settle down. In April he became twenty-one and in May he became a bridegroom, marrying Judy Page, eldest daughter of the Honorable John Page of North River. His father had some reservations about the match and remarked to Rowland Hunt:

> I have received the case of Instruments for Hugh, who is just married, for which I know in your Heart, you will blame him and me too, though your Complaisance will not let you tell us so much, however, having lost Mr. Dudley by death I must take him into the store to assist me: and if I find him disposed to do Business properly, it may be better for him.[76]

Besides the start in trade, the father gave his second son slaves and plantation property in Frederick and Fauquier counties.

The newlyweds lived in the big brick house with his parents, and Judy had to make the transition from calling her new mother-in-law *cousin* to a more endearing term. The elder Nelson house seemed almost empty while Hugh and Robert and the Burwell boys, Nathaniel and Carter, were away at college. Now the young couple, with young Billy, who would start school in Williamsburg in the summer, with Tom's two older boys, William and Thomas, made the house come alive again.[77]

By midsummer, Judy Nelson knew she would have a baby before March of next year. She might have kept this news a secret for awhile, but she solicited her father-in-law's help in repairing her valuable old heirloom watch. Mr. Nelson wrote Rowland Hunt that he would be sending the timepiece to London in the Hunt ship, *Prince of Wales*, and he asked him to select a "skillful Hand" able to put "every Part into the completest Order." He insured the watch and chain for eighty-four pounds.[78] It is doubtful whether Judy's expensive watch would have been entrusted to Charles Jacob even if his shop in York Town had been open at the time. Though he advertised that he could repair "Clock & Watches in the neatest and most approved Manner, and at the most reasonable rates," colonists were always confident that the mother country had the most expert craftsmen.[79]

✦ ✦ ✦

In all probability Tom saw John Hatley Norton when he went to Williamsburg, for the young English merchant was visiting his cousin George Wythe, who was building a small house and had sent his invoice for four dozen brass-jointed rings, side hinges, and rising joints for shutters.[80] All three men might join the crowd at Chowning's or the Raleigh escaping the oppressive heat. Sultry July days would sharpen their thirst for claret, rum, or sherry. As the groups gathered, they discussed the abandonment of the Non-Importation Association and the drastic results of the recent flood. John Hatley, a member of the association, was aggrieved that so many planters had lost their tobacco in the flood, but he had more personal problems on his mind. He was pulled in two directions: loyalty to his father in England and his love and allegiance to the choice of his heart in the Colony.

Back in York Town, Tom took stock of his supply of spirits at the Swan Tavern, for business was brisk when ships pulled into the port of entry to be loaded with the huge tobacco hogsheads throughout the summer.

Expenditures were rising for the British merchants. The tough terms that had been imposed were stated to his son by John Norton. Though he was determined not to exceed fifty pounds to engage the *Lyon*, he was obliged to give the owner one hundred pounds.[81]

George Goosley of York Town was so desirous to command a fine ship that he had consented to contribute fifty pounds toward the charter. Robert Cary had to meet the same terms to secure the *Brilliant* and Samuel Athawes had agreed on the *Pitt*, a ship of five hundred hogsheads with Captain Jonathan Punderson at its helm. This change caused Mr. Nelson to comment, I "suppose he has left poor Lilly in the lurch." He then questioned Samuel Athawes, "You parted with Lilly for the expensiveness then what will you think of Punderson's bill paid for all the staves?"[82]

The Nelson firm shipped more tobacco in 1771 than it had for several years. Writing to Samuel Athawes, William said, "My Crops have proved more plentiful than for some time past."[83]

To the Hunts he wrote, "My Fear is that you will have more Tobacco consigned to you than you seem to desire."[84]

It was a notable day for the Norton firm in London when its new vessel was launched from the English shore on its maiden voyage to the Virginia Colony. Captain Moses Robertson wrote John Norton on August 8, 1771, of his arrival, "I have to say for the *Virginia* that she does everything that can be Expected of a Ship and is Certainly as fine a Merchant Ship as can be built."[85]

John Page of Rosewell was anxious to view the vessel and assured Mr. Norton that "it was late in the Evening when she went down; so that I had but just a Glimpse of her. However if she does not sail in two or three Days, I will go to York & see her. She is by all Accounts the most elegant, & best Ship we have had in the Trade in Virginia."[86]

Captain Robertson had mishaps with crew and cargo. He lost his chief mate and a seaman of the *Virginia* to bilious fever. All the sailors were sick and two were so ill that they had to be discharged. He had only six in good condition for the run home, including the new mate "at 10 Guineas & 5 Gallons of Rum." The captain was unable to put more than 563 hogsheads aboard and had to leave out almost 300 tobacco casks. The lack of iron for ballast also detained him.[87]

Several other ships ran into a streak of bad luck in the next few months. Although man-made troubles were feared, they could be fought; weather was the unpredictable foe. In split seconds a storm at sea could snap sails, twist rigging, and send carronades across the deck.

Samuel Waterman must have been dejected, even though Mr. Nelson expressed to him that the loss of the *Latham* was "An Event beyond the Reach of Human Power to prevent and therefore must be submitted to."[88]

Hugh was learning the operations of the family firm by helping out in the store. He discovered that more than 250 hogsheads of tobacco stamped with the Nelson name were loaded into ships from May to November. He was angry with Samuel Athawes for "halving his Wife's pins," as he called the short order that had arrived. Tom and his father talked with him on the subject but since Hugh was in "such a Disposition" about the matter William Nelson had felt that it was necessary to notify the London merchant that a friendly letter from him to Hugh might straighten out the trouble.[89]

Tom was pleased when William Reynolds stepped into the Swan Tavern soon after his arrival in August, for he was impressed with the improvement of the young man during the three years he had been in England. Anyone could see at a glance that Billy was not the same ungovernable boy who had bothered David Jameson so much that he had hurriedly sent him to London to learn the trade under John Norton. Young Reynolds was now an adult with a goal: to settle in trade and seek a suitable wife. Being "greatly in want of a good hair dresser in York" did not deter Reynolds from fervent courtship of a number of comely ladies upon his return.[90]

Tom told him that his brother Hugh had married in May and his cousin William, the Secretary's son, the previous November. Then with a bit of pride he spoke of the additions to his own household. A fifth boy had been born since Billy had been away and also a baby daughter who would be one year old in December. When Reynolds visited Tom, however, he was more intrigued with the Grymes girls than with the five boys and feminine toddler in the Nelson home.

According to Mrs. Goosley, at whose home he boarded at first, he was soon "violently smitten with a Miss Grymes."[91] A few months later Billy wrote to his friend George Norton about Miss Grymes:

The sweetness of that Young Lady's disposition joined with a Character in every degree amiable made no small impression on my heart but believe me I have not the least expectation of marrying her nevertheless I am much indebted to you for your kind wishes on that head.[92]

In September Reynolds was living in his family's house near the Swan Tavern and was angry that Mrs. Robertson, his tenant, had let hogs tear down the fence pales and ruin the garden that his mother had so carefully tended. "I had not the Civility to call upon her,"[93] he wrote Courtenay Norton in London.

Nevertheless, he was "so happy as to have my female Neighbours to drink tea with me"[94] (including the Nelsons and Grymes), he confided to Mrs. Norton, that he instructed the Norton merchants to send him several dozen spoons, sugar tongs, ladles, dessert knives, and forks marked with his crest in a mahogany case, and a "Mahogany Tea Chest & Canister" by the very first ship sailing for York Town.[95]

Billy found the neighbors exceptionally kind in asking him to dine with them, especially the Secretary with whom he ate at least once a week. In these social gatherings, he garnered a good deal of information that was interesting to the Norton family in England.

John Hatley Norton often was the center of conversation. Several persons were convinced that the climate of Virginia was harmful to his health. He was well when he went to Hanover the first of August, though the drought was as "fatal to the high lands as the Freshes were to the low grounds,"[96] but the dryness aggravated his ague and fever. Back in York Town in early October, Dr. Riddell was able to reduce the fever by a special remedy.

Martha Goosley informed Mr. Norton, "I have left nothing unsaid in my power to persuade him to return to England for eighteen Months past & it was my desire your friend the President wrote you upon the subject."[97] (Doubtless there was much betting by village wits that her nagging would drive John Hatley to depart.)

President Nelson had written to Mr. Norton in May:

You want your Son at home, & I heartily wish him with you, For since last Fall, his health has generally been bad, & always precarious: insomuch that I don't think this Climate will do for him long, I have urged him as far as I decently can to go to you this summer; to which I find him averse, and I am of Opinion that Nothing less than your Parental Authority can overrule his Inclination to Stay longer.[98]

Since John Hatley Norton had turned twenty-six years old September 4, his father realized that he was not a boy under his roof and it was more difficult to deal with his independence.

Before a month had passed after his arrival in York Town, William Reynolds had already ascertained that young Norton would not embark for England. In a long letter to George Norton, he stated:

> I am told by Robertson (who see him three or four days since) & several others that he seems to have no thoughts of returning, he very often says that unless he cou'd do as he wou'd wish why shou'd he want to live, to tell you the truth I believe his regard for Miss Nicholas is too deeply rooted ever to be eradicated. . . . I have been in the Company with the Lady since my Arrival, she is one of the most agreeable, sensible Girls I ever convers'd with.[99]

Meanwhile Billy Reynolds was considering his own plans:

> I am determined within myself as soon as I get settled to look about me for an agreeable companion, you will say my sentiments are alter'd. . . . so they are. . . . wasting time with wanton women . . . is odious. . . . a Moth in a garment, for they not only ruin Fortune but constitutions. . . . believe me my Friend a virtuous Woman is ever a blessing to a Man.[100]

Billy was also concerned about John Hatley's romance with Sarah Nicholas, "They cannot yet bear the sight of each other without great Emotions,"[101] Reynolds wrote Mr. Norton on August 19.

On November 26, William again wrote the father, "but I must tell you plainly I believe he has not the least thought of returning & I have good reason to think he has again renewed his suit with Miss Nicholas."[102]

Reynolds was right. The romance had reached a climax. Risking parental censure and the vagaries of the Virginia climate, John Hatley Norton made up his mind, and the newspaper noted:

> Married—On January 26, John Hatley Norton, Esquire, to Miss Sally Nicholas, eldest Daughter of Robert Carter Nicholas, Esquire, Treasurer of this Colony.[103]

In the next few weeks, the bridal couple received congratulations and gifts from the Norton family. His father seemed reconciled to the event, yet still reproved his son, "hope that you will be a little more steady when you have entered the Matrimonial Estate."[104]

Soon Sally would have a dozen teaspoons and "new Fash'ble Ear Rings" that would go well with the broach John Hatley had commissioned for his bride, but his brother advised that a locket for a lady was "much in vogue" in London and more appropriate.[105]

◆　◆　◆

It was sweltering in July when the Assemblymen started arriving in the capital for the special session called to consider relief for the victims of the flood.

On Thursday, July 11, President Nelson stood before the assemblage. Beneath his high forehead, the administrator's expressive eyes peered at his associates. He was aware that summoning the representatives from all over the region in the midst of summer was inconvenient but said that the "Circumstance of the Country" made the meeting imperative, and he asserted, "I feel so sensible for the Sharers in this Melancholy Catastrophe . . ." he said, and the Assemblymen agreed to his suggestions that they be "instrumental in alleviating their Distresses." [106]

Tom served on a committee to "examine the state of accounts and losses" [107] caused by the flood.

On Friday, July 12, and Saturday, July 13, several accounts and petitions were presented concerning the damage done to the public warehouses at Shockoe's, Rocky Ridge, Byrd's, Warwick, Falmouth, and Dixon's. By Tuesday, July 16, the committee presented its findings. Richard Bland reported they found a total loss of 2,375,511 pounds of tobacco, a shocking figure. The legislators voted to pay for the tobacco losses by an emission of a sum of money—to be redeemed by December 10, 1775—not to exceed £30,000. Taxes imposed on exported tobacco, wheel carriages, ordinary licenses, and writs would provide payment. [108]

President Nelson was pleased that the Assemblymen had acted with the "Attention and Application" that he desired. In additional business, John Norton was commissioned to secure a sculptor in London to order an "Elegant statue of his late Excellency with proper Inscription"; [109] the statue was to be finished in twelve months. Norton had four medallions made, "exceed'g good likeness of Lord Botetourt," [110] which he presented to President Nelson, Treasurer Nicholas, Speaker Randolph, and one for his son John Hatley Norton. [111]

A front page story July 18, 1771, in the Rind *Virginia Gazette* contained appreciation to William Nelson from the Assemblymen for his conduct of office as Acting Governor; essentially the same appeared in the official minutes:

> Permit us to express our satisfaction in the great attention you have paid to the Affairs of the Government. . . . And we think our Country happy in having a native of your distinguished Abilities, and long Experience in business to preside over us.

This same issue of the paper announced that the Non-Importation Association had been disbanded. President Nelson had already predicted the demise of the organization to the Secretary of the Colony, Lord Hillsborough, stating:

> The Spirit of Association which hath prevailed in this Colony for some time past, seems to me from the defection of the Northern Provinces, to be

cooling every day. Meeting to be held 14th but so few Associators met that they did nothing but adjourn such until next summer such lukewarmness convinces me that this engagement will soon die away and come to naught.[112]

Because the Burgesses were in Williamsburg and most of them were members of the association, they met July 15 to discuss the dissolvement. They still recommended that the colonists refrain from importing painters' colors, glass, and paper of foreign manufacture; and they particularly asked the citizens not to purchase tea since the tax remained on that item. They complained that newspapers had undermined the association's purpose, frequently publishing negative stories, questioning the detaining of persons and destruction of goods by the arbitrary decision of a few individuals.[113] One outraged citizen observed that sensible people of Virginia were displeased over the strict adherence to the association since so few inhabitants were primarily interested in trade. These attacks influenced public opinion against the organization.

◆   ◆   ◆

President Nelson, through correspondence with Lord Hillsborough, had known for months that a new Governor had been appointed for the Colony and that Lord Dunmore was reluctant to leave his New York post, in fact, had begged Britain to allow him to remain in New York. The monarch and ministry ignored his importunings, although he stemmed from the royal line of Stuart and after his name, John Murray, could sign the titles of Earl of Dunmore, Viscount Fincastle, and Baron of Blair, Moulin, and Tillymont. The nobleman bowed to the inevitable.[114] Rolling down the countryside by coach until he reached the Eastern Shore, the royal official boarded a vessel for the rest of the voyage to Virginia.

William Reynolds, returning from an eastern trip, sailed on the same ship with his Lordship and informed his friends about the incident. "I had the honour of crossing the Bay with him and introducing him at York, he appears to be quite Affable & is Complisant enough to say he likes Virginia,"[115] Reynolds noted.

Since it was late on Tuesday night of September 24 when the captain steered the ship near the shore, the entourage disembarked the next morning. President Nelson and the Secretary rode to the dock to greet the Governor.

Tom scrutinized the new Governor as his father proffered the formalities. Lord Dunmore held his head erect and his reddish hair gleamed in the bright sunlight. Above the small mouth was a long, sharp nose and his dark eyes passed over the people in a cursory glance.[116]

William Nelson was charitable in his first appraisal of the administrator and noted on November 19 to his friend Samuel Athawes, "I believe from appearance we shall be happy with him, for I think I discover many Good Qualities in him."[117]

Returning to the capital, the coach was crowded with the Governor, his secretary, Captain Foy, the two corpulent Nelsons and John Page. They arrived in Williamsburg to be greeted by Councilman Robert Carter. Then they all repaired to the Palace.

That night the town was illuminated with lanterns hung from the parallel rows of catalpa trees along the lanes that led to the Palace. Even a suave Stuart descendant and sophisticated Scotsman like Lord Dunmore must have been warmed by this welcome and "testimony of joy" from Williamsburg's cordial citizens.[118]

As the autumn leaves changed in color, and the citizenry settled down under Dunmore, William Nelson and the Secretary grieved to see John Blair's life ebbing away. Then on November 7, 1771, the newspaper announced to the public:

> On Tuesday last died in the 85th Year of his Age, the Honorable John Blair. . . . The virtues of his private Character have been but rarely equaled and perhaps never excelled.[119]

By that time the Assemblymen realized that Lord Dunmore had no intention of cementing cordial relations with the Virginians. He had prorogued the General Assembly on his arrival and a private conversation with Robert Carter Nicholas and George Wythe's advising him to be more approachable had not helped. Local residents grumbled that his secretary, Captain Foy, was more military in bearing than helpful in administration.

Richard Bland was candid in his caustic comments of Governor Dunmore, saying, "We entertained a very Disadvantageous Opinion of him from the accounts brought us from New York." Tavern goers shared the story that one night Dunmore and some inebriated companions had dragged the chief justice from his coach, demolished the vehicle, and yanked on the horses' tails. This cruel act was beyond the pale of horse-loving Virginians.[120]

Though Governor Dunmore had deferred the General Assembly, Colonel Washington—still soliciting support for the land claims of Virginia veterans—was in Williamsburg in October and dined with the Council members, Speaker Randolph, and Treasurer Nicholas.[121]

Governor Dunmore issued a proclamation again on October 12, 1771, to prorogue the General Assembly until the second Thursday in January. According to custom, the representatives ran for re-election in December. Dudley Digges and Thomas Nelson, Jr., were duly returned to the House to represent York County, but Dunmore postponed the assemblage again until

February when the Old Dominion lay covered under the severest snowstorm in memory—"up to the breast of a horse" according to Washington.[122]

On Tuesday, February 4, 1772, William Nelson, Thomas Nelson, Richard Corbin, William Byrd, III, Philip Ludwell Lee, John Tayloe, Robert Carter, Robert Burwell, George William Fairfax, John Page, James Horrocks, and Ralph Wormeley, Jr., the twelve Council members listed in the *Journal of the House of Delegates*, took their oaths.[123]

It was not until Monday, February 10, that business began for want of a full complement of representatives. Washington had set out on February 25 but did not reach the capital until March 2.[124]

Governor Dunmore addressed the Assembly and asserted that he desired his "Administration be marked with useful services to the country. . . . regulate and encourage Agriculture."[125]

Thomas Nelson, Jr., was appointed with Robert Carter Nicholas to draw up a reply. Reappointed to the Committees of Religion, Privileges and Elections, and of Propositions and Grievances, Tom's assignments gave him as much committee service as any other Burgess. All through the spring, until the Assembly adjourned on Saturday, April 11, the thirty-three-year-old lawmaker helped to prepare and present bills, taking them to the Council for concurrence.[126]

Tom made a mental note to remember to tell Lucy that her brothers, John Randolph Grymes and Philip Ludwell Grymes, were transferring land for sale. Edmund Pendleton and Tom were appointed to prepare the proper forms.[127]

In addition to their attendance at the Assembly, the Nelsons had another interest in the capital for the Nelson boys were in school there as well as the Burwell boys, and Tom was already thinking of sending little William there soon for instruction.

◆   ◆   ◆

Very few educational endeavors had been made in Virginia until 1693 when the College of William and Mary was established in Williamsburg, with three men credited for its founding. Colonel John Page instituted the idea; Governor Francis Nicholson supported it. The Reverend James Blair perhaps constituted the most important promoter of the project. With a graduate degree from the University of Edinburgh, the dynamic minister came to the Colony in 1685 and married a Virginia woman who was also determined in manner. (Sarah Harrison Blair startled the assemblage at her wedding when she spoke up and stated, "No obey." The embarrassed rector repeated the vow and the obdurate lady reiterated, "No obey." After the third futile attempt, the cleric continued with the ceremony.) Appointed commissary of the Colony by the Bishop of London, Blair went to England in 1691 to secure a charter for the College.[128]

Despite his numerous positions—college president, commissary, rector for Bruton Parish Church, and Council member—the versatile Blair found time to indulge in the "Sport of Kings." He owned a private track and was so infatuated with horse racing that he organized a Jockey Club for the capital.[129]

The Nelsons knew that John Blair had reason to remember his remarkable Uncle James with gratitude. When no children were born to the James Blairs, John received their attention and funds. When Dr. James Blair died in 1743, he left his nephew John £10,000, bequeathed his books to the College, and left a gift of £500 for the institution.[130]

The College of William and Mary had its adherents and its critics. There was a difference of opinion concerning the institution and its instructors. Although most of the patrons were pleased that the curriculum centered on divinity courses, languages, and philosophy, others thought the subjects too limited; yet when the Reverend James Maury suggested in 1762 substituting the study of geography and history for Greek and Latin, there was a howl of heresy.[131] Jefferson praised two of the college professors: George Wythe, the eminent law teacher, and William Small, who taught mathematics.[132]

Evidently John Page considered his colonial education excellent when compared with the schooling that his cousin Robert Carter, III, had secured abroad. After Robert returned, John remarked that he was "inconceivably illiterate, and also corrupted and vicious." (Later on John changed his opinion of Robert's attainments and asserted that he "conversed a great deal with our highly enlightened Governor Fauquier . . . from whom he derived great advantages.")[133]

Landon Carter, too, made light of an English education:

> I believe that everybody begins to laugh at English education: bring back only a stiff priggishness with as little good manners as possible.[134]

Robert Carter, who resided in the capital for over a decade, took his family to live at Nomini Hall on the Potomac in 1772 and relinquished his role as a legislator. The next year he engaged Philip Fithian to teach the Carter children. Five daughters and three sons, ranging in age from five to seventeen years, were placed in the care of the young Princeton graduate. On his journey to take up his duties, Fithian noted the towns he encountered as he rode from Greenwich to Baltimore, through Stafford, and on to the Northern Neck listing the taverns and checking the cost of his trip. After arriving at Colonel Carter's domain on Thursday, October 28, he jotted in his journal, "Distance appears to be 260 miles, perform'd in seven Days. And my whole Expence appears to be 3 £ 6s 6d."[135]

The Nelsons certainly knew that there were irregularities from time to time at the College. Yet all three men had developed an objective viewpoint on the question. William Nelson and the Secretary served on the Board of Visitors for the College and recommended improvements.[136]

The quartet of older Nelson sons had many relatives and friends in their classes at the College. Thomas at twenty-three was the oldest of the group. His younger brother John, third son of the Secretary, had been born in 1750, so he and Nathaniel Burwell were the same age. Uncle William had praised both his nephews as promising youths and had attested that Nat was an amiable young man who applied himself to his studies, particularly in mathematics. When pupils were puzzled over a knotty problem, Nat could quickly supply help. Bob Nelson was next in line as to age but was two years the junior of John and Nat. Since he and Nathaniel were enamored with Mary and Susanna Grymes, they had another bond in common and could confide in each other the trials of courtship.[137]

Edmund Randolph was a first cousin of the girls and a college classmate of the boys. When the young ladies drove over from York Town for a visit at his home, it was fun to be the first to inform the fellows. It didn't take them long to rush to his house, albeit on foot because college authorities forbade students to keep horses at the College.[138]

Eighteen-year-old Edmund was a serious student of philosophy. He was the third generation of Randolphs to attend the College. His grandfather, Sir John Randolph, had been enrolled there in the early part of the century, then had studied law at the Temple in London. Peyton and John Randolph followed in their father's footsteps studying at the local College and then pursuing their legal training in England. Peyton had been Attorney General and his brother John held the post at present. In the future the mantle would fall on the shoulders of Edmund.[139]

Although Nat was interested in math, he was intrigued with Susanna. Three of his sisters had already married and now Alice, his fourth sister, wed the Reverend James Maury Fontaine in Williamsburg. All through the spring, summer, and autumn, Nathaniel pondered the possibility of continuing in college or stopping to marry and settle down.[140] He was advised to deliberate because there was some question that his sisters might be "entitled to the surplus profits of the estate and *not the sons*: tho I think this opinion not defensible,"[141] according to William Nelson. Then when Hugh Nelson married in May 1771, Nat wished to wed his lady love, but after careful thought decided to stay in school "to pursue his studies at the College until October 1772, a most commendable Resolution," Mr. Nelson observed, adding this was an "Instance of Prudence and Good Sense."[142]

Nelson sons were registered on the College rolls from the start of their studies in the grammar school on through graduation. Hugh attended from February 1769 through March 1771, buying his cap and gown in February

'72 and leaving March 25 of that year.[143] His father had consulted Parson Camm on his course of study, and books, globes, and instruments had been ordered from abroad to aid in the instruction. After Whitsuntide in 1767, Hugh and Charles Grymes, Lucy's younger brother, had been promoted to the Moral and Mathematics School. John, Philip, and Benjamin Grymes were also listed as boarders at the College. In 1760, Philip Ludwell and John Randolph Grymes went to England to further their education.[144]

By the 1770s, more Nelson boys were enrolled at the College of William and Mary. Bob and Nat Nelson and their cousin Carter Burwell had been taught to read and write by a tutor in York Town before they were sent to Williamsburg. Eleven-year-old Billy Nelson, youngest of the boys, had studied the fundamental subjects, too, and all had learned Latin. Probably the sons of the Secretary, Thomas and John, received the same preparation in their home town before starting their advanced courses in the capital. The school's accountant listed a balance of £/13/7 against the two students on September 25, 1770. (Entries are recorded for John as early as 1754. Since he was only four at the time, the statement seems erroneous, but "Son of the Secretary" was affixed to the account as a designation.)[145]

No wonder William Nelson, the Secretary, and Tom could be seen walking toward the Wren Building on the campus whenever they were in Williamsburg.

While his father and uncle talked with Preacher Camm and Professor Gwathkin, Tom talked with his three brothers and two cousins. The elder Nelsons and the teachers stepped upstairs to a room set aside for instructors to read, relax, or receive guests. The Secretary might hear that Thomas, his second son turning twenty-three and the eldest of the Nelsons then registered on the rolls, had been removed to the Philosophy School. Billy, who had started his studies in the spring of 1771, seemed adjusted to the routine. The sons attended compulsory chapel services where the roll was checked each morning and evening.

Being boys of the aristocratic class, the Nelson sons and the Burwell boys looked forward to a future filled with privilege and promise. Thomas and John had heard the Secretary speak of the troubles of the tax turmoil and Bob and Nat knew William Nelson struggled to straighten out the debt situation, but they all had high hopes that the economic entanglement would soon be settled. Tom had been an active member of the non-importation agreement, yet he had admitted that the ban on British goods hadn't brought the mother country around. Still, they expected to inherit estates and live in ease. Visions of riding to hounds through the vast areas of the countryside came to their minds. They talked of building big houses and bringing their brides home. No prophet could predict the forthcoming political upheaval. When the colonies broke their bonds with Britain, the boys became the soldiers and statesmen of the new nation.

Nathaniel Burwell was awarded a Bachelor of Arts degree at the commencement in August 1772. A newspaper announcement informed the public that the occasion commemorated the establishment of the College and that a "Number of Gentlemen in the City and Neighborhood attended by Invitation." [146]

Congratulations were in order for President Camm, too, since he had received "Letters appointing him the Lord Bishop of London's Commissary for Virginia." [147]

Highlight of the graduation for the Nelsons and Burwells came the moment Nathaniel Burwell was awarded the gold medal established by the late Governor Botetourt for the "Encouragement of Students in Philosophic Learning." James Madison from Augusta County received the other reward "after which the whole Company sat down to an Entertainment provided for the Occasion, and spent the Day in decent Festivity." [148]

CHAPTER TWELVE

Deaths, Depressions, and Debts: 1772–1773

Mr. Nelson Dies ✦ *Attention to Accounts* ✦ *Bankruptcies in Britain* ✦
Counterfeit Crisis ✦ *Credit of the Colony* ✦ *Lucy and the Ladies* ✦ *Affairs
of the Asylum* ✦ *Tradesmen in York Town*

Tom could not relax when he returned to York Town from Williamsburg though his activities in the April Assembly had been the most arduous since he had been a Burgess.

At home he related to Lucy some of the remarks he had written in reply to the Governor's address, and she was anxious to learn about the land transactions of her brothers.

Since his father suffered a recurrent illness off and on throughout the summer, Tom's assistance as eldest son was needed more than ever. Attention to accounts and correspondence at the store, checking with plantation overseers at nearby Penny's and Terrapin Point, as well as the lands in the remote regions and the Hanover tract, all took time. Managing the mills and caring for the crops also crowded Tom's calendar so that little time was left for the tavern. Coming to the conclusion that he could not continue to operate the ordinary, he placed this advertisement in the Purdie-Dixon *Virginia Gazette* of May 21, 1772:

TO BE LET: The well Accustomed SWAN TAVERN in York Town.

In the evening, Tom enjoyed puffing on his pipe. His father had informed the factor the previous fall, "Pray send me a box of elegant smoking Pipes; for though I am a poor hand, my son is very fond of an Evening Pipe; which I think does not hurt him, as he is now about as fat as I am."[1] When it arrived, William wrote that it was "plain," but lack of design did not affect the draw.

Twenty-seven years' experience in buying British goods had developed a discerning eye and discriminating taste in the York Town merchant. Inferior merchandise irritated William Nelson, and he had cautioned Tom and Hugh to check cost and correctness in the commodities for stocking the store. William wrote the factors about such discrepancies as millstones not being uniform, pencils arriving without the slates, and a piece of fustian cloth as "different as fine broadcloth from Drab."[2] Notifying the English merchants about poor products made them more scrupulous in filling orders, he believed.

The Nelson ladies inspected the fine fabrics whenever they visited the store. While Lucy selected a thick holland-type linen for her boys, Judy chose the thin white cambrick cloth to make dresses for her baby daughter. Elizabeth fingered the expensive silks with their changing colors. Merchant Athawes thought the material too costly and William agreed it was extravagant and "much dearer than intended."[3] Elizabeth was particularly proud of the new mahogany cistern, but Mr. Nelson had commented such "Elegancies are so many Incidents to Luxury, to which the Virginians are best too prone."[4]

He had indulged his own desire for artistic paintings by the Collets. The father excelled in landscape scenes but had retired and turned his brush and easel over to his son. William Nelson wished to encourage the young man so he ordered prints, paying as much as twenty to twenty-five guineas. When they arrived in the late summer, William wrote Samuel Waterman he was pleased with the pictures yet the artistic canvases were so similar to former purchases.[5]

The best claret came from Cary and Company, good thick cheese from Norton, and porter was procured from several London tradesmen with the stipulation that it must be shipped only by a York Town ship since "Nothing is so subject to Plunderage as bottled liquor coming from another river."[6]

Samuel Athawes had shipped Elizabeth some "Hose Bottles of Porter," and he was assured, "when emptied shall be sent to Martin's Hundred" as he desired. The special bottles would be a gift for Nathaniel Burwell from the English agent.[7]

The Burwell boys were becoming men of business, growing and shipping their own tobacco. Athawes was advised to take care to add the letter C to the family mark for Carter's tobacco to "distinguish it from his brother's."[8]

Tom listened to Billy Reynolds in the sultry summer as he discussed the trade situation. Billy had been sickened at the thought of settling in York Town at first, so he had visited Philadelphia and New York to determine if business prospects were better in the North. He had concluded that a stranger would be at a disadvantage in those cities; he really longed to return to England to assist the Norton associates and asserted, "for in England Business is pleasure but here it is Slavery. . . . Trade at present is dull throughout the Country."[9] British merchants were also suffering losses through stagnation of trade so bankruptcies had forced several firms to close.

Martha's son William Goosley, however, was living in London evidently oblivious to an economic crisis. A communication attested that his quixotic antics had led him to expend £1,000, one extravagance being a bountiful "Public Breakfast at Bath," which cost £27; and he had spent £100 to bedeck himself in a splendid suit that would dazzle the colonists. George Goosley, his brother, was bothered by these expenses. Captain George left London in March and sailed into York harbor in May with a cargo for Reynolds.[10]

Another Goosley son, Cary, asked Mr. Nelson to assist him in securing the post of Naval officer and William had written the authorities in England that the young man had presented a rough sketch of the profits of the position and proposed to pay the agents £50 Sterling clear. If agreement was reached, Mr. Nelson promised: "I will take care to have a proper security; not only for the annual payments to you, but also for the faithful discharge of the Duties of the Office."[11]

After agreements were reached, the York Town sponsor advised the agents abroad of his trust in Cary in a February communication, "I am confident that he will conduct himself with the strictest propriety & Justice in the Office; and, if he should attempt anything contrary to his Duty, Mr. Ambler under whose eyes all the Business of the Customs is transacted, and who does everything as it might be done would not suffer it."[12]

The promising young gentleman had barely made a beginning in his new post when he lost his life. Cary had been staying with Billy Reynolds and was in his store the last of June. Captain George Goosley, Cary's brother, and Billy had gone to Williamsburg on business. Since Captain George anticipated making just one more voyage from Virginia to Britain before quitting the trade, he had several details to check on in the capital.[13]

Leaving the store, Cary had saddled up his horse for a Saturday ride through the country. The Purdie-Dixon *Gazette* reported Cary's tragic accident in its July 2 issue: "Misfortune to be thrown from his unruly Horse, which taking Fright, and his Foot hanging in the Stirrup, he was so much bruised, and otherwise hurt, that he expired in a short time after being taken up."

Billy Reynolds recorded his impression of the melancholy occurrence more candidly to George Norton on June 30 after the mishap, "Poor Cary Goosley was imprudent enough to attempt to ride a race on a horse of his wch; threw him & killed him instantly, his poor Mother was up at the Treasurer's & in a miserable state of health, and am apprehensive this Affair will shorten her life many days."[14]

The authorities in London were also acquainted of the accident by Mr. Nelson and apprised that Governor Dunmore had appointed Dr. George Riddell, "with my Approbation" to fill the post. A deposition was required for the deputy as in reality he held the place "for the Benefit of Mrs. Goosley, a very worthy Good Woman and Mother of Cary Goosley; to whom £50 year is very convenient; and for this Reason I shall be glad of your approbation of the appointment."[15]

✦   ✦   ✦

At the store on the main street, Tom and Hugh Nelson looked at the large seine and talked of the countless fish they could catch with the huge net if they just had time to stretch it across a tributary of the York Town. It was "of 4 strand Twine, forty fathom long, 12 feet deep, 10 feet to each End Herring Mesh well fitted with Corks and Leads and a Coile of white rope 2½ inches round."[16]

Both Nelson sons were passing up the pleasant pastimes of hunting and fishing to devote more time to their many duties. They were saddened to see the stress their father labored under all through the summer as he struggled with a stomach disorder. Some days he was forced to rest completely; other days he felt somewhat recovered from what he called his "indisposition" and would engage in routine endeavors. Attempting to answer the innumerable letters from his merchant correspondents was quite a task, Mr. Nelson confessed in his communication of July 3, 1772, to Samuel Martin:

> I am now in my sixtieth year, and find I cannot carry some attacks on my health so easily as I could formerly; indeed how should I since this is Course of Nature, but . . . I will submit . . . with the Philosophy and Religion I can call to my Aid.[17]

The last business letter William Nelson wrote was addressed to Rowland Hunt on September 14 and concerned a cargo of arrack:

> My customers insist that it is not genuine, but a composition of French brandy and Lisbon wine in consequence of which, some of it has been returned to my hands. What is to be done with such unsaleable and a very costly article?[18]

The meticulous York Town merchant thought the Hunts had also been tricked so he continued:

> . . . that the culpable person (whoever he is) may not be censured unjustly Captain Clark will deliver you a bottle of Arrack that the Judges on your side the Water may give their opinion upon it; that it is not such I had last year and for many years before I am well convinced. . . .

With prescience that he would not recover from his condition, William Nelson turned his attention to his personal affairs. On October 6, 1772, he filed his will. Dudley Digges, David Jameson, and Lawrence Smith, Jr., were present at the court of York as witnesses.[19] Mr. Nelson suffered intestinal

191

trouble all through autumn, and his complaint eluded the curative efforts of the York Town physicians, as Tom would explain later in his letters to English friends. A bill for £200 sterling, to be paid to Dr. Corbin Griffin from London merchants who owed William Nelson, probably represented payment for much of the medicine and treatment for the patient.

When Hugh returned from his September trip to the upcountry plantations, he found his father in a sad state of health.[20] A somber stillness pervaded the household. Elizabeth sat by her husband's bedside. Judy cuddled her baby daughter close to stifle her crying. Lucy kept her boys from running across the street, and the servants cared for them when she went over to the big brick house. Seven-year-old Thomas felt especially forlorn since he missed his brother William at school in Williamsburg since October. Tom felt sorry for his second son.

Well-meaning neighbors came to call on the ailing Nelson with an assortment of soups and stews, spirits and suggestions. Martha Goosley, remembering his generosity to her family, surely reciprocated by dropping in with some food, although she was embroiled in a feud with John Hatley Norton over rent. (When her former boarder and business merchant had sent her an account of the debts of her son Cary, she poured out her woes to Mr. Norton in London. Mr. Ambler and Mr. Jameson had different opinions regarding the rent; the former felt £25 was right; Mr. Jameson thought £30 a good sum provided the house was put in "Tenantable Repair." She also consulted Colonel Digges, who looked at the dwelling and diplomatically suggested that £27 and 10 Shillings should be the sum, "which I am willing to Pay," Mrs. Goosley declared. She was determined to live on "friendly terms" with John Hatley despite his threats of turning her out and she affirmed, "nor shall any provocation draw me into a quarrel with you my regard for the family you are connected with is yr Security."[21] Her son William Goosley was far from patient about payment and was lashing out at the Nortons with libelous statements. Thomas Everard wrote John Norton on November 30, "I never saw so much Malevolence ridiculous threats and Bombasts from any one and this without provocation or just cause for resentment. I am satisfied the Youth will miss his Aim he will not prejudice you or raise his own reputation by it.")[22]

The news that Mr. Nelson was seriously sick had spread to the capital and Council colleagues, though scattered throughout the Colony, heard of his grave illness. Landon Carter recorded in his diary on Friday, October 9, 1772, "I understand by my daughter Lucy, just come, that President Nelson is now in great danger."[23] Later on friends of the interested families would remark that Eleanor Tayloe of Mt. Airy became the bride of Ralph Wormeley, Jr., on November 19, 1772, a day of beginning for the couple and the close of life for William Nelson.[24]

Word reached Williamsburg rapidly when William Nelson died Thurs-

Nelson-Galt house, Williamsburg, Virginia, was purchased by William and Secretary Nelson in 1749. Courtesy of the Colonial Williamsburg Foundation.

day, November 19. The two newspapers assigned much space to tributes to the long-time legislator; both publications praised his private character and public career. Said Purdie-Dixon:

> We cannot help condoling with the Public for the loss of so Benevolent Member of Society, so firm a Patriot, and so upright. Judging our Affection and Respect would lead us to draw this Excellent Character at full Length, but we are certain his Virtues have made too deep an Impression on his Countrymen to need the Assistance of Panegyrick.

Editor Rind was more explicit in his esteem:

> As a Magistrate his Abilities were unrivaled. Justice, Humanity, and Impartiality, dictated all his decisions; and as a Man he was an Ornament to his Species his Breast animated by a general Philanthropy, each Day was counted lost, that was not marked by some Benevolence.

Tom recalled his father's relinquishing of English property after discovering another relative had a better right to the land as well as innumerable

193

instances of his generosity to individuals and groups. To encourage worthy enterprises, William Nelson had contributed to institutions and industries. His name led the list of gratuities given to a school run by charity in Maryland.[25] An act to encourage arts and manufactures was passed during the French and Indian War with prizes to be given for perfecting products. As much as £500 would be awarded for ten hogsheads of superior wine, with subscribers paying for the premiums. After the ten-pound contribution of Governor Fauquier, Mr. Nelson followed with a five-pound donation. Of more than one hundred sponsors, only two other gentlemen matched the pledge.[26]

The *Virginia Gazette* remarked that Nelson's "liberality softened all the Rigours" of the poor and stated that his death would deprive people of a generous benefactor. As President of the Court of Directors for the hospital at Williamsburg, the writer continued, Mr. Nelson had demonstrated his interest in the deranged. His bequest of £100 was the first for the asylum. Reporter Rind concluded his obituary by saying Mr. Nelson had "Grown old in all the well earned Honours which his Country could bestow, and still more conspicuous for his Virtues than his Exalted Station."[27]

The Nelson boys—Robert, Nathaniel, Billy, and Thomas's little William—left the College for York Town's observances of William Nelson's death. Tom sensed that his son was bewildered by the strange silence that surrounded the Nelson households as a stream of people came and went for days offering condolence and bringing food. Two daughters-in-law oversaw the servants' cooking of chicken, hams, and roasting rounds of beef. Relatives arrived in the six-day interval before the funeral rites and were housed with Elizabeth and her boys, at Tom's three-storied house or with the Secretary. People were accustomed to sharing space and none expected a private room. "How fortunate Elizabeth was to have five sons to lean on," the neighbors thought. Though Billy was only twelve, the others were grown. Nathaniel was seventeen and Robert, twenty; Hugh had turned twenty-three in the spring, and Tom almost thirty-four. Elizabeth's brother, Robert Burwell, was surely by her side as well as the Burwell nephews and Lucy Burwell who had married Captain Lilly and lived in York Town.

Carriages from Williamsburg delivered the families of Peyton and John Randolph, Elizabeth Harrison Randolph, Robert Carter Nicholas and his wife, Ann Cary, George Wythe, John Blair, Jr., the Page relatives. Peyton and John Randolph were Lucy Grymes Nelson's uncles, and Elizabeth Harrison Randolph, Peyton's wife, was a first cousin to Elizabeth Nelson. Their mothers, Anne Harrison and Elizabeth Burwell, were sisters, daughters of "King" Carter. A close connection had always existed among the Carter clan.[28]

Robert Carter Nicholas might have been accompanied by his wife, Ann

Cary, who would have wanted to see Mrs. Goosley. (Their new son-in-law, John Hatley Norton, however, would have avoided the vexatious lady.)

The Page relatives would have had to cross the York River to reach the seaport town. If the wind and weather were favorable, John Page and his wife, Jane Byrd, Judy's parents, might have sailed down the bay. Frances Burwell, another niece of Elizabeth's, and her husband, John Page, Jr., could have arrived by the river from Rosewell. Rebecca Burwell Ambler and Jacquelin, who lived down the street next to the Custom House, would have been on hand to lend assistance to the family. Near neighbors in attendance would have included Dudley Digges, who (just like the Secretary had married an Armistead sister) had been a Burgess for nearly a decade before Tom returned from England. Digges was ten years older than his colleague.[29] David Jameson and his wife, Mildred Smith (descended from seventeenth century settlers), might have been joined by William Reynolds, the merchant entrusted with the task of settling the estate for William "Billy" Reynolds four years before.[30] Dr. Thomas Powell lived just beyond the Jamesons. (He and Dr. Corbin Griffin had decided to dissolve their partnership that year, and Dr. Griffin was continuing to practice in the desirable downtown site parallel to the Court House in a shop rented from William Nelson.)[31]

As the Williamsburg contingent gathered for the funeral, they brought news that letters for the ship *Lun and Loyd* had been stolen from in front of the Raleigh where a box had been placed for the convenience of correspondents. Some "wicked disposed persons" had broken into the box and scattered the letters on the street. James Southall, operator of the ordinary, was offering twenty pounds reward to apprehend the "authors of the atrocious act." Lawyer Peter Lyons, who was provoked by the "vile Rascals" who had taken six packets of his own communications, took time to write to the merchant Norton that "The chief Ornament of this Country is gone—our President died last week, respected and lamented, and is to be buried this Day."[32]

The group gathered at the residence on Wednesday, November 25, for William Nelson's funeral. Children were not excluded nor house servants, who hovered in the back while others stood in the yard sometimes shivering in their thin shalloon. Some mourners wore black broadcloth, crape bows, and left arm bands, mourning gloves, watch papers, rings, and gold and silver lockets inscribed with the initials of the deceased.[33]

Well-to-do families often used black velvet to cover the wooden casket. Black crape bows were fastened to the corners of the dark draping. Yet a simplicity of style would have been observed in the obsequies, for Mr. Nelson had stipulated in his will, "My Body I desire to be interred as my Executors shall think fit, in a decent but not pompous manner."[34]

Genuine regret marked his passing and the mourners present agreed with the sentiment expressed by Robert Carter Nicholas, "He died as he had lived, one of the best Men & the best of Christians. This Country has sustain'd a Loss not easily to be repair'd."[35]

The Reverend Mr. Camm preached a "most Excellent sermon" for a gentleman whose life had been dedicated to duty and whose character was so laudable in his love of God and his feeling for his fellowman that it was difficult to decide in which accomplishments his endeavors were the most exemplary. The rector remarked, "There seems by his Fall a large Gap to be left in Society."[36]

An imposing cortege of carriages followed William Nelson's hearse to the church cemetery where William Nelson was lowered next to the elaborate tomb of his father, "Scotch" Tom Nelson.

◆　　◆　　◆

On November 20, the day after William Nelson died, Williamsburg merchants, under old Andrew Sprowle's chairmanship, met to shore up their lagging sales. David Jameson later related to Tom the group planned to meet quarterly on the twenty-fifth day of January, April, July, and October, publishing notices three weeks ahead of time in the Virginia, Maryland, and Pennsylvania *Gazettes*.[37]

Another circumstance that interested and involved the close-knit clan was the culmination of Nathaniel Burwell's and Susanna Grymes's long courtship:

> November 28, 1772—Marriage Bond—Nathaniel Burwell, James City County—Susanna Grymes, Middlesex, Philip L. Grymes, Security.[38]

The alliance had the approval of Lucy, her sisters and brothers, and also of the Burwells. It added another link to the intermingled blood connections. William Nelson had been Nathaniel's guardian. His mother was Lucy Grymes Burwell of Brandon, a sister of Philip Grymes, Susanna's deceased father, thus making Nathaniel and Susanna first cousins.[39]

According to custom, banns were announced three times. People who missed the declaration in church saw the notice in the Purdie-Dixon *Virginia Gazette* on December 3:

> Marriage, Nathaniel Burwell, Esquire, of Merchant's Hundred to Miss Sukey Grymes, a Daughter of the Hon. Philip Grymes, deceased.

A congregation of the immediate family met on December 21 to hear the reading of William Nelson's will with executors Tom, the Secretary, Robert Carter Nicholas and Tom's younger brother Hugh. The will, proved with Dudley Digges, David Jameson and Lawrence Smith, Jr., allocated £5,000 sterling to his wife, Elizabeth, with other stipulated amounts; Nathaniel and

Billy, the younger sons, were also assigned £5,000 each; Hugh and Robert were allotted £2,000 each. The patients of the insane asylum received £100 and the poor of York-Hampton Parish, £50. Mary Nelson Berkeley, William's sister, was bequeathed £25 annually during her life and Cousin Hepsibah Nelson, £20 a year. Elizabeth became heir to the house and all its furnishings for her lifetime; then Hugh would inherit it. The gardens, stables, coach, chariot, cart, horses and harness, all liquors and provisions, town cows, and ten house servants were willed to his wife as well as his watch, jewels, rings, snuff boxes, and clothes and "new goods she shall *chuse* out of Store up [inventory] three younger children 150 pounds Sterling, prime cost." The plantations in Warwick and James City counties called Cheesecake and the Pennys, the Terrapin Point properties, and the Dowsings tract, with slaves and stock, were apportioned to Elizabeth. She was to be provided with beef, pork, wheat, and corn, firewood and "£100 sterling paid yearly to her by Thomas out of estates to him," with £75 paid annually out of the estates set aside for Hugh and Robert.[40]

Hugh had already been given the lands and slaves in Frederick and Fauquier counties. The mulatto woman Aggy and her children were assigned to him and a half partnership in the store with Tom. The plantation in Albemarle County was shifted from Thomas to Robert. Nathaniel and William received shares in the Dismal Swamp scheme. All the sons were bequeathed prized personal possessions: Thomas, a Virginia amethyst seal set in gold; Hugh, a gold watch and chain and carnelian seal; Robert a gold stock buckle; Nathaniel, a sword and pistols; and Billy, the best "Garnett sleeve buttons sett in Gold."[41]

Tom received Hannah, the mulatto woman, with her children, and all the rest of the estate, including the extensive Hanover plantations, lands in Louisa, Prince William County, York County holdings, all slaves and stock, capital, and half interest in the family firm.[42] Immediately, he took up the task of informing different factors in England about his father's death. Through the dreary days of January he sat in the store at the big desk with sheaves of papers stacked in piles—letters, accounts, lists. He dipped his quill pen into the ink frequently, sanding the parchment often as he continued the necessary chores. To Samuel Martin he wrote of his father, "His life was exemplary, being blessed with public and private virtues."[43]

To his cousin William Cookson he commented, "Let it suffice to say that he lived by all beloved and died by all lamented. . . . My poor Mother, as you may imagine, is under a deep affliction, to which, I fear, she gives way too much, but I am in hopes time will effect a cure."[44]

In checking the accounts, Tom and Hugh discovered that their father had demonstrated his usual perspicacity. Several of the British tradesmen owed the Nelson firm, but the York Town enterprise was indebted to the Hunts over £1,500. In fact, Tom wrote Messrs. Thomas and Rowland Hunt on

January 21, 1773, "I make the Balance due you £1571:13:3 instead of 1574:7:9 as you make it."[45]

Since the ship *William* had to have several new timbers laid and £120 expended on repairs, Tom remarked:

> This gave the Alarm of her being an improper Vessel to trust a cargo in. . . . it might appear presumptive in me to hint you purchase a ship of about 450 hhds . . . receive my private crops exclusively. I confess to you there is something of self at the bottom of this, for I should be sorry to trust so great a share of my property in such chartered ships as are generally sent here and indeed almost every House of note trading from London to the River has a ship belonging to it except yours, so that it is in some measure for your honor that I mention this.[46]

The correspondent mentioned to the various merchants that he, his brother Hugh, the Secretary, and Robert Carter Nicholas were the executors of his father's estates, and Tom also notified the tradesmen that he and Hugh "proceed to carry on the Business of the store in partnership." Communications were sent to William Cookson and Samuel Martin pertaining to the property in Penrith that he desired to sell. Since he had five sons, he explained, "I would rather purchase a tract of land in this country which would make a very good provision for any of them."[47]

Attempting to straighten out the accounts was a tedious task. Books could not be balanced until collections came in from local customers, and sterling was scarce so people put off paying their debts. The liabilities in the ledger for the clientele of the Colony indebted to the Nelsons totaled twice as much as the amount the family firm owed the Hunts. Already an appeal had been published in the press to comply with the terms of the will of the testator:

> The late Honorable William Nelson—All persons indebted to him will endeavor to make as speedy Payments as Possible. Those who have Accounts open on his Books, and who cannot immediately discharge the Balance are desired to give their Bonds. This Request is the more necessary as most of the Legacies bequeathed by the Testator are to be paid in Sterling Money, and he has directed that his younger Sons Fortunes shall be paid out on Interest upon undoubted Securities, as soon as it can be done. Those who have any Demands are desired to make them immediately.[48]

Few prompt payments were forthcoming, but William Digges, the younger, paid £80, and Tom included it with five other bills of exchange from the foreign firms and sent them to the Hunts. On February 16, Tom wrote a short letter and listed the drafts: Samuel Athawes—£383:8; Samuel Waterman—162:9:2; John Norton & Sons—264:6:8; Maurice Griffith—120:6; George Maynard—59:43:3; and William Digges, the younger—£80.

He reckoned the total at £1069:8:7 (which was incorrect) and entrusted the communication to Captain McCunn, commander of the *Juno*, and stated, "with the Tobacco that you have in your hands, will I hope be sufficient to discharge the Balance due to you."[49]

While Tom was persevering with the pen, John Norton's son, George Flowerdew Norton, was keeping his brother abreast of affairs in Britain. The tobacco trade was not flourishing, selling as low as 9d, he stated, ending the epistle with the comment, "The market falls daily & the French have discontd. buying." He also observed on the Goosley attacks on the Nortons:

> The Bustle made by Goosley, & his Mother I think was extraordinary as unexpected. I think we have made them of too great Consequence by replying to their Allegations, Mrs. Goosley has wrote my Father two of the most scurilous Letters that ever I saw from *a woman*, & particularly one that can't be ignorant of the Kindnesses My Father, & Mother have done for her, & hers. tho' nothing is strange nowadays when Ingratitude, & every other Sin predominates over our Passions, & smother almost every spark of Virtue remaining in us. . . . they are beneath our Notice, therefore hope you will act the prudent Part, & not put your Life in Competition with W. G.'s."[50]

Long before the letter could reach John Hatley Norton, William Goosley had become a bridegroom so perhaps romance blotted out his resentment against the Nortons.[51] The announcement of the nuptials appeared in the Purdie-Dixon *Virginia Gazette* of January 21, 1773: "Marriage—Mr. William Goosley, of York, to Miss Ludwell Harrison, of Wakefield in Surry."

Captain George Goosley was not so lucky in love. On January 20, Tom wrote John Norton about his father's death and the accounts. Then he relayed the romantic involvements of the Goosley brothers, but with discretion did not disclose the name of the young lady who rejected George:

> Captain Goosley has been disappointed of his Marriage; the young Lady having changed her mind before his Arrival; the effect that a long absence too apt to produce: His brother William was the other day join'd in wedlock to Miss Harrison, a daughter of Colo. Harrison of Wakefield in Surry. I am sorry to hear from all hands that the price of Tobo. is so very low; many of the Scotch Childs, as well as some of our own Country Men, I fancy have burnt their fingers by their last Years purchase.[52]

Mr. Norton notified his son about the slow sales caused partly by poor quality, dry rot, and "stinking like a dunghill and not worth a farthing." Nearly 100 hogsheads of trashy tobacco had arrived in the *Virginia*, fit only for the French. Business was bad and bankruptcies were rife. Several brother traders had "split on the rock." Three hundred ninety-eight names with outstanding obligations on the books of Norton & Sons created a £63,856.7.5 worry for Mr. Norton.[53]

The commercial concerns, money matters, and tobacco trade were not Tom's only interests. He decided to seek the Council seat vacated by the death of his father, and had already requested the required recommendations from the Governor, noblemen in England, as well as influential friends in the Colony and important factors in Britain. Several candidates wanted the post; Governor Dunmore eliminated Joseph Watson stating that Watson had no "connections or influence," and recommended the appointment of either John Page or Thomas Nelson.[54]

Robert Carter Nicholas wrote John Norton his estimation of Tom:

> Perhaps you may think me partial to him, as he is a near Relation, but I really think his Pretensions are superior. . . . he had a liberal & expensive Education at Cambridge . . . that proved a Foundation for him to build a Stock of manly Sense on; I believe he has as good a Heart as any Man living; his morals are sound; his Conduct steady, uniform & exemplary; & in point of fortune, which necessarily gives a Man an Independency of Spirit, he is inferior to very few.[55]

Nicholas enclosed letters for Norton to deliver to patronage dispensers and in January approached the Duke of Beaufort and Mr. Montague, the agent of the Colony, on behalf of Colonel Nelson.

The influential connections and important contacts of other candidates had not been idle. Colonel Byrd had close bonds with Britain, and presumably he pulled some strings for his brother-in-law, John Page of North End, whose wife was Jane Byrd. The royal official was aware of a growing restlessness in some of the Burgesses, and Tom was numbered among the progressive group. Sensing that an undercurrent of disquiet could sweep away the status quo, Governor Dunmore sought to stem the tide with conservative subjects. The administrator admired Councilors Corbin and Wormeley whose attachment to the Crown and affection for the Empire was paramount in their actions and expressions.

John Norton summed up the situation to his son John Hatley in his letter of March 20, 1773:

> Before this reaches Virga you will no doubt have heard Mr. Jno. Pages appointment to the Council, Lord Dunmores Interest was too powerful for any opposition.[56]

Indeed, Tom Nelson lost to his senior opponent, but harbored no grudge against the winner. John Page was his brother Hugh's father-in-law, an affinity that assured courteous acceptance.

Early in 1773 Tom was chosen a vestryman for the York Town church.[57] The religious influence from his parents helped to prepare him for the post, and his wife's strong faith was a factor. Accorded this distinction at thirty-four, Tom seemed destined to follow in his father's footsteps.

◆　◆　◆

Calamity struck the Colony at the beginning of 1773 with the revelation that counterfeit money was being circulated. Treasurer Nicholas notified the public through the press that the five-pound paper notes issued in 1769 and 1771 were false. He explained the forgeries were cleverly executed but careful examiners could detect the spurious bills.[58]

Governor Dunmore called together the Council for advice. To catch the criminals, the men proposed a one-hundred-pound reward for apprehending those passing the counterfeit pounds and a reward of five hundred pounds for the arrest of the forgers. An informer soon reported a well-organized counterfeit ring operating in Pittsylvania County near the North Carolina border. At least fifteen Virginia violators were involved and the executive later confirmed, "some of them people of fortune and credit in the Colony."[59]

Five of the counterfeit criminals were arrested, but despite the dispatch with which Governor Dunmore had caught the culprits and placed them in the Williamsburg jail, criticism surrounded his procedure. The criminals had been tried before the *York County* court rather than in Pittsylvania where the accused men had been arrested.[60]

Richard Bland read the Burgesses' address of thanks to Lord Dunmore for his vigor in bringing the forgers to justice, yet pronounced with candor:

> The Proceedings of this case, my Lord . . . are nevertheless different from the usual mode, it being regular that an examining court on criminals should be held, either in the County where the fact was committed; or the arrest made.[61]

Dunmore was annoyed at the Assemblymen for questioning his authority, and mistakenly commented, "There was but one person who has the least knowledge of the laws of this Colony."[62] Not only were there several lawyers in the Virginia Assembly who were authorities in citing their legal rights under the British constitution but also many laymen among the legislators who could quote sections to strengthen their stand.

◆　◆　◆

On March 4, Thomas Nelson, Jr., attended the special session of the Assembly summoned by the Governor.[63] Since he had not seen several of his associates in many months, they offered him sympathy on the loss of his father. Some of the men grumbled about the inconvenient call of the spring meeting as it was time to start planting. Others questioned John Hobday's claim that his new invention could separate 120 bushels of wheat from straw in a day. Since he had substantiated his claim by demonstrating the device before numerous spectators, Jacquelin Ambler, David Jameson, Secretary Thomas Nelson, and John Page of Rosewell had gone on record as recommending the improved invention. "We have examined a Model and are of the Opinion [it can be] easily carried into Execution."[64]

John Page was intrigued with inventions. He had asked David Jameson to import two instruments from London patterned after a contrivance he had devised to measure moisture, and the two gentlemen were excited about the experiment in which they were engaged. Every day they inspected the instruments and noted in their journals the exact amount of rain or dew. On July 21, Mr. Page would convey in a communication: "I had also supposed that not only our Crops, but our Health must be greatly affected by this Inequality of Moisture, & that both must depend on a certain due Proportion of Heat & Moisture." The machine was so minute in its measurements, he said, that after thirteen months of observing the elements the results were at Rosewell "40–346/1000," at York Town "41–32/1000."[65]

Fifty-one representatives did not appear at the opening of the Assembly in March. Nine new Burgesses replaced men who had died, and younger men were receiving more recognition. John Blair, Jr., became acting clerk of the Council, and Tom helped count the votes that placed Edmund Pendleton, Jr., in the position of clerk of the House.

Once again Tom sponsored the salary recommendation for Peter Pelham as jailkeeper and also served on a special committee to consider increasing the size of the jail. Tom was assigned with others to examine the bill to check the right of possession ("to dock the intail") of lands and slaves belonging to his cousin, Lewis Burwell.[66]

The principal business of the Burgesses, however, was the enactment of proper legislation to re-establish the Colony's credit. The Assembly authorized Treasurer Nicholas to borrow sufficient specie to redeem the 1769 and 1771 emissions, to call them in, and to issue new notes of about £36,000.[67]

On Friday, March 12, the House of Burgesses resolved itself into a Committee of the Whole. Thirty-year-old Dabney Carr, brother-in-law of Thomas Jefferson, presented some resolutions "to remove the uneasiness and to quiet the minds of the people"; eleven Burgesses should be elected to communicate with sister colonies up-to-date information on any actions by the British Parliament that concerned the colonies—a Committee of Correspondence. The House adopted the resolutions unanimously and the representatives were pleased with the progress of the eleven-day session.[68]

In his report to Lord Dartmouth, Governor Dunmore brushed the resolutions aside with the remark, "Your Lord will observe, there are some resolves which show a little ill humour in the House Of Burgesses, but I thought them so insignificant that I took no matter of notice of them."[69]

He explained more fully the emission of new money:

> I may not have been empowered to pass any new Act for emitting paper Money, yet as that instruction empowers the Governor to pass an Act for

emitting ten thousand pounds, and Mr. President Nelson, during his Administration passed an Act for emitting the sum of Thirty thousand pounds, which was approved by His Majesty, all of which by Act of Assembly are redeemable in the year 1775 considered in a new Emission by the substitution.[70]

The administrator admonished the Burgesses in his farewell address:

I recommend to you to use your endeavours in your several Counties to abolish the Spirit of Gaming, which I am afraid but too generally prevails among the People and to substitute in its place a love of Agriculture.[71]

Plantation gentry, who had been procuring vast tracts of territory by patent and petition, certainly agreed that the art of agriculture should be encouraged, but they didn't agree that a love of the land could be substituted for the sport of a turn at the tables.

❖ ❖ ❖

Tom slowed his pace to a stroll as he and the Secretary proceeded from the Capitol. Though his uncle was only in his mid-fifties, his nephew, like other colonials of the time, thought of him as an old man. The Secretary suffered from gout and was plump, so his gait was deliberate. As they rounded the corner, they glanced toward the shop of Peter Pelham where the industrious gentleman sold sundry articles in addition to his duties as jailkeeper, organist and, occasionally, dance teacher.

Along the street stood a succession of sturdy frame houses with steep slanting roofs set with dormer windows and with T-shaped chimneys at either end. Each home had stables, the necessary, a well, a laundry, smokehouse and kitchen nearby.

There were signs of spring all along the thoroughfare. The tap of hammer and sound of the saw mingled with the thud of lumber being stacked and scrape of bricks as carpenters repaired the dwellings.

Light rains had brushed the evergreen bushes to a shining brightness so that the leaves of the cherry laurel, coralberry, and dwarf box shrubs sparkled in the soft sun. Council colleague Colonel Byrd lived in a handsome brick house just past the intersection of Queen Street. Just beyond, on the corner of South England facing Francis Street, was Robert Carter Nicholas's big frame dwelling. A close companionship existed between Tom and his step-uncle, and the young man had a high regard for his relative's counsel.

When the gentlemen glanced at the magazine where the military supplies of the Colony were stored, Tom recalled that "Scotch" Tom had been a strong supporter of Governor Spotswood, who designed the arsenal. (Lucy's great grandfather, Philip Ludwell, II, had just as strongly opposed Spotswood.)

The men slowed next to observe construction at the hospital site. Eight lots had been bought from Dr. Thomas Walker of Albemarle County; the required 200,000 well-burnt bricks had been made on the spot and thousands of planks were piled in the plot ready to finish flooring, doors, and window sashes.[72]

On May 7, the Court of Directors' minutes of the hospital had recorded:

> The Honorable Thomas Nelson, Esquire, unanimously elected President of this Court in the room of the late Honorable William Nelson, Esquire, deceased.[73]

George Wythe's resignation as trustee of the hospital organization had been filled by Reverend John Camm. Benjamin Harrison of Berkeley and Nathaniel Burwell of Martin's Hundred replaced William Nelson and Dr. James Blair, deceased. The Secretary's and Tom's interest in the hospital never flagged and they were to serve as trustees all of their lives.

At the College Tom and the Secretary observed President Camm's house, built in the first third of the century.[74] Young Betsy Camm, not yet twenty, had filled the mansion with life . . . despite tongues wagging over her marrying a man three times her age.

Besides Robert, Tom's other brother, Nathaniel, and Billy were registered at the College. Nat evidently excelled as a scholar and was employed to tutor pupils as the records reveal he received "Salary as a student." Though little Billy was only in his thirteenth year, he was showing signs of liking law and would later practice that profession.

Carter Burwell had a new guardian since Mr. Nelson's death. His stepuncle, Robert Carter Nicholas, was to administer his affairs until he became twenty-one. Carter did not seem so strong as his cousins; but if he needed a special diet when sick or "tea to be made and sent by the housekeeper and wine whey," he could pay for it as required by the College rule.[75]

The College had its struggle with finances although revenues came from quitrents and taxes on tobacco. Pupils paid tuition fees and furnished their books and even "Fewel and candles to be provided at own expense."[76]

Apparently, the Nelson boys were well adjusted or, if they participated in any pranks, they were not publicized. Henry Harrison, however, was proving a handful for the Secretary, for President Camm had approached him about the boy's antics. He would not attend dinner in the supper hall regularly, and the housekeeper was not supposed to "send victuals to room except sick." The recalcitrant truant was squandering his time in idleness.[77]

❖   ❖   ❖

Perhaps an asthmatic attack curtailed Tom's correspondence in April and May, for only three letters appear in the accounts during those months.

Bankruptcies in Britain that spring made merchants fearful of furnishing supplies to colonial storekeepers. Thomas and Rowland Hunt were hesitant about shipping goods to York Town tradesmen; the Nelson firm was indebted to the English establishment about £2,300.

John Norton notified his son John Hatley about the crisis in the market:

> I am credibly informed the Hunts are on demur whether to supply the Nelson's store or not, fears of disappointments in Remittances & splitting on the same Rock many others have done, have caused a general Alarm among all our Merchants here.[78]

Norton cautioned his son to practice circumspection with no further tobacco commitments since the price of the product had fallen to 12 shillings from its former 20 to 25.[79]

Letters from the Hunt brothers to Tom echoed these sentiments and indicated that the order probably would not be filled. In irritation, Tom immediately contacted Robert Cary and Company:

> You will we dare say, be greatly surprised at this Letter, as it encloses an order for Goods to the amount of about £1200 Sterling, from Men with whom you have very little connections."[80]

Letters of recommendation had been written for the family firm, and the correspondent candidly stated, "We some time ago sent an order for Fall Goods to Messrs Thomas and Rowland Hunt but by Letters that we have lately received, we have reason to think they will not ship them."[81]

Communications with the Hunts were candid. Tom reproached the brothers by repeating some of their remarks: "Regard we always had for your Father and our correspondence with *him* for years past . . . induced us to execute your Order. . . . We candidly inform you that it would have been more agreeable to us not to ship the Goods."[82]

Tom questioned their six-months' interest terms and said all other businessmen allowed twelve months for the charge.

Despite the "Difference" and "Indifference" that the Englishmen had exhibited toward the Nelson enterprise, in December Tom declared:

> Now Gentlemen, let the Hatchet be buried, and we will acquaint you fully upon what Terms we can import Goods from you. R. H. must know what an extensive Credit our Father used to give; from eighteen months to two years; often longer; and our customers having been so long indulged will not be brought at an instance to pay within the year; so that unless we can import goods on twelve months credit, it will not answer.[83]

Tom rode out to the nearby plantations to check on the crops. While tobacco was the principal product, his men planted corn and wheat to furnish food for the family. His Uncle Nicholas had told him of the bad luck he had had with eggshell wheat imported the past spring, stating, "I suppose not one grain in a hundred vegetated." [84]

In May Captain Esten delivered the statue of Lord Botetourt, carefully packed and protected, on board the *Virginia*. John Hirst, a stonemason, came to set up the statuary in the Capitol. The sculptor was so apprehensive an accident might mar his work he had spared Hirst for the voyage to Virginia though the trip "was very inconvenient to him." [85] The colonists were proud of the elegant carving and satisfied with the expeditious manner in which the mason placed it in position.

Though the summer was sweltering with its "extraordinary hot & dry weather," Tom forced himself to stay in the store to catch up on correspondence and check the accounts. He often confessed to the merchants he wrote that warm weather just aggravated annoying business matters. [86]

Thomas Everard, distressed over the condition of his daughter suffering with severe fevers, explained the effects of the heat had "Injured her health, has reduced her greatly & disabled her from using her Pen." [87]

Mr. Norton received another epistle from Mr. Nicholas relating to the mason who set up the Botetourt statue who was "very fearful of the Effects of our hot weather, & withall anxious to return to his Family, proposes taking his Passage in a Ship of Mr. Backhouse's." [88]

On August 4, Tom wrote briefly to Mr. Backhouse in Liverpool and enclosed a "Bill of Loading for 10 hghds. Tobacco and Bills of Exchange for £293:18:5, which I hope, with £15 due to my Father's Estate will fully reimburse you for the Goods that I expect from you." [89] When the goods arrived in the autumn amounting to £390:15:8, the Nelson firm would still be in arrears. Then in November Tom explained to Backhouse:

> India Dimity, Irish Linen, and 25 yards of blue cloth were made out at £4:11:4 instead of £4:9:7, which though trifling, yet we would wish to adhere strictly to the rules of doing business, we thought proper to acquaint with. [90]

Ships lined the seaport's shore all through the summer. The *Arnold* arrived on July 29 and thirty-five hogsheads were put aboard the vessel for Mr. Waterman. In September, Waterman was consigned ninety-four hogsheads from Tom, seven of his mother's, and eighteen belonging to the estate of Armistead Lightfoot, "a pretty tolerable lift to the *Neptune*," Tom noted.

Athawes, as usual, was pessimistic about the product so Thomas probably took pleasure in penning on July 21, "despairing as you seemed to do of getting your ship loaded at all, you will be greatly surprised to find that she will go home full. . . . Tobacco in general is of good quality." [91]

Though the *Rising Sun* had been unable to take any of Tom's tobacco, fifty hogsheads had been sent down to the hold of the *Hansbury* and Robert Cary was alerted, "I do not look upon this Tobacco in the light of a remittance, but as a small return for the favor that I expect you have done me, by paying off Messrs Hunts and shipping a cargo of Goods."[92]

After this July communication, Tom attempted in August to explain the complicated entanglement of affairs to the London agent:

> It gives me great concern that I cannot, by this opportunity make you a remittance in Bills of Exchange; the great disappointments that I have met with in collecting money puts it quite out of my Power. I have endeavored to borrow a sum sufficient and have obtained a promise from Colonel Corbin, but he has not yet been able to raise it, though he hopes to do it by the time Captain Punderson will sail, when you shall receive all I can possibly get.[93]

Troubled that his credit was suffering, Tom affirmed, "a person who may have Thousands due to him can command so little. . . . may I say nothing."[94]

Tom became edgy over the economic entanglement and threw in testy thoughts to the Hunts:

> I cannot help thinking but you are tired of the Virginia Trade and prefer the Jamaica and Dominica; if so, speak out . . . [and the business could be handled] not with more integrity, yet with less grumbling. . . . I tell you freely that unless a Merchant will upon occasion advance goods, he is not the man for me. You have on board the *Hope* only 12 hhds of my Tobacco a smaller number than you expected to receive, and that I intended to have shipped before I saw your letter; for this you may Thank yourself.[95]

Thomas was one of nearly four hundred Virginia debtors who owed the firm of John Norton, but his business relations with him were on a more cordial basis.

His August 7 correspondence read in part:

> The Merchants of this Country are not yet collected together to transact business; tho' most of them had bound themselves under penalty to meet on the 25th of July. This must be attended with very great inconveniences as many Ships are gone without remittances & this prevents my discharging the Balance against me on your Books by this Conveyance.[96]

Concerning the floor cloth and anchovies that he had ordered, he continued:

> The Cloth is injur'd by being rol'd before the paint was dry; the Anchovies are very fine, for which Mrs. Nelson returns you her particular thanks.

Money was so tight that British merchants protested the bills of men who were noted for the highest integrity in business transactions.

The House of Hansbury pushed George Washington too far in this type of remonstrance concerning the Custis estate; he ended his commercial connection entirely with the English company.[97]

Athawes, always apprehensive, protested a draft of Tom's for £180, and at the end of the year Tom wrote him:

> I will not be out of humor with you though you have protested my Bill to Cocke for £180, but I think you might as well have paid it when you had 90 hghds of Tobacco . . . which most certainly overbalanced our Accounts.[98]

By September when the rest of Tom's tobacco was rolled to the dock and stored in the *Neptune,* he had consigned more than 340 barrels of the leaf to British merchants. He mentioned that 24 hogsheads had been purchased, probably a few more had been bought, but certainly most of the considerable cargo bore the Nelson stamp since he had made the remark, "this by no means a Time to purchase."[99]

Before Captain Punderson set sail, he was given an important order to Mr. Waterman:

> My Mother desires you will send her a genteel Chariot with six harness to be painted of a grave color and the Coat of Arms of our family, the whole to cost about £100 Sterling.
>
> In Memory to my Honored Father, I must beg of you to send me a genteel black Marble Tomb Stone with the enclosed inscription engraved on it: If you have no objection, I should be glad to have it bespoken of Oliver in Cannon Street; he has sent me three for our family and will therefore know what sort of one I want.[100]

September 14 Tom went to Williamsburg to attend a meeting of the hospital trustees; the building was complete, accomplished at a cost of £592:12:11¾ according to builder Benjamin Powell, and ready to be inspected. The trustees hired James Galt keeper of the asylum and placed advertisements in the newspapers announcing the hospital would receive patients October 12.

Tom and Secretary Nelson, with their neighbor Dudley Digges, joined kinsmen Peyton Randolph and Robert Carter Nicholas, and Thomas Everard and John Tazewell for the tour.

The brick building stood two stories tall with balanced windows, a centered cupola atop the roof, and tall chimneys at equal distance on either side. The seven men scrutinized the stone steps and window gates imported from England, then inspected the twelve-room floor plan on the lower level and ascended the staircase to the second story to view rooms provided for trustees' sessions and the custodian's quarters.

Tom attended the hospital's opening October 12 when 'Jeremiah Cassidy' of Hanover County was admitted "of unsound and disordered mind" after being detained in the public jail since the previous February, his stay there having been paid for by the court. According to regulations, the sheriff of a county called the justices together to make inspection of and inquiries about prospective patients. If confinement was recommended, the sheriff and guards brought those afflicted to Williamsburg and was paid twenty shillings for summoning the justices, five pounds of tobacco per mile for transportation. Deputies received the same sum as to the distance.[101]

◆   ◆   ◆

His uncle, Robert Carter Nicholas, had a personal pleasantry to tell Tom, since a baby girl had just been born to Sarah and John Hatley Norton. On October 15, the proud grandfather notified the Norton grandparents, "Our Son & Daughter are both extremely well; Sally about a Fortnight ago presented us with a Jolly Girl, who is named after yr. Lady."[102] The typical sentence summed up the status and customs of colonial times. John Hatley's name came first though he was the son-in-law and even if his daughter had just experienced the pangs of childbirth, she was "extremely well" and the baby was named after the father's mother.

Thomas Everard, however, had distressing news about his daughter, Mrs. Horrocks: "My poor Dear Fanny has been very ill for two or three months past," he declared and hoped that after the excessive heat of the dry summer had passed that the "fine and pleasant" fall weather would help her health. That was not to be so, and she died in December.[103]

The colonists continued to order many things from England. Lucy, Tom's wife, Mrs. Lightfoot, and the Berkeley ladies ordered lists of personal and household items in the autumn. They were not so demanding as the avid fisherman about whom Tom wrote Mr. Waterman enclosing a sample "Hook . . . to be carefully returned":

> An acquaintance of mine, who is very fond of fishing particularly for sheepsheads has desired me to send for a gross of hooks of a peculiar kind so that he may not be disappointed has given me a pattern which is to be strictly observed."[104]

Young Ralph Wormeley, married just over a year, commissioned Tom to order a chariot supplying explicit directions for Robert Cary and the coachmaker. His wife, Eleanor Tayloe, reared at Mt. Airy, was accustomed to riding in an elegant carriage so her husband wanted the handsome equipage for her by spring.[105]

Not all colonists ordered their conveyances from abroad. While in New York, Governor Dunmore had been satisfied with the work of Elkanah

Deane, an Irish emigré, purchasing a two-wheeled chaise, a four-wheeled enclosed coach, and an open phaeton from Deane.[106]

However, continuing to order carriages from England rather than patronizing a local coachmaker was typical of the colonists. In January, 1774, Tom wrote John Norton, "I had the misfortune to have my Chariot broke to pieces the other day and shall be obliged to you to send me a neat plain post chaise with four Harness and two spare glasses."[107]

The day after the "Vile Rascals" had robbed the letter box at the Raleigh, Peter Lyons started to rewrite some of his orders and asked John Norton to send "a small, neat, light post Chariott, that may be drawn in Summer with two small Horses and will just hold two Ladies & carry Trunks & ca." This November note was followed by another in December explaining that the chaise was "for the use of my Wife, who was so puny that she could not venture to ride out in an open Carriage"; however, Mary Power Lyons never lived to ride out in the little chaise for her husband informed the English factor, "No doubt you heard of my misfortune in the loss of Mrs. Lyons, who died in February & left me the care of seven Babies."[108]

Nevertheless, the Irishman who was making a name for himself as an attorney had found another companion by the end of the year. The Purdie-Dixon *Virginia Gazette* announced on December 30, 1773:

> Married—Peter Lyons, Esq., of Hanover, to Miss Judith Bassett, of this City, a Lady of Great Merit.

Despite their debts, Tom's peers were not parsimonious. Invoices for luxurious items, fine fabrics, grand furnishings, condiments, and spirits accompanied letters to London.

Lord Dunmore stocked his pantry from England: "100 lb. Rice, 100 lb. split peas, 50 lb. Maccaroni, 100 lb. Currants, 50 lb. Jar Raisins, 30 lb. Almonds, and 12 Do. of small pickled Cucumbers." For the cellar he ordered "3 Hogshead of Porter, 15 Do. of Ale, and 15 Dozen bottles of Strong Beer."[109]

One hundred of Lady Dunmore's guests could lift perfectly matched glasses since she had ordered 144 from abroad, as well as 72 tumblers, 72 quart bottle decanters with handles, and 36 two-quart decanters. A retinue of forty or fifty servants were brought from Britain; all wore imported clothing. Footmen were outfitted in blue and brown uniforms; grooms wore striped flannel waistcoats. Six imported caps covered the postilions' head; two dozen livery hats were ordered and fifty coarse hats for the field hands as well as "12 Pieces of Oznabrigs, 150 yds. blue plains, 100 Strong Coarse Stockings, and 100 pair Strong large Shoes for Negroes."[110]

Lord Dunmore's wardrobe required enough fabric to make three coats of green, three in brown, scarlet, and gray, one brown "Casimere," one green and one gray of medium weight cloth, and one black. Dunmore wanted, in addition, a chamber organ and a "very Small Organ for teaching birds."[111]

◆　　◆　　◆

Late in the afternoons Lucy walked down the sloping terrace on the western side of the house to stroll around the large lawn. Thick clusters of blue, purple, and white larkspur were scattered among the yellow-orange marigolds that blossomed from July to late fall. Already the cardinals and thrushes were searching for ripened berries among the well-tended shrubs and trees surrounding the area. Just before four o'clock, Lucy would send for the tea table to be set under the honey locusts and lindens. Her sisters would gather in the garden. Elizabeth was now in her twelfth year, quite a young lady, and Hugh's wife, Judy, would join the group. The elder Mrs. Nelson was still depressed and often wouldn't stir from her house across the street although Lucy's and Tom's latest offspring, baby Elizabeth, became an effective inducement for a visit. Even a year later Tom was making excuses for his mother for not answering the letters of the Athawes's ladies, explaining, "for though she has in some measure recovered the severe shock, which she felt some time ago yet she has not yet the spirits to intermix with society or concern herself with the affairs of this world."[112]

Women didn't talk of trade or money matters as they sipped their tea, but of fads and fashions. Articles in the *Ladies' Magazine* suggested ways to enhance beauty: For whitening teeth it advocated taking a half-ounce of hyssop, thyme, and mint, then a dram each of alum, salt, and hartshorn, to be placed in a pot over burning coals with pepper, mastic, and a scruple of myrhh. This was to be dissolved in rose water, and the toothpaste rubbed on the teeth each morning, then the mouth rinsed with warm water. To check telltale lines of age, the magazine recommended a cosmetic for the complexion: Strain some barley water through line cloth, drop in some balm of Gilead and "shake the bottle incessantly for ten or twelve hours" until the balsam was thoroughly blended. After washing their faces in rain water, women were advised to apply the precious fluid.[113]

Courtship and marriage fascinated both sexes. The public thought unmarried people peculiar, often a burden in the residence of relatives. The law imposed extra taxes on bachelors, and the papers poked fun at spinsters. The *Virginia Gazette* even published "The Picture of An Old Maid":

> Mrs. Mary Morgan has lived to the age of Fifty-five, unmarried, but she merits no blame on account of her virginity, for she certainly would have entered into the marriage state if any man had thought proper to make his addresses to her. Nature has bestowed on her no beauty, and not much sweetness of temper: the sight of a married one hardly supportable . . . inwardly tortured with her own ill nature, she is incapable of any satisfaction

but what arises from teasing others. . . . she has read just enough to render her distinguishingly pedantick, but too little to furnish her mind with any useful knowledge.[114]

The caricatured woman had a case for a slander suit; no record of one exists. The title "Mrs." used by old maids after fifty often confused folk when "Miss" was correct.

The Grymes girls were not going to be caught in such a predicament. Susanna had started the marital trend the preceding fall when she wed Nathaniel Burwell. In 1773, two of the brothers married. Bob Nelson had been paying court to Mary for a long time, and their relatives believed the couple had an understanding.

Philip Ludwell Grymes had married in June. As he was in his late twenties, next to Lucy in age, the sisters declared him old enough to settle down. Lucy turned thirty in August. By eighteenth-century standards, she was not thought of as a young woman but a mature matron, married eleven years, and the mother of six children. Her figure had filled out to some plumpness even when she was not in a "delicate situation," as the colonials called a pregnant condition.[115] If she began to lose a few teeth in bearing so many babies, that fact, too, was to be expected.

The newspaper printed Philip's announcement in big letters—probably to indicate the families' prominence:

PHILIP LUDWELL GRYMES, Esq. of the county of Middlesex, to Miss JUDITH WORMELEY, daughter of Ralph Wormeley, Esq.[116]

A few observant persons realized that publishers were not pointing out the fortunes of the bride as had been done formerly. Even social announcements were being affected by the economics of the times.

Autumn brought a respite from the sweltering heat but no surcease from the debt situation.

"The Difficulties attending the Collection of Debts in this Country, is almost inconceivable & I fear they will increase," wrote Robert Carter Nicholas to John Norton,[117] and as Treasurer of the Colony his testimony was indisputable. Besides authorizing him to borrow £36,000 pounds, the Assembly had adopted a measure to provide copper halfpence coins as a convenience for transacting business.

Tom and his brother Hugh learned that a working day lasted from dawn till dusk. So many people owed the firm considerable amounts, "but I cannot command it," Tom had to admit to the agents abroad. "It is as disagreeable to me to be behind with you, as it may be inconvenient to you to be out of your cash."[118]

After deliberation, the brothers decided to ask Augustine Moore to aid them in the family firm. Many factors in England were informed about this arrangement and that the new concern was to be called Thomas Nelson, Jr., and Company. A typical message about Moore mentioned, "This Gentlemen—was brought up under my Father with whom he afterwards lived and conducted himself in such a manner as to gain the esteem of all that knew him but particularly his Patron."[119]

Sometimes Lucy and Tom had time to talk sitting in front of the fireplace in their big bedroom on the second floor—the same size as the spacious drawing room on the floor below. In addition to the bedstead with blue "morrain" curtains, there were Windsor chairs and several tables creating a comfortable setting. A nursery adjoined the room.[120]

The couple spoke of plans to enroll Thomas, who would turn nine on December 20, at the College in Williamsburg with his brother William, his Nelson uncles, and various cousins. They did not consider an English education for their sons because of the expense and the risks of an ocean voyage.

Life in London or the lure of foreign lands might be more fascinating than the pleasures of America, but there were other compensations in the Colony. The many marriages of late made Tom remember the remark of his father, "You know that warm weather in Summer & little to do in Winter naturally dispose men to Matrimony in this part of the World."[121]

Lucy's brother Benjamin, fourth son of Philip Grymes, had married Judy Robinson of Middlesex County.[122] Like his brother Philip Ludwell, Benjamin had selected a young lady from his own county and of an old family.

Tom's cousin Robert Page of Hanover had married Molly Braxton, eldest daughter of Colonel Carter Braxton.[123] Tom's grandmother, Elizabeth Carter Burwell, and Colonel Braxton's mother, Mary Carter Braxton, were half-sisters, both daughters of "King" Carter. Carter Braxton was just two years older than Tom.

Tom and Lucy's cousin Charles Grymes married Anne Lightfoot of York ousting all other rivals.[124] The bride was Tom's first cousin, sister to Rebecca Ambler.

Judith Carter was not so fortunate in her romance because of her father, Landon. When she eloped with her cousin Reuben Beale in the next spring of 1774, Colonel Carter promptly announced his disapproval. The rector intervened for the couple and attempted to have the parent repent of his enmity, penning on the outside of the envelope, "Don't fling this in the fire as there is gold in it."[125] Landon Carter answered the appeal with a two-page communication on the rightness of his position. Reuben's father, Captain William Beale, also tried to appease the testy colonel and sent two dozen trout for his table. In his diary on May 2, 1774, Landon affirmed:

> I thank him in their behalf and ordered a bu. of Bernard Creek oysters to be returned. I shall not eat of these fish but have only behaved consistent with my determined reflections to have no intimacy or connection with them.[126]

Young "Jackie" Custis also had his mind on marrying. Colonel Washington had exerted every effort to educate his stepson. While he was making plans to enter the boy at King's College in New York, eighteen-year-old Jack became engaged to Eleanor Calvert of Maryland. The clandestine pledge frustrated his mother and "Papa," but they accepted the arrangement with good grace. Yet the marriage was not to be solemnized until Jack consented to attend college. Washington accompanied Jack to New York and enrolled him the last of May 1773. In June, "Nelly" Calvert visited her prospective in-laws at Mount Vernon with other guests. On the nineteenth, the colonel sat at the head of his table as a hospitable host for the numerous visitors. Suddenly Jack's sister, Patsy Custis, suffered an epileptic seizure and died instantly. Mrs. Washington was prostrate with grief. Overwhelmed at his sister's death, Jack started school but soon begged to stop and wed Nelly immediately. Against his discretion, Washington conceded, and on February 3, 1774, John Parke Custis married Eleanor Calvert at Mount Airy, her Maryland home.[127]

Tom thought wedlock brought innumerable blessings. His and Lucy's happiness made him advocate marriage even to agent Samuel Athawes, who must have been astonished to read Tom's advice:

> Mount mares and gallop to some acquaintance's House where there are a parcel of pretty girls and chat with them for an hour or two. . . . You old Bachelors are strange beings, why don't you get a wife? . . . many solitary hours you must pass. I should detest the thoughts of going to bed alone so often as you do.[128]

◆　　◆　　◆

Merchants of the town agreed with Tom that they could discharge their debts if they could collect obligations. The four executors of William Nelson's estate appealed to his debtors in newspaper ads that appeared through 1773 and up to April 21, 1774. Hard-pressed planters were implored not only through the paper and by personal persuasion but also by letter threatening a court case. Imprisonment for indebtedness was the ultimate punishment.

Billy Reynolds recalled his feeling of frustration upon his return to York Town two years before when he heard about the inhabitants who were involved in the complicated money crisis. It was common talk around town that Armistead Lightfoot had drunk himself to death after being compelled to sell slaves and land. Jacquelin Ambler had been disturbed by his brother-in-law's dissolute course.[129]

"Betting" Byrd was still addicted to gambling and his antics were bandied about in the taverns. Yet the York Town friends might not think it fitting to discuss his financial difficulties with Hugh since his mother-in-law was a sister to William Byrd, III. The men had noticed in the November 4 Rind *Gazette* that the sale of the "Honorable William Byrd's land, advertised in this paper to be on the 4th instant, is postponed until Thursday the 25th."

There was nothing novel about this announcement since Byrd had already been pushed to part with much property of his enormous estate. Sales were often postponed because the gentlemen engaged to sell the lottery tickets had not secured sufficient purchasers.

All through the autumn, John Blair, Jr., had been attempting to settle the estate of his father and of his brother Dr. James Blair, both deceased, and had advertised a dwelling house with furnishings to be sold September 14. Since only six months' credit would be allowed, the period was too short for many prospective buyers.[130]

Tom hadn't worried his wife by discussing the long drawn out debt entanglements of her uncle, Benjamin Grymes. Mr. Grymes's name had appeared in numerous announcements to sacrifice large land tracts to satisfy his creditors: fifty-one slaves and about three thousand acres in Spotsylvania County; regions along the Rappahannock and Mattapony rivers with 200 to 2,500 acres plus lots and the wharf in Fredericksburg; finally, the forge and furnace. A debt due to William and Thomas Nelson dragged on until 1775 when 2000 acres were mortgaged for £800.[131]

Several gentlemen gathered in the Swan Tavern undoubtedly discussed their distinguished neighbor-to-be, Lord Dunmore. The previous summer he had ordered 85,000 nails, 2000 brads, four dozen spades, files, hatchets, and scythes as well as a "Chest of Carpenter's Tools." The official intended to build a brick mansion similar in structure to Porto Bello, a seventeenth-century dwelling bounded by Queen's Creek between Williamsburg and York Town.[132]

Tom sold to Billy Reynolds the buildings and lot adjacent to the Swan Tavern for £550, and purchased 120 acres near the town, then advertised for sale a tract of about 600 acres situated on the Charles River. Although part of the property was marshy, a prospective buyer might not concur with the seller's statement that "it may be drained with very little expense. It lies upon a river that abounds with oysters and fine fish, particularly sheepheads; it is within 200 yards of a mill and 2 miles of a church. My reason for selling is my having bought a tract of land more convenient for me."[133]

Dudley Digges told Tom he had received a firsthand report of Parliament's plan regarding tea. John Norton had secured copies of the acts and his reply to a query was pessimistic as he affirmed there were "strides toward despotism . . . with respect to the East Indian Company as well as America, that we have too much reason to dread bad consequences from such proceedings." Norton added that great quantities of tea would be shipped to Boston, New York, Philadelphia, Virginia, and South Carolina, informing the factors, he had "advised the gentlemen not to think of sending their tea till

Government took off the duty, as they might be well assured it would not be received on any other terms."[134]

Parliament pushed through its plan. To prevent the waste of millions of pounds of tea crowding the warehouses of the East Indian Company, the minister and monarch maneuvered a monopoly, eliminating English and colonial middlemen. The company was empowered by the government as the sole seller to consignees in the colonies. Even with a three-pence tax, tea would be cheaper than the colonial merchant or Dutch smugglers charged. Restraint of trade roused the colonists' ire all up and down the Atlantic coast. Consignees resigned their posts except in Boston where the sons of Governor Hutchinson had received this patronage plum.

Boston merchants were in a frenzy; the Sons of Liberty were at fever pitch. Sam Adams had a rallying cry to unite the Whigs. The *Dartmouth* sailed into Boston Harbor the last of November 1773. When the *Beaver* and *Eleanor* pulled into port, the three ships had a total of 343 chests of tea on board. December 16 was a dark, drizzly day. By dusk more than one hundred "Indians" with faded blankets and red and black smeared faces rushed to the wharf; they swarmed over the ships, smashed the tea chests, and hurled the tea into the harbor. They met no resistance from the authorities. Riders started toward other seaport towns to report their action.[135]

In Philadelphia and New York, the colonists refused to accept their tea. The angry folk of Annapolis fired on the ship carrying theirs, and the citizens of Charleston confiscated the tea chests. By the last of December, Tom and his fellow tradesmen read the critical remarks of editor Rind: "That bane to America, that poison to health, the East India Company's tea."[136]

CHAPTER THIRTEEN

Resistance, Remonstrance, and Representation: 1774–1775

Routine Responsibilities ✦ *Hospital Trustees' May Meeting* ✦ *Governor Dunmore Dissolves Assembly* ✦ *Representatives at Raleigh* ✦ *Eighty-nine Burgesses Sign Association* ✦ *Brilliant Ball* ✦ *June 1 Fast* ✦ *Bad Business Orders* ✦ *Thomas Notifies British Merchants* ✦ *Speaks to York Town Freeholders* ✦ *August Convention* ✦ *Non-Importation Association* ✦ *Delegates to Congress* ✦ *Two Tom's Tie* ✦ *Death of Mr. and Mrs. Page* ✦ *Autumn Activities* ✦ *Robert Nelson Marries Mary Grymes* ✦ *Merchants Meet* ✦ *Richmond Convention* ✦ *York Town Tea Party* ✦ *Mary Is Born*

Tom attended to his correspondence and accounts at the large walnut desk in the southwest study. His desk provided four cubby holes above the wide writing space and a secret, locked drawer. Ornate brass handles adorned the handsome secretary. As he worked, he recalled his late father's shouldering of numerous responsibilities. Tom had turned thirty-five in December and needed to take stock. Had he discharged his duties to his family and friends faithfully? Had he attended to the affairs of the church and the activities of the Colony diligently? Had he done all he could to collect the large sums owed the store in order to cancel his own obligations? His problems were not singular but the ones faced daily by other planters and merchants.

Lucy's sister, Mary Grymes, would soon move across the street after she married Robert Nelson, Tom's brother. Her erstwhile beau, Billy Reynolds had at last found an amiable lady in Nancy Perrin of Gloucester. Since three years had elapsed before he wed, he had won his wager with Mrs. Norton that he would not remain single a year; but he had forgotten the bet.[1]

Reynolds and his bride settled in the cottage next door to the Swan. Doubtless the Nelson clan entertained the couple as Reynolds had regularly supped with the Secretary before his marriage. When the Reynolds reciprocated, Nancy could be proud that her husband had equipped the kitchen with "a Carving Knife & fork, a neat Mahogany Tea Chest & Canisters, 1 soup Ladle, 1 punch Ladle, & pr. Sugar Tongs, a Cream Bucket & Ladle—all marked with the Crest." Also included was a supply of over three dozen different types of spoons.[2]

◆   ◆   ◆

On Monday, January 24, 1774, Tom and the Secretary rode to the colonial capital to attend a routine session of the hospital trustees to determine the state of the patients confined and give directions toward the institution's future management.

A free mulatto woman from Richmond County who had spent six months at the hospital was released because the examiners testified she was "restored to her perfect senses."[3] The records do not reveal a follow-up on the case, what work she secured or where she lived.

◆   ◆   ◆

Tom derived a special satisfaction from straightening out the business breach with the Hunts. A difference of opinion had started years before between the Hunts and his father. On May 3, Tom answered three of their letters and acknowledged:

> To find that the Harmony that had subsisted so long, between the two families, is likely to be renewed upon a permanent basis, gives me the greatest pleasure, and had our Intentions been clearly understood at first as they are now, the little fracas, would never have happened. You are now, I hope, thoroughly convinced of my early designs to reimburse you the cash that you had advanced for the partnership by my selling my property at Penrith. . . . Before the end of the year, I am in great hopes I shall make matters square with you on my private Accounts; and with respect to the Store account we shall take care that our Orders shall very little; if at all, exceed our Annual Remittances.[4]

With this business seemingly settled, the representative made ready to attend the Assembly called for May 5. On May 4 he awakened to find that a silvery frost had spread across the area, so thick that at first many folk thought snow had fallen. What damage had been done to the wheat and corn crops? The flowers, sprung up in the last few days, looked like glass with their frozen coating.

Washington waited until May 12 to leave for Williamsburg in order to check the damage to his crops.[5] The Purdie-Dixon *Virginia Gazette* of May 12 announced, "Accounts from various parts Country giving Melancholy distress Injury late Frost severest ever remembered." Colonel Landon Carter received word from his son that there was "dismal prospect of a famine—everything seemed destroyed by the frost."[6]

Such adversity would not stimulate the sale of land. On Thursday, May 5, as the Assemblymen arrived in the capital, they noted another advertisement of Tom's in the newspaper: twelve months' credit allowed on the purchase of 412 acres.[7]

Although Lord Dunmore had proclaimed the previous October that he would convene the Assembly May 5, 1774, the legislators would not have been surprised if the session were postponed. Rumors flew until John Blair, Jr., clerk of the Council, issued a notice on April 21 published in the newspaper:

> Doubts having arisen, it seems, in many parts of the Country about the Time of the Meeting of the General Assembly, I have Authority to assure the publick that the Day appointed for that Purpose is the first Thursday in the ensuing month.[8]

The Assembly gathered before the Governor on Friday, May 6, when he asserted in his address that he had "Nothing to require of them." George Washington had not arrived, but he would have been agitated that Dunmore did not mention territorial disputes and Indian troubles on the frontier. Tom surveyed the members of the spring session and noted some changes. John Page of North River had been advanced to the Council. John Randolph had been elected a Burgess for the College. John Page of Rosewell could not have been pleased over this event as he had opposed Randolph for a visitor for the College, stating that his "disposition and character were not of the moral and religious" nature needed for the position.[9]

The colleagues had offered condolence to Thomas Jefferson grieved over the loss of his brother-in-law and cherished friend, Dabney Carr of Louisa County. Young Carr had been a capable and convincing speaker who, some men said, rivaled Patrick Henry. The thirty-year-old legislator had proposed the creation of the Committee of Correspondence the year before.[10]

Robert Wormeley Carter, eldest son of Landon, was representing Richmond County now along with Francis Lightfoot Lee. It is likely that Tom knew his Carter lineage well enough to know that Robert was a step first cousin to his mother. The happenings in the House for the first few days bored Carter, and he commented on the dull routine to his father. Livelier items of personal interest were reported of the activities at Rippon Hall plantation and the antics of the overseer and slaves. On May 8, Robert Carter requested that a horse be sent to him from the nearby manor as "his had been badly kicked by that of Nat," Landon Carter's servant. Two days later he wrote that William Jackson, "the overseer at Rippon" had pursued a wench to Williamsburg because she had been derelict in her duty. The angry supervisor had snatched the girl and "he turned up her clothes and whipped her breech; I checked him for his mode of correction and made the matter up between them," the son informed his father perhaps wanting to impress his parent with his serious behavior. "Wild" Bob, as some folk called him, hit the bottle, and he and his father oftentimes had bitter battles.[11]

Sitting on the straight backed benches with the Burgesses, Tom tried to relax as the routine petitions were read. Clementina Rind appealed to the legislators to appoint her "printer to the public" in place of her deceased husband, William. Her competitors, editors Alexander Purdie and John Dixon, also coveted the post. A few days later Richard Bland announced that Mrs. Rind had received the majority of votes to become the public printer. Whether it was from courtesy, compassion, or her capability, the good woman was gratified to know that she got sixty ballots from the Burgesses, with five cast for Purdie and two for Dixon.[12]

So far there seemed little business for the Burgesses to undertake. They considered increasing the fine for horse stealing. They allowed John Hobday £300 reward for inventing a wheat machine. John Armistead appealed for the sale of some land for proportion of debts due the estates of his deceased father. Benjamin Grymes, Lucy's uncle, still struggling with his debts, presented a petition for reasonable satisfaction for his slave frostbitten while confined in the "Gaol for hog stealing." Richard Henry Lee presented a number of petitions in his resonant voice making even routine matters sound important; Tom was especially interested in two bills relating to the defense of the Colony.[13]

Claims for cures of diseases interested the colonials, and petitioners recommended their drugs and slaves to the representatives for rewards just as the inventors of machines expected payments.

On Wednesday, May 11, the record contained a "Petition Charles Hunt had discovered . . . in his opinion a remedy cure Dropsy, Nervous Cholic, and Hectic Fevers." The discoverer of such a panacea would reveal it to the parliamentarians upon receiving a reasonable reward.[14]

The papers also advertised potions and tinctures for treatment. In the Purdie-Dixon *Virginia Gazette* of April 14, 1774, Tom read:

> Dr. Hammond's strong specifick pills are an invaluable cure for the yaws, in every Stage; even the most inveterate; also for the remains of the Venereal Disease, by bad cure; or frequently contracted Both these disorders will be entirely eradicated, even where salivation fails.

While the routine bills of the Burgesses evinced no particular expression, the whims of the weather caused excitement. The plantation representatives had not fully evaluated the damage done to their crops by the severe frost of May 4. On Saturday, May 14, about five o'clock in the evening a "most extraordinary Storm of Hail struck, some of the stones being as large as Pigeons Eggs, great damage to windows and shingles knocked off several houses."[15]

The session dragged along until the nineteenth of May when those assembled received the provision of the Boston Port Act.[16]

As soon as Tom heard the stipulations, he sensed the hand of Lord North in the harsh measures of reprisal. Boston was going to pay for its tea party.

English critics of colonial protests were incensed over the incident. Playing Indian and throwing away valuable tea was the last straw, so Parliament passed its "Intolerable Acts" that indicted the innocent as well as the guilty. The seaport town would be closed to trade, the capital of Massachusetts was moved to Salem; British officers would control all courts, and criminals would be transported to England for trial. Troops would be quartered in Boston to enforce the regulations; town meetings were forbidden. In sweeping aside the guaranteed rights of the colonial charter by a stroke of the pen, Parliament pushed the conservatives to join the ranks of the radicals.[17]

John Adams and Sam Adams, highly indignant, organized effective resistance. Now their patriots' party had a common cause. In their fiery resentment they assigned couriers to the port towns with broadsides explaining the Boston Port Bill and its consequences.[18] The Virginians soon ascertained they would be affected by the stipulation that large areas in the Ohio Territory would be annexed to Canada. This provision astounded land speculators and soldiers who by patent and petition had laid legal claims to the vast tracts.

Tom knew well the gentlemen still serving in the Council or House of Burgesses who were venturers in various land schemes. It seemed a coincidence that the two great land companies had been granted their charters on the same day twenty-five years ago.[19] The Lees, Washington, and John Tayloe had thrown their lot with the Ohio Company. The late William Nelson, the Secretary, Colonel Byrd, Richard Corbin, and Edmund Pendleton had become subscribers to the Loyal Company. All these gentlemen would be questioning the right of Parliament to uproot people residing in the outlying regions.

Thomas Nelson, Jr., had strong sentiments regarding the rights of the colonists. To one of his English factors he wrote:

> To be subject to the impositions of an Arbitrary Parliament and thereby suffer our property to be taken from us without our consent, we cannot, we are determined not to submit it as let the consequences be ever so fatal.[20]

In these May evenings men were on the move in Williamsburg gathering in small groups along Duke of Gloucester Street, then drifting into the taverns to talk of the new threat. Tempers flared over the topic of monopoly and tankards thumped the tables. If Parliament could push tea down their throats through a favored company, would an exclusive control of all commodities be next? The tobacco trade already had enough restraints.

Tom realized that the so-called "old guard" were becoming as vehement over their rights as the more restless representatives.[21] Peyton Randolph, powerful in physique as well as political stature, was changing his philosophy about the British demands. Since former protests to Parliament had been disregarded, shouldn't the resistance of the colonists now be more rigorous?

Robert Carter Nicholas was shocked that a Protestant Parliament contemplated establishing the Roman Catholic religion in Canada. Furthermore, he proclaimed that they should not tolerate the unjust provision to annex vast tracts of the Ohio territory to the northern provinces.[22]

Two other lawyer legislators, who had faced each other as opponents in the court room, agreed on their interpretation of the "Intolerable Acts." Neither tall Edmund Pendleton with his penetrating blue eyes nor slender George Wythe with his sharp gray eyes approved of criminals' being transported to England for trial. This provision violated a person's inherent privilege to be brought to justice before his own vicinage.[23]

The more militant members of the House of Burgesses met together at Council chambers May 23 to devise some vivid incident or occurrence that would focus Virginians' attention on the plight of Boston. Thirty-one-year-old Thomas Jefferson, youngest of the progressive politicians, rummaged through Rushworth's *Historical Collections* searching the pages for a precedent.[24] Patrick Henry, indifferent to dress but inflamed with the implication of the moment, was ready for drastic action.[25]

Scions of an aristocratic family, Richard Henry Lee and his younger brother Francis Lightfoot Lee shocked the Tidewater gentry by their sympathy for the Boston mobs. A slender patrician who spoke in smooth, melodious tones, Richard Henry felt an affinity for Sam Adams and the two men agreed that a general congress with delegates from all colonies should be called to consider the crisis. Francis Lightfoot Lee lent his sturdy support to every protest against the arbitrary acts of the British ministry.[26]

Though George Mason was not a Burgess, he was in Williamsburg in May on business and a guest of the session. Assemblymen sought his advice, since he had formulated the preceding plan of the Non-Importation Association.[27] The progressives planned to urge another boycott of British goods as well as a day of prayer.

Patrick Henry and Richard Henry Lee, the Assembly's two foremost speakers, agreed with political sagacity that the group "wait until next morning on Mr. Nicholas whose grave and religious character was more in unison with the tone of our resolutions and to solicit him to move it."[28] This strategy was a master stroke of diplomacy by the delegates.

On Tuesday, May 24, Robert Carter Nicholas presented the following proposal to the House of Burgesses:

> This House being deeply impressed with apprehension of the great dangers to be derived to British America from the hostile invasion to Boston in our sister Colony of Massachusetts whose commerce and harbor are, on the first day of June next, to be stopped by an armed force, deem it highly neces-

sary that the first day of June next be set aside by the members of this House as a day of Fasting, Humiliation, and Prayer, devoted to implore the Divine interposition for averting the heavy calamity which threatens destruction to our civil rights; and that the minds of His Majesty and his Parliament may be inspired from above with wisdom, moderation, and justice, to remove from the loyal people of America all cause of danger from a continued pursuit of measures pregnant with their ruin.[29]

The Assemblymen approved the proposal by a unanimous vote, then continued its routine session. Just after three o'clock on May 26, John Blair, Jr., clerk of the Assembly, appeared and announced the Governor's command to "attend his Excellency immediately in the Council Chamber."[30]

Governor Dunmore had heard of the liberal members' maneuvers and their plans to protest the Boston Port Act. Landon Carter affirmed that there was "Great alarm in this country. The Parliament of England having declared war against the town of Boston and rather worse . . . this but a prelude to destroy the Liberty of America." He also intimated that John Randolph had informed Lord Dunmore that a resolution would be presented. Dunmore then consulted the Council on whether to dissolve the Assembly and three times they "observed profound silence." Though adverse to the Governor's action, the Council thus gave tacit assent.[31]

Despite disagreements between the Assemblymen and the administrator, social amenities continued. Governor Dunmore entertained George Washington as a dinner guest at the Palace May 25. The next morning the two gentlemen rode to the royal retreat of Porto Bello where they ate breakfast.[32] Washington then returned to the session summoned with the group before an irritated Lord Dunmore the very next day, May 26.

> Mr. Speaker, and Gentlemen of the House of Burgesses, I have in my hand a paper published by order of your House, conceived in such terms as reflect highly upon His Majesty and the Parliament of Great Britain, which makes it necessary for me to dissolve you; and you are dissolved accordingly.[33]

Tom glanced at his associates and knew they, too, were recalling a similar occurrence of May 1769, when Governor Botetourt had dissolved the House over the Burgesses' opposition to the Townshend taxes. Now the representatives repeated their previous performance. They strode from the Capitol in the May sunshine and congregated at the Raleigh Tavern, where both conservatives and radicals crowded into the Apollo Room in a rage over Governor Dunmore and Parliament's treatment. The next day they voted to form an association explaining their resolves in the newspapers that day.

> To secure our dearest rights and liberty from destruction by the heavy hand of power lifted against North America. . . . our dutiful application to

Great Britain for the security of our ancient and constitutional rights have been disregarded . . . subjecting them to the payment of taxes imposed without the consent of the people or their representatives.[34]

The delegates declared that the act to deprive Boston of its commerce was disgraceful and "a most dangerous attempt to destroy the constitutional liberty and rights of all North America."[35]

The Committee of Correspondence was to communicate with the committees in other colonies "on the expediency of appointing deputies from the several Colonies of British America to meet in general congress, at such place annually, as shall be thought most convenient."[36]

Eighty-nine Burgesses signed the document. Speaker Peyton Randolph and Treasurer Nicholas led the list and conservatives Richard Bland, Archibald Cary, Benjamin Harrison, Edmund Pendleton, and George Washington supported the agreement.

The progressives eagerly signed: Patrick Henry, Richard Henry Lee, and Thomas Jefferson; then Tom affixed his signature to the resolution.

✦　　✦　　✦

Earlier in the year the people throughout the Colony of Virginia had anxiously awaited the arrival of Lady Dunmore, and the newspapers had kept them informed. The February 24 Purdie-Dixon *Gazette* had announced that "The Right Honorable Countess of Dunmore and Branches of that noble family set out from New York the 2nd of this Instant, and may be hourly expected at the Palace in this City."[37]

The March 3 issue noted that "Last Saturday evening the Right Honorable Countess of Dunmore, with Lord Fincastle, the Honorable Alexander and John Murray, and the Ladies Catharine, Augusta, and Susan Murray accompanied by Captain Foy and his Lady arrived at the Palace in this City."

By this time, the colonists had also learned that the titled couple had lost their second son, ten-year-old, William, the preceding year. Other sons, Alexander and John, were enrolled as students at the College of William and Mary upon their arrival. One observer had commented that Lady Dunmore was quite "elegant" and described the three daughters as "sprightly, sweet girls."[38]

The Council was also effusive in its expression to the executive saying, [we] "congratulate your Excellency on the safe arrival of the Countess of Dunmore, and your Family, in this Country, an Event, while it adds greatly to your Lordship's Domestick Felicity gives us a pleasing Earnest of your Intention of continuing among us."[39]

Upon reading these polite remarks, a visitor to Virginia would have concluded that perfect harmony existed between the executive and the people. The Council was striving to maintain the status quo, not questioning the prerogatives of the Crown and the power of Parliament. It was their bold brothers in the House of Burgesses who were stirring up the strife.

While the Burgesses were busy with the plan to boycott British goods and the proposal to convene a general congress, the royal representative was thinking about social conventions. He planned to set up an official court for the colonial capital. On May 26, the same day the resolutions were printed and Governor Dunmore dissolved the Assembly, the special rules of precedency for the provincials to follow appeared in the newspaper. The President of the Council, Secretary Nelson, and his wife ranked next to Lord Dunmore and his lady, followed by the other Councilors and their wives, the chief justice, the Treasurer, other judges, the Attorney General, the Burgesses, and then lesser dignitaries.[40]

Some colonials had disliked the kingly coach and splendid symbols displayed by Governor Botetourt. The rules of precedency also received criticism, provoking mutterings among some men that royal trappings were an unnecessary show of pomp.[41]

Presumably Thomas Nelson, Jr., read the regulations and might have mused that the colonials would have a chance to participate in the imposing procession the next night. The Assemblymen had made arrangements to honor Lady Dunmore with a brilliant ball on Friday, May 27. Just because her husband had dismissed the House of Burgesses was no reason, the representatives argued, to abandon their courtesy.[42]

As hosts, the Burgesses were holding this celebration at the Capitol where a cavalcade of coaches crowded the circular approach to the building on Friday evening. His Lordship and Lady Dunmore, with the sons and daughters, formed a receiving line to greet the guests. Some of the sixty yards of silver lace the official had ordered no doubt adorned the ball gowns of the ladies. The Governor could choose from his wardrobe of twenty new "superfine" coats.

According to the rules of precedency, Secretary Nelson and his wife were the first to enter since he was the acting president of the Council. He was tall and portly and hoped his plagued gout wouldn't act up so he could step through the grand procession. Colonel Tayloe also had attacks of this disease, as did Richard Henry Lee who would appear later in the line with the other Burgesses.

Robert Burwell, who had served in the Council since 1762, was still looking about for a third wife, so this festive affair seemed promising to him.

Richard Corbin had been the Receiver General of the Colony for twenty years. Since he lived lavishly at Laneville he would not be overawed by the ostentation of this occasion. He admired the showy style set by the Crown official. (Colonel Corbin and his wife sometimes ignored each other for an interminable time.)

Another long-time Councilor was Colonel William Byrd, III. Deep in debt, he continued to gamble for high stakes, selling vast tracts of land to recoup his losses. He liked fine liquor and detested conflict. As an heir to political prominence and social prestige, the powdered heads still turned when he escorted his wife, Mary Willing, to such an entertainment.

When Colonel John Tayloe entered the hall, he attracted attention by his air of self-assurance. Lady Dunmore might have noticed his keen eyes and deeply clefted chin as he bowed low over her hand. Big jeweled buttons flashed from his splendid suit.[43]

Philip Ludwell Lee had been appointed to the Council in 1757 when he was thirty years old, the same year that Colonel Tayloe started his service. Scion of the outstanding Lee family, Philip Ludwell was the eldest of six sons and a bachelor when appointed. The brothers didn't rush into matrimony so Stratford remained without a mistress until his marriage to Elizabeth Steptoe. He was thirty-seven when baby Matilda was born in 1763.[44]

Francis Lightfoot Lee was thirty-five when he wooed and won the hand of seventeen-year-old Rebecca Tayloe in 1769. His brother William had married their first cousin, Hannah Philla Ludwell, in London the same year leaving bachelor Arthur to moan, "I am now the only unhappy or single person in the family; nor have I any prospect of being otherwise."[45]

Though Philip Ludwell lacked the grace and eloquence of Richard Henry Lee (who married twice) and was wanting in the witty charm of Francis Lightfoot, he bound his brothers together into a close-knit clan that had much political power.

Some of the social company might wonder why Councilor Carter had not attended the Assembly so was not present at the prestigious affair. Mrs. Carter, who was "cheerful and chatty" and looked lovely even when overcome with extreme heat would have enjoyed the gala gathering.[46]

If scholarly Richard Bland attended the affair, he might have had to wear his green shade to protect his blurred eyes from the bright chandeliers. Handsome Edmund Pendleton towered above muscular Archibald Cary of middle stature.

This grand celebration with its coterie of Council and the aristocrats of the Colony was the last splendid soiree. Although the Palace and Capitol were opened on other occasions, an era was ending. A new spirit was rising, and the influence of the English landed gentry was losing its luster. Deep indebtedness and a growing resentment over British restrictions were paving the road to revolution.

The ball did not divert the Burgesses from the business at hand. Though many members rode away from Williamsburg over the week end, the Committee of Correspondence met on Monday, May 30, when Peyton Randolph called together twenty-five of the remaining representatives.[47]

Tom attended the ten o'clock session when the committee proposed cutting all commercial dealing with Great Britain and recommended forfeiting debts owed by the colonial citizens to English businesses. Although the obligations Tom owed to English firms were enormous, he felt the debts should be honored so he stated that he intended to settle his own accounts. George Washington agreed with him.[48]

The delegates agreed to inform all their associate Burgesses by letter of their deliberations and to ask them to come to Williamsburg on August 1 to consider further steps since, "Things seem to be hurrying to an alarming crisis, and demand the speedy, united council of all those who have a regard for the common cause."[49]

On Wednesday, June 1, in accordance with the resolutions, a special day was set aside for a fast and the representatives proceeded "with the Speaker and the mace to the church in this city."[50] Peyton Randolph and Robert Carter Nicholas led the legislators into Bruton Parish Church for the solemn ceremony. Reverend Mr. Gwathkin "excused himself" and asserted that he was "afraid he would not be able to participate in the service."[51] The Reverend Mr. Price substituted and stood before the Assemblymen to "read the prayer and preach a sermon suitable to the occasion."[52] Many people were pleased to hear of the rector in Richmond County who relinquished "God Save the King" in favor of the patriotic sentiment "God preserve all the just rights and liberties of America."[53]

George Mason was anxious that his children observe the occasion. He wrote, "should a day of prayer and fasting be appointed in our County, please tell my dear little family that I charge them to pay a strict attention to it, and that I desire my three eldest sons and my two eldest daughters may attend church in mourning, if they have it, as I believe they have."[54] This was a polite request to his family since Mrs. Mason had died in 1773 so the father knew that the children had mourning clothes.

On the other hand, Councilor Carter, who had been absent from the May Assembly, opposed the observance and ordered that his household at Nomini Hall disregard it and affirmed, "No one must go hence to Church, or observe the Fast at all." Yet the colonel conceded that tea should not be served and coffee was substituted at the table.[55]

Much later Edmund Randolph would remember that "The fast was obeyd throughout Virginia with such vigor and scruple, as to interdict the lasting of food between the rising and setting sun."[56]

✦   ✦   ✦

Tom acquainted Hugh with the actions of the Assembly as the brothers checked on the stock at the store. Both young tradesmen were impatient with several shoddy articles that had arrived.

In a letter to the Hunts, Tom stated,

Mr. Davis's Calamanco Shoes are so unreasonable large that they will fit none but now and than A Country Girl who have been accustomed to go barefoot from her childhood . . .

6 horns [were sent] in liue of Tin Lanthorns which we ordered and having more of them already on hand than we can dispose of, we shall get the favor of Captain Clark to take back.[57]

The correspondent for the family firm sometimes wrote communications that did not relate to shipping tobacco, ordering supplies, or returning inferior goods. Members of the community called on him for aid. In asking a favor for a friend, he affirmed to Athawes that it was his conviction

that part of every Man's Time and Thoughts ought to be devoted to the interest of others . . . Tom Nelson supported that belief with his actions and often his financial aid despite growing responsibilities with the business and increasing concern over England's behavior tword the colonies. He wrote Mr. Athawes requesting £50 "on my account" for Samuel Sheild, a young man seeking holy orders from the Bishop of London. (After his ordination, Sheild returned to Virginia in 1775 to become rector of Drysdale Parish and husband of Miss Mary Hansford, whose sister had married preacher John Camm). In another generous move, Tom and Nat Burwell went security for £300 in Captain Lilly's imprudent ship-building venture. On behalf of Lucy's sister he wrote Samuel Athawes June 6 seeking items for her wedding apparel, and a month later again wrote noting he had failed to send the stays measurement for Miss Grymes who was to give "her heart and hand to my Brother Bob." He complained of the heat saying, "I am so relaxed that I have not resolution to go through the letters that I have to answer," yet the weary writer continued his task for several more communications that July day.[58]

◆　　◆　　◆

Tom notified the freeholders of the county to attend the meeting on July 18, while Dudley Digges told the inhabitants of York Town. A posted broadside read:

ALARMING CRISIS DEMANDS SPEEDY, UNITED COUNCILS OF ALL THOSE WHO HAVE REGARD FOR THE COMMON CAUSE.[59]

When the citizens of the county convened at the Court House on the appointed day, they unanimously chose Thomas Nelson to moderate the meeting; he addressed the crowd with a stirring speech:

Friends and Countrymen—We are met today upon one of the most important matters that can engage the attention of men. You are all acquainted with the Attacks which have been lately made by the British Parliament upon, what is dearer to Americans than their lives, their liberties. . . . You have heard of the Acts of Oppression wich have passed against a Sister Colony, under which it is now actually groaning, and must be sensible that this is only a Prelude to the Designs of Parliament upon every other part of this wide extended Continent.[60]

To consider their course of action in this crisis, Tom explained that the Assemblymen had agreed to call a convention for August 1, in the capital duly reported in the July 21, 1774, Rind *Gazette:*

> You all know what it is to be Free men; you know the blessed Privilege of doing what you will with your own, and you can guess at the Misery of those who are deprived of this Right. We have found already the Petitions and Remonstrances are Ineffectual and it is now Time that we try other Expedients.

So that the oppressors would feel the "Effects of their Mistakes," the orator announced that representatives from the counties had recommended cutting off all commercial intercourse with Great Britain, which the citizens could do without great inconvenience.

The speech secured the desired results and the freeholders of York County adopted strong resolutions regarding their rights:

> As the fountain from whence all power and legislation flow, a right coeval with human nature, and which they claim from the Eternal and immutable laws of nature's God.[61]

Dudley Digges and Thomas Nelson, Jr., were chosen to represent the county at the general convention called for August 1 at Williamsburg and were counseled by the citizens "To put a stop to that growing system of ministerial despotism which has so long threatened the destruction of America."[62] The delegates were also instructed to declare that no man should be taxed except by the Burgesses chosen to represent them. Colonists all over the Old Dominion read the remarks of Thomas Nelson, Jr., and the resolves passed by the citizens of York County on the *front* page of both the Rind and Purdie-Dixon papers.

When the York Town legislators arrived for the convention in the capital city, they found a large number of their colleagues already assembled. As Tom mingled among the gentlemen, he glimpsed his Burwell kin, Carter cousins, Randolph relatives, and his cousin George Washington. Thomas Jefferson was missing—suffering from dysentery that forced him to stay at Monticello. Jefferson was keenly disappointed but sent two copies of a special composition to Peyton Randolph and Patrick Henry. Speaker Randolph placed the paper on the table where some of the representatives read "A Summary View of the Rights of British America," a lengthy treatise with far-reaching thoughts, and they had it published. Peyton Randolph was so impressed by the paper that he invited some representatives to his residence to hear it read aloud.[63]

Tom listened attentively to Jefferson's contention that the Crown should be the connection between the mother country and the colonies, but this concept of a commonwealth system of nations was too advanced for the time. The liberal ideas were too progressive for the legislators to endorse.

The members of the convention accomplished two acts of consequence. Firstly, they adopted a strong Non-Importation Association, and the newspaper printed the resolves on its front page:

> We do hereby resolve and declare that we will not, either directly or indirectly, after 1st November next, import from Great Britain any Goods, Wares, or Merchandise whatsoever; Medicine Excepted; nor will we, after that Day import any British manufactures, either from the West Indies or any other place. . . . the detestable Tea, which laid the Foundation of the present Sufferings . . . we view with HORROR. and therefore resolve, we will not from this Day, either import Tea of any Kind whatsoever, nor shall we use, or suffer any of such of it is now on Hand to be used, in any of our Families.[64]

No slaves would be bought after November 1. Then the representatives warned the British government that unless American grievances were redressed by August 10, 1775, no tobacco would be exported to England.

Secondly, the convention decided to send delegates to a general congress to convene at Philadelphia on September 5. It chose seven deputies to carry the resolutions of Virginia to the first Continental Congress: Peyton Randolph, Richard Henry Lee, George Washington, Patrick Henry, Richard Bland, Benjamin Harrison, and Edmund Pendleton, in order of the number of votes each received. These men were the representatives of the House of Burgesses who had presented bills. All of them were trained in the law, except Washington. He had fought on the frontier and was noted for coolness and courage.[65]

Some of the representatives gave their reasons for selection on their ballots. Edmund Randolph stated in his history that some men had mentioned "that Randolph should preside in Congress; that Lee and Henry should display the different kinds of eloquence for which they were renowned; that Washington should command the army, if an army should be raised, that Bland should open the measures of ancient colonial learning: that Harrison should utter plain truths, and that Pendleton should be the penman for business. Perhaps characters were never better delineated."[66]

Thomas Nelson, Jr., tied with Thomas Jefferson as next in rank in the balloting. They were the two youngest members of the group. Edmund Randolph would also comment about his cousin, "Mr. Jefferson, however, was disappointed in a seat at the first session of Congress."[67] Doubtless Tom was disappointed too, but he surely had a sense of pride in his standing in the poll even though he was not a winner.

Back in York Town by August 7, Tom picked up his pen and expressed his sentiments to his two closest merchant friends in Britain.

His communication to agent Athawes commenced:

> Poor America is greatly distressed at this time, and every man's thoughts are taken up in endeavoring to form some plan to prevent the impending Yoke that the British Parliament are determined to rivet about her Neck.
>
> . . . if you profess a regard for America, as you are a friend to Liberty, to bestir yourself in these affairs: It will not be sufficient to say that you never meddle with Politicks, when so many thousands people are concerned. . . . every man ought to insist on a redress of grievances . . . beset both houses of Parliament, Petition the King and though he may reject your Petitions even until seventy times seven, do not cease.[68]

In a long letter to the Hunt brothers, Tom wrote:

> The Parliament of Great Britain have taken such extraordinary steps toward America. . . . arbitrary System which has been so iniquitously adopted to enslave us. . . . the whole Continent of British America is unanimously determined to break off all commercial intercourse, with Great Britain unless the oppressive Acts are repealed by the tenth of August 1775.
>
> To enumerate all the Acts of Oppression would take up more time than I have to spare. Suffice it then, to mention the Boston Port Bill, by which 1500 people are punished for the violence of a few.
>
> The Ministry are going to establish the Roman Catholick Religion in Canada and just barely tolerate Protestinism; was there ever such thing done by a Protestant Parliament?[69]

Those assembled raised a subscription to relieve the plight of Boston's people; and despite debts and short crops, the citizens of York County contributed funds and food. Tom gave 100 bushels of wheat and secured an additional 118 bushels of wheat and 20 of corn to the 403 bushels of wheat and 115 bushels of corn on board a ship ready to sail to Massachusetts Bay.[70]

Through the summer and autumn, Tom shipped over 300 hogsheads of tobacco. A high percentage of the cargo consignments had been bought, and with the uncertain market and the poor price for the product, he lost money.[71]

Tom and Hugh entered into a new enterprise with several of their friends who bought shares in the agricultural company that Philip Mazzei had organized. Growing grapes for wine was the principal endeavor, but the business intended to branch out with experiments for improving plants, extracting oil, and producing silk. Tom purchased a share for £50 as did Jefferson; Governor Dunmore bought four shares in the scheme. Mann Page, Jr., and Hugh bought one share together.[72]

Routine activities of the Nelson family were abandoned in August as the relatives rallied around Judy Nelson in the loss of her mother, Jane Byrd Page on August 11.[73] This daughter of Colonel William Byrd, II, had wed John Page at seventeen and borne fifteen children in twenty-eight years of marriage. Four of the babies had not survived infancy.[74] The mourners speculated on whether Mr. Page could manage with his small brood or would parcel his progeny out among relatives. In a similar situation Tom had opened his doors to Lucy's three sisters. Hugh might hesitate with the offer since he and Judy were living under his mother's roof, yet they were related since the children's paternal grandmother, Judith Carter Page, was Mrs. Nelson's aunt. Before any definite decision could be reached, John Page died September 30. Hugh had a heavy heart as he watched his wife endure the affliction of losing her mother and father in less than two months.

The Purdie-Dixon paper of October 6, 1774, praised John Page:

> He was one of his Majesty's Council of this Colony, and a Gentleman not more remarkable for his Sweetness of Temper and other amiable Qualities, than for the Integrity and Abilities with which he filled his Place at the Council's Board.

On October 8, Tom wrote John Norton a short letter about the death of Mr. Page which caused a vacancy on the Council:

> I must give you the trouble once more, of the care of a Letter to Lord Stamford, upon the old Subject of a Seat at his Majesty's Council. . . . vacancy having happen'd by the Death of our worthy friend Mr. Page of North River, who died of a Bilious complaint on 30th of last Month.[75]

His appeal to Athawes for assistance in the matter was more personal. It was also written on October 8:

> Dear Sam—You tried your luck once to have me appointed of his Majesty's Council, but was too late. A vacancy has lately happened by the Death of Mr. Page . . . if I do not succeed, I will give it over and confine myself to my Farm, where I find a vast deal of happiness, perhaps more than I shall in the more exalted Station.[76]

The last of the tobacco shipments for the Nelson firm shipped October 10 with 184 hogsheads sent to the Hunts, a "good lift," and 33 for Athawes.

In addition to checking cargo, ships' captains had to search their vessels for runaway slaves. Two of Tom's relatives might have joined him on the docks to look for stowaways. Lewis Burwell had an escaped slave who could read and would try to pass as a free man. Charles Grymes, who had won the hand of the widow Lightfoot, was looking for Johnny who had stolen clothes and was "fond of liquor, fond of cock fighting, card playing . . . he could also read and write so would attempt to pass as a free man," the captains were warned.[77]

Tom read the papers and received reports from various people pertaining to the seven Virginia delegates in Philadelphia. After the August convention in Williamsburg, the deputies had just a few days to attend to personal affairs before starting for the Continental Congress.

Patrick Henry had a heavy burden to bear. His wife, Sarah Shelton Henry, had lost her sanity. Baffled and bewildered by such a problem, Henry had confined her in the basement of Scotchtown with a Negro attendant. He was aware of the whispers in the neighborhood, but the fiery patriot could not miss the important meeting.

Henry had left his home in Hanover County to join Edmund Pendleton in Caroline. The two gentlemen were guests of the Washingtons at Mount Vernon on August 30. Then the three horsemen left the next morning for Philadelphia, reaching their destination on September 4. Peyton Randolph, Richard Bland, Benjamin Harrison, and Richard Henry Lee had already arrived.[78]

Sometimes Tom took time from his correspondence to step onto the wharf to watch the vessels coming and going. One ship that sailed into the seaport in the fall had a special significance for the family. The wedding attire for Mary Grymes, who was marrying Tom's brother Bob, had arrived. Slaves piled the portmanteaus, bags, and boxes on a cart and started up the sloping street to Tom's residence where Mary had help from Lucy and Elizabeth to unpack the trousseau.

While the ladies bustled about with the fine apparel, food preparation, and directing the servants' extra cleaning, Bob went to the York County Court House to secure bond on Thursday, October 20, 1774, and the record reads:

> Robert Nelson, brother of Thomas Nelson, Jr., to Miss Mary Grymes, spinster, Security—Thomas Everard.[79]

St. George Tucker, who was present at a ball honoring the couple just before the marriage, attested that he was "Remarkably happy that evening in meeting with all my York friends, assembled together spent the evening in the utmost pleasure and satisfaction."[80]

Governor Dunmore made more enemies in the autumn. He deferred the November Assembly, ignored the 1763 proclamation ceding the Ohio territory to Canada, and in a martial mood rode off with a regiment toward the region to conquer the Indians.

Colonel Andrew Lewis had marched his militia to Point Pleasant, where

on October 10, the colonial soldiers clashed with Cornstalk and the Shaw-
nees. The Virginians won after an all-day encounter, and Dunmore dismissed Lewis's division causing disgruntlement among the ranks.[81]

The Virginia delegates at the Continental Congress were anxious to attend their own Assembly in the autumn. Unaware of Dunmore's postponement, the deputies left Philadelphia before the October 26 adjournment.

Tom and Lucy read with especial interest the notice on the front page of
the Purdie-Dixon *Gazette* in the November 3 issue:

> Last Sunday morning arrived in town from the General Congress the
> Honorable Peyton Randolph, Esquire, Chairman thereof with Colonel
> Richard Bland and Benjamin Harrison, Esq., of Berkeley, two of the Dele-
> gates from the Colony. These Gentlemen left Philadelphia 24th of October
> and the Congress was expected to break up in a day or two.

Tom was in Williamsburg during the first days of November for the meeting of the merchants.[82] He probably dropped by the Randolph residence, as
he did frequently, to hear Uncle Peyton Randolph and his cousin Ben Harrison explain that the articles of the Non-Importation, Non-Consumption,
and Non-Exportation Agreement taking effect December 1 would mean orders arriving between December 1 and February 1, 1775, were to be sent
back or settled by the local committee.

Williamsburg was crowded. The newspaper might have exaggerated the
number in its statement that between "4 to 500 merchants" were in town,
but the citizens were aroused to the point of determined resistance.

At the request of Secretary Nelson, acting president of the Council, the
upper Assemblymen had convened although Governor Dunmore had not
returned from the Ohio region. These men of the minority meeting had
weighty matters on their minds.[83] Doubtless they spoke of the death of John
Page and the absence in England of George William Fairfax, which reduced
their number. Colonel Byrd, clergyman Camm, Richard Corbin, and Ralph
Wormeley had strong royalist sympathies. At an informal gathering the gentlemen probably indulged in ingenuous inquiries. Did they ask Philip
Ludwell Lee why his brothers Richard Henry and Francis Lightfoot were so
passionate in their protests? Why couldn't Colonel Tayloe talk sensibly to
his son-in-law, Francis, because he knew that a balky horse needed a tight
rein and firm hand? Would Secretary Nelson and Robert Burwell explain
how their nephew Thomas Nelson had such fervent feelings on the issue?

This group was baffled, and its succinct statement in the Purdie-Dixon
Gazette on November 10 contrasted sharply with the coverage devoted to
the delegates to the Continental Congress: "This day the Honorable President with advice Majesty's Council prorogue General Assembly to first February next."

On that day all British invoices were to be disregarded.

There was general acceptance of the Association all over the Colony. The devotees of horse racing made a sacrifice and reported that the "Jockey Club had postponed the Dumfries Races scheduled for the 29th, in conformity to the 8th Article of the Resolves," and the newspaper affirmed that the reward for the gentlemen would be "Honour and Glory in place of guineas."[84]

The turmoil over tea caused an eruption in York Town. When Captain Howard Esten sailed the *Virginia* into port on Friday, November 4, the inhabitants soon heard that there were two half-chests of hyson tea on board.[85] Quickly the word spread. When the rumor reached across the river to Gloucester, groups gathered while citizens of York County crowded into the Court House. What course of action should they take? Tempers flared as the townspeople converged at the dock to view the vessel with its odious cargo. Remember the Boston resistance! Why shouldn't we throw the tea overboard? Among the milling throng, cooler heads wished to resist until their representatives, Dudley Digges and Thomas Nelson, Jr., in Williamsburg could be consulted for a course of action after meeting with the Burgesses. Some enraged citizens "went on board the said ship where they waited some time" for word from Williamsburg;[86] lacking that, the impatient patriots tossed the tea into the river. They then returned to shore and informed the excited crowd that "no damage was done to the ship or any other part of her cargo."[87]

The York Town tea party stirred up a tempest. On the following Wednesday the county court drew up resolves criticizing John Norton for shipping the tea, censuring Captain Esten for transporting it, and condemning Prentis and Company of Williamsburg for not countermanding the order.

"We intend to convince our enemies that we never will submit to any measure that will endanger our liberties," the court contended and also declared that it had directed the captain to sail the ship out of York Town in twenty days.[88]

John Norton and Captain Howard Esten explained through print that the *Virginia* had left London before they had received a copy of the resolves. John Norton's apology was published in the Dixon *Gazette* on May 6, 1775:

> It gives me infinite concern to find that I have fallen under the heavy displeasure of the Gentlemen of the Committee of York and Gloucester— the two half chests of tea were shipped inadvertently . . . for which I am heartily sorry.

Norton stated he believed Great Britain should not tax America. Thus one tradesman well known to many Virginians made an abject apology. No one escaped suspicion. Even the trustworthy Treasurer was charged with concealing tea.[89]

Merchant Prentis also made excuses and explained his position pertaining to the York Town tea throwing incident:

> It gives me much concern to find that I have incurred the displeasure of the York and Gloucester committees, and therby the public in general, for my omission in not countermanding the order which I sent to Mr. Norton for two half chests of tea.[90]

The county committees were arduous in their assignments. Merchants cringed and complied with the articles of the Association, some with conviction, others from fear of the consequences.

✦ ✦ ✦

The Purdie-Dixon supplement of December 8 announced the birth of a daughter, Virginia, to the Countess Dunmore at the Palace and on December 19, the Thomas Nelsons became the parents of another daughter, the seventh child Tom listed in the family Bible.[91] A still-born baby had filled the interim between the infant and almost four-year-old Elizabeth. Following the colonial custom of giving names, they called their second daughter *Mary* after Lucy's deceased mother.

The Nelson family had another occasion to rejoice. Robert Carter Burwell, twice a widower, married his third wife the last day of the year. Mrs. Mary Blair Braxton, the forty-year-old widow of George Braxton, became his bride. Colonel Burwell was the only living brother of Tom's mother and was fifty-four years old.[92]

The last of the month Elizabeth was saddened by the death of her nephew, Armistead Burwell, but life was made up of marriage, birth, and death.[93] Tom met the demands of these everyday events connected with his family and friends with equanimity.

✦ ✦ ✦

A military mood existed among the men of York Town. When Colonel Nelson mustered the militia, he noticed the unit marched with a new briskness. Companies of citizens were drilling all over Virginia, and plans were made to outfit the volunteer forces with uniform shirts and special sashes for the officers. The gentlemen freeholders who composed the regulated militia very subtly resolved that such organizations would relieve Britain of having to provide a standing army for the protection and defense of the colonies.

Money matters also demanded attention as colonists exchanged treasury notes of the scarce silver or gold coins for copper currency. Five tons of copper half-pence pieces had arrived the previous February so Treasurer Nicholas notified the public through the Dixon-Hunter *Gazette* on February 27, 1775: "Those who have Demands, PROPERLY AUTHENTICATED, may receive what proportion they please in Copper . . . office open every day except Sunday."

Across the Atlantic, two eminent peers in Parliament spoke in support of the colonial cause. William Pitt, now Lord Chatham, argued in the House of Lords against the acts of his government toward the American colonies, reasserting that only the local assemblies should impose taxes:

> Taxation is theirs; commercial regulation is ours. . . . abandon the idea that you can crush a brave, generous, and united people with arms in their hands and courage in their heart—three millions of men, the genuine descendants of a valiant and pious ancestry driven to those deserts by the narrow maxims of a superstitious tyranny.
>
> Every motive, therefore, of justice and of policy, of dignity and of prudence, urges you to allay the ferment in America by removal of your troops from Boston, by a repeal of your acts of Parliament, and by a demonstration of amicable disposition toward your Colonies.[94]

The ministers rejected his resolutions.[95]

In the House of Commons, Edmund Burke also advocated that the colonies be allowed to tax themselves. Since it was impossible for the Americans to appear in Parliament to represent themselves, certain concessions must be accorded them. The act that would transport persons to England for trial was particularly "obnoxious," the orator declared. His speech toward reconciliation was cast aside.[96]

The last of the month York Town was crowded as citizens responded to a request published in the paper to meet at the York County Court House "to elect delegates to attend the Convention at the Town of Richmond on Monday 20 day of March next."[97]

The brick building was filled with freeholders and the court-yard crowded with farmers as Dudley Digges and Thomas Nelson, Jr., moved among the men. There was a steady stream of customers stepping across the street to the Swan Tavern. Conservatives hoped for reconciliation and were heartened by such statements as that of Captain Hunter, lately returned from London, who believed "the unhappy disputes with colonies will be amicably settled when the new Parliament meets."[98]

Parliament, however, had already passed over the colonial petitions and protests that Lord North had placed before the body. The prime minister admitted that he had not read the papers.

Though the voters of York County continued to voice their grievances against the policies of the home government, they promptly attended to the purpose of their convening, as noted in the newspaper:

Last Monday the freeholders of York County unanimously elected Dudley Digges and Thomas Nelson, Jr., Esquire, their delegates to represent them in general convention to be held at Richmond 20 March next.[99]

Richmond had been selected as the site for the spring convention to elude interference from the royal executive. Delegates dragged in for two or three days from the remote regions of Virginia. They were disappointed in the village and soon discovered that the inns and taverns did not compare with the ordinaries of those in the capital.

Forty years before William Byrd, II, had been an enthusiastic press agent when he advertised the site of Richmond as a "pleasant and healthy situation, a little below the Falls."[100] High on the hills above the James River, sixty-five-foot wide streets had been laid out marked with numbers, a device later copied by several cities. Yet the sprawling town lacked a spacious hall to accommodate an assembly of more than 120 members. Thus St. John's Church, a sturdy white-framed structure standing high on a hill, was selected for the session. The sprouting grass in the churchyard cemetery and the lustrous leaves of the bending tree branches proclaimed the serenity and the sweet promise of the season.[101] But soon the walls of the sanctuary reverberated with the stormy session.

Thomas Nelson, Jr., and Dudley Digges could cover the sixty-five-mile trip from York Town in one arduous dawn-to-dusk trip, but probably chose to stay one night at Doncastle's ordinary about sixteen miles past Williamsburg.

As George Washington rode down from the Potomac country, he paused along the way to inspect the marching and drilling of the Dumfries Independent Company. Thomas Jefferson came to the conference from the western Piedmont section of the Colony. Patrick Henry of Hanover County and Archibald Cary from Chesterfield, adjoining counties to Henrico, had a shorter distance to reach their destination.[102]

All the counties had sent at least one delegate to the special session and most of them had elected two. John Randolph was absent. Representative for the College of William and Mary, his royalist sympathies were already separating him from the popular cause of the people. The representatives elected Peyton Randolph chairman of the convention and John Tazewell, clerk. They then unanimously approved actions taken by the delegates to the Continental Congress the previous fall in Philadelphia. "A resolution was offered, considered and adopted, returning the thanks of the Convention and the Colony to the Virginia delegation in Congress."[103]

Edmund Pendleton presented a resolution to thank the Jamaica Assembly since this body had petitioned the Crown on behalf of the American colonies. The conservative statesman alleged that they all wished "to see a speedy return to those halcyon days when we lived a free and happy people."[104]

Robert Carter Nicholas seconded his resolution and asked, "What days were happier than those of the near past, when Virginia, under the best of Kings (all heads did not nod with approval at this avowal) enjoyed a generous prosperity."[105]

Patrick Henry, losing patience with the appeasers, arose in his dark red wig, his shoulders stooped, but his blue-gray eyes burning. Agreeing with the vote of thanks to Jamaica, he affirmed, "That address was noble and inspiring, but, in my opinion, it is absurd to rest quietly expecting a return of the halcyon days of old."[106] The men sat up straight and turned their eyes toward him as he proposed measures to strengthen the military position of the Colony:

> That a well-regulated militia is the natural strength and only security of a free government. . . . insecure in this time of danger and distress to rely that any provision will be made to secure our inestimable rights and liberties from the further violations with which they are threatened. . . . That this Colony be immediately put into a state of defense.[107]

Seconding the resolution, Richard Henry Lee proclaimed:

> We use but a natural right in making provision for our protection. . . . I hate to contemplate the possibility of collision with the mother country, and I know our weakness.

He also reasoned that England had a vast disadvantage in transporting troops across 3000 miles of water, and he quoted Scripture and Shakespeare: "The race is not to the swift, nor the battle to the strong. Thrice is he armed that hath his quarrel just."[108]

The Assembly was aroused as these two ardent leaders led the fight to arm the Colony against any hostility, but arguments were offered in opposition. Benjamin Harrison pronounced the resolutions as "rash and inexpedient." He pleaded for the representatives to wait until a reply could come from England to their latest petition and asserted, "I am as warm a friend of liberty as any man in this Convention, but I deprecate any step which will stop the production of tobacco and corn and reduce the people to starvation."[109]

Then Peyton Randolph recognized his kinsman who represented Albemarle County. Thomas Jefferson apologized to his friend from Charles City County but alleged:

> Sir, the Colony should be prepared. I recognize no allegiance to

Parliament—only to the King of England. . . . I regard these acts of Parliament—attempting to tax our people and shutting up the port of Boston, as the acts of a foreign power which should, by all means in our power, be resisted.[110]

Edmund Pendleton made a passionate argument for patience and forbearance. Believing that the unjust acts would be righted when the ruling party in England was ousted, he questioned:

> Are we ready for war? Where are our stores? where are our arms—where are our soldiers—where our money, the sinews of war? Great Britain was A nation ready and armed at all points; her navy riding in triumph in every sea; her armies never marching but to certain victory.[111]

Cautious Robert Carter Nicholas remarked that he considered the resolutions "hasty, rash, and unreasonable." Yet if the Colony should resort to arms, he thought that only trained troops could protect the province. In the French and Indian War, he said "Virginia was envied by the other colonies for its two regiments of regular troops under the command of a distinguished gentleman present here."[112]

Colonel Washington did not move a muscle. A militia force was wholly insufficient if arms were necessary and Nicholas recommended raising an army of 10,000 men.

"Short enlistments [as Patrick Henry had contemplated] will prove the bane of war," Nicholas contended.[113]

How often Washington must have recalled these prophetic words later during the dark, distressing days of the Revolution.

Thomas Nelson, Jr., could not temporize with tyranny. He was ready for resistance and rose in the crowded church to speak. Though he had not debated on the floor of the House of Delegates against the leading legislators, he exclaimed:

> I am a merchant of York Town, but I am a Virginian first. Let my trade perish. I call God to witness that if any British troops are landed in the County of York, of which I am lieutenant, I will wait for no orders, but will summon the militia and drive the invaders into the sea.[114]

Men of moderation in the Assembly were astounded. Several gentlemen rose from their seats. Peyton Randolph pounded his gavel. The young York Town legislator had cast his lot with the liberal leaders. Still harboring hope for reconciliation, the conservative combination were disconcerted, while the progressive patriots preparing for a fight were pleased. The speeches of those sustaining the resolutions were pointedly brief, while the opponents' objections were longer.[115]

Patrick Henry made his final plea March 23. Starting to speak in a subdued tone, calm and composed, he discussed the conduct of the British ministry toward the colonies. Reaching a climax in his review of abuses, his delivery became more dramatic as he declared: To be free is to fight! An appeal to arms is all that is left! Strength cannot come by inaction; the battle was not only for the strong but also to the vigilant, active, and brave. Like a prophet he cried:

> The war is actually begun. The next gale that sweeps from the North will bring to our ears the clash of resounding arms! Our brethren are already in the field! Why stand we here idle? What is it that gentlemen wish? What would they have? Is life so dear, or peace so sweet, as to be purchased at the price of chains and slavery?[116]

Then drawing himself up to his full height Henry electrified his hearers:

> Forbid it, Almighty God! I know not what course others may take; but as for me, give me liberty or give me death![117]

The atmosphere was hushed. Then the representatives realized that they had heard the thunderous rumbling of a revolution. The momentous events of that March day were etched forever in their memories. When the president called for a vote, the resolutions passed. The progressive patriots had won a victory in their plan for preparedness. In a few months the inspired Virginians would continue the issue and advocate independence from Great Britain.

Their roles were denoted by distinctive titles. Patrick Henry, Thomas Jefferson, and George Washington were designated as the *tongue, pen,* and *sword* of the American Revolution.

Since Richard Henry Lee spoke eloquently in classic style and was versed in language and literature, he was compared to the outstanding Roman orator and was referred to as the "Cicero of the Revolution." Thomas Nelson, Jr., was also complimented. As the crisis continued and his love of liberty made him as unselfish in sacrifice and as dedicated to duty as the illustrious Roman legislator, he was called the "Cato of the Convention."[118]

CHAPTER FOURTEEN

Men on the Move: 1775

April Activities ✦ Desperate Dunmore Removes Powder ✦ Vehemence and Violence ✦ Peyton Randolph Returns from Philadelphia ✦ Royal Family Flees to Fowey ✦ Second Richmond Convention ✦ Rumors and Reflections ✦ Virginia Chooses Commanders ✦ York Town Astir ✦ Thomas as Delegate ✦ Washington Commander ✦ The Nelsons Leave for Philadelphia

Governor Dunmore, desperate and distracted, sat sulking in the Palace while the Assemblymen deliberated measures to defend the Colony. Left alone by the legislators, the official had time to consider retaliation. By his vested powers from the King, he issued a proclamation March 28, 1775, to prevent the appointment of deputies from Virginia to attend the Congress.[1]

Then he turned his revenge toward veterans and patentees of the territory to the northwest. Dunmore charged the surveyor of the land lacked the appropriate credentials. Washington, worried, wrote the executive a lengthy letter detailing the land developments. He received a curt reply from Dunmore.[2]

In April rumors were adrift that Governor Dunmore had sent soldiers to remove the locks from the guns at the public arsenal where the Colony stored arms and ammunition. A volunteer force gathered for guard duty several nights but finally discounted the report and disbanded April 20. Dunmore grasped the opportunity.[3]

Captain Henry Collins, commander of the royal armed schooner *Magdalen,* and his soldiers slipped into the storehouse and seized the gunpowder. Fifteen marines piled about twenty barrels of the explosive powder from the magazine on waiting wagons and rushed down the road in the dark toward the James River where the kegs were put aboard H.M.S. *Fowey.*

Next day the public read the *Virginia Gazette:*

> This morning between 3 and 4 o'clock, all the gunpowder in the magazine to the amount as we hear of 20 barrels, was carried off in his Excellency's the Governor's waggon. . . . soon as the news of this manoeuvre took wind the whole city was alarmed and much exasperated; and numbers got themselves in readiness to repair to the Palace.[4]

The inhabitants were incensed; murmurs grew to loud mutterings when men realized the executive had endangered public safety. The Williamsburg Volunteers rushed out with rifles.

Captain James Innes, usher of the grammar school at the College, headed a group of townspeople to patrol the thoroughfares. Wives watched anxiously from the windows. Citizens crowded the capital shouting up and down the streets to attack the Palace and assault the Governor.[5]

Peyton Randolph and Robert Carter Nicholas confronted the crowd attempting to calm them. The governing body formulated a protest, and the group pushed up the double drive to the Palace where Speaker Randolph presented the declaration to the irascible Dunmore and proclaimed:

> Inhabitants of this City were this morning exceedingly alarmed by a report that a large quantity of gunpowder was . . . removed from the public magazine of this City and conveyed under escort of marines, on board one of his Majesty's armed vessels lying at a ferry on James River.[6]

The Speaker asked why Dunmore had removed the powder and when it would be returned. Randolph stated the powder was stored in the public magazine to secure the safety of the people in an emergency and especially against a slave insurrection. The Governor claimed he had heard reports of a slave uprising so the powder was conveyed to a safer spot. Although some men considered the Governor's answer an absolute lie, his explanation avoided an attack.

Word spread rapidly from Williamsburg newspapers and couriers to other regions of the Colony where outraged colonists erupted over the powder occurrence. Men met, and militia marched. A group from Gloucester vowed to capture the Governor. By the last of April, several companies of cavalry from counties in the area convened at Fredericksburg.

Hugh Mercer wrote to Washington that the men were unwilling to submit to such an insult.[7] Fourteen Troops of Light Horse with about 600 men were ready to ride to Williamsburg but waited on word from Peyton Randolph. Mann Page, Jr., consulted with the Speaker about the crisis. Editor Purdie in the Wednesday, April 28, *Virginia Gazette* announced:

> Yesterday about one o'clock Mann Page, Jun., Esq., one of the representatives from Spotsylvania, arrived here in 24 hours from Fredericksburg being charged [to] inquire whether gunpowder been replaced.

Randolph urged the cavalrymen to use restraint because he believed violence would produce ruinous results. Before returning to their plantations, the riders drew up some forceful resolutions that concluded with, "We do now pledge ourselves to each other to be in readiness, at a moment's warning to reassemble, and by force of arms; to defend the law, the liberty and rights of this or any sister Colony, from unjust and wicked invasion."[8] A change from "God save the King" to "God save the liberties of America" expressed the new essence of freedom.[9]

Other Virginia leaders agreed with Randolph that rash action should be avoided. Pendleton and Washington, preparing for the second meeting of the Continental Congress in Philadelphia, wrote letters advising against a precipitate clash. Even progressive Richard Henry Lee recommended caution in the crisis.[10]

Impetuous Patrick Henry had different ideas, for he was irritated that the Fredericksburg men had been restrained. His prophetic cry about a clash of arms predicted at Richmond six weeks before had become a reality. Blood had been spilled on the grass at Lexington Green in Massachusetts.

Ten days later the colonists of Virginia read of the event in their Dixon-Hunter *Virginia Gazette* of April 29, 1775:

> This morning arrived an express from the northward with the following advice to all friends of American liberty be it known, that this morning, before break of day, a brigade consisting of about 1,000 or 1,200 men landed at Cambridge marched to Lexington where they found a company of our Colony militia in arms up they fired without any provocation.

The Purdie *Virginia Gazette* stated the same day:

> It is now full Time for us all to be on our Guard, and to prepare ourselves against every Contingency. The *Sword* is *now drawn*, and God knows when it will be sheathed.

Ranks of British redcoats firing upon the small patriot force further incensed Patrick Henry. Summoning the militia of Hanover County to meet him at Newcastle on May 2, he inflamed the volunteers with a fiery plea to recover the powder Governor Dunmore had seized in Williamsburg. Reprisal was the solution. The company responded with shouts and cheers, and other companies joined the cavalcade. When word reached Williamsburg of his plan, riders hurried to restrain the hotheads, but the men advanced. Henry was determined to accomplish his mission and had detached a force to contact Receiver General Richard Corbin at Laneville in King William County to demand payment from the Crown treasury for the powder. Corbin was not at home but in Williamsburg at the request of the Governor.[11]

The group of gentlemen who responded to the Governor's frantic call had dwindled to half a dozen. Dunmore, desperate, urged the Council to back his decisions. With temper flaring, Dunmore faced acting President Thomas Nelson, Richard Corbin, William Byrd, III, John Tayloe, Ralph Wormeley,

Robert Carter, Robert Burwell, and Clerk John Camm.[12] (One critic noted that Corbin was "slightly affected with palsy, and *grievously afflicted with the love of money*" and asserted that he was afraid.)[13]

Henry's volunteer force of 150 men had stopped at Doncastle's ordinary about sixteen miles west of Williamsburg where the fiery commander dispatched a courier to Williamsburg to discover the whereabouts of Corbin in order to collect money for the purloined gunpowder.

Carter Braxton, Corbin's son-in-law, acted as agent and turned over £330 drawn on a London bank to Patrick Henry, declaring that the determined leader preferred that payment to a bill of exchange on a Philadelphia bank offered by Secretary Nelson. Both Robert Carter Nicholas and the Secretary had ridden to the tavern to reason with Henry, for neither of these moderate-minded men could sanction Henry's strategy. By patience and perseverance, they convinced him that his object had been accomplished with the payment and that peace would be restored to the Colony when he returned with his company to Hanover County.[14]

Many Tidewater aristocrats criticized Patrick Henry vehemently for his rash action. In response, Henry published in the paper that he had received "330£ compensation for the gunpowder, which money I promise to convey to the Virginia delegates at the General Congress."[15]

On May 6, Governor Dunmore issued a proclamation against the fiery incendiary to the effect that Patrick Henry was stirring up sedition and that he and "his deluded followers were exciting the people to join in these outrageous and rebellious practices . . . strictly charging all persons; upon their allegiance, not to aid, abet, or give countenance to the said Patrick Henry."[16]

The declaration failed to have the desired effect. Some of Henry's admirers admitted he had been hasty in his resistance but insisted that his heart was right. Because rumors were flying that Dunmore would arrest Henry on May 11 when the popular patriot was ready to ride to the second session of the Continental Congress in Philadelphia, men all along the upper regions swung into the saddle and accompanied him across the Potomac to the safe shores of Maryland.[17]

The Governor was on his guard. Where once the royal residence had rung with laughter and music, its elegant rooms now echoed with marching men. Dunmore summoned sailors from the British ships and marines from the men-of-war to protect the Palace. Servants and Shawnee hostages were armed. Primed rifles and cannon were placed on Palace Green. Lady Dunmore and the children hastened aboard the *Fowey* which removed to the York River.[18]

The Nelson family and their friends were drawn into the turmoil of these disquieting days. The angry May 2 session when Dunmore had defended his deeds doubtless made Secretary Thomas Nelson reflect on how different Dunmore was to his predecessors. Although Fauquier and Botetourt had differed with the colonial delegates, they had been artfully diplomatic in voicing their disagreements.[19]

Governor Dunmore detailed his difficulties to Lord Dartmouth in candid communication on May 15:

> There is scarce a County of the whole Colony wherein part of the people have not taken up arms and declaring their intentions of forcing me to make restitution of the Powder. . . . country every where arming and disciplining Men, even in the place where I live drums are beating, and Men in uniform dress with arms are continually in the street.[20]

When the frigate *Fowey* appeared in York Town harbor with its cargo of gunpowder, the townspeople congregated at the waterfront to stare at the armed ships ringing their shore. Idle curiosity was replaced by genuine alarm as the sailors faced their cannon toward the town.

Captain Montague, commander of the man-of-war, notified the Honorable Thomas Nelson that a report had reached the ship of persons threatening to attack Governor Dunmore at the Palace. Therefore, the officer was sending a detachment from the ship to "support his Excellency. . . . Therefore demand you make use of every endeavor to prevent the party from being molested and attacked as in that case I must be under a necessity to fire upon the town.[21]

This threat sent the town into an uproar. Husbands warned their wives to stay back from the windows and to bolt the doors. Servants hauled children in from the yards. As Tom and Dudley Digges walked down the street, they were surrounded by townspeople wanting to understand; Jacquelin Ambler, David Jameson, and William Reynolds were among a crowd gathered at the Court House. The committee Nelson and Digges headed secured a copy of the letter from Montague and drew up yet more resolutions. (By the time the Secretary received the letter, it was too late for him to use his influence. He was exerting his endeavors to placate Henry at the time. Secretary Nelson would have been a principal sufferer if Montague had bombarded the port.)

> To threaten to fire upon the town has testified a spirit of cruelty unprecedented in the annals of civilized times—added insult to cruelty considering the circumstances already mentioned of one of the most considerable inhabitants of said Town. He has discovered the most hellish principles that can actuate a human mind.[22]

The committee recommended people show no mark of civility to Captain Montague.

The defiant Governor in his determination to crush the designs of the "enemies of order and government," blundered from one mistake to another.[23] Dunmore would never admit that his unwarranted action in seizing the powder had triggered the trouble. In retaliation to the seething unrest, he had fortified the Palace. He had ordered a special spring gun be set up in the powder horn as a protection against would-be intruders. Early in May some of the young men in Williamsburg, just as resolute as the royal executive, entered the octagonal arsenal. The spring gun went off injuring the patriots, thus causing more condemnation of the Governor.

Later in June a group of young men invaded the royal residence to remove arms. Theodorick Bland, Richard Kidder Meade, James Monroe, George Nicholas, and Harrison Randolph rushed into the grand house to haul weapons from the walls.[24]

Nature also acted violently toward the end of May, with hailstones and heavy rains throughout the town. The Palace and College lost three hundred panes of glass.[25]

Although Dunmore had not experienced much satisfaction from the Council which he had called to the capital on May 2, he decided to summon the House of Burgesses into session the first of June. He was aware of the proceedings of Parliament relating to affairs in America as were Virginians who had read the remarks of Lord Pitt and Edmund Burke in their local papers. Lord North, the Prime Minister, had also presented a proposal to Parliament, incorporating in his "Olive Branch" conciliation a plan of self-taxation by the Assemblies of the Colonies, though Parliament would still have the power to allocate amounts and to veto legislation by local governments. The Governor intended to dangle Lord North's proposal before the delegates.[26]

Peyton Randolph was in Philadelphia at the second Continental Congress, but when word reached him that the General Assembly of Virginia would convene June 1 at Williamsburg, he left on the twenty-fourth of May to attend the local meeting. The newspaper gave a glowing account of his entry into the city:

> The Williamsburg Volunteers in uniforms well mounted and equipped set out in regular military procession to meet the Honorable Peyton Randolph, late President of the Grand Continental Congress . . . his presence being requisite at our General Assembly now sitting here. On Tuesday about noon Troops of Horse met that Gentleman at Ruffin's Ferry.[27]

Colonel Carter Braxton and militiamen marched out two miles to escort the entourage into town at sunset and "bells began to ring . . . unfeigned joy of the inhabitants, on this occasion, . . . harmony and cheerfulness, . . . several patriot toasts."[28]

Thomas Jefferson was the alternate for Randolph at the Continental Congress, but the veteran legislator had informed his young kinsman to await

247

him in Williamsburg. The Speaker was scheming for a strong pen to reply to the plan of the Prime Minister.[29]

The Assemblymen's attire astonished the Governor at the June gathering as much as their attitude and actions. Many of the men, abandoning their silks and satins, were sporting hunting shirts, and several of the fellows entered with rifles on their shoulders.

Governor Dunmore presented Lord North's "Olive Branch" proposal but the Burgesses rejected his proposition. They appointed Thomas Jefferson to write their reply.[30]

The philosopher-patriot asserted that the proposition was irrational and insidious. The British government had disregarded American grievances. Parliament and the Prime Minister had not relinquished their practices of taxing and restraining trade; neither had they renounced their intention to transport persons to England for trial or surrendered the stationing of troops on American soil. Americans could not accept such a proposal.

The session became a sparring contest between Dunmore and the local representatives. Though the charges were couched in the usual obsequious style, their accusations were clear when the Assemblymen affirmed, "We feel very sensibly, my Lord, the Weight of the Insinuations in your Message."[31]

Thomas Nelson, Jr., played an important part in the special session. On Friday, June 2, he was appointed along with Treasurer Nicholas, Thomas Jefferson, Henry Lee, Francis Lightfoot Lee, and others to draw up an address to the Governor.[32] The group censured the executive for the existing economic conditions since the "occlusion of our Courts of Justice can be only abscribed to a Combination of untoward and distressing Incidents [which] explains the necessity of the suspension of commerce. . . . We are desirous that the courts should be opened."[33]

Through the hot, humid days of June, Thomas was a busy member of the House of Burgesses as he attended his assignments on the committees of Religion, Privileges, Propositions and Grievances. He also reviewed "All Things relating to the Trade of the Colony" and later recommended that the building of the Cape Henry lighthouse should start.[34] The York Town legislator was fortunate to have the house on Francis Street just around the corner from the Capitol. Doubtless he often invited his colleagues Tom Jefferson and Frank Lee to the residence for refreshments.

The rival editors of the *Virginia Gazette* applied for the position of public printer. Tom carried to the Council the name of Alexander Purdie for the post after Purdie had overcome his competitors—John Pickney, Dixon, and Hunter to secure the job.

The rift between the representatives and Dunmore reached a climax the first week of June. Assemblymen assured Governor Dunmore that he was in no danger and the Burgesses affirmed their pride in and respect for the Palace, yet his Excellency was not appeased. John Randolph insisted the administrator had no reason to be apprehensive as almost every day His Lordship had been at the Randolph home about one and one-fourth miles from the Palace, yet there had been no insult or injury as he passed to and fro. In spite of reassurances, Dunmore threatened to retire to York though the people's representatives protested to him, "how inconvenient and improper it would be for the House to adjourn to York Town."[35]

Nevertheless the descendant of the House of Stuart deserted his post and fled to his family already aboard the frigate *Fowey*. A message he left indicated he and his family were in constant danger of an "unnecessary fury which has unaccountably seized upon the minds and understanding of great numbers of people."[36]

The Burgesses began to bear down on the most important bit of business on Monday, June 5. They appointed Hugh Mercer, Thomas Nelson, Jr., Robert Carter Nicholas, and Thomas Jefferson to a twenty-one member-committee "to examine the public magazine and report on the stores."[37] Hugh Mercer, a practicing physician in Fredericksburg, had seen military service on the Scottish moors and fought on the American frontier.[38] Colonel Nelson had commanded the York Town militia for a dozen years and was interested in battle strategy and military tactics. The militia had regular drills on the Court House lawn and had learned to load their muskets in record time.

The committee had to confront Dunmore to secure the key to the storehouse. When the official objected, the Assemblymen were adamant. Since all of them were "known to his Excellency," they were indignant over the delay. Three days later they gained entry to the arsenal and discovered glaring deficiences. Of the 527 old muskets, they reported the "Barrels were very rusty and the Locks almost useless; the 150 Pistols were old; 108 New Muskets were without Locks; and 35 small Swords were in bad order. Nineteen halberts and 157 trading guns were in good order" as well as 1,500 cutlasses with scabbards, the type of sword used by sailors on war vessels.[39]

To their disgust, the gentlemen saw only one hogshead of good powder and five barrels buried in the ground—ruined by the late rains. Afterwards they succeeded in getting private citizens to return weapons removed from the arsenal and agreed that gentlemen of the town would guard the magazine. Then they informed the Governor again that his action concerning the arms and ammunition had aroused the inhabitants because the Burgesses had made the "minutest and strictest inquiry as to the Cause of the disturbances."[40] Then the delegates declared that the "Country had been in a State of Tranquility till received Account of your Lordship's removal of the Gunpowder." They requested the powder be returned against the "probability of an Indian invasion or Insurrection of Slaves. . . . order 2,000 Stand arms, 5 Tons Powder, 20 Tons lead, and a sufficient quantity of military stores immediately to provide for the Defense of the Colony."[41]

Though Lord Dunmore had abandoned the government, the delegates did not desert their duties. They sent couriers to the vessel in York Town appealing for his return, but Governor Dunmore was adamant; he had no thought of resuming his responsibility in Williamsburg.

The Assembly was not ready to adjourn so the House of Burgesses proclaimed Secretary Nelson, as President of the Council, was empowered to perform all functions as the governing official. The last Assembly under the authority of the Crown ended as the representatives of the Colony grasped the reins to guide a new government. The body completed its business and dissolved on June 24.

York Town was astir through the summer months over these unexpected events, its citizens restless and uneasy over the Governor's presence there. On the waterfront they stared at the armed ships in the York River and studied the *Fowey* to catch a glimpse of the Dunmore sons, removed from College, their three older daughters, and the six-month-old baby, Virginia, huddled with Lady Dunmore aboard the vessel with Lord Dunmore.

No respite awaited Thomas Nelson, Jr., when he returned to York Town the last of June for he realized that he had been neglecting his private affairs. Whenever Colonel Nelson stopped in at the Swan Tavern, citizens plied him with questions. How far would the Colony go to retain its rights? Would the embargo on British goods make England rescind the tea tax? Was the Governor just going to stay on the ship? Patiently, Tom tried to supply some answers; he realized he had only a few days at home with his family before he must leave for Richmond to attend the Assembly session Peyton Randolph had scheduled for July 17.

At home young Elizabeth no longer enjoyed the spotlight as the youngest Nelson since Mary had usurped that position six months earlier. William and Thomas were already attending the College's grammar school, and Tom had hired Dr. Jacob Hall as a tutor for the younger boys—Philip, Francis, and Hugh. Hall wrote his sister later about his employer and position:

> Colonel Thomas Nelson, one of the delegates to Congress, a gentleman of the first Fortune and Interest in the Colony. He allows £10 apiece for each of his 5 sons, with the Liberty of taking 4 or 5 more, gives me my Board and Accommodation, a servant to wait on me, and makes a Compliment of their Board to the Boys in my Favor—I have the Benefit of his Library which is a fine collection, make no doubt I shall live as Comfortable as these troublesome times will admit.[42]

Hall's £50 salary was a generous sum; it was more per student than the

£60 his cousin Robert Carter of Nomini Hall had paid Philip Fithian to teach eight children.[43]

✦   ✦   ✦

The colonists were informed in the June 30 issue of Purdie's *Virginia Gazette:*

> Early yesterday morning sailed from York Town his Majesty's ship *Fowey* and the *Magdalen* schooner; which last, we are informed proceeds to England immediately, with Lady Dunmore, and the rest of the Governor's family, attended by his Lordship's chaplain, the Reverend Mr. Gwathkin.

Gwathkin was the instructor who had inspired Nat Burwell to excel in mathematics yet would not participate in the June day of prayer and fasting. With the present upheaval, the professor didn't understand his pupils or the patriots. He was glad to be going home.

Governor Dunmore paced the deck impatiently, but the *Fowey* did not actually depart from York Town until July when the *Mercury*, a twenty-four-gun man-of-war sailed into the harbor to relieve the vessel.

In Philadelphia statesmen at the Continental Congress experienced a new spirit of unity. Richard Henry Lee wrote that a "perfect unanimity" existed and that the men exhibited a "firmness of union and determination to resist."[44]

Since Parliament had proclaimed the Colony of Massachusetts in a state of rebellion, their representatives resolved to raise a force of 13,600 men for protection.[45]

George Washington was appointed chairman of a committee to plan the defense of New York City as British regulars were en route to the port. Though he had been a member of the Congress in 1774, this responsibility was the first recognition that Colonel Washington had received.[46] He would soon be accorded another honor.

John Adams had decided that a southerner should command the army of the colonies to show united support. Adams canvassed the constituents and discovered that Edmund Pendleton was not in favor of Washington for the post. John and Sam Adams worked together for the nomination and on June 15, 1775, the Congress chose George Washington by unanimous vote to be General and Commander-in-Chief of the Continental Army.[47] Tom and his family and friends in Virginia were gratified at the choice.

✦   ✦   ✦

In mid-July, Tom and Dudley Digges rode together to Richmond for the Virginia Convention—Tom, more passionate in his protests on the tea tax;

his older colleague was convinced that the Colony must act. Representatives from all across Virginia answered the roll call in the sweltering heat of July 17, their wrinkled clothes clinging to their bodies. Peyton Randolph presided.[48]

Richard Bland, as a senior statesman and a recognized authority on the rights and privileges of the provinces under the British constitution, made a report the following day. Since bloody clashes of the colonials had already occurred with the British regulars around Boston and Governor Dunmore had deserted his post, the resolution declared, "We are determined to defend our lives and property, and maintain our just rights and privileges at even the extremest hazard."[49]

Rumors were afloat that British regiments would soon land on Virginia shores although the *Fowey* had sailed from York Town and the *Mercury* remained in port. On the third day a committee was appointed to prepare an "ordinance to raise an armed force sufficient for the defense of the Colony."[50]

Colonel Tom Nelson, who was gaining a reputation as a gentleman versed in military matters, agreed to serve on this committee with Richard Bland, George Mason, and his cousins Carter Braxton and Robert Carter Nicholas.

The Virginians pledged to "disband such forces as may be raised in this colony, whenever our dangers are removed, and America is restored to its former state of tranquility and happiness."[51]

Yet the times were so troubled that even Richard Bland did not escape suspicion. Stranger still, his long-time associate in the Assembly and fellow congressman, Edmund Pendleton, was gullible enough to believe charges of Bland's disloyalty. Reverend Samuel Sheild, rector of Drysdale parish in Caroline County where Pendleton worshiped, spread the rumors about Bland, who rose before the body to acknowledge "certain false and scandalous reports, highly reflecting on him and his public character had been circulated."[52]

The Burgesses found there was no middle ground; a man was a friend or a foe. When his loyalty to liberty was questioned, a gentleman countered injustice through the columns of the press. Richard Bland called the clergyman's bluff and requested a full inquiry. His accusers admitted in print on August 5 that their accusations had been "false and groundless" and they further affirmed that Richard Bland was a "friend of his country and uniformly stood forth as an able assertor of her rights and liberties."[53]

Bland had served the Colony for over three decades, and the venerable Virginian tendered his thanks for the Assemblymen's confidence in re-electing him to the Continental Congress but, because of his age and blindness, he declined to be a delegate again.

At the spring session the delegates had appointed a central committee to set up an armed force and one or more volunteer companies of infantry and horse troops had been recommended for each county. Regulations stated that the rank and file of militia would consist of sixty-eight men, one captain, two lieutenants, one ensign, four sergeants, four corporals, and a drummer. Each man should be equipped with a rifle and bayonet, cartouche box, tomahawk, one pound of powder, and five pounds of rifle ball. Special hunting shirts would make up the uniforms.[54]

Since Congress had already selected George Washington as Commander-in-Chief of the Continental Army and sent him to Cambridge, Massachusetts, the Old Dominion was denied the services of its most distinguished soldier. The Assemblymen considered possibilities for selecting the military leader for Virginia. Thomas Nelson, Jr., colonel of his county militia, had marched the men, held rifle practice, and set up target training for the troops. He had some aptitude and interest in military affairs but was not a seasoned soldier. Hugh Mercer, the foremost military man of the Colony, was a veteran soldier—but not a Virginian. At the battle of Culloden in 1746, the Duke of Cumberland had destroyed the forces of Bonnie Prince Charlie under whose banner Mercer had fought. The young Scottish surgeon had been wounded but escaped to America. As a captain under General Braddock in the French and Indian War, Mercer had also been wounded and at Fort DeQuesne he had witnessed Braddock's disastrous defeat. Patrick Henry had often roused the sentiments of his peers and had also experienced commanding the volunteers' advance on Williamsburg in May to retrieve the gunpowder. He was ready for new laurels and his friends felt he would like to command the colonial force.[55]

On August 5, the body voted for officers. On the first ballot, Mercer received forty-one votes; Henry, forty; Nelson, eight; and William Woodford, one.[56] Since Mercer had not polled a plurality, a second count was in order. Nelson withdrew his name and advocated the election of Mercer because of his wide experience in military matters. Other men admitted that the surgeon soldier from Fredericksburg had an outstanding record, but objected because he had been born in Scotland. Practical politics came to the forefront in the controversy, and Henry was chosen to command the First Regiment. The patriot could certainly incite his followers even if he knew nothing of firearms. Washington was not the only man who had misgivings concerning the choice and mentioned it was a "mistake to place him in the field." Thomas Nelson, Jr., was selected to head the Second Regiment, William Woodford to lead the Third. Mercer was overlooked.[57]

The delegates met from seven in the morning until ten at night. A pleasant change in the routine occurred on August 9, when the gentlemen greeted four of their representatives who had returned from Philadelphia and appeared in the Assembly.[58] Patrick Henry was complimented on his new command of the First Regiment. Thomas Jefferson was also commended, for his fellow legislators had learned that his pen had been employed to explain the reasons for raising an army "against violence actually offered" by the British.[59] Tall Edmund Pendleton and plump Benjamin Harrison were presumably received with cordiality and coolness. Friends would flock to grasp their hands but some representatives were reserved in their greetings. Colonists who were fond of George Washington would pull Pendleton aside to question him on why he had opposed the choice of his Virginia comrade to be Commander-in-Chief. Admirers of the "Old Antiquary" were angry over the slanderous rumors circulated about Richard Bland and wondered why Pendleton who was so perceptive had swallowed such reports.[60]

Richard Henry Lee arrived at the Assembly on Friday, August 11, just in time to be re-elected to the Continental Congress that day. Because of poor health, Edmund Pendleton had requested that he be relieved from service and Washington's and Patrick Henry's seats were now vacant. Peyton Randolph led the list again in the voting followed by Lee, Thomas Jefferson, Benjamin Harrison, Thomas Nelson, Jr., Richard Bland, and attorney George Wythe. It was an honor for thirty-six-year-old Nelson to rank fifth in the election. With the exception of Jefferson, he was the youngest member among these men of intellect, talent, and training.[61]

Richard Bland received the plaudits he desired and the confidence he coveted; but he declined the post. Francis Lightfoot Lee and Carter Braxton were nominated to fill his place and Lee was elected to the position.[62]

Money and military matters were foremost on the Assemblymen's agenda. They resorted to issuing £350,000 of paper money to be secured by the property of the Colony. Though the patriots found Parliament's taxes odious, the Virginia lawmakers had to lay levies on land, licenses, carriages, and tithables. The convention had already petitioned John Norton of London to lend the Colony £5,000 sterling to replenish the gunpowder supply.[63]

When rumors reached Richmond that Lord Dunmore was collecting a force and a fleet, committees from York and James counties agreed to "pay particular attention" to his activities; if he attempted to land soldiers in Virginia, the volunteer companies were to be called out to "repeal such Troops by force." Nelson was given leave of absence on Monday, August 14, to relay the word to Williamsburg and ready the York Town militia for such a contingency.[64]

The delegates appointed a Committee of Safety as the central authority of government for the Colony. This body had broad powers to provide for the public safety in enforcing resolutions of the Convention, to raise regiments, furnish funds for arms and ammunition, and stock supplies. Edmund Pendleton was chosen chairman of the committee and George Mason, John Page, Richard Bland, Thomas Ludwell Lee, Paul Carrington, Dudley Digges, William Cabell, Carter Braxton, James Mercer, and John Tabb were named as members—generally, men of moderation.[65]

Because Thomas Nelson, Jr., had resigned the command of the Second

Virginia Regiment after he was chosen a delegate to the Continental Congress, the convention appointed William Woodford from the Third Regiment as colonel of the Second and agreed that the military complex for the Colony should consist of these two regiments, with two companies to be forwarded to the frontier, minute men troops to be trained, and Virginia divided into sixteen districts.

Nelson had already left Richmond for York Town when the Assembly jubilantly announced that Otway Byrd, Esq., "on account of his attachment to American liberty, resigned his provision and prospects in the British Navy, and may be destitute of employment."[66] Therefore the representatives recommended that General Washington promote the young recruit, for they realized that his father, Councilor William Byrd of royalist sympathies, would disinherit his son. Shortly thereafter, the press announced that Byrd had been appointed aide-de-camp to Major General Charles Lee at Cambridge. The newspaper noted that Lee was not related to the Northern Neck family.[67]

Tom had approximately two weeks in August to attend to his affairs before leaving for Philadelphia. It was discouraging to examine the debit entries on accounts at the store. The Nelsons were still indebted to the Hunts, and local customers owed obligations to the firm. Hugh and Bob had found pressing their clients for payments a disheartening and hopeless chore. Since December, the boycott of British goods by the Association had business at a standstill. The Custom House was quiet.

According to the terms of the Association, an embargo on exports was to become effective September 10 if Parliament did not repeal the tea tax. Therefore, tobacco cargoes would soon cease; vessels were leaving Virginia before the deadline date. The Continental Congress's faith that the economic edict would compel a concession from England had failed. The British ministry had ignored the measure just as Parliament had paid no attention to the various appeals of the Americans. Captain Howard Esten had secured only some lumber as ballast for his vessel. Captain Robertson had been trying to secure tobacco for the Norton ships as ". . . apprehensive that the Exports wou'd be stopt Every day . . .", but by August, the Captain informed his employer that the *Liberty* would not be loaded as only 350 hogsheads had been obtained and the commander commented, "had not the times have been so Critical Might have gone Near to have loaded . . . ."[68]

Although Tom had advertised the Swan Tavern for sale three years before, no bid had been taken so he was still operating the ordinary. Hugh had to keep an eye on the enterprise in Tom's absence and care for the plantations. The family felt grateful that dependable George Dabney was still directing the huge Hanover estate.

Tom was also concerned whether the local militia company would measure up to the standards set by the two Richmond conventions so he checked on the arms and ammunition supply. Rumors still persisted relating to British regulars invading Virginia. It was possible the former Governor might return with a fleet and force.

Since Lucy would have to leave the children for an indefinite length of time, she had to be persuaded to take the trip to Philadelphia with Tom. Relatives assured her that they would care for her family. Grandmother Elizabeth would look after little Elizabeth and eight-month-old Mary. The tutor had the boys in his charge. She finally agreed to the journey taking pleasure in Peyton Randolph's company in their carriage. This would be the third trip for her Uncle Peyton to Philadelphia, where the veteran Virginia leader had been chosen chairman of the Continental Congress. Ever popular with the people in Virginia, he had become a symbol of statesmanship during the difficulties with Governor Dunmore. The experienced Speaker had summoned the conventions at Richmond to consider the state of the Colony and the steps of resistance against British tyranny.[69]

Lucy was distressed to discover that her uncle, John Randolph, was not immune to implications. Colonials compared his earlier Loyalist leanings with the strong stand his brother Peyton had shown against Britain. Such a furor was stirred up that John Randolph felt called upon to clarify a conversation held in his own house. Someone had accused John of saying "the merchants would not meet, because they were afraid of being robbed of their money by Patrick Henry."[70]

Randolph resorted to the press: "I take this opportunity to declare upon my Honour, that I never said or thought any such thing, and that the person who charges me with uttering such expressions must be mistaken my Words or inferred from a meaning never intended to be."[71]

John Randolph, disheartened, unable to compromise with the changes, renounced his position and property to become an exile in England. After listening to the debates between his father and uncle, John Randolph's son Edmund rallied to the patriots' standard although he incurred the wrath of his parent.[72]

On August 12, the Dixon-Hunter *Virginia Gazette* announced:

> Mr. Edmund Randolph, of this city, is appointed, by the General Congress to be Muster Master General of the Continental Army, with £200 per annum, and is gone to the provincial camp near Boston.

His leavetaking preceded the departure of his father who informed the public through the Purdie *Gazette* on August 25, "I intend to leave the colony for a few months." John Randolph had no foreknowledge that he would never again set foot in Virginia for he thought the struggle would soon be settled. He announced that John Blair, attended by the Attorney General, would act for him in affairs.

The Randolphs had chosen their separate courses and would never see one another again.

◆   ◆   ◆

The Nelsons left York Town the last week of August and completed the first lap of their long trip by rolling up in front of the Peyton Randolph residence on Nicholson Street in Williamsburg. Servants crammed more bags and boxes under the carriage seats and stacked portmanteaus on the back of the coach. The Purdie *Virginia Gazette* of September 1, 1775, noted their leavetaking:

> Since our last, the Hon. Peyton Randolph, Col. Thomas Nelson, and George Wythe set out for Philadelphia to attend the General Congress on the 5th of this instant, accompanied by their several ladies.

The Nelson vehicle was heavily loaded with luggage and crowded with its corpulent quartet, for "queenly" Betty Randolph and her husband, Peyton, were portly and Tom and Lucy were also plump.[73] The group rode the principal highway paralleling the York River until they reached Doncastle's ordinary about sixteen miles above Williamsburg. Wythe's driver followed the front carriage, and the coaches then continued, crossing by ferry the curving Pamunkey that flowed left from the York River. A few miles along, the travelers crossed Todd's bridge spanning the Mattapony River and continued to Bowling Green and on to Fredericksburg. This 100-mile distance required a few overnight stops, although Speaker Randolph mentioned that Mann Page, Jr., had made the journey on horseback in twenty-four hours to consult Randolph about the gunpowder incident.[74]

From Fredericksburg the passengers proceeded through the Potomac region toward Alexandria, then crossed the curving Potomac River into Maryland, where an unfortunate accident damaged the Nelson carriage considerably but left its occupants merely shaken up. Editor Pinckney in his September 14, 1775, *Virginia Gazette* noted:

> We learn that our worthy Delegate, Thomas Nelson, Esq., has been much fatigued and embarrassed in his expedition to Philadelphia, his carriage having broke down just as he got on the Maryland Side, which was so much injured that he could not under a considerable time have proceeded had it not been for the Kindness of a gentleman in the neighborhood, who supplied him with another.

Peyton and Betty Randolph in all probability rode on to the Philadelphia capital with the Wythes, as their arrival was announced in the Philadelphia paper on September 6, later copied by the *Virginia Gazette*.

The Nelsons reached Philadelphia less than a week later and secured quarters with Benjamin Randolph where the Wythes and elder Randolphs also rented rooms. Thomas Jefferson was also lodging there, but his wife was too ill to make the trip with him.[75]

CHAPTER FIFTEEN

Congress, Constituents, and Canada: 1775–1776

Philadelphia ✦ *John Adams Describes Delegates* ✦ *Nelson with Funds* ✦
Conservatives and Radicals ✦ *Military Matters* ✦ *Lucy and Ladies* ✦ *Feuds
and Defections* ✦ *Peyton Randolph Dies* ✦ *Virginia Events* ✦ *Battle of
Great Bridge* ✦ *Christmas* ✦ *"Common Sense"* ✦ *Homecoming* ✦ *Nelsons
in Service*

Thomas Nelson, Jr., stepped out from the Randolph residence on Chestnut Street and threaded his way through the throngs of people. Scores of shopkeepers, mechanics, traders, clerks and merchants moved with the stream. Privateers and riggers hurried to the dock on the broad Delaware River. Grand carriages and humble carts thumped along the cobblestones. Peddlers hawked their goods at every corner. Somberly dressed Quaker gentlemen mingled with more elegantly adorned lawyers and legislators striding toward the State House.

In the well-planned capital, stores, coffee houses, narrow taverns, markets, livery stables, printers' shops, and warehouses filled the two-mile stretch of land lying between the Delaware River dividing Pennsylvania from New Jersey and the narrow Schuykill River. Municipal street cleaners and garbage collectors kept the city neat and clean. Christ Church's steeple rose above the rooftops of other buildings on High and Second streets. Many of the Congressmen climbed its tower to view the city. Some delegates lost their way in the biggest colonial city in America, for Philadelphia boasted a population close to 40,000 people. New York and Boston had about half that numbers. Tom, educated in England and used to London's more than a million people, found Philadelphia laid out like the smaller Richmond, where the Virginia Assembly had adjourned in August. Both contained straight numbered streets running parallel to a river. The avenues that cut across the Quaker City were named after fruit and forest trees—Apple, Chestnut, Pear, and Walnut.[1]

Tom's distress about his late appearance at the Congress on Monday, September 11, 1775, was relieved when he realized several other representatives had not yet arrived. These men, who were preparing to engage in a contest with the greatest empire on earth, had plausible excuses. After the August 1 adjournment, numerous Congressmen had made a trip from Philadelphia to Cambridge just outside of Boston where they had observed the American army under the command of General Washington.[2]

John Hancock delayed by "a touch of gout" did not arrive at the Assembly until the thirteenth of September; the disease was so prevalent among parliamentarians their conversations were laced with complaints and remedies. Yet the sufferers rose at dawn, wore their heavy clothes through the warm weather, and sat in the sessions day after day attending to their duties from ten to fourteen hours.[3]

The Committees of Correspondence, first suggested by the Virginia Assembly, had strengthened the chain of resistance to Britain's arbitrary acts. These committees communicated with one another on the procedures of Parliament, growing grievances, resolutions on rights, and by common consent, a call to the convention.[4]

The authority of the Congress had been administered through the Association and the provisions of the Non-Importation, Non-Consumption, and Non-Exportation Agreement had not only prohibited buying British products but had also sought to encourage the economy of the colonies through cultivation of more food crops, promotion of manufactures, establishment of infant industries, and the advancement of arts and crafts. Sacrifices were required of the rebels since the documents stated diversions and extravagances such as shows and horse racing should be discouraged. With patriotic fervor, the devotees of horse racing in the Old Dominion had already foregone the pleasure. Although the boycott of British goods had not had serious impact on England, the colonists were feeling its effects as scarcity of products made prices rise.

Delegates composing the Continental Congress decided a Committee of Safety should set up a system of defense with each colony appointing such a committee as the acting civil authority. The committees were arduous in their activities—intercepting mail and challenging different citizens. Britain had also started seizing letters sent to the mother country. British customs officials employed informers to spy on colonial smugglers and now the tables were turned. No one was immune from suspicion. Now the patriots inspected stores and interrogated merchants. Suspected Loyalists were ridiculed in print and punished.[5]

When Tom first approached Pennsylvania's State House for convention meetings, he was attracted to its tall tower with its large bell inscribed, "Proclaim liberty throughout the land, and unto all the inhabitants thereof."[6] The building faced Chestnut Street and was flanked by the planetarium and Philosophical Hall.[7] A lobby and two 40' x 20' rooms formed the first floor of the big brick building; the spacious gallery on the second floor stretched a full one-hundred feet. September sun streaked through the high windows bouncing light from its white-paneled walls; horseflies swarmed through the openings.[8] Jefferson had already warned Tom to watch out for the pests that flew from the livery stable close to the State House. Delegates within the House were safe from electrical storms as one of Benjamin Franklin's remarkable lightning rods protected them from harm. The versatile Dr. Franklin and his erudite colleagues of the American Philosophical Society had been delving into scientific phenomena for three decades and their discussions ranged from diagrams for submarines to the possibility of men living on the planet Mars.[9] The venerable Dr. Franklin now nodded during the long deliberations in the Congress.

John Adams often chafed under the carpings and commented sharply about the "nibbling and quibbling" of the different controversies.[10] He jotted down his impressions of the delegates, noting that three new representatives from Virginia had arrived: "Thomas Nelson is a fat Man, but alert and lively for his Weight. He is a Speaker." He also evaluated George Wythe as a "Lawyer, . . . of the first Eminence," and Francis Lightfoot Lee as "sensible and patriotic, as the rest of his family."[11]

Adams described Delaware's Caesar Rodney as "the oddest looking Man in the world; he is tall—thin and slender as a Reed—pale—his Face is not bigger than a large Apple, yet there is Sense and Fire, Spirit, Wit and Humour in his Countenance."[12]

The previous year at the First Continental Congress when the representatives were entertained so royally, Adams had attested:

> Spent the evening with Lee and Harrison from Virginia, the two Rutledges, Dr. Witherspoon, Dr. Shippen and other gentlemen; an elegant Supper, and We drank Sentiments till eleven O'Clock. Lee and Harrison were very high. Lee had dined with Mr. Dickinson, and drank Burgundy the whole afternoon.[13]

As an arch rebel anxious to sever British ties, Adams was vexed at the hesitant tactics of Benjamin Harrison and vented his annoyance by commenting in his diary that Harrison was "indolent, luxurious, heavy gentleman of no use on Congress or committee, but a great embarrassment to both."[14]

In the same journal he described Randolph as "well looking," Lee as "tall, spare" and Bland as "learned, bookish."[15]

The chronicler decided that "To the Virtue, Spirit, and Abilities of Virginia We owe much—I should always therefore from Inclination as well as Justice, be for giving Virginia its full Weight."[16]

At one sumptuous dinner the diarist declared that the host had served "Every thing which could delight the Eye or allure the Taste. . . . Flummery, Jellies, Sweetmeat of 20 sorts, Trifles, Whip'd Syllabubs, floating Island, . . . and then a Dessert of Fruits, Raisins, Almonds, Pears & Peaches—Wines most excellent & admirable. I drank Madeira at a great Rate and found no inconvenience in it." [17]

After the sessions of the Second Continental Congress started, the delegates were diligent in their duties. They often began their discussions before breakfast, then sat through debates and deliberations all day, and many members met with special committees at night to complete their assignments. [18] No business was too minute for the men to mull over or problem too petty to consider. The colonists had endured indifference and indignation from the Crown and their petitions and protests to the British Parliament had been spurned and scorned, but the representatives were patient and persevering. Schemers and solicitors took up time. Inventors presented plans with incredible claims, but Congress was interested in an invention that could blow up the British Navy. [19]

Thomas Nelson, Jr., felt at ease among the Congress's lawyers and merchants, planters and physicians—men who had served in the assemblies of their colonies. By 1775 the delegates had developed a new dimension; they were rebels—bold enough to risk poverty and ruin. [20]

There were distinct contrasts among the half-hundred constituents. They differed in their method of planning or presenting resolves at the meetings, in their physical bearing, in their manner. [21]

John Hancock was handsome, wealthy and regal in bearing, a Boston merchant with power and prestige. At thirty-seven he had married Dorothy Quincy the previous summer. Boston society had conceded that the animated Dolly, ten years younger than her husband, was a proper choice for the merchant prince. He fancied fashionable attire and fine foods (in spite of his gout). [22]

Secretary Thomson represented the rags-to-riches story. Left an orphan at ten in the new land, the indomitable Scotch-Irish lad was self-educated and became a recognized classical scholar. From teaching to trade, the enterprising Thomson had profited. As the convention's only salaried official he sat at his desk in plain dress, tall, thin, and serene, recording the proceedings. (Thomson was to serve in this role for fifteen years, watching the patriots struggle for independence, witnessing their resolute strife, and seeing the birth of a new republic.) [23]

Thomas Nelson, Jr., was appointed to the Committee of Accounts and Claims on Thursday, September 14. [24] All through the fall his committee convened at eight in the morning and stayed until nearly ten at night, Silas Dean wrote his wife, poring over preceding resolutions passed by Congress in order to make proper recommendations. Resolutions had already passed in the summer that three million Spanish milled dollars be minted for expenses and Congress expected the colonies to redeem the bills of credit for Congress was confronted with clothing an army, paying for arms, ammunition, stores and supplies. [25]

Dr. Franklin, the sixty-nine-year-old patriarch of the parliamentarians, informed an English friend that the Committee of Safety sat from six o'clock in the morning until nine at night "to put the province in a state of defence." Other groups gathered in morning meetings before all the members assembled in the downstairs hall for regular sessions that lasted until late in the afternoon.[26]

Virginia, as the most populous province and richest in resources, led the list of colonies required to levy taxes in support of the specie to be issued.[27] Even the most optimistic person realized that the government could operate only by the guarantee of the Thirteen Colonies, yet the printing press was not a cure for financial ills, as some of the Founding Fathers pointed out.

The Continental Congress had set salaries for officers, appointed Dr. Benjamin Church as Surgeon General, employed two treasurers with wages, and had elected Benjamin Franklin as Postmaster General at one thousand dollars a year though the Congress had no legal sanction to levy funds; however, there was no escaping the fact that money was necessary to keep men in the field with stores and supplies.[28]

Nelson took the floor of the main hall on September 23 to move for needed clothing and equipment for the Continental force and recommended "5,000 Sterling be advanced to the Quartermaster General to be laid out in Cloathing for the Army. . . . 263 kettles, canteens, & spoons supplied to soldiers, be charged to the Continent."[29]

Sam Adams seconded the motion. Two decidedly different Connecticut delegates favored the measure in debate. Silas Deane with a Yale degree spoke easily and confidently. Roger Sherman, a rural Yankee in plain clothes and a self-educated man, was "as badly calculated to appear in such a Company as a chestnut-burr for an eyestone," according to his colleague Deane.[30] Yet Sherman would continue to serve his country throughout the Constitutional Convention. He thought a soldier should supply himself but agreed with Deane that sutlers had taken advantage of the troops.

Benjamin Harrison believed that the money should be advanced.[31] Samuel Chase of Maryland declared: "A Soldier without Clothing is not fit for Service. . . . it would not be proper to make purchases in Philadelphia since the city had broken the Association and raised prices 50 per cent."[32]

John Adams agreed that "The Army must be clothed; or perish. . . . We ought to look out that they be kept warm and that the Means of doing it be secured." Nevertheless when the bill passed he couldn't resist remarking, "Colonel Nelson and Colonel Harrison indulged their Complaisance and private friendship for Mifflin and Washington to carry."[33]

Thomas Mifflin had been elected a delegate from Pennsylvania to the First Continental Congress, and he was destined to be a delegate to the convention that ratified the Constitution. When the representatives had arrived in Philadelphia, the warlike Quaker wined and dined them at his

Statue of Thomas Nelson, Jr., at the monument of Washington on the Capitol grounds, Richmond, Virginia. Courtesy of the Virginia State Library.

handsome house. In June, Major Mifflin had been appointed an aide to General Washington. Now, as the quartermaster general, he would receive the order to clothe the troops and be allowed five percent for his trouble.[34]

❖   ❖   ❖

While Thomas Nelson, Jr., was involved with the intricacies of finance during the sweltering September days, Lucy Nelson, Rebecca and Frank Lee, Elizabeth and George Wythe, and their servants had been inoculated against smallpox as eastern cities had experienced smallpox epidemics and Philadelphia had been struck in 1774. Through the years, opposition to inoculation had lessened and by the autumn of 1775, the two Dr. Shippens had performed the process many times. Dr. William Shippen, Jr., had married Alice Lee of Stratford, so he was a brother-in-law to Richard Henry and Francis Lightfoot Lee.[35] Evidently the Virginians submitted to the ordeal as soon as they settled in the city since Purdie in his *Virginia Gazette* of October 6, 1775, gave this account:

By a letter from another Gentleman in Philadelphia, dated September 25, We have the agreeable intelligence that Mrs. Nelson, Mr. Wythe and his Lady, Mr. Francis Lightfoot Lee and his Lady, with their several servants, are safely through the smallpox.

The *Virginia Gazette* of Dixon-Hunter on August 26 presented a realistic picture of wartime conditions that was a contrast to the visions of John Adams and other gentlemen conjuring the glories of gallant battle charges. Above the columns titled "Prospect" and "Bunker Hill," people could ponder the comparisons: At Prospect, seven dollars a month; at Bunker, three pence a day; fresh provisions in plenty at Prospect; rotten salt pork at Bunker; on Prospect, health; on Bunker, the scurvy; Prospect provided freedom, ease, affluence, and a good farm; Bunker offered slavery, beggary, and want. Yet the editors apprised the public that there were Englishmen who praised the patriots for their bravery:

The Lords Rockingham II, Shelbourne, and Chatham, and their friends, it is said intend to erect a monument in Westminster Abbey, to the memory of the Americans who were killed in the battle of Lexington.

Representatives at the Congress recognized that resistance to attack and relations with foreign alliances were of prime importance. To stabilize the money situation, cut red tape, and expedite handling of accounts, many of the constituents thought a special committee should be granted the central authority. Roger Sherman, awkwardly clutching his fists, stood rigidly on Monday, September 25, to propose that one member from each colony should constitute this committee of central control. Samuel Adams seconded the motion. Querulous Benjamin Harrison wondered if this was the proper way to thank the colonies for their services in training troops and equipping rifle companies; Adams explained that there was no reflection on the riflemen. The motion carried.[36]

Two days after proposing that £5,000 sterling be advanced for clothing, Tom again stood to move that $20,000 be placed in the hands of the newly formed committee to settle the accounts.[37]

Expenses seemed endless. As the committees tackled the accounts, Silas Deane commented, "the eleven hours' sitting is too much for my Constitution. . . . only one dish of coffee at six in the morning." Other members attested that Sam Adams ate little, slept little, but thought much during these days.[38]

Congress established the special committee Sherman had suggested composed of one member from each colony. Thomas Nelson, Jr., became committeeman for Virginia, a mark of respect for his character and conscientiousness. He was appointed to chair a committee of three assigned to examine all the funds of the Continental treasury to form an estimate of the public debts already contracted. A report was due by June 1 of the following year.[39]

Thomas Cushing, of Massachusetts, and James Duane, of New York, constituted the committee with Tom. Cushing had come to the first Congress in September 1774, with the two Adams and Robert Treat Paine. As he had observed opposition building between radicals and conservatives, Cushing had moved that prayers be read every morning, hoping they might set the mood for accord. Delegates immediately objected to the measure because of the different religious faiths represented. Sam Adams, a Congregationalist, approved and Reverend Jacob Duche, an Episcopal rector, was chosen chaplain. His opening prayer from Psalm 35, particularly pleased militant members: "Plead my cause, O Lord, with them that strive against me. Take hold of shield and buckler, and stand up for mine help."[40]

James Duane had allied himself at the first Congress with the conservative faction. Consequently, he clashed with progressive John Adams on the floor, who commented that the New York lawyer was "squint-eyed," and "sly and surveying," but Adams also stated he was "sensible and artful." A prolific penman, Duane is credited with recording that "Congress" and "President" had been decided by the delegates to be the official titles used by the organization. Unemotional in expression, restrained and reasonable in style, Duane nevertheless recognized that the colonists had just grievances. When he worked on the Declaration of Rights, he reiterated that the inherent claims of life, liberty, and property were privileges; that assembly, petitions, and trial by one's own peers were guarantees not lost when people migrated from the mother country to a new land.[41] These ideas were later incorporated in the Declaration of Independence.

Realistic Congressmen had recognized for months that their own Association was tying up trade. The provisions of the Non-Importation and Non-Exportation Act impeded their progress in defense preparations, and they knew patriot troops had been forced to retreat from Bunker Hill because they ran out of powder. In the summer session the statesmen resolved to allow American vessels to export produce in exchange for weapons, the exports to equal in value the imports. Whether to open the ports to world trade was discussed, but the question was postponed. By the last of September the subject was considered again, and the Virginia Congressman took a prominent part in the proceedings.[42]

A cautious Philadelphian, Thomas Willing, declared that the terms of the Association were detrimental to the trade and he desired some indulgence for the mercantile class.[43] Though a merchant himself, Thomas Nelson, Jr., stated that "the merchant should not be indulged more than the farmer." There would be no end to the humoring, he continued, if any group were granted particular favor.[44]

Silas Deane declared:

> Whether we trade with all nations except Britain, Ireland, and the West Indies, or with one or two particular nations, we cannot get Ammunition without allowing some exports. The merchants have neither money nor bills and our bills will not pass abroad.[45]

Richard Henry Lee was a strong advocate for opening the ports to foreign trade. All through October he voiced his opinion that "all should suffer equally" and the various colonies should be on the same footing to remove "jealousies and divisions."[46]

Meanwhile, Lord Dunmore had sent British ships and seamen to spy along the shores near Norfolk. Lee appealed to the Congress to assist his Colony by raising "a force by sea to destroy Lord Dunmore's power. . . . He is fond of his bottle, and may be taken by land, but ought to be taken at all events."[47]

George Wythe, concurring with his Virginia colleague concerning trade, tactfully stated, "It was from a reverence for this Congress that the Convention of Virginia neglected to arrest Lord Dunmore."[48]

Closer to the fact was the tempered stand of the Committee of Safety in Virginia made up of moderate men who, favoring an orderly system of government, restrained hotheads from rash action. The diffuse Loyalists were deceived and did not form a powerful Tory party.[49]

Massachusetts was under military rule. British General Thomas Gage kept the King's regiments on the move from morning to night. Tory spies ferreted information from indifferent or greedy folk who wanted the British guineas. A large segment of Loyalists lived in New York; rich Philadelphia families and those throughout Delaware and Maryland favored the royal standard; Scotsmen in the mountains of North Carolina were true to the throne; and Tory support was strong in South Carolina and Georgia.[50]

The Committee of Safety in each colony promoted the patriots' cause. These committees were well organized, closely knit and led by men who had served in local legislatures.

Dr. Joseph Bartlett and John Langdon, both staunch supporters of the colonial cause, represented sparsely settled New Hampshire in the Continental Congress. In October, their citizens requested the statesmen to seek the counsel of Congress to start a civilian administration since affairs were in a "convuls'd state." Delegates who dreamed of a great democratic nation were elated over this entreaty. On November 3, Congress passed the important resolution:

> That it be recommended to the provincial Convention of New Hampshire, to call a full and free representation of the people, . . . establish such a form of government as in their judgment will best produce the happiness of all the people."[51]

In secrecy Sam and John Adams wrote letters to spread the word. As proponents of popular government, both men noted that every colony would soon see the necessity of such a step for the "states," a term John Adams preferred instead of "colonies." He succeeded in having "mother country" dropped from the language but "colony" held on. Sam Adams cut up his letters, bit by bit, so that no one could be involved, but his younger cousin John wrote constantly and saved every scrap.

John Adams continued to characterize his fellow delegates. He penned a sharp portrait of the Rutledge brothers of South Carolina as "uncouth and ungraceful speakers—both spout language in rough and rapid torrents, but without much force or effort."[52] He further commented that John Rutledge had "no keenness in his eye, no depth in countenance,"[53] and he asserted about the younger brother that "Young Ned Rutledge is a perfect Bob-o-Lincoln—a swallow, a sparrow, a peacock."[54]

John Rutledge, however, had served as the chairman of the committee that drafted the recommendation to New Hampshire, and he made a similar request to South Carolina if the "Convention of South Carolina shall find it Necessary."[55]

The Congress had previously created an army now camped at Cambridge and now it sought to outfit ships for service.[56] Though the representatives realized that the Royal Navy ruled the seas, the rebel patriots were imbued with purpose. The legislators had learned that the British were sending two ships to Canada loaded with guns and ammunition. Alert to attack, John Adams advocated outfitting American vessels. Opponents believed it was a "fantastic, sheer folly, wild, and impossible and preposterous plan."[57] The Virginia delegates felt the plan was valuable and their powerful influence was brought to bear in favor of the proposal.[58]

George Wythe challenged the Congressmen with an impassioned plea:

> Why should America not have a Navy? No maritime power near the coast can be safe without it. The Romans suddenly built one in their Carthaginian war. . . . Colonies abound in natural resources, firs, iron, ore, pitch, and turpentine the necessary materials for ship construction.[59]

By the last of October the members had authorized a navy of two sailing ships, one with ten guns and the other with fourteen, and crews of eighty men. On the thirtieth they commissioned two larger vessels, one with twenty guns, the other not to exceed thirty-six. The infant fleet had specific instructions to cruise for three months on the sea eastwardly to prey on the English enemy.[60]

The naval committee, with John Adams as chairman, gathered in the dark November nights at Tun Tavern on the dock near Walnut Street wharf. The waterfront was lined with warehouses, squat stores, shops, ordinaries, and fish markets. Riggers, sailmakers, shipwrights, and whalers wandered up and down. Big ships sailed up the Delaware River, sloops and cutters crowded the harbor. Curses and oaths were loud as the seamen complained of the squeeze in shipping. Crewmen stared curiously at the Congressmen discovering these were the sharp fellows who raved about the tea tax and England's trade monopoly, for the Congressmen cornered all who frequented the tavern to talk of freedom and liberty.

Fifty-one-year-old Christopher Gadsden, a rich merchant from Charleston, was the only radical representing the South Carolina colony. He fought to strengthen the fighting forces, and Silas Deane asserted "He is for taking up his firelock and marching direct to Boston."[61]

In January the next year he would take command of South Carolina's First Regiment.

✦　　✦　　✦

While their husbands were making history in the Congress, Lucy Nelson and the other wives were learning about Philadelphia. Handsome residences ranged her tree-lined thoroughfares. The Quakers were establishing institutions of learning to stamp out illiteracy, and the Scotch-Irish Presbyterians were also enthusiastic about education, surpassing all other sects in starting schools. Students could learn more languages in Philadelphia than in any other city. Apprentices could advance their skills by attending classes offered at night by private academies. Street lights were provided. Dr. Benjamin

Franklin had formed the Junto Club and the American Philosophical Society with the objective of stimulating intellectual inquiry.[62]

The Virginia ladies had attended many brilliant balls and the theater. In fact, the first theater had been established at Williamsburg and plays had been popular in the colonial capital. The Quakers frowned on such frivolities as balls and theaters and had passed laws to prohibit revels and sports, yet dancing schools had been started and strolling players were no longer confined to the periphery of Philadelphia.[63]

Since the city had a conglomerate population, prejudice against various religions was not prevalent. The Lutherans had placed the first organ in their church just after the century started. The simple structures of the Quakers contrasted with the classic construction of the Anglican Christ Church. Many members of the Virginia Established Church had never before entered the church of a dissenter, but Alice Shippen took Lucy to hear the eminent Dr. John Witherspoon, president of Princeton, who preached at the Presbyterian Church. Witherspoon was no stranger to Virginia since his 1769 visit to Williamsburg had netted a contribution of £66 for Princeton.[64]

Sometimes the women strolled through Market Square inspecting the work of Philadelphia's skilled silversmiths, glassblowers and cabinetmakers. Alice Shippen was a good guide for her sister-in-law, Becky Lee, and Virginians Lucy Nelson, Betty Randolph, and Elizabeth Wythe, because her father-in-law, Dr. William Shippen, had helped to found in 1765 the first medical college in the colonies. Laymen in Philadelphia were learning about anatomy by paying five shillings to attend the physician's popular lectures.[65]

◆　　◆　　◆

Though the delegates had been cautioned not to divulge the deliberations of the Congress, some of the representatives could not refrain from revealing proceedings to family and friends. British intelligence was well informed through letters intercepted from the "scoundrels," as critics called the colonial patriots. The Tory press printed rollicking satires on the rebels. Eventually, by experience and painful embarrassment, the delegates grew more discreet and their enthusiasm for the cause was complemented by skillful statesmanship.[66]

John Adams was so provoked that John Dickinson had drafted a second petition to the Crown that he confided in a friend, "A certain great Fortune and piddling Genius, whose fame has been trumpeted so loudly, has given a silly Cast to our whole Doings. We are between Hawk and Buzzard."[67] The British seized the secret communication and published it, so Adams and Dickinson had not spoken to each other since July. John Hancock was also avoiding the Adamses. He had been humiliated when they had sponsored Washington for Commander-in-Chief, an honor Hancock courted.[68]

All three members had been misled by their Boston associate, Dr. Benjamin Church, the Continental army's Surgeon General. No delegate had doubted the loyalty of his colleagues in spite of differing viewpoints; consequently, they were in an uproar when General Washington reported that Church had delivered, through his mistress, an uncoded message containing military secrets to General Gage. Under pressure she had admitted that Church was the author of the communication.[69]

Only in retrospect did the Massachusetts representatives piece together his treachery. Church had composed political poems for the patriots, but no one paid any attention then to similar parodies published by the Tories. The doctor was always in debt; but he had constructed a handsome house, cared for his family, and supported a mistress in style. Dr. Church had been a boon companion to the Boston club crowd. When a student apprentice discovered the doctor had hundreds of bright British guineas, he was amazed. But his astonishment could not surpass that of the Boston companions in the Congress when they found out the deception. Church was jailed in Connecticut "without the use of pen, ink, and paper," and paroled after a short time in prison. Eventually he escaped to a vessel sailing for the West Indies and the ship was lost at sea.[70]

The Congressmen experienced another shock by the unexpected demise of their first president. Peyton Randolph died of a stroke on October 22 while a guest of Henry Hill in the country near the Schuykill River. In her hour of sadness, Elizabeth Harrison Randolph turned to Tom and Lucy for help. Duties would ordinarily have devolved on her brother, Benjamin Harrison, but they became Tom's because Harrison was away inspecting the Continental army at Cambridge.[71]

The Nelsons shared her sorrow since Tom and Betty were second cousins and Peyton was Lucy's uncle. The young York Town representative realized that his own political career had been aided by family connections. No opprobrium was attached to nepotism in the eighteenth century since patronage for relatives was the accepted practice in politics.

On Monday, October 23, the Congress resolved to attend Randolph's funeral with crape around each left arm and continue in mourning for one month. To handle funeral arrangements, Congress appointed a committee composed of Samuel Hopkins of Rhode Island and Samuel Chase of Maryland as well as South Carolina's Henry Middleton, who had served as president in May when Randolph had been indisposed.[72]

Although the Association required that costly mourning symbols be eliminated, the representatives buried Peyton Randolph with impressive rites. His draped casket was removed from Benjamin Randolph's residence on Chestnut Street and drawn in a slow procession toward Christ Church where the bells were silenced. Three battalions of artillery—with muffled drums and furled flags—lined the streets. The military presence testified to Randolph's high rank. Respect for the former president was also shown by the retinue of gentlemen following the cortege. John Hancock and members of the Congress formed a large contingent followed by the clergymen and vestrymen from Christ and St. Peter's churches; six magistrates supported the pall. One correspondent commented it was the "greatest collection of people he had ever seen."[73]

The Reverend Jacob Duche, rector of the combined churches and chaplain of Congress, preached the funeral service, praising the late president for his integrity, intelligence, capability, competence, discernment and diligence. Randolph was laid to rest temporarily in Christ Church cemetery until his body could be removed to Virginia.

◆   ◆   ◆

Early in November Benjamin Franklin, Thomas Lynch, and Benjamin Harrison returned from their eleven-day trip to the Continental army and its commander in Cambridge, Massachusetts. Their message to Washington from the Congress had been one of total confidence in his courage and wisdom. By his discretion, Washington should decide whether to attack the enemy at Boston before British reinforcements arrived. As a consequence of recommendations worked out by Washington and his visiting committee, Congress changed the Articles of War on November 4. More men were to be recruited for service until the fighting force totaled in excess of 20,000 troops. Militiamen were to re-enlist for another year. Violators would meet stricter penalties; deserters, mutineers, and traitors would be shot.[74]

Nelson and several statesmen opposed the parole of a British officer, who promised to return to Scotland and never serve in America again; however, sufficient men approved the application so that it passed.[75]

Lynch wrote Washington of his pleasure that Congress had passed the recommendations of the committee, raising the pay for officers even beyond the proposal. A major general had received $166 per month. Thinking that some officers had seemed indifferent to duty, Lynch advised the Commander-in-Chief to forbid his men "to sweep the Parade with the skirts of their Coats or bottoms of their Trousers, to cheat or mess with their Men, to skulk in battle or sneak in Quarters."[76]

The overworked delegates continued to meet mornings and nights to catch up on their committee assignments while attending all-day sessions at the State House. Benjamin Franklin nodded in his straight-backed chair as his bifocals slipped down his nose; yet items of importance did not escape him. Aged Stephen Hopkins rapped his hickory cane with restless impatience at remarks he considered irksome. Thomas Nelson and some of the other more corpulent gentlemen welcomed the cool hint of winter winds but grew irate at George III's refusal to receive the most recent colonial petition. Further, he had declared the colonies to be in a state of rebellion; abettors and perpetrators were to be severely punished.[77]

His royal proclamation spurred the fight for a fleet. On Friday, November 10, 1775, the Congress resolved, "That Two Battalions of Marines be raised, experienced seamen to be enlisted and commissioned to serve for and during the present war between Great Britain and the Colonies."[78]

The word *war* was used openly for the first time, not *controversy, disagreement,* or *dispute.* Now the delegates were determined to fight for freedom. Congress commissioned a navy of thirteen ships, established wages (commanders would receive $32 a month), drew up rules regarding meals, behavior, disease, and death.

Manifesting a fatherly concern for the morals of the seamen, Congress directed commanders of the ships to call together the "United company and take care that divine service be performed twice a day on board; a sermon would be preached on Sunday unless bad weather or other extraordinary accidents prevent." Sailors who swore, cursed, or blasphemed would be forced to wear a wooden collar around the neck or "some other shameful badge of distinction." Officers would forfeit one shilling for each offense. Drunken seamen would sit in chains until sober. Inebriated officers would forfeit two days' pay. Delegates lightened the punishment of flogging; no more than twelve lashes with a cat-o-nine tails would be applied on the bare back.[79]

While some colonies were breaking the bonds with Britain, New Jersey was trying to build stronger ties to the throne. Thousands of Tories there, led by their Loyalist Governor William Franklin, illegitimate son of Benjamin Franklin, were faithful to the Crown. Nearly a score of years earlier, Benjamin Franklin had sailed to England to plead the cause of Pennsylvania in a tax case. William accompanied his father and remained in England until he earned an M.A. degree from Cambridge. At thirty-one he received his appointment as Governor of New Jersey and twelve years later he was determined to remain in the royal fold.[80]

On November 27, the legislators in the New Jersey Assembly had prepared a petition to the King to intercede in the colonial dispute to prevent further bloodshed. The Congress reacted quickly by passing a resolution "That in the present situation of affairs, it will be very dangerous to the liberties and welfare of America, if any Colony should separately petition the King or either house of Parliament."[81] On December 5 John Dickinson of Pennsylvania, George Wythe of Virginia, and John Jay of New York, all able attorneys, addressed the New Jersey Assembly and reviewed the case against Britain, emphasizing that unity could solve the colonists' problems. They accomplished their purpose, and Governor Franklin wrote in his report to Lord Dartmouth:

A Committee of the General Congress at Philadelphia came in great haste to Burlington, desired admittance into the Assembly, which was granted, they harangued the House for about an hour on the subject, and persuaded them to drop the design.[82]

The Virginia delegates in Philadelphia kept up to date on the activities in their Colony with accounts from the newspapers and communications from the eleven-man Committee of Safety. Nelson had three close associates serving on the eleven-man committee: Cousins Carter Braxton and John Page, and Dudley Digges, a longtime neighbor and colleague.

The committee had gathered in Richmond the last of August, about the time Thomas was leaving to attend the Congress, and resolved to raise two regiments. At the September convention in Hanover Town, it had arranged for officers and formulated a schedule for provisioning the regiments. The group moved to Williamsburg on September 30.[83]

Companies from areas surrounding Williamsburg—Amelia, Caroline, Culpepper, Elizabeth City, Gloucester, Lancaster, Princess Anne, and Prince William counties—were encamped around the capital. The men had brought blankets but some were sleeping in the open as sufficient tents had not yet been supplied. Soon companies from Henrico and Mecklenburg counties joined the contingent.[84]

Chairman Edmund Pendleton informed Richard Henry Lee at Philadelphia that the Virginia companies lacked arms and ammunition, a situation that had been predicted by Robert Carter Nicholas. Pendleton implored the representatives of Virginia to ask the Congress to relax the terms of the Association so that needed arms and ammunition could be imported.[85]

The close-knit Lees were fiery rebels in the fight for freedom. Thomas Ludwell served on the Committee of Safety and communicated with Richard Henry and Francis Lightfoot Lee at the Continental Congress. The two youngest brothers, William and Arthur, who lived in London, aided the American cause there. William had already predicted that the dispute between the colonies and Britain would lead to independence and Arthur was urging the colonies to unite so that the British government could not pull the provinces apart piecemeal.[86]

Virginia's delegates in Congress received reports that Lord Dunmore was determined to destroy the rebellion. His sailors and seamen were pillaging the seacoast towns for supplies. Hampton inhabitants had heard their town was to be torched. Reacting to rumors George Nicholas had fired a shot at the British supply tender in Hampton Bay on October 26.[87] Although the Colony had no ships to prevent Dunmore's forays, military companies were forming in the Tidewater counties and setting up camps in the area. Colonel Patrick Henry's troops manned the College of William and Mary. The Committee of Safety met in Williamsburg as the acting authority of government.[88]

Almost one-third of the population fled Norfolk early in November when Governor Dunmore issued a proclamation decreeing the Colony under martial law and offering freedom to indentured servants and slaves who were "willing and able to bear arms." The governor vowed death to traitors and commanded "every person capable of bearing arms to resort to his Majesty's standard."[89]

Loyalists supported Dunmore in his determination. Although Scottish shipper Andrew Sprowle had once signed the Non-Importation Agreement, the colonists' drift toward separation alarmed Sprowle and many other Scotsmen who maintained their allegiance to the Crown.[90]

The anxious citizens left in Norfolk, caught in the middle, appealed to the Committee of Safety which responded with assurance that they could "support and protect the persons and properties of all friends to America. . . . no foundation to the rumor that troops would destroy property. . . . army aforesaid being instructed, particularly to support and protect."[91]

The Congress continued to name committees, send forth fact-finding commissions, and compose correspondence. Since their work for the cause took precedence, husbands apologized to their wives for not writing home more often. (Lucy relieved Tom of this responsibility plying his mother and her sister Mary with questions about the children; she missed her family. Hugh had turned seven the last day of September; Thomas, her second son, would be eleven years old December 20; Elizabeth, five on December 26, and Mary would celebrate her first birthday on the nineteenth.)

To seek aid from and alliances with foreign countries, the Congress had appointed a Committee of Secret Correspondence. It contacted Arthur Lee in London to ascertain what help could be expected from European powers.[92]

It was especially important to convince Canada that its interests were entwined with the colonies so the courtship of that sparsely settled territory had begun. It became the duty of General Philip Schuyler, a New Yorker who had served in Congress, to induce Canada to support the colonies and even send delegates to the Continental Congress.[93]

Brigadier General Richard Montgomery, a former British officer now leading a colonial force of recruits, was to move toward Montreal. Colonel Benedict Arnold, commanding a thousand volunteers, would advance to Quebec. The colonials' march in late autumn took its toll with raging torrents, thick snows, and starving men. Captain Daniel Morgan's Virginia riflemen survived to fight on through the Revolution. The veteran commander had pushed his volunteer company from Virginia to complete a 600-mile march in three weeks. The military objective to conquer British forts and the political goal to persuade the people of Canada to become the four-teenth colony and set up a new government was doomed to failure.[94]

Thomas Nelson, Jr., and his two committee members, James Duane and Thomas Cushing, understood perhaps better than anyone the financial picture was not a promising one. Cushing, having served on the rules and regulations committee for the army realized the true cost of providing for a force in the field. The Canadian campaign was a prime example of lack of preparation, food, equipment, and funds. Duane, a sensible and logical lawyer, understood that unlimited currency would quickly depreciate. On December 26 the committee suggested to Congress that needed sums be borrowed. The group strongly recommended Congress stop printing paper money as this led to inflation. Congress, however, continued its issue of paper money.[95]

The strain of the sunrise to sunset schedule tired the statesmen so that short tempers and frayed nerves gave vent to impatient outbursts. Eliphalet Dyer of Connecticut was not the only constituent complaining about being cooped up too long in the city. Thomas Jefferson was worried about his wife, Martha, recovering slowly from pregnancy and sorrowing over the loss of a second daughter just before the Congress had convened in September. John Adams was so swamped with committee work for the last six weeks of the session he penned neither impressions of the parliamentarians nor their remarks.[96]

Dyer, Jefferson and John Adams departed for their homes in December.

✦ ✦ ✦

Meanwhile, General Washington wrestled with the problem of expiring enlistments. Scant clothing, lack of barracks, frigid cold, poor pay, and inactivity were not conducive to re-enlistment. The enrollment time for six Connecticut regiments expired December 1, and the generals guessed that only one-half to two-thirds of the officers would stay on. Results of a count from the Eighth Regiment of Connecticut revealed a discouraging fact when a lieutenant recorded, "After breakfast, we called out the Company and made a trial to see who would stay in the service till the 1st of January, but not a man would engage."[97]

The Virginia Congressmen had read the disheartening news in Purdie's *Gazette* of August 26, 1775, that Dunmore had a "new ship just launched Burthen about 4,000 Tons and a Brig But for what purpose is not certainly known." Dunmore's flotilla controlled the harbor at Hampton at the broad mouth of the James River across from Norfolk.

Edmund Pendleton had called Lord Dunmore old "Wronghead" and now Dunmore lived up to the title. Incensed over criticism in a Norfolk newspaper, he ordered the printing press seized and hauled to his vessel where he issued his own version of events. The commercial seaport with its 6,000 population had a Loyalist faction that rallied to the royal standard. Dunmore's biggest blunder, however, was arming slaves. Putting guns into their hands pulled their vacillating owners into the patriot cause.[98]

The Committee of Safety sent Colonel William Woodford and the Second Virginia Regiment to Norfolk for military maneuvers. Since Colonel Patrick Henry was Commander-in-Chief of the Virginia forces and colonel of the First Regiment, the oversight was conspicuous. Henry was indignant and his followers incensed. They cursed Pendleton for his partisanship and attacked the chairman with charges of envy against his political rival. The civil authorities readily acknowledged that Henry led in forensic fire but gunfire was a different matter. Building breastworks, commanding a charge, and facing a barrage of bullets required experience. Richard Bland, Carter Braxton, William Cabell, John Page, and John Tabb supported Colonel Woodford as the better qualified commander.[99]

The Second Regiment reached Suffolk on November 25 with more than 400 men. Five companies of the Culpeper militia wore green shirts inscribed across the front with "Liberty or Death." Lieutenant Charles Scott and Major Alexander Spotswood commanded the minutemen companies.[100]

Lord Dunmore had collected a contingent of 1,200 troops composed of the British Fourth Regiment of sailors and marines, Loyalists, and two slave companies with nearly 300 Negroes. Dunmore had invested the corps with dignity by designation and dress, outfitting the black regiment with uniforms emblazoned "Liberty to Slaves," but white officers commanded the black troops.[101]

Dunmore chose Great Bridge—about twelve miles south of Norfolk—as his key defense and fortified the narrow wooden structure that spanned Elizabeth River's marshy swamp with cannon and sent slaves to burn the houses nearby. News of Dunmore's maneuvers reached the Committee of Safety. Thomas Ludwell Lee was worried when he wrote, "Our Army has been for some time arrested in its march to Norfolk by a redoubt or stockade or hog-pen."[102]

Impatient with the progress of the patriot soldiers, John Page said, "Woodford has been hitherto prevented from passing Great Bridge, on his way to Norfolk by a body of Negroes headed by Scotchmen and a few Regulars."[103]

Colonel William Woodford, however, surprised the blacks in their burning raid and routed them, killing one or two Negroes, wounding several, and capturing several prisoners. Woodford then moved his men toward the south end of the bridge, built breastworks, and stationed his "shirtmen"—so called, perhaps, because shirts were the extent of their uniforms—on good ground. He waited for reinforcements from North Carolina, but they did not arrive until after the engagement. Three companies from Colonel Henry's detachment had been directed to the peninsula with 500 pounds of powder and 1,500 pounds of lead shot. Resentment flared between the regiments, and the First Regiment declared its reception was cooler than the winter weather as they were not "invited to eat or drink." Dunmore reassured his force they had nothing to fear since the rebels had not faced King's regulars. Woodford tried the old military trick of sending out a slave who pretended he was running away. Dunmore captured the servant and believed the story that rebels numbered no more than 300 men.[104]

On December 9, British Grenadiers marched precisely six abreast onto the narrow bridge while guns from the ship *Otter* pointed toward the patriots. The rebels held their fire until the Englishmen came within 150 feet. Then rebel riflemen poured shot at the column. British soldiers crumpled; Colonel Fordyce fell. The English suffered over sixty casualties and the patriot shirtmen did not lose a single soldier. The Battle of Great Bridge was a great victory for the Virginians as it crushed the Loyalist movement in the Colony.[105]

Desperate, Lord Dunmore boasted that he would burn Norfolk on New Year's Day, but his fleet lacked fresh food and water and foraging parties made tempting targets for the patriots. Filth on the ships bred fever and disease took its toll. Every day bodies were dropped overboard.

Nevertheless, early on January 1, 1776, Dunmore turned the British guns toward Norfolk. Shot split the wooden structures along the waterfront. Frightened civilians, running out into the cold, were mowed down. Redcoats rushed into homes with flaming torches. The noise of bombarding cannon was deafening; running mobs pounded the cobblestone pavements, and looters screamed as they sacked the stores. Tobacco casks smoldered; overturned tar barrels added to the tinder. All day British cannon boomed across the bay. Tory troops began the catastrophe, but colonial forces finished the destruction and over 900 houses were destroyed. Since Norfolk had contained the clerks, officials, Scots factors, and tradesmen true to the Crown, Dunmore had fired on friends as well as foe. (Andrew Sprowle, old and discouraged, did not survive the shock of destruction and loss of property. He died aboard a British vessel.) The Governor succeeded in alienating loyal Virginians by arming the slaves and burning the prosperous seaport city. The richest, most populous, and the first Colony of the British Empire in America was lost forever.[106]

✦　✦　✦

Christmas was not a day of celebration for the colonists in 1775, and it was a particularly quiet period for the Nelsons at Philadelphia. Lucy and Tom, away from their children for the first time, were homesick and saddened by the death of Peyton Randolph. Still the couple felt fortunate to be among friends. The Frank Lees and George Wythes were still with them at the Benjamin Randolph residence on Chestnut Street where their own servants tended to the cooking and cleaning. The Shippens had also opened their hospitable home to the Virginians.

Christmas Eve fell on Sunday. Although most colonists were churchgoers, the clergy observed that their congregations were more crowded than usual on December 24. The spacious brick building with its fine woodwork, wide windows, and grand organ could accommodate its regular worshipers as well as the Congressmen and their wives. The Reverend Jacob Duche, following the ritual of the Established Church for December 24, read Psalm 50 proclaiming the majesty of God and revealing that the Heavenly Father derived pleasure from the faithful obedience of the people and not from mere ceremony. Special services were held again on Christmas Day, and Lucy derived inspiration and strength in the worship service, but Tom was back in Congress the next day, making a report for the Committee of Accounts and Claims that had recommended no more paper emissions. Again the proposal was bypassed.[107]

◆　　◆　　◆

Thomas Nelson, Jr., and his colleagues in Congress on January 11, 1776, passed a resolution that pinpointed the fiscal crisis:

> That if any person shall . . . be so lost to all virtue and regard for his country, as to refuse to receive said bills in payment, or obstruct or discourage the currency in circulation . . . such persons shall be . . . treated as an enemy of his country." [108]

Two of the members who had served with Nelson on the Committee of Accounts and Claims had asked for leaves of absence. After John Langdon had returned from the difficult Canadian mission in December and reported the poor preparations for the northern army, he had gone to New Hampshire to enlist men for service. Langdon was replaced by his associate, Dr. Josiah Bartlett, who favored the cause of independence. Sam Adams replaced Thomas Cushing.[109]

Sam Adams had a dream of an ideal democracy. He was prematurely gray and his palsied hands shook, but fire was in his eyes when he said, "If America is virtuous, she will vanquish her enemies. It is my duty to oppose to the utmost of my ability the designs of those who would enslave the country." [110] Subtle and scheming, he was often distrusted; conservative Congressmen were dismayed at his fervor.

Nelson was just as impatient with the fainthearted delegates as Adams was and he poured out his feelings to his cousin, John Page, in Virginia:

> We cannot expect to form a connexion with any foreign power as long as we have a hankering after Great Britain. . . . absurd to feel affection for

people carrying a savage war against us. Independence, confederation, and foreign alliances are as formidable to some of the Congress, I fear a majority, as an apparition to a weak enervated woman.[111]

Then Nelson implored Page to sound out the viewpoint of Virginians upon the "grand points of confederation and foreign alliances." Many rumors indicated Britain was sending over peace commissioners to discuss reconciliation with the Congress, but Nelson distrusted the motive if it were true and remarked:

We are now carrying on a war and no war. . . . they seize our property wherever they find it, either by land or sea: and we hesitate to retaliate, because we have a few friends in England who have ships. Away with such squeamishness, say I.[112]

Concerning the clergy, he commented:

What think you of the right reverend fathers in God, the bishops, One of them refused to ordain a young gentleman, who went from this country because he was a rebellious American: so that unless we submit to parliamentary oppression, We shall not have the gospel of Christ preached among us, but let every man worship under his own fig tree."[113]

There was no vacillation on Nelson's part. He believed that independence was the right course for the colonies to follow; his stand was firm for uniting the Thirteen Colonies into a confederation.

Nelson attempted to convince three colleagues on the now five-member finance committee to become more active in the cause of separation. James Duane, the well-to-do lawyer from New York, was conservative in his stand; Richard Smith of New Jersey, had his doubts about independence; and Thomas Willing, a Philadelphia merchant, also was against the move. Elbridge Gerry, small in stature, weighing only a hundred pounds, but strong in his feelings for complete independence, was a new representative from Massachusetts.[114]

On January 2 the Congress condemned the "execrable barbarity" of the enemy in burning defenseless towns although news of the Norfolk bombardment had not yet reached Philadelphia. Falmouth, Massachusetts, had been devastated the previous fall by invading British who bribed the Indians, committed murder and cast innocent people into gaols "without regard to age or sex."[115]

The disastrous defeat of the Canadian campaign had occurred the last of December, but the legislators would not learn about the fall of Quebec until January 17. Although sobered over the loss in Canada, the delegates kept trying to secure a stronghold to the north. Major General Charles Lee, third in command under General Washington, was chosen to head up the Canadian campaign. An experienced English soldier who had professed his patriotism, Lee knew the French language and could write well.[116]

Since there were only a few hundred Protestants in the Canadian provinces, the diplomatic mission was strengthened by including Charles Carroll, a rich Maryland Catholic, and his brother John, a priest. Benjamin Franklin, who spoke French fluently, and Samuel Chase of Maryland, were also envoys.[117]

Thomas Nelson expressed his ideas on the recent events in his letter of February 4 to his friend Thomas Jefferson:

Dear Jefferson:

I had written to you soon after the repulse of our Troops in Quebec . . . a true state of that unfortunate affair; but upon comparing it . . . with one I saw afterwards, I found they differed so materially that I burnt my Letter and determined to leave you to the Newspapers for your intelligence.

We have late advice from England, which you will see in the enclosed papers. I would rather send you a dozen Ledgers and Evening Posts, than transcribe three paragraphs of them. But I have good News for you, which neither of these papers contains. A Vessel arrived two nights ago with 60 Ton of Saltpetre, 13 Ton of Gun powder and 2,000 Stand of Arms and we are in daily expectation of 25 Tons more of Gun powder.[118]

The small fleet of American ships had sailed in February for the West Indies and had seized supplies of gunpowder from Nassau.

Big news from Boston soon excited the Congress. In the darkness of Monday night, March 4, American forces had pulled the cannon captured at Ticonderoga onto Dorchester Heights and placed them in a commanding position over the port city.[119] Astounded at this unexpected turn of events, Sir William Howe decided to desert the town and the "Tories were thunderstruck!" Before evacuating Boston, redcoats created chaos—plundering stores, smashing supplies, pitching food into the streets, scattering salt, and ransacking homes for jewels and silverplate; however, the Americans were amazed to find British fortifications almost wholly intact with guns and cannon. The British also left behind much-needed medicines and blankets. When Howe and his troops sailed from the harbor on March 17, over one thousand Loyalists left for Halifax, Nova Scotia.[120]

On Monday, March 25, 1776, the representatives in the Congress received gratifying news from General Washington. Nelson notified Jefferson of the military maneuvers in a long letter:

Troops are marching every day from hence to support the remains of our Army before Quebec, The Eastern governments are raising Men for the same purpose. One Battalion has already marched from Connecticut, so that we are still in hopes of reducing the Garrison before it can be relieved in the Spring.

General Washington has sent Major General Lee to New York at the head of 1,200 Volunteers from Connecticut to defend that province against a detachment from Boston. . . . The Committee of Safety of New York however sent a remonstrance to Lee, who sent it on to Congress . . . .

The letter and remonstrance being read, a violent debate arose on one side as to the propriety of an armed force from one province entering another without express orders from Congress. . . . On the other side was urged the absolute necessity of securing that province, the loss of which would cut off all communications between Northern and Southern Colonies and which if effected would ruin America.[121]

It was clear that Congress did not intend to leave a single doubt that the elected delegates to the body formed the civil authority.

Continuing the communication, Nelson added some personal comments:

You would be surpri'd to see with how much dispatch we have done business since Dyer and Gadsden left us. The former you know was superseeded and the latter was ordered home to take command of his Regiment.[122]

Nelson's opinion concurred with that of John Adams who stated, "Eliphalet Dyer is long-winded and roundabout, obscure and cloudy, very talkative and very tedious, yet honest; means and judges well."[123]

Nelson concluded his letter to Jefferson:

I have much more to say to you but the person who carries this to you is impatient to set out on his journey. He is one of the County Men by the name of Blanc. You must certainly bring Mrs. Jefferson with you. Mrs. Nelson shall nurse her in the small pox and take all possible care of her. We expect Braxton every day and then I shall beat a march for a few Weeks. I have not the time to add more than to desire my compliments to Mrs. Jefferson and to beg that you will believe me

Your sincere friend and hble. Servt.

P.S. I send you a present of 2 shillings worth of Common Sense. I had like to have omitted to send you a present from the Quakers also.[124]

Packing up the newspapers and pamphlets for Jefferson and being pushed by the impatient person conveying the correspondence kept Nelson from commenting on *Common Sense* or on the Quaker tract. While few folk perused the treatise entitled "Ancient Testimony and Principles of People Called Quakers, Renewed, with Respect to the King and Government," all kinds of colonists were reading "Common Sense," the forty-seven-page pamphlet that had been printed anonymously. Its authorship was attributed to various Assemblymen but guesses favored Dr. Franklin, who was acquainted with the actual author, Thomas Paine. Paine, who had been befriended by Franklin on arriving in Philadelphia in 1774, edited the *Philadelphia Magazine*.[125] Paine had arranged with a Scots printer, Bobby Bell, to print 500 copies of "Common Sense" priced at two shillings. The public ordered 2000 copies one week after publication; then demanded thousands more. Franklin purchased fifty copies for his friends and then asked for fifty more but had to wait for delivery. The printer hired assistants and ran his presses at night. By the end of 1776 more than 120,000 copies of "Common Sense" had been printed. The dynamic document burned with patriotic frenzy:

> O ye that love mankind! Ye that dare oppose not only tyranny, but also the tyrant, stand forth![126]

The pamphleteer implored people to seize the opportunity for independence:

> The sun never shined on a cause of greater worth. 'Tis not the affair of a City, A County, or a Province or a Kingdom; but of a continent—at least one-eighth part of the habitable globe. 'Tis not the concern of a day, a year, or an age; posterity are virtually involved in the contest, and will be more or less affected even to the end of time, by the proceedings now.[127]

How could there be reconciliation after April 19, 1775, the author asked, when the royal sovereign of the mother country had sent his soldiers to slaughter his children? The path of separation would be filled with suffering and destruction, but sloughing off a despotic government was the shining goal:

> Everything that is right and reasonable pleads for separation. The blood of the slain, the weeping voice of nature cries, 'TIS TIME TO PART.
> These are the times that try men's souls: The summer soldier and the sunshine patriot will in this crisis, shrink from the service of his country; but he that stands it Now, deserves the love and thanks of man and woman. Tyranny, like hell, is not easily conquered; yet we have this consolation with us, that the harder the conflict, the more glorious the triumph.[128]

Even the taciturn Commander-in-Chief commented that the "flaming argument" of the treatise had raised the soldiers' spirits.[129]

Three Frenchmen appeared in Philadelphia denying any diplomatic connection with the French court. A secret committee of Congress played along with the game negotiating contracts for needed gunpowder. Congress then decided to send a secret agent to France to strengthen foreign ties and chose Silas Deane, a Connecticut lawyer not re-elected to the Congress. He continued the spirit of intrigue acting the role of an American merchant while attempting to acquire arms, ammunition, and clothing for 25,000 soldiers.[130]

The forward-moving men in the Continental Congress were in favor of forming a confederation of the colonies, facing the issue of independence, and securing foreign aid and alliances. Yet the conservative constituents employed moderate methods and were putting their trust in compromise. Tom's cousin, Carter Braxton, arrived as the replacement for Peyton Randolph and presented his credentials to the Congress on Friday, February 23, 1776. The Nelsons planned to leave Philadelphia for Virginia as soon as he was settled.[131]

Some thought the conservative Tidewater section of Virginia had sent the new constituent to the Congress to check the movement for separation from Great Britain. Some believed the representative had Loyalist leanings since his father-in-law, Richard Corbin, was steadfast in his support of the Crown. Of the six delegates from the Old Dominion, only Harrison was holding back in breaking the bonds with Britain. Jefferson, the two Lees, Wythe, and Nelson were progressive patriots impatient with the appeasers and ready to pursue action. Carter Braxton could not accept their liberal viewpoint. He looked upon democracy with disdain and had no bright dream of a new republic.[132]

◆　　◆　　◆

What a happy homecoming the Nelsons had in early March. Their five boys rushed from the house, Elizabeth running close at their heels followed by fourteen-month-old Mary. As the couple hugged the children, the servants surrounded them with welcoming grins. Soon the grownups gathered to welcome the travelers: Elizabeth and her daughters-in-law Judy and Mary, from across the street, then Hugh and Robert from the store. Lucy was looking forward, too, to seeing her sister Susanna and her son, about the same age as Lucy's Mary.[133]

The Nelsons read in the Purdie *Gazette* of March 8, 1776, two death notices of persons closely connected with the family:

> Death—Carter Burwell, Esquire, at London who some time ago went there for the recovery of his health. He was the youngest son of the late Colonel Carter Burwell, in his twenty-first year; after a lingering illness.

No doubt the Secretary had already dropped by to mention that the mother-in-law of his eldest son, William, had passed away.

> Mrs. Elizabeth Chiswell, relict of the Late Colonel John Chiswell, at William Nelson's, Esquire, Caroline. She died in her fifty-fourth year, and was a most amiable Lady, from her door, the needy were never turned away.

Tom found the shelves in the store almost empty from the effects of the embargo, and customers complained about the cost of goods. Even coarse cotton and ordinary duffel were difficult to obtain and commanded a high price. The Committee of Safety strove to secure oznaburg for the troops. Salt and sugar were so scarce that the articles cost ten times over the former price, and rum had jumped from two to twelve shillings. The Committee had suggested that the ground in smokehouses be sifted for salt, and the Congress had also sent out a resolution:

> Proprietors of tobacco warehouses in Virginia and Maryland have earth of the floor worked for salt petre . . . that tobacco stalks and trashy leaves should be spread on the light and loose dirt so that the soil be impregnated with nitrous particles.[134]

Landon Carter wrote in his diary on Friday, March 1, that "John Wormeley is making his people make up bread with salt river water." Carter had also sent a servant to the river to boil down the water for salt, securing "half a coffee cup."[135]

March was a month of military activity for the Colony. The drum beat summoning Williamsburg's able-bodied to muster captured the imagination of Tom's twelve-year-old William and eleven-year-old Thomas who believed they were big enough to begin drilling. The boys' inexperienced eyes did not detect what John Page saw in the armed men ". . . a handful raw, undisciplined, and indifferently armed, wretchedly clothed without Tents & Blankets."[136]

Thomas Nelson reviewed the ranks of the local militia. Dr. Corbin Griffin and Reverend Robert Andrews, serving on the county's committee of defense raised two companies of minutemen with fifty men in each unit. (Dr. Griffin had married Mary Berkeley, daughter of Mary Nelson, Tom's aunt, who had married Edmund Berkeley, so he was considered kinfolk.)[137]

At the Swan Tavern, Dudley Digges told Tom that regiments were being raised as well as a five-vessel navy to protect the several rivers of Virginia. Thomas Lilly, an experienced captain, would command one of the ships. William Reynolds was purchasing the necessary equipment for the Eastern Shore Battalion and was to receive £200 to be "paid in continental money in three months." Another townsman was active for the county forces and the clerk had recorded funds would be furnished to "Captain William Goosley of £231.3.4 for the pay and provisions of the Company at York."[138]

The convivial associates at the Swan agreed that Hugh Mercer was a mighty fine fellow not to bear a grudge against the government. Six months before, the veteran soldier had been by-passed by the voters who had placed Patrick Henry at the head of the Virginia army. Now the Dixon-Hunter January 13, 1776, issue of the *Gazette* had announced that Hugh Mercer had accepted appointment as colonel of the Third Regiment.

Three of Secretary Nelson's sons had volunteered their services. William, 30, clerk of Caroline County, had been commissioned a major in the Seventh Virginia Regiment and Thomas, 28, was chosen a captain of the unit for which he was conscripting men. His brother John, 26, was busy purchasing horses for his cavalry, with an allotted £750 for "arms, horses, and accoutrements."[139]

Spring brought the usual number of weddings for Lucy and Tom to read about in the newspapers.

> Marriage—Benjamin Harrison, Jr. Esq, of Berkeley to Miss Sukey Randolph, oldest daughter of Colonel Richard Randolph of Curles.[140]

Colonel Landon Carter recorded in his diary before riding to the wedding of Mann Page, Jr., and Mary Tayloe that he hoped with a "hearty and devout Prayer that I may keep my Tongue." Whether Colonel Carter kept his promise not to make caustic remarks is not known. He disliked the bride's father and doubtless disagreed politically with other gentlemen attending the affair.[141]

Newspaper columns were crowded, too, with the notice of sales. Boats, slaves, and property had to be sold by the indebted planters. Jacquelin Ambler planned to sell his house in York Town:

> Commodious four rooms above and four below, brown stone house, well cultivated gardens, stables, kitchen, and wash house in good repair.[142]

He also advertised other property about two and one-half miles from town of about one hundred acres of cleared high land and fifteen acres of meadow that would be a convenient farm for any gentleman.

◆   ◆   ◆

To solve the colonial crisis, the Crown had instructed the governors to choose commissioners from the Loyalists to act as intermediaries between the sovereign and subjects. Lord Dunmore chose Richard Corbin as his envoy in Virginia.[143] The Committee of Safety returned a pointed reply. Virginia would not treat individually with the throne; Continental Congress had the sole power of negotiations. Dunmore was incensed, especially since General Henry Clinton with his suspicious disposition was on hand to hear the curt refusal. General Howe had selected Clinton to be in charge of the British campaign in the South, and the stocky commander was headed for Charleston, South Carolina.[144]

On March 1, the Congress had created a Southern Department of the Continental army, and Major General Charles Lee arrived in Williamsburg the last of March to assume command. The egocentric former British officer had displayed his concern for the colonial cause so aptly that several delegates had been disposed to elect him commander-in-chief. Fortunately, practical politics had placed George Washington in the position instead of the unstable Lee. Some of his associates had dubbed Lee as arrogant and obscene and the colorful character continued to cut a wide swath, issuing orders without the sanction of higher authority and wasting time on the way to Williamsburg with wanton women.[145]

Displeasing townspeople, General Lee set up headquarters in the elegant palace in Williamsburg, and a pack of dogs trailed him on all his rounds. Criticizing the army arrangement throughout the Tidewater district, he said he was surprised some men hadn't been stationed in every house for security!

To General Washington he confessed "I am like a dog in dancing school, I know not where to turn myself."[146]

Without consulting the Committee of Safety, Lee changed the College into a military hospital and pulled in the troops from the river areas. It was inevitable that the eccentric commander would collide with cool-headed Edmund Pendleton. The chairman informed the general that his conduct had been improper and inconsistent. Lee changed his mind and asserted, "The Convention and Committee of Virginia are certainly a most respectable body."[147]

A current surging toward separation swept Virginians along as the old Council members dwindled in power and personnel. Death had claimed John Page of North River in the fall of 1774 and Philip Ludwell Lee in the early part of 1775. George William Fairfax was living abroad. Secretary Nelson was still president of the Council but ailments of age made him long to retire from political life. Since his three sons were serving in the Virginia regiments and his numerous Nelson nephews were lovers of liberty, the Secretary's sentiments were swayed to support the colonial cause. William Byrd, III, had protested when his son Otway joined the American army. Robert Burwell took the oath of allegiance, but he tried to maintain a middle course.

Robert Carter, residing at Nomini Hall and attending to his 70,000 acres, profited during the war period by selling food and supplying tons of iron from the Baltimore Iron Works to the troops. In the political upheaval, economic interests impelled Colonel Carter to abandon allegiance to the Crown. In April 1776, his sons, Benjamin and Robert Bladen Carter, volunteered for service in the Fifth Virginia Regiment.[148]

Richard Corbin was repelled by the fervent patriots who proclaimed rights for all men, since he believed privilege and power were the especial prerogatives of the plantation aristrocrat, yet even he must have struggled with his conscience and reasoned that the rebels had right on their side since Landon Carter stated, "Heard Old Corbin would be a patriot if his wife and children would let him."[149]

In the tumult of the times, the Reverend John Camm was the most violent Tory of them all. His ties with England made him intensely subjective in his views.[150]

The slightest signs of disaffection sparked the rebel patriots to react, and

Tory sympathizers with indiscreet tongues were questioned, suppressed, ridiculed, and punished.

Ralph Wormeley, Jr., had written John Grymes on April 4 that Lord Dunmore wished Wormeley to join him. Wormeley affirmed,

> No man hears the accursed tyranny that is erected with more impatient mortification than I do. . . . If there were a corner on the face of the earth that I could support myself in, and enjoy that freedom that I am now violently deprived of, I would, for gratification of my own happiness, fly to it.[151]

Since exportation of products was prohibited and patriots used his wheat, flour, and corn for the colonial army, the unhappy Wormeley stated he could not support himself in any other place.

The Committee of Safety intercepted the letter, and on April 22, Ralph Wormeley, Jr., appeared before the committee. The authorities charged statements contained in the communication were "full proof of the inimical disposition . . . Against the rights of America and showing a readiness to join the enemy of this Colony."[152] Wormeley was required to post £10,000 bond, not to correspond with the British, be confined to the Colony, and appear at any time that the convention might call him before the committee.[153]

CHAPTER SIXTEEN

Inclination, Independence, and Individuals: 1776

Virginia May Convention ✦ *Tory Trials* ✦ *Patrick Henry and Thomas Nelson* ✦ *Resolutions on Independence* ✦ *Constitution for the Commonwealth* ✦ *Arguments on Articles of Confederation* ✦ *Declaration of Independence*

The first week in May found a variety of Virginians winding their way to Williamsburg. There was a difference in the delegates from former days. The complexity of change was apparent not only by the full attendance of the constituents at the Convention but also by their appearance, attitude and actions. Several counties such as Cumberland and Charlotte had directed their delegates to declare for independence.[1]

York County had re-elected Thomas Nelson, Dudley Digges and William Digges, who had served in the sessions while Thomas had been in Philadelphia for six months.

Adherents of Patrick Henry were on hand, still grumbling over another affront to their hero. The local committee had brushed aside Henry the past December to lead the attack at Great Bridge. The Continental Congress had overlooked the patriot as overall commander of Virginia's troops, appointing Andrew Lewis, a frontier fighter, to the position. General Washington had put in a good word for Lewis, his old comrade in arms, whose courage had been tested on the battlefield. Patrick Henry had resigned as colonel of the First Regiment after Lewis's appointment.[2]

At this May meeting, Henry's supporters from the upper region intended to avenge the affronts by sponsoring another candidate for chairman of the Convention, even though Edmund Pendleton was the natural choice for the post since he had served as chairman of the Committee of Safety and had the support of the Tidewater section.[3]

Nelson spoke to the old stalwarts still serving their countrymen. Richard Bland, his faded blue eyes almost blind and his form stooped with age, was in attendance, as was Archibald Cary, who lived at Ampthill in Chesterfield County and operated an iron foundry. Cary was intolerant of the Baptists and hated Patrick Henry; since his stand on questions was so unyielding, constituents called him "Old Iron." Robert Carter Nicholas, was there, still wrestling with his conscience on the issue of independence even though the citizens of James City County had instructed him to declare in favor of the great question. Nelson also noted his cousin, Lewis Burwell of Gloucester County, among the one hundred men attending the significant Assembly.

Tom recognized Lucy's handsome twenty-three-year-old cousin, Edmund Randolph. Nearly six feet tall, he towered over twenty-five-year-old James Madison, just at five feet six inches; these precocious young men gained attention and respect with their profound intelligence. Dark-eyed Edmund liked poetry and philosophy. His pale colleague, a Princeton graduate, would continue his studies of the classics until summoned to create a constitution for the new nation.[4]

At the formal opening of the Convention Monday, May 6, Richard Bland, rising above the suspicion Edmund Pendleton had cast on his character the previous summer, nominated him as chairman; Archibald Cary seconded the motion. Henry's followers proposed Thomas Ludwell Lee for the position but their opposition was short-lived and Edmund Pendleton became chairman of the Convention noting at the outset: "Time was truly critical . . . since the administration of justice, and almost all powers of government have now been suspended for now two years. . . . Subjects of the most important and interesting nature require our serious attention."[5]

Thomas and the members of the Privileges Committee on Tuesday, May 7, were "empowered to examine the conduct of such persons inimical to the rights and liberties of America."[6] The next day they interrogated John Tayloe Corbin, of the Loyalist family, who had made derogatory remarks about the decisions of the county Committee of Safety. Corbin claimed "he was determined to submit and came with his aged father to Williamsburg, but upon arrival he was arrested and confined in the guard house." He made an abject apology, but the lawmakers were not in a mood to tolerate lack of loyalty. Bond was set at £10,000 for John Tayloe Corbin, who was to remain in custody in Caroline County.[7]

Although Ralph Wormeley, Jr., had been questioned by the Committee of Safety in April, this wealthy proprietor of vast plantations, was summoned to appear before the Assembly. The river baron had written that he was bearing the Committee of Safety's "accursed tyranny" with "Impatient mortification" and must have been embarrassed over the second charge. The royalist expressed regret for his remarks, but the representatives were not impressed and set sentence of £10,000 bond and confinement to his holdings in Frederick and Berkeley counties. Wormeley posted bond and went into exile on his estate.[8]

Nelson worked with Nicholas and Cary on a project to produce salt, saltpeter, and gunpowder desperately needed for the Colony's defense. They ordered the public printer to produce one hundred copies of a pamphlet on

"The Art of Making Common Salt" for distribution among the people.[9]

After the day's meetings, Patrick Henry and Thomas Nelson lingered in the late afternoon sun discussing the colonial crisis. Henry had reservations about a resolution for immediate independence feeling that America should first secure official aid from France and Spain.[10] Nelson figured Virginia should hazard the venture and have faith that France would enter negotiations with the colonies through the plan proposed by the Congress. He was to state in the Assembly, shortly thereafter: "Americans have been oppressed and had humbly supplicated a redress of grievances which had been refused by insult. It is absurd to be abject to a sovereign who has sent soldiers to our shores to suppress us."[11]

Most Assemblymen nodded in agreement as they were acquainted with George III's proclamation for the purpose of "Suppressing Rebellion and Sedition" with its demanding provision that "All Officers, Civil and Military were to suppress such rebellion and bring the traitors to justice."[12]

With his contempt for the Crown, Patrick Henry proclaimed to the group "The King had proved himself a tyrant, rather than a protector of the people. . . . Parliament . . . have lately passed an act approving of the ravages that have been committed on our coasts . . ."[13]

Thomas Nelson sat up late the evening of May 8 to compose a special communication on the subject of independence:

> Since our conversation yesterday, my thoughts have been sorely employed on the great question, whether independence ought, or ought not to be unanimously declared? Having weighed the argument on both sides, I am clearly of the opinion that we must, as we value the liberties of America, or even her existence, without a moment's delay, declare for independence.
>
> I can assure you Sir, that the spirit of the people (except a very few of them in those lower parts, whose little blood has been sucked out by mosquitoes) cry out for this declaration, the military in particular, men and officers, are outrageous on the subject; and a man of your excellent discernment need not be told how grievous it would be in our present circumstances to dally with the spirit, or disappoint the expectations of the bulk of the people.[14]

Richard Henry Lee wrote Patrick Henry from Philadelphia urging him to push for independence in the Virginia Convention. Since Virginia had led in important affairs before, Lee attested:

> Ages yet unborn, and millions existing at present, must rue or bless the Assembly . . . the spirit, wisdom, and energy of her Councils will rouse America from the fatal lethargy . . . our clearest interest, therefore, our very existence as freemen, requires that we take decisive steps now, whilst we may, for the security of America.

He clinched his summary with a quote from Shakespeare, "There is a Tide in the Affairs of Men, Which taken at the Flood leads on to Fortune."[15]

Still Patrick Henry preferred to wait on the proposal in the Convention until the surge for independence swept the people in its favor.

Tom had heard Richard Lee expound on independence both in conversation and on the floor of the Congress and knew the path of revolution would be filled with risk and ruin. Despite the dangers, he had concluded his public address of May 8 with the pledge, "I may venture to affirm, that no man on this continent will sacrifice more than myself by the separation."[16] This assertion proved to be prophetic for the ardent patriot.

The influence of fasting and prayer was not overlooked by the patriots who instructed the printer to republish the resolutions of the Congress recommending a fast. The Convention set aside Friday, May 17, as the day for a public fast and instructed the chaplain to preach at Bruton Parish Church on that date.[17]

Military matters occupied the minds of men all over the Old Dominion. When the overseers of Chesterfield County had sent an entreaty that they be excused from drilling with the county militia, the Convention refused the request since the men were "able bodied" and could add "considerable strength" to the service.[18]

Thomas Nelson read a request from Major General Charles Lee asking the representatives to raise 1,300 militia and minutemen from the various counties to assist North Carolina since an attack by the British was anticipated in that area. On paper the regulations were precise, with two battalions to be formed with a full complement of officers. Each unit was to elect a surgeon and a mate, and the Assembly planned to advance each soldier a month's pay. In practice, the troops lacked sufficient supplies and many of the men marched away without blankets or tents.[19] Lee wrote Congress, however, and complimented the Convention for its attitude and aims:

> There is a noble spirit in this Province, pervading all orders of men; if the same become universal, we shall be saved. I am fortunately, for my own happiness, and I think, for the well being of the community, on the best terms with the Senatorial part, as well as the people at large. I shall endeavor to preserve their confidence and good opinion.[20]

During one week the delegates discussed the important issue of independence inside the Capitol and outside in groups gathered on the lawn, considering three propositions which would be placed before them formally May 14.[21]

Eccentric Meriwether Smith of Essex County, sometimes called "Fiddle" or "Fiddlehead" by his colleagues, first criticized British actions by saying "Lord Dunmore has assumed a power of suspending by proclamation the laws of this Colony . . . legalizing every seizure, robbery and rapine." Then he stated that the royal government should be dissolved. He offered a two-paragraph resolution calling for independence and recommending that a Declaration of Rights be prepared and a system of government be established to "secure substantial and equal liberty to the people."[22]

Chairman Edmund Pendleton presented the second proposition. Pendleton presented his experiences as chairman of the Committee of Safety, acting authority for the Colony during Governor Dunmore's unprecedented acts recalling the "inhuman and cruel manner King George the third had withdrawn his protection pursuing with utmost violence a barbarous war against the Colony in violation of its civil and religious rights." The conservative leader concluded that the "union between Great Britain and the American Colonies should be totally dissolved and thus the inhabitants were discharged from any allegiance to the King."[23]

Patrick Henry's paper was more inclusive than the two drafted by his colleagues. It comprised a long list of grievances against the British government and advocated a unity for the colonies not contained in the Smith or Pendleton proposals.[24]

The tide for independence was running strong, with political strategists sounding out the statesmen on their stand for separation and a confederation of the colonies. When the second week of sessions started on Monday, May 13, anticipation engulfed the delegates. The progressive patriots realized the time was ripe for the resolution. As the leader of the popular party, Patrick Henry could count on support from the representatives of the upper region on the presentation of his formal resolve, but would the members of the old oligarchy oppose the motion? His friend, Thomas Nelson, had fervent feelings on independence and was a rich aristocrat allied with the Tidewater gentry. Could Nelson be the catalyst to cement the various views if he spoke in favor of the important issue?[25]

On Tuesday, May 14, the different drafts were offered by the authors and debated by the delegates for two days. They also studied Robert Carter Nicholas's conservative viewpoint. The respected treasurer thought that the American colonies could not carry on such an "arduous contest" against Great Britain, and he had the "fortitude to yield to his fears" in voicing his convictions.[26]

Thomas Nelson, Jr., was not apprehensive about the assignment Patrick Henry persuaded him to undertake, although Nelson made no pretense to oratorical powers. Inspiration stemmed from his ardent feelings against the actions and insults perpetrated by the monarch and the British ministry. The hall was hushed as the York Town delegate declared that the colonial petitions to restore peace had been ignored. Instead of a redress of grievances, the goal of the royal government was oppression. Such a vindictive administration, by its arbitrary acts, would effect the total destruction of the colonies. The animated patriot asserted that the colonies could choose either abject submission to the arrogant tyrants or total separation. Nelson moved that the Virginia Colony absolve all allegiance to the Crown and declare its independence.[27]

The issue of independence was re-enforced by the forensic fire of Patrick Henry who inflamed the officials by his eloquence. As a skillful parliamentarian, Edmund Pendleton revised all the resolutions in a polished presentation. The clerk recorded, "There were 112 members present on May 15, who voted unanimously for the resolution," even Robert Carter Nicholas.[28]

The final form of this momentous resolution for independence read:

> That the delegates appointed to represent this colony in General Congress be instructed to propose to that respectable body all allegiance to, or dependence on the Crown or Parliament of Great Britain; and that they give the assent of this Colony to such declaration, and to whatever measures might be thought proper and necessary by the Congress for forming foreign alliances, and a confederation of the colonies, at such time, and in the manner, as to them shall seem best; provided, that the power of forming governments for, and the regulations of the internal concerns of the Colony, be left to the respective legislatures.[29]

Clerks made copies of the resolutions to send to all the other colonies with a circular letter urging them to unite with Virginia on this significant step.

Thomas Nelson, Jr., was presented a legible copy to convey to the Continental Congress, and he did not linger with his family at York Town but left for Philadelphia on horseback May 17 with the valuable papers tucked safely in his saddlebags.

The enthusiastic citizens of Williamsburg celebrated the event by hauling down the British banner from atop the Capitol and hoisting the Continental standard, the first such flag to fly in any colony. With cheers and cries, the citizens continued merrymaking throughout the day ringing bells and beating drums. The militia marched before the dignitaries in the spring sunlight. After parading, the soldiers discharged artillery and arms. Gracious gentlemen by a "handsome collection" treated the troops to fine food and sparkling spirits. Toasts were drunk to the "American Independent States," the "General Congress of the United States and Their Respective Legislatures," and to "General Washington and Victory to the American Arms." Editor Purdie pictured the pleasure of the people in his *Virginia Gazette* of May 17, 1776:

> The soldiers partook of the refreshments prepared for them by the affection of their countrymen. The evening concluded with illuminations and other demonstrations of joy; everyone seemed pleased that the domination of Great Britain was now at an end, so wickedly and tyrannically exercised

for these twelve or thirteen years past, notwithstanding our repeated prayers and remonstrances of redress.

As Tom rode along the route traveled twice in the past six months, he thought about his participation in the Convention proceedings. It had been exciting to present the motion for independence in the Convention, a momentous step for the Virginia Colony, the first, largest, and most powerful of the thirteen American colonies to sever connection with Great Britain.

Another progressive patriot in Philadelphia was deliberating on the decision of the Virginia delegates. Thomas Jefferson divulged his desire to participate in the proceedings to Thomas Nelson, Jr. The correspondent began a letter on May 16 but did not complete the communication until May 19 with a dismal postscript: "Yes, we received disagreeable news of a second defeat at Quebec. . . . General Wooster had the credit for this misadventure."[30]

Jefferson was back in his old lodgings at Benjamin Randolph's house on Chestnut Street but he said that he would "endeavor to move to the outskirts of the town away from the excessive heat!" This plan was not executed, but on the twenty-third he rented rooms from Jacob Graff, a bricklayer who had built a new brick house on the southwest corner of Seventh and High streets (now Market). He had been detained six weeks longer than intended by his "inveterate headaches," but he notified Nelson that "In future you shall hear from me weekly while you stay, and I shall be glad to receive Conventional as well as public intelligence from you. . . . I am here in the same uneasy anxious state in which I was last fall, Mrs. Jefferson could not come with me."[31]

George Mason had missed the first week of the May meeting in Williamsburg, for the representative wrote to Richard Henry Lee on May 18, after he had arrived in the Assembly:

> After a smart fit of the gout, which detained me here for the first of the session, I have at last reached this place, where, to my great satisfaction, I find the first grand point has been carried. . . . in all probability, have a thousand ridiculous and impractical proposals concerning the framework of a constitution. . . . Mr. Nelson is now on his way to Philadelphia, and will supply your place in Congress by keeping up the representation of the Colony.[32]

In a communication from Williamsburg on May 24, Edmund Pendleton revealed to Thomas Jefferson the moderate conservative party's position in the Virginia Convention:

> You'll have seen your Instructions to propose Independence and our resolutions to form a Government. The Political Cooks are busy in preparing the dish, and as Colonel Mason seems to have the Ascendancy in the great

work I have Sanguine hopes it will be framed so as to answer its end, Prosperity to the Community and Security to the Individual, but I am yet a stranger to the plan.[33]

Patrick Henry began a long letter to Richard Henry Lee written from Williamsburg on May 20:

> Ere this reaches you, our resolution for separating from Great Britain will be handed you by Colonel Nelson. The grand work of forming a constitution for Virginia is now before the convention, where your love of equal liberty and your skill in public counsels, might so eminently serve the cause of your country.
>
> I wish to divide you, and have you here. . . . A confidential acc't of the matter to Colonel Tom, desiring him to use it according to his discretion, might greatly serve the public, and vindicate Virginia from suspicions. Vigor, animation, and all the powers of mind and body, must now be summoned and collected together in one grand effort.[34]

Patrick Henry did not name Carter Braxton and Benjamin Harrison as the delegates he wished to imbue with more determination against British aggression, yet these legislators lacked the strong spirit for separation that inspired Nelson, Jefferson, the two Lees, and George Wythe. Since Thomas was cousin to both Braxton and Harrison, Henry wanted the York Town representative to reason with the two gentlemen.

Attorney Wythe had asked John Adams to set up a suitable plan of government for the states to follow, and Lee, in an April letter to Henry, had approved the form with a few changes as a practicable guide for the Virginia Convention.[35]

A pamphlet printed in Philadelphia had appeared in Williamsburg proposing a plan of government for Virginia. It was written by "A Native," but pointed to the pen of Carter Braxton whose views on the virtues of aristocratic rule were advanced. In it, a lower house of representatives would be elected by restricted voters and then it would select a governor, judges, and a treasurer. The upper senate would serve life tenure.[36]

Patrick Henry and the progressive liberals were against power by oligarchy so he opposed the proposition. Henry described the difficulty to John Adams in a letter dated May 20:

> My most esteemed republican form has many and powerful enemies. A silly thing, published in Philadelphia, by a native of Virginia, has just made its appearance here . . . .
>
> His reasons upon the distinctions between private and public virtues, are weak, shallow, and evasive and the whole performance an affront and disgrace to this country; . . .
>
> Before this reaches you the resolutions for finally separating from Great Britain will be handed to Congress by Colonel Nelson. I put up with it in

the present form for the sake of unanimity. 'Tis not quite so pointed as I could wish.[37]

Henry and Lee both favored consolidating foreign alliances and establishing a confederation of the colonies before proclaiming independence.

Richard Henry Lee wrote a long letter to Edmund Pendleton on May 12 from Philadelphia:

> Before this reaches you I hope much progress will have been made toward the establishment of a wise and free government, without which neither public or private happiness or security can be long expected.[38]

Though Lee was considered a liberal and had demonstrated a progressive stand in debates against British tactics, his next remarks show his concern for moderate men in the new Virginia government:

> Would it not be well to appoint Mr. President Nelson, the first Governor if he would accept, since he possesses knowledge, experience, and has always been in a dignified position?[39]

The old guard who were not ready to relinquish political power agreed with this position, but Patrick Henry and his adherents advocated a progressive candidate for the position.

Another communication from Lee on the twenty-eighth to his brother, Thomas Ludwell Lee, conveyed some important information:

> Colonel Nelson is not arrived, but I suppose he will by this time Sennight, about which time I shall set out for Virginia, and after resting at home a day or two, will attend the Convention at Williamsburg. The sensible and spirited resolves of my Countrymen on the 15th has gladdened the heart of every friend of human nature in this place, and it will have a wonderful effect on the misguided Councils of these proprietary Colonies.[40]

According to the official record, Nelson arrived in Philadelphia and presented the resolution on independence from the Virginia Convention to Congress on May 27.[41] (Perhaps Lee misdated his letter of the twenty-eighth or continued the correspondence afterwards without correction.)

The resolute patriots of Virginia had voted on the issue of independence and sent Thomas Nelson to the Congress with the draft to direct their delegates "to propose to that respectable body to declare the United Colonies free and independent States."[42] Then the representatives in the Old Dominion began to prepare a document to express the fundamental principles of political freedom and to formulate a constitution for the evolving Commonwealth.

George Mason meditated upon the proposition in the evenings, his portly frame leaning toward the table, his keen black eyes scanning the sentences that flowed from his pen.[43]

Edmund Randolph recorded the developments through the June days citing the parliamentarians' steadfast purpose: ". . . a perpetual standard should be erected, around which the people might rally. . . . Many projects of a Bill of Rights and Constitution" were drafted.[44]

By June 12, the Virginians advanced a second significant step toward freedom for the individual when the Declaration of Rights received the support of every representative. The basic principles of democracy and the essence of individual rights permeate its passages with the guarantee of government to protect its people:

> That all Men are by Nature equally free and independent, and have certain inherent Rights, of which, when they enter into a State of Society, they cannot, by any Compact, deprive or divest their Posterity; namely, the Enjoyment of Life and Liberty, with the means of acquiring and possessing property, and pursuing and obtaining Happiness and Safety.[45]

Provisions were set forth for separate legislative, executive, and judicial powers, for free elections, taxation by consent, a well-regulated militia, judgment by jury for civil and criminal cases, and freedom of the press. Then the democractic compact concluded with a caution:

> That no free Government, or the blessings of Liberty, can be preserved to any People but by a firm Adherence to Justice, Moderation, Temperance, Frugality, and Virtue, and by frequent Recurrences to fundamental Principles.[46]

The document comprised the fundamental laws of a democractic form of government and eleven years later became the basis of the Bill of Rights for the Constitution of the United States.

Jefferson, intensely interested in what occurred at the Convention, yearned to have his democratic concepts considered and confided to Nelson:

> It is a work of the most interesting nature, and such as every individual would wish to have his voice in. It is the whole object of the present controversy; for should a bad government be instituted for us in the future, it had been as well to have accepted at first the bad one offered to us from beyond the water without the risk and expense of contest.[47]

He felt that the legislators in the Convention should not draft a permanent constitution at that time but should elect special representatives to do so. Jefferson persuaded Edmund Randolph to present his objections, but the delegates decided that if they had the power to declare independence, they had the authority to adopt a constitution, which they did on June 29, 1776. This constitution was the first written instrument ever formed by an independent state.[48]

The election of the first executive for the Commonwealth brought forth the partisan factions of the Old Dominion. Tidewater conservatives led by Edmund Pendleton persuaded Thomas Nelson, Tom's uncle, to run for the post. He had served as Secretary since 1743 and as President of the Council and acting Governor after the desertion of Lord Dunmore.[49]

Representatives of the upper region, anxious to change the aristocratic control, chose popular radical Patrick Henry. The constituents of the Convention chose a Governor on the same day that they adopted a constitution. Aging Secretary Nelson received forty-five votes; one ballot was cast for John Page; Patrick Henry polled sixty votes and became the first Governor of the Commonwealth.[50]

Not happy with Henry, the old-guard gentry reacted with caustic verbal and written comments. Landon Carter recorded in his diary Wednesday, July 3, 1776, that at the Court House meeting on Monday, "Mr. Page there gave me an account that Pat. Henry was chosen Governor. . . . I see and condemn, but as the multitude of my city has done it, I say nothing but can't admire the choice."[51]

On this same date another opponent observed, "At a time when men of known integrity and sound understanding are most necessary they are rejected and men of shallow understanding fill the most important posts in our country. What but inevitable ruin can be the consequence of this?"[52]

Secretary Nelson was selected to serve as one of the eight Councilors to assist and advise the Governor, but he declined the position on account of his age. At sixty, having spent more than half his life serving his Colony, he was ready to retire. Sons of the old oligarchy chosen for the Council included John Page, Jr., and John Blair; Edmund Randolph was elected Attorney General.[53]

The deliberating body decided to reduce to five the number of delegates from the new Commonwealth to the Congress; on June 20, George Wythe, Thomas Nelson, Jr., Richard Henry Lee, Thomas Jefferson, and Francis Lightfoot Lee were elected representatives. They dropped Carter Braxton and Benjamin Harrison whose viewpoints were too conservative for the militant members of the Convention.[54]

While the representatives at Williamsburg were setting up a state government, Lord Dunmore was still cutting a wide swath in the waters of the Chesapeake during the warm June days. Since some of his ships had sailed up the Potomac River, reports reached the delegates that the ex-governor was plotting to seize Mrs. Washington and devastate Mount Vernon and

Gunston Hall. After the danger subsided, George Mason informed his friend and neighbor General Washington about his fear and action in the situation:

> Dunmore has come and gone, and left us untouched except by alarm. I sent my family many miles in the back country, and advised Mrs. Washington to do likewise as a prudential movement. At first she said, "No; I will not desert my post"; but she finally did so with reluctance, rode only a few miles, and plucky little woman as she is, stayed away only one night.[55]

Dunmore had anchored the British flagships off Gwynn's Island and had built a barricade of breastworks on the 2000-acre area. He crowed that he could crush any "crickets" sent against him although his 500-man force was diminished every day from disease and death that ravaged the ranks.

Brigadier General Andrew Lewis accepted the assignment to oust the official and marched several hundred militia to the margin of the mainland in July erecting emplacements with several cannon at strategic sites. Lewis had reason to despise Dunmore since the bitter battle at Point Pleasant when the Governor and his forces failed to appear to fight against the Indians. On July 8, Commander Lewis stepped up to the eighteen-pound cannon to fire the first volley that struck its target by blasting Dunmore's ship. A second shot smashed into the quarters and killed three sailors and a third ball crashed into the cabin hitting Dunmore in the leg, breaking his valuable china collection and causing the Lord to cry, "Good God! that ever I should come to this!" The last royal executive of Virginia hoisted sail and escaped to New York.[56]

◆　　◆　　◆

When Thomas Nelson, Jr., arrived in Philadelphia the last of May and presented his dispatch on independence from Virginia to the Congress, the delegates were discussing the disastrous defeat of the American army at Quebec. The investigating committee had returned in early June with a report of "an Army broken and disheartened, half of it under inoculation . . . many great abuses . . . shocking mismanagement."[57]

General Washington had received the calamitous news of the Canadian campaign at his headquarters in New York. Congress called in the Commander-in-Chief for a conference on the military crisis, and Washington rode into Philadelphia on May 23, after a two-day trip. (Mrs. Washington had preceded him to the Quaker City to be inoculated for smallpox.)[58]

Despite defeat, the army committee, with the Commander-in-Chief's counsel, determined to continue the contest. Approximately 30,000 militia were to be recruited for service until December 1 with the general apportionment of sending 6,000 men to reinforce the garrison on Richlieu River in Canada; 13,000 soldiers to serve under Washington to defend New York;

and 10,000 troops to compose a "Flying Camp" of regiments held in reserve.[59]

Doubtless Colonel Nelson had some conversation with his cousin Washington before the general departed for New York on June 4. When the men were in a hurry, they patronized Fountain Tavern just across the street from the State House; with more leisure, they gathered at the fashionable City Tavern on Market Street. The Bunch of Grapes Tavern was also a popular gathering place for the patriots. Nelson could report to Washington about the heated debates and the unanimous resolution in Virginia for independence. The general was gratified that his Colony had come to this conclusion for he was convinced, "We have nothing more to expect from the justice of Great Britain . . . ."[60]

The Commander-in-Chief and the Congressman were well aware that the King and his subservient cabinet had purchased mercenary soldiers from six German principalities.

Washington would always have worries about expiring enlistments, but the British government also had its military headaches. The monarch and his ministers had discovered that Englishmen were reluctant to battle Americans. Lord Effingham, Lord Keppel, and General Amherst refused to fight the rebels. British fighting forces were spread on foreign fields and many men were needed to crush the rebellion of the colonies. King George III asked Catharine the Great of Russia for her experienced troops, but the Empress turned a deaf ear to the British entreaty. Nearly thirty thousand soldiers were eventually sent by German princes who wanted British gold. Since the bulk of almost 17,000 soldiers came from Hesse-Cassel, the term Hessian was applied for all the alien units. When the parent country bought foreign troops to quell her progeny in the family quarrel, the breach was only broadened. Gentlemen with sentimental attachment for the royal regime were disenchanted, and men who were trying to steer a middle course swerved toward separation.[61]

The burning issue of independence engaged the thoughts and engulfed the talk of all the delegates in Philadelphia during the hot July days. Crowds of Congressmen gathered in groups outside the State House in the open courtyard to thrash out the pros and cons of the thorny topic.[62]

Nelson, Jefferson, Wythe, and the two Lees agreed that declaring for independence was simply enforcing a fact that already existed. The staunch support of these patriots prompted Elbridge Gerry to exclaim, "Virginia always depended upon; as so fine a spirit prevails among them that, unless you send some of your cool patriots among them, they may be for declaring Independence before Congress is ready."[63]

Thomas Nelson, Jr., observed the reaction of conservatives to the disturbing document he had brought from Virginia. The draft for independence had lain on the table ten days. Some merely glanced gingerly at the paper while other representatives read the resolution meticulously and pondered its meaning. John Dickinson was determined to postpone consideration of the proposal and could count on Robert Livingston of New York and Edward Rutledge of South Carolina to help him to delay the vote.[64]

On Friday, June 7, the representatives ranged around the green-covered tables, settling down for a routine session, when Richard Henry Lee rose to speak. A special silence pervaded the room and all eyes looked toward the tall legislator from Virginia who gestured so gracefully, his crippled left hand covered in black silk. The hall resounded as the orator offered a resolution with three propositions:

> That these United States are, and of a right ought to be free and indepen-
> dent States, that they are absolved from all allegiance to the British Crown,
> and that all political connection between them and the State of Great Brit-
> ain is, and ought to be totally dissolved.
> That it is expedient forthwith to take the most effectual measures for
> forming foreign alliances.
> That a plan of Confederation be prepared and transmitted to the respec-
> tive Colonies for their consideration and approbation.[65]

The bombshell had burst, but decision on the question was delayed, so the factions gathered their forces. All day Saturday until seven o'clock in the evening debates ensued.

John Dickinson, as usual, was the member in the forefront of the fight resisting the measure. He contended lack of military might and foreign friends were cogent factors to consider. Though "slender as a reed" and "pale as ashes," according to John Adams, the representative from Pennsylvania reasoned that the move was premature and pled persuasively for its postponement. Declaring that Delaware, Maryland, New Jersey, New York, Pennsylvania, and South Carolina were "not yet ripe" for the resolution, and indeed the delegates of these six colonies had been instructed to defer independence, Dickinson was strongly supported in his claims by his conservative Pennsylvania colleagues, Robert Morris and James Wilson.[66]

Morris had been born in England although he had lived thirty of his forty-three years in the colonies. The prosperous Philadelphia merchant had made his mark in the Congress by his financial advice. Contending that the issue of independence was presented at an improper time, he would be absent with Dickinson a month later when the draft of the Declaration of Independence was brought before the body. The outspoken financier finally signed the document; John Dickinson never did.[67]

Opposition to independence was offered by another Pennsylvania statesman. Thirty-three-year-old James Wilson, born in Scotland and an able attorney, was well versed on the question. Six months earlier the Congress had asked Wilson to draw up a draft relating to independence, and he had done so, but his work had been eclipsed by the eloquence and emotional appeal of the pamphlet "Common Sense" printed in January.[68]

Thirty-year-old Robert Livingston of New York, a direct descendant of Lord Livingston, once guardian to Mary, Queen of Scots, took the conservative side with his friend from South Carolina, twenty-six-year-old Edward Rutledge. Considering the proposal not only precipitous but also ridiculous, Rutledge moved to postpone the vote until July 1, and the motion passed. On June 8 he had written John Jay to hurry back from New York to help block the measure: "I trust you will contribute in a considerable degree to effect the Business. . . . Clinton has abilities but is silent. . . . Floyd, Wisner, Lewis & Alsop tho good men, never quit their chairs."[69]

The conservatives were pleased about the postponement, but the progressive faction also scored success by proposing the appointment of a committee to draft a declaration of independence just in case Congress approved the measure; their proposal passed. Massachusetts and Virginia advanced arguments for immediate adoption of the resolve. Although its foes had presented some forceful points, the proponents still had their sights on the goal of representative government and were ready to launch the ship of state.

Two of the rebels were early risers. John Adams rose at four o'clock to write reports, carry on correspondence, and record his impressions of the people and proceedings. While his green case was crammed with communications, Sam Adams tore up his notes with his trembling, palsied hands. As the organizer of the first Committee of Correspondence, the gray-eyed propagandist had penned hundreds of letters to rally men toward revolution. Politics was his profession. Residents in Philadelphia recognized the cousins as they walked toward their rooming house near Arch and First streets. Forty-year-old John, short and stubby, was trailed by fifty-three-year-old Sam, seedy, with graying hair, and seamed face. Their determination was matched by that of Virginia's delegates, who dreamed of a great democracy evolving from the Thirteen Colonies.[70]

Forty-four-year-old Richard Henry Lee had offered the motion for independence and by his eloquent oratory had emphasized the need to cement foreign alliances, form a confederation of the colonies, and absolve allegiance to the Crown. Who could deny that the King had denounced his colonial subjects, purchased mercenaries to crush the rebellion, and proclaimed a policy of complete conquest? Lee often stated British tyranny was still hanging over their heads like a flaming sword.[71]

George Wythe argued that independence already existed since forces were in the field and American lives had been lost in conflict.[72]

The supporters *for* independence stressed that *no Assemblyman* had argued *against* the fact that the colonies had just cause for separation. Nelson and other merchant members felt that restraints on trade and taxation without consent had brought them to the breaking point.

Political contriving played a part in the selection of the drafting commit-tee. Lee was overlooked because the conservatives suspected him. The pro-gressives hated Harrison, so Thomas Jefferson became the compromise choice. On June 11, John Adams, Benjamin Franklin, Roger Sherman of Connecticut, Robert Livingston of New York, and Thomas Jefferson were selected for the task. It was a competent committee. The men met for dis-cussions, jotted down ideas, and then asked Jefferson to put the paper in proper form.[73]

Thomas Nelson did not see much of his friend during these last days of June, for he spent much of his time bent over his especially-built mahogany writing box in the two-room suite on Seventh and Market streets. He was to draw many ideas from his reading of liberal philosophers and his own reflec-tions on government.

Congress continued to advance as though the issue of independence would become a certainty and appointed two committees on Wednesday, June 12, that related to the resolution. The record reads "That the commit-tee to prepare and digest the form of a confederation, to be entered into between these Colonies, consist of a member from each Colony."[74]

Thomas Nelson, Jr., was chosen to represent Virginia, and the list also included Josiah Bartlett of New Hampshire, Samuel Adams of Massachu-setts, Stephen Hopkins of Rhode Island, Roger Sherman of Connecticut, Robert Livingston of New York, John Dickinson of Pennsylvania, Thomas McKean of Delaware, Thomas Stone of Maryland, Joseph Hewes of North Carolina, Edward Rutledge of South Carolina, and Button Gwinnett of Georgia.[75]

The lukewarm legislators of New Jersey were overlooked but on July 15, the patriot representatives of New Jersey dismissed the Loyalist Governor, William Franklin, and elected different delegates a few days later.[76]

Thomas Nelson surveyed some of the statesmen serving with him on the Committee of Confederation and attempted to assess their position. Never doubting that independence must be declared, Nelson was aligned with the arch rebel Sam Adams, the supreme strategist in pulling political strings.

On June 17, Josiah Bartlett summed up the situation in a letter to former colleague, John Langdon, who was fighting with the colonial forces:

> Affair of Confederation of the Colonies is now unanimously agreed on by all the members of the Colonies. . . . As it is a very important business, & some difficulties have arisen, I fear it will take some time before it is finally settled. The affair of voting; whether by Colony as at present or otherwise, is not declared and causes some warm disputes![77]

There was no doubt that Dickinson was determined to delay the vote and that he would be backed by Livingston and Rutledge. Delaware's Colonel McKean could be counted on the affirmative side. Stephen Hopkins, though sixty-nine, was a liberal. Nelson knew that Roger Sherman, despite his questions, was ready to support the resolve. Joseph Hewes of North Carolina had been added to the Treasury Committee as had Thomas McKean so Thomas knew both of them better than some others. Hewes, one of the two bachelors in Congress, had overcome his previous doubts and now supported separation. His worries were evident in his epistles:

> I see no prospect of a reconciliation. Nothing is left but to fight it out, and for this we are not well provided, having but a little Ammunition, no Arms, no money, nor are we unanimous in our Councils. We do not treat each other with that decency and respect that was observed heretofore. Jealousies, ill-natured observations and recriminations take the place of reason and Argument.[78]

As the controversy continued, Pennsylvania asserted itself and agreed to the issue of independence. Delaware instructed its delegates to declare in favor, and Maryland parted with its popular Governor, Sir Robert Eden, with compunction. Samuel Chase and Charles Carroll, having returned from their mission to Canada, met with the county committees in Maryland, and Chase wrote numerous letters to various leaders. He finally announced Maryland's approving vote to John Adams: "Our people have fire if not smothered."[79] Adams responded by changing his mind about Chase, declaring he no longer was so "violent, boisterous, tedious upon frivolous points. . . . [but was] active, eloquent, spirited, and capable."[80]

In spite of the second defeat in Canada, Congress intended to pursue the contest to win the province from the Crown. General David Wooster was charged with the failure of the campaign, but that was not his only crime, according to his critics. A tale was circulated that the Connecticut commander had demanded the stripping, tarring, and feathering of a camp follower and then had the woman and the guilty soldier driven about in a cart with directions that the accused couple must continue their embraces in public.[81]

Horatio Gates, a former British officer living in Berkeley County, Virginia, who had sided with the colonists and was serving as adjutant general for the Continental army, became the new commander for the Canadian campaign. According to some delegates, their decision on June 17 vested the general with dictatorial powers.[82]

Thomas Jefferson showed his general draft of the Declaration of Independence to his fellow committee members during the last days of June. The rangy Virginian visited Dr. Franklin in his Market Street residence where the wise philosopher recommended a few minor changes. "We hold these truths to be sacred and undeniable" became "self-evident." The phrase "equal creation" was improved to read "that all Men are created equal." Franklin suggested that "from preservation of Life and Liberty and the pursuit of happiness" should read "that among these are Life, Liberty, and the Pursuit of Happiness." The seventy-year-old statesman was impressed, however, by the elevating style and inspired ideals of Jefferson.[83]

John Adams was equally impressed with the document. Although like Jefferson he was opposed to slavery, he, too, knew that the Southern representatives would offer objections to an abolition statement so, after making a few minor changes, Adams vowed to Jefferson that he would stand behind the manifesto.[84]

Roger Sherman, attired in his plain Puritan dress, meditated on the noble concepts in the document and was so moved by its lofty sentiments he made no suggestions.[85]

Robert Livingston, the fifth member of the drafting committee, had proclaimed that a declaration of independence was premature and presumptuous. The aristocratic young lawyer left Philadelphia and returned to his palatial residence in New York without reading it. The document was placed on the table at the front of the assembly room on Friday, June 28. Jefferson, who was seated with Dr. Franklin at the side, scrutinized the faces of his colleagues as they read their copies. Gestures by the gentlemen and overheard snatches of conversation intimated to the author, who was sensitive to criticism, that the instrument, if adopted, would be cut by the Congress. (During these anxious days, Jefferson went on a buying spree. He bought a special map, some spurs, a thermometer, a new straw hat that cost ten shillings, and seven pairs of gloves for his wife, Patty.)[86]

Tom polled his cousins on the declaration with predictable results. Braxton complained he was being lugged into independence and wanted to wait until the British peace commissioners arrived.[87] Benjamin Harrison was hesitant because he believed a confederation should be formed first and foreign alliances secured before separating irrevocably from Great Britain. Francis Lightfoot Lee and his brother Richard Henry (who had left on the thirteenth to attend the Virginia Assembly) were strong for severing all ties with England.

On Monday, July 1, as the delegates arrived at the State House, Jefferson recorded the temperature at 81.5 degrees just before nine in the morning.[88] President Hancock and Secretary Thomson were in their places at the front of the room as the clock in the tower chimed nine. The chairman banged his gavel, and the humming of the statesmen stopped.

A request by General Washington for additional reinforcements to resist an attack was granted. Joseph Hewes, however, was not the only member who realized that it was "a melancholy fact that half our men, cannon, muskets, powder, clothes, and the rest, is to be found nowhere but on paper."[89]

After routine reports were read and the representatives had returned from the midday recess, the chairman turned the chair over to Benjamin Harrison, and the House was convened into the Committee of the Whole.

Thomas Nelson sensed that the differences of the two opposing leaders on the question went deeper than just political opinions. John Dickinson hadn't spoken to John Adams in the year since Adams's statement criticizing Dickinson had been intercepted by the British and published in their press.

Dickinson rose and delivered a long discourse against declaring for independence. The time was not ripe and the rash move would result in many commonwealths, causing a calamitous civil war, the Pennsylvania lawyer pointed out.[90]

Nelson observed that the Congressmen fidgeted and were not so attentive as the sultry afternoon wore on and the recital continued. His cousin Ben Harrison shifted his bulk in the chair and mopped perspiration from his face. By now, he and Carter Braxton knew that the Virginia voters had not re-elected them as representatives to the Congress.[91] William Ellery from Rhode Island was sketching caricatures of his colleagues. Colonel McKean was restless and praying that the express rider could reach Caesar Rodney in time for the Delaware delegate to return to cast a vote in favor of the resolution. Jefferson sat on the right side of the hall by the window to catch the light as he took notes on his portable writing case. Dr. Franklin was dozing. Sam Adams was worried, and old Stephen Hopkins tapped his cane with impatience. John Adams listened attentively to the conservative floor leader as he knew it was his task to oppose him by advancing the affirmative position for the patriot cause.[92]

One fortunate incident had occurred in the afternoon. The doorkeeper had just handed Adams the approval of the Maryland assembly that had arrived by special courier from Samuel Chase.[93]

While Dickinson droned on, the blue sky turned black and the clouds burst with piercing thunder and peppering rain. Pages hurried to pull down windows and light candles. Dickinson concluded his remarks.

Now it was up to John Adams to rouse the representatives to vote for independence. He was not so polished a speaker as his Philadelphia opponent, but his feelings were fervent and his convictions sincere. The arch rebel reviewed the reasons for an immediate declaration of independence. As he later recalled, "nothing was said but what had been repeated and hackneyed in that room a hundred times over for the six months past."[94] The Continental army was in the field; the King, ignoring their petitions had denounced the Americans as traitors and had transported thousands of red-coat troops and hired Hessians to crush the rebellion. If the colonies would declare independence, foreign allies would come to their assistance, Adams alleged. The voice of the people cried for freedom and the world was waiting for the colonies to cast off the shackling chains of oppression.

Before Adams summed up his speech, three new representatives from New Jersey appeared in the Assembly, the Reverend John Witherspoon, Judge Richard Stockton, and Francis Hopkinson. Though rain-drenched, these delegates desired to hear a review of his presentation. Adams was averse to a repetition of the arguments as it was late and the legislators were weary, but the Presbyterian preacher pressed the spokesman so the rebel leader gave a resumé of the points of separation, and ended his summary with an emotional appeal:

> All that I am, and all that I hope for in this life, I stake on our cause. For me, the die is cast. Sink or swim, live or die, to survive or perish with my country, that is my unalterable resolution.[95]

There were smiles of satisfaction from the progressive patriots and surprise on the faces of the conservative colleagues when the trial vote on the resolution for independence, confederation, and foreign alliances was taken. The representatives of New Hampshire, Massachusetts, Rhode Island, Connecticut, New Jersey, Maryland, Virginia, North Carolina, and Georgia voted *aye*. New York abstained awaiting instructions. Pennsylvania and South Carolina cast *no*, and the two delegates from Delaware were divided; George Read was opposed while Thomas McKean voted in favor. At the end of the nine-hour session young Ned Rutledge astonished the delegates by proposing a postponement until the next day suggesting that South Carolina might swing to the affirmative side.[96]

Tuesday, July 2, dawned with a gray dullness. A brisk rain blew as the summer storm continued from the night before.

When Tom hurried down the rain-soaked street toward the State House, he noticed the mud-spattered carriages of the representatives rolling along the thoroughfare. President Hancock rode like a prince in his great coach from the Widow Graydon's mansion. He was a merchant prince; some folk said the richest man in New England.

The crusading Adams's cousins had only a few blocks to walk from Arch Street and both looked primed for battle. Sam wore the black broadcloth suit his Boston friends had bought for him, and John had just had his hair cut. Thomas Jefferson lacked sleep. He had sat up late in the night writing letters, one in answer to a communication received on Monday, which revealed his concern over his re-election to the Congress. He stated that "The omission of Harrison and Braxton, and my being next to the lag, gives me some alarm."[97]

Nelson had no such fear as he had been second in total votes for Congress following George Wythe and before Richard Henry Lee. Jefferson was fourth, and Francis Lightfoot Lee was the fifth delegate elected from the Old Dominion. Jefferson had also made copies of his draft to send to Patrick

Henry, Lee, and Wythe who were in Virginia at the Convention at Williamsburg.[98]

In the lobby Nelson doubtless spoke to the newly arrived group from New Jersey. He knew John Witherspoon, who had visited Virginia in 1769, and was glad to meet Judge Stockton, who was strong for separation. A young man closely associated with the New Jersey members paused to greet them. Just six months before, Dr. Benjamin Rush had married Julia Stockton, the judge's daughter. Upstairs the liberal contingent from Pennsylvania was electing Dr. Rush a delegate. The following week he would present his credentials, but the young physician now hurried out to attend to his numerous patients.[99]

Colonel McKean was waiting impatiently for Caesar Rodney. As soon as the Delaware rebel had received the message, he had rushed into the thunderstorm and hurried his roan mare over the muddy roads into the night, then mounted a fresh horse the next morning and rode on toward Philadelphia. The radical delegates employed delaying tactics while they waited for Rodney, requesting the Secretary to read again the resolution that Nelson had brought from the Virginia Convention. Finally, the legislators could detain no longer so the Secretary was directed to call the roll for the vote. The representatives from New Hampshire, New Jersey, Massachusetts, Connecticut, and Rhode Island voted *aye* for independence. As they had the day before, New York delegates abstained. Pennsylvania had only five delegates present since John Dickinson and Robert Morris had absented themselves. Charles Humphrey and Thomas Willing voted against while Dr. Franklin and James Wilson voted in favor. John Morton broke the tie when he stood to support the resolution and carried Pennsylvania for the affirmative column. The rebels looked up with relief as Caesar Rodney, his green scarf covering the cancer on his face and his clothes dripping wet, walked into the room in time to cast a decisive vote. (Delaware then had two votes for and one against.)[100]

Virginians Thomas Nelson, Jr., Thomas Jefferson, and Francis Lightfoot Lee gladly called out their aye votes. Then the delegates from Maryland, North Carolina, South Carolina, and Georgia swung their states in support. Twelve colonies had declared for independence. Adjournment was quick and laughter broke the strain, with hand clasps and back slapping adding to the exultation.

John Adams was anxious to convey the tidings to his wife, Abigail:

> The second day of July, 1776, will be the most memorable epocha in the history of America. I am apt to believe it will be celebrated by succeeding generations as the great anniversary Festival. It ought to be commemorated as the day of deliverance, by solemn acts of devotion to God Almighty. It ought to be solemnized with bonfires and illuminations from one end of this continent to the other, from this time forward, forevermore."[101]

On Wednesday, July 3, Secretary Thomson was directed to read the complete draft of the declaration before the assembled delegates, but two more hectic and hot days of debate followed before the document was finally adopted. The full title, "A Declaration by the Representatives of the United States of America in General Congress Assembled" had a grand ring and especially gratified the progressive rebels like John Adams who had struggled to have *States* substituted for the term *Colonies*.[102]

Versatile Francis Hopkinson, just arrived in the Congress from New Jersey, was gratified since his essay "A Prophecy" had predicted that independence would be declared. As the grievances against the royal government were being read, he had reason to recall the brush-off the British had given him a decade before when he was in England. Though recommended by Franklin and related to Lord North by marriage, Hopkinson had not received the political post he sought. Now as a constituent of the revolutionary Congress, the thirty-eight-year-old statesman scanned his associates and drew pen portraits of the delegates during the two days of controversial debate on the draft. He also responded to the request of General Washington to draw a pattern for a permanent American flag.[103]

Tom, like his associates, was anxious to push through the preliminaries on Thursday, July 4, and move on to the principal proceeding of approving and adopting the Declaration of Independence.

Members of Congress were disgruntled that the New York delegates were holding back, waiting on instructions. A British fleet of more than a hundred ships surrounded Staten Island. General Washington lacked soldiers and supplies, and the Tories were active in the area. The Commander-in-Chief had communicated about the laxness of the provincial leaders to President Hancock: "Subject is delicate . . . we may therefore have [we] internal as well as external enemies to contend with."[104]

When Thomas Nelson read the preamble to the Declaration of Independence, he thrilled at the grandeur of Jefferson's style. The natural rights of mankind were well-emphasized as the impelling reason to break the old political bonds and form a new government:

> When, in the Course of human Events, it becomes necessary for one People to dissolve the political Bands which have connected them with another, and to assume among the Powers of the Earth, the separate and equal Station to which the Laws of Nature's God entitled them, a decent Respect to the Opinions of Mankind requires that they should declare the Causes which impel them to Separation.

The York Town representative read the second paragraph, with its delineation of the relation of men to government:

> We hold these truths to be self-evident, that all Men are created equal,

that they are endowed by their Creator with certain unalienable Rights, that among these are Life, Liberty, and the Pursuit of Happiness—That to secure these Rights, Governments are instituted among Men, deriving their just Powers from the Consent of the Governed, laying its Foundation on such Principles, and organizing its Powers in such Form, as to them shall seem most likely to effect their Safety and Happiness.

Then he read the long list of grievances against the King. Though the colonists had sent countless protests to Parliament concerning injustices, the author concentrated on the crimes of the Crown in his indictment of George III.

The Congressmen trimmed the condemnation of slave traffic since they concluded that the issue was out of focus for the document. They eliminated some of the accusations casting George III as the chief criminal. References to the Scotch mercenaries were also removed.

During the humid days of July 3 and 4, when the changes were being made in the document, wise Dr. Franklin leaned toward his young colleague and told a tale of human foibles to console the author, but only with time did Jefferson see the humor. He never admitted, even in old age, that the additions and omissions improved the declaration. Yet a minute comparison of the draft and the final copy reveals that the revisions were justified. Strict grammarians changed *it's* that Jefferson used for the possessive *its*, started sentences with capital letters, and corrected his poor spelling.[105]

The three premises presented in the original motion for independence were included by the Congress: absolving allegiance to Britain, forming foreign alliances, and setting up a system of confederation for the colonies.

Roger Sherman moved that the final, corrected form of the document be read in its entirety to the delegates. Then late in the afternoon of July 4, the secretary was directed to call the roll of delegates to vote on the declaration.

Thomas Nelson listened intently and looked at his fellow legislators as they stood to cast their votes. His colleague on committees, Dr. Josiah Bartlett of New Hampshire, had said it was a "good document," and he was the first to vote in the affirmative for adoption. Next came the three militants from Massachusetts, Samuel Adams, John Adams, and Robert Treat Paine, who cried out loud ayes. Their fourth member from the Bay Colony, Elbridge Gerry, was absent on this Thursday but became a Signer. Sixty-nine-year-old Stephen Hopkins and his forty-eight-year-old fellow legislator, William Ellery, stood for Rhode Island. Four constituents from Connecticut concurred: Roger Sherman, Samuel Huntington, William Williams, and Oliver Wolcott.

The five new radical representatives from New Jersey were anxious to vote *aye* for independence: Judge Richard Stockton, Reverend John Witherspoon, Francis Hopkinson, John Hart, and Abraham Clark. All five later suffered from British subjection.

The four representatives from New York, Francis Lewis, William Floyd, Lewis Morris, and Philip Livingston had to remain silent again, but by July 9 their Assembly approved independence and the express arrived in Philadelphia on July 15 with the solemn commitment.

The Pennsylvania delegates had been divided in their stand on the measure. James Wilson had objected to the term "Scotch mercenaries," but the lawyer pamphleteer had overcome his feelings of opposition to vote for independence. Benjamin Franklin took no part in the debate on the floor but had worked privately for passage. After John Morton wrestled with his conscience and broke the deadlock on July 2, he supported the motion, but his family and friends shunned him for the decision.

The Maryland men had been rebellious against the especial privileges of the proprietary type of government in their colony. The extensive efforts of Samuel Chase and Charles Carroll of Carrollton, scion of a ten-thousand-acre estate and called the richest man in America, had pulled the people of Maryland toward popular rights. William Paca followed the lead of Chase, a lifelong friend, and Thomas Stone, trained in the law, was strongly allied with his associates. Chase, Carroll, and Paca were absent on July 4, but all of them arrived in time to sign the document in August.

Richard Henry Lee and George Wythe were in Virginia on the day of decision, but both men had fought on the floor for opening the ports to promote trade and to obtain commercial connections. They considered foreign aid and alliances essential factors for colonial victory. Francis Lightfoot Lee did not engage in debate, but he was in favor of independence. The philosopher-patriot Thomas Jefferson, with his deep conviction about the natural rights of man, had denounced the despotism of royal rule. Inspired by the writings of John Locke, he had a vision of freedom for all mankind.

Thomas Nelson was a man of action, audacious in efforts to advance the colonial cause. Forthright in his fight against aggression, he had alarmed his friends when he proclaimed that his "trade might perish," but if any British troops landed on the shores of York County, he intended to "summon the militia and drive the invaders into the sea!"[106] The fervent Virginian was proud to cast a vigorous voice vote in favor of independence.

Benjamin Harrison and Carter Braxton, reluctant rebels from Virginia, even reactionary to the surging sentiment rising for separation, signed the document in August before leaving for Virginia.

Joseph Hewes had startled the statesmen three weeks before by his dramatic shift for independence and the lone legislator from North Carolina stood again to call out *aye*. His two associates, William Hooper and John Penn, were absent on July 4, but they arrived later to become Signers.

South Carolina's four delegates were aristocrats, Cambridge-educated, from large plantations. Family prestige had pulled them into public service. Thomas Lynch, Jr., and Arthur Middleton succeeded their fathers in the

Congress. Thomas Heyward had replaced the fiery Christopher Gadsen who was serving his state as colonel of the First Regiment. Edward Rutledge, acknowledged leader of the moderate legislators, had argued against independence; his brother John had left the Congress to serve South Carolina as provisional Governor. Only after the indictment on slavery was stricken from the declaration did Rutledge lead the South Carolina delegation to support the document. Middleton, absent July 4, signed later in the summer.

The Georgia constituents serving in the Second Continental Congress were transplanted citizens of the thirteenth colony just as were the three delegates from North Carolina.

Georgia had no representation at the First Continental Congress and the colony had refused to adopt the Articles of Association embargo on English goods. Dr. Lyman Hall, who had been born in Connecticut and had a degree from Yale, had settled at Sunbury, in St. George's Parish, Georgia. The minister-physician fought for the measure and persuaded his parish to sever trade relations with Britain. When he appeared in Congress in May 1775, as a delegate from the county rather than the colony, the statesmen were in a quandary over the singular situation. After the British armed the Indians along the Georgia borders, people swerved to the colonial cause and the provincial body in February 1776 had elected Button Gwinnett and George Walton to join Dr. Hall in Philadelphia. Button Gwinnett was influenced by Hall to favor independence and to become a Signer.

George Walton had been born in Virginia to poor parents and was left an orphan as a child. While working as an apprentice to a carpenter, he acquired some education. Through ability and with the assistance of a Georgia attorney, the ambitious man had become a lawyer and had been elected to serve in the Second Continental Congress. He had reached Philadelphia in July 1776, just in time to cast his affirmative vote on the issue of independence and to become included with the immortal fifty-six Signers of the Declaration of Independence.[107]

On this great day, the exhausted delegates desired to rush from the room but, dutifully, they stayed to resolve that the Declaration of Independence should be printed.

Secretary Thomson handed author Jefferson the corrected copy. Copies would be sent to the states, Committees of Safety, officers of the militia, and to the clergy to be read at the conclusion of divine service. A special courier would convey the document to the Commander-in-Chief at New York. Only President Hancock signed the authenticated copy attested by the signature of Secretary Thomson. The officials knew they were marked men by the British.

Printer John Dunlap spent all night struggling with the marked-up manifesto. All day Friday the printing shop hummed with the presses turning out broadsides of the Declaration of Independence. That afternoon clerks and congressmen picked up copies, and in a few days the delegates were enclosing them in envelopes sent by special couriers to officials, family, and friends.

President Hancock wrote General Washington on Saturday, July 6:

> Sir, the Congress for some Time past, have had their Attention occupied by one of the most interesting and important Subjects that could possibly come before them or any other Assembly of Men.[108]

Compared to the excited expressions of other representatives relaying the event, the report of the President was reserved and an understatement of the significant step. The Commander-in-Chief directed that the Declaration of Independence be read to the Continental army on July 9.[109] There were bells and bonfires, cheers and beating drums, and that night in New York a crowd of citizens hauled down the equestrian statue of George III. Later the four hundred pounds of lead were cast into bullets for the patriot troops.

On Monday, July 8, members of the Congress participated in a celebration to proclaim the Declaration of Independence to the people of Philadelphia. Church chimes pealed and the big Liberty bell in the State House tower rang. Dignitaries and delegates struggled up the steps of the twenty-foot high circular platform of the planetarium, about sixty feet south of the state house. Chubby John Adams puffed in the climb. He had already stated that the dais was ridiculous. Lanky Thomas Jefferson and sturdy Roger Sherman helped gouty Benjamin Franklin mount the stairs. The day was hot and humid but a crowd of patriotic citizens collected. Plain people for the most part heard the proclamation—bakers and butchers, mechanics and merchants, apprentices in leather aprons, carpenters and coopers in coarse cotton, sailors from the ships down on the docks, a sprinkling of women and children—all mingling in the yard. The Tories were not there, but at home, silent and sulking, biding their time for revenge, and the gentry of the city had gone to their grand estates in the country.[110]

The Declaration was read again in the afternoon to the regiments. The soldiers fired thirteen salutes to the states though powder was scarce. The militia marched, and with bells, bonfires, and illuminations the celebration continued into the night. The citizens pulled the symbols of royal authority from public buildings and tossed the emblems of the Crown into the fire.[111]

Thomas Nelson noted that the makeup of the Congress had changed with the climax on the issue of independence. Three of the irreconcilable constituents from Pennsylvania were gone. Although he had led the opposition to the measure, no objective person doubted the patriotism of John Dickinson. There were even genuine regrets that the able attorney had failed of re-election. Desiring to serve his country, the Quaker rebel then donned the militia uniform and as a colonel rode northward with his regiment to fight for the colonial cause.[112]

Charles Humphrey had also been replaced by the provincial Pennsylvania body. Thomas Willing, with whom Nelson had worked on the five-member committee to examine the treasury accounts, was not re-elected. He and Robert Morris, both well-to-do Philadelphia merchants, had been accused the year before by some of their associates of profiteering on gunpowder contracts. George Clymer, James Smith, George Taylor, and Dr. Benjamin Rush had been chosen as the new delegates from Pennsylvania. Joseph Alsop of New York, who believed the Tory press accounts that British peace commissioners were coming, had resigned his seat.[113]

Work was by no means over. The delegates now must design a charter for union. The committeemen were confronted by the perplexing questions pertaining to taxes and trade, representation and voting. Since Virginia was the largest and most populous state, Nelson pondered the problems, as her sacrifices would be great. The Virginia Colony not only had claims to the area across the mountains to the mighty Mississippi River but also had titles to the territory that extended to the vast northwestern region. The land controversy, type of taxation, viewpoints on voting, and kind of representation were thorny topics battled back and forth in the committee and on the floor through the sweltering weeks of summer. Distrust fostered difficulty since the smaller states feared the larger ones would smother them and usurp control.

Though the colonies had banded together under the Congress to resist British tyranny, restraints, and restrictions, the several states were setting up governments under their own constitutions. The representatives were reluctant to relinquish certain rights to central control. The lawmakers, with intense loyalties and interests were apprehensive of too much authority for a large administration. The legislators were willing to form a league of friendship, but each state would retain its "sovereignty, freedom, and independence."[114]

On July 12, just one month after the committee had been appointed to prepare a plan of confederation, however, the proposal was presented on the floor of the Congress. Debates lasted longer than the discussion on the issue of independence. A motion was passed that eighty copies be printed secretly and sent to the states to study the plan. This bit of business was about the only progress on the proposition. No representative in the summer of 1776 realized that the report would be shelved for over a year. It was November 15, 1777, before the Articles of Confederation were adopted.[115]

The doubts and disputes over the Confederation were still being discussed on Friday, August 2, when the delegates attended to the act that was considered a secondary matter by members of the Congress. The engrossed parch-

315

ment of the Declaration of Independence was ready for the representatives to sign.[116] This deed destined them to be exalted by the republic and enshrined by posterity while other officials have faded into oblivion.

These promoters of the American Revolution paid a price for their principles. They became marked men, and only those inspired by faith in their fight for freedom could have endured what ensued. Congressmen were captured, family members imprisoned, and officials made to flee as fugitives to escape the English enemy.

Sacrifice and suffering stalked the Signers throughout the colonial conflict, but not a single statesman defected on his decision.

CHAPTER SEVENTEEN

Correspondence, Celebrations, and Crises: 1776–1777

Williamsburg Celebrates Independence ✦ *Divided Families* ✦ *Nelson and News from Virginia* ✦ *Changes in Congress* ✦ *Departing Delegates* ✦ *Nelson Home and Back to Congress* ✦ *Congress Adjourns to Baltimore* ✦ *Baby Lucy Is Born* ✦ *Family Firm Closes* ✦ *Congress Again in April* ✦ *Nelson Suffers Stroke*

As each city and county along the coast received its copy of the Declaration of Independence, printed in July 1776, and delivered by skilled horsemen, each celebrated its own way.[1] The citizens of Williamsburg joined the jubilee, its Council directing printers of the various *Virginia Gazettes* to publish the Declaration and instructing the "sheriff in each county in this commonwealth proclaim the same at the door of the court house the first court day after he shall have received the same announcement."[2]

Broadsides were printed and distributed to the public. Customers and shopkeepers along Duke of Gloucester Street clutched their copies and read the stirring expressions of human freedom. Editor Purdie reported in his paper on July 26 that the "Declaration of Independence was solemnly proclaimed at the Capitol, the Court House, and the Palace, amidst the acclamation of the people, accompanied by firing of cannon and musketry, the several regiments of Continental troops having been paraded on that solemnity."[3]

Williamsburg was warm that July day with heat and humidity and the atmosphere was charged with the citizens' ardor. The sound of rifles, drums, and bells filled the air as plain folk and planters, tradesmen and tavern keepers, thronged the streets moving up the double drive under the spreading catalpa trees toward the Palace. Eyes strained to glimpse the first Governor of the Commonwealth step from his handsome house, but Governor Henry was sick at his home, Scotchtown, Hanover County where he was to remain from June 29 to the middle of September.[4]

Colonel Landon Carter despised Henry and rejoiced at the rumor of his demise. Hearing that guns had routed Dunmore's troops from Gwynn's Island and that the Governor had died, the old aristocrat recorded gleefully in his diary July 13, "We ought to look on those two joined as two glorious events. Particularly favourable by the hand of Providence."[5]

Editor Purdie stated his opinion in the August 2 *Virginia Gazette*, "We have the pleasure to inform the public, that our worthy Governor, who is now at his seat in Hanover, is so much recovered from his late severe indisposition that he walks out daily, and it is hoped will soon be able to return to . . . attend the duties of his high and important office."

Lieutenant Governor John Page presided over the Council with competence and had the able assistance of long-time legislators during Patrick Henry's six-week absence. The group could rely as well on the counsel of experienced Secretary Nelson returned to his old post on July 23.[6] The Assembly was swamped with requests. Congress required the state to bolster regiments of the flagging Continental forces with more soldiers and military supplies. The Council also had to consider the defense of its vast territory by strengthening the outposts of the frontier and fortifying the ports along its lengthy shoreline. Cannon at Gloucester and other sites were ruined by salt water since the guns had been sinking in the sand.[7]

Thomas Nelson heard about the happenings at home from family and friends and was happy to note that the name of Nelson occurred repeatedly in the public records. Just the day before the Secretary was sworn into office, Lieutenant William Nelson, of the Third Regiment, had received four pounds, ten shillings to purchase a tent for the troops.[8] It seemed unbelievable to the Secretary that his nephew was sixteen and certainly Thomas would hardly have known his baby brother, "Pin-basket Billy," as their father had called him, now grown and an officer of the militia company organized by the students of the College of William and Mary.

The Secretary's sons were occupied with military matters all through the summer season—recruiting men for the regiments and securing supplies. In June, the deputies had directed that a "Large Rifle gun" be delivered to Major William Nelson "for the use of the Seventh Regiment," and on July 30 the *Journal* listed that a warrant for "1,229 pounds, 2 shillings, and 10 pence be issued for the pay roll of the Seventh Regiment."[9]

Thomas, the Secretary's second son, was serving as captain under his brother, Major William Nelson, of the Seventh Regiment. Third son, John, had been commissioned a captain in June commanding the Sixth Troop of Horse. The authorities had allowed £750 to the cavalry unit to purchase horses, accoutrements, and 660 feet of plank to construct stalls at York Town.[10] Dixon and Hunter notified the public in their July 6 *Gazette:*

> Wanted immediately to mount the Sixth Troop, a number of Horses either Bays, Browns, Sorrels, or Chestnuts, from four to seven years old, and under 14 hands high. I'll give a good price for each, such as shall answer the Purpose they are intended for.
>
> JOHN NELSON

When the unit secured its mounts, the cavalry was a colorful group and the thud of horses' hooves, din of drums, and thump of marching feet excited the envy of the York Town boys. The classics and cyphering could not compete with the martial sounds pervading the town. Tutor Hall, at the Nelson house, sometimes let his students have a half-holiday to watch the proceedings. William celebrated his thirteenth birthday August 9, and he was beginning to feel much older than his brothers. He liked to stay at the store with his uncles, Hugh and Robert, to hear the men talking about beating the British.

There was no middle course for a man to choose in the colonial crisis. Virginia's patriots were not patient with those who vacillated and intently questioned indifferent citizens. A man was either a friend or foe. Loyalists who criticized the cause were brought before the active Committee of Safety to answer charges. The press abetted the rebels in their efforts to expose the offenders.

Lucy was distressed that dissension had divided her family and was embarrassed to read in the Pinckney *Gazette* of July 5 that Benjamin Grymes was "Accused of Toryism." Captain Gabriel Jones had complained that her uncle had spoken disrespectfully of the Convention committee and that Grymes was guilty by confession, for the complainant quoted, "That he in conversation with the said witness did say, that his nephew John Grymes was an innocent man; that he had been unjustly treated by the Committee of Safety."[11]

John was Lucy's brother and, according to Jones, her uncle had stated that the "Committee instead of suppressing riots and mobs was encouraging them. . . . Congress and Convention did nothing right—that the Convention (were a) pack of rascals."[12] John Randolph Grymes joined the Tory troops and served as major in the Queen's Rangers under Colonel John Graves Simcoe.[13]

Sometimes Lucy and her sister-in-law, Judy, Hugh's wife, discussed the divided loyalties. William Byrd, Judy's uncle, was not sympathetic to the patriot cause and was staying at Westover instead of in Williamsburg, watching and waiting for the political winds to shift while trying to survive financial adversity. The plantation owner had lost a big bay horse and offered £205 reward to any person returning the animal and five more if the thief were convicted, the amount indicating the inflationary price of the period.[14]

John Randolph, Lucy's uncle, had departed for England with his wife and daughters the previous fall; but his son Edmund had remained in Virginia to become a rebel soldier and had served in Boston as muster master for the American army. The sudden death of Peyton Randolph in October 1775, had required Edmund to return home to administer his uncle's affairs. The Attorney General had just been appointed one of the judges of the Admiralty Court. The Dixon and Hunter *Virginia Gazette* of August 9, 1776, complimented the justices on their work toward "the establishment of a government."

By the end of the month, Edmund had taken a bride:

> Marriage—Edmund Randolph, Attorney General of Virginia, to Miss Nicholas, a young lady whose amiable sweetness of disposition, joined with the finest intellectual accomplishments, cannot fail rendering the worthy man of her choice completely happy.[15]

Editor Purdie was not so effusive as the Dixon-Hunter press in his statement:

> Marriage—Edmund Randolph, Esq., Attorney General, to Miss Betsey Nicholas, second daughter of the treasurer.[16]

Lucy knew Tom would be interested in the news of the couple since the groom was her first cousin and the bride a step-cousin to Thomas. Several other announcements in the August papers attracted Tom's attention. His brother Hugh, his cousin Charles Carter of Shirley, and Henry Fitzhugh had forewarned all persons through the press against "hunting or ranging on our lands in Fauquier County, which we have found to be a practice very destructive to our flocks, sheep, cattle, etc. . . . Mr. James Collins having often trespassed is forbid doing so again at his peril."[17]

Editor Purdie, caught in the economic pinch, appealed to the public in his August 9, 1776, newspaper: "Notwithstanding several applications to customers to pay subscriptions at the end of last year, I find there are upwards of One Thousand who have never paid me a single farthing."

Newspaper columns were crowded with notices of men stating, "I intend to leave the Colony."

Checking the political news, Tom noticed that his neighbor David Jameson had been elected to serve as a Senator from the districts of Elizabeth City, Warwick, and York counties, while Dr. Corbin Griffin had become one of the delegates in the county of York.[18]

Editors voiced their personal viewpoints in the August papers; Purdie optimistically reassured readers that confidence in American arms would bring success. On August 9, 1776, his *Virginia Gazette* stated pertaining to ammunition

> We have just got a supply of 290 half barrels of gun powder and 90 stand of arms; and 436 barrels with 18 chests of arms, arrived safe some little time ago."

One week later he noted,

> From undoubted authority, we can assure the public that 15,000 wt. pure

lead have been got from our mines in the back country; which, after being cast into bullets, we hope will be unerringly directed against our enemies.

Another item that intrigued the patriot readers related to the erstwhile royal executive:

> . . . we learn that last Wednesday morning the Right Honourable Earl of Dunmore, Viscount Fincastle, and Baron Murray of Blair, Mouilli, and Tillimet, after dividing the fleet, and burning ten or a dozen vessels, took leave of the capes of Virginia, where he has; for more than twelve months past perpetrated crimes that would even have disgraced the noted BLACK BEARD.[19]

Plain folk in the taverns poked fun at the long title and guffawed about the fatuous chief as they guzzled ale.

During the long summer days, the post riders pounded the different roads from Philadelphia in all directions. These hardy men followed regular routes, often covering sixty miles from dawn to dusk, as their sturdy but swift-pacing horses sped northward to New York, Boston, or southward to Baltimore or Williamsburg. All types of correspondence crammed their saddlebags: letters to family and friends as well as messages in military code. Correspondence from the delegates of Congress crowded the mail containers. Statesmen wrote their wives about the drudgery of their days, their wearisome duties, and their desire to return home if even for a short stay.

George Wythe went home to Williamsburg in June and on the thirteenth, Richard Henry Lee wrote General Washington, "This day I sett off for Virginia."[20] The master of Chantilly escaped capture by the English enemy while at home and on July 21 advised Landon Carter of the adventure:

> Last night I was engaged with a party of militia expecting a visit from four of the enemies Ships and 3 Tenders that appeared off this house about sunset.[21]

Having attended the convention sessions in Williamsburg until the Assembly adjourned on July 5, he commented in a letter of July 6 to Samuel Adams, "Our Devil Dunmore is as he was, but we expect shortly to make him move to his quarters."[22] A month later this accomplishment had been achieved.

Francis Lightfoot Lee implored his brother to hurry back to the Congress as Carter Braxton had departed for Virginia just after the signing of the Declaration of Independence on August 2, and five members were required to maintain the state's representation.[23]

Early in August evenings, the four remaining representatives from Virginia might meet at the city's most famous restaurant, the fashionable City Tavern on Market Street chosen for its fine food and sparkling spirits. Delegates stopped there often since mail was delivered to the tavern.[24] There was no dearth of conversation among the quartet. Thomas Jefferson, reticent thus far in public, was a clever conversationalist in private. He felt disconcerted at Braxton's leave taking because it compelled him to remain longer in Philadelphia. Jefferson was worried about his wife's illness and had informed Patty that his intent was to leave for Monticello on August 11; he realized, however, that he would have to wait for the return of Colonel Lee and George Wythe.[25] Forty-two-year-old Francis "Frank" Lee was satisfied to stay in Philadelphia since his young wife, half his age at their marriage seven years earlier, was with him in the city. The couple had no children. Ben Harrison, not re-elected as a delegate to the Congress, also planned to head for home when Wythe and Richard Henry Lee returned to the city.[26] Young Tom Nelson, not quite so corpulent as his cousin Harrison, was candid and cheerful in disposition. He had made several short reports in the Congress often using similes to make a point.

The group enjoyed discussing ways for the Congress to put democratic principles into practice and knew a committee was working on a plan "to encourage Hessians and other foreigners to quit the iniquitous service."[27] The colonists had resented the Crown's hiring of mercenaries to fight against Americans and many moderate citizens had swung to the side of the colonial cause as a result of royal action. Seventeen thousand troops supplemented the royal regiments. Officials in Philadelphia were not oblivious to the fact that an ordinary hired soldier had no stake in the patriots' struggle. Therefore, the revolutionary government offered enticements to the foreigners—land grants and opportunities in various occupations.

After the British had sailed from Boston, six hundred Scottish Highlanders had arrived in the seaport city and were captured by two colonial companies. These prisoners had been parceled among the Thirteen Colonies to be absorbed in the life and activities of the citizens. Richard Henry Lee pictured a promising future for them in Virginia:

> The 217 that have fallen to our shore are distributed thro' this Colony, a few in each County, and permitted to hire themselves out to labour, thus to become Citizens of America instead of our enemies.[28]

Military matters were of foremost concern for the Congress to consider. The delegates from Virginia had been present on Thursday, August 13. The Congress authorized that the Eighth Virginia Battalion should receive retroactive pay from May 25, and the salaries for the men of the Seventh were set from June 17. The war effort was being stepped up with encouragements of retroactive pay and promotions. Since Nelson had an avid interest in military affairs, he was especially attentive to the defense act and acquainted with many officers of the Virginia companies. His two first cousins, William and Thomas, served as major and captain in the Seventh Regiment. By official order, Colonel Hugh Mercer, of the Third Battalion, was promoted to brigadier general; George Weedon was commissioned a colonel; and Alexander Spotswood was advanced to lieutenant colonel.[29]

+   +   +

As Acting Governor of Virginia through the summer months, John Page was burdened with the business of a beginning administration. He often apologized to Tom and Thomas Jefferson for not writing more often. On July 6, Page began his epistle to Jefferson with this paragraph:

> When I wrote last week to Colonel Nelson, I promised to write to both of you this Post, a circumstantial Account of the State of Things here, but the whole Week has slipt away in the Hurry of Business and I am now as much in Want of Time as ever, the post being about to set out in a few hours.[30]

The young executive described his exacting duties in his communication of July 15:

> Our Governor is still so sick that he cannot attend to Business. I am presiding member and am so pestered with Letters and answering them I have not time to add but few words more.[31]

Five days later Page wrote:

> Give my love to Nelson. Tell him I have not Time to write another Line being beset with the Governor's Business who is still unable to attend.[32]

The two Congressmen in Philadelphia eagerly exchanged items of interest from their mutual friend. The Convention in Virginia had acted with alacrity to confiscate the Porto Bello property of Lord Dunmore and had arranged for an auction to sell his slaves and personal estate. The patriots had also resolved to strike from the church litany references to the King and the royal family. The York Town legislator had probably heard Page's description of the defense problem facing his government in his statement, "Colonel Stephens is fortifying Portsmouth, but we are in want of Cannon to mount on the Works necessary to command the whole Harbour of Norfolk."[33]

Probably Jefferson also shared with Nelson a pointed remark made by Edmund Pendleton pertaining to the two representatives that had not been re-elected to the Congress. Carter Braxton and Benjamin Harrison were Nelson's cousins, and he knew the progressive faction in Virginia had defeated them both as delegates. Pendleton summed up his opinion of the vote, stating he was "not surprised when Braxton was left out" but felt that the omission was an "unmerited, cruel degradation to Colonel Harrison."[34]

On August 13, Thomas Nelson wrote to John Page a factual picture of the military situation:

> I wish I could, by this Letter confirm the report that prevailed some weeks ago, of thousands of men going into New York daily; but alas! that like most news was not above half true. We received a letter from the General yesterday, by which we find that he has not above 12,000 effective men . . . three thousand being sick and unfit for duty. . . . The militia that went from this Province . . . are deserting by companies. . . . They cannot bear the thoughts of those who are left behind, reaping all the benefit from the very extravagant price that Goods are sold at. . . .
>
> I was not very fond of the two Regiments being ordered from Virginia, because I did not think they would arrive in time to be of service to New York but when we considered that you had no great probability of an attack being made upon you and that to oppose a proposition of that kind would savor strongly of self we agreed to it.[35]

Nelson informed Page that the Committee of Safety had forwarded accounts of the Colony with a letter requesting that vouchers be sent. As the accounts were now in his possession and would remain there until the vouchers were received, the conscientious Congressman ended his letter with an urgent appeal:

> Do my Dear Sir, attend to this matter, for it is extremely disagreeable to me, to be entrusted with business and not give it that dispatch which is expected and which the notice of affairs requires. There were 200,000 dollars sent to the paymaster a fortnight ago, which I hoped has been received before this. We will endeavor to get an advance of part of the money upon account and advise you with one success, but the vouchers must be sent to us.
>
> Thos. Nelson, Jr.[36]

After the culmination of adoption and approval of the Declaration of Independence, an anticlimactic atmosphere took over Congress; absenteeism was prevalent. When the delegates had created an army and navy, they had sanctioned strict controls for the services; now they concluded its own body would benefit by more orderly conduct. Jefferson was a member of the committee that composed the rules and regulations and the report was read to the representatives: "No member to be absent without leave of House—Every person sit when not speaking—No person to walk while question putting—No person to read printed papers."[37]

Nelson no doubt smiled to recall that the new regulations would not affect Joseph Alsop, who had rattled the pages of the New York papers during the sessions. After independence had been declared, Alsop had resigned his post and left for New York. Tom wondered if the rules might prevent Francis Hopkinson from sketching portraits of the statesmen or William Ellery from scribbling epigrams or Rhode Island's Stephen Hopkins from tapping his cane so impatiently. Unlike his militant colleagues from Massachusetts, Robert Treat Paine had voiced so many objections to various measures that his cohorts called him the "Objection Maker" so his opposition would not be missed.[38]

As the August days slipped into autumn, Nelson was still calling together the committee of accounts to check drafts drawn on the treasury to pay the bills. So many delegates continued to depart during the last of the summer session that the committee had a constantly changing personnel. Wealthy Philip Livingston of New York, wary of the liberal Whigs, and George Read of Delaware, cautious and conservative, joined the group in July; and George Clymer, one of the new patriots from Pennsylvania, who exchanged his gold for Continental currency, was also appointed a member.

Thomas Nelson reported on Tuesday, August 27, when the Congress had resolved itself into the Committee of the Whole that his committee had considered the matters referred to them and made "sundry amendments to the plan of treaties." He was grateful that Richard Henry Lee, returned from Williamsburg the last of August, was appointed to the group.[39]

Jefferson left the city on September 1 to journey to Monticello and Ben Harrison also headed for home. Francis Lightfoot Lee was appointed to the Board of War on September 11 in Ben Harrison's place.[40]

Through the warm days of September, the weary members struggled with amendments to set up a system to expedite the war effort. Three times Tom reported that the committee had not come to a conclusion, but on Monday, September 16, Nelson attested that "88 battalions were to be enlisted as soon as possible," with Massachusetts and Virginia furnishing fifteen each.[41] The troops were to stay in service for the duration of the war unless discharged sooner by the Congress. Land grants were to be given the soldiers, with the states distributing disbursements. A colonel would receive 500 acres; lieutenant colonel, 450; major, 400; captain, 300; lieutenant, 200; ensign, 150; each non-commissioned officer and soldier, 100 acres. General officers for the regiments were to be appointed by the Congress but the states had the power to appoint officers for the regiments raised and to fill vacancies. The recommendation read: "Every state was to provide arms, cloathing, and every necessary for its quota of troops. The expenses of the cloathing to be deducted from the pay of the soldiers, as usual."[42]

The strain of the long sessions and the stifling humidity of summer heat had taken its toll of the Congressmen; several were sick and others were departing from Philadelphia throughout the autumn days. Old Stephen Hopkins was forced to return to Rhode Island. Joseph Hewes, an overworked official, often the only one in attendance from North Carolina, was worn out and wrote friends he would return home.[43] Even twenty-six-year-old Edward Rutledge was exhausted and exclaimed on September 23, "I have been so much on the Wing that for some Weeks past it has been impossible for me to put pen to paper."[44]

Sam Adams and John Adams, who had attended continuously, were also tired. On August 12, Sam left for Boston leaving only John Adams and Robert Treat Paine, who was ill, to represent Massachusetts. Always a persevering penman, John Adams had written long letters to his wife, Abigail, and to the authorities on a plan for choosing Congressmen that would allow each legislator leave every three or four months. He also asked his wife to send horses for the trip to Massachusetts which he finally started October 10, when he wrote in his journal:

> Sat out from Philadelphia towards Boston, eated at the Red Lyon, dined at Bristol, crossed Trenton ferry, long before Sun set, drank Coffee at the Ferry House on the East Side of Delaware, where I putt up—partly to avoid riding in the Evening Air, and partly because 30 miles is enough for the first day as my Tendons are delicate, not having been once on Horse back since the Eighth day of February.[45]

Thomas Nelson left Philadelphia after September 21 for home. As he rode through Virginia, he noticed a martial air throughout the state. Men were mustering on court greens, and York Town was astir with military activities. Hugh and Robert were still training the local troops. John Nelson was securing horses for the Sixth Troop of cavalry and the screech of saws and tapping hammers sounded as carpenters constructed stalls for the mounts. Tom's cousins, William and Thomas, had been sent to New York in September attached to the command of Colonel George Weedon. Because he handed punch around to his regiment in gourds, he was often called "Joe Gourd." President Hancock had warned Weedon to avoid Philadelphia because of the smallpox. After the Third Regiment left Williamsburg in August for New York, the Fourth, Fifth, and Sixth regiments also marched northward to join General Washington.[46]

On September 13, Captain John Chilton recorded in his journal, "Great joy was expressed at our arrival and great things are expected from the Virginians."[47]

Thomas Nelson had heard the news of the military action around New York just before he headed home. Panic-stricken patriots attempting to surrender had been shot by the Hessians; however, the next day three rifle companies from the Third Virginia Regiment and reinforcements from Maryland helped the rebels send the redcoats from the fields. More royal troops were then brought in and twelve British squadrons forced the American army to retreat across New Jersey. A conflagration swept New York City on September 20 and 21. British blamed the rebels for the burning and royal patrols seized civilians and meted out drastic punishment. Some of the suspects were pushed to their deaths in the raging fires.[48]

Since he was at home only through October, Tom had little time to spend with his family. Lucy was plump again with pregnancy but cheerful. The two girls were growing fast, and the five boys were thriving. Chosen once again as a representative, Nelson left for Williamsburg as he had done countless times in years past. Nelson had a chance to talk with his friend Governor Henry, back in the capital after his illness, as well as Dudley Digges, John Page, and Benjamin Harrison. Like the Congress, local lawmakers were involved with military matters. The House of Delegates resolved that six new battalions of infantry should be raised for Continental service. The legislature also passed measures to alleviate tobacco losses.[49]

On October 11, 1776, Editor Purdie announced in his *Virginia Gazette:*

> On Monday last the General Assembly of this commonwealth met at the Capitol, agreeable to adjourning, and the plan of government adopted to the late convention when the Honorable Archibald Cary, Esq. was elected Speaker of the upper House, or Senate, and the Honorable Edmund Pendleton, Speaker of the House of Delegates.

That same day the Dixon-Hunter paper also had an item pertaining to the political setup:

> Sunday last Thomas Jefferson, Esquire, a delegate for this Colony in Continental Congress, arrived here from Philadelphia, and on Tuesday set out for his seat in Albemarle. We hear that Benjamin Harrison, Esquire of Berkeley, is chosen a Delegate to Congress, in the room of Thomas Jefferson, Esquire, resigned.

Jefferson was dissatisfied with the constitution that the Virginia Convention had approved in June, so he planned to launch his reforms.

Since Tom left for Philadelphia again around the first of November, he missed the spirited maneuvers that Jefferson proposed, but the first reform to abolish entail and the primogeniture system passed.

When Nelson stepped into the state house at Philadelphia on November 10, 1776, he sensed a somber mood among the members. He found many familiar faces missing. The four New York representatives had returned to their state. The British had already wrecked Whitestone, Frances Lewis's handsome house and seized his wife as prisoner. The property of William Floyd and Philip Livingston was ruined and the British later burned Morrisania, Lewis Morris's estate. All the wealthy rebels were paying a dear price for the principle of freedom.[50]

Maryland's members were also absent. Although the conservative element in Delaware defeated Caesar Rodney for re-election to Congress, the patriot had recruited men for Maryland's colonial regiments. The Georgia Congressmen had also gone home. Therefore, the Continental Congress lacked the nine states required to compose the body.[51]

Frank Lee summed up the situation in his letter of November 9 to Colonel Landon Carter:

> All not well in Congress. Only the members grow weary, go off, and leave us to think, which obliged us to call for them. There are some, my dear Colonel who wish the Congress to be divided and contemptible; as that can't be accomplished, the next thing is, to make the world think it is so.[52]

Nelson realized these remarks were all too true. During the drizzly days of November, gloom engulfed the statesmen. They were discouraged over the New York defeats and depressed about the deaths and desertions that had depleted the American army. Lack of arms and ammunition was disheartening, the scandal in the supply system disgraceful.

Defections in their ranks also added to the distress. The three Allen brothers switched sides. Nelson wrote Jefferson about the turncoats and also showed his aversion to the action of John Dickinson:

> Your friends, John, Andrew and William Allen are with General Howe; and Dickinson is they know not where, but it is imagined he is on board the Roebuck. This Gentleman, after giving his Vote repeatedly in Congress, for the emission of Continental Money, wrote to his Brother not to receive any of it in payment for his Debts, and his letter was intercepted by the Council of Safety. What does he deserve?
> The Allens have hamm'd themselves finely for when they went to Howe, there was little doubt, but he would shortly have been in possession of Philadelphia, as indeed he might, had he played his Cards well; but now I am in hopes that will not take place, and that they will be treated as they deserve. There are some of the Vilest Rascals in the City and neighborhood of Philadelphia that ever existed.[53]

The Commander-in-Chief and the Congress had one problem in common. Their projects were strong and resourceful on paper but fell far short of their goals in reality.

Upon his return to the Congress, delegate Nelson had been disappointed to realize that the representatives had resorted to a lottery scheme to raise five million dollars. He had no faith in securing funds by such a method and thought it just a "game," but the ten million dollars that the Congress had allocated in the spring for the 1776 campaign was gone by the end of October.

As acting chairman of the Committee on Ways and Means empowered to pay for military supplies and to establish the credit of the Continental currency, Tom faced a tremendous task. On Friday, December 6, he was forced to report on matters of the treasury that his committee's plan was not "perfected" and therefore desired to sit again. The members of the committee realized all too clearly that raising revenue by issuing more paper money was causing inflationary conditions.[54]

The Congress rebuked citizens who were profiteering by selling products for British gold while the patriot soldiers suffered in the field. The delegates also discussed the usefulness of cavalry units even before they had heard of the terrible thrust employed by the English. In its first formal attack of the war, the Seventeenth British Dragoons had swept rapidly through the rebel ranks at Chatterton's Hill hacking the soldiers with sharp swords.

On Friday, November 29, five men were appointed to prepare a "proper method of establishing and training cavalry" for the American army: Richard Henry Lee and Thomas Nelson, Jr., two skilled horsemen from Virginia; Robert Treat Paine of Massachusetts, sick and serving his last term; Arthur Middleton, the rich young planter from South Carolina; and William Floyd, the wealthy New Yorker whose property the British had plundered.[55]

In November, Edmund Randolph had been in Philadelphia attending to the removal of the remains of his uncle, Peyton Randolph, back to Williamsburg so that his body could be buried in the family vault at the College chapel. Though busy with countless details and duties in the Congress, no doubt Nelson assisted the nephew with the arrangements as he had done the previous autumn when the parliamentarian passed away in Philadelphia. Edmund could tell Thomas news of Lucy and the children and relay how Aunt Betty Randolph was striving to settle the estate. People were slow in paying debts, and she was also begging people to bring back the books they had borrowed from the Speaker. Young Randolph told Tom that Robert Carter Nicholas, Edmund's father-in-law, planned to resign the position of Treasurer so that he could devote more time to his duties as a delegate in the Virginia Assembly. George Wythe had resigned from the Congress and he and Jefferson were studying legal tomes and tracts to recommend revising the laws of the Virginia constitution. Mann Page, Jr., of Mannsfield had been elected as the new representative.[56]

The officials knew of rumors circulating in Philadelphia that the rebels were ready to surrender. Tories were thronging the taverns and toasting the King, bragging about his Majesty's units crushing the colonial upstarts and boasting that one hundred British ships were sailing toward the city. Frenzy gripped the populace at Philadelphia and it was common talk among the people on the streets that the Congress would abandon the Pennsylvania capital. Panic-stricken patriots wondered whether to remain or leave, and an exodus started from the city in December.[57]

Cornwallis was in close pursuit of the Continental army in these dismal days. Washington and the straggling patriot soldiers struggled on in the drizzling rain and cold. With men heading home in the face of the foe, General Washington judged his troop strength at about 3,400 men. The military effectiveness of the American army was at its lowest ebb.[58]

Marching with the Pennsylvania militia on the retreat, Thomas Paine penned his view of the crisis:

> These are the times that try men's souls: The summer soldier and the sunshine patriot will, in this crisis, shrink from the service of his country; but he that stands it now deserves the love and thanks of man and woman. Tyranny, like Hell, is not easily conquered. Yet we have the consolation with us, that the harder the conflict, the more glorious the triumph.[59]

The words carried no weight with some impatient rebels, who, disheveled and discouraged, continued to drift away.

The Congress adjourned on December 12, voting to assemble at Baltimore on the twentieth of the month.[60] Lord Howe was delighted with developments: rebel forces had fled; Lee was captured; the Congress was leaving Philadelphia; New Jersey Loyalists were flocking to the royal fold. The confident Howe felt assured the rebel cause was ready to collapse. Lord Cornwallis was allowed leave to sail home soon to see his sick wife. "Sir Billy" Howe left for New York and his lady love, Mrs. Joshua Loring, whose husband was in charge of war prisoners. General Howe closed the campaign for the winter season after stationing approximately 14,000 British troops throughout New Jersey. He gave strict orders that the Crown forces were to protect the inhabitants and their property, but the redcoats and Hessians seized crops, cattle, and horses without paying. Rape of the women turned some of the Tories toward the American side.

Thomas Nelson described some of the devastation to Thomas Jefferson in a letter of January 2, 1777, written from Baltimore:

> They play the very Devil with the Girls and even old Women to satisfy their libinous appetites. There is scarcely a virgin to be found in the part of the Country that they passed thro and yet the Jersies will not turn out. Rapes, Rapine, and Murder are not sufficient to rouse the resentment of these People. If that be not sufficient provocation, I despair of anything working them up to opposition.
>
> The General was informed a few nights ago that a conspiracy was formed by some people in Bucks County near his Camp to kidnap him as poor Lee was, but he has more prudence than to be caught in that manner, however the disposition of the Inhabitants of that County appears to be inimical to our cause which you knew before.[61]

George Washington contemplated neither inactivity nor capture in the winter weeks but was planning an attack on the enemy at Trenton. At dusk on Christmas Day, the rebel regiments rowed across the Delaware River toward Trenton where Hessian outfits taking their ease after a grand dinner with much drinking were stunned by the three-pronged thrust of the Continental troops. Over nine hundred prisoners, thirty officers, and other high-ranking officials capitulated. Washington's men captured a thousand muskets, several cannon, drums, and colors. His strategy had been successful. The Continentals had won a complete victory in two hours without losing a single soldier.[62]

Thomas Nelson conveyed the news to Thomas Jefferson in Virginia:

> We have at last turned the Tables upon those Scoundrels by surprise, as you'll see by the enclosed paper. . . . The Number of prisoners exceeds what the General makes them by 500. He is always very moderate. Could we but get a good Regular Army we should soon clear the Continent of these damn'd Invaders.[63]

The patriotic Congressman was but echoing the sentiments that the Commander-in-Chief had expressed. The postscript of Nelson's letter informed Jefferson of losses suffered by two of the Signers:

> Our little friend Hopkinson has suffered greatly by these Freebooters; They have destroyed all his furniture, Cabinets of Curiosities, and his fine Harpsichord, which I am told was the best that ever came to America. You have little chance for the Tellescope. Old Witherspoon has not escaped their fury. They have burnt his Library. It grieves him much that he has lost his controversial Tracts. He would lay aside the cloth to take revenge of them. I believe he would send them to the Devil, if he could, I am sure I would.[64]

Representatives of the Congress had ridden to Baltimore before December 20 carrying important records and securing a residence for its sessions. Built for a tavern, the dwelling had a long room and two fireplaces, but it was not so comfortable as the Philadelphia State House chambers. The delegates disliked Baltimore for recent rains had turned the unpaved streets into streams of mud; several members called the place a "dirty boggy hole."[65]

On Tuesday, December 24, Thomas Nelson, Jr., and William Ellery were appointed to the Treasury Board. Ellery, a Newport, Rhode Islander, was versed in various languages as well as the law and was especially interested in commerce and naval affairs.[66]

Congress adjourned for December 25 and Christmas in a strange town was dismal for the delegates especially without the company of their families. Lucy had been with Thomas at Philadelphia the preceding year, but in 1776 he was away from his wife and separated from his children. The Lee brothers were the exception for both had brought their wives with them to Baltimore. (A new Virginia delegate, Mann Page, Jr., had been delayed in attendance by the sickness of his bride, the former Molly Tayloe, who had made him a brother-in-law to Frank Lee.) John Adams, dining with these delegates at the home of a prominent Baltimore merchant, was impressed by the bracelets the ladies wore. He wrote:

The Virginia Ladies had ornaments about their wrists, which I don't
remember to have seen before. These ornaments were like miniature pictures, bound round the Arms with some Chains.[67]

On Friday, December 27, five members were appointed by the Congress
to execute a plan to conduct the executive business of the body in a better
manner. Seamaster William Whipple of New Hampshire, lawyer James
Wilson of Pennsylvania, shipper Elbridge Gerry of Massachusetts, planter
Thomas Nelson of Virginia, and merchant Robert Morris of Pennsylvania
were selected to serve on the committee although Morris was remaining in
Philadelphia to manage necessary matters for the military.[68]

On that same day, the Congress conferred on General Washington broad
authority to conduct the war with complete powers. The government
granted the Commander-in-Chief the jurisdiction "to take, wherever he
may be, whatever he may want for the use of the army, if the inhabitants will
not sell it, allowing a reasonable price for the same; to arrest and confine
persons who refuse to take the continental currency."[69] The statesmen had
taken a significant step; some legislators felt it was a giant leap—an emergency wartime measure effective for six months.

During the last few days of December, Congressman Thomas Nelson was
so swamped with committee assignments that he was hardly aware of the
dampness, yet the air rising from swampy marshes made him choke and
cough. He and Richard Henry Lee were enthusiastic over establishing a
cavalry unit and pored over plans for the project.

One item indicated the rising inflation, "To Colonel Nelson, for expences of an express, the sum of £170-4 84/90 dollars."[70] Finding funds was a
perpetual problem and sessions with the Treasury Board were not promising.
Thomas was also meeting with the members of the recently appointed committee to expedite the executive business of the Congress. A letter to General Horatio Gates dated December 31 reveals another aspect of his
activities: "Being one of the committee appointed by Congress to prepare a
plan for establishing a Board of War and Ordnance, and not having a thorough Knowledge of the Duties of your Board . . . furnish me with such a plan
as you think best adapted to answer the designs of Congress."[71]

The last day of the year ended on a brighter note for the delegates when
the victory dispatch of the Trenton triumph was read, lifting the morale of
the members and renewing their faith just as it had raised the spirit of the
soldiers in the revolutionary cause. The royal regiments had been appalled
by the American assault at Trenton. Lord Cornwallis, embarking for England, had his leave canceled.

General Washington planned another ruse against the redcoats. Leaving
fires in the Continental camp, sleepy rebel soldiers stumbled over frozen
roads and covered cannon were pulled away in a nocturnal march toward

Princeton. Since the British guards reported seeing glowing fires, they believed the rebels were still encamped.

General Hugh Mercer commanding the vanguard encountered the enemy about sunrise on a summit outside Princeton. Although British reinforcements pushed the patriots back, Mercer, refusing to surrender, was clubbed, shot, and stabbed five times by British bayonets. Thirty years before the Scottish soldier had served as a surgeon at the brutal battle of Culloden, and he had survived wounds suffered in the French and Indian War. The veteran fighter was left bleeding on the battlefield near Stony Creek, but by a miracle he was still alive. General Mercer was removed to a nearby residence and Lord Cornwallis allowed General Washington to send an aide to attend the officer. Dr. Benjamin Rush cared for the surgeon-soldier, but the battle-scarred veteran fighter died from his severe wounds on January 12, 1777.[72]

◆　　◆　　◆

Though Thomas Nelson was busy throughout the day, in the evenings he pulled his chair close to the hearth to read letters from home. On January 2, Lucy had a third daughter whom she called Lucy. If Tom had the time, he might have pondered the notice of Colonel Byrd's death. The former Council member and prominent planter, who had remained faithful in the royal fold, received a terse announcement in Purdie's January 3, 1777, edition. Formerly, an obituary notice for such a rich representative would have been long and complimentary.

> Deaths—Yesterday morning, after a short illness, the Honorable William Byrd, esquire, at his seat of Westover.[73]

◆　　◆　　◆

After the successful attacks of the American army on British troops at Trenton and Princeton, Congress published the Declaration of Independence January 18, 1777, with the names of the Signers and sent copies to all the states.[74] The Articles of Confederation had not yet been adopted, and some of the Congressmen wondered if constituents from the large and small states could ever compromise their ideas on the issue.

Nelson was wrestling with the constant worry of paper emissions and rising prices. He wrote Robert Morris on January 25 pertaining to the financial problem:

> My dear Sir. . . . The great demand for Money from every quarter has kept our Treasury so low that I have not had it in my power to send you any; There will however be 200,000 dollars sent in two or three days at farthest. . . . When I could give satisfactory answer to Congress upon a requisition being made for a Sum of Money, I took the greatest pleasure in transacting

the business of the Treasury Board, but of late we have been so circumstanced that I had almost as leave go to Jail as go near the Treasury.

Harrison and Hooper have taken to their Horses. The former when mounted looks like a commander in chief. The latter would make a good Aide de camp for him; He has leave of absence on account of his health.[75]

In a few days Hooper wrote to Morris in Philadelphia relating to his own health and mentioned that of Nelson:

I am now recovering, and God willing propose moving southward in a few days. Nelson by advice of a physician goes tomorrow. He is in a bad state of health. Harrison is still ill and unless he is more attentive to Exercise and Regimen I fear the consequence will be serious.[76]

The Congress adjourned on February 27 and the representatives packed for their return to Philadelphia.[77] Before he left Baltimore, Nelson probably had a visit with the Virginians passing through the town to the north. In January, various issues of the *Virginia Gazette* had informed the public that four companies of Light Horse Troops commanded by Captains Lees, Nelson, Jameson, and Temple arrived in Williamsburg on their way to join General Washington in New Jersey.[78]

Departing from Baltimore rather than Philadelphia, the York Town delegate could save at least two days' traveling time as he moved toward Virginia. Yet the trip could not have been pleasant for a person feeling ill as the February winds blew across the slippery rain-washed roads.

Thomas Nelson was the center of attention in his family during his days of convalescence. When the sun filtered into the master bedroom, he sat by the fire and cuddled little Lucy on his lap. The five boys, Elizabeth, and Mary had hurried visits. Lucy realized that it was difficult for an active man like Thomas to rest and relax. He read the papers and was distressed to learn that rebel prisoners were being mistreated.[79] It was disturbing to find out that sixteen men had run away from the Seventh Regiment, yet there were courageous Continentals of the unit fighting the English enemy. The members of the Nelson family were proud to learn that Major William Nelson led a force of 150 men to attack the British garrison, and the Americans "routed them and took the whole prisoners, among them a Major, Captain, and three Subalterns with 70 stands of arms."[80] For this conspicuous service, William Nelson was advanced to colonel and attached to the Eighth Regiment under Peter Muhlenberg, the "Fighting Parson" who had been promoted to brigadier general of the new brigade.[81] When the Secretary came to visit, Thomas congratulated his uncle on having three sons serving the cause of their country.

Conversation with Hugh and Robert was not such an enjoyable exchange when they talked about the family enterprise. Nelson admitted frankly that he had neglected private matters for public affairs. The brothers had been trying to operate the mercantile establishment under the onus of embargoes and economic conditions that had ruined commerce. The shelves of the store were empty and stacks of bills went unpaid. Diminished stock and uncollected debts gave evidence of the decline of a once bustling business.

Seventy years before, "Scotch" Tom Nelson had started the store. William Nelson had expanded the enterprise through nearly three decades, but the war had wrecked the market so Thomas and his brothers were forced to close the concern. Augustine Moore, who had been indentured to William Nelson and had continued to assist the sons in the operation, put the following advertisement in the papers:

> The Partnership of Thomas Nelson, Junior and Company, of York being at an end, all Persons indebted to them are requested to settle their Accounts as soon as possible, and those who cannot conveniently discharge their Balances it is expected will give Bond for the same. If any have Demands against the Partnership, they are desired to bring them in, and they shall be paid.[82]

The family firm had made this same appeal after the death of Mr. Nelson in the autumn of 1772 and many of the same debts were still on the books.

An announcement in the Dixon-Hunter February 14 issue saddened Tom's mother; "Deaths—Honorable Robert Burwell, at his seat at Newington, in King William." The loss of her last brother, two years younger than she, was difficult for Elizabeth Burwell Nelson. The Councilor's passing added an extra burden for Thomas since he was appointed executor of the estate.

✦   ✦   ✦

Congressmen had returned to Philadelphia from Baltimore the last of February renting rooms in the residences along Chestnut, Market, and Walnut streets close enough to the State House so the statesmen could walk to the Assembly.

Sessions started March 12, 1777, and by the first week in April, representatives had arrived from all the states. When Nelson reached the hall and presented his credentials, he was aware that many members of the Congress were present who had been absent during the winter.[83]

Nelson learned from his cousins, Mann Page, Jr., and Benjamin Harrison, as well as the Lee brothers, that the issue on Confederation had been resumed; but when the delegates discovered that the draft intended to strip the states of some power, an amendment was prepared regarding the sovereignty of the states. Two days of debates and discussions had ensued.[84]

Richard Henry Lee had spoken against the amendment and supported the authority for Congress, but the concept of a strong central government was too liberal for the legislators. Eleven states voted "that all sovereign power was in the states separately."[85]

While the statesmen had sidestepped the settlement of Confederation temporarily, the power struggle continued. Congress recognized the services of her patriot commanders by promotion and pay—a move that pleased some soldiers, incensed others who felt they had been overlooked.

The statesmen were courted in the spring by numerous foreign adventurers arriving in Philadelphia to offer their service to the American army. European officers expected a top commission in the Continental corps. Even before General Washington wondered what to do with the foreigners and stated that his own soldiers would find it difficult to serve under strangers, the delegates decided to stop the flow. On Thursday, March 13, Congress resolved:

> That the Committee of Secret Correspondence be directed forthwith to write to all their ministers and agents abroad, to discourage all gentlemen from coming to America with expectation of employment in the service, unless they are masters of our language, and have the best recommendations.[86]

The executives conceded that diplomacy should be displayed in dealing with foreign soldiers of fortune. Artillerists and engineers were needed and the officials were happy to hear the report duly recorded in the *Journal* that the French ship *Mercury* had arrived at Portsmouth, New Hampshire, in March with the following supplies:

> 12,000 firelocks, 11,987 fusees, 11,000 gun flints, 1000 barrels of powder, 48 bales of woolens, 9 bales of handkerchiefs, two cases of shoes, 1 box buttons and buckles, 1 case sherry oil, 1 box lawn, and 1 case needles and silk neckcloths.[87]

The delegates remembered the dead during their long, busy days. The body of General Hugh Mercer, brought from Princeton to Philadelphia, was buried with military honors at Christ Church. On April 8, the representatives recommended that the Congress erect monuments to the memories of the two patriotic physicians who had died in defense of freedom: one to General Joseph Warren to be placed in Boston, Massachusetts; one to General Hugh Mercer, to be raised at Fredericksburg, Virginia. In further gratitude to the Generals, the government stipulated "that the eldest son of General Warren and the youngest son of General Mercer be educated, from this time, at the expense of the United States."[88]

From Morristown, New Jersey, General Washington's dispatches to the Congress revealed that the burdens of building an American army increased rather than lessened. Expiring enlistments reduced the ranks to a thousand men in January. Smallpox swept through the remaining troops. At this low ebb in the Continental camp, General Howe could have routed the ill and shivering rebels with one strike and ended the American Revolution. Fortunately for the patriot troops, "Sir Billy" Howe was kept busy with the pastimes of New York City and his paramour there so he did not push the campaign.

Captain John Taylor gave an account of the military conditions on April 13 to his uncle, Edmund Pendleton, the Speaker of the Virginia House of Delegates. Thrown from his horse that month and needing time to recover, Pendleton had time to ponder the communication:

> The desertions from our army are to the last degree alarming; some companies having lost 300 odd men; of these many go to the enemy . . . Hope for the best, but at the same time fear the worst; I wish, I wish from my soul we had more Virginians than are, but as we have not, the honour of preserving America must be acquired by one alone.[89]

Taylor remarked that one-sixth of the men were naked and one-third were without blankets. He felt the officers' low pay had led to fraud and that much dissatisfaction resulted from the fact that the Congress had failed to keep promises made to the men.

The Congress continued to urge the states to call out militia units in full strength and forward the regiments to the American army. It counseled muster masters to produce complete certificates with the correct number of noncommissioned officers and soldiers.

On Wednesday, April 13, Nelson was appointed to a committee with two of his former colleagues, Samuel Adams and Elbridge Gerry, and a new member, young William Duer, of New York, to "Confer with the commissary general means obviating an ill consequences ensue from the losses of provisions at Danbury."[90] Delegate Duer was an Englishman with a degree from Eton and had been in the colonies a decade. As a manufacturer of cotton cloth, he could estimate the cost of the materials.

A British detachment had destroyed the inland supply base of the American army at Danbury, Connecticut, in a surprise attack plundering supplies, burning public and private dwellings, and ransacking 1,700 tents desperately needed by the Continental troops. Old General David Wooster pulled together a patriot force to follow and harass the British. The general was killed in the skirmish and some of the representatives recalled with regret that Wooster had been charged the year before with incompetence in the Canadian debacle though he was afterwards cleared.[91]

On Friday, May 2, Thomas Nelson suffered a mild stroke that affected his memory at the time. His associates were alarmed about his condition and realized that the delegate had just returned after a two months' absence to recover his health. Now the York Town legislator needed a long leave that was obtained on Thursday, May 8. Eight days later the representative was resting at his residence Offley Hoo in the rolling hills of Hanover County, Virginia.[92] On May 16, he wrote George Wythe, Speaker of the Virginia House of Delegates:

> Sir—A total inability to attend to business, having oblig'd me to quit the Congress, I beg leave, thro' you, to Acquaint the Assembly with it, that they may appoint another Delegate; and I will take the liberty to advise, that this be immediately done, because the Congress are now engag'd in forming the Confederation, in which Virginia is deeply interested.
>
> Nothing but necessity could have induced me to leave Congress at this critical time, and I hope I shall stand excus'd.[93]

CHAPTER EIGHTEEN

Recovery and Refuge, Reforms and Recruitment: 1777–1778

Nelson Home to Recuperate ✦ *May Assembly* ✦ *Patrick Henry Elected Governor Again* ✦ *Henry Courts Dorothea Dandridge* ✦ *Nelson Appointed Brigadier General* ✦ *Drills for Defense* ✦ *Washington and Nelson Correspondence*

Thomas Nelson, Jr., recovered his health in the deep silence of the Hanover hills. Within the residence, only servants moved quietly. (Patrick Henry, too, often sought refuge in those hills from the pressures he was experiencing. In April he had been in the area to attend the funeral of his uncle, the Reverend Patrick Henry, an Anglican clergyman for over half a century.)[1]

During the days of his recuperation, Thomas reflected on the changes in his life. War had brought ruin to his own business and shifted the fortunes of his friends and family. William Byrd, III, had died in January 1777 leaving an estate encumbered by debts. Mrs. Byrd, as executor, advertised in April that "100 Virginia born slaves well clothed" would be sold at auction. The Dixon-Hunter *Gazette* of the eighteenth also announced that the handsome house was for "sale . . . a good brick dwelling house with four rooms on each floor situated in Williamsburg lately occupied by the said William Byrd and at present by the Reverend John Bracken, convenient outhouses and several lots adjoined." Bracken, who had married Sally Burwell, a cousin to Tom, had purchased the property.

Later in August and September, Mrs. Byrd was compelled to auction furnishings, fashionable plate, cattle, horses, sheep, a coach, chariot, and several blooded colts. The family library of nearly 4000 volumes remained intact.[2]

As executor for the estate of his uncle, Robert Carter Burwell, Nelson knew his task would be difficult and tedious. Burwell, like Byrd, had made bad investments and his holdings had been heavily involved for the past decade.

The stress of the war produced short tempers and anger at real and *imag-*

ined slights. Nelson noticed in the newspapers that the non-commissioned officers and soldiers stationed at York Town had resented the removal of Dr. Corbin Griffin in favor of Dr. Matthew Pope as the director and physician of the hospital. By address and published protests, the group had aired its grievances about Griffin's being replaced and had gone to his home to tender its thanks for his "unwearied attendance" and the "salutary prescriptions" he had prepared for the sick men of the garrison "committed to his care."[3]

Thomas had just missed the short visit of Nicholas Cresswell to York Town since the Congressman had been back in Philadelphia in April before his sickness compelled him to resign. The English visitor had viewed the village and Nelson estates and expressed in his journal on Tuesday, April 29, that York Town was a pleasant town on the river, navigable for the largest ships.

"Close to the town there were several very good Gentlemen's houses built of brick and some of their gardens laid out with the greatest taste of any I have ever seen in America," the admiring traveler commented. He then continued candidly, "By now almost ruined with disorderly soldiers, and what is more extraordinary their own soldiers, the guardians of the people and the defenders of their rights. Houses are burned down and others pulled to pieces for fuel. Most of the gardens are thrown to the street."[4]

Cresswell also observed the economic stalemate stating, "Everything is in disorder and confusion and no appearance of trade. This melancholy scene fills the minds of the itinerant travelers with gloomy and horrid ideas." He lodged at the Sign of the Swan and on Wednesday, April 30, noted, "Had honor of breakfasting with his Excellency." Though Secretary Nelson was hospitable to the visitor, he paid no heed to the entreaty of the Englishman who avowed, "All that I could would not procure me permission to go on board his Majesty's ships in the Bay."[5]

As Thomas's recuperation progressed, he became anxious for activity. By May the freeholders of York County had expressed their confidence by again electing him a delegate to the Virginia Assembly. The constituents of Fauquier County chose Hugh Nelson as their representative.[6]

As soon as a quorum was present, Nelson presented a bill to quarter troops in tents and barracks because York Town citizens had complained about the soldiers' destructiveness. To regulate the troops' behavior, commanding officers and their men were made responsible for damages and repairs.[7]

Nelson found many new faces among the Assemblymen with newcomers representing the upper regions. These rangy frontiersmen favored the reforms and revisions Jefferson proposed. The seeds of religious dissent had been stirring for over a decade giving impetus to the reforms.

George Mason had incorporated the principle of religious tolerance in the Virginia Bill of Rights with the thought, "That religion . . . can be directed only by reason and conviction, not by force or violence; and therefore all men are equally entitled to the free exercise of religion, according to the dictates of conscience. . . ."[8] Nonconformists had flooded officials with petitions outlining the right to worship when and where they pleased. They were strong in their stand for separation of church and state and resented paying taxes to support the Established Church.[9]

Carter Braxton, Robert Carter Nicholas, and Edmund Pendleton, all conservatives, supported the colonial church and its rights to privileges and power. Aligned with Jefferson as proponents of progressive reform were the philosophic George Mason, George Wythe, and James Madison.

On Thursday, May 29, Thomas Nelson gladly cast his ballot for Patrick Henry to start his second term as Governor of the Commonwealth.[10] Henry turned forty-one on that day; twelve years before on his twenty-ninth birthday he had roused the House of Burgesses with his bold resolutions against the Stamp Act.

On May 30, 1777, the Dixon-Hunter *Virginia Gazette* announced Henry's election:

> Yesterday the General Assembly of this State agreeable to the Constitution, or form of government proceeded to the choice of Governor and Council for another year, when his Excellency Patrick Henry, Esq., was unanimously chosen Governor and all the members of the Privy Council are continued in office, except the Honorable Meriweather Smith, Esq., in whose room the Honorable Thomas Nelson, Esq., is appointed.

Edmund Randolph was re-elected Attorney General and John Page was again selected Lieutenant Governor. Thomas Nelson, Jr., felt honored to be elected to the executive branch (the old Council) and would have enjoyed his association but declined the post at the end of June because of his recent illness.[11]

In June, Henry rode to Hanover County to propose marriage to Dorothea Dandridge although he was several years her senior. Eighteen years before he had dropped by the home of his friend Colonel Nathaniel West Dandridge, ready to play his fiddle for the young folk, and had met Tom Jefferson there, a rangy, red-headed sixteen-year-old on his way to attend the College of William and Mary. Both men had made their mark since that time, and baby "Dolly" had grown into a comely young woman whose reddish hair framed a pretty face. The bride-to-be had an aristocratic background, as her mother was a daughter of colonial Governor Alexander Spotswood. Her father was first cousin to Martha Dandridge, who had made two fine marriages, first to Daniel Parke Custis and after his death to George Washington.[12]

A visit by Mrs. Washington to Williamsburg inspired authorities to celebrate her arrival with appropriate ceremonies. The press informed its readers:

> Last Thursday about eleven o'clock in the forenoon, arrived here from the seat of Burwell Bassett, Esq.'s in New Kent, Lady Washington, the amiable consort of his Excellency General Washington. Upon her arrival, she was saluted with the firing of cannon and small arms, and was safely conducted to Mrs. Dawson's in this city, and intends setting out for the northward in a few days.[13]

The paper also reported that the authorities had a high regard for "General Washington's merit as the illustrious defender and deliverer of his country," and city officials resolved that a gold medal should be executed and "presented to the General's Lady."[14]

After the Assembly's adjournment, the delegates scattered in different directions across the state. When the afternoon heat subsided Thomas would visit the Swan Tavern. Although brother Hugh was up in Fauquier County and his brother Billy was at College in Williamsburg, Robert would be there, and also Nathaniel, now in his twenties and courting "Jeanie" Page. The long-time neighbors, Dudley Digges, David Jameson, William Reynolds, and Dr. Pope gathered to imbibe apple or peach brandy. Pope had advertised his property for sale without a description of the house and lots in York Town, but the doctor declared, "It is presumed no one will purchase without first viewing the premises, it is therefore needless to say any Thing about them or their situation."[15]

Their talk often turned to changes so different from former carefree days. York Town was filled with troops—exciting for the young—but too boisterous and sometimes destructive for the mature citizens of the town.

Nelson was in charge of militia units again as of Monday, July 21, by the "recommendation of the York County Court," the Governor's commission. He was expected to resolve the situation that had caused so much complaint. Patrols were posted. Regulations restricted the movements of slaves and servants; rioters were clapped in jail.[16]

The campus was in a turmoil with the antics of Tory John Camm, who had been elected to the presidency of the College in 1772. Patriotic professors and students resisted his royalist principles. When authorities of William and Mary had weighed the evidence of "neglect and misconduct" against Camm, they evicted the preacher.[17]

Billy Reynolds, who managed the York River Company, reminded members to attend the meeting at "Mr. Southall's in Williamsburg, or depute some person to vote for them, as it is proposed to increase the stock."[18]

Dudley Digges told the group that the Council had acted August 15 in Governor Henry's absence to call out more militia, since Lieutenant Governor Page had been alerted that several British ships were off the Virginia shores. Nelson knew of this alarm and on August 15 had written General Washington:

An express arrived yesterday from the Eastern Shore with intelligence of a large Fleet of Ships being seen off Matonken on the Sea Board of that Country. What their Purpose is, we know not; though I believe not to pay a Visit by their playing on and off. . . ."

Should they chuse to amuse themselves here, they will have it in their Power to do almost what they please in the lower Parts of this State; for I am sure there never was a People worse prepared for Defence than we are. However I am determined to cast every Nerve to make a Stand against them should they land.[19]

The writer apologized to the Commander-in-Chief "for not complying with my promise of writing weekly; but such is the condition of my weak Head, that I have never attempted a Letter without experiencing violent Pain in it for Hours after." On the back of the communication Nelson noted, "At nine o'clock last night upwards of one Hundred sail of Vessels were seen standing in the Capes."[20]

The fleet sailed on to Maryland, but the authorities considered the alarm of such import that additional defense preparations were undertaken. On August 29, when Governor Henry had returned to the capital, His Excellency, with the advice of the Council, appointed Thomas Nelson, Jr., Esq., brigadier general and commander-in-chief of the military forces of the Commonwealth.[21] In the August 22, 1777, *Virginia Gazette*, Editor Purdie praised the selection of Nelson for the post with these statements:

The appointment of a gentleman so universally beloved and esteemed for his zealous attachment to our sacred cause, cannot fail of giving of the most unfeigned pleasure to every friend of his country, who reflects that, except our noble general to the north, there is not a native in America to whose standard so great a number of warm friends and respectful persons would rather repair as to that noble and worthy gentleman's. . . .

. . . that the worthy general has accepted the command upon the most disinterested motives as he has refused a salary. . . .

Such instances of genuine patriotism mark the most generous attachment to his country, and its liberties.

General Nelson wrote General Washington that the Governor and Council had honored him with the command of 4000 militia and affirmed that it was "an appointment that was unsolicited, unexpected. . . . I confess my want of military knowledge; but by assiduity and attention, I hope to make myself a soldier." Nelson explained his plan of defense and distribution of the citizen soldiers and stated that Portsmouth was the seaport where ships could be built "there being at this Time two Frigates upon the Stocks, I shall garrison that Post with 1,200 Men, who, upon Danger of an attack are to be reinforced by the militia of the adjacent Counties. The other Forts are Hampton, York, and Williamsburg, where I shall endeavor to make the best Disposition of the remainder of the Troops." His latest information on the British Fleet was that they were past the Potomac on the eighteenth. He stated that he was exceedingly concerned for their friends on the Eastern Shore and didn't know how they were to be protected.

> What can be done in a Country so divided by Water courses as this is, with only 2,000 men badly trained and worse armed; and the Difficulty of commanding Militia you are well acquainted with. Nothing but the immediate Danger into which . . . we were likely to fall and a Desire to extricate my Country from it, should have induced me to undertake the arduous Task.[22]

The last of August marching feet, shrill fifes, and beating drums resounded in crisp rhythm through the capital. The Dixon-Hunter *Gazette* of August 22 notified the public, "Yesterday evening the troops in this city, both regular and militia, were reviewed on the College Green by General Nelson who expressed himself much satisfied with their readiness to attend on the present occasion, and made a most animated speech to them on the present prospect before them." It was wise of Nelson to compliment the corps rather than reveal the real condition of their predicament.

On September 2, General Washington wrote General Nelson a long letter to congratulate him on his appointment, stating that it gave him great pleasure:

> The want of Military experience you mention, is no obstacle to you to serve your Country in the capacity in which you have undertaken. In our infant state of war, it cannot be expected, we should be perfect in the business of it. . . . your zeal and assiduity will amply supply any deficiency. . . .
>
> It is without a doubt a disagreeable task to Command Militia, but we must make the best of circumstances, and use the means we have. That they are ill armed too, is a matter of great concern, every attention should be paid to putting them upon as respectable footing as possible. It is of the first importance."[23]

Rather than station a considerable force at Hampton and York where they might be cut off by the English enemy sailing up the rivers, Washington suggested that the patriots throw up a few redoubts and keep parties of men at several places. This tactic would intercept retreats and retard movement of the British troops.

General Nelson was pleased that his seventeen-year-old brother, Billy, had been elected second lieutenant of the College company; the Reverend James Madison was the captain of the corps. On August 15 they had participated in the celebration of the founding of the College. The Reverend James Madison had led the prayer and had given the sermon; William Nelson had delivered an oration on the question, "What government is most favorable to public virtue, and the arts and science."[24]

In his new post, General Nelson was empowered to appoint his own secretary, aide-de-camp, and brigadier major, if necessary. He selected the Reverend Robert Andrews from the College faculty, professor of Moral Philosophy, as his secretary and set him to work immediately writing letters to all the county lieutenants in charge of militia.[25] The commander informed his officers of impending enemy attacks and instructed the lieutenants to train the troops for any emergency, check arms and ammunition, and promptly return reports on strength and supplies. With characteristic energy, Nelson analyzed the accounts that arrived and set up a defense system for the Commonwealth. Ten days after his appointment, on Thursday, August 28, General Nelson "laid before the Governor and Council an arrangement of the several companies of militia lately ordered upon Duty so as to form 8 Battalions and Infantry consisting of 500 men each."[26] Garrisons would be established in the seaport towns along the exposed coast as extra soldiers were sent to guard Hampton, Portsmouth, and York.

Earlier in the year, Nicholas Cresswell, visiting from England, had made adverse comments about the York Town cannon and corps of artillerymen in his diary of April 29, 1777.

> Here is a battery of twelve pieces of heavy cannon to command the River and a company of artillerymen stationed here, but they make a sorry appearance for so respectable Corps, as the military ought to be.[27]

William Mitchell, son of the late Stephen Mitchell who had operated the Swan Tavern for Nelson, was the new quartermaster, empowered to employ twenty-five Negroes to finish the river fortification.

In September men with muskets and powder horns slung over their shoulders were on the move across Virginia, marching to the capital and coastal cities. Trails of dust arose about them, and loose shirts stuck to sweating bodies in the humid heat.

General Nelson endeavored to drill and discipline the regiments into a force capable of resisting the redcoat columns. A constant clamor of rolling drums, brisk orders, and rifle blasts filled the air. Mounted couriers clattered back and forth from Williamsburg to Hampton, Portsmouth, and York Town with communications from the general to the colonels in charge of the coastal garrisons. An attack on the seacoast towns seemed imminent.

✦　　✦　　✦

While General Nelson pursued his military preparations to protect York Town against the English threat, his cousin Thomas Nelson, was thinking of romantic conquests.

Young Thomas Nelson, second son of the Secretary, had advanced his courtship of Sally Cary by correspondence but had appeared in person to ask Colonel Wilson Miles Cary for the hand of his daughter in marriage. Captain Nelson had served with his Virginia regiment in the eastern campaign and had asked Washington for a discharge from the army.[28] Young Nelson had noted that the corps had a greater proportion of officers than was necessary and asserted it had not been his intention to remain long in the service. Washington discerned the real reason of his desires when he replied to the request to leave:

> You plead so powerfully and urge so many reasons . . . that I cannot refuse your request. The principal cause of your application, however, you have not explicitly stated, but yet I presume my conjecture respecting it, are just and right. I suppose it is your marriage to Miss Cary.[29]

The nuptial notice for the couple appeared in the September 26 issue of the Purdie *Virginia Gazette:* "Marriages—Thomas Nelson, Jrn., Esq., Captain of the First Virginia Regiment, to Miss Sally Cary, eldest daughter of Wilson Miles Cary, Esq., of the County of Fluvanna."

A few days later in early October Patrick Henry paid £2 for a marriage license that enabled him to eliminate the three Sunday announcements. Governor Henry and Dorothea Dandridge were wed in the regular ceremony of the Episcopal Church in Hanover County. Citizens of the Commonwealth heard of the event as family and friends spread the word. Strangely, newspapers in Williamsburg did not print any statement about the Governor's wedding. Patrick Henry had wooed Miss Dandridge earnestly throughout the waning weeks of summer and into fall. Apparently his attentions had effectively eased the romantic memory of John Paul Jones whose charms and attractiveness had earlier dazzled Dorothea. Fate had intervened to bring about the departure of the engaging fugitive.[30]

General Nelson kept abreast of the activities of the American army in the East. If he could have viewed the Virginia soldiers in the two-hour parade through Philadelphia on August 25, he would have recognized many men who had a prominent place in the procession. Close after General Washington and his aides appeared the cavalry regiments of two Virginia colonels, George Baylor and Theodorick Bland. Three other Virginia brigades were in the forefront of the Continental forces. His cousin, Colonel William Nelson, was serving in the First Brigade under the fighting clergyman, General Peter Muhlenberg. Then followed the brigade units of General George Weedon and General William Woodford, veteran Virginia commanders.[31]

On September 9, the rebels and redcoats clashed at Brandywine Creek. The Continental army suffered twice as many casualties as the British in this bitter battle. Congress departed from Philadelphia and several thousand Crown troops marched in like conquering heroes.[32]

General Nelson received a long letter from General Washington relating the events:

> The action . . . you will have heard of. I have not time to give you the particulars. A contrariety of Intelligence in critical and important points contributed greatly, if it did not entirely bring on the Misfortune of the day.

The Commander then stated that the storm along the Schuykill River affected the next action:

> . . . frustrated by a most severe rain. . . . changing Route rendered Arms unfit destroyed almost all the Ammunition in the men's pouches. General Howe in two days fell down toward Schuykill near the Valley Forge. . . . last advices Germantown it is probably that some of their parties have entered the City, and their whole Army may, if they incline to do it, without our being able to prevent them.[33]

The Germantown defeat was another disaster for the patriot soldiers. When victory seemed almost in sight, confusion in murky cloudiness caused the Continentals to mistake their own men for the enemy and fire into their own ranks. Panic-stricken rebels ran through the thick fog in retreat.

In a communication to General Nelson on November 8, General Washington wrote, "It is in vain to look back on the 4th Instant at Germantown. We must endeavor to deserve better of Providence, and, I am, persuaded, she will smile on us."[34]

General Washington's prayer that Providence would smile on the patriots' cause became a reality in a few weeks.

Genial "Gentleman Johnny" Burgoyne was in a mellow mood, drinking champagne with his current mistress, and recalling the bet to beat the rebels by Christmas. Instead of concentrating his redcoat column in upper New York, he divided his 5000 British troops into three divisions out of sight of one another. Colonel Daniel Morgan's Virginia riflemen, hidden behind fences and perched in trees, picked off the British officers with rapid firing.

On October 7, the second battle of Saratoga started as the British drums beat an advance. The Americans for once outnumbered their opponents two to one. General Burgoyne made a valiant effort to pull his Crown elements together, but his forces were routed. On Friday, October 17, General Burgoyne rode to the American headquarters. About ten o'clock the drums rolled as 5000 royal troops trudged by in sullen silence to stack their arms.

The significance of the surrender at Saratoga was stupendous.[35] Its impact inspired anew the spirit of the American people and the conquest influenced France to recognize the infant republic formally. On January 8, 1778,

King Louis XVI notified Benjamin Franklin in Paris that his country would enter into a Treaty of Alliance with the United States.[36]

Williamsburg celebrated the Saratoga victory with pomp and a parade. Instructions were issued for the officers at the garrison to "see that the men shall be clean, shaved, their hats cocked, and their guns and accoutrements in good order." For the special occasion each soldier was to receive a gill (four ounces) of rum. At three o'clock on October 30 the ceremony began as the forces filed from their barracks to form a battalion. The martial music of the drum and fife beat the tempo as the troops started from the north end of town and were joined by the city militia. The platoons rounded the corner by the Capitol, marched down Duke of Gloucester Street, and proceeded with military precision to Court House Green. Since the Assembly was in session, the speakers of both houses and the delegates were honored guests gathered at the Court House.[37]

General Nelson reviewed the troops. Thirteen discharges of cannon boomed a salute; the infantrymen fired three volleys, and three loud huzzas from all present rang out to hail the victory. The newspaper account of the parade and festivities noted that the "joy and satisfaction upon the occasion was evident in the countenance of everyone and the evening was celebrated with ringing of bells, illuminations, etc."[38]

In reality Thomas Nelson, Jr., had no official capacity as brigadier general of the state militia. Because the threat of invasion had passed, the Council had discharged the servicemen on September 30, putting an end to Nelson's position and showing their appreciation to him by affirming, "Board being highly sensible of the Activity, Diligence, & good Conduct of that gentlemen in the Discharge and Trust reposed in him, recommend to his Excellency the Governor to give him the most honourable Testimony thereof."[39]

General Nelson had notified George Washington of the military change:

> The Governor and Council have thought proper to dismiss upwards of 1,000 of the militia and talk of discharging more of them. I believe on account of the scarcity of provisions, which has been occasioned by our thinking ourselves too secure from any attack from the Enemy, and selling vast quantities of salted provisions which at this time are much wanted.[40]

Although disappointed by the action of the authorities, Nelson affirmed, "I must acquiesce."[41]

When the Council convened on Friday, October 10, Lieutenant Governor Page presided (since Governor Henry was on his honeymoon) and read the communication that General Nelson had received from General Washington:

> I am inclined to think General Howe's objective is so fixed that Virginia will have but little cause to apprehend an Invasion this Campaign. . . . If my

conjectures on these head are right, the keeping on the Militia, that are first assembled, would incur a heavy expense without any necessity for it.[42]

Because he had taken a trip to Hanover after the militia had been discharged, Nelson had not read this dispatch as soon as he otherwise would. He was disturbed that the delegates had been late in arriving for the General Assembly session scheduled to start October 19. Military and money matters had been of primary concern to the conscientious official for three years, but not enough members appeared to make a quorum until the end of the month. Thomas was serving as chairman of a committee to find funds. Rich planters dipped into their own pockets to help the state, and Secretary Nelson lent several hundred pounds toward the project. Property taxes were increased, slave rates raised ten shillings a hundred pound valuation, and hikes made on horses, mules, and cattle. Levies were added on liquor, marriage licenses, carriages, and permits to operate ordinaries. The delegates even proposed a five-shilling tax on certain dogs, but this impost seemed too far-fetched and did not pass.[43]

While attending the autumn assembly, Nelson wrote Washington from Williamsburg on October 24 pertaining to the military plans:

> That the aid to be afforded by militia is no means desirable, provided other could be procured, I am very sensible, but indeed my dear General, I am sorry to tell you, that you are in future, to expect only drafted Militia or volunteers for the time from this State.[44]

A plan permitting a man to send a substitute soldier in his place "had induced many to give as high as £100 for a recruit, which has effectually put a stop to the enlisting business for a bounty of twenty dollars."[45]

In addition to approving tax measures and answering innumerable claims, the Assemblymen observed the amenities with appropriate courtesy. The House of Delegates paid honor to Thomas Nelson, Jr., on November 3, as Speaker George Wythe stated:

> Resolved that the thanks of this House be given to General Nelson for his services to the Commonwealth, as commander of the forces thereof. . . .
>
> General Nelson, the representatives of your country are ever disposed to pay proper attention to your distinguished merit. Your acceptance of the appointment to the command of forces of the Commonwealth, in the manner you did, showed you to have been activated by noble principles and generous motives; and your exemplary diligence and alertness in performing the duty were such as become a virtuous citizen, and a good officer.[46]

General Nelson responded graciously to the tribute:

> Mr. Speaker—so honorable a testimony that my conduct hath been approved by my country, will make a lasting impression on me. I assure the

House, that it is my chief ambition to deserve the good opinion of my fellow citizens, so it shall be my study and endeavor to secure a continuance of it, by faithfully discharging my duty in any office, civil or military, they may think me worthy of.[47]

Property was changing hands frequently. Nelson was acting as a trustee with his Burwell cousins to dispose of land belonging to the late James Burwell, and he was still trying to settle the estate of his late uncle, Robert Carter Burwell. In the fall of 1777, his uncle Robert Carter Nicholas wanted to sell his Williamsburg property, as well as five hundred acres six miles from Powhatan Swamp. Nicholas had advertised that the numerous stores in town were detached from the other buildings with "eight lots with large gardens dwelling house large and commodious with four rooms on front and in good repair . . . a fine spring."[48]

John Parke Custis had written George Washington pertaining to a planta-tion in King William County. His stepfather informed Jack he could have the dower estate with his coming of age "if agreeable to his Mother, except the breeding Mares and Fillies," but since Washington was too far away to discuss the matter effectively, he advised Jack to consult some "impartial Gentlemn unconcerned with valuation—General Nelson, Colonel Braxton, George Webb, Esq. I mention these Gentlemen because they are persons of character, and because no time may be lost in the Appointment."[49]

The representatives at the autumn Assembly recognized the seriousness of the money situation and raised the Governor's salary from £1,000 to £1,500. In 1778 the stipend was doubled to £3,000, but even with the in-crease in his income Patrick Henry discovered he could barely pay his bills with the depreciated dollar.[50]

The currency crisis caused many men to leave the army to look after their families. Colonel William Nelson wrote General Washington on October 13, 1777, his reasons for resigning from the Continental army:

> Sir, Lest you should be at a loss to conjecture on what principles I was induced to decline the command of the Regiment which you have been pleased to do the honor to proffer to me thro' Colo. Meade, I take the liberty of informing your Excellency, that as a variety of interesting Circumstances, among which personal Indisposition and the present peculiar delicate situa-tion of my Family & private affairs are by no means the smallest, has ren-dered it impossible for me to continue for any time in the military lines. . . . I have to request the permission of resigning my Commission and of returning to Virginia, where concerns of the utmost tenderness & importance to me demand my immediate presence.[51]

On that same day his wife, Lucy Chiswell Nelson, penned a remarkably revealing letter to Thomas Jefferson. She declared that her husband had defended his country in the conflict and been advanced to a lieutenant colonel and asserted:

> As he has a Family who very much want his presence, he is desirous of the Command of the last Battalion of Artillery which is to be disposed by the Assembly at their next meeting; not that his Ardour is in the least abated but he thinks he can serve his Country as effectively here; and attend to his own Affairs which suffer much by his absence. You know my situation, with three young Children, must make him anxious for a success on this occasion; and as you have a good deal of Influence in the House, you will oblige me exceeding by giving him your Interest.[52]

Jefferson's answer to this appeal, written from Williamsburg on October 24, was politic and opened with statement, "Colonel Nelson's merit and his present command place him in my judgment without a competitor for the post to which him appointed."[53] Jefferson then voiced the viewpoint that people had been "deceived by overrating" his influence and that nothing but "force of personal merit" could assist in promotion. Many officers, however, would have disagreed sharply with his opinion. Before Lucy Chiswell Nelson could receive the reply from Jefferson, her husband had resigned his commission in the American army.

The Congress had decided to shift the duty of supplying the soldiers with clothing to the states, for the delays and deficiencies of outfitting the units had been disgraceful. Cloth from France failed to reach the army because the British ships blockaded the seaports. When Washington communicated with friends and officials, his correspondence noted the nakedness of the Continental troops. One of his letters to Nelson, dated September 27, had listed the lack of bare necessities:

> Here, I must remark our distress for want of Shoes is almost beyond conception, and that from this circumstance our operations and pursuit have been impracticable.[54]

Then on November 8 the Commander-in-Chief had written Nelson from White Marsh concerning the militia the local leader had wanted to enlist:

> I now wish I have given more into your generous proposal; but the distance, and uncertainty of keeping Militia in service any length of time were obstacles . . . which seemed too great to counterbalance by the advantages of your coming . . . but the glorious turn to which our affair to the North have since taken, makes a new plan, and Winter campaign, if we can get our ragged and half naked soldiers clothed.[55]

The Assembly of Virginia authorized Governor Henry to seize shoes, stockings, linens, and woolens from any person hoarding goods, as speculators planned to sell supplies out of state for high profit.[56] The commanding officers of the county militia were asked to secure from citizens a pair of shoes, stockings, and gloves for each soldier serving in the Continental army. Nelson was diligent in this duty and dipped into his own funds to help furnish outfits.[57]

Encouraging re-enlistments and raising recruits remained a constant problem. General Washington, expressing his ideas on enlistment to General Nelson wrote: "If our Regiments were once compleated and tolerably well Armed and Clothed, the calls upon Militia afterwards would be rare; and 'till these measures are accomplished, our expenses will be enormous."[58]

General Washington was worried that the enlistment time for the first nine Virginia regiments would expire in a few weeks and wondered how many men would re-enlist.

Congress finally approved the Articles of Confederation on November 17, 1777, and forwarded the compact to the thirteen states for ratification.

Nelson had represented Virginia on the committee appointed in the Congress on June 12, 1776, to prepare a plan of government under central control. As he read the complete document printed by Dixon-Hunter in the November 28 issue of the *Virginia Gazette*, Nelson recalled the long debates over the Confederation in the stifling summer days of 1776 and was pleased to cast his affirmative vote for the compact. He was gratified that his associates in the December Assembly approved the articles unanimously. By the following July, nine states had adopted the Confederation and three others soon followed with a favorable vote. (Maryland delayed its ratification until March 1, 1781 when the states owning large lands to the West ceded their claims.)

The Nelson family and other citizens of York Town in December were concerned with the smallpox scourge that had swept through the soldiers' camp. On December 15, the York County Court asked Secretary Nelson to confer with the Governor and his Council to order the officer of the garrison to send infected soldiers south of town. The worried lawmakers also wanted sentinels posted to prevent the spreading of the disease. Dr. Pope, as the physician in charge of the hospital, soon set up a place where persons were inoculated against the disease.[59]

On January 20, 1778, Nelson wrote General Washington from Williamsburg about the plans for inoculation and told of some citizens' opposition to the procedure:

> Your favor of the 15th ult. should not have remained so long unanswered, had I not been obliged by an indisposition, to absent myself from the business of the House of Delegates, for a fortnight past. . . . for I am well convinced that General Howe would offer more by a few Phials of small pox matter, than he could his whole train of Artillery; and yet so perverse are

our Countrymen in general, that they would hazard almost American Independency rather than submit to a temporary ill.[60]

Despite his public duties and private concerns, Nelson did not neglect his correspondence with the Commander-in-Chief. The rapport that existed between the two men resulted from mutual esteem, and their involvements in military matters, as well as their family relationship.

After Nelson had asked the Commander-in-Chief about the strength of the American army, the General replied that this question "Is of so important nature, that although I have the fullest confidence in you, I dare not trust the particulars to paper for fear of accidents. This much I can assure you, that our numbers have always been much exaggerated and that the Enemy have constantly exceeded our Continental force."[61]

With desertions and disease taking toll, militia coming and going, regimental officers resigning, and a shortage of staff aides, in reality the Commander-in-Chief could not keep an accurate and up-to-date account of the army.

General Nelson envisioned a regular army enlisted for a period of three years. With longer terms of service, the detachments could be disciplined adequately to defend the country and to pursue the conflict with Great Britain to a victorious conclusion.

Strangely, General Washington did not agree entirely with the expectations of General Nelson:

> Although it is devoutly to be wished that Soldiers could engage for three years of the war, yet I am perswaded it would not be consistent with good policy to attempt it at this time; consequently, that the plan of drafting for twelve months only is a wise measure.[62]

The Commander-in-Chief, like others, deplored the fact that representatives of the Continental Congress had diminished in strength and statesmanship. He expressed his views to Nelson in Virginia.

> You gave me reason, my dear Sir, to believe, I shall see you at Camp in the spring. I shall rejoice at it, or to hear of your being in Congress, again, as I view with concern the departure of every Gentleman of independent spirit from the grand American Council.[63]

In all probability, Nelson heard about the conspiracy called the Conway Cabal against the Commander-in-Chief. Rumors reached Williamsburg in December. Since he had a high regard for the Commander-in-Chief, he defended General Washington against malicious talk. So did Governor Henry when he received a long unsigned letter crowded with criticisms of the Congress, the supply system, and the hospital setup. The anonymous author reached a climactic point by praising Gates, Charles Lee, or Conway as capable commanders who could save the country. Patrick Henry claimed he could not recognize the writing but enclosed the correspondence with a letter to General Washington. The Commander-in-Chief identified the handwriting of Dr. Benjamin Rush in the extremely critical epistle and informed Henry.[64]

The men who maligned Washington failed in their efforts to replace him, but relationships among them simmered with furious undertones.

The Continentals in camp at Valley Forge had a more pleasant incident to talk about in January. Captain Henry Lee, attached to the Light Dragoons of his kinsman Colonel Theodorick Bland, and seven of his cavalry companions had scattered two hundred Englishmen in a skirmish at Spread Eagle Tavern when the redcoat column attempted to steal horses. Lee would turn twenty-two on January 29, so the deed was a fitting birthday celebration. Washington invited the captain to become one of his aides, but Lee preferred action in the field. He was promoted to major for his heroic feat and permitted to raise two companies of cavalrymen. Later "Light Horse" Harry gained further fame and recognition in rank as the bold and brave leader of Lee's Legions.[65]

Lucy and Thomas Nelson were naturally interested in the news of this expedition. The young captain was Lucy's third cousin; his mother shared the name *Lucy Grymes*. George Washington also might have looked at the lad with more than official interest for young George had been among the many beaus courting his mother, known as the "Lowland Beauty."

CHAPTER NINETEEN

Allegiance, Arguments, and Arms: 1778–1779

Oath of Allegiance ✦ Sequestration ✦ Nelson's Volunteer Cavalry Corps ✦ Cavalrymen to Philadelphia ✦ Congress Disbands ✦ English Evacuate Philadelphia ✦ Baby Robert is Born ✦ Nelson Returns to Congress ✦ Deane–Lee Feud ✦ Complaints and Charges ✦ Nelson and Two Lees Leave Congress ✦ British Threat to Virginia ✦ General Nelson and Mobilization ✦ May 1779, Assembly

Nelson was indisposed the last of December 1777, and the sick spell caused him to miss the meetings of the House of Delegates until the twentieth of January 1778. Petitions poured into the Capitol from every direction as citizens and the military sought help. Typical of these was the one presented in the House of Delegates by General Nelson for Nathaniel Gist that stated, "He did render essential service and ought to be paid £50 for his trouble."[1]

Captain Nathaniel Burwell, commanding the troops quartered at Portsmouth, complained that the commissaries had failed to furnish the "Garrison with flour," and his appeal to the authorities was only one of countless complaints.[2]

When the gentlemen gathered in the taverns during the winter weeks, their talk turned to taxes and trade. The General Assembly had accepted the recommendation of Chairman Nelson to raise revenue and had increased taxes on property, stock, and licenses. Owners of large estates declared they would have to dispose of some of their holdings to pay the taxes.

Merchants worried about the loss of trade. Shopkeepers on Duke of Gloucester Street in Williamsburg agreed with the complaints of their disgruntled customers; prices were exorbitant. Even well-to-do women refused to pay fifty shillings a yard for linen or to buy English broadcloth at four pounds a yard. Sixteen ounces of tea cost twelve pounds.[3]

The House of Delegates since May 1777 had been diligent in ascertaining the political ideology of its constituents. At that time, lawmakers had passed legislation requiring every male citizen over sixteen to renounce his loyalty to the British government and assert his allegiance to the Commonwealth.

Clerks kept lists of citizens who complied and those who did not. County judges were kept busy offering the oath of allegiance.[4]

Lord Thomas Fairfax, the sixth earl by the name, however, because of his age, was allowed to remain on his land but required to pay double tax on his extensive estates and tithables. He lived at Greenway Court near Fredericksburg and was holding in fee and entail about five million acres between the Rappahannock and Potomac rivers for the Fairfax heirs. He was one of the few recusants in Virginia remaining quietly in his residence. If Lord Fairfax had taken the oath of allegiance to the patriotic government, he would have lost his vast English lands. The Fairfax family had befriended young George Washington a quarter of a century before, but fortunes of war had broken the bonds.[5]

In addition to making British-loving people renounce their loyalty to the Crown *and* sign a loyalty oath, the statesmen next determined to sequester the lands of the Loyalists. The delegates also decided to ease its citizens' debts to English creditors by permitting them to pay British merchants in the depreciated paper money.

Nelson had been in attendance in the autumn Assembly of 1777 when Jefferson first introduced the issue, but he had not been present in January when the resolution was first read. The Sequestration Act appealed to debt-ridden representatives entangled in an economic crisis brought on by the conflict. Assemblymen argued that the state's sagging economy would be strengthened whenever the "lands, slaves, stocks, and implements belonging within this Commonwealth together with the crops now on hand or hereafter to accrue and all other estate of whatever nature not herein otherwise provided for of the property of any British subject, shall be sequestered into the hands of the commissioner to be appointed from time to time by the Governor and the Council for each particular estate."[6]

Citizens owing money to a British subject could pay the sum into the loan office and the creditor would receive a certificate showing he had discharged his debt.

Thomas Nelson, Jr., certainly had as much cause as his colleagues to cancel his increasing indebtedness by such a method. He had been forced to close his firm because business had been so bad, but his integrity, sense of justice, and moral principles made him oppose the measure and determine to pay his debts in full.

Nelson stood in the Assembly to remind the representatives that their debts had been incurred in a previous period under prior laws. In policies of trade the contracting parties had reciprocated a mutual trust, and in his opinion the obligations were still binding. Proclaiming that British merchants had often proved to be the colonists' benefactors, he considered the bill a breach of contract. The act would not only bring about "injustice to the innocent," but would also show a spirit of "gross ingratitude" to English creditors. He declared with fervor, "For these reasons, Sir, for these reasons, I hope the bill will be rejected; but whatever its fate, by God, I will pay my debts like an honest man."[7] Despite his rational defense, the delegates passed the provision on January 22.

On the next day, the Assemblymen, with the approval of Governor Henry and the Council, appointed Thomas Nelson, Jr., and Alexander Spotswood, brigadier generals to command the troops of the Commonwealth. Nelson was considered an expert in military matters by his colleagues, and Colonel Spotswood had been a major in the Second Virginia Regiment, had served in the Continental campaign in the North and been commissioned a colonel.[8]

To raise revenue the Assemblymen issued more paper money, but as the pasteboard bills rolled from the press, their value depreciated daily. The rate soon became five to one.

Jefferson, satisfied with the passage of the Sequestration Act in January, headed home for Monticello in the Albemarle hills after four months in Williamsburg.[9]

Those who stayed in the Assembly realized not enough Virginians were volunteering for service in the Continental army and instituted a draft system to be set up under the administration of the county courts. Authorities were directed to prepare pieces of paper with "Service" written on some slips and "Clear" on others. On an appointed day all eligible men were to appear at county court houses throughout the state and draw for the draft.[10]

General Nelson was concentrating his energies on encouraging recruits for the ranks. He presented a bill proposing a volunteer regiment of 5000 Virginians be raised promptly to serve for six months, but the bill was rejected because the representatives thought such a move would check regular recruitment.

A new opportunity for service was soon opened for General Nelson when the Congress passed a resolution Monday, March 2, 1778:

> That it be earnestly recommended to the young gentlemen of property and spirit [all the states were listed] to raise a troop or troops of light cavalry, to serve at their own expense [except in the articles of provisions for themselves and forage for their horses] until 31 December next.[11]

When the resolution reached Virginia, Nelson was enthusiastic over the chance to command a cavalry corps. With characteristic energy, he began contacting eligible men from his family and friends to enlist in the light horse troop. His brothers Hugh and Robert answered the call, but Nathaniel had matrimony on his mind and didn't join. Cousin Lewis Burwell, from Gloucester County, became a member of the corps and put up £100 for the project.

Editor Purdie praised this generous gesture in his May 1, 1778 *Virginia Gazette:*

> When gentlemen of the first rank and fortune set so noble an example, we can hardly entertain a doubt of General Nelson's Corps being soon able to march to join their illustrious Commander in Chief with a complete and well appointed regiment.

The Assembly passed an act appointing General Nelson to raise the Regular Horse unit of 350 volunteers. Members voted £12,000 to supply arms and £4,000 to buy mounts for the men who could not furnish their own horses. The bill provided that purchasing horses should not exceed £150 for each animal.[12]

General Nelson published an address in the Dixon *Virginia Gazette* April 24, 1778, urging young gentlemen to enter the cavalry corps:

> True sons of Liberty, of such, and of such only, the corps must be composed. There are many gentlemen in this state, whose fortunes will enable them to equip themselves. They should step forth and set an example. . . . We have among us noble spirited young men whose patriotic zeal would prompt them to join us, did not their inability in point of fortune prevent them. . . . To enable such, therefore, to enter this service, I propose that such should be furnished with a horse and accoutrements by subscription in their respective counties, and surely those who remain'd at home, enjoying all the blessings of domestic life, will not hesitate to contribute liberally for this purpose.

Nelson was not one to ask the liberty-loving citizens to contribute without doing so himself; he dipped into his own funds to outfit the forces. Young volunteers gathering for the cavalry troop discussed possibilities for their uniforms. High helmets with plumes, colored facings with bright buttons, polished boots, and shining swords were favored dress for light dragoons. Editor Dixon's paper informed the public with the patriotic fervor:

> Several young Gentlemen in this city having offered themselves Volunteers for General Nelson's Light Horse provided they could be equipped, a subscription was immediately set on foot for that purpose, and upwards of £300 subscribed in a day or two.

Regarding recruitment, Nelson wrote General Washington on May 5 [I] "am endeavouring to promote . . . raising Volunteer Cavalry. . . . Several of the first gentlemen in the country having engaged as privates, who will equip themselves . . . others by subscription."[13]

Nelson declared he would use all dispatch to get the cavalry equipped and asked General Washington for instructions on this point. By the end of the month, the Commander-in-Chief replied, "I Thank you for your exertions to raise a body of Cavalry for reinforcing and relieving those belonging to the Army, which by the severe service of the last campaign are much reduced . . ." and counseled Nelson not to wait upon the carbines. Then General Washington referred to the Treaty of Alliance with France and commented that it "must have been more galling and degrading to the pride and ambition of Britain than anything she has experienced since she was a Nation. . . . Matters abroad appear to be in as favorable train as we could wish."[14]

The Congress had stipulated in its resolution regarding the corps that at least twenty and not over sixty should sign, but the ambitious Virginia Assembly had set 350 in its act. General Nelson worked tirelessly through the spring and summer to secure the number, but only one hundred Virginians rode up to the rendezvous at Port Royal on the Rappahannock River. Under Nelson the detachment drilled through suffocating June and July days with temperatures often soaring above one hundred degrees learning to mount quickly, form, wheel, and spur across the field in a fighting charge. George Nicholas was elected first lieutenant and Hugh Nelson became the second lieutenant of the corps.[15]

Although General Nelson desired more than the one hundred volunteers, others thought the number sufficient and Edmund Pendleton stated the ranks were filling up.

Recruitment for the ranks was becoming more difficult in the third year of the war. Although few could quote the figures, every family in the Commonwealth seemed to have a soldier in service. In 1778, over twenty-four thousand men were either members of the county militia forces or had served with one of the nine Virginia regiments in the Continental army.[16]

Since Nelson put his patriotism above profit, he was disappointed that men were averse to fighting in the army but were alert in mercantile endeavors. He expressed to General Washington that the "number of resignations in the Virginia line is induced by the officers, when they have returned, finding that every man who remains at home is making a fortune, whilst they are spending what they have in the defense of their Country."[17]

The Commander-in-Chief answered this communication with these thoughts:

> I am sorry to find such a backwardness in Virginia in the service of the Army. I am convinced that you have left nothing undone, of encouragement, for the increase of your Corps, or that could be of advantage to the service; and shall be happy to see you with such number as you have collected as soon as their condition will admit of their joining the army.[18]

By the end of July, General Nelson and his horsemen crossed the Rappahannock River to ride through the rolling Maryland countryside toward Baltimore. Count Casmir Pulaski was in the city striving to secure men for an independent cavalry corps. The twenty-nine-year-old Polish nobleman had proved a problem to the Commander-in-Chief and the Congress in clamoring for top rank. After being promoted the previous September to chief command of the Continental cavalry and being commissioned a brigadier general, the dapper, swarthy count still caused controversy and resigned the post in March. The Congress then permitted Pulaski the privilege of recruiting his own Light Horse troop, but he ran into trouble again with the authorities by enlisting prisoners and deserters. When Pulaski reviewed the volunteer Virginia corps, through his interpreter he commended the gentlemen for "high gallantry" and their "excellent condition."[19]

General Nelson's "body of Virginia gentlemen elegantly mounted as Volunteer light horse" pushed on to Philadelphia and arrived August 5, according to the *Pennsylvania Packet* in its August 6, 1778, issue. He was anxious to visit the Congress but distressed to learn the British had dumped corpses and debris in pits so close to the State House that the session did not start until July 7. The delegates had the area cleaned before convening. Although few Signers were still serving, the statesmen had celebrated July 4 with an appropriate public ceremony, and the group had attended Christ Church on Sunday to give thanks for the divine guidance that had supported the independence of the states.[20]

The excited young gentlemen from Virginia hardly had time to view Philadelphia—the planetarium, Philosophical Hall, vocational schools, fashionable City Tavern—before the changeable Congress decided their corps was not needed. The blow was not softened by compliments from the Congress.

> A Volunteer Corps of Cavalry from the State of Virginia, under the command of the honorable General Nelson, who are now in this city, on their way to the army, under the command of General Washington, and, whereas the removal of the enemy from this state renders the employment of this corps at present unnecessary; Resolved, that it be recommended to the said corps to return, and that the thanks of Congress be given to the Honorable General Nelson and the officers and gentlemen under his command for their brave, generous, and patriotic efforts in the cause of their country.[21]

It was also recommended that the "inhabitants imitate the virtuous conduct of the Volunteers from Virginia." The men's dreams of winning honors were crushed. General Nelson was keenly disappointed by the decision of the Congress to disband his corps, but he called the troops together and tried to cheer the downcast cavalrymen. Glancing at his group, he readily understood that some of them lacked funds. With his usual generosity, he told them, "If anyone here is in want of money, let him repair to my quarters and I will supply him myself."[22] Many of the men accepted the offer, some of them probably thinking it was a present rather than a loan, for the expedition proved to be an expensive project for General Nelson.

Before the cavalrymen started through the countryside on the return home, Nelson made another generous gesture by the gift of a fine horse to the Commander-in-Chief. He sent a short letter to General Washington on August 11, from Philadelphia:

> I have been informed that you have had the misfortune to lose your favourite Horse and that you are not mounted at present as you ought to be. . . . sending you a Horse that will suit you better than any one in America. . . . insist that he be accepted as a present.[23]

On August 20 a response came from General Washington in White Plains:

> My dear Sir—In what terms can I sufficiently thank you for your polite attention to me, and agreeable present. . . . with what propriety can I deprive you of a valuable and favourite horse? You have pressed me once, nay twice, to accept him as a gift; as a proof of my sincere attachment to, and friendship for you, I obey. . . . I am heartily disappointed at the late resolution of Congress for the discontinuance of your Corps.[24]

◆   ◆   ◆

When General Nelson and his cavalrymen returned to Virginia in August, they found the state drenched by heavy rains, wheat and corn crops beaten down by the deluge. Tom's cousin Landon Carter wrote in his diary, "rain nothing but rain," "more rain than a planter could tell what to do." (He also complained of colic that "drove him out of bed till broad day," intermittent fevers and swollen feet, yet he stated, "I was able without spectacles to read a note," written just before his sixty-eighth birthday on August 18.[25]

In the late autumn evenings after the Nelson household settled down for the night, Lucy had time to tell Tom about the activities of family and friends. Nathaniel had married Jane "Jeanie" Page, Hugh's sister-in-law in June. Editor Purdie had published the notice in his *Virginia Gazette* June 12, 1778:

MARRIAGES—NATHANIEL NELSON, ESQ; to Miss Jeanie Page, third daughter of the late Hon. John Page of North River.

On August 2 Patrick Henry's bride of ten months presented him with their first child, a daughter, whom they named Dorothea Spotswood Henry. The new arrival was Governor Henry's seventh child but the first baby born to his second wife.[26]

361

Lucy would soon present Tom with another son. Robert was born on October 14, their ninth child, the sixth son. William had celebrated his fifteenth birthday on August 9, and Thomas would turn fourteen on December 20.[27] The teenagers liked the parade of troops and the tempo of martial music, but their mother had other plans for her sons.

Tom no longer owned the Swan Tavern, having sold it for £1,000 of depreciated currency. York Town merchants could agree with Billy Reynolds in his remarks that "the Company I was concern'd in has been rather unfortunate. . . . John Hatley Norton has been very successful this War & must have made something very clever."[28]

Nelson and his neighbors regretted the death of John Norton October 25, 1777. Because of the stoppage in shipping and the acts of Parliament preventing correspondence with Americans, letters were either late or did not arrive at all. Several letters extending sympathy did not reach the Norton family until the fall of 1778.[29]

The older men reminisced about the passing of another Englishman whom they could remember by reputation. William Pitt, Earl of Chatham, had opposed the arbitrary policies of Britain toward America.[30]

Dudley Digges had a bit of bright news for Nelson since the Council had voted several warrants to reimburse General Nelson for the various charges of the cavalry.[31]

Patrick Henry had been re-elected Governor of the Commonwealth for his third one-year term on Friday, May 29.[32] Through much of June, however, ill health prevented the executive from presiding over the Council so Lieutenant Governor Page was chairman and the members had passed the special act regarding the cavalry.

The Commander-in-Chief had notified Nelson that the "hand of Providence has been conspicuous" in a change of circumstance for the Continental army. A surge of martial spirit had swept through the military camp at Valley Forge.[33]

General Charles Lee, who had wasted time indulging in indiscretions and writing criticisms about the Congress and General Washington, had been captured by the British several months before. Released on parole, he was escorted back to his camp where rumor said he had entertained a worthless woman at night in his room which was next to Mrs. Washington's sitting room.[34]

British General Richard Prescott had been exchanged for General Charles Lee. Captured first in 1775, he had been exchanged, and seized a second time in 1777 when he left Newport to lodge with the ladies of the evening nearby. Rebels dragged the British general from his warm bed.[35]

General Nelson was active in the Assembly all through autumn. Many petitions were referred to Nelson's committee; one of his volunteer cavalrymen asked for £100 for the loss of his valued mare which had died from the "excessive heat." Another gentleman needed compensation for "nursing and maintaining the soldiers for service." The Assemblymen allowed "40s for his trouble and expense—10d per day for 312 days amounting 151.10s for maintaining and nursing" two soldiers that would be charged to the United States of America.[36]

Purdie asked for remuneration as the public printer and by Tuesday, October 20, the representatives had resolved to pay the editor £1,500.

Nelson served on committees to check provisions and supplies and another charged with securing information about the Virginia troops in Continental service.

In November, Nelson, Mason, and Nicholas prepared a bill empowering the Governor to "seize and take all grain and flour necessary to support the French squadron." This same committee had worked on a bill for "impressing wagons and horses" and had written a bill to amend the act of sequestering British property, which Nelson read for the first time on Thursday, October 22.[37]

Some of the representatives became restless listening to the list of repetitious pleas. The record mentioned that George Mason, Thomas Jefferson, and Philip Grymes were all taken into "custody" and brought back into the hall. Small fees collected from the tardy members as a fine did not help the coffers very much.[38]

In October couriers pounded into Williamsburg from the coastal towns with intelligence that British ships had been sighted in Chesapeake Bay. Congress urgently requested Virginia to send militia units to South Carolina and Georgia. General Nelson reported that the committee recommended sending 1,000 troops to give aid to the two states. Then a report came that the English fleet had sailed back northward.[39]

Princess Anne County residents complained that numerous inhabitants of Norfolk were still supporting the royal standard. The delegates passed a proposal "to expel from the Commonwealth, and to prevent in future the return of persons who have shown themselves inimical to the liberties of America."[40]

A more pleasant piece of news was an announcement from Colonel George Rogers Clark. Two years before, the rugged, red-headed explorer had convinced Governor Henry and the Council to provide powder to protect the state's western region. With black eyes flashing, he had succinctly stated, "If a Country is not worth protecting, it was not worth claiming."[41] He and his 175 men had traveled more than a hundred miles through thick forests to reach Kaskaskia and capture the garrison there. Fort Cahoika also succumbed to a surprise attack. Father Gibault assisted the twenty-six-year-old Clark in gathering the French settlers at the post to take the oath of allegiance to the Commonwealth of Virginia. Clark and his warriors pushed on in a few weeks and conquered the fort at Vincennes seizing redcoat prisoners. The American flag was hoisted over all three forts. The Virginia Assemblymen were gratified that they had authorized the expedition and delighted to hear Clark's dispatch describing the successful captures.[42]

In the previous year several members from Virginia had served in the Congress for only a few months and then left, disillusioned about the economy and losses to the British. The bickering of the body over the Deane–Lee controversy, the suffering of the soldiers at Valley Forge, and a seeming lack of loyalty were causing rifts among the representatives.

On leave from the Congress, Richard Henry Lee wrote Governor Henry from Chantilly on November 15, 1778, about the discouraging conditions with the comment that the "division among ourselves, and the precipice on which we stand with our paper money, will, I verily believe, [be] the source of their [the enemy's] hope. . . . my anxiety arises from the clear conviction I have that loss of liberty seems at present more likely to be derived from the state of our currency than from all other causes."[43]

In December 1778, General Washington confided some of his deepest concerns to Benjamin Harrison in a lengthy communication, asserting "that America never stood in more imminent need of the wise, patriotic, and Spirited exertions of her Sons than in this period." He implored Harrison to use his influence to save his country by "sending your ablest and best Men to Congress. . . . in the present situation . . . I cannot help asking: Where is Mason, Jefferson, Nicholas, Pendleton, Nelson, and another I could name."[44]

The Virginia Assembly had already acted in accordance with the advice and had re-elected Thomas Nelson, Jr., on December 8 to represent the Commonwealth in the Congress in place of John Harvie who had resigned. The resolve stated that the delegate "be elected to that office without the formality of a ballot." It was the consensus among his colleagues that Nelson's nomination added strength to the state delegation because of his political experience and patriotism.[45]

Since Tom had spent many months in the Congress serving on committees to secure funds, he was well aware of its financial problems. Stopping inflation and stabilizing the currency were thorny topics. Previous proposals to burn the bills had been rejected, but in December 1778, the Assemblymen approved a measure to take some certificates out of circulation.

Tom knew his own funds were dwindling and his debts increasing. Before leaving for Congress again, he sold 600 acres of his York County property for £1,200.[46] If Lucy wondered why her husband would consent to serve in the Congress again so soon after his severe illness, she would not remonstrate with him. Some men would have held a simmering resentment over the summary dismissal of his cavalry corps in Philadelphia the previous spring, but Lucy knew Tom's resolute belief in the colonial cause would keep him in the service of his country.

After the icy snows slipped away and the incessant rains subsided so the rivers could be crossed, Thomas Nelson rode the familiar route once again toward Philadelphia to present his credentials to the Congress on Thursday, February 18, 1779.[47] Nelson found the financial situation depressing. Formerly, his committee had recommended to stop printing paper money as specie and to borrow from a foreign power, but the Congress had kept the presses rolling. Day by day the value of the issues declined and prices soared. Speculators and profiteers contributed to the crisis. A hundred pounds of flour cost up to fifteen pounds and hay for horses ranged from ten to thirty pounds per ton, General Washington had written. By June 1 the representatives had approved another thirty-five-million-dollar issue.[48]

Tom discovered that dissensions among the statesmen this session made earlier debates about independence and confederation pale in significance.

On March 23, Nelson wrote to General Washington from Philadelphia commenting on the dangers of the currency crisis.

> I am happy that my taking a seat again in Congress meets with your approval, and I shall be still more happy, if by my advice and assistance, America shall be relieved from the present distresses; for in my opinion she has not . . . been in so much danger as she is now, and principally from the state of our finances . . . in a strange confusion. What may be the result . . . calling in the Emissions of April and May 1777 and 1778 I know not; but the present effect is very contrary from what was expected. . . . I fear it has given a deadly slap to the credit of any Paper Money that may hereafter [be] issued by Congress.[49]

The Commander-in-Chief had been in Philadelphia the last of December and in January 1779 to present plans for the Continental army's proposed spring campaign. General Washington declared if he were called on to draw a picture of the delegates, "I should in one word say that idleness, dissipation, and extravagance seem to have laid fast hold of most of them."[50]

Several of the representatives reasoned that because the English enemy had evacuated Philadelphia, it was possible they might pull out entirely from the continent. The Commander-in-Chief was astounded at such thinking. The body did pass the bounty encouragement that stipulated each soldier who re-enlisted for the duration of the war should receive more money but not to exceed 200 dollars.[51]

Philadelphians found much to gossip about when General Benedict Arnold arrived in the city as military commander. He set up headquarters in a handsome house and lived lavishly. Silas Deane resided there, and rumors spread that Arnold, Deane, and Robert Morris were getting rich on government contracts. Rebels were incensed that Loyalists received lenient treatment and Tory belles danced at the city's balls. Although a leg wound kept him from dancing, Arnold, dressed in his bright uniform, enjoyed watching graceful Tory Margaret Shippen whirl around the floor. Because Arnold was friendly with the British, the Congress staged an investigation but lacked sufficient evidence for a conviction. After a whirlwind courtship, Arnold proposed to Margaret Shippen and, despite parental disapproval, the eighteen-year-old girl became the bride of General Arnold on April 8, 1779. The thirty-eight-year-old bridegroom bought the splendid Mt. Pleasant mansion as a wedding gift for his wife, and his grand gesture touched off more talk about his funds.[52]

Nelson soon noticed that the feud between the followers of Silas Deane and the adherents of Arthur Lee had split the Congress into two antagonistic factions. The delegates from Virginia were divided on the dispute. Richard Henry Lee and Francis Lightfoot Lee believed their brother Arthur Lee, while Meriwether Smith stood with the conservative statesmen from the middle and southern states who defended Deane. Deane had been sent to France to secure aid; and Dr. Arthur Lee, living in London, was asked to sound out foreign sentiment on the colonial cause. Dr. Benjamin Franklin was then appointed a commissioner to join Deane in France. The trio were at odds with their opinions and personalities. Deane was garrulous and Lee contentious. All through the autumn of 1778, the Congress questioned Deane on his agreements and accounts concerning French aid. They found it difficult to ascertain whether supplies from France before the official alliance was signed were a gift or whether the new nation was indebted for the items. Deane claimed the supplies were to be charged; Arthur Lee declared they were a gift. Conrad Alexandre de Rayneval Gerard, the French ambassador to the United States, was caught in the crossfire of the feud.[53] The controversy became so involved that Congressmen neglected the country's interests. Debates raged for months pertaining to a peace settlement and representatives split according to regional interests.

March was a busy month for Nelson as he served on several committees to "consider the circumstances of the southern states and ways and means for their security and defense and report to Congress without delay."[54] Then he worked with four other members to consider measures for the defense of South Carolina and Georgia.

Washington wrote of his feelings to Nelson on March 15.

> Our Affairs, according to my judgment, are now come to a Crisis, and require no small degree of political skill. . . . Unanimity in our Councils, disinterededness in our pursuits, and steady perseverance in our national duty, are the only means to avoid misfortunes.[55]

While General Washington had innumerable worries with plans to win the war and communicated his perplexities in his correspondence, there were some light moments at Middlebrook where he was headquartered. On

February 18, 1779, a ball was held in an attractive enclosure in Artillery Park to celebrate the anniversary of the French alliance. The seventy ladies did not lack for partners as several hundred gentlemen attended the affair.[56]

General Greene and his charming wife, Catherine, gave a ball at their brick residence on the Raritan. General Washington got plenty of practice on that March evening swinging through the rhythmic steps. Greene wrote of Washington, "His Excellency and Mrs. Greene danced upwards of three hours without sitting down. Upon the whole we had a pretty little frisk."[57]

The animosity emanating from the Deane–Lee controversy continued to keep the Congressman on edge. The record of Wednesday, May 24, 1779, is filled with charges against both Silas Deane and Arthur Lee with corroborating evidence. The resulting dissension caused several representatives to call on their respective states for a replacement. Nelson also asked for a leave of absence and was back in Virginia by the middle of May, soon followed by the two Lee brothers.[58]

On May 8, a British fleet of thirty-five ships, half of them large-armed vessels lined with guns and filled with two thousand troops, had sailed into Chesapeake Bay. The raiders swarmed ashore in the Hampton Roads harbor destroying Fort Nelson and looting Portsmouth guarded by only one hundred Virginia militia. The British burned rebel barges and boats and set the torch to three thousand hogsheads of tobacco, then swept on toward Suffolk killing and capturing cattle, smashing patriot supplies, and burning twelve hundred barrels of pork.[59] Governor Henry's proclamation of May 15 to the citizens of Virginia stated that the English enemy had invaded the state and had taken ". . . the fort at Portsmouth and also destroyed many vessels and committed horrid ravages and deprivations . . . plundering and burning houses and exercising other abominable cruelties and barbarities."[60]

General Nelson gathered together the available militia in the area, sending his own slaves to work in some neighborhood fields while the men mustered. He established a garrison at York Town to guard against an impending attack and stationed smaller forces along the shore.[61]

General Charles Scott had been raising two thousand recruits throughout the state to be sent to the relief of South Carolina, but in the local crisis the old commander requested the Assembly to bring the regiments back to Virginia. Colonel George Baylor's cavalry camped at Winchester and was sent to Williamsburg to protect the capital.

General Nelson received a report from Colonel Thomas Marshall, dated May 26, stating that "The enemy's fleet are now under full sail and stand out at Hampton, but whether they mean to have us altogether, or only to move to some more defenseless quarter, where they may ravage and destroy with impunity, is a question out of my power to determine." The young commander continued, saying they would "watch and give earliest intelligence if [they] turn up by or York River, join you with all my troops."

I cannot conclude this letter without mentioning the activity and zeal, with which the Gentlemen of the light horse, under Captain Nelson, have shewn on all occasions they really are an exceeding useful Corps, and have set a most laudable example.

Colonel Marshall then commended the "college volunteers" for their "cheerfulness to duty" and affirmed that "never in my life saw troops fly to arms with more readiness."[62]

By May 26, the British ships sailed away from the Virginia coast and General Scott with the recruits from the Commonwealth marched into South Carolina to assist the colonials in defending Charleston against the Crown forces.

Nelson was elected again as a delegate to the Virginia Assembly by the voters of York County and appeared in the Assembly the end of May. Governor Henry was looking forward to leaving office. He needed relaxation, as he had suffered through the spring with periodic feverish spells and had missed several sessions of the Council. When Thomas had a chance to talk with his friend, he found him disturbed over the controversies in the Congress, and he probably discussed the divergent trends in his own administration. Nelson was aware that the forces of liberalism and conservatism had already divided the Assembly into distinct factions.[63]

Jefferson had led the liberal combination to support his progressive reforms. Arguing against primogeniture, establishing the separation of church and state, and fighting the Sequestration Act had incurred the wrath of the influential aristocracy. For the past three years, Jefferson had recommended the removal of the capital to Richmond. On May 28, 1779, he was appointed to a committee to consider shifting the seat of government from Williamsburg to a more centrally located site. Then on Saturday, May 29, a proposal was presented and read for the first time. By June 3, this goal had been accomplished.[64]

The election of a new executive was also a foremost matter. The progressive forces of the Piedmont region, deriving strength from Patrick Henry partisans, sponsored Thomas Jefferson for Governor. The conservatives from the Tidewater section supported two candidates for the gubernatorial post: John Page, who had gained first-hand experience as the presiding official in the absence of Governor Henry, and Thomas Nelson, Jr., who had followed his father William Nelson and his uncle Secretary Thomas Nelson into a family tradition of civil service. Tom had represented his country in the local legislature for years as well as the Commonwealth in the Congress.[65]

The three candidates who were friends connected by close family ties, did not campaign for the governorship, but their partisans canvassed the county delegates who would elect the Governor. The campaign centered on the division between the conservative aristocratic class and the emerging liberal representatives who were ready to wrest control from the oligarchy. On Tuesday, June 1, Thomas Jefferson polled a plurality of fifty-five and the Tidewater statesmen split, casting thirty-eight votes for John Page and thirty-two for Thomas Nelson. The record of the House of Delegates read, ". . . neither of these persons balloting for a majority of both houses, the House proceeded to ballot between Thomas Jefferson, Esq., & the Honorable John Page." On the second ballot Page received sixty-one votes and Jefferson sixty-seven. Page and Nelson congratulated Jefferson and the election did not appear to damage the men's friendship.[66]

◆   ◆   ◆

Aristocratic gentlemen who mistrusted Jefferson grumbled about his familiarity with German prisoners—the cultured ones—quartered in barracks near Charlottesville. He befriended especially Baron von Riedsel and his wife. When Jefferson entertained the educated English officers and higher ranking German officers the Baroness would amuse the assemblage with a spicy story caricaturing rustics or an Italian song. She wrote in her diary, "The Virginians are most indolent, which is ascribed to their hot climate, but with the slightest inducement, they are ready in an instant to dance."[67] (Although she enjoyed Jefferson's hospitality on several occasions, she did not mention the family once in her diary.)

Thomas enjoyed conviviality with family and friends during the stifling summer days. He and Lucy often visited his mother and the large family clan that filled the household across the street. All the Nelson sons had brought their brides home to live under the parental roof. Tom and Lucy had lived in the William Nelson house over five years; their first four boys had been born there before they moved to the mansion that "Scotch" Tom Nelson had built. Robert Nelson and his wife, Mary Grymes, sister to Lucy, would celebrate their fifth wedding anniversary in October. Hugh and his wife, Judy Page, had two daughters, Jane Byrd and Lucy. Nathaniel and his bride, "Jeanie" Page, shared the home as well. (In four years the couple would become parents of Betsey, William, and another boy whose name was not later listed in his father's will.) Only the Nelsons could keep from confusing the repeated family names and manage to identify all the occupants of the dwellings. Nineteen-year-old William, the youngest of the five Nelson sons, was still a student at the College of William and Mary where he served as a second lieutenant of the College militia unit.

Just recently the Reverend James Madison, president of the College, had married Sally Taite of Williamsburg. The nuptials caused no especial excitement, as the wedding of the Reverend John Camm had a decade before when he had defied the rules to take young Betsey Hansford of York Town as his bride. Life's fitful fever was now over for the Reverend John Camm, for death had claimed him during the early part of the year. The militant minister might not have been mourned greatly by the patriotic citizens of the York Town community, but the Nelsons and their neighbors had been shocked to learn in the May 22, 1779, Dixon-Nicholson *Virginia Gazette* of the death of twenty-five-year-old Betsey Camm, who left five motherless children.

Elizabeth Nelson was grieved over the loss of her nephew, Lewis Burwell of Gloucester, who had died in the spring. Since he had married Judith Page, also a relative, the ties were close. Burwell had been born in 1737, just a year before Elizabeth's eldest son, Thomas.[68] Nelson had been notified in Philadelphia of the passing of his cousin, but now he had time to talk with his mother and read the eulogy that their mutual friend, St. George Tucker, had written about the sad event. The close associates of the Flat Hat Club at the College mourned the passing of their fellow member. Colonel James Innes wrote to St. George Tucker on March 20, 1779:

> I was with him the Day before he died—just time enough to have the happiness of performing the last friendly act for him. . . . he retained his senses most perfectly to the last moment—and met Death . . . with the utmost Serenity, Confidence and Composure. His Exit has given me a much better opinion of that Religion—to which he was most enthusiastically attached—than I have for some time entertained.[69]

Innes had asked Tucker to compose an ode to their companion and the elegy had been published in the paper. Young William Nelson was a member of the Flat Hat Club and was entrusted with the books and papers of the organization.

◆   ◆   ◆

Like other folk, the numerous Nelson tribe had been amused at the antics of the College students in their persistent plans to honor the Commander-in-Chief at a festive affair in February at the Raleigh Tavern. The College crowd and some citizens contacted the Governor concerning a banquet and ball to celebrate Washington's birthday but were denied their request since, the executive explained, he was against "rejoicing at a time when our country was engaged in war."[70] The petitioners then called on Councilor Dudley Digges; he also dismissed the group. The party planners, however, continued their project, sparked by spirited Colonel James Innes, over six feet in height. The twenty-five-year-old leader directed that two pieces of cannon be dragged up to the Raleigh so the celebration could be saluted with booming salvos. Captain Ned Digges sent his subordinate with a platoon to remove the cannon. Colonel Innes refused. The revelers plied him with punch. Captain Digges rushed to Governor Henry about the situation, but the official tossed the problem back to Digges. The captain marched with sixty men and, brandishing his bayonet, demanded that Colonel Innes surrender the cannon. A curious crowd of spectators lined the street to badger and cheer the combatants. Innes faced the contingent shaking his cane at Digges and declaring he would hit him if he did not depart immediately. The captain threatened to fire if the guns were not surrendered. Innes repeated his threat and ordered his cohorts to discharge the cannon with brickbats. After some delay, Captain Digges retreated, and that evening the College students had their ball.[71] The Dixon-Nicholas newspaper of February 26 duly notified the public of the festive event:

> On Monday 22 instant a very elegant entertainment was given at the Raleigh Tavern by the inhabitants of this State, to celebrate the Anniversary of that day which gave birth to GENERAL GEORGE WASHINGTON, Commander in Chief of the Armies of the United States, the Saviour of his Country, and the brave asserter of the rights and liberties of mankind.

✦   ✦   ✦

The citizens of York County met the last of July to discuss the currency crisis. As the group gathered on Court House Green, talk centered on prices. Shoes were selling for sixty dollars a pair; coffee cost twenty dollars a pound and tea was marked twelve pounds for sixteen ounces. Customers complained to the innkeepers about a common meal costing as much as twenty dollars.[72]

Nelson headed a committee of fourteen persons, among whom were experienced merchants Augustine Moore and William Reynolds, to study the situation.[73] The committee proposed setting a ceiling on the cost of certain products and a list was published in the July 31, 1779, Dixon *Virginia Gazette:* "Wheat per bushel, 6; flour per hundred, 20; brown sugar per pound, 1; West India Rum a gallon, 10; and French Rum per do, 6."

The same paper informed the public that the inhabitants had "entered into several resolutions well calculated to aid the exertions of the Governor in restoring its just value to our paper currency. The rates were the same as those fixed by the town meeting of Williamsburg, a few articles excepted."

An optimistic press resolved the matter favorably, but the freeholders soon found out otherwise when the Congress informed the citizens that no city, county, commonwealth or even the Congress had the power to impose a restriction on rates. Congress certainly didn't want lesser bodies usurping power it did not possess.[74]

When Thomas Nelson rode to Williamsburg to attend the autumn Assembly, the session did not start on Monday, October 4, because the delegates were slow to arrive. Tuesday, Wednesday, and Thursday slipped by and on the seventh the clerk recorded in the official *Journal* that "forty-one members besides speaker failed to appear"; a long list of the legislators were named to be taken into custody.[75]

By Wednesday of the following week, Nelson had again been appointed chairman of the Propositions and Grievances Committee and his table was soon stacked with pleas for damages "praying to be paid." In one such case, the representatives acted to relieve the "distressed circumstance" of the widow and children of Lieutenant Colonel John Seayres, who had fallen on the field at the battle of Germantown, so the sum of £250 was allocated to the family. Tory John Fisher was allowed to take the oath of allegiance because he had expressed his "attachment and interest in the American cause." The petition of David Ross, who professed his feeling for the patriots, was passed and the delegates granted his desire to become a citizen of the Commonwealth.[76]

The authorities turned a deaf ear to Peter Pelham's request for an additional tobacco allowance to care for the prisoners. He was not intimidated by the notorious Henry Hamilton confined to his quarters. Hamilton, former British Governor of the Northwest Territory, had insinuated that his jail keeper was "a Character beneath other people's notice." The previous February, Hamilton had been forced to surrender the fort at Vincennes to Colonel George Rogers Clark. News of the indiscriminate murder of women and children and the cruel atrocities by Indians preceded Hamilton's arrival in Williamsburg where a curious crowd gathered to stare at him and his subordinates. His policy of giving rewards for scalps had earned him the name "Hair-buyer" and the fear and hatred of loyal citizens.[77]

The Commonwealth experienced difficulties with its delegates to the Congress. James Mercer stayed only three weeks. Edmund Randolph, William Fitzhugh, and Meriwether Smith, elected in June, wrote letters of resignation in the fall.[78]

The statesmen in the autumn Assembly struggled with money matters and military measures. George Mason, Thomas Nelson, and Patrick Henry were appointed to check into the condition that some sheriffs were "misapplying money and taxes."[79] Mason and Nelson worked together on a petition to divide the parishes in Drysdale, Caroline, and King and Queen counties.[80] They also were empowered to present a bill for the regulation of importing salt and laying a limited embargo on the article.[81] On the proposal to put off a bill of "regulating militia," the two officials voted on opposite sides; Nelson voted against delaying the matter; Mason voted in the affirmative and the measure was postponed.[82]

On Tuesday, November 2, General Nelson presented a bill "for more effectively securing to the officers and soldiers of the Virginia line the lands reserved for them."[83] Settlements northwest of the Ohio River were to be discouraged.

General Nelson had Patrick Henry, Carter Braxton, and Nathaniel Burwell on his committee to prepare, explain, and amend the act concerning officers, soldiers, sailors, and marines serving in the forces. By Friday, November 26, he was ready to read the resolution that "all officers and soldiers as citizens of the Commonwealth belonging to any corps or contingent (actual service to the State) entitled to state provisions, clothing, bounty or other emoluments."[84] The provision included land or money with six months' pay to enable and to encourage soldiers to stay in service. This act was intended to ease the existing discontent among the commissioned officers. Colonels Bland and Baylor, commanding dragoons, had protested that state provisions of clothing and bounties had been denied their detachments.

The executives were emphatic in the resolution that "All persons in the State possessing arms, horses, cattle, and other property United States be compelled to deliver to Continental officers on demand."[85]

Chairman Nelson and a fifteen-man committee were involved with the investigation of persons antagonistic to the patriot party. The committee softened the Sequestration Act by granting leniency to citizens of the Commonwealth who were in England for their education and also to those persons who had gone to Great Britain to be with their families.[86]

The petition of Lucy Ludwell and her husband, John Paradise, attesting their allegiance was gratifying to Thomas so he could assure his wife of a favorable outcome for her cousin.[87]

Lucy longed to hear news of her uncle John Randolph and his family in England. She wanted to know more about her brother, John Randolph Grymes, who had resigned from the Queen's Rangers and sailed for England in 1778 where he married his first cousin Susannah Randolph.[88]

Nelson noted with satisfaction that members of the Norton family were complying with the oath of allegiance and returning to Virginia. Miss Frances Norton had married John Baylor in London on November 18, 1778, and three days later the couple set sail for Virginia.[89]

Throughout the fall session General Nelson presented a variety of petitions ranging from establishing ferries, incorporating the town of Alexandria, and supporting delegates to the Congress, to recommending a foundry be built at Westham. On December 10, he reported that the "Sum of one million five hundred thousand pounds arising from the sale of sequestration British estates be applied to payment of the requisition made by Congress to this State."[90] This figure indicated the inflationary trend of the times.

To meet the rising costs of operating government, the debt-ridden representatives raised taxes on slaves, spirits, and vehicles; and the officials present were as hard hit by the tax hike as any group of gentlemen. A tax of six pounds on all slaves over twelve years old except those exempted by age and infirmities was imposed; three pounds on a free male person above twenty-one years of age, with officers, navy men, and soldiers exempted. A forty-pound tax on coaches and chariots was to be collected by March 1, 1780; thirty pounds were placed on phaetons, stage wagons, and four-wheeled chaises; and ten pounds charged on two-wheeled chairs. Ordinary licenses cost forty pounds; eight shillings were to be collected on gallons of rum and brandy distilled in the state, with ten shillings for the imported spirits.[91]

On Thursday, December 16, the statesmen were still struggling with military matters and the delegates directed the Governor and Council to inquire about the militia that had marched to South Carolina and "did not return," lacking the permission of the commanding officer. The parliamentarians voted forty pounds for every non-commissioned officer and private in addition to his usual pay.[92]

◆   ◆   ◆

When the autumn Assembly adjourned December 24, Thomas Nelson rode home to spend Christmas with his family reflecting on the past four Christmases since the rebellion began. In 1775 Lucy had been with him at Philadelphia missing their children; in 1776, he had spent a dismal day away from his family in Baltimore. Although Thomas had been at home for Christmas in 1777, the smallpox scare that swept through York Town had made the season miserable. In December 1778, he had been re-elected to serve in the Congress which left him little leisure as he had struggled to sell more property to provide for his family during his forthcoming absence.

Once again the holiday was not devoted to gala diversions, but Lucy managed a good meal for the household. The flour shortage cut down on the family's pastries and puddings, but baked ham, chicken, apples, potatoes, relish, and pickles provided delicious fare.

Seated at the head of the table, Thomas offered thanks on the occasion, grateful to be surrounded by his six sons and three daughters. His wife, seated at the other end of the table was flanked by her sister Elizabeth, now nineteen. Robert, at fourteen months, and Lucy, who would be three in January, fidgeted from the clutches of the servants. Since three of the children had been born in December, the dinner could also have served as a birthday celebration. Thomas turned fifteen on the twentieth of the month and felt he was catching up to his sixteen-year-old brother William in studies and sports. Five-year-old Mary had been born on December 19, and the day after Christmas Elizabeth would be nine, when the master of the household turned forty-one. The third boy, Philip, had entered his teens in March; Francis turned twelve in June, and Hugh became eleven the last day of September.

During the dark winter weeks, Nelson meditated on the miserable conditions of the Commonwealth. He could not find a solution to his personal indebtedness any more than the state could solve its accumulated accounts. In the past two years paper dollars had depreciated so much in purchasing power that it took ten times the Continental currency to buy products in 1779 as it had in 1777. Confronted by these grim facts, his usual optimism failed him. Nelson recalled with distress the committee reports he had made to the House of Delegates that pinpointed the financial plight of Virginia. The economic decline had not been eased, as expected, by the sale of British estates. In his letter of November 29 to the Commander-in-Chief, Nelson had noted that the Ways and Means Committee had considered "measures to meet the requisitions of Congress," but in reality he could not be reassuring about the outcome. One astute observer had estimated the debts of the state at £26,000,000.[93]

Crop failures in the fall also contributed to the general distress. The price of wheat had skyrocketed because of scarcity. To stop speculators from supplying foodstuffs to the British, authorities had recommended an embargo on the exportation of "beef, pork, wheat, Indian corn, pease, and other grains."[94] Citizens of the Commonwealth first read the announcement of the proclamations as it appeared in the Dixon-Hunter *Virginia Gazette* on January 15, 1780.

Nature also created hardships with several weeks of wretched weather. About the middle of December, severe snows and icy storms began to cover the countryside and continued into the New Year. Old timers remarked that temperatures were the lowest they could remember in over thirty years. Poor people and slaves perished in the cold. Stock disappeared in the snow drifts several feet deep. Rivers froze. One York man informed newspaper editors ". . . several men crossed the river yesterday from Gloucester to that place, upon the ice, an instance of which is not remembered by the oldest person now living."[95]

In December 1779, the Governor and Council had approved a service recruiting plan submitted by the Board of War. The recruits were to report at designated places in the several counties by January. Colonels William Nelson and Samuel Griffin assisted James Innes, chairman of the War Board, in this endeavor. The trio, realizing the inclement weather would hamper their efforts to recruit soldiers, issued new orders from the war office at Williamsburg on February 4, postponing the days of rendezvous.[96]

Citizens living along the coastal counties were again apprehensive about an invasion by the English enemy. General Nelson certainly knew that Virginia, with many rivers running inward from the sea along a lengthy shoreline, would be difficult to defend. General Washington had written Governor Jefferson on December 11, "that a very large embarkation [said to amount to 8,000] . . . was at the Hook on the point of sail; and destination *reported* to be for Chesapeake Bay."[97] Fortunately, the news was premature, and the Commander-in-Chief soon conveyed that fact to Jefferson.

Their worries, however, were real. In November General Nelson and many others had been bitterly disappointed about the stunning loss of Savannah to the British although his remarks were mild in his November 29 letter to General Washington, "You have heard about the misfortune at Savannah."[98] Misfortune and confusion contributed to the defeat and failure of the American force to destroy the British fort at Savannah and oust the foe from Georgia.

CHAPTER TWENTY

Money Matters and Military Measures, Traitors and Turncoats: 1780

Nelson Pledges Funds As Security for State ✦ *Resignations of Officials and Officers* ✦ *Governor Jefferson's Frustrations* ✦ *Susanna Is Born*

Through the winter, wind whipped the stark trees and whirled the powdery snow. As the York River slowly thawed, gray slush beat upon its sandy beach. Twisting swirls of smoke from York Town chimneys filled the sky.

Virginia's desperate financial situation called Thomas away again from his family. Because of the economic crisis in the Commonwealth and the quotas required by the resolution of the Congress, the officials had floated a £5,000,000 loan. Returns of revenue were so inadequate, however, that the legislators petitioned individuals to lend funds to the government. With his characteristic patriotism, Nelson pledged his financial assets as security and joined in the endeavor to solicit subscriptions, riding to the plantations of family and friends during the chilly days to borrow money. Although not all owners opened their pocketbooks willingly, they did fling wide their doors in welcome, for they recognized Tom as a man of principle and loyal patriotism; Nelson succeeded in raising £10,000 for the cause of the state.[1]

The same economic depression was sweeping through all the states like an epidemic. Delegates at the Congress also faced the difficulties of increasing indebtedness, spiraling prices, and the decline of the dollar. Expenses were so exorbitant in Philadelphia that representatives resigned their posts. Three of the Virginia representatives had returned from Philadelphia in the fall.[2]

In December Congressman Cyrus Griffin had asked permission to return home, but his request was denied since he was the only delegate from Virginia at that time. Because he could not "maintain his house at the market prices," he had requested articles from the Continental stores, receiving a barrel of beef, pork, and a few barrels of flour, "but was so unlucky" not to get any good products. Nevertheless, he was criticized for his requisition.[3]

As a member of finance committees in the Virginia Assembly as well as the Congress, Nelson knew the overall picture. He had no faith in the lotteries, realized that counterfeiting by the enemy and local forgers only contributed to the paper currency crisis, but was perhaps most incensed at profiteers and speculators who monopolized the market in disreputable deals.

Patriots of Philadelphia had questioned the accounts of General Benedict Arnold after his appointment to the administration of American affairs in the reoccupied city. He was found guilty of conveying his private property in public wagons and allowing the *Charming Nancy* to sail from port without permission.[4]

Whenever a need arose for funds for the forces, as for his cavalry corps in 1778, Nelson demonstrated his devotion to the colonial cause by donating his own money. As a member of the Congress in 1775, 1776, 1777, and again in 1779, he knew the Continental Congress, with its vague control under the Articles of Confederation, could not compel, only persuade, the states to raise sufficient funds for the revolution.

Nelson and other statesmen studied the requisition for Virginia:

> 40,000 hundred weight of beef, 1,278 barrels of flour, 10,700 bushels of salt, 400 tons of hay or corn blade, 200,000 bushels of corn or short forage and equivalent, 6,000 hogsheads of tobacco, and 100,000 gallons of rum.[5]

Only Pennsylvania was called on for the same number of bushels of corn and the Commonwealth was to send more tobacco than any other state. Since there had already been a scarcity of salt in the state and a shortage of grain crops in 1779, Nelson knew the Commonwealth would have to be combed to its far-flung frontier to meet the emergency.[6]

Congress had to assure the French ambassador, the Chevalier de la Luzerne, and the French allies that the United States could bring into the field a force of 25,000 men for the spring campaign.[7]

General Washington wondered when and where that number of recruits could be raised although he concurred with the Congress that thousands of troops were needed to win the war. During the heavy snows of the winter, the soldiers at Morristown had suffered severely. Scantily clad, shoeless, often without food, the forces struggled at their tasks.[8]

In January 1779, the Congress had required the states to pay £15,000,000 into the Continental treasury. Printing presses rolled. By December of the year, the rate of exchange dropped to twenty to one; in 1780, forty to one; then sixty to one. On April 4, 1780, the authorities boldly set forth the situation,

> There is no money in the treasury, and scarce any provisions in the public magazines. The states are greatly deficient in the quotas of money, they have been called for. More than fifty millions of dollars of the quotas that have

come due to this time, remain unpaid. Silver and gold may be received as payment at the rate of one Spanish milled dollar in lieu of forty dollar bills now in circulation.[9]

Thomas Nelson not only kept up with his friends and relatives engaged in the maneuvers of the militia units but also checked on the news about the Virginians fighting the enemy in the Northeast.

Colonel Daniel Morgan had resigned his command in July suffering from rheumatism and—perhaps worse—lack of recognition.[10]

Colonel Theodorick Bland finally received confirmation to resign his command in the cavalry corps in the autumn. In November 1777, the cavalryman had attempted to leave the Continental army, but the Commander-in-Chief had declined to grant the discharge at that time.[11]

The liberal revisers of the constitution for the Commonwealth of Virginia led by Jefferson had established a Board of War and a Board of Trade to expedite enlistments, secure supplies, set up a defense system to stabilize the economy. Although the new Governor was a staunch supporter of the powers of the people through their representatives, Jefferson soon discovered that additional advisers increased his difficulties. Despite the bounties and premiums offered as an inducement to men to enlist in the service so that eleven battalions could be raised as required by the Congress, the state failed to supply its share of soldiers during Jefferson's administration.[12]

Thomas Nelson could not catch up on the news of his neighbors so frequently as formerly. David Jameson was busy commuting from York Town to the capital serving in the Council; Dudley Digges had moved to Williamsburg as a more convenient place to attend his Council post.

When John Page resigned from his Council post in the spring, Digges became Lieutenant Governor. In his letter of April 7, 1780, Page explained to his lifelong friend Thomas Jefferson that he had often mentioned the matter of retirement but had stayed on because of the report of an enemy invasion. The master of Rosewell continued in his communication:

> As I find the Obstacles to my Attendance on the Board greatly increased, beg leave to retire. . . . nothing but the particular Situation of my private and domestic Affairs which have suffered extremely by a four years and a half almost total Neglect of them could induce me to retire from the Service of my Country during the war.[13]

Governor Jefferson was disappointed about the decision. By May, Jacquelin Ambler, who had married Rebecca Burwell (the fair "Belinda" young Jefferson had courted), had also resigned.[14]

Digges and Nelson observed the social amenities by offering congratulations to the new bride and groom who added another connection for the two families. Another of Tom's numerous Burwell cousins took Martha Digges as his wife, and the *Virginia Gazette* of Dixon-Nicholson had announced the nuptials in its March 11, 1780, issue: "Marriages—Captain Nathaniel Burwell, of the Artillery and Miss Patty Digges, daughter of the Honorable Dudley of this city." The groom was from King William County and though Thomas thought of Patty as a youngster, she was a grown-up lady of twenty-two.

An announcement of more widespread interest to the Assemblymen was the March 25, 1780, Dixon-Nicholson notice that the executive offices were being removed from Williamsburg to Richmond, the Convention to commence in the new capital April 24. Thomas Nelson and other legislators from the lower coast would have more miles to cover, but Thomas had no intention of deserting his duty. Lucy would be having another baby in the fall but he knew she could face the birth with composure. Though the Nelson household was crowded to capacity with six sons and three daughters, there was always room for another cradle.

Governor Jefferson had been away from the capital from February 20 until March 14. When he returned to Williamsburg, he read the circular letter from President Samuel Huntington of the Congress dated February 10, 1780, that had arrived in his absence.[15]

The Congress had authorized a Continental army of 32,211 men "exclusive of commissioned Officers" for the next campaign. This number had been upped by 10,000 from a former proposal. As Jefferson studied the communication, his blue eyes fixed on the figure of 6,070 as the quota set for Virginia to recruit. Massachusetts was required to raise the same number; Pennsylvania, 4,855; Delaware, just 405 men.[16]

In addition to enlisting men for the campaign in the Northeast, the Commonwealth of Virginia was raising regiments for the Carolina campaign. At a meeting of the Board of War on March 13, the members had requisitioned 126 hats, 50 uniform coats, 50 vests, 219 shirts, 219 pairs of shoes, 264 overalls, 132 stocks, and 132 knee garters to outfit 60 volunteers from Virginia, 132 non-commissioned officers and privates for the expedition to South Carolina. Lieutenant Governor Page and the Council replied to the recommendation by advising the Board to exercise its own judgment pertaining to the price and purchase of the articles.[17]

At last the harsh winter that had gripped Virginia was brushed away by the warmth of spring. Townsmen in Williamsburg threaded their way to Burdett's ordinary, the Red Lion, and Marot's near the Capitol, or to Chowning's close to the Court House near Market Square Green. Shoppers at Davidson's or Tarpley's found depleted wares on shelves once filled with condiments, raisins, and tea.

Men and women gathered along Palace Green to see forty-nine crates of furnishing, books, paintings, lamps, china, silver, and various ornaments being moved from the Governor's mansion into a procession of carts and wagons. The gossips wondered, "Should the once-royal residence be stripped of every item?" Governor Jefferson's enemies questioned his motives. The gossip grew until wagging tongues implicated James Innes as an accuser of the executive's conduct regarding the removal of Palace furnishings. A report was sent to the Governor. Innes wrote Jefferson denying any part of such "Cowardly and envious attacks."[18] Jefferson had achieved his objective in changing the capital city. The mansion's furnishings were installed in an ordinary wooden house on a hill in Richmond and representatives across Virginia were packing for the ride there for the spring session. Seasoned statesmen who had attended the special Assembly called there in 1775 alerted their new colleagues that the accommodations at Richmond did not compare with the comforts of Williamsburg.

Thomas Nelson had traveled from York Town to Richmond numerous times and realized it would take him more than eight hours of hard riding to complete the sixty-five-mile trip. Although the General Assembly opened its doors in the plain wooden structure which served as the State House on May 1, it wasn't until May 9 that a quorum of delegates was reached. Thomas Nelson rose in the first session to recommend Benjamin Harrison for the position of Speaker, and Harrison was elected without opposition.[19]

Nelson was again appointed to the Propositions and Grievances Committee and also Privileges and Elections with Richard Henry Lee, his cousins Carter Braxton and the second Landon Carter, son of the old colonel who had died December 17, 1778.[20]

General Nelson had a chance to become better acquainted with two military-minded men, James Innes and Robert Lawson, as they served together on the special committees concerning defense and discipline for the forces. Another plan of defense for the eastern frontier was to be set up, as Virginia was vulnerable to attack by the British aggressors.[21]

On Friday, May 12, General Nelson was appointed chairman of a committee to bring in a bill to regulate discipline for the militia forces and to plan workable measures to withstand invasion by the English as well as insurrection from within by Loyalists in the state. Thomas was dwarfed by his committee colleague, James Innes, who was so heavy that he could not sit on an ordinary chair. Reclining his bulk on the floor, the younger man often amused Nelson with his warm wit as the two representatives bent their heads over regimental bills.[22]

On Monday, May 15, the delegates voted to send arms that could be spared from the public magazines for the assistance of North Carolina. By Friday the officials stated 1,500 stand of arms should be secured and stationed at strategic points along the James River and the lower part of Virginia.[23] The state had supplied sixty officers to serve at Charleston and requisitioned "180 yards Broad Cloth and trimming for sixty suits of Clothes; 300 Linen Shirts; 50 yards Cambrick for Ruffles; 60 pairs Shoes; 90

handkerchiefs; 270 yards Jeans for summer Vests and Breeches; and 60 Hatts."[24] Whether the requisition could be fulfilled remained the question.

Two troops of Major John Nelson's cavalry were being readied for the South Carolina trip. A report of May 2 listed twenty-three soldiers engaged for temporary enlistments and forty-one men being signed up for the duration of the war. The corps was attached to Colonel Charles Porterfield's infantry numbering 218 recruits enrolled for the Carolina campaign.[25]

On Saturday, May 20, General Nelson received a majority vote to chair the important Ways and Means Committee. Although his old friends Patrick Henry and Richard Henry Lee served with him on the nine-member committee, the two men had opposing viewpoints concerning the currency crisis. Nelson was caught in the middle. The Assembly eventually adopted a plan proposed by the Congress to call and destroy old certificates and to reissue new money.[26]

On Wednesday, May 24, Thomas Nelson recommended before the Committee of the Whole that a force of "5,000 men for succouring our southern friends and for defending this State on its eastern frontier . . . be formed with provisions, arms, military stores and all other necessaries for that number of men, ought to be procured."[27]

On that same day the majority votes for the new members of the Council were counted by General Nelson and a committee. Thomas took three names to the Senate for approval: General Andrew Lewis, the rugged frontier fighter who had defied Lord Dunmore and driven him from Gwynn's Island; George Webb, who had served as Treasurer; and Jacquelin Ambler, well-to-do landowner and customs official. Lewis, Webb and Ambler would fill vacancies caused by the resignations of John Page, John Walker, and James Madison, the latter two gentlemen having been chosen to represent the Commonwealth in the Congress.[28]

Feeling the strain of arduous sessions, on Friday, May 26, Nelson asked for a one-week leave of absence; Patrick Henry obtained leave on June 7 to return to Leatherwood where he remained. Both members missed hearing another request from the Congress.[29]

On May 30, Speaker Harrison presented the proposal to the House of Delegates from the national Assembly asking the State of Virginia to raise $1,953,200 for support of the huge French fleet and force that would be stationed on the coastal shores. Already overburdened with debt, depressed by the depreciation of their currency, and overwhelmed by spiraling prices, the delegates wondered how they could raise the revenue. The rate of exchange had soared sixty to one requiring stacks of bills to purchase a pound of salt or sugar. The treasury of the Commonwealth was as empty as the coffers of the Congress.[30]

Just before Nelson returned to the General Assembly the first week of

June, the representatives had resorted to the same solution employed in February—borrowing funds from individuals. Gentlemen lending the government money for the emergency would receive six per cent interest to be repaid in December or the amount could be discounted from their taxes. Nelson was appointed one of the solicitors on the seven-man committee to secure the loans. State tobacco was also to be sold to answer the appeal of the Congress. On June 8, Governor Jefferson wrote to Speaker Harrison, "According to the advice of the General Assembly, we have proceeded to take Measures for selling six hundred Thousand weight of the public Tobacco."[31]

The legislators empowered the executive to seize surpluses of stock and stores for public use from the individuals in case of invasion. Families would be allowed sufficient articles for subsistence and certificates for goods would be paid by the Commonwealth. On June 20 the authorities passed a bill to impress horses and wagons to furnish mounts and to haul materiel for the Maryland men marching through the state to aid South Carolina.[32]

All summer long the delegates to Richmond had debated the cumbersome and time-consuming commissions of the Board of War and the Board of Trade, finally abolishing these bodies. They appointed a commercial agent, a commissioner of war, and one for the navy to expedite military emergencies.[33]

While the statesmen struggled, the tramp of marching feet and thud of horses' hooves had echoed through the Tidewater region as soldiers moved toward the Carolinas.

General Clinton reinforced his redcoat regiments with 2,500 British regulars brought down from New York and seasoned soldiers stationed at Savannah that the royal contingents had captured. Crown troops totaled over ten thousand, compared to about five thousand patriot forces. Only 800 were regular Continental troops, half of which were Virginians, and the rest of the American army was composed of militia units.[34]

On May 12, 1780, General Benjamin Lincoln surrendered the South Carolina fort at Charleston—defeated by the incessant bombardment of April and May, scarce provisions, insufficient reinforcements, and no means of escape. Thomas Nelson and his fellow delegates were downcast when the dismal news reached them at Richmond. The members gathered in groups talking of soldiers killed by Tarleton's Tories. Some of the officials realized it would be their responsibility to notify the families and friends of the misfortune. In addition to those killed, hundreds of Virginians had been seized as prisoners and shipped to a British stockade in New York.

Colonel Matthews headed the Virginia officers of the line held in captivity on Long Island—including three majors, seven captains, twelve lieutenants, and eight ensigns. He wrote Governor Jefferson describing the deplorable conditions of "irksome confinement . . . left to struggle with calamities of indigency and want." Some patriot prisoners had been in custody several years. Nathaniel Pendleton, nephew of Edmund, had been a British prisoner since the fall of Fort Washington. Repeated appeals to the Continental Congress for relief had brought only promises for the prisoners. The petitioners asserted they had demonstrated "patience and perseverance becoming a Soldier and the Citizen." The Virginians vowed this appeal was their last resort and enclosed a complete list of the names and rank of the officers.[35]

Colonel George Baylor and Captain John Spotswood were on parole in Virginia. Robert Randolph was also on parole but was required to return to the Long Island prison.

In addition to worries about the prisoners of war, the Governor was impatient about delayed intelligence concerning the Charleston disaster. He wrote the Congress on June 9, "Our information from the Southward has been at all time defective, but lamentably so on the late occasion. Charleston had been in the hands of the enemy 24 days before we received information of it."[36]

On June 2, James Madison had written Governor Jefferson from Philadelphia about the surrender of Charleston. This letter should have reached Richmond around the tenth of the month.[37]

Governor Nash of North Carolina, in his communication dated May 30, notified the Virginia executive of the surrender at Charleston and enclosed the Articles of Capitulation. On June 9, Governor Jefferson transmitted the terms to Speaker Benjamin Harrison and stated that the letter had "just come to hand."[38]

This serious lack in the intelligence service prompted the administrator to assert to his Commander-in-Chief on June 11, 1780, "I Shall immediately establish a line of expresses from hence to the neighborhood of the army hope conveyed rate of 120 miles in 24 hours."[39]

James Monroe became a messenger for the Commonwealth in the summer. The twenty-year-old lieutenant was at loose ends after leaving the Continental army. He had been in the forefront of the fight at Trenton, was shot in the shoulder, and later fought at the battles of Brandywine, Germantown, and Monmouth, but no post had been offered him with the state troops.[40] The young man was considering law as a career since the College of William and Mary had just opened the first school of law in an American institution on December 4, 1779, under George Wythe, appointed professor of the course.[41] Monroe was guided in his decision, however, to become a courier by his uncle Joseph Jones, just re-elected to the Congress from the Commonwealth. Politically wise, Judge Jones counseled Monroe to cultivate Governor Jefferson. Monroe did, fulfilling his mission faithfully in securing information on British maneuvers in the Carolinas and forming a lifelong friendship with Jefferson that later would push him up the political ladder to the presidency. (Although Thomas Nelson might have met the courier at this time, his fifth son, eleven-year-old Hugh, would come to know the serious-minded Monroe well in future years. Hugh would serve his state as a delegate and a representative to Congress and the United States as minister to Spain—appointed by President Monroe.[42])

The Governor instructed young Monroe on June 16 to proceed with other rider/messengers and made arrangements to provide messenger stations—one every forty miles with reliable riders ready to take the places of any who became ill. He cautioned the couriers to travel by night and to observe British movements. Monroe met Governor Nash of North Carolina at the end of the month. He also questioned two patriot soldiers from General Woodford's brigade who had escaped from the Charleston prison and had reached North Carolina, then sent a report to Governor Jefferson that redcoat regiments had sailed from Charleston leaving about 800 troops there; 2,500 were encamped at Camden; and 600 cavalrymen were on call. Monroe was uncertain as to the objective of British operations but believed the English forces might land in Virginia.[43]

An atmosphere of frenzied activity to find men and funds filled the Assembly during the summer. All across Virginia recruiting officers were striving to swell the ranks while representatives struggled to raise revenue. General Nelson endeavored to secure subscriptions from private citizens. Congress had allocated nearly two million to be raised by Virginia. Through the hot days, Nelson traveled the dusty roads through the counties south of the James River. He asked his family and friends in the York Town area for assistance and implored individuals throughout the Tidewater territory for aid. Since the Exchecquer was exhausted and the Commonwealth's credit had crumbled, distrust engulfed the people; cautious Virginians refused the request. Some thought there were not enough shillings in the state to fill the sinking hole of the treasury. Pledging his own resources again as well as funds from the Robert Burwell estate, Thomas Nelson impressed many inhabitants with his integrity and high principles. Some lent the government money on Nelson's guarantee. His vigorous efforts raised £41,000 toward the contribution required by the Congress from the Commonwealth.[44]

On June 30, 1780, Governor Jefferson wrote Samuel Huntington, the President of Congress, "You will receive a part of the requisition of $1,953,200 Dollars . . . there remaining a deficiency 522,960$\frac{1}{9}$ which I hope to be able to send within four weeks from this time."[45]

There was no respite for the representatives or rest for Nelson. On that same day a courier reached Richmond alerting the authorities that British ships had sailed into Chesapeake Bay and thence into Hampton port. The

Governor and Council informed Thomas Nelson immediately he would again be appointed brigadier general of the militia and instructed him to rush to the coastal region. Nelson wrote John Page July 8:

> I came away from Richmond in so great hurry of the late alarm, that I did not bring the certificates of any of the money down. The treasurer had been so much engaged for several days that he had not made them out, but gave me a general receipt, specifying the gentlemen's names and the sums they had lent. This general receipt Mr. Reynolds has, together with the certificates for the individuals and Colo. Lewis shall have his through you, as soon as it comes to hand.[46]

Through the humid days of July, the devoted patriot met county militia commanders throughout the Tidewater area, tallying the number of men available in the area around the York and James rivers, urging unit leaders to train their troops adequately to withstand an attack and studying the accessible stores. Nelson encouraged voluntary enlistments from the plantations for the troops of cavalry the representatives proposed to raise. When the British ships sailed from Hampton without invading the state, the representatives concentrated on outfitting soldiers to send southward, collecting arms and ammunition, finding food for the forces, and providing transports for the troops.

Governor Jefferson's terse statement, "The want of money cramps every effort," became a resounding cry repeated by all the fatigued representatives in their endeavors during the emergency.[47] Military forces began to lose their faith in the government, and militiamen complained about marching away from home ill supplied. Two regiments stationed in York Town refused to proceed southward without pay and provisions. With characteristic ardor for cause and his usual generosity, General Nelson advanced the necessary sums.[48]

A wave of discontent surged through the war-weary citizenry all over the country. Raucous cursing of lost battles and bankrupt conditions could be heard in the taverns above the clanking mugs by men voicing their grievances.

Half-fed and hardly clothed, men deserted the Continental forces in alarming numbers. Two detachments of Connecticut soldiers paraded in protest; mutiny occurred at Morristown in May. As turncoats switched sides, the British boasted that the American rebellion was crumbling.[49]

Through the summer, Governor Jefferson, frustrated by the situation, suffered more and more from migraine headaches. More bad news came when he learned Loyalists in the western region ruined the works at lead mines in New River. Colonel Preston informed the executive that he had summoned the militia from Washington, Montgomery, and Botetourt counties to suppress the insurrection. Colonel William Campbell, frontier fighter and brother-in-law of Patrick Henry, was already in the area to quell the Cherokee and Chickamauga Indians. The Governor ordered Campbell to raise 500 volunteers and stop the insurgents.[50]

On August 16, the Continentals could not stem the tide of experienced English soldiers at Camden. The untrained recruits fumbled their unused bayonets and fled, but the seasoned Delaware and Maryland men tried to stop the scarlet troops. Lord Cornwallis was the victor and General Gates the vanquished in the disastrous defeat.

Gates's hasty escape—180 miles from Camden, South Carolina, to Hillsborough, North Carolina—and abandonment of what remained of the patriot regiments caused adverse comments by both civilians and military men.[51] Alexander Hamilton, General Washington's ambitious young aide, was caustic in his censure.[52] Engaged to marry Elizabeth Schuyler in December, daughter of the aristocratic General Philip Schuyler, Hamilton's criticism of Gates fanned the flames of an old feud between the two generals. The Congress and the Commonwealth of Virginia planned courts of inquiry concerning the conduct of General Gates. Because of the urgency of military preparations, however, the Congress postponed questioning. Replaced by General Greene, Gates retired to his home in Virginia, depressed and disillusioned at being denied an opportunity to defend his position and saddened over the death of his only son.[53]

After the defeat at Camden, Governor Jefferson admitted that men, materiel, and fortified positions were inadequate to withstand invasion by the English but maintained hope that General Clinton would hold the British regiments in New York and, the powerful French fleet could protect Virginia from attack.

In late August, the accumulated pressures of administrative affairs, and the poor health of his wife, made Governor Jefferson contemplate resignation.

> The application requisite to the duties of the office that I hold is so excessive, and the exertions of them after all so imperfect that I have determined to retire from it at the close of the present campaign. I wish a successor to be thought of in time who to sound Whiggism can join perseverance in business and an extensive knowledge of the various subjects he must superintend. Such a one may keep us above water in our present moneyless situation.[54]

One veteran legislator of Virginia was quick to voice his opinion concerning obligation to public service. Conservative Edmund Pendleton, who had opposed the policies of the young liberals, had censured Patrick Henry for resigning a seat in the Congress; when he heard that Governor Jefferson also intended to resign his office, Pendleton commented, "It is a little cowardly to quit our Posts in a bustling time."[55]

Another conservative statesman who had served the Colony and Commonwealth practically all his life passed from the scene in September. A notice in the newspaper on the thirteenth: "Last Sunday was interred in the churchyard of this place ROBERT C. NICHOLAS, ESQ: of Hanover County after a lingering illness." [56] Grandson of "King" Carter, reverent and highly respected by his colleagues, Robert Carter Nicholas had symbolized the aristocratic oligarchy. He had stood solidly with Pendleton against the progressive reforms of Jefferson in changes for the Established Church.

Thomas Nelson regretted the death of his relative and reflected on the counsel and consideration he had received from his stepuncle since 1761 when, as a young man just returned from England, he had been elected as a representative from York County to the House of Burgesses. Nicholas had been a Burgess with Dudley Digges from the county from 1756 to 1761. Then young Nelson was selected from York County and Nicholas from James City County to serve in the House of Burgesses. In 1766, Robert Carter Nicholas became the Treasurer of the Colony and served in that post until 1776.

Thomas comforted his mother, saddened at the loss of her stepbrother, yet even the amenities were curtailed during the troublesome times. The threat of enemy invasion loomed like a thunderous cloud over the Commonwealth.

As General Nelson rode on an inspection tour of the defense posts along the lower peninsula, he found that supplies fell far short of requirements for the local regiments to resist effectively a British attack. Willoughby Point on the tip of the entrance to the broad-mouthed James, Norfolk and Portsmouth, Hampton and Newport News, York Town, on its bluff above the York River, Gloucester Point—all these seaport towns needed to be strengthened.

Like other officers of the Virginia forces, Major John Nelson had written a letter to Governor Jefferson describing the dire needs of his cavalry detachment. On September 8, 1780, Jefferson answered the appeal saying, "I have directed Cloathing to be got ready for your men," but finding twelve horses would be quite difficult, for the merchants would sell only for "ready money, which we have not." [57]

The General Assembly had empowered the executive to impress supplies, but the administrator was afraid of too much authority being concentrated in one person, even in himself. Jefferson further demonstrated his great regard for the representatives of the people to establish policy in this reply:

> With respect to the officers going into continental service we can have no objection to putting two of the troops altogether on the continental establishment, but that it transcend our power. The assembly alone can do this with the consent of Congress. [58]

The delegates agreed in principle with Governor Jefferson yet felt that desperate conditions demanded drastic measures; many members wanted the executive to exert more authority in the administration.

Seasoned officers were being called back into Continental service. Destiny and time resolved the old difficulties among the leaders. For three years, Generals Scott, Muhlenberg, Weedon, and Woodford had competed for top command. After the American army had settled on the slopes of Valley Forge in the winter of 1777–1778, the Commander-in-Chief was lenient in allowing leave. General Scott, General Muhlenberg, and General Weedon left for Virginia on furloughs and the full responsibility of the Virginia regiments fell on General Woodford. Then in March the Caroline County commander had been granted permission to return to the Commonwealth. Dissatisfied over conditions, General Woodford wrote a letter of resignation and consequently lost his commission, renewing the rivalry in rank among the remaining trio. It was accelerated when Woodford decided to rejoin and was willing to serve as a junior officer under General Weedon. When an overall commander for the Carolina campaign was being considered in late 1779, however, General Woodford was chosen to lead the contingent so the burning controversy among the Virginia officers burst into a flaming feud again. General Scott was out of the wrangle since he had returned to Virginia in the spring of 1779. The representatives of the Assembly had awarded the Virginia veteran with a fine gelding, completely caparisoned, as a token of appreciation for his war services.[59]

General Weedon, old "Joe Gourd," who had been at his home in Fredericksburg since 1779, refused to be a subordinate to General Woodford although he had retained his commission. When the Congress and the Commander-in-Chief asked him to encourage enlistment in the Commonwealth, the tavern keeper responded affirmatively and engaged in recruiting men for the ranks in 1780.

At the capitulation of Charleston, General Woodford had been captured and sent with the Continental prisoners to New York. The courageous commander died in the crowded encampment on November 13, 1780, just a month after his forty-sixth birthday.[60]

General John Peter Muhlenberg, the fighting parson, stayed in the service and was also re-enlisting recruits for the regiments in Virginia as well as signing up soldiers who had deserted their detachments. The authorities of Virginia had suggested to the Commander-in-Chief that rebel deserters would "willingly return" to the service if they were not imprisoned. Accordingly, newspapers printed over and over a proclamation by General Washington:

> In order therefore to take from them every possible pretext for absenting themselves longer from their duty, I hereby offer and declare a free pardon.[61]

On October 15, 1780, Congress at last recognized the valuable contributions of Daniel Morgan, promoting him to brigadier general. He began to pull together his rough and ready riflemen. Later in the fall, he led them southward to combat the British when the dreaded invasion of Virginia became a reality.[62] Commodore George Rodney steered a fleet of fifty-four British ships into Chesapeake Bay, transporting 2,500 Crown troops under the command of General Alexander Leslie. When a courier conveyed the news to Richmond, General Nelson rushed to defend Virginia with the disordered militia of the counties.

From Hall's Mill on October 21, General Nelson informed Governor Jefferson:

> Sir, I was this morning informed that the Enemy had landed a party of light Horse . . . on their way to Great Bridge, which I fear they have taken possession of by this time. . . . no Militia collected. . . . I hope you will lose no time in ordering a body of Men down, that we may at least attempt an Opposition. I shall endeavor to collect a force from these Counties, but the Confusion is so great that much cannot be expected. . . . horses being unfit for that service. . . . The Cattle . . . fallen into the enemies hands . . . from their Ships and bringing Light Horse with them, I suppose they mean to make their Winter Quarters in this State.[63]

General Nelson went back to Williamsburg to pull together more militia units while General Muhlenberg moved to the south side of the peninsula with a patriot force. Despite the danger of British occupation, recruits straggled in slowly. From a parade of about 400 men one day, only 60 volunteered for duty.

On November 3, General Nelson informed General Weedon, "The militia have appear'd in such small Detachments, that it has been impossible to make any proper arrangements." Nelson discovered that "two Companies from King and Queen County" were totally without weapons.[64] No one in Williamsburg could repair rifles so General Nelson urged General Weedon to send two men from Richmond for that purpose. The veteran Virginia leader was informed that medicines were lacking.[65]

Despite the deficiencies, Nelson had sent detachments to General Muhlenberg and managed to organize one complete regiment which he placed under the command of Colonel William Nelson. His report to General Weedon stated, "He will take his Station somewhere below York, tho' not so low as to be in Danger of being surrounded." Boats were to be brought down from the shipyards to Burwell's Ferry to transport troops. Colonel Southall was sent to Hampton and a detachment of his troops was directed to forestall the residents from fraternizing with the enemy. Nelson called Southall "a man of discretion," able to ". . . discriminate between those People who are attached to the Enemy by principle & those who may have been compelled through timidity to surrender themselves, he will treat them properly."[66]

Thomas Nelson, Jr., paid for provisions for the troops from his own pocket.[67]

During the autumn days, the approach of the enemy had so absorbed General Nelson and Governor Jefferson they had hardly been aware of baby daughters born to their households. On October 3, 1780, infant Susanna Nelson made her entry, the couple's tenth child. (All their children lived to maturity—a record for colonial days.) Lucy Elizabeth Jefferson was born November 30, 1780, but lived less than five months.[68]

Thomas Nelson, Jr., missed the autumn Assembly because his time was devoted to raising more recruits, but the response was discouraging. Thomas heard more talk about inflation than independence. The first warm fervor for liberty was cooling and had been replaced by a spirit of inaction and indifference. With the thousands of troops that the Commonwealth had furnished the Continental forces, every family seemed to have someone in the service. Soldiers who had slipped away from the royal grip in the Carolinas straggled back into the state with tales of terrible suffering. Miles of marching without shoes, with empty stomachs, rusty rifles, no ammunition—and no pay—were only some of their grievances.

The representatives were later than usual in arriving at Richmond to attend the October Assembly. The quorum required for the session had been reduced to fifty. Because the British were occupying the James River outposts, delegates living along the peninsula had to make preparations to protect their families and property. It was November before the legislators convened in the capital city, and General Nelson soon learned that his friend Patrick Henry had been appointed to his old post on the Propositions and Grievances committee.[69]

By the third week of November, the enemy had not moved up the rivers and General Nelson wrote General Weedon from Rich Creek on the twenty-second:

> I had the pleasure of receiving your Letter of the 19th yesterday afternoon on my arrival at this post. What the devil these fellows can be waiting for I cannot conceive. They have had two or three fair winds and still remain in Hampton Road. They have an Idea on board the fleet that I am three thousand strong. Let them continue to think so. It is certain that they do not care to trust their Boats on shore. Several Negroes have gone to them from this Neighbourhood. If the intelligence of Cornwallis is true, the Campaign will end gloriously for us, notwithstanding the misfortune of Charleston & General Gates.
>
> I am glad to hear your Brigade is so very tractable. Mine is so detach'd that I have hardly been able to do anything with them yet. They are station'd at York, this Post, the Halfway House & Hampton, so that I have not many at any one of these places.[70]

General Nelson's cousin Nathaniel Burwell, from Isle of Wight County, had been robbed by the British in a privateer piloted by one of his escaped slaves. Sixty invaders plundered his property, seized nine Negroes, took Burwell's watch, and stole some silver plate.[71]

A report on the rebel triumph over the Tory troops at King's Mountain in South Carolina on October 7, 1780, had reached the camp and caused General Nelson to comment optimistically to General Weedon about the intelligence of Lord Cornwallis.[72] This victory of the rugged overmountain men instilled a new vigor and spirit into the sagging Continental cause all across the South.

General Cornwallis and his British regiments then beat a retreat southward to Winnsboro, South Carolina. General Leslie in Virginia entreated the Earl for instructions concerning a rendezvous for the two forces, entrusting the message to a trained spy. When patriots intercepted the intelligence agent, he popped the rolled-up silk paper missive into his mouth, but the rebels recovered the report and the plan was revealed. By the end of November General Nelson noted that the English fleet was standing out on the capes and the ships sailed out to sea. Virginia was saved from further ravaging, but the respite was short lived.[73]

CHAPTER TWENTY-ONE

Invasion and Infringement, Insurrection and Indifference: 1780–1781

British Ships in Chesapeake Bay ✦ *General Nelson Mobilizes Militia* ✦ *Traitor Arnold Invades Virginia* ✦ *Refugees Leave Richmond* ✦ *General Steuben and General Nelson Discuss Defense* ✦ *French Fleet* ✦ *Affair at Westover* ✦ *Marquis and the Menace* ✦ *Special Strategy for the South*

In the damp, dark days of December the dismissed militia of the Commonwealth were marching back across the coastal region to their homes.

General Nelson was welcomed by his wife and children at York Town. Baby Susanna was oblivious to the commotion, but her father cuddled his new offspring and recorded her name in the family Bible, then went across the street to see his mother and talk with his brothers about fall crops, promising this year in contrast to the poor harvest of the previous year.

He was happy to be home with his family for the holiday season although there were only quiet celebrations centered around the church and family gatherings. Christmas Eve fell on Sunday in 1780 so the pews at York-Hampton church were crowded with numerous Nelsons for the special service. The Reverend Robert Andrews, professor of moral philosophy at the College, was rector; he had served as an aide to General Nelson and would soon be called back to the same capacity.

Just five days later, the hulls of a twenty-seven-sail flotilla appeared on the horizon of Chesapeake Bay. Surmising that the ships comprised a hostile fleet when he sighted them off Willoughby Point, Commodore James Barron of the Virginia navy sailed into Hampton port in the late afternoon to alert Jacob Wray of the danger. The local merchant then sent the message to General Nelson.[1] Since no lookouts had been posted and the postriders had been disbanded, Nelson had to find someone to take the intelligence to Governor Jefferson in Richmond sixty-five miles away. Governor Jefferson received the news at eight o'clock the next morning, December 31, but he wanted definite information from another dispatch that the fleet was, in fact, the enemy, and two days later wrote to General Nelson, "None such having come within fifty Hours, the first Intelligence totally disbelieved."[2]

William Tatham, an English-born adventurer who had come to the Colony in his teens and had been a cavalryman under General Nelson in his volunteer corps, recorded his impression of the incident. The twenty-eight-year-old young man had been ready to ride from Richmond down the James River when Nelson's courier had rushed into the city. Curiosity caused Tatham to delay his journey, so he jogged over to see Jefferson where he found the Governor walking in his garden. The executive affirmed his opinion that the fleet "might be nothing more than a foraging Party, unless he had further information to justify the measure, he should not disturb the Country by calling out the Militia."[3]

Governor Jefferson asked Tatham that day to deliver a message to General Friedrich Steuben at Wilton, six miles south on the James River: "27 sail of vessels, 18 of which were square rigged, were yesterday morning just below Willoughby's Point, no other circumstance being given to conviction and force or destruction, I am able to dispatch General Nelson into the lower country to take such measures as exigencies require for the instance, until further information is received here."[4]

The Baron then sent the inquisitive courier to General Nelson, who asked Tatham to become an aide.

Jefferson did not call the Council until Monday, January 1, 1781, when David Jameson, William Fleming, Andrew Lewis, George Webb, and Jacquelin Ambler arrived and heard the report about the ships in Hampton harbor. The executive suggested setting up an express system; the Council approved the action and adjourned. The British were busier than the deliberative body of Virginia.[5] Further intelligence reached Richmond Tuesday, January 2, from Colonel Nathaniel Burwell that he had sighted the strong fleet moving up the James River. The county lieutenant noted that "23 Sail, including two men-of-war, and a number of Flat-bottom'd boats. . . . ships full their men"[6] comprised the flotilla flying the British flag.

The Governor and Council, alerted again to the alarm, at last realized that the royal fleet was not simply a "foraging party" but a raid. The members stirred themselves to pass resolutions that should have been acted upon two days before or put into effect by the executive in the wartime emergency. General Nelson was sent a commission with blanket authority to call out the militia from the counties along the coast and place men at the points he thought proper. The officials ordered one-half of the militia from the counties close to Richmond and Petersburg to turn out and one-fourth from the more distant counties above. Jefferson and his advisers affirmed, "We mean to have 4,600 Militia in the Field," and they asserted that a "Separate Corps" would be formed by "Those who bring rifles and Accouterments."[7]

General Nelson hurried to Williamsburg after receiving his commission and attempted to bring some order there. Since the courier service had been discontinued, Governor Jefferson asked the delegates at Richmond, just adjourned in late December, to deliver the directions to the different counties regarding the militia reporting for duty.

The delay was a further detriment to the defense system. As the men, dressed in diverse clothes, carrying heavy muskets and rifles, collected in Williamsburg, General Nelson tried to form an adequate force to oppose an enemy attack. Some of the gentlemen had good hunting guns, but had never fought and there was no time to train the troops in bayonet thrust, concerted charge, or deployment. Assisted by Colonel James Innes and Colonel Samuel Griffin, both former members of the Board of War and men experienced in battle, Nelson led the small contingent across the swampy stretches to Jamestown.[8]

Renegade Benedict Arnold leading the redcoat regiments moved up the James River on Wednesday, January 3. With an experienced English force of 1,200 troops, the turncoat was confident he could crush rebel resistance. Arnold intended to impress the British brass with his command. He summoned General Nelson to surrender, but the spirited leader defied the direction.[9] In a lengthy letter to Colonel Bland, John Page complained about the lack of proper supplies for Virginia's citizen soldiers but commented with pride on their stand against the foe:

> I must however in justice to the militia of Williamsburg and James City, which first turned out under General Nelson and Colonel Innes, and that of Gloucester, which I had the honor of leading out to re-inforce those gallant few, not omit the virtues they displayed on that occasion. Nelson and Innes with 150 of the first mentioned militia, opposed Arnold's landing at Burwell's Ferry, and beat off his boats, after returning a verbal answer of defiance to his written letter, which you will see in the Richmond paper.
>
> The same noble spirit actuated above 330 of our Gloucester Militia, who live much exposed to the enemy—they readily turned out and joined Nelson, who with a handful of men, badly provided with ammunition, had been endeavoring to get in between Arnold and Richmond, but in vain.[10]

George Wythe and some gentlemen who were hunting partridges in the river region took some pot shots at the royal ships, but made no mark on the moving vessels.[11]

That night Governor Jefferson received a report that Arnold had reached Jamestown. Another courier clattered into the capital by five o'clock the next morning, Thursday, January 4, with news that the English fleet with fair wind and favorable tide had passed Hood's Point. General Steuben fumed, recalling that his recommendation to reinforce the fort had been ignored.

At 3:00 P.M. on January 4, 1781, General Nelson wrote to Jefferson from Pierres, twelve miles above Williamsburg:

I have just received an enclosed letter from Wmsburg which give the best account of the Enemy's force that I have yet obtain'd. Their intentions are higher up the River, either at Petersburg or Richmond, which they will make a bold push for, if not check'd; on their landing if they discover a determination in the Inhabitants to oppose them, they will move with caution, and perhaps return to Hampton with disgrace. They will proceed as high up as the River as they can for fear of desertion among their Troops, to which they are much dispos'd.

I remain very weak having receiv'd no reinforcements from the Neighboring Counties yet. Our Expresses behave most infamously and in what manner to act with them I know not. Unless some rigorous measures are taken with them, we shall have no regularity.[12]

The Council had convened and advised the executive to call out all the militia from the counties around the capital. The dispatches instructed the detachments to come promptly, with or without a full complement. About 100 men reported to Major Charles Dick at Richmond. It was distressingly obvious to the officials that no effective defense of the capital could be established. A stream of refugees started leaving the city, their possessions packed in carts and coaches. Through day and night wagons crammed with military stores and public papers creaked to Westham six miles up the river. Governor Jefferson sent his family to his boyhood home, Tuckahoe, in Goochland County northwest of Richmond.[13]

General Nelson moved his little band up to Byrd's Tavern in the evening. At eight o'clock his second letter of the day to Governor Jefferson listed his latest intelligence:

On my way here this evening I received Information that the Enemy had landed their whole force at Westover, and were marching for Richmond. I have ordered the whole strength of King William, King and Queen and Gloucester to rendezvous at Bacon's Ordinary 6 miles above New Kent Court House, whence I shall march them as will appear best for the Service. The whole Militia of New Kent are now turning out.[14]

To General Steuben, the Continental commander, Nelson noted:

I shall to Morrow march what Force I can collect by the Route to Holt's Forge, and thence as the Movements of the Enemy shall direct. I expect my Force will by to Morrow Noon be about 350. It will give me Pleasure to receive from you as frequently as possible such Advice as you shall think proper to communicate.[15]

General Steuben was also attempting to collect citizen soldiers. As the old professional martinet reviewed the recruits, his rage erupted. Disgusted with the endless delays of the democratic process to supply soldiers with basic needs, he cursed in a mixture of good German, fluent French, and broken English. When he found the militia from Chesterfield County pitiably naked, the Baron sent them back to the barracks.[16]

While the slow-moving mobilization in the Commonwealth continued, Benedict Arnold was informed by his intelligence that the rebels were too weak to resist. The daring commander entered the capital with 900 trained troops on Friday, January 5, in the early afternoon. The Governor and Council had gone. Major Dick and his 100-man detachment came down to join General Nelson and his militia units near the Chickahominy River.[17]

In the raid on Richmond, the British burned buildings, plundered property, and seized slaves. Ten of Governor Jefferson's servants were stolen. Black George eluded the captors and cleverly concealed the family silver in a feather bed. (When later freed by his master, the slave stayed on with the household.) The raiders swarmed through the deserted city ruthlessly destroying stores, smashing tobacco hogsheads, and damaging wine casks. The soldiers enjoyed the spirits and so did roaming swine. Redcoats and tipsy hogs staggered down the sloping streets of Richmond.[18]

British Lieutenant Colonel John Simcoe with fast infantry and thirty horsemen, followed the patriot wagons to Westham. He demolished the mill and magazine with dispatch, then burned the foundry where, unfortunately, Council records had been placed despite Governor Jefferson's instructions to leave the records at the river landing for removal across the James to a safer position.[19]

Arnold took his British troops back to Westover the next day. Rain deluged the region and prevented the patriots from pursuing the royal force. General Nelson expressed his disappointment to Jefferson:

> I am pained to the very Soul that we have not been able to prevent the Return of the Enemy, but even the elements have conspired to favour them. On Saturday night I intended a blow at their Rear, when the Gates of Heaven were opened and such a flood of Rain poured down as rendered my Plan abortive by almost drowning the Troops, who were in Bush Tents, and by injuring their Arms and Ammunition so much that they were quite unfit for Service that they may not go off without some Injury. I have offered two pieces of Cannon to be planted at Kennon's where I am; am told we may do them Mischief. These Cannon I propose to defend by Infantry as long as I can. Should they overpower us, it is better to lose the Gun than not to attack them somewhere.[20]

Nelson directed Major Charles Dick and his detachment to watch the enemy moving inland on the river and to march his men toward Williamsburg. If the enemy did not embark, General Nelson planned to push closer to them by way of Charles City Court House. He posted patrols along the James River to report on the maneuvers of the royal regiments. There was plenty of talk in the neighborhood by people curiously concerned about the movements inside the Westover mansion. Benedict Arnold was enjoying the elegant hospitality of his hostess, Mrs. William Byrd, III.[21] While the entourage dined, the rebels wondered about the lady's loyalty; they knew her late husband had revered the Crown and that her family in Philadelphia were Loyalists. Mary Willing Byrd was also a cousin to Peggy Shippen Arnold. Was she imparting information inimical to the colonial cause?

Citizens across the Commonwealth also criticized Jefferson for the disgraceful event of the English invasion. In one week the enemy had despoiled public property with only token resistance. The Governor had been ousted from the capital and proud Virginians felt that Britain's success had shamed the state. Why hadn't the militia been called out immediately? Why had the postriders been abolished? Why were there no lookouts along the river ports?[22]

General Nelson's aide William Tatham, a man of many interests—agriculture, the law, surveying, science—described his exploits as an express-man at the time in his journal, "ridden down several fine horses . . . General Nelson ordered him to obtain the best horse available and be ready for particular service as various reports were rumored about the Governor and Nelson desired dispatches of the utmost importance"[23] be delivered to his Excellency immediately. Tatham was urged to avoid risks by passing through the country around Newcastle. The messenger found the chief executive in the residence of Dr. Evans in Manchester and stated that he spent part of the evening very pleasantly with the two gentlemen.[24]

Governor Jefferson returned to Richmond on Monday, January 8, 1781; a wintry wind blew a cheerless cold over the capital. Only George Webb and Jacquelin Ambler attended the Council sessions that day, but they started to assess the situation, and the executive wrote General Washington and the Congress explaining the events of the past week. He estimated that the enemy had 1,500 infantry and 50 to 100 cavalry in their force. Hood's Point had to be abandoned by the fifty men stationed there, and the Governor stated simply, "As the orders for drawing the militia hither had been given but two days, no opposition was in readiness."[25]

He made no explanation of his failure to act promptly on the intelligence he had received from General Nelson. The day the redcoats marched into Richmond Governor Jefferson attested, "only 200 militia here too few to do anything effectual. The enemy's forces are commanded by the parracide Arnold."[26]

Jefferson estimated the troop strength of the patriots as 300 militia at the Forest six miles above Westover under Colonel John Nicholas; 200 with General Nelson at Charles City Court House eight miles below Westover; Colonel Gibson commanded 1,000 militia; and Baron Steuben had 800 men on the south side of the James River. Governor Jefferson listed the principal losses sustained by the public as the Council records, five brass field pieces, and four pounders hidden in the river. Among the items damaged or destroyed by the English were 150 arms, 5 tons of powder, 150 wagons, tools, cloth, linen, and 120 sides of leather. The rebels later recovered about 300 stand of arms from the river.[27]

On Wednesday, January 10, with a favorable southeast wind, the enemy embarked from Westover. General Steuben, stationed on the south side of the James River, rushed toward Hood's Point to stop Arnold but did not reach the post in time. General Nelson notified Governor Jefferson that the British fleet had reached Sandy Point the day after Steuben's departure. The executive agreed with Nelson's evaluation of the ineptness of the express system and stated, "I have not heard a tittle of the Enemy since your information that they were at Sandy Point."[28]

Lacking intelligence might be fatal to the military defense so he informed General Nelson that expresses were "to be stationed at Bottom's Bridge, another at New Kent Court House, a third at Bird's Tavern, a fourth at Williamsburg, a fifth halfway between that and Hampton and a sixth at Hampton . . . if necessary be put into motion every day." Each rider would have about fifteen miles out and back on his run.[29]

On January 13, 1781, General Nelson wrote Jefferson regarding the progress of the British ships:

> This day the Enemies Ships passed Burwell's Ferry and have fallen so far down the River that I think they intend nothing further on the North side of the James River at present.[30]

British troops had landed at Surry, and Arnold was believed to be with them. Nelson surmised the redcoats intended to march through Smithfield and Suffolk and push on to Portsmouth and said, "I shall order part of the Troop under me to attend the motions of the Enemy down the River and give Protection to the Country."[31]

About 1,000 militia were concentrated at Williamsburg and York Town but many men had no arms. Despairing cries for arms and ammunition from the patriot commanders covered Jefferson's desk. Many Colonels exclaimed that not one-half or even one-fourth of their men were equipped.

General Steuben asked the administrator for 1,000 stand of arms[32] and received the reply from Governor Jefferson that some arms "had been sent down to different places to be put into the hands of the militia coming in. . . . I fear it will be impossible to furnish the thousand stand of arms you desire."[33]

When the Prussian soldier also received a report that General Nelson and his detachment were in desperate "want of Ammunition for 20,000 Cartridges,"[34] Steuben recalled some arms collected for General Greene's southern army.

Some of the militia wanted leaves of absence and local leaders felt their grievances were justified since they had been hurried from their homes leaving their families unprotected.

The lack of arms made Governor Jefferson write General Nelson on January 15, "As I suppose . . . you may have more Men than Arms, and there are no more Arms fit for use remaining in the public stock, economy will require that the surplus Militia be discharged. This measure is the more necessary, as the law for raising new levies remains unexecuted while the Militia are from their Co."[35]

New militia units, totaling 4,650 men, would be drawn from twenty-four counties. The moving in and out of camp continued like a merry-go-round. Men without guns and those with expiring enlistments left as new levies came in. Soldiers were shifted from one post to another.

The detachments of the Commonwealth consisting of approximately 3,700 militia were distributed in three distant encampments: General Weedon at Hunter's Works near Fredericksburg; General Steuben at Cabin's Point on the south side of the James River; General Nelson with contingents at Williamsburg and York Town.

Major John Nelson had ninety-four cavalrymen on the southern side of the river, and the French adventurer Charles Armand was in the area with a corps of horsemen. Official orders directed that two hundred pairs of boots should be obtained for the mounted men. Instructions were also issued that boats—anything capable of moving arms and men—should be collected and sent to General Nelson.

Governor Jefferson received communications from General Nelson written on January 15 and 16:

> This afternoon I have intelligence that it was on its way again, and said for Newport yesterday about twelve o'clock, the Enemy were seen from this Shore to land a Number of Men on a point below the Mouth of Pagan Creek, and soon afterwards heavy firing commenced, the Issue of which has not yet reached me. Very few men have joined me from those Counties, whose Militia, according to yours of the 15th, were to compose the Armament for our Defense on this Occasion for which reason it will be immediately in my Power to comply with your Instructions.[36]

Governor Jefferson informed Nelson that some of Richmond's prominent men had decided to enlist; Nelson was to form them "into proper troop, settling the commands as shall be most agreeable to themselves"—an indication of the executive's belief in the privileges of the individual.[37]

Horses had been stolen at Westover by some of the soldiers from Charles City so the administrator urged General Nelson "to take the most coercive measures for compelling a restitution" of the animals.[38]

Benedict Arnold's British armada composed of the forty-four-gun *Charon*, twenty-gun *Fowey, Amphitrite, Iris,* and *Thames,* brigs, frigates, and sloops filled with royal forces arrived in Portsmouth January 19. Hessians in green and redcoat regulars swarmed through the streets of the seaport town.[39]

General Steuben crossed the river and went to Williamsburg January 20 to confer with General Nelson. Steuben was impressed with Nelson's martial manner and ardent zeal. The fifty-year-old Baron bowed, his grayish-brown eyes sweeping the countenance of his forty-two-year-old colleague. Steuben sensed in Nelson's steady eyes and amiable disposition a devoted patriot who would make sacrifices to defend his state. The two portly commanders studied the military situation from every angle. They tallied troop strength, noted the terrain, checked available arms, and scrutinized food supplies in an endeavor to mount an offensive attack. Nelson conveyed their conclusions to Governor Jefferson January 21:

> He is of the opinion with Colonel Senf who surveyed that country and many other Officers acquainted with the ground, that we are not in a situation to undertake such an Enterprize.[40]

The principal operation of the patriot forces would be a defensive position to prevent further enemy incursions. Steuben estimated a regimental strength of 2,700 men, exclusive of volunteer horse and Nelson's and Armand's corps of cavalry, would be sufficient to protect the peninsula.

General Steuben returned to Richmond to expedite enlistments leaving General Muhlenberg in command on the south side of the James River above Portsmouth; General Nelson was in charge of the militia above the river.

Since Arnold had moved up the James toward Richmond, the Continental commander again recommended that Hood's Point be fortified. Engineer Senf prepared a detailed list of requirements for eight mounted field pieces, barracks, and redoubts to be built, so bricklayers, carpenters, laborers, and slaves would be needed for the construction.[41]

General Steuben and Governor Jefferson became embroiled in a wrangle over obtaining the workmen. The Prussian thought that militia or slaves could be summoned to construct the stronghold. The executive claimed that under the Constitution of the Commonwealth a free man could not be compelled to work without his consent or a slave conscripted unless his master approved. Steuben carped to General Washington, "The executive power is so confined that the Governor has it not in his power to procure me 40 negroes to work at Hood's."[42]

As the state was stymied without funds and in desperate need of military supplies, the Assembly appointed Speaker Benjamin Harrison a special emissary to present these problems to the Congress. James Madison resented the mission as a reflection on the efforts of the representatives already serving Virginia.[43] Harrison encountered financial difficulties on his journey to Philadelphia in exchanging state money for Continental currency. On February 12, after his arrival, he wrote to Jefferson, "The Expence of transportation I must pay out of the money you entrusted me with, there being not a shilling in the Continental Treasury."[44] The new money of the Continental Congress was exchanged at a rate of 75 to one.[45]

Harrison's report was not encouraging:

> It appearing Congress cannot command Men or quantity necessary to furnish them in the field . . . abundant cloathing can't procure without money or tobacco.[46]

In these dreary days General Nelson continued to seek ammunition and food for his citizen soldiers. He wrote the Governor on January 22 that he could procure "240 Stands of fine arms at Baltimore for £190 a Stand which is much below the Price allowed for them this State."[47]

> I would also take the liberty of suggesting another Matter to you, that is the Necessity of calling the Assembly. From disagreeable experience I am convinced that the Defence of this Country must not rest on the Militia under its present Establishment. They have been so much harassed lately that they would give nearly half they possess to raise Regulars, rather than be subjected to the Distresses they fear at leaving their Plantations and Families.[48]

His men had been subsisting on corn meal, but General Nelson felt that some flour should be on hand and also thought the men might have some rum allowed with their rations. Much corn had been spoiled during the long haul from the Cumberland to Newcastle by water and Newcastle to Richmond by land.

Nelson explained the difficulties of the discharge plan to Jefferson:

> We have been obliged to call out the whole of the Militia from several Counties, some of whom I have not been able to discharge for want of Men to relieve them. I am ordered by Baron Steuben to keep in this Neck 1,000 to 1,200 Men, and were I to discharge the Men who were on Duty the last Invasion, which I confess they have a Right to claim, I should not have one third that Number. Many of the paroled men of Elizabeth City have taken up Arms, and others will do so if they are supported. This I am about to do with a light Corps. There are many those which the Service requires to be done, which cannot be effected for the Want of Money.[49]

General Nelson might wonder at the welfare of his own family at York Town. Since his brothers and cousins were engaged in the war effort in and out of the seaport village, only venerable Secretary Nelson was on hand as the head of the clan. Former neighbors were away serving the state. David

Jameson and Dudley Digges were members of the Council. Dudley Digges wrote Governor Jefferson from Ruffin's Ferry on the 19th, "I am thus far on my way to Williamsburg to collect the scattered remains of my property which was hastily distributed in such places as were deemed secure." He added he was pained that some days would elapse before he could attend the Assembly.[50]

Dr. Matthew Pope, appointed chief surgeon for the state, had the same money problems as other officials. He wrote Governor Jefferson that "the orderly, his wife, and Negro woman at the York Hospital who had been in the service since July last . . . never received a single shilling . . . they were suffering from want of pay long due them." Because they had borrowed money to live, the surgeon surmised the trio would be tempted to "help themselves" to stores and supplies.[51]

The appeals of General Nelson were answered by Governor Jefferson on January 25 with the information Nelson would receive his flour and the arms from Baltimore. Jefferson agreed the price was a bargain if the arms were good and promised to find means to pay for the shipment. As to the application of spirits for the soldiers he stated, "Baron Steuben informed me in conversation that spirits would not be allowed as a part of the daily ration but only on particular occasion." He then announced that the Assembly would convene on March 1.[52]

Continuing their close correspondence, General Nelson conveyed some encouraging news in his communication of February 3 written from Williamsburg to the Governor:

> I have visited the Posts below this Place and am happy in informing your Excellency that the paroled People require nothing but Assistance to make them very spirited Friends to their Country. They have in general destroyed their Paroles, and have formed a very fine Company to join Troops sent down.[53]

The apprehensive people in the area had accepted paroles, a form of promise for protection, from Benedict Arnold on condition that their property would not be damaged. As British plundering continued, however, the pledgers shifted to the patriot side.

The Governor and General Nelson were engaged in two special schemes: to burn the British fleet and to capture Benedict Arnold. Both ventures required boats and bold men.[54]

Adventurer Beesly Edgar Joel, a British officer and deserter, was selected to secure an old ship to be fired and sent amidst the British fleet at Portsmouth. Instead of obtaining an old hulk, Joel had taken the *Dragon* from the Navy Yard. This ship was appropriated by the Assembly so General Nelson regretfully canceled the project. Captain Joel had not only taken the wrong ship but also talked about the scheme, as the commander explained to the executive, "it being known all the low Country and probably by the British before this day."[55]

Joel was furious and complained to the Governor that he had "condescended to the meanest employment of a common Sailor" and even avowed that he had injured his constitution in the fatigues involved.

Jefferson approved the action of General Nelson and attested, "Your suspension of Captain Joel's enterprise against the Enemy's fleet seems to have been well grounded. It was become so universally known leave doubt enemy apprised."[56]

Despite the efforts of General Nelson to establish a fighting force with the raw recruits, the restless militia clamored for leave. Nelson wrote Jefferson February 7:

> I have discharged the militia that were down on the last Invasion. Numbers have deserted and others from various circumstances have been permitted to go home so that the force on this side of the river is much short of what was allotted. Neither the Caroline nor Essex militia have been called out. They would afford a good reinforcement.[57]

Although General Nelson had difficulties with his dwindling force, the hardships were not comparable to reports that reached camp about "Mad" Anthony Wayne's men rebelling and rioting.[58]

It was encouraging to hear good news from General Daniel Morgan's efforts at Cowpens, North Carolina. Morgan had planned a different kind of deployment in his battle maneuvers with picked riflemen for the advance guard, militia to form the first and second lines, firing two shots at the enemy then falling back to reload and returning by the right wing of the Virginia veterans. The main line of defense on the crest was composed of Continental regulars with cavalry at the rear. The strategy worked. When the Crown's columns advanced in perfect line formation, patriot forces poured rifle shot at their ranks. The "Old Wagoner" had beaten Tarleton. Victory was sweet for the Virginian, but he realized that when Lord Cornwallis learned of the loss, he would be as restless as a lion stalking its prey. In the drizzling rain, the rebels raced across the countryside to the Catawba on January 23 covering one hundred miles in five days.[59]

The action between the British troops and the American army in the Carolina campaign affected affairs in the Commonwealth of Virginia. The authorities were aware that General Nathanael Greene and his force formed the bulwark between the state and the British foe. To stop Lord Cornwallis from advancing into Virginia, more soldiers had to be sent southward to strengthen the Continental units. Not only General Greene but also Virginia commanders sent appeals to Governor Jefferson to reinforce the rebels in North Carolina.[60]

Jefferson issued instructions after the middle of February for militia to be called out from Rockbridge, Rockingham, and Shenandoah counties for relief, "provided they can be induced to go willingly the length of their march heretofore and having been some time in the service seems to give them a right to be consulted."[61]

General Steuben doubtless cursed again since he often proclaimed that some Virginians seemed to think that the war was being fought on another planet!

On February 17, Governor Jefferson notified General Greene that additional militia from Washington, Montgomery, Boutetourt, and Bedford counties had been ordered for his Continental regiments as well as riflemen recruited from Henry and Pittsylvania.[62]

General Nelson had been striving to maintain his militia called up from the coastal counties to protect the peninsula. Feeding his force and finding shelter for the soldiers through the winter weeks had been a monumental task. He had received numerous letters from General Steuben who felt that granting flags of truce to people to recover their property had resulted in perilous consequences. On February 3, General Nelson conveyed to the Continental commander:

> Orders respecting flags strictly adhered. . . . Our force here . . . is now insufficient for the protection of this Neck; . . . ought to be particularly attended to, both on account of the advantages which the Enemy would derive from the possession of it, and the peculiar situation of Many of the Inhabitants, whose attachments to and confidence in their Country have induced them to destroy their paroles.[63]

General Nelson was engaged in a scheme to capture Benedict Arnold by luring him aboard either of two small boats Nelson had secured by exhausting effort. William Reynolds was watching the vessel at York; the other boat was moored in Gloucester County where Nelson believed some of the paroled men could act as intermediaries in the plot. Governor Jefferson was anxious to seize the "scoundrel" and approved the plan. Governor Steuben was ready to help and General Muhlenberg had been asked to select a squad of tight-lipped mountain militiamen to prevent the "discovery of this design." Jefferson offered a reward of 5,000 guineas for "this greatest of all traitors," provided Benedict Arnold could be captured alive, 2,000 gold coins if Arnold was killed.[64]

General Nelson, however, gave up his plot when the French fleet arrived writing Governor Steuben, "There will be no occasion now for the boats I had engaged,"[65] figuring the French fleet would accomplish the protection needed.

Colonel Charles Dabney sighted the fleur-de-lis adorned flags at 3 A.M. February 15 and reported immediately to General Nelson, who exultantly sent a dispatch to the Continental commander:

What you expected has taken place. I give you joy with my soul. Now is the time. Not a moment ought to be lost. I intended to have crossed the James River this day, but I shall first wait on the French Commodore and then cross to afford you every assistance in my power. I have represented to the Governor the necessity for dispatch in our operations.[66]

General Nelson and his staff rode rapidly toward Hampton Harbor on the sixteenth to confer with Captain Armand de Tilly in charge of a sixty-four-gun ship and two frigates, each equipped with thirty-six guns. The commander spent two days discussing the defense situation of the state. The French allies were anxious to plunge into an offensive operation against Arnold but rejected the plan of Jefferson and ranking officers of the Commonwealth. Because the state lacked artillery to launch an all-out attack, the Virginia authorities desired de Tilly to sail his ships with their superior gun strength up the Elizabeth River to block the British. Militia forces would be summoned to the area. The French Commodore objected; the waterway was too shallow for his squadron to enter, but he promised to cruise off the Cape to intercept any supplies from reaching the English enemy.

General Nelson wrote a long letter to Governor Jefferson on February 18 concerning the vital conference. One observation was particularly pleasing to report:

> This Fleet brings intelligence that three seventy-fours of the enemies Northern Fleet were lost, rendered useless and missing, the *Culloden* of seventy-four Guns, a copper bottom'd Ship was entirely lost, the *America* was missing, and the *Bedford* dismasted and no means of repairing her.[67]

Despite the English fleet's difficulties, de Tilly feared British ships would sail into the bay and bottle up his smaller squadron.

General Nelson returned to Williamsburg and wrote Jefferson:

> Commodore Tilly having determined to sail with the first fair wind, the Enemy will be left at Liberty to make use of all the Advantages which their Command of the water gives them over us. They will probably be inclined, for some losses they have sustained since the Arrival of the French Squadron, to wreak their Vengeance on the Parts of the State most Exposed Hampton and the adjacent Country have particular Reason to dread the Effect of their Resentment, having furnished our Allies with Pilots, and testified the greatest Readiness to afford them every other kind of Assistance. It gives me the utmost Pain that I find myself unable to give them the Protection they merit; the Force at present under my Command amounting to no more than four hundred Effectives.[68]

The French squadron had seized eight enemy vessels including the *Lord Cornwallis* and another privateer; other prizes were expected. General Nelson requested the French Captain, ". . . assist the State with Arms or any

Military Stores that he could spare from the captures or otherwise." [69] He also hoped that his promise of a proper return would be approved by the authorities.

On February 20, General Nelson sent the following information to Governor Jefferson:

> By intelligence received last night, the French Fleet had fallen below the old Fort on Point Comfort. The prizes they have sent round to York, and I fear from their present weakness they will not be safe there. [70]

An incident that involved the civil and military authorities of the Commonwealth at this time erupted into an explosive controversy. Traitor Arnold's seizure of slaves and stock from Westover touched off the fiery situation. Mrs. Byrd appealed to General Steuben, and the commander agreed that the servants and horses could be returned by a British ship flying a flag of truce. Lieutenant Hare had set sail on February 10, in H. M. S. *Swift* to move up the James River on this mission, but Virginia patriots prevented the vessel from reaching Westover. In his communication to Governor Jefferson on February 18, General Nelson stated:

> A Flag Vessel from the enemy, in which was Lieutenant Hare formerly detained at Hampton has been stopped at Sandy Point. The enclosed papers will inform you of the business and the extraordinary Conduct he has observed. His abuse of Characters in this State has been general and his Expressions concerning your Excellency have been such, as from any other mouth but that of an enemy and at the same time a person of very little consequence in any point of View would be extremely injurious. His insinuations were that you had received gold from New York. I mention this not as a Circumstance which can affect you but which may perhaps in him be deemed justly a Violation or an unwarrantable abuse of his flag. An officer who was sent aboard saw in the Fire something which had the appearance of Letters just consumed. [71]

Colonel Innes was more vehement in his version of the incident and stated to General Steuben that the ship had been stopped because the vessel had "Attempted at an unreasonable hour of the night, to pass the posts on James River, refused to come to when hailed and fired upon the Guards." [72]

The suspicions of Major Turbeville, who stopped the ship, were further aroused when Lieutenant Hare refused to admit the rebel officer into the cabin to search for questionable papers. The patriot commander pushed into the room and "found several packages of papers in flames, and other evident marks of letters, which had been destroyed—in the vessel were discovered several Articles of merchandise, such as Brandy, porter, port wine, China, Linnen, Broad Cloth & c & c & c." [73]

Though Lieutenant Hare claimed these supplies were sea stores, the articles clearly demonstrated to Colonel Innes that clandestine trading had transpired.

Tempers flared. Numerous interchanges filled with invectives kept the express riders on the run. General Steuben was enraged at Jefferson, as usual, and angry with Colonel Innes and Major Turbeville. In his opinion the officers had overstepped their authority. The strict Prussian soldier desired Governor Jefferson to discipline the insubordinates, but he declined to interfere in a position he considered a military matter. On the other hand, Steuben tossed the problem of the illegal traffic with the enemy into Jefferson's lap as a civil concern and refused to resolve the entangled complications. While the participants sparred, the tongues of the citizens continued to wag about the antics at Westover.

General Nelson's exposure during the damp days confined him to camp with a severe cold. Secretary Andrews wrote General Steuben that by February 20 Nelson was so much worse that he could not do business.[74] The Prussian soldier was worried because he planned to separate the militia from the regulars and had instructed General Nelson to take command of all the militia regiments in the southern region. General Muhlenberg was to return to Richmond to take charge of the Continental troops but had to be left in the area until Nelson recovered.

The local militia commander had mentioned to Jefferson that the units from Albemarle and Fluvanna counties were in such distressed condition for clothing that they should be discharged. When Colonel Innes was appointed to take temporary charge of Nelson's militia force on February 21, he immediately informed Governor Jefferson that most of the men were "totally destitute of the necessary cloathing to protect them from the Inclemency of the weather. They are lousy dirty and ragged, and from these Circumstances becoming every day more sickly. . . . Apprehensive of a mutiny, unless some assurance can be given of a speedy relief." Innes then confirmed that "General Nelson is at present confined to his Chamber with a violent pleurisy."[75]

Though the officers were troubled about the wretched state of the troops, more militia were being called to form regiments for the Carolina campaign. While indisposed, General Nelson received a dispatch from Jefferson dated February 22, which reported that one-fourth of the militia from Loudon, Fauquier, Prince William, and Fairfax counties had been called to march immediately to Williamsburg. The contingent would comprise 1,090 men, and General Nelson had been ordered to expedite the execution of the order. Jefferson sanctioned Nelson's securing arms from Commodore de Tilly. He enclosed an extract of a letter from Virginia's delegates to the Congress and asserted, "Should Arnold not be recalled by positive orders, he may possibly come up Appomattox either to attempt a junction with Lord Cornwallis or to divert our reinforcements to General Greene, and place him between two fires. Lord Cornwallis had not crossed the Dan on the 19th." He ended the February 22 letter on an optimistic note: "Our accounts of the militia turning out to reinforce General Greene are flattering."[76]

At the end of the month, Jefferson had encouraging news from Washington:

> I have put a respectable detachment from the Army in motion. It is commanded by Major General and Marquis de La Fayette. It will proceed by land to the Head of Elk, at which I calculate it will arrive the 6th of March at farthest, and will fall down the Chesapeake in Transports.[77]

Another French fleet under Admiral Destouches was on the way, General Washington wrote, to co-operate with the Commonwealth in capturing Arnold and blockading the British in the bay.

Messages from Lafayette also arrived for the authorities, and the executive and officials of the state redoubled their efforts to strengthen the defense system. General Nelson had been informed by Governor Jefferson that he was "anxious to prepare for cooperation with our Allies, and for providing for their support."[78] Since York Town was the most effectual port to prepare for their vessels, he was sending engineer Colonel John Christian Senf down and artillerist Colonel Harrison to establish cannon and General Nelson was asked to use his "influence" in securing the necessary laborers, tools, and equipment to expedite the project. The executive stated to General Steuben, "I hope General Nelson's influence may have enabled him to procure hands for this purpose. The four battery pieces with their carriages, and one mortar, with its beds are got on board today."[79]

The Baron went to Williamsburg camp from Chesterfield Court House on March 6, and he sent off a dispatch to Governor Jefferson the next day with the disappointing announcement, "no appearance of the French fleet"[80] as yet.

By March 13, however, young General Lafayette arrived in York Town aboard the *Dolphin* having left a light infantry force of 1,200 men at Annapolis. Steuben, Nelson and Lafayette conferred on the defense system of the state and exchanged several letters with Jefferson, "The interest being Common to All engaged in this Cause, and the interest of Virginia being particularly Concerned in this Expedition, I do not More Question the Good Intentions of the State than I do My own on this Occasion," Lafayette wrote on March 16.[81]

The twenty-three-year-old Marquis had developed more diplomatic finesse in dealing with democratic forms of government than General Steuben, managing a proper balance between deference and decision in his consultations with the fifty-year-old Baron. As Lafayette reconnoitered the area, he discovered the handicaps others had found—a "great deficiency of Horses," and a lack of "ammunition in camp" at Suffolk which had prevented a foray against the foe.[82] General Lafayette and the lookouts along the coast had scanned the sea for the arrival of the French fleet but instead of seeing the flags of France, they sighted English ships off the capes.

When the Marquis and his staff returned to Williamsburg on March 20, General Weedon wrote Jefferson that the young Frenchman had reported the sighting of British ships with "great mortification."[83] In a few days intelligence informed General Lafayette that British Admiral Arbuthnot and his ships had scattered the French squadron. On March 27, Lafayette wrote Jefferson, "Since the return of the British fleet in the Bay, with a Number of Vessels supposed to be Transports from New York, I have entirely lost Every Hope of an immediate Operation against Portsmouth."[84]

General Steuben wanted General Nelson to attend the spring session scheduled for March 1. Unfortunately, Nelson had not recovered his strength sufficiently and General Weedon wrote the Baron, "General Nelson has been with me since you went away. He has been exceedingly unwell, and still is much indisposed."[85]

Surprisingly, the statesmen from across Virginia arrived at Richmond by March 2, a most unusual occurrence for the officials. The legislators elected Richard Henry Lee Speaker.[86]

The pockets of the delegates were crammed with petitions from constituents clamoring for restitution for slaves, stock and other property stolen by the British. The war-weary citizens protested high prices, impressment, recruitment, and raids.

General Morgan's message to Governor Jefferson attested to the Frederick County citizens' widespread resentment: "When I arrived home, I found the people in a ferment about the Taxes, and some went so far as to say they would not pay them."[87]

The representatives sympathized, but they were caught in the same economic squeeze. After the members grappled each morning with governmental measures of militia, materiel, and money, the statesmen paid for their noon meals in nearby taverns with stacks of paper money. A hot dinner cost thirty dollars, but an abstemious delegate could save ten dollars if he chose a cold plate. By the spring of 1781, West India rum had risen to thirteen dollars a gill (four gills to the pint); peach brandy cost twelve dollars; apple and good whiskey sold for eight dollars.[88]

The authorities were frustrated over their failure to trap Arnold in February when de Tilly appeared with a few vessels and had continued their appeals for French aid, writing spirited letters to Washington and the Congressmen at Philadelphia.

General Nelson was impatient that his illness kept him incapacitated through March. Confined to his room, he had time to recall the French allies whom King Louis XVI had sent to aid the rising republic. When the French force under Comte de Rochambeau and Admiral de Ternay had arrived at Newport, Rhode Island, the previous July, American authorities inadvertently had not been present with a proper salutation. Townspeople had not greeted their Gallic associates with a warm welcome—only stared bleakly at the newcomers from broken windows, but their indifference soon changed. The citizens were charmed by the genial manner of General Rochambeau, a handsome fifty-five-year-old professional soldier (with more than forty years fighting for France), and by his army of 5,000. Four infantry regiments were outfitted in bright uniforms: the Bourbonnais in white uniforms with black bands; the Santonge in white and green; the largest unit, the Royal Deux-Ponts in blue with bright yellow facings; and the Soissonnais bedecked in white broadcloth coats with crimson or rose-colored facings and white, plumed hats. The cavalry under the Duc de Lauzun clattered along the cobblestones in blue jackets, yellow breeches, gold braid, and fur shoulder capes. The Duc de Lauzun and his legion, filled with fiery exiled Poles, were equally at ease at a soiree as in the saddle. The gallantry of the visitors made every village girl feel like a *femme fatale*. Rakish Count de Fersen, rumored to have been Marie Antoinette's lover, bent over the women's hands with grace. Count de Fersen, who served as aide to Rochambeau, observed that aristocratic consciousness of class still prevailed in America, although her leaders proclaimed individual rights as the ideal. Both de Lauzun and de Fersen lived dangerously and died courageously. (During the French Revolution, through a false accusation, Count de Fersen was murdered by a mob and the Duc de Lauzun was put to death by a revolutionary tribunal.)[89]

Another observer, Nicholas Cresswell penned an astute comment about Washington in his journal:

> General of a Republic, he does not have that imposing ostentation of a Marshall of France giving an order; hero of a Republic, he excites another sort of respect, which seems to give birth to but one idea—that the salvation of each individual is attached to *his* personality.[90]

Frenchmen were accustomed to spirits, but they were amazed at the interminable toasts of the Americans and astonished at the endless cups of tea that the ladies and gentlemen drank. The soldiers were relieved when they discovered they could refuse politely to consume the refreshment by placing their spoons across the top of their cups.

Some Congressmen caroused at the celebrations and slipped into the State House the next day with drowsy indifference. When General Nelson heard rumors of the revelry, he remembered the duties of the delegates back in the first years of the Continental Congress when he had served his state. As a legislator, he had spent long hours from daybreak until late at night laboring on workable laws to weld the colonies together for the common cause. The fervent spirit shown by the statesmen of 1776 in their love of liberty and the fight for freedom had faded.

General Steuben traveled to Richmond the last of March to lobby with the legislators to pass his military plan. It was his conclusion that 2,000 select militia be chosen for the Carolina campaign. The Baron desired to march with the men as their commander.

Governor Jefferson and his advisers from the Council considered the military measure, and on March 29 they rejected the plan stating that in their opinion the "proposition seems to be founded upon very probable principles, yet the number of arms that such a Detachment would necessarily carry with them bearing a very great proportion to what will afterwards remain in the State, it will be a measure unjustifiable in the present circumstance of affairs the enemy having lately received a great reinforcement."[91]

On March 15, General Greene had already faced the enemy at Guilford Court House, North Carolina. His army had been augmented by militia flocking in irregularly, so the force fluctuated. With about one-third of his 4,200 seasoned Continental soldiers, Greene crouched in the forest and peppered the redcoat ranks as they approached. Hard-riding horsemen charged on the field, and the fight became a tangled mass of men. Lord Cornwallis turned his cannon on the field to break up the troops, thereby killing British as well as Americans. General Greene concluded that he could not gamble his whole army in a concerted all-out attack and retreated after two hours.

The British commander was master of the battlefield at Guilford Court House, but his triumph was bought at a terrible price. Casualties included one-fourth of his force, nearly one hundred soldiers killed and over four hundred wounded. A dozen officers had been lost and twice that number wounded.

General Greene lost seventy-eight men killed in the conflict; fewer than two hundred were wounded.[92]

CHAPTER TWENTY-TWO

Governor and General: 1781

Discouraging Drafts ✦ *Chagrins for the Commander-in-Chief* ✦ *Resistance to Redcoats* ✦ *General Lafayette Arrives in April* ✦ *Cornwallis Advances into Virginia* ✦ *Convention at Charlottesville* ✦ *Jack Jouett's Ride* ✦ *General Nelson Elected Governor* ✦ *Return to Richmond* ✦ *Defense and Depredations* ✦ *French Fleet Arrives in August* ✦ *Trouble with Troops* ✦ *General Washington Arrives in September*

General Nelson began to improve from his illness in April. From his window in Williamsburg, he could see a wave of color spreading over the old capital as grass thickened, bulbs flowered, and tiny buds began to fill the tree branches. Yet the sweetness of spring could not dispel the dread of an approaching attack by the English enemy. Coaches, carts, and hastily loaded wagons rolled inland as residents made their way from the coastal regions.

General William Phillips had brought to Portsmouth 2,500 redcoats in English vessels crowded with artillery and cavalry.[1]

To meet this menace, General Nelson issued calls for all the men in counties around Richmond to be in readiness and for half the militia to muster in the outlying counties, but results were disheartening even though the enemy was camped on the coast in full force. In Kent County, adjacent to the capital, only 9 men appeared out of 104 who were supposed to report. Volunteering in Virginia was at a low ebb; men who had served three months were demanding discharges.[2] General Nelson, not defeated by the depletion of his detachment through discharges, desertions, and disease was ready to train more raw recruits.

General Steuben was complimentary to General Nelson, praising him for his zeal, but the inadequacy of military supplies and indifference of the people to imminent danger irked the commander so that he carped at the Governor and his government. The professional soldier advised the Assembly that the patriots should make an audacious counterstroke against the enemy by collecting private and public boats to sail down the streams to block the British; the representatives refused to pass the plan.[3]

Nelson received a communication from Washington asking him to give his "advice and assistance" to Monsieur Camus, a French naval officer who had arrived to command an armed ship in the York River. The Commander-in-Chief ended his letter with the appeal, "You will therefore oblige me by rendering him every service in your power."[4] General Nelson was elated since the news indicated French aid was on its way.

General Lafayette's division had been reduced by desertion and disease. Unpaid and without uniforms, the New England units grumbled that they would rather be "struck one hundred lashes than go South." The brigades reached Baltimore on April 16, and the officer outfitted his detachments with blankets and books securing the promissory notes with his own signature. A gala banquet and ball tendered by the French officers was turned into a sewing bee by the winning ways of General Lafayette who convinced the women to give up dancing to make shirts for the departing soldiers.[5] The Marquis had a strong personal incentive to pursue General Phillips who commanded the British force in Virginia. When Lafayette was only two, Phillips had killed Lafayette's father at the battle of Minden, Germany, during the Seven Years War. He had often been told of his mother's grief realizing her son would never know his father.[6]

Leaving soldiers not strong enough to travel, tents, and artillery in Maryland to catch up later, General Lafayette marched his troops twenty-eight miles through intermittent spring rains the first day; half the men rode while the others marched and then the procedure was reversed at regular intervals. On April 21, the Continental division crossed the Potomac and arrived at Alexandria. It was here the Marquis heard angry citizens tell how Lund Washington, the manager of Mount Vernon, had hobnobbed with the enemy in an effort to retrieve slaves the British had talked into fleeing the plantation. General Lafayette felt that friendship had its duties so he wrote General Washington on April 23 his distressed feeling:

> Mr. Lund Washington went on board the enemy's Vessels and consented to give them provisions. This being done by the gentleman who in some measure represents you at your house will certainly have a bad effect, and contrasts with spirited answers from some neighbors who had their houses burnt accordingly.[7]

As soon as he received the report, General Washington wrote to his remote cousin the regret over the property loss:

> But that which gives me the most concern, is, that you should go on board the enemy's Vessels, and furnish them with refreshments. It would have been a less painful circumstance to me, to have heard that in consequence of your non-compliance with their request, they had burnt my House, and laid the Plantation in ruins. You ought to have considered yourself as my representative and should have reflected on the bad example of communicating with the enemy. . . . to communicate with a parcel of plundering Scoundrels, and request a favor by asking the surrender of my Negroes, was exceedingly ill-judged.[8]

The tale spread rapidly through the Tidewater region since it embellished the tale about the appeal Washington's mother made to the General Assembly for financial aid. Speaker Benjamin Harrison, realizing that the request was a whim of a capricious old woman rather than a case of real want, had checked action by the Assemblymen so that General Washington would not be subjected to needless humiliation and notified his old friend of the situation.[9]

General Steuben admitted that he had no answer to the gnawing question of whether the British army would assault Petersburg or attack Richmond again. He decided to combine his militia with General Muhlenberg's men and directed the fighting parson to bring his division from the Tidewater peninsula to Petersburg making a combined force of about 1,000 men to oppose several thousand soldiers of the British army.[10]

With only token opposition left in the lower Tidewater, General Phillips, who had smarted under prison confinement, and Benedict Arnold seized the opportunity to strike. Eleven British square-rigged ships sailed up the James River on April 18. Patriot patrols reported the progress of the impressive fleet. By 7:00 A.M. Friday, April 20, at least twenty ships had been sighted and at 2:00 P.M. royal troops were landing on the Jamestown shore. Virginia riflemen fired at the five hundred English infantrymen but were forced to fall back. On Sunday, fourteen British ships and sixteen flat-bottomed boats sailed up the Chickahominy River. Arnold burned the rebel boats touching off a raging fire that swept through the shipyard to consume a twenty-gun ship under construction.[11] The patriots, however, took pride in Major John Nelson and sixteen cavalrymen's surprise attack and rout of 600 British regulators.[12]

On April 25 General Steuben and General Muhlenberg, with a thousand rebels stationed at Blandford Church at Petersburg, bravely resisted two thousand English troops under General Phillips and Benedict Arnold but were compelled to retreat. General Steuben later wrote General Greene: "I must confess I have not yet learnt how to beat regular troops with one third their number of militia."[13]

Colonel John Banister wrote an account of the enemy action to Colonel Theodorick Bland:

> After our militia had gained the hill, they retreated toward Chesterfield Court House, where they halted the next day. This little affair shows plainly the militia will fight, and proves if we had force to have occupied the heights, they [the enemy] would not with that force [have] entered the town.[14]

The British had not yet burned all the Banister mills, he asserted, "but have taken all the bread and flour, to the amount of £800 or £1,000, eleven of my best negroes the first time, and how I expect they will get the rest."[15]

General Nelson had instructed Colonel Innes and his militia to move toward Richmond. Riders brought reports that Crown troops were traveling through Charles City County on a rapid march toward the capital. General Phillips pushed a division to Chesterfield Court House and destroyed rebel barracks, while Arnold took a detachment to Osborne about fifteen miles below Richmond and scuttled the patriot ships. With heavy artillery, the traitor directed fire at the *Alert, Renown, Tempest,* and *Jefferson.* Since the *Liberty* escaped the enemy fire, people thought it a prophetic sign that the fight for freedom was not lost.[16]

General Phillips had issued instructions that private property was not to be plundered, especially the Bland family plantation as a favor to Colonel Theodorick Bland, who had shown civility to British prisoners confined at Charlottesville. Yet the redcoats, in a violent raid, stormed Bland's home breaking up furnishings and stealing slaves and stock. The royal regiments moved on to Manchester on April 28 just across the James River from Richmond. Now the officials of the Commonwealth had no doubt as to the objective of the British foe. The Governor could easily see the English encamped across the James River from Richmond.

General Nelson and his militia arrived in Richmond to resist the redcoats. Governor Jefferson reported to General Steuben about 200 patriots with arms and 300 without presented a dismal prospect for defense of the capital.[17]

General Lafayette and his detachment rose at dawn Sunday, April 29, to reach Richmond by the afternoon, just in time to help save the city from the invaders. He conveyed his exuberance in a May 4 communication to General Washington:

> General Phillips was amazed at our celerity and flew into a violent passion and swore vengeance against me and the corps I brought with me.[18]

General Lafayette was not so excited when he reviewed the meager rebel militia units at a parade in Richmond. Minus uniforms, without weapons, insecure, the men could not make an impressive appearance or present arms properly. Letters from the Governor to Lafayette had apologetically explained that his exertions and the authority of the Assembly had been ineffectual.[19] Poring over plans with General Steuben and General Nelson, General Lafayette distributed the patriot detachments to defend the state. The Prussian drill master was to ready recruits for the Southern campaign. Two brigades of militia numbering 1,200 to 1,500 were to be divided between General Nelson at Williamsburg and General Muhlenberg on the south side of the James River. Colonel Innes would command the York Town fort and the Gloucester garrison. The Continental troops under General

Lafayette would encamp on the Chickahominy River about sixteen miles below Richmond.[20]

The British raided Jamestown May 7, then unexpectedly changed course to push upstream. General Lafayette responded with alacrity and on May 8 marched his men to cut off the foe. Stopping at Osborne, the patriots slept in the encampment the Englishmen had just evacuated. The French nobleman reclined on the same bed General Phillips used fighting a rising temperature. After reaching Petersburg, the old officer could not direct his detachments as he lay with a raging fever. He died on May 13.[21]

Meanwhile, Lord Cornwallis, acting on his own authority without consulting General Clinton, asserted that the Carolinas could not be conquered as long as Virginia was able to arm the Southern Department. The last of April he moved his British regiments of 1,400 men from Wilmington, North Carolina. Among them were the Twenty-second Guards, Thirty-third West Ridings Guards, Twenty-third Watch, Seventy-first Highlanders, Eighty-second Light Infantry, Hessian units, and Tarleton's Tories.[22]

War hysteria was intensified by the cry that Cornwallis was coming.

Not enough representatives assembled at Richmond May 10, as requested, to make a quorum. The few delegates who did attend rushed about the rambling Capitol at Fourteenth and Cary Streets piling records in carriages. They decided to convene at Charlottesville on May 24, believing the community to be a safer refuge from the redcoats.[23]

Governor Jefferson rode away from Richmond on May 15, remaining at his Tuckahoe residence a few days before moving on to Monticello. Panic gripped the general population as people recalled the previous raid and scurried to pack family and possessions into all available vehicles. The cavalcade moved down the thoroughfares exiting from the town, carriage wheels grinding deep into the dusty roads.

At Wilton, on the James River, General Lafayette let his Continental troops cut off their long coats to be more comfortable in the warm weather. Clothes were cleaned, kettles scrubbed, and rifles repaired while the balmy river breeze blew up the bank.

After General Phillips's death, General Lafayette refused to recognize Benedict Arnold as head of the British brigades. A rider sent to Petersburg by General Nelson returned in the evening of May 16 with an angry retaliation from the traitor. Arnold threatened to send the captured Continental officers to the West Indies; ten American officers were held prisoners at Petersburg.[24]

General Nelson reported to General Lafayette that no British regulars had crossed to the south side except a few sailors who had landed in the lower part of Charles City and stolen corn from the citizens. Reinforcements from Fredericksburg and the adjacent counties had not arrived in Williamsburg. The Continental commander and the local leader realized that the rebels would have to rely on strategy rather than troop strength to resist the foe. General Lafayette needed an effective cavalry to combat the enemy; John Nelson's corps was weary from long service to the state.[25]

Horses suitable for cavalry were at a premium. Farmers angered at the methods of impressment agents from the Southern Department had been planting food for their families and withholding their horses from the rebels. The price of no other product had become so precious as brood mares and stud stallions. The Virginia Assembly set the value of a cavalry horse at $150 in hard currency, which translated into $150,000 in Continental paper money. Governor Jefferson had been warned by General Daniel Morgan that a satisfactory system of supplying the patriot cavalrymen should be established or the British would buy the horses with gold guineas. Jefferson replied to the "Old Wagoner" that only Assembly members had the power to pass such an act. While Jefferson waited for the representatives to approve the recommendations according to the Constitution, royal solicitors purchased thoroughbred Virginia horses for Tarleton's and Simcoe's cavalry corps.[26]

After reconnoitering the position of the British boats at City Point, General Nelson wrote to Governor Jefferson on May 10 from Four-Mile Creek:

> I am informed that the Light Horse under Colonel Call are discharged in eight days from this time, which will put us entirely in the power of the Enemy, already an overmatch for us in Cavalry unless others can be induced to enter in from the Counties whence the reliefs of Militia coming. I mention this matter that measures may be adopted to remedy the great inconveniencing that will arise from the discharge of the Corps. It will be impossible to give you further intelligence of the movements of the Enemy without more cavalry or Expresses. The cavalry that we have are obliged to be constantly on the Enemy's lines.[27]

Major John Nelson, also vitally interested in the same subject, informed the Governor about the conditions of his cavalry in a letter from Hanover Town on May 25:

> The reduced situation of my Corps had induced the Marquis to order me to this Place, for the purpose of recruiting the Horse & getting equipt as fast as possible.[28]

The major had conferred with Lafayette at Wilton and been assured of supplies, so he had applied to Mr. Ross in Richmond and received, "two Hundred prs. of Over all & one Hundred stable Waistcoat of Light Canvas, upon a promise from me to obtain an Order from you for them; he has also sent out Agents to procure Boots, Spurs, & Army Combs for us."[29]

His letter continued:

As to our Saddles & Bridles, they were never good for Any thing—tho' I shall have as many fitted as possible, but it will be better to have a new Set made complete, as what we have, with all the repairs we can give them, will not last long, & to let you know the true situation of the Horses, they were never fit for Dragoons & are so much worn down with hard service, that I should despair of getting many of them in Order in Six Months & when in the best Plight, they are only fit for Express and Waggon Horses—the Marquis has ordered some to be purchased on Continental Account.[30]

John Nelson believed that horses should be bought despite the high cost. Although the enemy outnumbered the patriot cavalry, not a single animal had been secured.

Lord Cornwallis and his Crown columns reached Petersburg on the Appomattox River by May 20. The commander assumed charge of the British regiments, and royal reinforcements consisting of two British brigades and two Anspacher battalions augmenting his army to a total troop strength of 7,200 soldiers. The superior Royal Navy pulled into Portsmouth, cruised along the Chesapeake area, or sailed up the Tidewater rivers at will since the rebels were too weak to offer resistance.[31]

Arnold, despised by the Americans and distrusted by the British, was recalled to New York. The traitor and his wife, Peggy, left for London in the latter part of the year where only a cool reception, scant recognition, and no coveted peerage was tendered the turncoat.[32]

In less than a week, Cornwallis, who was anxious for action, started the scarlet-clad columns toward the capital to catch General Lafayette. The redcoats crossed the James River near Westover about thirty miles below Richmond. Patriot patrols alerted the Continental commander in Richmond and General Nelson at Williamsburg. General Muhlenberg and a 500-man detail moving ammunition over the Appomattox River were alarmed at the approach and General Steuben drilling 500 recruits for the Carolina campaign moved to protect supplies stored at Point of Fork.[33]

With the imminent threat throughout the Tidewater region, citizens of York joined the travelers escaping from the coast into the upper countryside. For the second time during the year, Lucy Nelson became a refugee and left her home for the Hanover plantation. Baby Susanna was bundled up against the spring breeze and two-year-old Robert was caught on the run. Elizabeth, Mary, and Lucy at ten, six, and four, could be guided into assistance. Twelve-year-old Hugh lugged his books, while thirteen-year-old Francis, and Philip, who turned fifteen in March, wondered if they might become drummer boys with the troops. Their strong-willed mother settled this question quickly. When the carriages drove into Williamsburg, seventeen-year-old William and sixteen-year-old Thomas, drilling with the College detachment, were directed to step into the family coach, and the vehicles rolled through Richmond toward the hills of Hanover County.[34]

General Lafayette concluded that his force of approximately two thousand militia scattered at various sites and only nine hundred Continental soldiers could not beat the British brigades—more than double their numbers. To evade the enemy until his regiments were reinforced, the Marquis managed to evade Cornwallis by moving his men seventy miles above Richmond to the Rapidan River to await General Wayne. In a letter to General Washington, Lafayette lamented:

> Were I to fight a battle, I should be cut to pieces, the militia dispersed, and the arms lost. Were I to decline fighting, the country would think itself given up. I am therefore determined to skirmish, but not to engage too far, and particularly to take care against their immense and excellent body of horse, whom the militia fear as they would so many wild beasts. (I am not strong enough even to get beaten!)[35]

Lord Cornwallis failed to follow up his first advantage of splitting the patriot troops, but contingents of Crown detachments destroyed the bridge at City Point and captured some of the militia in Chesterfield County. Cornwallis chased after the Continentals but halted at North Anna River because his supply base was stationed on the sea.

General Nelson and his militia unit moved into the Hanover County region to harass the British. While in the vicinity, the local commander stopped by Offley Hoo to see his family. He was worried about their welfare since the redcoats were swarming through the territory. While the pursuer and the pursued maneuvered across the area during the last of May, General Lafayette sent a frantic appeal to General Morgan to raise a rifle corps of Virginia volunteers. Lafayette also decided that the desperate situation in the state justified his holding the troops that General Steuben was training to send southward to General Greene.[36]

General Weedon had been instructed to transfer the supplies at Hunter's Iron Works near Fredericksburg inland away from the reach of the redcoat soldiers. On June 1, he wrote General Lafayette about his situation:

> I intended moving tonight with the small handful of men in this place, but not being able to remove the stores and disperse the tobacco, as mentioned to you this morning, have risked your censure for the completion this object, well knowing that a few men added to your operating force have but small weight in anything decisive.[37]

Only a few representatives of the General Assembly, scheduled to be in Charlottesville by May 24, had arrived in the mountain village even by the last of the month.[38] Benjamin Harrison, Speaker of the House of Delegates, and Archibald Cary, who served in the same capacity for the Senate, were Governor Jefferson's guests at Monticello. Patrick Henry and John Tyler soon joined the group. The colleagues, discussing conditions in the Commonwealth, sensed the Governor's dejection and realized he wanted to relinquish the reins of government. His term expired on June 1.[39] On May 28, Jefferson had written to General Washington:

> A few days will bring to me that period of relief which the Constitution has prepared for those oppressed with the labours of my office, and a long declared resolution of relinquishing to abler hands has prepared my way for retirement to a private station.[40]

When recollecting the events of these fateful days later on, Jefferson wrote:

> From a belief, that under the pressure of the existing invasion, the public would have more confidence in a military chief, and that the military commander being invested with the civil power also, both might be wielded with more energy, promptitude and effect for the defence of the State.[41]

Delegates who had drifted into town were contacted, and the representatives resolved to set up a ballot for electing a Governor on Saturday, June 2, but they postponed the vote until Monday. After Jefferson made his exit, William Fleming of the Council handled the gubernatorial duties for the Commonwealth during the first few days of June.

Lord Cornwallis, concluding that he could not catch Lafayette, whom he called "The Boy," now turned his attention to a two-pronged thrust ordering Tarleton and 250 of his Tories to capture the Virginia officials at Charlottesville. On Sunday, June 3, the horsemen galloped across the Hanover hills looking like a hugh green wave. The cavalry commander planned to push the mounted men seventy miles in twenty-four hours, but on reaching Cuckoo Tavern in Louisa County, the riders stopped to rest. At the ordinary, twenty-year-old militia captain Jack Jouett, who had been at the inn overnight, discerned that the dragoons were headed for the temporary capital. Slipping out of the tavern in the late evening, the six-foot-four-inch, two-hundred-pound Jouett stripped a British soldier of his uniform, mounted his bay horse and rushed toward Charlottesville. Using an old river road across the wooded region, riding over ravines, and darting through branches that scratched both rider and mare, Jouett's horse lived up to her reputation as the fleetest of any racer in seven counties, traveling the fifty-mile distance to Charlottesville, where he was able to warn the Assemblymen who adjourned to meet in Staunton forty miles to the west. Along the route in Louisa County, Tarleton and his legion lingered to burn a twelve-wagon train filled with clothing for General Greene's Continental troops.[42]

While Captain Jouett clattered through Charlottesville before sunrise on Monday morning calling out, "The British are coming," Mrs. Walker of Castle Hill a few miles east of town was delaying the British by serving the soldiers a hearty breakfast. The charming, twice-widowed hostess had been mistress of the mansion only six months as the third wife of sixty-six-year-old Dr. Thomas Walker. Regardless of the hospitality of his host and hostess, Tarleton instructed his troops to seize Walker's guests.[43] Colonel John Syme, the elder halfbrother of Patrick Henry, frightened even the English fighter as he was dragged from his bed in a disheveled state. Delegate Newman Brock-enbrough was in bad health and never had a chance to serve his constituents after being captured. He was released but not re-elected a representative in the fall. Judge Peter Lyons, who had traveled in his carriage to Castle Hill from Hanover County to attend the Assembly was taken into custody as were Daniel Boone, printer James Hayes, Robert and Hugh Nelson, Tom's brothers, and Congressman Francis Kinloch of North Carolina.[44]

Captain Jouett moved on through Milton in the early morning and up the rugged ridge to Monticello to warn Governor Jefferson and his guests that the redcoats were on their way to Charlottesville. The messenger delayed at Monticello only long enough to drink some sweet Madeira before rushing on with his mission. Before leaving, the legislators ate a leisurely breakfast. Governor Jefferson sent his wife and girls to Colonel Carter's plantation, then walked outside to stare down the slope toward town through his long spy glass. Seeing no special stir there, he started back to the house; glancing once again at the town through the telescope, he glimpsed Tarleton's galloping troops. As Jefferson hurried to join his family, an advanced detail of English dragoons under Captain McLeod entered the estate. Remarkably, Tarleton reversed his usual tactics and forbade his men from plundering the Jefferson property; not a paper was touched. (Servants Martin and Caesar had been placing silver plate under the porch as the redcoats rode up the summit. Caesar got caught in the cellar and spent the long day in the dark.)[45]

General Edward Stevens, brave on the battlefield, deceived the enemy by dressing in ragged clothing and riding on an old nag. As the British pursuers pushed past him on the road, he must have smiled, for he recognized the faces of many regulars he had faced on the field in combat.[46]

In a communication written from Chantilly on June 12, to the commander, Richard Henry Lee assessed the situation in the state:

> The Governor has resigned his office, but no successor had been appointed, and Mr. Digges, the Lieutenant Governor it seems has been made a prisoner and released upon parole. . . .
>
> Thus, we remain without a government at a time when the most wise and most vigorous administration of public affairs can alone save us from ruin determined for us by the enemy.[47]

The veteran Virginia lawmaker was so depressed that he decided General Washington should return to the state and assume dictatorial powers. Others held the same opinion. The printing press at Charlottesville had been seized and Lee lamented the loss as the patriots would be prevented from publishing important public papers. He affirmed, "Every thing in the greatest possible confusion, the enemy far superior in force to that with the Marquis, and practically every thing that force and fraud can contrive."[48]

While the representatives rode the rough trail through Rockfish Gap toward Staunton, men with muskets poured from the mountains to protect the pass. Clouds of dust covered the foliage as militia units marched eastward to meet the enemy, and members of the legislature moved westward to re-establish the government. Families fled to the hills as the forces formed.[49]

Benjamin Harrison, Patrick Henry, and John Tyler, pushing toward Staunton, paused at a mountain cabin about dusk to seek some refreshment. They received a rebuff rather than hospitality from the old lady of the hut. Thinking her visitors had abandoned Charlottesville while her husband and sons had rushed to defend the town, she cried out to the group of gentlemen, "Ride on ye cowardly knaves!" Amazed to discover that Speaker Harrison and Patrick Henry were two of the delegates escaping from the English, the woman was finally convinced that the representatives had good reason to run. Only then were the statesmen invited into the house for supper.[50]

The old woman was not the only patriot who complained about the Assemblymen's and the Governor's escape. Betsy Ambler, Rebecca Burwell Ambler's daughter, expressed her disdain for the delegates' flight:

> Such terror and confusion you have no idea of, Governor, Council, everybody scampering. . . . But this is not more laughable than the accounts we have of our illustrious Governor, who, they say, took neither rest nor food for man or horse till he reached C——r's Mountain![51]

Conversely, the lady saw no humor when her father, Jacquelin Ambler, was forced to hide in a coach to evade the clutches of the British while a servant slipped food to him in the long hours.[52]

The second phase of Lord Cornwallis's military plan to smash the patriots was not really successful. Colonel John Graves Simcoe, commanding the cavalry of the Queen's Rangers and reinforced by the crack Seventy-first Highland Regulars, did surprise General Steuben and 500 soldiers guarding the garrison at Point of Fork. Simcoe instructed the Rangers to light campfires all along the river bank to indicate that a full force was ready to swoop down on the defenders. The ruse worked and General Steuben ordered the rebels to retreat, abandoning arms and ammunition. The Baron was blamed for the fiasco; Speaker Harrison avowed Steuben would not fight. The House of Delegates, despondent and edgy over enemy incursions, decided on an inquiry of the affair.[53]

General Nelson, commanding the Second Line under General Lafayette, moved his corps to Brock's Bridge during the first days of June to ferry across the North Anna River. The brigadier general aided Lafayette in confusing the English by fanning out the patriot forces; local militia came forth to defend their soil and baffle the British. Lord Cornwallis was determined to destroy the patriot   supplies at Albemarle Court House, but Tarleton was thwarted in the attempt and his express to the English Earl was intercepted by rebel intelligence.[54]

Though involved with military maneuvers in Virginia, General Nelson was interested in news of the Carolina campaign. Many militiamen straggling home through the spring as their enlistments expired were well known to the state commander.

General Greene, despite dwindling numbers, had moved into South Carolina drawing the English enemy. The British had built a series of stockades that stretched through the state along the rivers and tributaries. Greene relied on Light Horse Harry Lee's and Colonel William Washington's cavalry to cut communications of the British columns. The rugged fighters led by General Francis Marion, the "Swamp Fox," and General Andrew Pickens harassed the royal regiments, too. General Thomas Sumter and his collection of Carolinians were to assist Greene in the assault against Camden.

The Continentals had a formidable foe in Lord Francis Rawdon. The twenty-six-year-old English leader was lank, dark, and dubbed the ugliest fellow in the royal forces, but he was a fighter. Since Bunker Hill, the British commander had led his Irish Volunteer Corps in tough campaigns.

Lee's legion and Marion's men were successful in swamping Fort Watson. With an improvised platform of towering logs, the patriots pushed to the post with peppering rifle fire and captured 100 British prisoners in the surrender. The aristocratic cavalry commander of Virginia and the ragged partisan rebel of South Carolina worked well together to beat the British. They moved on a brick and stone mansion formerly owned by widow Rebecca Motte. The redcoats had confiscated and fortified it so successfully not even a six-day rebel siege evicted the British. Frustrated, the patriots planned to fire the structure and smoke out the foe. An ardent rebel, Mrs. Motte handed the fiery arrows to the Americans for their attack, but the English evacuated the handsome house and the blaze was extinguished. That evening the engaging hostess entertained the victorious and the vanquished officers at dinner.[55]

Gradually, the American commander of the Southern Department obtained his objective since British forts were abandoned or battered by the rebel forces.

Summer rains delayed until June 10 General Anthony Wayne's arrival in Virginia with three Pennsylvania regiments of one thousand men to augment the American army. Four colonels commanded the contingents whose horses had dragged six cannon over the rolling countryside. "Mad" Anthony attracted attention, for the thirty-six-year-old commander was a fearless fighter as well as a handsome man with fine features, dark hair, and discerning brown eyes.[56]

Colonel Richard Butler brought along his notebook to record his impressions, and so did Captain John Davis and Lieutenant William Feltman. Davis recorded in his diary on June 10, "Join'd the Marquis's this day, made a march of 23 miles, pass'd a body of Militia, 1,800 Men." Feltman noted the march had been severe.[57]

In the middle of June, Lord Cornwallis attacked Elk Hill, Jefferson's plantation on the James River, burning barns, killing cattle, and ruining corn crops. He took horses for the British troops and cut the throats of two young colts. Silver plate was stolen and slaves seized. Jefferson felt he could have excused the enemy if the slaves had been emancipated, but their destiny became "inevitable death from the smallpox and putrid fever then raging in his [Cornwallis's] camp."[58]

The British regiments reached Richmond June 16; the rebel forces followed. Reinforced in number and bolstered by the chase of the retreating redcoats, the spirit of the Continental soldiers rose, although some of the troops were marching without shoes. General Lafayette and his legion swung over the South Anna River. On reaching the plantation of Colonel Nathaniel Dandridge in Hanover County, the patriots halted to pitch camp. As the detachments moved southward shadowing Lord Cornwallis, a courier from across the state caught up with the contingent on June 16, presenting General Nelson the news that on Tuesday, June 12, Thomas Nelson, Jr., Esq., had been elected Governor by a joint ballot of both houses of the Assembly, receiving a majority vote.[59]

By education and experience, the York Town leader was trained for the task since he had served the state for twenty years as a Burgess, Congressman, and member of the House of Delegates. He also understood the needs of the military system; yet Nelson must have had a feeling of foreboding when he contemplated the complex situation he had to face. Riding toward Staunton, General Nelson must have pondered the problems of his new position and questioned his role in guiding the reins of government. Could he inspire the war-weary citizens to make more sacrifices to end the conflict successfully? Could he secure the supplies so necessary to win the war?

General Washington would soon write to his stepson, John Parke Custis, concerning the election:

> I am much pleased with your choice of a Governor. He is an honest man, active, spirited and decided, and will, I dare say, suit the times as well as any person in the State.[60]

Arriving at Staunton on June 18, the forty-two-year-old Thomas Nelson

425

was greeted by former colleagues and kin who had crowded into Trinity Church for the convention. William Fleming (acting executive authority since June 3), Andrew Lewis (frontier fighter), and George Webb (caretaker for Virginia's finances) were the only Council members in attendance. Joseph Prentis and Dudley Digges had resigned in May. John Tyler had declined to serve in the body but reconsidered.[61]

General Nelson also recognized other representatives: John Page, Archibald Cary, and John Tyler, Patrick Henry's brothers-in-law Colonel William Campbell and Colonel William Christian, Patrick Henry, and his old friend and close neighbor, David Jameson.

The following day Samuel Hardy, Samuel McDowell, and William Cabell were chosen as members of the advisory board, but Cabell declined to serve and Nelson would again see two of his cousins in the cramped quarters: Benjamin Harrison, long-time legislator, and George Nicholas, son of the late Treasurer Robert Carter Nicholas. The twenty-seven-year-old George Nicholas from Albemarle County stirred the statesmen in the first few days of discussion with two provocative topics. A little more stooped, Patrick Henry could still speak persuasively and took a prominent part in the raging controversy. With the tenseness caused by the incursions of the enemy, the desperate delegates had engaged in a bitter debate concerning the establishment of a dictatorship.[62] It was reminiscent of the wrangle in the dark days of 1776 when the remnants of the American army had retreated into New Jersey from the conquering British foe and the Congress fled from Philadelphia to Baltimore. The flagging spirit of patriotism, however, filtered through the country and penetrated the Virginia Assembly where the discouraged parliamentarians had considered electing a dictator. It was then that the irascible Mr. Cary had confronted John Syme, Patrick Henry's half brother, with the threat:

> I am told your brother wishes to be a dictator; tell him from me that the day of his appointment shall be the day of his death—for he shall feel my dagger in his heart before the sunset of that day.[63]

The Assemblymen did not forsake the democratic form of government in 1776 but gave the Governor and Council more authority to act during the military crisis.[64]

The second discussion of the constrained delegates during the early June 1781 session set off a sharp dispute and started a rift between Patrick Henry and Thomas Jefferson that never healed. George Nicholas moved in the House of Delegates that an investigation be conducted to examine Jefferson's efforts during his one-year term the previous twelve months. A special committee was appointed to study the charge that Governor Jefferson had been delinquent in providing an adequate defense against the English.

Henry supported Nicholas in the charge. When Archibald Cary's communication concerning this action caught up with Jefferson at Poplar Forest, he was extremely hurt by the accusations.[65]

These explosive issues reflecting the uneasiness, unrest, and recriminations of a wartime period had settled to some extent by the time General Nelson reached Staunton. For a second time, the representatives did not resort to setting up a dictatorship yet, in effect, such enlarged powers were extended to the new Governor and his Council, so that they had arbitrary authority.

On Wednesday, June 20, 1781, magistrate Sampson Matthews of Augusta County administered the oath of office to Thomas Nelson, Jr., who became the third Governor of the Commonwealth of Virginia.

The representatives passed strict resolutions to protect the safety of the state. To oppose the enemy strenuously, laws were to be executed promptly so the executive and his advisory board were empowered to call out forces and impress food, horses, wagons, ships, slaves, or any necessary supply to prosecute the war. Regulations added six months' service to militiamen who failed to answer the first summons and death was the penalty for desertion. Persons resisting the rules to strengthen militia regiments would have their property seized and redistributed. Martial law was set up in a twenty-mile area surrounding American and enemy camps. Tories were to be banished without trial. Continental officials would administer quarters and provisions for the troops. The authority of the local courts was augmented to the same power as those of the General Court of the Commonwealth so that the enforcements could be expedited. The representatives realized that requirements for the recruits must be lowered to enlarge the ranks so the lawmakers passed a resolution that men five-feet four-inches tall could enlist "if they were able bodied, sound in mind, and not subject to fits."[66]

In his dual role as Governor and General, Nelson issued instructions immediately to the lieutenants of Frederick, Berkeley, Hampshire, and Shenandoah counties in the northwestern section to summon two-thirds of the militiamen to march to join General Lafayette. Directions noted their detachments must number at least 200 men. Officials of the other mountainous counties received orders to raise riflemen in Buckingham, Augusta, Pittsylvania, Henry, Rockbridge, Botetourt, Albemarle, and Amherst. These recruits of not less than 200 men in a company were to come "mounted, armed, and accoutered" and move toward the main army.[67]

The authorities had already asked General Daniel Morgan to recruit riflemen and command the corps against the British adversaries he had faced on the field of battle. In Winchester on June 15 the "Old Wagoner" was ordered to remove redcoat prisoners into Maryland to avoid recapture by English dragoons. Major John Nelson attended the conference and was combing the countryside for decent horses for his cavalry.

On June 20, Governor Nelson answered the report just received from General Morgan with these words:

> The readiness which you show to assist our invaded Country gives general Satisfaction, and I doubt not but this Letter will meet you far advanced on your march to join the Marquis with such volunteers as you have been able to collect. I am sensible of the great inconvenience arising to the People by being called out at the approach of Harvest, but I have my hopes that some capital Blow may be struck time enough to enable the Commander of the Troops to dispense with their Services at that Time.[68]

Mention was made that measures would be taken to care for the accounts of necessaries furnished by the tradesmen to Major Nelson's corps.

The Governor had the advice of Councilmen William Fleming, Andrew Lewis, George Webb, Samuel Hardy, and Samuel McDowell during these days of momentous decisions. The officials were concerned about the recent insurrections that had occurred in Rockingham, Augusta, and Hampshire counties, but the board believed that only a few disaffected persons were involved. They recommended that Governor Nelson offer pardons on the condition that the ringleaders and deserters were delivered up and then be returned to duty as citizens. If the culprits refused, the whole strength of the counties would be called out to bring them to justice.[69]

Toward the last of June Governor Nelson and the delegates repacked state papers and started to ride the rutted roads back to Charlottesville where they assembled Monday, July 2. On that day Governor Nelson began a letter to General Weedon:

> An indisposition that attack'd me on the road from Staunton, has prevented my answering your dispatches before.
>
> Your vigilance and ability to search out and to apprehend the Tories in the borders of Rappahannock meets with the thanks of the Executive. If I can be aided by yourself and others in that quarter, and by persons equally zealous, in the other parts of the State, I have great expectations of ridding the Country of these people. The Assembly have vested the Executive with extensive powers, and they will not, I hope, be afraid to exercise them for the security of the State.[70]

Two letters written by Colonel William Nelson on June 18 and 19 to General Weedon from Leeds Town on the Rappahannock had already reached Weedon at Fredericksburg. Governor Nelson would have been happy to hear the news, as the communications related to prisoners the colonel had taken and their trials. William Nelson observed, "Unless they are closely confined, they will certainly escape, as few possess more cunning or a greater inclination to Villainy than these Men . . . ." Nelson was complimentary of his station:

In the Course of my Military Life, I had never so pleasant a command as this: The Officers are Gentlemen & the Men Soldiers; no idling or drunkenness, but the most perfect obedience to the most minute of my orders. I am forming the Legions of Westmoreland & Richmond in order to furlough the rest of my Command: the latter county hath already a Body of Horse raised, but I much doubt the possibility of raising Horse in the former, in which tho I fail, then a company of Infantry must do the business alone.[71]

In his second letter Colonel Nelson discussed the trials:

We are here deeply engaged in trying some vile Rascals: The Ct. sat all day yesterday and went through one trial only. This affair has already produced the most happy Effects: Deserters, & every other sort of villain, come in daily for mercy. . . . we must stay here embodied for a Month, if the trials last as long, after which I beg your permission to go and assist one of the most distressed Families in America; my own, who, to the number of six are at this moment without food, raiment or lodging, except what they receive from the bounty of others I know not where.[72]

There were rumors that the redcoats had burned many houses on the north bank of the Potomac, none on the South side, but many robberies had been committed by the enemy privateers even after an American flag vessel had gone up to Alexandria. The colonel suggested that this matter needed an inquiry. Although he had contacted the lieutenants of two counties, he commented in the postscript of his June 18 letter, "My Express has returned from Northumberland and Lancaster, without a single line from either of the Lieuts. not so polite you will say, but no bad News I presume is stirring there, or perhaps they might have condescended to have written."[73]

Governor Nelson was glad to greet Jacquelin Ambler, a former colleague and cousin by marriage, who resumed his duties on the Council at Charlottesville in July when the administrators agreed to re-establish the government at Richmond. While the representatives were riding to the capital, Governor Nelson took the opportunity to see his family in Hanover County and survey the damage to his plantation.[74]

The rebels and redcoats had covered much territory from the middle of June into the first few days of July. As Cornwallis moved eastward to enter Richmond on June 16, the French nobleman had followed with but a twenty-mile distance between them. Lord Cornwallis had been disappointed in not destroying the Continental stores at Albemarle Court House, yet with seven thousand troops the aggressive commander still had a decided advantage over the Americans. He could have turned at any time in an offensive attack. Now the Continental army had been supplemented by riflemen under the command of Colonel William Campbell whom Governor Nelson had called up from the mountain counties and with the arrival of the 450 levies Baron Steuben had brought into camp on June 19. There were nearly

1,600 men in the New England light infantry and Pennsylvania Line under General Muhlenberg and General Wayne. Approximately 1,300 men composed the Virginia brigades commanded by General Edward Stevens and General Robert Lawson. Militia came and went as they always had, but Lafayette had a total troop strength of nearly 4,500 soldiers, counting the small cavalry of about 120 to 200 artillerists who were in charge of eight cannon. The Marquis managed to deploy the men about so that British spies would be deceived. Camp was shifted constantly yet unit officers understood the plan for quick concentration. As the troops tramped over the dusty trails in the humid heat, the soldiers suffered from thirst and hunger. Rebels rushed into the orchards along the route for ripe fruit. Dysentery often resulted from the gorging.[75]

The soldiers' bare feet became bruised. On July 3, General Lafayette had sent a dispatch to Colonel Davies for needed supplies, stating "As many of the troops are entirely without shoes, I must request you to use your best endeavours to procure and forward supply of that article."[76] Rather than be delayed in joining the troops, the commander suggested that the dragoons come into camp with hunting shirts.

Captain John Davis recorded in his diary June 22, "through Richmond, in 24 Hours after the enemy evacuated it—it appears a scene of much distress!"[77]

His friend Lieutenant William Feltman commented in his diary that day, "Marched at 2 o'clock through a well inhabited country, though I can give no account of the people, as I have not been in the inside of a house [only] ordinaries."[78]

On Sunday, June 24, Captain Davis described the speedy trial of a deserter:

> A fine morning, we lay on this ground all day enjoy ourselves and cooking. The quiet of the camp was soon disrupted and Thursday one of our soldiers taken deserting to the Enemy 4 o'Clock he was tried, and Executed in the evening. March'd at dark in order to surprise Tarleton, 12 miles, he got wind of our approach and retir'd.[79]

Lord Cornwallis evacuated Richmond on June 20—having burned some houses and left some tobacco hogsheads in the street to be torched—and advanced to New Kent Court House on the twenty-third.[80]

The patriots marched a stenuous twenty-two miles in pursuit but could not strike. General Lafayette explained to Governor Nelson in a letter from Rawson's ordinary on June 26:

> Lord Cornwallis was at Bird's yesterday, from which place he retired with his main body into Williamsburg. We have been pressing his rear, with our light parties, supported by the army, but his Lordship has proceeded so cau-

tiously, and so covered his marches with his cavalry, that it has been, under our circumstances, next to impossible to do him any injury.[81]

On that same day a brisk skirmish occurred at Spencer's ordinary between the British and a special Continental corps. John Simcoe, with some green-coated Jagers and Queen's Rangers, had been roaming in the region seizing cattle, smashing stores, and planning to burn patriot boats. General Wayne was directed to send a detachment to intercept the raiders and chose Colonel Richard Butler for the mission with Major McPherson. The men marched all night of the twenty-fifth but at daybreak the Major mounted fifty infantrymen with the cavalry for the close chase. As patriot companies from General Wayne advanced to reinforce the rebels, Simcoe called on Cornwallis for assistance. When the full British force moved forward from the old capital, fighting ceased.[82] The British returned to Williamsburg where Cornwallis had ensconced himself in the Reverend James Madison's house on the campus of the College of William and Mary despite the fact the Madisons had lost their infant son fairly recently. Cornwallis provided quarters on the College grounds, but Nelson's friend St. George Tucker attested to the treatment of the Madisons: "They were refused the small privilege of drawing water from their own well."[83]

In ten days the redcoats wreaked havoc through the town seizing servants and leaving several inhabitants without help, among whom was Mrs. Peyton Randolph who did not have "a human being to assist her in any respect for several days." The English threw refuse along the streets so that flies were a plague and it was "impossible to eat, drink, sleep, write, sit still, or even walk about in peace on account of their confounded stings." Worse was the spread of smallpox by raiding troops through the region. It reached such "a crisis throughout this place so that there is scarcely a person to be found to nurse those who are most affected with it. . . . As the British plundered all that they could, you will conceive how great an appearance of wretchedness this place must exhibit. To add to the catalogue of mortifications, they constrained all the inhabitants of the town to take paroles." St. George Tucker summed up the ruinous situation with the succinct statement, "Pestilence and famine took root, and poverty brought up the rear."[84]

Although Governor Nelson's communication to Lord Cornwallis concerning ship passports and tobacco currency could not have taken effect by July 9, Tucker mentioned that patriot prisoners captured at Charleston were being exchanged and paroled and noted, "A Flag from Charlestowne came to Jamestown the night before last (July 9). I went thither immediately and was happy enough to hear that my Brother is actually arrived at Hampton being on board a hospital ship."[85]

The returned prisoners presented a problem. General Lafayette notified Governor Nelson later in the month:

The exchanged and paroled officers went to join their respective lines or states.—Many citizens taken as militia must either remain here to go to Philadelphia until Carolina is reconquered. Such as are exchanged must at least get out of the enemy's way—They will want money horse, and waggons—the liberal sentiments that actuate the State of Virginia will no doubt prompt her to take an equal care of Every American who has suffered for our noble cause.[86]

Governor Nelson was generous in granting sums of money and supplies to the needy officers.

By early July the Continental forces were fanned in closer formation than usual a few miles from Williamsburg. Colonel Campbell's riflemen were in front of Byrd's Ordinary. Four miles back, Colonel Christian Febiger, the courageous Dane who had fought in the colonial conflict since the Canadian campaign, was in charge of the eighteen-months' men of General Steuben. The Baron had retired to Charlottesville for a rest. The divisions of General Muhlenberg and General Wayne were back another mile. Detachments of General Lawson and General Stevens formed the rear guard.[87]

While encamped along the York River where the soldiers washed clothes and waded, the Philadelphia Line lost one of its surgeons. Captain Davis recorded in his journal on July 1, "Unfortunately, Dr. Downy drowned, supposed by fit of cramps."[88]

The fifth anniversary of the Declaration of Independence was celebrated with ceremony on July 4. General Lafayette reviewed the troops on parade and salutes were fired with gusto. To observe the occasion, he gave a dinner for his officers.

John Davis described the day:

A wet morning, clear'd off 10 o'clock. This day we had a Fudejoy in celebration of the Independence of America. After that was over, Pennsylvania Line perform'd several maneuvers, in which we fir'd.[89]

The soldiers were in good spirits. While cooking their meals, the men talked about their maneuvers in the continual chase up and down the state. The rebels were confident the redcoats were on the run. They had heard Cornwallis's forays from the Carolinas to Virginia had been extremely costly, and their own increasing troop numbers gave them confidence. Cornwallis may, indeed, have paused when he considered that two colonial commanders whom he might face had already beaten the British. General Campbell and the frontier fighters had crushed the Tory force at King's Mountain; General Morgan and his rangers had triumphed over Tarleton at Cowpens.

Lord Cornwallis, acting on his own initiative, had previously ignored General Henry Clinton, but now he listened to the urgent letters of his commander who had learned through intercepted intelligence that the patriots under General Washington were planning a siege against New York. Clinton ordered Cornwallis to send three thousand British reinforcements to him promptly and the Earl was to take a position at Old Point Comfort in Virginia. On July 4, the scarlet wave of British regiments started rolling away from Williamsburg toward the James River to set sail for Portsmouth.[90]

As soon as the Continental camp was notified of this news, General Lafayette moved his men on July 5 along the Chickahominy to keep Lord Cornwallis from crossing the river. General Wayne advanced with seasoned detachments of infantry, riflemen, and cavalry, and the patriots pushed on to Green Spring plantation July 6 just a half mile away from the British outpost.

Crafty Cornwallis surmised that his clever young adversary would attempt an attack, so the Earl sent spies to spread the rumor that the main British army had crossed the river; the ruse worked. Only the British baggage and Simcoe's Rangers had been rowed over to the south side.

"Mad" Anthony swept up with his men to engage in a skirmish. Tarleton's riders retreated according to Cornwallis's strategy to pull the patriots toward the tangled woods where the enemy lay in wait. The precision firing of the rebel riflemen picked off three British officers. General Lafayette was impressed with the skill of the patriot sharpshooters, but he became suspicious of the sturdy resistance of the royal pickets. He surmised that strong support was back of the van, and a personal reconnoitering revealed that the British regiments were in reserve in the wooded area.

Lord Cornwallis commanded his redcoats to move forward in the lines with the Forty-third, Seventy-sixth, and Eightieth regiments formed to the left supported by the Twenty-third, Thirty-third, and Hessians for the second line of defense, ready to repulse the rebels.

Afraid that a general retreat would cause a rout, "Mad" Anthony ordered the Americans to advance quickly, firing rapidly. A sharp exchange ensued before dusk. Three artillery pieces poured forth shot. General Lafayette lost a horse, and all the artillery animals were slain. The English flanked the rebel force, but General Wayne averted a disaster by skillfully withdrawing his colonial soldiers. Continental casualties amounted to four sergeants, twenty-four rank and file killed, five captains, one captain-lieutenant, four lieutenants, seven sergeants; eighty-two men were wounded, twelve reported missing. (The riflemen's fates remain unknown.) The rebels had to abandon their cannon. Lieutenant Feltman was wounded in the left breast but stayed with his patrol. The British lost seventy-five men killed or wounded in the Green Spring skirmish.[91]

Tarleton was ready to pursue the patriots, but Lord Cornwallis decided against a chase in the dark. That night the Continental troops moved toward Chickahominy Church. The next day Lord Cornwallis crossed to the south side of the James River and headed toward Suffolk and Portsmouth. Tarleton was sent across the state as far as Bedford County to destroy patriot stores, but General Wayne's detachment and Morgan's riflemen chased him from his goal.

In the hot and humid days, General Lafayette moved his men to Malvern Hill above the marshes where wells with adequate drinking water helped to make a comfortable camp. Several reports were sent to General Nelson along the route. Copies of the commander's public letters were enclosed with the communication written on July 10, in which the officer observed:

> It gives me pleasure to think that while the enemy were anxious to fight, not one gun was fired, but the moment they declined coming to action, we made it our business to force them to partial engagements followed by general retreats.[92]

From Holt's Forge on July 12, Lafayette's message concerned the cavalry and began:

> Captain Rudolph the bearer of this has been sent to me by General Greene, with the most pressing and particular request to have Colonel Lee's Legion completed. The General is apprehensive of the worst effect of the enemy's superiority in horse; and that everything ruinous to the Southern States is to be feared from this cause. He wishes therefore that as many horse may be impressed as will mount the whole of the Cavalry. . . . I would request an impress warrant to seize or procure 100 horses . . . permission for him to enlist 100 dragoons, 100 infantry and 60 rifle men.[93]

From his headquarters at Long Bridge, the next day Lafayette wrote Nelson another long letter concluding that "The enemy in this quarter, pointing one quarter towards Portsmouth; with their legions on the route towards South Carolina, makes me conclude that the latter are at least intended to unite with Rawdon."[94]

Because of the critical situation, Lafayette had started rebel soldiers to the relief of General Greene, consisting of General Wayne's Pennsylvanians and about 800 new levies of Virginians. Since this force was inadequate to the emergency, Nelson was implored to order out one thousand militia to rendezvous at Taylor's Ferry on the Roanoke to march with General Wayne. The Marquis affirmed:

> There are other reasons however to induce this measure. If we do not want them beyond the Roanoke, we may in this Quarter. The enemy has not left the State. And should he again turn himself this way, we shall certainly want not only them, but a much greater number.[95]

The express was instructed to ride day and night to deliver this important dispatch.

❖   ❖   ❖

When Governor Nelson returned to Richmond July 16 to re-establish the executive office, he was confronted with a financial crisis, insufficient stores and supplies, inadequate arms and ammunition, and an indifferent attitude by the inhabitants to a strong defense system. Conferences with the Council concerned claims, accounts, paroles, applications, prisoners, and adjustments. Through the stifling summer, he struggled to solve the endless problems.

Local courts received commissions to conduct trials for treason and the authorities were empowered to inflict penalties for "certain crimes, injurious to the independence of America during the present invasion of the Commonwealth."[96]

The people had no confidence in the currency, Major David Ross commented in a letter of July 22 to the Governor. Since the rate of exchange had risen 350 to one in the Commonwealth, Ross was embarrassed over handling the fees and expressed that it was entirely too high for many.[97]

The dollar continued to depreciate. On August 1, Charles Dick noted in his communication from Fredericksburg to the Governor that the rate was 500 to one; consequently, he had great difficulty in trying to keep people working at the gun factory.[98]

Writing from Philadelphia where he was a delegate to the Congress, Theodorick Bland had described the economic plight of the representatives in the city:

> The long expected and long wished for remittance which was to have come through the hands of Mr. Braxton has afforded us no relief and has evaporated into smoke. My Finances are as well as my Credit entirely exhausted, my Private resources in Virginia Cut off by the Enemy, and I am at this moment without the means of buying dinner or procuring money even to purchase a bait of oats for my horses. I have even offered my Horses for sale (but cannot meet with a Purchaser) in order to procure a present subsistance for my Family.[99]

Complaints from the county lieutenants concerning the difficulties with the draft came in daily; the local leaders stated simply that the militia companies ordered by the Marquis failed to march.

Although he said he would try to comply with the demand, Colonel William Preston was plain spoken about the men in western Montgomery County answering the call to arms to assist General Greene:

> I am convinced it is impossible. Enemy there in February could not draw out but a third did oppose. The backwardness of our militia Arises, in my opinion, from the Causes Disaffection of more than half of the People,

which appears to me to be gaining ground every day. . . . The Tories cannot be drawn into the Service by any means whatever, and the Whigs, who would render any Service, are afraid to leave their Property and connexions to the former. The second reason that prevents our men from going out is the exposed situation of our frontier to the savages facts that worthy Gentlemen of Board no stranger to.[100]

Militia from the Northern Neck did not respond to Lafayette's call for help, according to Colonel William Davies, since they believed the British might move up the Potomac; they needed to be in constant readiness for an enemy call and in consequence "nor is there any draft from them for the Marquis's army, except only counties of Culpeper, Fauquier, and Loudon, who are required by regular rotation to keep a fourth of their militia under him, till farther orders."[101]

A letter also arrived from General Robert Lawson, the veteran leader who had commanded Virginia troops in the Carolina campaign, concerning the want of weapons. Written from Prince Edward's Ferry on July 26, where the officer was raising recruits to march southward, Lawson stated that the local lieutenants could not arm the militia, that it was not practicable as rifles had been taken and not returned. Referring to Lafayette's request, General Lawson wrote:

> . . . sound out people in area about march complain irregular length distresses them greatly . . . not conceal from your Excellency many have openly avow'd it as their determination to serve as six months within the State, rather than perform this service. The horrors of southern climate are so strongly magnified & the fatigues of marching so seriously impressed on their minds that few considerations could induce them to engage in the undertaking with alacrity.[102]

Governor Nelson received a similar report from his cousin Lewis Burwell in Mecklenberg County:

> It is not in my power to arm them as frequent calls by Executive on this county for arms, confident every gun fit for use was collected. We could not arm about 50 men. People . . . determined to hide their arms, part with lives rather than give them up.[103]

Commodore Barron conveyed some important information concerning British ship movements to Governor Nelson on July 30:

> This morning early the Sail of the Fleet weighed from Hampton Road having on board a number of Horse Troops, with twelve large Barges full of Men and stood down toward the Cape having got at the proper channel.
> From every movement I think they are bound up the Bay they have left 20 Sail in the Ford and also men of war. This Fleet must contain near three

thousand Troops as they were full. The wind has just shifted far to go up the Bay shall be able to inform you by next what course they take. One of the transports is aground on Willoughby Point though I don't think if they were bound for sea they would wait for her.[104]

Governor Nelson instructed Colonel James Innes to take charge of the encampment at Williamsburg and to establish a post of protection for the peninsula area. When the commander had arrived on July 24, he found the old capital in a state of confusion. The British had left a trail of devastation. Ninety sick men in the hospital were suffering for lack of bedding, blankets, straw, medicines, wine, spirits, and necessaries. The citizens of the community were apprehensive. Paroled persons were in a quandary over their position. Recruits were not reporting. Disorder and disobedience prevailed in the "miserable place," for the official discovered "that there are no persons, the Commissioners excepted, who think they are obliged to obey orders." Colonel Innes thought straightening out the situation "would require at least Twenty thousand pounds cash—15 waggons and as many horses." Conditions had not improved five days later so the discouraged commander notified Governor Nelson, "Unless I am properly supported in the command to which I have been called, I beg Yr: permission to retire."[105]

Nelson answered Colonel Innes immediately:

> As I imagine it is still undesirable to make Williamsburg the Rendezvous of the Militia ordered to be embodied under your Command for the protection of the lower part of the Neck, you will appoint such place as your Judgment shall direct for that Purpose. The bad consequence of spreading the Small Pox, will not escape you, so that I shall suggest no caution on that score. Should any of the militia persist in pleading their Paroles as an excuse for not performing military service, which I hope no one will be so ignorant or unmindful of his Duty to do, it is necessary that he be proceeded against. . . . A strict adherence to this Order of Government may in some cases bear an appearance of cruelty, but the insidious Arts of the Enemy & and general welfare render it indispensable. It is, however, my Desire, that no Person be rigorously dealt with, when there is a Prospect of bringing back to a better sense of what is due to his Country.[106]

Colonel Innes moved his militia to the Gloucester garrison in August. Although the "Thunderbolt of War" was oftentimes impatient with the inadequacies of the service and had acted independently in certain situations, Innes organized an effective operation against the enemy. Patriots pushed close to the British camp to confine the Crown troops. Innes set up a system wherein spies, posing as tradesmen, entered the English camp from both sides of the York River. General Lafayette paid ten guineas from his own pocket to an espionage agent who could prove that he had penetrated British territory. The reward was increased when worth while information was secured.[107]

Private Charles Morgan acted his role convincingly. As a "deserter," he went to the British lines for protection and conversed with Lord Cornwallis. With raider Tarleton listening attentively, the "traitor" told that Lafayette had many boats ready to cross the river. Before departing, the patriot had persuaded five redcoats to leave the British regiments. As the contingent slipped away, they took prisoner a Hessian on patrol. Morgan refused promotion for the service requesting only that his old rifle be returned.[108]

Colonel Innes expressed his ideas on espionage activity to Sir John Peyton:

> It is sometimes absolutely necessary and politic to make use of small deception and finesse, you may therefore circulate in Gloster, that the Marquis has cross'd 5000 men over Ruffin's Ferry to sustain your little armament and annoy the enemy; that he is marching down on this side in person, with 8000 men, and that he will be as far advanced as New Kent Court house this even'g.[109]

General Lafayette had been unable to reinforce the rebel units as planned, but his letter to Nelson August 19 revealed pleasure at the pursuit of English detachments:

> Colonel Innes is now on the Gloster driving off the stock and making a forage. His force appears to restrain the enemy's small parties.
> On the 18th Colonel Innes made a forage toward Gloster, with a very inconsiderable loss: only three men and two horses were taken. I have ordered even all the cavalry (they will cross at Frazers tonight) and a regiment of the infantry to make a more general one, which I hope to effect, unless the enemy should move up in considerable force.
> I am much obliged by your attention to our want of waggons, and trust what has been done, and is doing will give us effectual relief.[110]

Various assistants had caused difficulties in securing the vehicles, especially Mr. Green, an assistant quartermaster, who returned Lafayette's warrants questioning the power of impress, so delay of delivery had resulted.

The messages from the Marquis ran the gamut of grievances: lack of men and money, arms and ammunition, stores and supplies. More militia left than came to camp, yet when recruits reported, there were not enough rifles. General Lafayette admitted there were abuses to the arms by the neglect of officers and also a lack of gunsmiths to repair the weapons.

Lafayette argued that reinforcing General Greene might compel Lord Cornwallis to detach a Crown division in that direction. In August the Marquis disclosed that the Earl might erect fortifications at York and Gloucester.[111]

All Continental commanders were conjecturing about the actions of their British adversaries. During the summer, General Washington wondered where and when Sir Henry Clinton would strike against the weakened American army. Twenty transports sailed into Sandy Hook August 12 with approximately two thousand German soldiers instead of the royal reinforcements that rebel intelligence reported. At least one anxiety was lessened when Washington realized the French fleet would move up from the West Indies to assist the allies in the Chesapeake area. Washington grasped the opportunity to organize an offensive operation against the British on a grand scale.[112]

Throughout the summer schooners had been sailing from Virginia to New York carrying communications between the two top British commanders. Their deep-seated resentment of each other was revealed in the correspondence. In detailed dispatches, General Clinton gave contradictory directions to Cornwallis who disdained his superior. Suffering from the extreme heat, Lord Cornwallis became more disgusted as he scrutinized orders from the oscillating official in New York. Instructions arrived for the commander to send soldiers to New York, to rush troops to protect Philadelphia; then General Clinton rescinded those orders and commanded Cornwallis to retain the regiments and select a suitable site along the seacoast for a British base; Clinton preferred Old Point Comfort as the defense post, but when the Earl and his English engineers surveyed the spot, they declared the channel untenable. The Crown fleet with a cargo of men and munitions pushed out from Portsmouth and cruised up the Chesapeake to York Town.[113]

Horses that the English had impressed from the Virginians hauled British baggage up the hills above the banks of the river. The rumble of their wagons, clanking cannon, and tramp of troops resounded across the ridges. Swirls of dust filled the air as the soldiers marched under the sweltering sun.

As the redcoats swarmed into York Town, civilians plied Governor Nelson for help. In his letter of August 15 to General Lafayette, the executive explained:

> Several of the inhabitants of York have applied to me for Flags, to endeavour to remove their families from thence. It would save much trouble, if some mode could be adopted for a general Application to Lord Cornwallis. For the present, however, I wish Mr. Reynolds and Mr. Gibbons could be indulged with one. I understand Colonel Matthews is at Byrds. He might send a Dragoon with these Gentlemen.[114]

From his Camp of Forks on the York River—where the Mattapony and the Pamunkey rivers flowed into the York—Lafayette notified Governor Nelson on August 19 that Lord Cornwallis wanted the families to move out by the twenty-second.[115]

On August 20 Layfayette wrote Nelson:

> Sir, From Lord Cornwallis's movements and the intelligence which I have received, it would appear that he is on the point of becoming active. As he has given time to us to collect and arrange our force it will no doubt make part of his policy to distract us as much as possible in order the better to cover his principal intention. Under these circumstances, as well as to guard against any sudden operation in our favor, I beg to recommend the calling out a body of 600 militia to rendezvous at Black River under the command of General Lawson. These should be complete in everything and in the most perfect readiness, either to reinforce me, or to act as circumstances require.[116]

The Governor endorsed this request received on the twenty-first and directed Colonel Davies to prepare letters for the corps of militia required.

It must have been a relief for Governor Nelson to read the statement "acquired a fondness for the Service" before perusing the rest of the report from his cousin Major John Nelson. The bearer, Mr. Tinsley, had volunteered for the cavalry and desired a commission. The major mentioned in his message, "He is well recommended by General Muhlenberg . . . join my Corps . . . we are in want of Officers." Then the cavalryman uttered the usual complaint of other commanders, that his unit was "destitute of every kind of arms, a number of which are still in the hands of Volunteers, collected put in hands of Men, who are enlisted for the war. Sure Necessity to arm every Dragoon, if, as we hear the Enemy have landed at Gloucester."[117]

On August 8, aide-de-camp James McHenry reported in detail on the needs of patriot regiments. Recommending that eight thousand be equipped for service, he remarked that the "number required equal number of muskets, bayonets, and cartouche boxes . . . but in these articles there is the most alarming deficiencies." General Steven's and General Lawson's brigades had only 1,339 muskets, 535 bayonets, and 1,106 cartouche boxes. No one knew better than Governor Nelson, as brigadier general of the state militia, what these figures signified.[118]

Nelson's dispatches contained, as well, reports of plundering and the taking of prisoners. A message from Colonel George Matthews at Williamsburg, written on July 23, reported a raiding party of 300 redcoats had landed at Mill Creek to plunder the inhabitants; Colonel Innes had not arrived in the area.[119] On that same day a letter from Lunenburg County described the damage of Tarleton's legion, striking suddenly and covering thirty to forty miles a day, destroying crops, wrecking provisions, and carrying away captives.[120]

A report on July 24 told how the enemy had taken Lieutenant Chandler and about thirty seamen as prisoners at Portsmouth:

> They were the best men we had in our service and many of them Colonel Barron informs me were at the capturing of above 500 men suffering all the calamities of war with ill usage, many been obliged enter Enemy's service.[121]

Through the dry days of summer, Governor Nelson stayed at his desk attending to public affairs. His corpulent frame filling the chair, his body bent forward as his bluish eyes scrutinized the stack of communications. Secretaries dipped their quill pens and produced mounds of correspondence requiring the Governor's signature. Nelson's own letters, cogently written, revealed his feelings. In a long letter to Colonel Josiah Parker commanding a detachment of 500 militiamen in Isle of Wight, Nansemond, and Southampton counties, Nelson explained:

> The late very critical Season of the Year has prevented the Marquis reinforcing you as could have been wish'd. I felt much for you, and the County under your immediate command, but circumstances rendered support impracticable. *Were the means of defending the Country equal to my inclinations to protecting it, not a spot should be subject to British depredations,* but we must make use of the abilities we have, and lament they are not more adequate to the purpose.[122]

Nelson was enraged over a brutal killing and incensed about the destruction caused by the English invaders:

> I am sincerely concern'd at the unhappy misfortune that has befallen Captain Nott. He was a firm Whig, and an alive, spirited officer, whose death will be severely felt by the friends to America in that part of the Country. The Villain who murder'd him I hope will meet with a punishment equal to the horrid crime he committed.[123]

Colonel Josiah Parker had served in the regular army with distinction but had resigned and then re-entered the state service in 1778. He tendered his resignation and Governor Nelson, regretting the decision, concluded his communication:

> I am greatly concern'd at your losses this Invasion, and am sorry to hear that you propose to leave us. Much as I wish you to continue in the field, I cannot insist on a measure that may interfere so greatly with your private Interest. At the same time I assure you that your Country will sensibly feel the want of your services in the field.

On July 27 Governor Nelson wrote to General Washington:

> As a bad apology would be worse than none, I will not attempt to make any for my long silence but rely on your goodness to pardon it.
> It is probable that you may have heard of the high honor my Country has conferr'd on me by electing me to govern them at this critical period. To have declined the appointment might have indicated timidity. I therefore accepted it with a determination to exert every power that I possess'd to give energy to Government and security to the Inhabitants of the State.
> The very extraordinary Maneuver of Lord Cornwallis into this Country

and his running up and down into different parts of it will I suppose make a great noise in Europe. But when the Geography of the Country and its circumstances are known I flatter myself the British Commanders will not have acquir'd so much military fame nor we shall suffer so much disgrace as may at first be attributed to both.[124]

The executive then stated that the enemy was superior to the state troops in arms, ammunition, and ships, yet the local militia had taken the field wherever feasible:

> Tarleton by sudden incursions into those parts of the Country that he knew were not in arms, has collected a number of Horses that have enabled him to run about paroling Citizens whom he has taken in their Beds.[125]

Governor Nelson attested that Cornwallis's marching through the Carolinas and into Virginia may give him "great eclat," yet he noted when the patriots had a force to oppose him, "he faced about and retreated with the greatest precipitation."

> That they done great injury both public and private is certain, but I have the consolation that he is further from the conquest of Virginia than when he enter'd it. I do not believe ten Men have join'd him, which must mortify him not a little. They have made Whigs of Tories.[126]

Nelson concluded the letter with complimentary expressions about General Lafayette affirming that the militia and citizens "have great confidence in his bravery and conduct. . . . character is held in the highest estimation by the Inhabitants of the State."

As soon as he received this report, General Washington wrote to offer his congratulations to the Governor General:

> Among your numerous friends, none will be found whose congratulations to your appointment to the Administration of the Affairs of Virginia, are offered with more Cordiality and Sincerity than mine.

Asserting that not half the men called to compose the army had arrived, Washington commented:

> After bringing you acquainted with this serious and important fact, I need not detail smaller matters of disappointment and difficulty to shew the irksomeness of my present situation.[127]

Governor Nelson endeavored to strengthen the military situation of the state by an appeal to the local leaders when he sent a circular letter July 31 to all county lieutenants:

The Harvest being over, I hope the Militia, which have been ordered into Service from your County, will take the Field with the greatest alacrity. There never was a Time when vigorous Measures were more necessary or when they promised greater Advantages. Every exertion will be made by the Enemy, if not to subdue, to gain Posts in this Country; a successful Opposition on our Part, which the Strength of this State is very capable of making, by frustrating their Expectations, will in all Probability together with this Campaign put a happy Period to the War.[128]

The promise that war could be won soon seemed overly optimistic to some commanders, yet the prediction became a reality in a few weeks. For several months, General Lafayette had recommended that cannon be mounted on traveling carriages for mobile transportation; no action had been taken on the plan but Governor Nelson directed Colonel Davies, in charge of the War Department:

Give the most pointed Orders for carrying this Business into immediate Execution. The Delay of a few Days may produce the most unhappy Consequences. I am sensible that the Public are not possess'd of Materials for this Work; for which Reason it will be necessary, disagreeable as impressing is, that Artificers, Tools, and every thing requisite be taken, wherever they are to be found, if not to be procured by any other means.[129]

Through extensive communications, the Governor alerted authorities along the coast to be aware of the "Enemy's movements" on shore and sea and with dispatch convey what they observed. Nelson complimented Commodore James Barron for his alertness:

We think it is a particular Piece of good Fortune, that a Gentleman in whom we can place the fullest Confidence, is so situated, as to be able to do us the most essential Service in this respect.[130]

To expedite communications, Nelson ordered two swift sailing boats for the use of government officials. On August 1, intelligence arrived from the bay side that British transports with about three thousand troops had embarked from Hampton Roads.[131] Governor Nelson informed Governor Thomas Sim Lee of Maryland:

The Wind & Tide were both unfavourable for their standing up, & they had come top from which we have Reason to apprehend their Object is up the Bay. I hope, should their Intention be to attack any Part of your State, that you will have Time to make some Preparations for their Reception.[132]

Nelson kept trying to secure stores and supplies by personal appeal and power of office, but often when goods were procured, the lack of wagons and horses to haul them where needed became the problem. Citizens complained continually about accepting the government certificates. Agents attested that Virginia farmers didn't want the vouchers for foodstuffs, grumbling that the receipts were not worth the paper they were printed on. The situation was so tense, public property was being looted even by rebel soldiers.

Washington had ordered Pennsylvania troops to march southward where he intended to join them, but the long march over rough roads left their clothing in rags. General Anthony Wayne thus allowed the men to appropriate clothing from the Commonwealth supplies stored at Chesterfield Court House. This action set off a series of protests. Colonel Davies, Commissioner of the War Department, was especially incensed since the Virginia units were desperate for the outfits. He voiced strong objections to the Governor reporting the loss of 16 pairs of boots, 237 pairs of men's shoes, and about 2,000 yards of oznaburg cloth.[133] Governor Nelson contacted General Lafayette immediately:

> I enclose . . . Papers received Yesterday, relative to a seizure of Stores, the property of the State, made by General Wayne. This Step will, in a considerable Degree, distress us, the Stores being intended for the use of our Troops now in the Field, which are in the greatest want of them. Besides, the Action, in itself, is of such a nature as is not to be tolerated where civil government is established, and regular modes laid down for procuring necessaries for our Armies. Other excesses are also said to be committed on the Property of Individuals by the Troops of the Pennsylvania Line.[134]

The Governor desired to think that these acts had not been countenanced by the officers, but he expected the Continental commander to examine and regulate the "conduct of all subordinate officers."

General Wayne wrote Governor Nelson from Camp Newcastle on August 19:

> From inattention, or some other cause the Commissary General of this State has suffered the troops under my command to experience great distress for want of almost every article of Provisions.
>
> We have been in the course of two weeks; six days totally Destitute of anything to eat or Drink except new Indian corn & water, we have neither salt, Spirits, beans or flour, which causes our people to fall sick very fast.[135]

Consequently, he took some corn from the fields at Bottom's Bridge but paid the owners by certificates. Wayne reminded the executive that the Congress had invested him with ample powers for this purpose. He offered no explanation regarding the seizure of the shoes, boots, and cloth.

Governor Nelson kept the delegates at the Congress informed abut events in Virginia. On August 3, he wrote the representatives at Philadelphia re-garding the British fleet's move:

> They have since moved round into York River and have landed both on the York and Gloucester Shores. The uncertainty we were in, with respect to their Intentions, had induced the Marquis to take a Position not far below this Place, that he might have it in his Power to march either Northward or Southward, as their movements should make it necessary.[136]

Because the British could transport their troops across the river with ease, they had committed devastation, he continued, "but I hope the measures we have taken for our Defence will effectually prevent, in future, their penetrat-ing far, or possessing long . . ." Nelson asked the delegates to apply for the exchange of Charles Tomkins and William Buckner of Gloucester, captured by Admiral Arbuthnot in March and confined in New York. Under a cartel agreement between the British and American commanders, prisoners taken before June 15 were to be released, so Governor Nelson noted, "They are entitled to their Liberty."[137]

Nelson had established a line of couriers so his communications to the Congressmen and to the Governors of neighboring states could be sent faster. He urged a continuance of mutual correspondence on a weekly basis.

To Governor Burke of North Carolina, he wrote about the great scarcity of salt. Since the provision could no longer be bought from Bermuda and other islands because of the British blockade, Governor Nelson asked his colleague to send a supply of salt to the Commonwealth:

> As it is probable this will be the Seat of War, we have very little prospect of being able to import any salt, and without it, it will be impossible to support the Army. I mention this matter for your Consideration, as, in my Opinion, the Interest of the South is deeply concerned in it.[138]

That same day, August 10, General Greene wrote a long letter to Gover-nor Nelson from his headquarters on the hills of the Santee. The six-page letter detailed procurements of soldiers and supplies as well as the state of the Virginia line:

> The ranks are thin, and the time of service will very soon expire. I hope every exertion will be made to fill up the line before the men get their discharge. . . . Your own experience no doubt teaches you the great impolicy of depending too much on militia.[139]

The southern commander stated that only regular soldiers could ensure safety, troops trained by discipline who could encounter danger and endure hardship. He thought men signed for only eighteen months were little better than militia and favored drafting for three or four years.

Major I. Burnett, an aide to General Greene, arrived in Richmond August 20; he was disappointed in not seeing Governor Nelson who had gone to Camp of Forks. The agent, relaying a favorable report to his superior, wrote, "The prospect for securing horses for the cavalry is flattering." Nelson had issued instructions for 200 horses to be impressed for the Third Regiment.[140]

With his knowledge of military matters and interest in the Virginia militia, Governor Nelson had been anxious to inspect Lafayette's units at the Continental camp. On his way to visit "West Point" at the Forks the third week in August, illness overcame the Governor. Exhausted by his endeavors to meet the endless demands of wartime, he went home to Hanover County to rest with his family for a few days. Long letters from Lieutenant Governor Jameson on August 24 and 28 to the Governor complained about the cavalry, absent Council members, shortages, disaffected citizens, and the accumulated business to be delayed "until your arrival."[141]

Governor Nelson rode to the river encampment the last of August for a conference with General Lafayette. The French leader had already received a letter dated August 21 from General Washington with the welcome news, "The Troops destined for the Southern Quarter are now in motion."[142]

While Nelson and Lafayette discussed the forthcoming campaign, couriers galloped into camp at the Forks with news of the French fleet's arrival in Chesapeake Bay. Writing to General Washington September 1 from his camp, the Marquis noted that the executive was so excited at the news that he jumped on his horse and rushed off to the Council.[143]

General Washington confided his military project to Governor Nelson in a communication from Chatham, New Jersey, under date of August 27:

A variety of Circumstances having concurred to induce me to change the plan of operation, which has been concerted for the Campaign; and to strike a blow at the Enemy in Virginia, I am now on my march for that purpose, with the whole of the French and a considerable Detachment of the American Army; the arrival of the Count De Grasse with a formidable Fleet and corps of land forces in the Chesapeake (which may every moment be expected) will I flatter myself (with proper exertion on our part) give a moral Certainty of succeeding in the great Object now in Contemplation. On so important and interesting occasion I can not entertain a doubt of receiving every possible aid and assistance from the State of Virginia; the Great Articles of Supplies which will be principally wanted are Salted Provisions, Beef Cattle, Forage and the means of transportation.[144]

After rushing back to Richmond, Nelson granted the authority by the General Assembly to handle the wartime exigencies, did not hesitate to exercise his powers. Throughout September, Robert Andrews and other aides drafted countless directions. The absent Council members were called to convene in the capital promptly. They sent appeals to authorities throughout the state to assist in securing "the very large supplies necessary for the armament lately arrived, and for the troops expected from the Northward." The executive implored all assistants to provide "fresh meats and vegetables" so vitally necessary to sustain the forces. He reiterated to the commissary general that the undertaking was so significant and would "require the most vigorous and unremitting exertions. . . . This will be an extensive business, and will demand many able and active men to execute it. Disappointment will be attended with the most fatal consequences." [145] Nelson asked the county lieutenants to urge the commissioners to act swiftly to find food and "to procure all the waggons that they possibly can." [146]

Governor Nelson extended a cordial greeting to Count de Grasse on September 2:

> Sir: The arrival of his most Christian's Majesty's fleet, under your command, in Chesapeake Bay, was yesterday announced to me while in the Marquis de la Fayette's camp. I take the earliest opportunity of congratulating you on your safe arrival, and of acknowledging this signal proof of the attention of our very great and generous ally, and the alacrity with which you, Sir, and the other officers of this fleet and army, execute his intentions in our favour. An armament so powerful and so competent to every purpose, will not only give a fortunate turn to our Military operations, but will convince the incredulous and disaffected who may still lurk amongst us, that his most Christian Majesty is, both sincerely determined, and fully able, to support the American United States, in vindicating their rights and maintaining their independence. [147]

The administrator pledged his authority and service of the state to the "speedy and successful accomplishment" of the great objective.

In a September 2 letter, Nelson wrote to Governor Thomas Sim Lee of Maryland:

> Sir: On the 31st of August, the French Fleet commanded by the Count De Grasse, consisting of 28 ships of the line and six Frigates, with 3,000 land Forces, arrived in Chesapeake Bay. They have made such dispositions as will prevent the British army, now at York, from crossing the James River below the Falls, should they attempt to escape to the southward. . . . In all human Probability, Lord Cornwallis has nearly finished his career, and will shortly receive his reward.

Explaining the great need for provisions, he asked that quantities of flour be sent down the bay. [148]

Substantially the same information was sent to Governor Burke of North Carolina September 3:

But what raises our Hopes and Joys to the most exalted Pitch, and which I have reserved to the last, to crown the political Feast which this letter will afford you, is a movement of our great general, who, on the 27th of the last month, was at Chatham, with all the French troops of the Northern Army, and a body of Continentals, on his march to Virginia.[149]

September 2 a short note was penned to Thomas McKean, then President of the Congress pertaining to the recent developments:

Sir: It is with great pleasure I inform you of the arrival of the Count De Grasse, in Chesapeake Bay, with a very powerful armament. We are making every exertion to improve this favourable opportunity of striking a blow, which will not only, for the present, relieve this State from the ravages of war, but will have the strongest tendency to bring our just contest to a speedy and happy conclusion.[150]

The Virginia official was optimistic about the success of allied operations against the enemy in his state and had concern for the campaign in Carolina. In a communication to General Greene September 5, Governor Nelson commented, "But notwithstanding the very flattering prospect here, I feel an uneasiness when I consider that your situation may not be so agreeable."[151]

General Greene was informed that the French force had landed at Jamestown and had joined Lafayette near Williamsburg:

The enemy have made no movement which I have heard of since this event, but continue in York, strengthening their Post. We have called out a very large Body of our Militia, which, when added to the forces already in camp, will enable us closely to invest York.[152]

Two other official documents were drafted the same day. To Robert Morris, a former colleague in the Congress who was Superintendent of Finance, Governor Nelson acknowledged the receipt of several reports and added:

A person has been for some time employed in liquidating the accounts between the United States and this State; another is engaged in settling the accounts of the Specific supplies furnished by this State. In general, I may observe that this State has far exceeded all requisitions of Congress in its advance and most of the Specific Supplies.[153]

On September 5, he set the seal of the Commonwealth on an official proclamation placing an embargo on the exportation of the following products:

. . . all Beef, Pork, Bacon, Wheat, Indian Corn, Pease, or other grain or flour or Meal of the same, to continue until it shall be annuled by proper authority.[154]

All mariners, masters, and commanders of vessels were strictly prohibited to export these provisions under severe penalties.

A summer drought had caused crop shortages, and the resulting dry streams produced a scarcity of meal and flour, for without the power the big wheels of the mills could not turn to grind the grain.

The Governor had been gratified to read a communication from his cousin Lewis Burwell of Mecklenberg County, dated September 9, requesting two dozen blank commissions for his unit and asserting, "I hope to have a hand in taking Cornwallis as I shall go down with our militia in a day or two."[155]

Colonel Burwell informed Colonel Davies on September 11 about the food situation:

> I applied to the Inhabitants of this County to furnish Wheat, Spirits, & Vinegar. Mr. Delony procured large quantity wheat but mills in this county dry. Get but little vinegar perhaps a hundred gallons.[156]

A message from Lafayette written to Governor Nelson on September 11 described the distressed condition in his camp: "There is not one grain of flour in camp either for the American or French army."[157]

The next day Governor Nelson noted to Commissary General Pierce, "What adds to the Distress is, that the Mills in this part of the Country have not water to grind the corn which can be collected."[158]

The express rider carrying the report from General Lafayette might have met the executive and his entourage on the way to Williamsburg. Governor Nelson had informed the Council that the increased operations against the opponent "induce me to take command of the Militia that are called out," and he advised the members to meet regularly, attending the board promptly to effect the necessary business.[159] After arriving in the old capital, the official observed to Governor Burke on September 11:

> I arrived here this day. Part of our troops are below, within eight miles of York. The French and most of the Continental troops lie still a mile or two above. Our force is daily growing stronger, and I flatter myself we shall very soon circumscribe Cornwallis within narrower limits than he has lately been accustomed to. We have had information of the arrival of the Northern Troops under his Excellency General Washington, at the Head of Elk. They were come down by water, and may be every minute expected. . . . a British Fleet . . . which drew out Count De Grasse . . . engaged, and that after a smart conflict, the Britons fled, and were pursued by the French. . . . I shall continue here until the fate of York is determined, unless the meeting of our Assembly obliges me sooner to leave the Field, and I expect to have the pleasure of communicating to you, from time to time, events of the most agreeable nature.[160]

General Washington had his worries over the whereabouts of the French fleet. The American army had started southward the third week of August and the French troops were also traveling in that direction as part of a grand military plan to trap Lord Cornwallis in the Virginia peninsula. The rebels had spread reports that the regiments were assembling to attack the British at Staten Island. To make the ruse credible, bread ovens were built at Chatham, New Jersey, for an encampment. Riders brought reports September 1 that the royal ships had sailed from New York. Washington feared the British squadron would block the French fleet.[161]

A cavalcade of allied columns moved on through Maryland. General Washington rode all day September 9 to reach Mount Vernon by dusk. He had not seen his home in over six years. The dining room was crowded with company for two days, as the hospitable host and Mrs. Washington entertained Generals Jean Rochambeau and Francois Chastellux and the military staffs at sumptuous meals. Leaving on the twelfth, Washington was met by a courier with news that Count de Grasse had battled the British on the high seas; but the lookouts had not seen the French fleet back in the Capes. After the allied armies had arrived at Williamsburg the middle of the month, General Washington received word from Count de Grasse; he was back in Chesapeake Bay with two boats captured from the British.[162]

Governor Nelson composed or dictated at least ten communications September 13.[163] Much of the correspondence mentioned the immediate need for flour and meal and empowered the noted citizens of the counties to impress the provisions. To Colonel Wills in Isle of Wight County, he wrote:

> You will take possession of Mills proper for your purpose, and you may assure the people that the Corn they advance on this occasion shall, if they require it, be replaced.[164]

To Commissary General John Pierce, he observed:

> The Vessel you dispatched from Richmond is not yet got down. This navigation is too uncertain and tedious for immediate purposes. Land Carriage would best answer them, if it is possible to make use of it. I am satisfied you will do everything in your power to send on supplies, and never were your exertions more necessary. Is there not Flour to be had at Petersburg, when it could be brought here?[165]

Governor Nelson alerted David Ross, acting agent for the state who was assisting the commissary, "The great distress the Army is now suffering from the want of Flour and Meal induces me to write to you, although I am persuaded you are exerting yourself in this business."[166]

He implored other officials to proceed up the James and Appomattox rivers to assist in procuring and sending provisions for the army. Vessels not engaged in public service were to be impressed for that purpose. Salt was desperately needed.[167]

Nelson asked General Robert Lawson to acquire the Commonwealth's horses from Captain Nelson's corps for transportation needs.[168]

Local commanders received instructions concerning enlistments:

> The men who came down are upon a regular tour of Duty, and cannot be discharged until that is expired. Such of them as are on the impressed horses must be annexed to the infantry of their county. Those who are mounted on their own horses, and are armed with swords, will be of service as dragoons, and may draw forage.[169]

Food for the forces received priority. Through perseverance, Nelson began to ease the shortages. That day he wrote of his difficult task to Governor Burke of North Carolina, but he could declare, "Our difficulties on this account seem now diminishing."[170]

Another thorny topic pertained to the petition of the Tory residents along the Rappahannock River. John Robinson, Philip L. Grymes, Ralph Wormeley, James Wills, Ralph Wormeley, Jr., Elizabeth Robinson, and Hugh Walker were the petitioners whose plantations had been plundered June 4 and 5 by Captain Ross and several privateers. The report related that twenty Negroes at Rosegill had joined the raiders and stolen silver plate as well as many other articles from the Wormeley residence. The petitioners proclaimed that "Hugh Walker had raised every person in the small town of Urbanna to oppose the robbers," but the slaves increased the force of felons so that rioters went wild, stealing and smashing through the plantations.

> They plundered . . . almost every article of value in the house, taking his own bed from under him, whipping one of his sons, and wounding one of his daughters . . . the vessel then proceeded around to Pianketank, . . . hearing that your petitioner Grymes with his family had returned to his old house plantation . . . and that his most valuable articles and plate were there . . . they took all the wearing apparel at your petitioner Grymes's wife, and all the plate they could find.[171]

Though Governor Nelson did not approve of his brother-in-law's loyalist attitude, he did not condone raids on private property.

Ralph Wormeley, Jr., and Philip Ludwell Grymes had secured a flag of truce and traveled to Portsmouth to await the arrival of General Alexander Leslie to represent the "illegal, unjustifiable" conduct to the British commander. The four-page petition notified Governor Nelson that some of the Negroes and articles had been sent back and were on board the flag ship. Nelson thought the Negroes, even those with smallpox, should be landed for attention.[172]

Problems that required determination by the representatives received short replies from Nelson. Major William Boyce, commanding a militia detachment at Surry Court House, had informed the Governor that Dr. Archibald Campbell had been court martialed for spreading smallpox through the camp. In his answer, Governor Nelson stated simply, "Until I can give it proper attention, and until further orders, you will keep Dr. Campbell in Custody."[173]

In his correspondence with Lord Cornwallis regarding the release of prisoners still confined on British ships, Governor Nelson was courteous but resolute in his reply to an August 5 letter. Cornwallis had assured the administrator that Messrs. Archer and Ryall would be relinquished, yet the men were still restrained, so on September 18 Nelson wrote to the English commander:

> I am, therefore, again to desire your attention to these gentlemen, and assure myself that you will order them released.
> I am informed that Major Arthur Dickinson, of the York County Militia, is in close confinement in your Provost. Your Lordship will oblige me by acquainting me with the reason of his being treated in this rigorous manner.[174]

Governor Nelson asked the English Earl to allow inhabitants of York to move their possessions under a flag of truce. He also questioned why Dr. Corbin Griffin was confined on one of the British prison ships. The governor had a personal interest as well as political concern in the physician who had married his cousin Mary Berkeley.

Governor Nelson did not tolerate defiance or disobedience among the troops. To Colonel Davies in Richmond, he wrote from Williamsburg on September 19:

> It is necessary when men so openly, on such interesting occasions, dare to disobey the orders of the Government, as in the instance of the Henrico Militia, that sure punishment should await their conduct.[175]

Davies was empowered to punish the offenders by measures he felt fitting for the misdemeanors. The Governor continued:

> The behaviour of Colonel Barbour in the highest degree is reprehensible, and I shall take that notice of it, which it deserves, and which I trust, will deter him and others from like practices in the future.

Colonel James Barbour, in his eagerness to equip his Culpeper County militia unit, had taken twenty-nine boxes of arms marked for the American army. Nelson was candid in his communication of September 19:

If we were to consider the Consequences of such Conduct, nothing could appear more criminal, or meriting more severe Notice. Suppose it to be general in the Counties through which public Arms pass, & no one County Lt. is more highly privileged than another, the Troops embodied would remain unarmed & the Force on which the immediate Salvation of the State depends, rendered incapable of acting. A great part of the Country would be exposed to inevitable Destruction.

Still however your general good Character inclines me to consider this Act, rather as intended to put your particular Militia into a good State of Defence, than to injure the Country at large.[176]

Governor Nelson's reprimand further ordered Barbour to collect and convey the arms to camp:

... with all possible Expedition ... as the Injury already sustained from the Detention is sufficiently great & I hope you will take Care that it not be increased by an unnecessary Delay in having the present Order executed.[177]

The action of other militia units gratified Governor Nelson who noted in his correspondence on September 12, "The alacrity with which the Militia is turning out on this Occasion, gives me great pleasure."[178]

Varied listings arrived with the letters. From faraway Fauquier County in the northwestern section of the state, W. Edmunds enclosed a tally of the troops: 887 men over 18 in the militia unit; 103 under 18, exclusive of officers. Edmunds described several eighteen-months men, "the chief of them unfit for military duty." Edmunds outlined his difficulties paying for provisions with certificates; his paper money could not compete with French solicitors who paid with gold pieces.[179]

Lieutenant Governor Jameson expressed the same feeling to the executive in a communication of September 13:

Sorry not in power to remedy Evils you mention. Every step within our power to forward supplies of both flour and meat has been taken.

I inclose you a Letter from Colonel Bland with two from your Sons.[180]

The Governor enforced strict penalties against Loyalist partisans. His opinion of them was expressed in a letter later to his friend John Penn of North Carolina:

The Tories seem on this Occasion to have been rather short sighted. A little British sunshine has called out these Serpents from their Holes before their winter was over; and I flatter myself it will only enable us more thoroughly to blast them.[181]

By Nelson's order, several violators were taken into custody and conveyed to the capital. Among the Tories transported to Richmond for trial were the Reverend John Lyon, rector of St. George's Parish in Accomac County, and three of his parishioners, John Custis, William Garrison, and Solomon Bunting, who had refused to serve in the rebel militia. In a communication to Governor Nelson, County Lieutenant George Corbin commented that the parson and parishioners "were showing marks of repentance for their action whether conviction or the arrival of the fleet of our generous ally," had caused the change of heart, Corbin was not sure. He was sending some large guns across by barge with a load of rum and brandy for the state:

> It gives me much satisfaction to find that your Ideas of our danger and defense on this shore agree with mine. . . . actions of the disaffected who privately and at length publicly joined their aid (with the enemy) to destroy our persons & property.[182]

The Reverend Mr. Lyon received preferential treatment, for the Governor informed Council member George Webb that the parson "may be permitted to reside in any part of the upper Country, at a greater Distance than twenty miles above Richmond, on giving responsible security for his good Behaviour."[183]

The executive doubtless felt some embarrassment over the arraignment of family friends and his brother-in-law Philip Grymes, but personal distress did not deter him from his duty. With the assistance of his cousin George Nicholas, who became an aide, and Professor Robert Andrews, Governor Nelson continued his efforts to outfit the troops and oust the enemies.

He wrote Colonel Innes from Williamsburg September 18:

> Sir, Information having been given me, that Ralph Wormeley, Ralph Wormeley, Jr., Philip L. Grymes, James Mills, Simon Frazer, Robt. Gilmore, Hugh Walker, & Jonathan Denison of the County of Middlesex, and Anthony McKittrick of Stafford County have been guilty of Conduct which manifest Disaffection to this Government & the Interest of the United States, you are hereby required & empowered to apprehend their Persons & Papers, & to have them conveyed to the Town of Richmond under proper Guard. You are authorized, for this Purpose to call upon the Militia of any County's you think proper, either of those in actual Service, or otherwise, to aid & assist you.[184]

There were grand moments of pleasure during these sweltering September days; Washington arrived September 14 after four o'clock in the afternoon. Although the approach to Williamsburg was not announced in time for militia regiments in the rear of the army to assemble, the French line west of the College formed proper ranks, and the Continental soldiers were able to step to attention with beating drums and cannon salute.[185]

Washington was accompanied by a small staff and several French generals as he rode along the well-known route into the old capital. Having traveled the thoroughfares of the College town innumerable times, the Commander-in-Chief recognized landmarks along the way. Among familiar faces was that of St. George Tucker who recorded:

> General Nelson, the Marquis, etc., rode up immediately after. Never was more joy painted in any countenance than theirs. The Marquis rode up with precipitation, clasped the General in his arms, and embraced him with an ardor not easily described. The whole army and all the town were presently in motion.[186]

General Washington set up headquarters at the Wythe house overlooking Palace Green and General Rochambeau was welcomed by Mrs. Peyton Randolph in her rambling frame house facing Nicholson Street.

General Saint Simon, commanding the French troops, conducted the entourage on a tour through the camp. The ceremony was continued at his headquarters that evening when Saint Simon entertained the officers at dinner. French bands performed classical tunes; Governor Nelson, attending the affair, was glad to announce that militia were reporting for duty with alacrity. Regarding food for the forces, he could reiterate his remark written the day before, "Our difficulties on this account seem now diminishing." His correspondence to Lieutenant Governor Jameson, Colonel William Davies, and Commissary General John Pierce announcing Washington's arrival had contained admonitions to exert every effort to secure food and forage for the huge force and their horses. The dispatch to David Jameson was dated 6:00 P.M.:

> Sir: His Excellency Gen'l Washington arrived here about two hours ago. The first division of his Army is coming down the Bay, and may be expected every moment. A very little time now will determine the fate of York, and with it probably that of the Continent. But what exertions will it require to subsist properly so great an Army? I feel the utmost anxiety on this account, and cannot forbear, though I am persuaded it is needless, pressing you to urge to the greatest and most unremitted activity and industry every Officer within your reach, whose business it is to provide forage or provisions for the Army. Beef, Flour, Corn, and the Means of Transportation, should be principal objects of attention, and the country cannot censure . . . encouragement . . . given to those who will lend their aid on this occasion. His Excellency appears to be in good health and Spirits.[187]

To the head of the War Department, Nelson had written, "Our Operations will now grow very serious, and it will be incumbent on us to exert ourselves that there may be no want of Ammunition."[188] To Commissary General John Pierce he reported:

The Provisions in Camp are scarcely sufficient to subsist the present Army for three days longer, and should the wished for reinforcements arrive before a fresh supply of provisions, Flour, at least, is received, it gives me Pain to think of the Situation we shall be in. Let me intreat you, therefore, to leave nothing untried which promises the smallest relief to us. Not only great quantities of Flour, but also Beef, will be wanted. All applications with respect to supplies of Provisions are made to me, and apprehensions I am under lest there should be a deficiency, create a perpetual uneasiness.[189]

The administrative authorities were expected to find forage for five thousand horses and to furnish at least thirty-five thousand food rations per day to the regiments. The Governor continued his exertions to accumulate arms and ammunition, spades, shovels, axes, hatchets, and hilling hoes for the anticipated siege. Couriers streamed from Williamsburg with official orders to assemble boats, collect horses, and obtain wagons. Nelson enclosed the power of impress so that enforcement could be expedited promptly.

Washington and all his subordinate officers breathed a sigh of relief when the riders brought the report that the French fleet had re-entered Chesapeake Bay. Governor Nelson informed the state authorities, his dispatch to Colonel Davies, dated September 16, 10:00 A.M., read:

The Count De Grasse has returned from pursuing the British Fleet. He has taken two Frigates, and is joined by the Rhode Island Fleet. In the latter came 600 Land Troops. Permit me once more to desire that you will press those whose business it is, to send on provisions with all possible expedition. I have just received information that 3,000 of the Northern Army are come into James River.[190]

To Lieutenant Governor Jameson he asserted, "No movement has yet been made by our Army. It is said that the Enemy are out as high as the half way house, in Force, this morning."[191]

Anticipation pervaded the camp and even the most indifferent private sensed imminent action.

Governor Nelson invited St. George Tucker to join his staff as an interpreter since Tucker spoke French fluently:

Our Acquaintance & the Circumstance of your being possessed of this Knowledge will make it particularly agreeable to me if you will accept this Appointment. I do not expect that you will give up the Command or rank you hold in the Line of Militia in actual Service. There will be no impropriety in your retaining them, & acting as one of my Aides on the present Occasion.[192]

Dispatches from Lieutenant Governor Jameson detailed his difficulties to Governor Nelson. He was disgusted with the inattendance of the Council in the capital and the indifference of the inhabitants throughout the countryside in selling supplies to the state. General Lewis and George Webb had left Richmond September 13 leaving only Jacquelin Ambler and Jameson to carry on the duties. In his letter of the fifteenth filled with laments, the Lieutenant Governor alleged, "I cannot consent to stay here longer to hear the daily complaints and reproaches of the people."[193] Jameson commented that his pleasure over the arrival of General Washington had been "lessened by reflection we are deficient on our part after all these exertions of our Friends to save our Country. The grand object may miscarry by the unaccountable neglect and indolence to say no worse of our people."[194]

With the daily depreciation of currency, prices kept rising. Farmers wanted gold coins the French agents offered them. Lieutenant Governor Jameson in his report of September 26 to the Governor remarked, "The people withhold their wheat in hope of receiving a present payment in Specie. It is absolutely necessary that something should be done, or our Army will be starved."[195]

Thomas Nelson answered these appeals with equanimity. In his dual office as Governor and General, he considered the circumstances, and because of the approaching battle with the British, he outlined his reasons for remaining with the army. In his reply to Jameson September 21, he said:

> Members of the Council give such bad attendance at a Time when Matters of so great Moment are in agitation. It is however impossible for me to quit the Army at this time,—at least the bad consequence which would result from it would not be compensated by any good which may arise from my attendance at the Council Board. The wants of the Army which are many, & which require the most instant Attention, are here represented to me on the Spot, & the most immediate Measures are fallen upon to supply or anticipate them.[196]

Explaining that the present military offensive plan should take precedence over other considerations, he believed that if the operation failed there would be only a "Shadow of Government." If it were successful, the structure of authority and administration would be strengthened. Thomas Nelson, Jr., was a man of action so he stayed with his forces at the battle front.

Compassion for the pathetic condition of Bellamy Crawford, clerk and paymaster of the South Carolina hospital, caused the executive to write:

> The case of Bellamy Crawford . . . is just represented to me. His Situation is such as excited Pity, & if it is at all possible, claims public assistance. He has a wife far advanced in her Pregnancy & is destitute of every thing necessary for a Woman in her Condition & without the means of procuring them. Exhausted as our Treasury is, I think we must on this Occasion spare something from our little stock.[197]

Although Governor Nelson understood the reluctance of the people to receive paper certificates for property and services, yet he advised his assistant on September 27:

> My opinion is, that they should receive the Depreciation current at the time of settling their accounts, and I look upon this measure which not only justice recommends, but Policy, and even necessity. I would also advise that no particular appropriations be made of the Paper State Money. . . . this money is fast approaching its end, and that our present business is, to look for a substitute. With good management, I think we have the opportunity to effect this, but it requires attention and address.[198]

David Ross had been appointed acting agent for the state and the authorities wished him to confer with the French agents to work out a satisfactory arrangement for purchases. He was in the camp near York on October 5 for that purpose; but before Ross's arrival, the executive had enlightened Lieutenant Governor Jameson about the situation on October 1:

> I received your letter, inclosing extracts relative to the French agents. The consequences of such proceedings, I have long foreseen, and have laboured to guard against by supplying forage, & c. I have met with much difficulty and vexation in the management of this matter arising, partly, from the unwillingness of the people to assist government, from which former treatment gives them, perhaps, too little reason to expect justice and partly from the desire of handling gold, which has too often been found to prevail over every other consideration.[199]

The French force and augmented American army crowded every available area around Williamsburg during the waning days of September. As temporary tents were raised for the thousands of troops, Nelson issued still more supply orders. A letter to Mann Page in Spotsylvania County is typical:

> You will be pleased to superintend the sending of Cattle from your County. To enable you to do this, you are hereby empowered to call for the public cattle, and also to seize on such as are proper for the Army.[200]

Richard Henry Lee had collected horses for the cavalry and communicated from Chantilly that Major Nelson had secured several horses in the neighborhood. Though ten horses had been received the last of September, five had to be returned as the animals were not suitable for military purposes. Aide Robert Andrews, writing for the executive, explained that the warrants were intended for more "extensive Distribution than your own County, but were enclosed to you as a Gentleman of Extensive Influence & Acquaintance with the persons to whom it would be proper to entrust them. . . . The Governor intreats that you will urge the Men employed in procuring

Provisions for the Army to the greatest Industry. Beef is much wanting."[201]

On September 25, Governor Nelson issued important instructions concerning the shipping of supplies:

> Stop all Vessels coming down either of the Branches of York River with provisions of any kind whatever, at Frazier's and Ruffin's Ferry, and if possible have them stored at those places: the danger attending Vessels coming down the River at this time being infinitely too great to hazard the Loss of any others—three having been captured by the Enemy this Day.[202]

Governor Nelson transmitted the power of impress to Sir Peyton Skipwith on September 26: "to impress Boats, Axes, Knives, & all other Articles requisite for the slaughtering of the Cattle collected at or near Hog Island, & transmitting them across the River."[203]

Sir John Peyton and Sir Peyton Skipwith were asked to be particularly careful in taking receipts for items furnished the French troops and to transmit them regularly to the Governor so he could settle accounts readily. Colonel Skipwith was soon asked to acquire two boats for communications between the two camps and to hire five or six good river pilots to go aboard the French vessels.

Colonel Lewis Burwell notified Governor Nelson September 30 that the militia from Mecklenburg and Lunenburg counties had marched by the official's orders, but high winds had delayed the detachment's crossing the river. Since the unit had but twenty indifferent guns, Burwell attested the troops would have to be armed.[204]

General Robert Lawson complained that the militia companies had only two colonels and two majors so the contingent did not make up a command. The veteran soldier wrote Governor Nelson September 29:

> Colonel Burwell has taken command of the militia . . . and regardless of the arrangements made by me, with the express approbation of your Excellency, is taking such steps as to derange my command, & disgust those officers, who have been appointed to command by the Executive. . . . I have no objection to Colonel Burwell. He may possess for what I know every talent that can make him great and serviceable in a military character. I wish only to preserve the system which has long been adopted and proceeded with success to the militia.[205]

Rivalry in rank always presented problems.

While Governor Nelson contended with the command situation, he had received two distressing reports. Rheumatism forced General Morgan to relinquish leading his rebel riflemen against the British. The Virginia veteran explained to Nelson in a letter dated September 20:

> I am in hopes we have that old fox Cornwallis pretty safe. Nothing this

side of heaven would make me so happy as to be at the taking him if my health would permit but I am afraid it will not, must therefore pray for your success which I shall most fervently do.[206]

News from North Carolina was oppressing.

Before this reaches you, you will have no doubt heard of Governor Burke's being taken prisoner by the Tories and carried to Wilmington. A circumstance to this State truly alarming . . . no possibility of furnishing with flour, salt, beef.

The message disclosed unfortunate news from the Eutaw Springs battle:

Colonel Campbell of your state was killed. The affair was obstinate and bloody. Several of the valuable Officers of Virginia and this State killed and wounded, our loss in private was considerable. . . . Colonel Washington and every officer with him wounded except Captain Parsons.[207]

CHAPTER TWENTY-THREE

The Siege and
the Surrender: 1781

Finding Food for the Forces ✦ Clothing for the Cavalry ✦ Express Established ✦ American Army and French Force ✦ English Evacuate Entrenchments ✦ Soldiers Shift Sides ✦ Secretary Nelson ✦ Storming Redoubts ✦ Conquest of Cornwallis ✦ Articles of Capitulation ✦ Surrender, October 19, 1781

Though Governor Nelson regretted taking necessities for the troops from the people of Virginia's ravaged land, he continued relentlessly trying to relieve shortages for the military forces. Gradually, improvements resulted from his indefatigability. Supplies began to trickle in for the allied armies though substitutes were often sent. Colonel Davies declared there was "no osnobrigs for bunks . . . but . . . cots sail duck may answer."[1]

Food was of prime concern, as was clothing for the Virginia militia "so that they may be enabled to make a decent if not a respectable Figure—: The Article of Shoes is peculiarly worthy of your particular Attention," Governor Nelson had noted to Colonel Davies on September 27.[2] When Commissary Davies ordered footgear for the French forces, he was surprised that almost two thousand pairs of shoes were still at Hampton but Davies promised to hurry them on by water. Misunderstandings of directions, as well as delays in delivery of articles, posed additional problems to the authorities.[3]

The Governor was grateful to receive a report from Governor Thomas Sim Lee of Maryland, dated September 21, disclosing that he had "Given directions to forward all Flour that can possibly be collected without delay upwards 2,000 barrels ready."[4]

A communication from Lieutenant Governor Jameson confirmed that after his daily calls on Commissary Pierce, "He thinks things are now in such a train as to keep the Army properly supplied with both Meat & Bread."[5]

After the wagons had finished hauling the artillery and military equipment for the allies' encampment being set up in an arc outside York, Nelson thought the conveyances would transport the foodstuffs he was collecting for the troops. He had sent off vessels to the Eastern Shore and up the James

River to secure corn and oats. The executive daily expected the return of the boats with barrels of corn.

General Washington wrote Governor Nelson October 14, 1781, concerning the inadequate clothing for the cavalry:

> Sir: From an impression made to me by Colonel White of the miserable condition of the men of the 4th Regiment of Dragoons for want of cloathing, I am constrained to apply to your Excellency to know whether it will be possible to procure any for them even of the commonest kind. . . . one hundred of the Men are literally naked at this advanced season. Could they be clothed properly, above one hundred fifty, who are mounted and tolerably equipped, might march immediately southward. A detachment of one hundred have marched from Ruffins to Richmond; they have nothing but stable Jackets, Shirts, and a few Caps, and consequently want Breeches, Boots, Stockings, Hats or Caps and either Cloaks or Blankets; perhaps Mr. Ross might, by an exertion procure the most necessary Articles if not the whole, for it will be a manner impossible to move them further than Richmond in their present condition.[6]

With the impending conflict nearing, Nelson established a chain of expresses to carry communications from the Camp of Forks at West Point to the capital. The line extended from the Brick House at New Kent across the Pamunkey River from West Point where two riders were to be placed, down to York. Two men were to be stationed at Byrd's Tavern on the way to Williamsburg, two at the old capital, and two in camp. In directing Major Day to take eight horses for the purpose, Governor Nelson declared:

> I do not require this of you as a part of your Duty, but as a most necessary and important Matter, which your Disposition to serve your Country will engage you voluntarily to perform.[7]

All through his numerous letters, Governor Nelson appealed to the recipients' patriotic ardor. His communications were courteous but direct in demands.

During the sultry September days, a comprehensive strategy began to take shape. On the seventeenth General Washington and General Rochambeau, accompanied by their aides, Jonathan Trumbull, Tench Tilghman, and Duportail, boarded the captured ship *Queen Charlotte* in the James and sailed down river into the Chesapeake for a conference with Admiral de Grasse aboard his flagship, *Ville de Paris*, a three-decked vessel outfitted with 110 guns.

When the six-foot two-inch Washington ascended the ship's ladder to step aboard, Admiral de Grasse kissed the American on both cheeks and exclaimed emotionally, "My dear little General!" Though de Grasse was six-feet, three-inches tall, the American aides could not control their amusement and Henry Knox guffawed.[8]

The meeting was a success for de Grasse promised to remain with his French fleet until the last of October and pledged to furnish reinforcements for the principal attack. General Washington notified de Grasse that Governor Nelson would send a "proper person" to reside aboard the Ville de Paris to check "legal passports" and thereby "abolish abuses."[9]

On the return trip the patriot party ran into a storm and had to abandon the rolling *Queen Charlotte* for another craft that could be maneuvered along the left shore of the river and rowed into College Creek.

On September 21, Governor Nelson reported to Lieutenant Governor Jameson at Richmond:

> The Reason of my giving you but little News, is because there has been very little to communicate. We have been waiting for Reinforcements & necessaries for commencing & carrying on the Siege. The General has been absent four Days, on a Visit to the Count De Grasse. He is every Hour expected back & as Part of the Northern Troops are in the River, it is probable the Army will very soon move down.[10]

This news referred to the rebel regiments that arrived on September 20. Young John Laurens also rode into the old capital after returning from his mission to France and brought word to General Washington, who had returned to Williamsburg on the twenty-second, that the French promised sufficient provisions to finish the war.[11]

Drums began to roll at dawn on Friday, September 28, to rouse 16,000 troops of the allied armies. The encampment around Williamsburg stirred with activity. Tents were struck, kitchen utensils packed on wagons ready to roll out of the city. Officers barked commands and soldiers started the thirteen-mile trek toward York under a fair sky. Rebel regiments and their French allies filed down on the sandy road.

The American army was composed of approximately 8,500 rank and file, including about 3,000 militia. There were three divisions of Continental detachments under the command of General Lafayette, General Steuben, and General Lincoln, the latter in charge of the American wing as second in command to Washington.

General Rochambeau commanded a French force of seven regiments composed of nine hundred men in each body divided into brigades under four major generals: the Baron de Viomenil, Chevalier de Chastellux, Marquis de Saint Simon, and Brigadier M. de Choisy. The Duc de Lauzun was in charge of a 600-horse troop and foot legion, and Colonel d'Abbville headed 600 artillerists. The French allies contributed approximately half the land force for the operation against the British.

Brigadier General/Governor Nelson had more than three thousand militia under his command. These detachments were divided into three regiments under the direction of General Weedon with 1,500 men, General Lawson and General Stevens each commanding 750 troops—all veteran Virginia officers who had encountered the English enemy in other expeditions. The Virginia militia presented a motley picture compared to the trim French troops, yet their spirits soared with anticipation.[12] Von Closen commented on the ragged regiments in a complimentary manner:

> What does it matter! an intelligent man would say. These people are much more praise-worthy and brave to fight as they do, when they are so poorly supplied *with everything!*[13]

Colonel William Lewis and his Campbell County riflemen were chosen to accompany the advance led by the First Brigade of infantrymen under the fighting parson, General Muhlenberg, preceded by Colonel Stephen Moylan and his dragoons. Moylan, a Catholic Irishman from Philadelphia in his mid-forties, had served in several capacities under the Commander-in-Chief who had confidence in the competent, talkative trooper.

About five miles out of Williamsburg the American wing swung right and the French followed the left lane to the seaport town. Governor Nelson and the Virginia officers commanding the militia moved to the right of Harwood's Mill. Fieldpieces were interspersed among the marching files in case the foe should attack. By midday the patriots met British pickets from Lieutenant Colonel Robert Abercrombie's Light Infantry, but rapid fire from the rebels sent them in retreat. Tarleton's Tory riders fell back to the British lines. A wave of allied armies continued through thick woods, cleared fields, and over the slopes around the seaport town.

General Steuben had Maryland detachments under his command, Virginia Continentals whom Lieutenant Colonel Gaskins had recently recruited, and General Wayne with his Pennsylvania regiments.

The New England soldiers in General Moses Hazen's battalions mopped their brows in the humid September heat. Men from Massachusetts, New Jersey, New York, and Rhode Island filled the marching columns. General Henry Knox's three hundred pounds held down his prancing horse as he watched the artillerymen moving the mounted guns over the rutty roads. There were several companies of sappers and miners, Delaware recruits, and dragoons among the troops.

The titled French officers viewed the approaching fight as another adventure. The green plumes of the chasseurs and red feathers of the tall grenadiers bobbed as the troops marched up the rising ridges. The Duc de Lauzun galloped rapidly ahead of his cavalry corps.

The allied armies established an encampment in a long semicircle outside the village running from the northwest side of the York River around the eastern end past Wormeley's Creek. The French regiments ranged from the river to the west crossing the Williamsburg Road up to Great River, a rivulet flowing north and south, also called Beaverdam Creek.

Washington had his headquarters back of the French artillery park with two tents, and General Rochambeau pitched his tents just above to the right. The American sector completed the campsite of the arc arrangement past swampy Great River with General Steuben and his soldiers stationed in front of the American artillery park and General Knox's post. General Lincoln's division and General Lafayette's detachments pitched camp back of Moore's Pond just left of Wormeley's Creek. General Nelson and his militia companies were bivouacked to the right of the French commander forming a reserve for the Continental regiments.

British riflemen positioned near Moore's Pond poured shot at the advancing Americans on Saturday morning, September 29, killing one soldier and wounding half a dozen men.

Lord Cornwallis had not been pleased with the British position at York Town. Sir Henry Clinton, however, had stated that it was absolutely necessary to hold a station in the Chesapeake.[14]

Lieutenant Frederick MacKenzie, of the Royal Fusiliers, recorded his impressions of the place and the people in his report:

> York Town on the South branch of the River stands high, is healthy, and contains houses sufficient for the accommodation of such an Army. On the left it is partly encircled by a Ravine with deep margins or Morass, which might be turned to advantage if the place was to be fortified. There is a Battery of Cannon, 18 pds. in front: only 9 were mounted when I was there. Tho' this place has the advantage of all others in Chesapeake Bay in depth of water, it is open to the E. & N. W. winds, therefore unsafe in the winter season. The people in and about it, influenced by the family of Nelson, are all rebellions [sic].[15]

On his arrival in August, Cornwallis had established a system of defense with a series of earthworks and entrenchments. Hundreds of captured slaves sweated in the scorching sun felling trees, trimming timber, and putting palisades on the ramparts. Three redoubts had been erected by the English engineers in the outlying line. Close to the York River in the western direction was the big star-shaped construction manned by the reduced but rugged Royal Welsh Fusiliers, who had fought from Bunker Hill through the Carolina campaign. Smaller stations had been set up near the rivulets to the east and the horn work transected the York-Hampton Road. A network of durable ramparts and redoubts formed the inner military fortifications. Fourteen batteries had been built to mount sixty-five guns, none larger than three eighteen-pounders. Ten redoubts completed the defense connections—all arranged with an abatis of projecting branches, barriers above a deep ditch. Two particularly strong positions of protection were Redoubts No. 9 and No. 10 situated just outside the principal British lines toward the east above the banks of the York River. The Union Jack flew above the defensive forts.

The forty-four-gun *Charon* and twenty-eight-gun *Guadeloupe* were pulled into port surrounded by a royal fleet of small sloops, supply boats, twenty-four transports, two frigates, and a few other vessels.

Across the river at Gloucester the British had built three batteries and four redoubts to protect the point. Colonel Thomas Dundas, who was the commander of the Forty-third, Seventh-sixth, and Eightieth brigades was in charge of the garrison and was supported by over four hundred cavalrymen under Simcoe and Tarleton.

Governor Nelson had already stationed General Weedon's regiments in the Gloucester area. In an epistle of September 19, Nelson explained to Weedon:

> The Reason, I imagine why no Relief has arrived in your Camp, is that the Militias of all the Counties, except King & Queen, which you mention, were ordered to come down on this Side; & the Militias of the Counties north of Pamunkey River to form the Gloucester Army . . . I have already given the necessary Orders respecting Ammunition, and shall take Care that your Force be made so respectable, as to enable you to awe the Enemy on your Side, & to act an offensive Part.[16]

The patriot columns were increased to 1,500 men, and Washington augmented the unit with the Duc de Lauzun and his dragoons. The contrast was striking between Weedon, the unaffected tavern keeper called "Joe Gourd," and the flamboyant French cavalryman.

Lord Cornwallis made a decision the evening of September 29 that caused consternation among his colleagues but delighted the allies. He abandoned the outer defense lines on Sunday, September 30. Tarleton scored his superior officer for the precipitate move and contended that every inch of ground should be contested. Disgruntled Germans complained over the surprise order and three soldiers from the Rhine deserted the camp that night. Eager Englishmen itching for battle grumbled at the retreat, the morale sinking. General Washington and many others wondered why the enemy had evacuated the exterior lines.

When Lord Cornwallis received assurances from General Clinton that British regiments would leave New York by October 5 to reinforce the York positions, the English commander determined to concentrate the Crown troops within the town and relinquish an offensive assault against the rebels.

Governor Nelson conveyed the news from his camp at York on October 1 to Lieutenant Governor Jameson at Richmond:

Our progress here has been more considerable, for the time, than could have been expected, and attended with less opposition and loss. Yesterday morning, it was discovered that the Enemy had evacuated their Out posts at Moore's Mill, Pigeon Quarter, and every other place beyond the Creek, except at Nelson's Farm. Our troops are today working on the grounds they relinquished. The French took possession of Pigeon Hill. There have been two men killed and six wounded.[17]

Exhilaration over the evacuation was marred a few days later by the death of Colonel Alexander Scammell, a seasoned officer who had served as aide to General Washington and as adjutant general during the severe winter at Valley Forge where his humor had often cheered the Commander-in-Chief.

As officer of the day for the allied armies Sunday, September 30, Colonel Scammell was surprised to observe the withdrawal of royal troops from the outer works. Gathering a patriot party, he led the group in reconnoitering the enemy redoubts. Suddenly, redcoat dragoons rushed from ambush to surround the rebel patrol. Colonel Scammell surrendered but was shot in the back by a British officer. Lord Cornwallis had Scammell's wounds treated by English physicians and then sent him back to the American army under a flag of truce, but he died in the hospital at Williamsburg October 6. The loss was felt throughout the Continental camp.

The allies advanced promptly into abandoned British posts. Preparations were made to proceed with a besieging operation against the opponent. Since General Steuben was the only officer present who had participated in extensive siege warfare, his advice on approaches and attacks was relied on heavily.

A sharp skirmish ensued on Sunday with Saint Simon and his French infantrymen pushing the English pickets back to the fusiliers' redoubt.

On October 1 the Commander-in-Chief walked over the battle ground with his aides and Major General Duportail, the thirty-eight-year-old experienced and energetic French engineer who had won the esteem of the Continental officials. Duportail would direct and determine the defense of the proper parallels. As the party advanced within three hundred yards of the principal British works, royal artillerists continually hurled shot at the colonial commission. Near the Poplar Tree Redoubt a cannon discharge sent the rebel detachment on retreat, except for General Washington. The calm commander kept his telescope trained on his target, observing the enemy. The officers continued their reconnaisance after orders were issued for alert pickets to protect the patriots.

Curious citizens of York Town roamed the fortifications until Washington was forced to issue instructions in General Orders on October 6:

The General forbids all those who are not required by their station or the Command of a superior Officer to employ themselves in reconnoitering the

Enemies works; the curiosity of such persons often interrupts the observation of Officers particularly charged with this business; the good of the service requires that each Officer adhere to the duty assigned to him.[18]

As soon as all the artillery and ammunition could be brought to the Continental camp, the problem of providing food for the forces could be expedited, Governor Nelson noted. He was exhausting every means to assist General Washington, who had requested 160 militiamen to assist General Knox in securing horses to drag the howitzers, and wagons to move the military stores. Nelson chose his friend Colonel George Dabney and his Virginia detachment to move field pieces, stores, and supplies from Trebell's Landing on the James River where the French fleet had unloaded them. Washington and other officers offered their mounts for the mission. Slow-moving ox teams were used to transport the heavy cannon across sandy stretches between the seaport towns. Patriot soldiers also struggled to move the equipment along the road. At the British post, regiments slaughtered horses they could not feed and cast the carcasses into the York River.

Governor Nelson regretted having to refuse wagons to General Choisy at Gloucester but reported to the French commander:

> All we have are employed in bringing on the heavy Artillery & Military Stores. Horses shall be instantly sent on, & though not at present so many as you want, yet in a short Time you will receive a sufficient Number & I have been assured by the Quarter Master General that as soon as the Harness coming down the Bay arrives you will be furnished.[19]

While the cannon moved along, thousands of troops were working on the first parallel for the proposed siege. The staccato sounds of spade, pick, and shovel rang in rhythmic tempo as the troops swung their entrenching tools into the sand or rock and swamp. The corps dug an encircling line of entrenchments two thousand yards long from the eastern end above the York River bluff around Wormeley Creek and across York-Hampton Road, to the western section below the town. They built five batteries along the breastworks and strengthened four redoubts. Twenty-five hundred armed sentries protected the workmen. Captain Davis described the action in his diary on October 2 and 3:[20]

> A continual firing from the Enemy Batteries all this day—our work goes on rapidly. . . . A deserter went in who informed them where our cover parties lay. They directed their shot from then the first kill'd three men and mortally wounded a fourth.[21]

As the fiery shells spewed across the sky, Colonel Butler recorded in his journal October 2 that he had counted 352 British balls exploding from dawn to dusk.[22]

Governor Nelson noted, "We have not returned a shot."[23]

In the darkness of October 6, French engineers directed the sappers and miners to finish digging ditches. A drizzling rain hindered the British blasts and hid the Continental corps. The next step was to set up the allied siege line. At most places the parallel line was approximately eight hundred yards away from the English encampment.

A few deserters shifted sides. One French soldier ran away from Saint Simon's regiment to the royal standard and probably divulged the plan of diversionary strategy from the French battery, since the English cannon began to concentrate on that position. Two deserters from the British camp said their forces lacked food and that smallpox had spread through the post. To prevent French vessels from pulling into port, Lord Cornwallis issued instructions to sink some British ships near the shore of York Town.

While 1,500 troops completed trenches and embrasures for the cannon, 1,200 men including militia units under General Nelson swarmed through the woods to cut saplings to strengthen the earthworks. The militia tied together bundles of brushwood making 2,000 fascines to fill the trenches and brace the walls; 1,200 gabions and saucissions—wicker-like cylinders filled with earth—were formed by 600 militia and 168 men to support the embankments. Soldiers sharpened points on logs for an abatis around the redoubts. Palisades and parapets were established as defensive barriers to protect the patriots from enemy fire.

October 3, Duc de Lauzun and his legion had routed Tarleton and his Tory riders at Gloucester in a brief but brisk engagement. When the French commander had closed in on the British camp, he encountered Tarleton and his dragoons guarding a British foraging detail. The two cavalry leaders charged each other and in the clash "British Benny" Tarleton was toppled from his horse. He was quickly surrounded by his men who were then backed by reserves. Colonel Mercer and his militia, supported Duc de Lauzun's men, poured shot at the surprised redcoats. One English officer was killed and several British soldiers wounded before Tarleton retreated.

Governor Nelson reported to the Congress two days later:

> This Evening will complete a Week, since we moved down from Williamsburg. The Enemy very quietly permitted us to invest them, & on the second Night fearful I suppose of a Storm, evacuated all their Outworks, except one on the Hill above the Creek on the Williamsburg road, which they will hold. We immediately took Possession of the works they left, which have been converted into covering Redoubts for the intended Approaches. These Redoubts are about half a mile from the Town—The Enemy endeavoured to retard these Operations by playing on our men who were at Work from their Batteries, but with little Effect, having killed in all only six men.[24]

The executive described the events of the Gloucester encounter:

> Tarleton was dismounted & wounded, a major who commanded the Infantry killed, near fifty Men killed & wounded, & the whole Party defeated. The Loss on our side of the Men under his Command behaved with so much Gallantry on this Occasion that the Commander in Chief thought proper to give them his Thanks in the Orders of Yesterday.[25]

Governor Nelson ended his report by entreating the delegates to secure for the state "its proportion of the Clothing lately imported for the Continental Army. . . . [the] few Troops we have now in the Field are not fit to be seen."

At sunrise October 7, British shot and shell sprayed the area, but the ravines and trenches protected the troops from the flames. With flying colors the American forces moved forward to beating drums, following the age-old tradition of opening formal operations. Twenty-six-year-old Colonel Alexander Hamilton, with his dark blue eyes scanning the scene, instructed Captain James Duncan to set the patriot standard on the parapet. The young officer obeyed immediately and was amazed that the slender colonel then commanded the full regiment to climb the rampart and execute the manual of arms. The British admired his bravado, so Duncan was relieved to report that not a man was lost in the maneuver.

Thomas Nelson described developments to the Lieutenant Governor in a letter of October 8:

> For some days after my last to you, our Troops were employed in making such things as are previously necessary to the opening of Trenches. On the Evening of the 6th we broke Ground, at the distance of 600 yards from the Enemy's works generally, though in some places rather nearer. The night was favourable & the Men had so far covered themselves, before the Enemy discovered what they were about, that although a heavy firing began about nine o'clock, & continued with little Intermission till the Morning, scarcely any Loss was sustained. The Fire was chiefly directed to the left where the French Troops were at work. Some Batteries I expect will be opened to Morrow.[26]

He was correct. His militia assisted the artillerymen in mounting the guns for the military operation.

On October 9 the French forces at the western sector finished setting their howitzers, four twelve-pounder guns, and six hugh mortars to open the bombardment at three o'clock against the British post. Fire was also hurled at the English fleet filling York harbor. The royal crew cut the *Guadeloupe's* anchor cables driving the ship to the less vulnerable Gloucester shore.

At the southeastern encampment, American artillerists had mounted six eighteen- and twenty-four-pounders, four mortars, and two eight-inch howitzers hauled in on special cannon carriages contrived by General Knox. At five o'clock the Commander-in-Chief touched fire to the first shot hurled toward the town. Eager rebels kept firing and the missiles hit their marks. British officers fell; the commissary general was killed, and the quartermaster adjutant wounded. Fragments of red-hot balls severed arms and legs of the English soldiers. As the cannonade continued, the few families who had not left fled from shattered buildings.

Secretary Nelson, however, remained in his home in the southeastern end of York Town, where Lord Cornwallis had established his headquarters. Besieging rebel batteries pierced the roof and walls of the sturdy brick house and window glass crashed to the ground. To prevent the royal artificers from repairing their guns, General Washington directed his artillerists to continue their assault through the night. Surgeon James Thacher recorded his impressions of the shelling:

> They are clearly visible in the form of a black ball in the day, but in the night, they appear like fiery meteors with blazing tails, most beautifully brilliant, ascending majestically from the mortar to a certain altitude, and gradually descending to the spot where they are destined to execute their work of destruction. It is astonishing with what accuracy an experienced gunner will make his calculations, that a shell shall fall within a few feet of a given point, and burst at the precise time, though at a great distance.[27]

On October 10, the French battery across the York-Hampton Road, with ten eighteen- and twenty-four-pounders and four mortars augmented by four eighteen-pounders of the Continental division, opened its attack on the English encampment.

Hessian trooper Johann Doehla wrote in his diary:

> Early this morning we had to change our camp and pitch our tents in the earthwork, on account of the heavy fire of the enemy. . . . Most of the inhabitants who were still to be found here fled with their best possessions eastward to the bank of the York River, and dug in among the sand cliffs, but there also they did not stay undamaged; for many were badly injured and mortally wounded by the fragments of bombs which exploded partly in the air and partly on the ground, their arms and legs severed of themselves struck dead.[28]

Although Doehla exaggerated the size of the shot and shell from the patriot and French fire, other recorders attested to the devastation. Another young German mercenary, Stephen Popp, wrote:

> The heavy fire forced us to throw our tents in the ditches. . . . We could find no refuge in or out of town. The people fled to the waterside and hid in hastily contrived shelters on the banks, but many of them were killed by bursting bombs.[29]

According to British historian Charles Stedman, by October 6 the allies:

> Made their first parallel at the distance of six hundred yards from the British works, and by the afternoon of the ninth, their batteries were completed, which immediately opened upon the town an incessant cannonade . . . And the continual discharge of shot & of shells from a number of heavy cannons and mortars, in a few days damaged the unfinished works on the left of the town, silenced the guns that were mounted on them, and occasioned the loss of a great number of men.[30]

Colonel William Nelson and Major John Nelson, serving with the Virginia forces, were worried about the welfare of their father, Thomas Nelson, and Governor Nelson was concerned for his uncle's safety. All three Nelsons solicited the Commander-in-Chief to seek a flag of truce from Lord Cornwallis for the Secretary's escape from his house. The request was granted and at noontime October 10, a white banner was hoisted from the British fort; firing ceased, and Secretary Nelson was helped to the American lines. The sixty-five-year-old gentleman still suffered from gout so he limped over his own land where he had often hunted woodcocks and wild game.

The Secretary confirmed to General Washington that the rebel cannonading had been devastating. Though the British were discouraged, Lord Cornwallis had received a communication from General Clinton with the promise that reinforcements would arrive in a few days to relieve the post.

Dining with St. George Tucker on Thursday, October 11, Secretary Nelson reported his impressions and the young soldier recorded them:

> He says our bombardment produced great effect in annoying the enemy and destroying their works. Two officers were killed and one wounded by a bomb the evening we opened. Lord Chewton's cane was struck out of his Hand by a cannon ball. Lord Cornwallis has built a kind of Grotto at the foot of the Secretary's Garden where he lives underground. A Negro of the Secretary's was kill'd in his House. It seems to be his Opinion that the British are a good deal dispirited, altho' he says they affect to say they have no Apprehensions of the Garrison's falling.[31]

Evidently, Governor Nelson was not informed immediately that the Secretary had been escorted into the Continental camp. With the opening of two additional batteries on the tenth, the allies had over fifty pieces of artillery focused to fire on the enemy enclosure. Their big guns rumbled, and swirling gray smoke filled the sky, but seasoned troops from Massachusetts to Maryland were accustomed to their clamorous boom.

On Wednesday, October 10, the American artillerists had mounted four eighteen-pounder guns and pulled up two mortar-type cannon that hurled projectiles at high angles. The patriots were proud of their military ma-

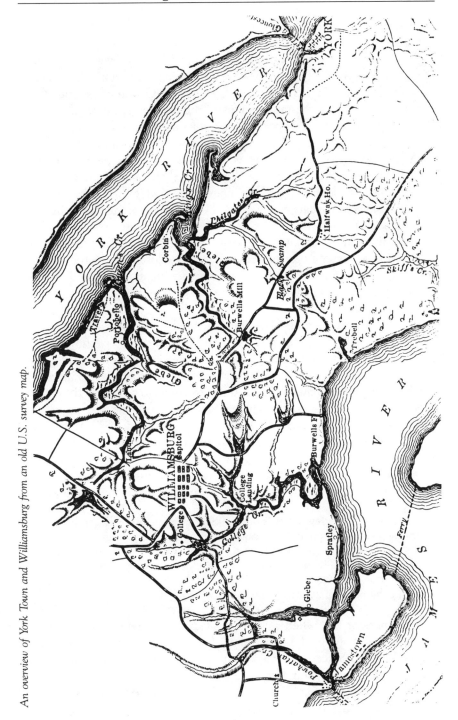

An overview of York Town and Williamsburg from an old U.S. survey map.

chines; the rebel gunners wanted to rival the accurate shells of their French counterparts.

As officer of the day, General Lafayette had asked Governor Nelson to attend the first firing of Captain Thomas Machin's cannon from the Second Artillery Company. In his dual role as General and Governor, Nelson was no stranger to officers or the rank and file of the regiments; the troops realized he had dipped into his own pocket to provide supplies for the forces and had supported the credit of the Commonwealth with his own funds.

As he rode across familiar fields toward the parallel, Nelson observed drastic changes in the area, but he did not dwell on damage already done to homes of family and friends and buildings in the town of his birth. War was a bloody business. Six years before, he had vowed to drive the enemy invaders into the sea, and his fervor at the time had shocked conservative colleagues. Despite discouragements with the defense system, or the indifference and disaffection of some citizens, Nelson had never lost faith in the fight for freedom. The flame of patriotism still burned in his heart, and Thomas Nelson, Jr., was still ready to make sacrifices with his purse and property for the colonial cause.

On that balmy October day when General Lafayette asked his advice about a particular target to point the artillery, there was no hesitation in Nelson's reply. The courageous leader indicated his own handsome brick house in the center of town. Reasoning that Lord Cornwallis had moved his headquarters there, General Nelson urged the units to discharge the cannon shot at the dwelling and proclaimed that not a particle of the property should be spared. He offered five guineas to the gunners who hit the house.[32]

Throughout the day the patriots had continued their bombardment of the British until by early evening, the air was choked with swirls of black smoke rising above the river. The French artillery had successfully struck the forty-four-gun *Charon;* Dr. Thacher described the occurrence:

> I had a fine view of this splendid conflagration. The ships were enwrapped in a torrent of fire, which spreading with vivid brightness among the combustible rigging, and running with amazing rapidity to the tops of the several masts, while all around was thunder lightning from our numerous cannon & mortars, & in the darkness of the night, presented one of the most sublime & magnificent spectacles which can be imagined.[33]

The spirit of the allied soldiers peaked with the promise of success. Friendly rivalry and brisk betting about beating the British amused American and French officers and men. With exaggerated politeness and enlarging the strength of their forces, General Steuben and French General Viomenil joined in, promising to aid each other if the British attacked. As a past master of bragging, Baron Steuben boldly informed his French associate that he would send eight hundred soldiers to his assistance. General Wayne remarked to the Prussian commander that he had only one thousand troops. The unabashed Baron agreed; "Mad" Anthony simply smiled and ordered his officers to back up the overstatement if the occasion arose.[34]

Lieutenant Feltman had already won a beaver hat from Captain Davis as the superior officer had bet on September 30 that the British would surrender the following Sunday. Captain Davis, however, was still optimistic. The two friends wagered again over winning the war. On October 8, Lieutenant Feltman entered in his diary, "This day I bet a pair of silk stockings with Captain Davis that Cornwallis and his army would not be prisoners of war by this day two weeks."[35] The lieutenant would lose this gamble, but he was glad to give up his silk stockings for such a glorious success.

On the ninth Lieutenant Feltman recorded:

> This morning 9 o'clock A. M. a deserter from the enemy's artillery came to us; he left them just as their piece fired, which was advanced in front of the Governor's house. He informed us that Cornwallis had given out orders to them not to be afraid of the Americans, that they had not any heavy pieces of ordnance except a few pieces of field artillery. He also informed the soldiery and inhabitants that the French fleet was inferior to him and were afraid to attack him; that they came to this place to procure a quantity of tobacco, and if they could not be supplied here, that the fleet would set sail in eight or ten days at the farthest, and leave the continent. Such are my Lord's addresses to his soldiery, but they have more sense than to believe in his weak expressions.[36]

Major Charles Cochrane managed to slip through the French ring of ships on October 10 in a speedy whaleboat with dispatches from General Clinton to Lord Cornwallis. The English commander assured the Earl that Admiral Graves would be leaving October 12 with reinforcements for the royal garrison. Lord Cornwallis informed General Clinton in his answer on October 11 that only naval action could save his situation and affirmed, "We have lost about 70 men, and many of our works are considerably damag'd."[37] Messenger Cochrane also became a casualty as he implored Lord Cornwallis to walk with him to the parapets to peer at the breastworks of the patriots; a rebel ball blew his head into a bloody mess.

The rebels knew British batteries had been severely damaged since salvos from the enemy's cannon had slackened. Washington extended the first parallel and began the second siege line for an all-out advance by the allied infantry. At dusk on October 11 men from General Steuben's and General Wayne's divisions moved forward to start the construction. Every soldier carried a shovel, spade, or grubbing hoe to dig the ditches; in addition, every other man lugged a fascine to fill the trenches. British gunners poured grapeshot and cannister fire at the patriots, but the real danger resulted from the cross fire and close range of the French firing at the enemy. Lieutenant Feltman recorded two men killed in his detachment and one badly wounded from the French batteries' shells, but the spades and shovels kept swinging while sentries watched for British balls to warn the workers. On October 12, Virginia militia and men from General Lincoln's division relieved the detachments. The diggers continued to build seven-foot wide entrenchments, three and one-half feet deep, while British cannon bombarded the rebel ranks; casualties were heavy. Particularly dangerous were five-inch projectiles the foe hurled, as these shells could not be seen until they descended.[38]

Two British strongholds close to the York River prevented the patriot forces from finishing the second parallel. Redoubt No. 9 was a five-sided fort strengthened with a surrounding abatis and manned by approximately 120 soldiers. Colonel McPherson commanded the British and Hessian troops inside the stockade. Above the bluff of the river stood the square-shaped No. 10 defense post, protected by a palisade and defended by Major Campbell and 70 redcoats. The allied command resolved to reduce the royal redoubts.

While they arranged for the attack, incessant cannonading echoed across the area from Cornwallis's experienced gunners, answered by a barrage from the American gunners and the French artillerists under Saint Simon.

General Rochambeau directed his division to hold fire for awhile. Taking his son and aide, the Vicomte de Rochambeau, the general stepped down to inspect the trenches. His French staff shuddered, but the pair returned without harm to inform Baron de Viomenil that the palisades still stood. By the afternoon of October 14, Washington and Rochambeau were alerted that the English encampment had been sufficiently raked with shot, their works so weakened that the surprise assault could proceed that night.

General Lafayette and four hundred light infantry were instructed to advance. Eager officers clamored for command of the expedition. When Lafayette chose former aide Chevalier Gimat to lead the attack, Colonel Alexander Hamilton formally objected.[39] The ambitious New York commander had seniority and appealed to General Washington; Hamilton won the assignment. The Commander-in-Chief discovered upon a visit to General Viomenil that the French commander had many requests from his own officers to lead the ranks on the night raid. Three daring young noblemen, the Comte de Damas, the Chevalier de Lameth, and the Comte de Vauban defied the refusal and accompanied the enterprise. Colonel William de Deux-Ponts led the regiment of four hundred French troops toward Redoubt No. 9 in the darkness after six rapid shots signified the advance. Lieutenant Colonel de l'Estrade, second in command with forty years' service, accompanied the four columns of chasseurs and grenadiers covering the ground quickly and quietly. A Hessian sentry on the rampart yelled, "Wer da?" and shot poured from the parapet. Axes, fascines, and ladders were lugged; but before the French could slash through the palisade, several soldiers were shot or stabbed. Colonel de l'Estrade was pulled back from the parapet into the ditch and two hundred men tramped over the officer in the onrush. Regiments rushed into the melee; Deux-Ponts shouted, "Vive le Roi!" and the troops in the trenches repeated the victory cry. After about a half-hour, the British surrendered the fort to the French force.

While the French soldiers had been subduing Redoubt No. 9, two detachments of four hundred troops under Colonel Hamilton and Colonel Gimat had accomplished their assignment in ten minutes. Advancing rapidly to the right end of the first parallel, they moved silently along the river bluff in the darkness. The unit carried unloaded muskets with sharp steel swords to bayonet the enemy. Gallant young Lieutenant Colonel John Laurens led eighty men behind the redoubt with Lieutenant Colonel Francis Barber and Major Nicholas Fish assisting in the attack. Halfway on the march, the troops halted and one soldier was selected from each company as the "forlorn hope," the brave man who was first to charge the fort. Captain Stephen Olney of Rhode Island, who had bolstered some wavering fellows of his company, reported later that all of them wanted to go on the risky mission. Sergeant Joseph Plumb Martin was in the front line with the sappers and miners moving up with their axes to chop the British barrier of abatis. He recorded:

> We arrived at the trenches a little before sunset. I saw several officers fixing bayonets on long staves. I then concluded we were about to make a general assault upon the enemy's works, but before dark I was informed of the whole plan.[40]

When they reached the redoubt, the challenge of the sentry went unanswered. Suddenly English volley exploded at the rebels scrambling to storm the stronghold. Colonel Gimat was struck in the foot and Captain Olney was stabbed and shot by the royal defenders. The sappers started slashing through the pointed sticks, and patriot soldiers pushed forward screaming and shouting as they tumbled through the palisades. Colonel Hamilton was boosted up as the British threw grenades at the assaulters, but the attackers rushed into the garrison with thrusting bayonets. Redcoats raced down the river embankment to escape. When Colonel John Laurens and his column climbed over the back rampart, British Major Campbell was wounded and realized further resistance was foolhardy. He tendered his sword to the courageous South Carolinian and surrendered the fort.

Continental casualties consisted of nine men killed and twenty-five wounded in the few minutes of furious fighting. Colonel Hamilton praised the patriot enterprise in his report writing that the rapidity and immediate success of the assault were a tribute to the troops. He complimented the officers for their cool expedition of the plan.[41]

With the capture of the two important redoubts, the allies grasped the advantage immediately.[42] Colonel Richard Butler, waiting in reserve with his rugged Pennsylvanians, instructed the soldiers to grab spades and shovels. Even though rain fell through the night, the rebels finished digging the second parallel by dawn encompassing the former British forts. Lieutenant Feltman in the fatigue party explained, "We were very much exposed in the enemy's fire, both musquetry and cannon balls and grape shot, and not a single man hurt."[43]

Later in the day, the details resumed their digging toward the enemy lines and were not so fortunate. Feltman stated the enemy kept throwing shells and "wounded a great number of men, especially the militia." Cannon, mortars, and howitzers were hauled forward encircling the English encampment about three hundred yards away from the British works.

Lord Cornwallis, communicating in code to General Clinton on October 15, assessed his predicament:

> My situation now becomes very critical. We dare not show a gun to their old batteries, and I expect their new ones will open tomorrow morning. Experience has shown that our fresh earthen works do not resist their powerful artillery, so that we shall soon be exposed to an assault in ruined works, in a bad position, and with weakened numbers. The safety of the place, is therefore, so precarious that I cannot recommend that the fleet and army should run great risk in endeavouring to save us.[44]

That same day the British fleet was standing off Staten Island as attempts to sail southward had been thwarted by a severe storm.

Lord Cornwallis was confronted not only by the superior strength of the combined allied armies ready to advance for the final siege but also by his own ranks reduced through desertions and disease. Hundreds of sick and wounded men crowded the hospitals. Diarist Doehla wrote repeatedly about desertions from the British regiments. Smallpox had spread especially among the slaves who had been seized. Though desperate, the British commander decided to act quickly. At a midnight conference of his officers, the staff planned a sortie. Colonel Robert Abercrombie was to choose 350 tough campaigners and with bayonets fixed, move toward the horn work at 3:00 A.M. October 15. The troops marched westward toward the junction of the allied line which they judged, correctly, would not be so closely guarded. Claiming to be a rebel relief column, the redcoats surprised the sleeping Agenale French force and stabbed many of the men.

Under cover of darkness, royalist troops used the same ruse to rush Colonel Henry Skipwith's one hundred Virginia militia who were guarding American guns. Their British officers yelling, "skin the bastards," the Englishmen succeeded in unmanning some of the cannon by plunging their sabers into the guns. But the Count de Noailles, Lafayette's brother-in-law, close by with a covering party of French grenadiers drove the British back. By noon the American artillerymen had removed the spikes and made the guns operable again.

General Nelson was alerted to the action at York Town by first-hand observation on the battlefield as well as by couriers. To expedite the attack, Nelson sent out countless expresses. Goods were being conveyed to General Choisy commanding the Gloucester garrison. On October 16, his Excellency instructed Colonel Godfrey of Norfolk County, in charge of the militia units:

> It is necessary that all Works thrown up by the Enemy in the Counties of Norfolk & Princess Anne should be immediately levelled. You will therefore call out a Proportion of Militia of your County, & enclosed are orders to the Commanding Officers of the Counties of Princess Anne & Nansemond to furnish you with a like Proportion, to execute this Work. For the greater Dispatch you are also hereby empowered to impress as many Negroes, Tools & other Requisites as will be sufficient for your Purpose.[45]

An explanation was sent to the commanding officers of Princess Anne and Nansemond counties concerning the assignment with the instruction, "As it is necessary that this Business should be instantly executed, you will comply with this requisite as quickly as possible."[46]

Governor Nelson also summoned the Virginia House of Delegates to meet at Richmond November 5. The previous session had been adjourned, "At which Time a sufficient Number of Members did not attend for the Dispatch of public Business, & the Exigencies of the Commonwealth require that an Assembly should be held as soon as may be."[47] The call for the meeting was sent to George Webb of the Council on October 17 with the direction, "Be so good as to have the seal of the Commonwealth affixed to the enclosed Proclamation and have a printed copy of it sent to the Delegates of every County, and to each Senator."[48]

Nelson described the events of the battle in his next paragraph to Webb:

> Since my last we took by storm two of the Enemy's Redoubts. The loss, on both sides, was nearly equal, and did not exceed one hundred. Our Batteries are now playing on their works at the distance of about 200 Yards. By noon, I am informed, we shall have seventy Pieces of heavy cannon planted against them which must soon reduce them to Terms. Unless they take a flight to Gloucester, which may delay their capture a few days. Yesterday morning, a little before day break, they made a sally, and got into one of our Batteries. They spiked 8 Cannon, which were immediately unspiked, and killed and wounded about 16 men. They were repulsed, and suffered nearly the same loss.[49]

The royal regiments were confronted with catastrophe. The British staff officers could not reprimand Lord Cornwallis or remind their superior that less than a week ago they had suggested evacuation of the position. Crowded in the cave headquarters beneath the river bluff, on the afternoon of October 16, the staff proposed a bold plan of crossing the York River to Gloucester. The columns would be joined by the English cavalry to surprise the patriots stationed there and move on to Maryland. British sailors brought sixteen ships into port, and that night the redcoats scrambled down the sloping banks to board. The first division was landed safely on the Gloucester side, and the transports had picked up part of the second detachment before midnight to row them over when a storm struck. Streaks of lightning zigzagged, thunder rumbled, and rain drenched the regiments, while the sailors struggled to control the craft, but their boats were blown back to the York Town shore, and the French captured two transports four miles down the river.

That same night allied soldiers had shifted more mortars into position so by early the next morning, October 17, missiles pounded the British post from a hundred guns.

Lord Cornwallis and General O'Hara went to the horn work to assess the situation and advised capitulation. Before ten o'clock a British drummer mounted the rampart and beat a parley, which was not heard above the din. A British officer joined the drummer waving a big white handkerchief. The cannon ceased. With the flag of truce came a concise message from Lord Cornwallis to George Washington:

> Sir, I propose a cessation of hostilities for twenty-four hours, and that two officers may be appointed by each side to meet at Mr. Moore's house to settle terms for the surrender of the posts at York and Gloucester.[50]

General Washington had anticipated such an appeal, but he was wise to the ways of his old adversary; there would be no stalling for time. Allied firing would cease for only two hours; proposed surrender terms must be submitted in writing. His courteous reply sent about 2:00 P.M. on October 17 read:

> An Ardent Desire to spare the further Effusion of Blood, will readily incline me to listen to such Terms for the Surrender of your Posts and Garrisons of York and Gloucester, as are admissible.[51]

Resenting the two-hour limit to compose a formal capitulation, Lord Cornwallis responded late in the afternoon with the surrender terms sketched but not specifically listed. Washington approved the proposals in essence, except the request that prisoners be paroled and returned to Europe. The English troops, including the marines and seamen, must be surrendered as prisoners of war and confined in America. Recalling the humiliation that

General Lincoln had endured in not being granted the honors of war when he surrendered Charleston to the British, General Washington expressed to Cornwallis on October 18 that the same conditions would be in effect.

While the American commander and the British chief were transmitting their communications under flags of truce for two days, thousands of troops were awed by the strange stillness. St. George Tucker wrote of the solemn silence comparing the meteors streaking across the clear sky to the fiery shells of the previous night, "happily divested of all their horror."[52] The rebel officers and their redcoat counterparts crowded the parapets to stare at one another across the scarred battlefield.

Many memories flooded the minds of these men, who had fought over six years from the battles around Boston through the York Town siege. The rebels had more retreats to remember than grand and glorious conquests. Yet the Continental soldiers had survived defeats and desertions, scant supplies and starvation, incompetence and indifference. They had outlasted the cruel campaigns of Canada, frustrations of the New York fight, disorder at Brandywine, confusion at Germantown, disappointment at Monmouth, and the bitter winters of Valley Forge and Morristown, to fight on doggedly for freedom.

The triumph at Trenton and the success at Saratoga were the bright spots of victory for these battle-scarred veterans. Some of the soldiers could recall vividly that on October 17 four years before General Burgoyne had surrendered a British army to the conquering Americans. With the capitulation of Lord Cornwallis at York Town, the struggle of the patriot revolutionists for independence was at last crowned with success.

The soldiers surveyed the devastation of the town. Homes were only shattered hulks. The Secretary's house was in poor condition with one corner blown off and the roof ruined. Rubble was strewn in the streets. Sick slaves turned loose from the British camp wandered into the town.

Baron Von Closen described the scene:

> One could not take three steps without running into some great holes made by bombs, some splinters, some balls, some half covered trenches, with scattered white or negro arms whole legs some bits of uniforms.[53]

On the river front, battered British boats lay along the shore. The redcoats had scuttled the twenty-eight-gun *Guadeloupe* so the great ship with twisted spars and torn rigging was slowly sinking. The famous old *Fowey* was among the damaged craft. If Thomas Nelson, Jr., had time to view the vessel, he would have recalled how Governor Dunmore had rushed to the royal ship for refuge, deserting post and Palace and angering the patriots by his antics.

Rebel soldiers, lacking much-needed sleep, stretched out on makeshift bunks in the Continental camp. In frustration, English infantrymen began tearing up tents, demolishing supplies, some drinking heavily.

Suddenly at daybreak on October 18, a British band sounded the skirl of Scottish bagpipes. In reply, French musicians assembled rapidly and the Deux-Ponts Regimental Band returned the tribute with a gay tune.

During the day, flags of truce waved in the breeze as couriers dashed back and forth between the camps. The peace commissioners were to meet in the house of Augustine Moore half a mile back of the first parallel of the American lines. Moore had served as an apprentice in the Nelson firm and had acquired a comfortable residence. General Washington had chosen Colonel John Laurens and General Rochambeau had selected the Viscount de Noailles as their representatives. Lord Cornwallis had appointed Colonel Thomas Dundas and his aide, Major Alexander Ross, to negotiate terms for the formal surrender. The British arrived in the afternoon; allied officers awaited them in the front parlor of the frame house. The final draft took several hours. Though Major Ross protested over the colors being cased and for the silencing of drums beating a British or German march, Colonel Laurens was adamant. The young South Carolina soldier had been captured at Charleston when the garrison had been forced to surrender to superior British strength and the Americans had been refused the honors of war. Now the tables were turned. The fourteen articles of capitulation stated that the British posts at York Town and Gloucester would surrender the troops, seamen, and mariners as prisoners of war. Artillery, arms, and accouterments were to be delivered to the allied armies. Ships and boats in the two harbors were to be delivered to the patriots after unloading private property. Lord Cornwallis and certain officers whom he chose would be permitted to sail to New York in the sloop *Bonetta,* provided no public stores were aboard. Then the ship would be returned to the Count de Grasse.

General Washington accepted the articles of capitulation the next morning with slight changes. After the final draft was corrected and copied, he wrote Lord Cornwallis that the terms should be signed by eleven o'clock on October 19 and specified that the British troops should file for a formal surrender at 2:00 P.M. Lord Cornwallis complied and returned the articles with his signature. The Commander-in-Chief, General Rochambeau, and the Count de Barras representing Admiral de Grasse, who had suffered an asthmatic attack, gathered in the captured British redoubt close to the river. Simply stating, "Done in the trenches before Yorktown, in Virginia, October 19, 1781,"[54] the general signed G. *Washington* to the document, and the other officers attached their signatures.

American details and French detachments were stationed to guard the British defense posts to prevent illegal persons leaving or entering the town. General Steuben roused the anger of the rebel soldiers again by grabbing the regimental flag from young Lieutenant Denny as he reached to place it on the British parapet; the Baron performed the ceremonious honor himself. Colonel Richard Butler was so incensed over the insult to his subordinate that friends had to keep him from fighting Steuben. But the rebels watched with amusement when Mr. Day, overseer for Sir Peyton Skipwith's Prestwould, confronted the ruthless Tarleton with a big sweet gum stick to claim his master's horse. "Bold Benny" simply relinquished the horse's reins to the astonishment and guffaws of onlookers.

The camps began to hum in the early afternoon with the hustle of preparations. Proud British troops polished their boots and donned new uniforms. Rum casks were opened and canteens overflowed. The trim French forces also had fresh outfits distributed and wrapped bright black gaithers around their legs. Officers sported plumes and gold braid trimming. Continental officers brushed dust from their blue and buff dress uniforms, but the troops still wore their hunting shirts.

Two weeks before, Governor Nelson had begged the Virginia congressmen to secure the state its proportion of clothing for the militia; nevertheless, on the momentous day, the men marched out in threadbare garments but with rifles polished to a bright gleam.

October 19, 1781, was a clear day with the soft sun spreading its warmth across the spectacular scene. French forces paraded toward the west side of the York-Hampton Road, the martial music of their Bourbon bands resounding with triumphant rhythms. Then the American troops stationed themselves opposite their allies on the surrender field. The patriots were not so perfect in formation and their regimental bands did not perform so grandly, yet these colonial soldiers were the symbol of a country that had conquered in its fight for freedom. They stood in long lines with the Continental forces in front and the militia units in back. Washington rode his favorite horse, Nelson, a light sorrel with white face and legs named after Thomas Nelson, Jr., who had presented the charger to the general in 1778.

As the group galloped down the lane between the allied armies, spectators studied the arrangement of American officers in the military formation. Solid General Benjamin Lincoln was second in command to General Washington. Corpulent General Henry Knox and handsome General Anthony Wayne were also in the forefront. Virginia citizens recognized the exuberant Marquis de Lafayette easily and were acquainted with the extravagant Baron Steuben arrayed in his bright medals. The crowd could not identify everyone, but they knew patriotic Governor Nelson, general of the militia, and the native Brigadier Generals Lawson, Muhlenberg, and Stevens of the Commonwealth.

General Rochambeau and his French entourage were aligned correctly across from the Americans awaiting the arrival of the British army. The allied columns were curious to catch a glimpse of Lord Cornwallis. At last they heard the rattling drums and the slow march of reluctant feet as the scarlet-clad British advanced from the town. The German mercenaries marched with precise order. Riding ahead of the defeated detachments was not Lord Cornwallis, but General Charles O'Hara, a handsome, ruddy Irishman of the Guards substituting for the sick and sulking earl. The deputy turned first toward General Rochambeau, but the Frenchman indicated General Washington as the guide, Count Dumas, interposed to point out the Commander-in-Chief. Unabashed, O'Hara smiled broadly, introduced himself, and made apologies for the absence of the British commander. General Washington then directed that his second in command, General Lincoln, would give the instructions for the formal surrender. The royal regiments were to proceed into the open plain where the French Hussars were encircled. British bands played the melancholy "The World Turned Upside Down" as the regulars moved slowly toward the surrender field. According to the terms, with flags cased, the embarrassed English and unemotional Hessian mercenaries marched with stuffed knapsacks, muskets, and rifles within the circle to ground their guns. Sullen soldiers were prevented from hurling their weapons down, but nothing could prevent the drunken ones from staggering through the maneuver. The British turned their eyes only toward the French victors, avoiding the American army. To capitulate to rebels infuriated the arrogant redcoats. Proud of the valiant patriots, General Lafayette signaled an American band to strike up "Yankee Doodle" and haughty English heads swung toward their conquerors. Observers of the occasion described in diaries that the British officers behaved rather badly, not facing the ordeal with fortitude but biting their lips, pouting, and crying. The victorious troops, they noted, were quite gallant to the vanquished, restraining from scoffing, slurs, and scorn.

The Commander-in-Chief invited General O'Hara to dinner that night, and the conquered general enjoyed the entertainment. Other Continental and French officers followed suit with a series of social affairs. A esprit de corps was established with the enemy with the approval of some officials and to the annoyance of others.

Washington offered congratulations to the allied armies in the General Orders of October 20. The French fleet and land forces were applauded first, as their assistance to the American army had been indispensable in achieving the triumphant victory. By blocking the British ships, the superior naval strength of the French vessels had clinched the colonial conquest.

General Washington wrote to Governor Nelson:

> . . . warmest terms his Excellency, Governor Nelson for the Aid he had derived from him and from the Militia under his Command to whose Activity, Emulation, & Courage much Applause is due; the Greatness of the Acquisition will be an ample Compensation for the Hardships and Hazards which they encountered with so much patriotism & firmness.[55]

Patrolling patriots still had their hands full to control rioting and looting by defeated, drunken redcoats.

Couriers rushed from camp with victory dispatches. The Congress first received the news from a report forwarded by Governor Thomas Sim Lee of Maryland that enclosed the express sent to Lee from Admiral de Grasse. It reached Philadelphia about 2:00 A.M. October 22. The Commander-in-Chief sent his restrained announcement by reliable aide Tench Tilghman, who sailed up the Chesapeake with the formal communication for the Continental Congress. Suffering from fever, the impatient young courier was annoyed because the boat ran aground and an unfavorable tide delayed him. The messenger hurried the last lap by horse, arriving with the official information October 24.

Governor Nelson also sent tidings to the Virginia delegates at Philadelphia. Dated October 20, 1781, the dispatch read:

> Gentlemen: It is with infinite pleasure I congratulate you on the Reduction of York & Gloucester, and the Capture of the whole British Army, under Lord Cornwallis. On the 17th, at the request of Lord Cornwallis, Hostilities ceased, & yesterday, the Garrison of York, amounting to upwards of two thousand and nine hundred effectives, rank and file, marched out and grounded their Arms. Their sick are almost seventeen hundred. The Garrison of Gloucester, & the men Killed during the Siege, are computed at near two thousand, so that the whole Loss sustained by the Enemy, on this Occasion must be between 6 and 7,000 men.
>
> *This Blow, I think must be a decisive one, it being out of Power of Great Britain to replace such a Number of Good Troops.* His Excellency Gen'l Washington's letter will inform you of the nature of the Capitulation, to which I must refer you, not yet having procured a copy of the Articles.[56]

Several aspects of the agreement pertaining to prisoners, refugees, the return of private property, and native persons who had joined the British forces fell to the civil authorities to resolve. Instructions were issued immediately by Governor Nelson, still exercising his extensive wartime powers. To Lord Cornwallis on October 20, Governor Nelson wrote:

> I have been informed that a number of Refugees from this State & also Negroes, are attempting to make their Escape by getting on Board the *Bonetta* Sloop of War. As they will endeavour to be concealed from your Lordship's Notice, till the Vessel sails. I have thought it necessary to make this Communication to you, that you may take Measure to prevent the State & Individuals from sustaining an Injury of this Nature.[57]

One of the defects of the British defense system at York Town had been insufficient officers, so Nelson knew the number should be small for those allowed to leave. Since the boat could hold about 250 people, it would be easy for a person to slip aboard the sloop unless Cornwallis stopped the exodus. Article 8 had stipulated that the British ship with its present captain and crew be put at the disposal of Lord Cornwallis to convey dispatches and such paroled soldiers that he chose to carry with him to New York.

The following day the Virginia Governor wrote Lord Cornwallis:

> I am informed that Lt. Col. Simcoe has refused to deliver up a certain Christopher Robinson, who now bears a Commission in his Corps, but who deserted from the actual service of the State.[58]

Robinson, a Middlesex County native, had been a student at the College of William and Mary when Benedict Arnold had invaded the state. He then left the College corps to receive a commission in Simcoe's Rangers. Nelson had no patience with Robinson's conduct, yet he refrained from expressing his personal opinion as he continued his letter to Cornwallis:

> The Articles of Capitulation cannot justify this Detention, and I shall by no means acquiesce in it. It is my wish to treat the Men, when the Fortune of War has put into our Power, with the Civility which (their situation claims) & it would give me Pain to be constrained in any Instance, to act in a different Manner.[59]

After the surrender of the Gloucester garrison, General Weedon had been occupied in rounding up refugees and taking in slaves that the British had seized. His report to Governor Nelson was answered with alacrity on October 21:

> The refugees you have taken may be sent over here, and also the negroes whose masters live south of York River, and you will be pleased to direct some person to give papers to such as belong to the north side, that they may be immediately returned to their owners. What we shall finally do with the sick and wounded prisoners, I have not yet determined. For the present, I shall order them to be guarded by the Militia of the County. All arms, except of the Guard Troops, are to be delivered to the conductor of the military stores.[60]

Nelson observed that the information Weedon reported "respecting negroes secreting themselves on board the Vessels" had already been relayed so orders had been given that all ships in the York River be searched.[61]

Over seven thousand British prisoners had surrendered to the allied armies on October 19. In a letter to General Lawson October 20, Governor Nelson instructed the officer:

> You will be pleased to take Command of the Militia ordered to conduct the British prisoners to their Stations. At Fredericksburg you will meet with the Garrison of Gloucester of which you will take Charge, together with the

Command of their Guard. One half of the Prisoners are to be stationed at Winchester, the other at Frederick Town, Maryland. Those allotted for Md., you will deliver to a Guard of that State on its Border; the other you will conduct to Winchester & so soon as Col. John Smith, Co. Lt. of Frederick can call out a sufficient Guard of the Militia of that & the adjacent Counties for which he has my Orders, you will deliver them up to him & discharge your Troops.[62]

The post script instructed the commander to use the power of impress if necessary to secure provisions.

CHAPTER TWENTY-FOUR

Postlude to Peace: 1781–1787

Citizens up and down the country celebrated the surrender at York Town with ringing bells, bonfires, illuminations, and cannon salutes. At balls and banquets people exulted over the event. Patriot officers observed the occasion with a festive *feu-de-joie*, drinking countless toasts to the triumph. In the minds of most men, as General Nelson asserted, the conquest of the British at York Town meant the end of the colonial struggle. General Washington, however, did not feel that the campaign had been concluded since the enemy still occupied New York and Charleston. In his opinion, the first great objective involved the American army's being able to take the field again; October 27, 1781, he wrote to Governor Nelson:

> I will candidly confess to your Excellency, that my only apprehension (which I wish may be groundless) is, lest the late important success, instead of exciting our exertions, as it ought to do, should produce such a relaxation in the prosecution of the war, as will prolong the calamities of it.[1]

Since the General Assembly of Virginia was to convene soon, the Commander-in-Chief suggested Governor Nelson urge the representatives to recruit more regiments to fill the quotas required from the state.

In the waning days of October while the executive attended to the endless duties of winding up the war, General Knox had been checking the British booty. According to the chief of the American artillery, his aides had counted over 7,000 arms and accouterments, 140 iron cannon, and 74 big brass and mortar guns confiscated from the enemy. Colonel Carrington, who had assembled artillery before for General Greene, chose suitable cannon for the southern commander. American army quartermaster Colonel Timothy Pickering requested cash to remove the captured stores from York Town, but Councilman George Webb remarked for the fourth time that the treasury of Virginia was exhausted by repeated advances to the Continental account.[2]

October 26 was so rainy and stormy that fatigue parties of the Pennsylvania Line could not fill in the trenches. Lieutenant Feltman and his friends played cards and drank wine through the evening, which was agreeable, but the diarist admitted the next morning, "I was very unwell from last night's carouse."[3]

The officers were to receive new outfits and were planning to purchase cloth from the merchants of York and Gloucester. By October 30, parcels of white superfine broadcloth and linens had been bought and the next day the agents were busy "completing our line with clothes," the lieutenant noted.[4]

According to his account, an accident on the afternoon of November 1 killed two men and wounded three soldiers. As a wagoner unloaded shells from his conveyance, the powder exploded killing him instantly and injuring an infantryman who died later.[5]

On the last day of October, General Lafayette wrote a letter of acknowledgment to Governor Nelson:

> Sir, Before leaving the State in which I had the honor to command the American Army I cannot refrain from presenting your Excellency with the homage of my gratitude and acknowledging the obligations which in a civil and military capacity I owe to your Excellency's assistance. The anxiety I feel to obtain the approbation of the people of Virginia induces me to request a very great favor from your Excellency. It is, that you would be pleased to lay before the honorable Assembly an account of my conduct in executing their recommendations for the impressment of horses. As this was done often in sight of the enemy, and sometimes, as it were from under their hands, it has been altogether impossible, in every occasion to preserve all those forms which I could have wished, but whatever has been done by my orders, will, I hope, appear to have been conducted in the best method which the moment could admit.[6]

The executive understood the exigencies of war required urgent action; he also realized that many citizens could not comprehend the demands necessary for defense.

Governor Nelson explained the instructions pertaining to the British prisoners to Governor Thomas Sim Lee of Maryland in a letter of October 21, so that he could make the "necessary preparations for their reception" and orders were forwarded to the commissary at Fredericksburg to "draw some days" provisions for the "approximate 6,000 captives."[7]

About two thousand British soldiers were sick and wounded, and the Governor ordered the county lieutenant at Gloucester to direct a militia detachment "under a discreet Officer" to guard the captives until some other disposition could be arranged.[8]

By November 3, British and German soldiers who had recovered from their wounds walked toward Fredericksburg escorted by Colonel Philip Van Cortland and the Second New York Regiment. About 1,300 sick and wounded men still remained in the hospital at Gloucester and were unable to march. This information was relayed to Governor Nelson by the Commander-in-Chief with an order to secure boats and wagons to convey the convalescents to Todd's Bridge and on to land at Fredericksburg or Hobbs Hole.[9]

The next day General Washington wrote the Governor to make arrangements to "Deposit all Arms & Ammunition for Musquetry brought from Northward & taken from the Enemy, at Westham in this State, or in its Neighborhood, supplies formed for the Southern Army, or issued to the State, in case of another Invasion."[10] He was advised to avoid the salt house, to station twenty-four men to secure the magazine, and to settle the stores in Richmond for the present.

This assignment would have to be handled by a subordinate as the extraordinary exertions of autumn had exhausted the Governor's health. Nelson had been indefatigable in his efforts toward winning the war. The overworked official went to Offley Hoo, his home in Hanover County, in November.

At Richmond the two remaining Council members were arranging for the meeting of the General Assembly on November 5; Jacquelin Ambler attended to the distribution of Governor Nelson's proclamation calling the convention, which for some unknown reason did not reach the Council chamber until October 26. Ambler wrote that he was pressed for time:

> The short Space of Time now remaining before the Day fixt on for the meeting . . . I have written pressingly to the printer to strike off three hundred Copies immediately . . . entreat you to have a sufficient number of Expresses ready in the morning in order to transmit them to the Counties.[11]

The only other Councilman on hand, George Webb, was worried about the overcrowded prison. There were forty-five prisoners, and the capacity of the structure was just half that number. Consequently, some captives were kept in the open yard "exposed to the Inclemency of the Weather, many of them must inevitably perish unless they can be put under shelter," he asserted to the commanding officer of the Henrico militia.[12] He asked the official to furnish a guard of sixteen men to assist in the safekeeping of the arrested men. Many of the captives in custody were Tories awaiting trial.

Webb wrote David Jameson on November 2 that he and Jacquelin Ambler had been the only Council members in the capital city for the past ten days and explained the resignations and removal of the other representatives:

Colonel Fleming has sent his Letter of resignation. General Lewis is dead. [The old frontier fighter had died September 26.] Mr. Hardy is gone to Carolina & Colonel McDowell left us with an intention to go to Kentucky and not return to the Board.[13]

He also revealed that Governor Nelson was suffering from a "very dangerous Illness," which would prevent his attending the Assembly for some weeks, Webb predicted.

Through November Governor Nelson was attempting to handle the public affairs of the state with the assistance of aide Robert Andrews.

Major John Nelson began his letter of November 3 to his cousin Thomas with this sentence:

> Your indisposition, when I was at your house the other day prevented my mentioning to you the many things relative to my Corps, the situation of which, at present, is truly distressing.[14]

The officer revealed that the recruits were naked and should receive winter clothing, and with the danger of smallpox felt that they should be inoculated. Lack of "clothes & Blankets without which they must starve at Winchester the cause of uneasiness principally arises from the appearance of the Small-Pox."[15]

Though his indisposition made the executive defer a decision that favored a certain firm, Governor Nelson wrote David Ross November 3 concerning the compensation for the soldiers of the state:

> It was my Intention that the State Officers concerned in the Siege not on Continental Establishment, should be equally benefited by the Capture of York with the other officers of the Army.
>
> I am also desirous that the Militia who were in Service during the Siege, & who contributed their Share toward the Reduction of York should receive some particular Compensation for the Fatigues & Dangers they may have undergone.[16]

As supplies were secured from the defeated enemy and would be sold, the executive desired the agent to make extensive purchases for the advantage of the militia.

Communications from county officials about accumulated cattle, work animals, wheat, and old rifles poured into the Hanover plantation. All the correspondents sought advice from Governor Nelson for the distribution of the articles. The quantity testified to the Governor's energy in securing supplies for the troops and to the efforts of the citizens in assisting the cause. Secretary Andrews sent numerous letters to the local leaders for his Excellency:

There being no longer a Necessity for making use of extraordinary Means for the Subsistence of the Army, the Governor has directed me to express to you his Acknowledgment for the Assistance you have given to the Public at a Time, when it was much wanted, & also to inform you that the common Methods of procuring Supplies are now sufficient to answer all Purposes.[17]

Among the long list of men who received commendation for their exertions were General Robert Lawson, Colonel Richard Henry Lee, and Colonel Barbour.

The executive received more reports citing grievances, uneasiness, and injustices that accompanied the inevitable aftermath of war. A typical example was the salary situation of the soldiers, as expressed by Captain Nathaniel Terry of the Tenth Virginia Regiment, who wrote the Governor from Halifax County November 4:

Sir—As I have not had a farthing of my wages since November 1779 (except 2/3 of a months pay) you will therefore readily suppose that I must be in great need. Your Friendship which I have so often experienced upon former Occasions, induces me, to hope you will continue your favors. Now Sir, if you can possibly procure my wages & transmit the Cash by Colonel Coleman, it will not only be serving a suffering soldier now a prisoner but lay me under everlasting obligations.[18]

In all probability Governor Nelson responded to this appeal by assisting the captain from his private funds, as was his generous custom. The executive had just expressed his concern for compensation of the soldiers of the state and was striving to relieve their condition.

The attention of the administrator was also directed to the hospital at Williamsburg. The elegant Palace, in which the executive had often dined and danced in the carefree days before the war, now housed the injured in a makeshift medical station that was understaffed and short of surgical supplies. It was crowded with war wounded from the York siege, making conditions for the troops intolerable. Governor Nelson was informed of these facts by Colonel Timothy Pickering, quartermaster general of the American army. In his mid-thirties, the tall, stern man from Massachusetts had served in the conflict since 1775 as militia commander, adjutant general, and member of the Board of War. The experienced soldier wrote from Williamsburg on November 8:

Upon arrival found Americans sick in a suffering condition. Wood and straw are most wanted at present. . . . upward 50 teams to transport & other stores & death of our working oxen have rendered it impossible to have a competent number of teams at this post for the supply of the hospital. Unfortunately too the subalterns command of Continental troops, which I requested might be stationed here for the service of the hospital were withdrawn when the camp broke up left sick to shift for themselves. Doctor informs me that there are three large rooms at the Palace destitute of fire places cannot remain in them unless stoves can be procured.[19]

Throughout October Governor Nelson and Colonel Thomas Newton of Norfolk communicated with each other about food for Count de Grasse and the French fleet. On November 2, Newton asked, "What to do with the cattle in pastures wasting daily expect many will die . . . horses also left by the enemy will perish if they are not sold."[20]

Two longer letters from Newton written on the tenth were filled with fury:

> The officers of Princess Anne County seem afraid to do their Duty. I think if some spirited steps are not taken & examples made of the Tories there, this County will neither get taxes or any thing else from them. Murder is committed there & goes unpunished, though, the Justices know the persons who did it; I do not wish to persecute, but if examples are not now made of several who have actually been in arms with the British, every person will find it their interest to be tories as they can then make money on both sides & too many in the lower parts lean that way.[21]

This serious situation weighed on his mind, as evidenced by his second letter:

> The Tories & refugees below are still unpunished to the great dissatisfaction of the well affected, many of them were in arms plundering & now live in affluence while those who were engaged in their Country's service are ruined.[22]

Governor Nelson received a three-page report from General Rochambeau at York dated November 6, outlining the plan of occupation by the French forces for the next few months. The commander had consulted Lieutenant Governor Jameson and reached agreement on the articles. Forage would not be taken from the people who only had a "sufficient quantity to feed their cattle" for the winter. Exact receipts would be given and an agent appointed to receive demands for forage and horses previously taken for the troops during the siege, though this matter would be difficult to straighten out since Lord Cornwallis and the American officers had also seized supplies.[23] The French commander stated:

> I have quartered the Legion de Lauzun at Hampton; I propose to put 4 batailloons in York and Glocester but as the British sick and prisoners, take up yet a great deal of room, I shall be obliged to put a batailloon at Halfway house, until the British hospitals be evacuated: Upon that object I earnestly beg your Excellency's assistance to have boats impressed, that they may be

transported to Tod's bridge and then to go upon Rappahannock river, according to the dispositions made by General Washington, for I confess to your Excellency, they are very bad company to keep with us, and I would wish to be speedily delivered of them. I will put 4 batailloons in Williamsburgh, with a part of the Corps royal of Artillery, the rest of that corps will go to Westpoint with the heavy artillery. I beg of your Excellency to send to Williamsburgh a trusty person to exercise the power of the State, in many little matters that may require it, and to be witness of the discipline we shall observe.[24]

General Rochambeau recommended that Colonel Dabney and his detachment remain at Portsmouth a couple of months "to observe on the coast the movements of the British and keep quiet the persons who may not be well affected to their country." He intended to establish two posts between Williamsburg and Richmond to expedite correspondence with "Your Excellency and to forward with more speed the intelligence you will receive from the Southward: I will likewise put two posts more; one at Ruffin's ferry, the other at Tod's bridge to correspond with the Bowlinggreen, Philadelphy, and General Washington."[25] He asked Governor Nelson to issue a proclamation to be printed in the public papers so the inhabitants would bring the provisions to the markets at Williamsburg, York, and Hampton and promised "full protection" to the sellers. A postscript of the dispatch disclosed, "Count de Grasse put to sea, on the 4th instant, at three o'clock in the afternoon."[26]

General Washington had attempted in vain to persuade the French admiral to assist the Americans in attacking the British encampment at Charleston. De Grasse only agreed to stay in the Chesapeake Bay area with his ships until a greater part of the American troops had been put on board transports. The Continental soldiers sailed away from the Virginia shore toward the north on November 3.

By November 5, General Washington was on his way to Williamsburg where he stopped to see the sick soldiers before riding to Eltham, Mrs. Burwell Bassett's (Martha Washington's sister) plantation approximately twenty-five miles north of Williamsburg near the Pamunkey and Mattapony rivers. Sorrow hovered over the household where "Jackie" Custis was suffering with a burning fever. In September Washington's handsome stepson had accompanied the Commander-in-Chief to his headquarters at York Town and had contracted camp fever. Sent to the residence of his aunt to recuperate, twenty-six-year-old John Parke Custis died a few hours after the arrival of his stepfather. General Washington grieved over his loss but faced the circumstance with forced calmness, comforting Custis's weeping wife left with four small children, and trying to console Martha Washington, now childless.[27]

A few days later, on November 11, a Peace Ball was held with festive ceremony at the tavern owned by General Weedon in Fredericksburg. Doubtless many prominent persons were present on the occasion, but neither General Washington nor General Nelson, nor their wives, attended the affair. The Commander-in-Chief had arrived in the town to see his mother, who was absent. Consequently, the capricious old lady was not led onto the floor by her famous son. The names of Governor Nelson and his wife were noted in the guest list, but certainly the couple would not have been able to attend the dance. General Nelson, ill throughout the month, was attempting to carry on the necessary correspondence for the Commonwealth through his aide.[28]

After receiving General Rochambeau's report with assurances to protect the rights of the people, Governor Nelson was distressed to read a detailed account about the destructive actions of foreign forces at York. A November 16 communication from his friend William Reynolds was filled with complaints against the French troops who had taken possession of almost all the houses in the town:

> Some of the Inhabitants are turn'd out and others with their family's confin'd to a room, a situation little better than a prison. Mr. Mitchell could not obtain part of your house on your order. Mrs. Powell let his family have two rooms at her house, But Count Veomenil who commands at this place turn'd them out of one. The Inhabitants in this Neck are plunder'd, and some of them left destitute of the necessary of life, corn. It gives me real concern to say our friends seem disposed to make the situation of the People more miserable than the British left them.[29]

The outraged citizen alleged that the action at York was not singular; consequently, he expected the executive would receive similar reports from other towns on this "disagreeable subject." Reynolds also predicted:

> Unless some measure is adopted to convince those Gentlemen that they were sent to assist, not distress us, we in this part of the Country may bid adieu to liberty, property, and every thing dear to Man—the Civil Power is done away, and a lock is no bar to the curiosity of a Petty Officer.[30]

The constant need to respond to these complaints was not conducive to Governor Nelson's recovery, and the muggy air of November aggravated his asthmatic condition. Between three and four in the morning, he was often awakened by labored breathing and a choking congestion in his chest. It was inevitable that he would not improve from his illness without complete rest. Toward the end of the month, the executive explained his situation in a short statement to his kinsman Benjamin Harrison, Speaker of the Virginia House of Delegates:

> The very low state of health to which I am reduced, and from which I

have little expectation of soon recovering, makes it my duty to resign the government, that the State may not suffer from want of an executive.[31]

Although Governor Nelson had called the autumn Assembly to convene November 5, not enough delegates arrived to make a quorum until two weeks later. Then a series of resignations confronted the lawmakers as well as applications for leaves of absence. Because of his health, Patrick Henry asked for leave on November 21 and left for Leatherwood.[32]

On Monday, November 26, a ballot was held to consider Nelson's resignation as well as the vacancies of three Council members: Andrew Lewis, deceased; William Fleming and John Walker, resigned. On Thursday and Friday the report was read again and Speaker Benjamin Harrison was elected Governor of the Commonwealth of Virginia.[33]

The representatives were still faced with the resolution passed during the summer at the Staunton session to investigate the conduct of Governor Jefferson in prosecuting the war. Jefferson's opponents, including George Nicholas and Patrick Henry, were not so avid at this time. Accusations of inaction when the enemy invaded Virginia and failure to act when he could not assemble the Council for advice had faded with the York Town victory. When the duly appointed committee met to consider the charges, Jefferson answered questions candidly and the Assembly voted to exonerate him.

During December, Virginia's citizens, weary of war, were incensed over the impressment of property. They censured Governor Nelson for his alacrity in seizing supplies. Some persons of Prince William County presented a petition accusing Nelson of impressing supplies without the advice of the Council and voiced objections to the embargo laid on various commodities. The delegates argued about the charges.

Word of the wrangling reached Thomas Nelson and despite his illness, he rode to Richmond from Hanover County on December 22 to answer accusations. After he had explained the actions he had taken to protect the state and supply the allied army and militia units, the members approved his actions during the crisis as "productive of the general good and warranted by necessity . . . Thomas Nelson be and hereby in the fullest manner indemnified and exonerated from all penalties and damages, which might have accrued to him from the same."[34]

Legislators with logical minds must have mused on the eccentricities of the electorate. Governor Jefferson had been censured because he would not decide on defense measures without the consent of the Council, and Governor Nelson had been criticized for acting with too much alacrity without the advice of the Council.

Thomas Nelson, Jr., returned to his home in upper Hanover County during late December. Lucy urged her husband to rest in order to recover his health and kept the children from disturbing him. Though his illness made him ineffectual, it was difficult for the active man to remain at home. Enforced relaxation gave him time to think, and his usual optimism faded into frustration when he assessed his situation. He had neglected private affairs for public activities. The family firm, which he had been forced to close, still showed thousands of pounds unpaid by creditors. By pledging his personal funds as security for the state, the zealous patriot had incurred heavy indebtedness. Considerable sums of money had also been lent to his cousin Carter Braxton.

In the wintry dusk, General Nelson sat by the roaring fire and reflected on his twenty years of service to the state. As Burgess, representative to the House of Delegates, member of the Congress, Brigadier General of the militia forces, and wartime Governor, he had answered the call of his country and reached the pinnacle of positions. In his dedication to duty, the forty-two-year-old statesman and soldier had made great sacrifices for the colonial cause, yet in the upheaval of the critical war period, many Virginians were perplexed and upset, so accusation, rather than appreciation, became the reward of an ungrateful republic to Governor Nelson.

While Professor Robert Andrews had been his aide, Thomas had talked with the teacher about further schooling for his sons. The College of William and Mary had closed during the conflict. Soldiers instead of scholars had crowded the campus. Consequently, the education of William, now past eighteen, and Thomas, seventeen in December, had been interrupted. Philip, Francis, and Hugh were all teenagers needing additional instruction.

Though Offley Hoo was not so spacious as the handsome Nelson house at York Town, there was no lack of hospitality in the home. Eminent visitors to the former Virginia executive testified to the cordiality of the family.

General Rochambeau and his aide Baron von Closen arrived after ten o'clock in the evening of February 17, 1782. They had lost their way along the rutty roads from Richmond. In his diary von Closen described their stay with the Nelsons:

> This worthy man gave us the most cordial reception possible: we were served an excellent supper, and immediately afterward retired exhausted fatigued.

The next morning the French official recorded:

> After an excellent breakfast, we inspected the farm and the approaches to the house, which is rather pretty. There are two others nearby and many Negroes cabins.
>
> General Nelson was one of the richest persons in Virginia, had 700 Negroes before the war, he has now only 80 or 100.[35]

(While Nelson had sold some slaves or lost a few to the royal raiders, he still owned approximately 400 blacks to work 20,000 acres of land.) The estimation of Thomas Nelson and his wife that von Closen continued was correct:

> He is a man of the greatest integrity, devoted to the cause of his compatriots and served his fatherland with zeal and disinteredness. Character of an upright man even at the cost of his fortune, which has been considerably reduced. At the siege of York Town he commanded the militia (the duty of every provisional Governor in America). He had two farms in the vicinity of the town, wch has been completely burned, pillaged and plundered. He is as good a Governor as he is a soldier, citizen, and father. His family is one of the happiest with wch I am acquainted: His wife, who is no longer young, has 13 living children and is respected for the upbringing she gives them. She is an excellent and thrifty housekeeper and provided very good meals for us. Although Virginians in general are noted for their hospitality and sociability, they particularly excel in these respects in the region along the James River.[36]

(Von Closen was confused on the number of the Nelson children as there were ten at the time.) The diarist then described Secretary Nelson:

> We met Governor Nelson's uncle, a worthy and respectable old man with white hair who had been the King's Secretary for the State of Virginia before the Revolution. He is regarded as one of the most learned men in his country in all fields of knowledge. He is generally revered and esteemed.[37]

He recorded that the Secretary's residence three miles from Hanover Court House was called the *Hornquarter* because at that quarter the horn blew to summon the slaves to start work in the fields. Von Closen was impressed by one of the pretty daughters-in-law at the home and drew picture portraits of the ladies. The house, located beyond the Mattapony River was not remarkable, he wrote, but had a charming garden. The stables were the best stocked for studs in Virginia and supplied superb horses for the countryside, the visitor noted.

Another generous characteristic of his host was revealed in the diary:

> Must note here how much we have appreciated the kindness of Governor Nelson, who, not content with having given us his carriage to travel in for 160 miles on rather bad roads even tried to press us to keep it as far as Williamsburg: but the General Rochambeau sent it back from Richmond.[38]

As General Nelson began to improve in warmer weather, he rode across the rolling hills to his plantations, Mont Air, Mallory's, Long Row, and Smiths. As he viewed the land in the spring with the grain crops depleted by the demands of the war, no doubt he wondered how many missives he had written to secure flour for the forces. Tiny shoots of green were sprouting from the corn slaves had sown in the soil. Nelson glanced at the numerous tobacco beds placed four feet apart and piled with brush to protect the plants. His holdings in Hanover County comprised about thirteen thousand acres. Tracts totaling more than seven thousand acres were located in Prince William, York, James City, and Loudon counties.[39] Several superintendents managed the properties, supervised about four hundred slaves, cared for the hundreds of horses, hogs, cattle, and sheep, operated the mills, and administered the accounts for the approximate twenty-thousand-acre undertaking. When William and Thomas accompanied their father on a trip to the fields, they learned that he relied on the opinions of the overseers relating to crops, slaves, and stock. The integrity of the persons hired to handle these huge estates was an essential characteristic for the enterprise to make a profit.

Another French visitor rode up the Virginia countryside to the Nelson residence in the springtime and along the way found forage wanting for his horse and the land wasted by the ravages of war. General Chastellux wrote in his journal that he set out on his journey at nine in the morning and reached Offley Hoo in the high hills at one o'clock in the afternoon. General Nelson was absent on April 10, so Lucy and her mother-in-law welcomed the stranger, "with all the politeness, ease and cordiality natural to the family, but as in America the ladies are never thought sufficient to do the honours of the house."[40]

Although the war had wrought changes in the household, one custom was continued by the Nelsons and the Chevalier commented there was "an excellent breakfast at nine in the morning, a sumptuous dinner at two o'clock, tea and punch in the afternoon and an elegant little supper." The dining routine "divided the day most happily," the diarist pronounced, "for those whose stomachs unprepared."[41]

Secretary Nelson was on hand with two of his sons and two of the General's brothers. The Chevalier commented that the Secretary "was an old man very gouty, who related with a serene countenance what the effect had been of the French batteries in front of Yorktown. . . . he had white locks, noble figure, stature."[42]

Young Mrs. William Nelson stayed in bed as she had suffered a miscarriage and her sister, Miss Taliferro, was also there to wait on the patient.

Stormy weather kept the company indoors for two days and the Marquis marveled, "It is worth observing on this occasion, where fifteen or twenty people (four of whom were strangers to the family or country) were assembled, bad weather forced inside—not a syllable about play." That astounded the visitor, as he attested when inclement weather forced crowds inside in France, games and gambling would have been their recreation. He complimented Miss Taliferro's singing: "Her charming voice and the artless simplicity of her singing, were a substitute for taste, if not taste itself." The diarist thought nothing but study was wanting to develop her natural talent.

Since the family lived in the forest, the chevalier concluded that the young lady had learned to sing from the birds when she could hear them above the howling of the hounds for her father was a great fox hunter. He scrutinized the shelves and noted that the library was well stocked with fine French authors as well as good British books.[43]

Chastellux also recorded that General Nelson was a "good and gallant man ever behaved with the utmost politeness to the French . . . conducted himself with the courage of a brave soldier and the zeal of a good citizen."[44]

The French official discerned that the former executive was worn out by the campaign but fatigue also resulted from the ingratitude of his fellow citizens, and Chastellux stated he was "sorry to add after Nelson called forth every resource exerted every means to furnish Washington with horses, carriages and provisions only recompense of labours hatred of a great part of his fellow-citizens."[45]

Entertaining foreigners was an exciting event for the Nelson family, but other company visited frequently. Representatives riding to Richmond for the spring session stopped by to see General Nelson. On Tuesday, May 8, 1782, the Convention opened. That same day baby Judith, the eleventh and last of Thomas and Lucy's children, was born.[46]

The long-time lawmaker soon heard news of the House of Delegates, where legislators were engaged in debates concerning the ceding of land from the Virginia territory to the United States. In January 1781, the state had agreed to cede the claims and afterward Maryland had signed the Articles of Confederation. Under its charter, the domain of Virginia extended from the Atlantic Ocean to the Mississippi River and stretched to the northwest around the lakes region; separate states were to be set up from that large land area. The General Assembly appointed a commission to study and survey claims to solve the boundary dispute between Pennsylvania and Virginia and asked General Nelson to serve on the committee. He declined and doubtless recommended his aide Robert Andrews for the duty; and the professor accepted the post.[47]

The Commonwealth was still trying to raise a satisfactory cavalry corps. On Thursday, May 31, a resolution was offered to organize the corps under Major John Nelson to be composed of sixty men supported by two infantry companies with one hundred men. On Monday, June 11, the formal bill to establish the corps was introduced.[48]

Since specie was still scarce, the Assemblymen passed an act to allow landowners to divide their taxes into two payments for the year, yet the officials still had difficulty collecting the duties, for debt and depreciation of the dollar still oppressed the people. Throughout the countryside the cry was the same as citizens complained about prices, and creditors clamored for repayment of money lent to the government.

As spring slipped into summer, General Nelson attempted to organize his own accounts, a tiring and frustrating task. He discovered little change in the long list of debtors on the ledgers of the family firm. The books still showed people owed thousands of pounds for goods bought before the war. Payment in paper money could not compensate for the original cost of the purchases, but tradesmen often reasoned that any type of credit column looked better than writing off an account completely.

The debt to the Hunts still hung over Nelson's head. Before breaking the bonds with Britain, Thomas had written the brothers in London that the Penrith property in Scotland would be sold and the funds marked for the English firm. Eventually, he was able to effect this plan.

When General Nelson scrutinized the papers stacked before him, he real-ized that his personal indebtedness had become quite involved. He had paid his own expenses while serving the state and had dipped into his own purse to help outfit the volunteer cavalry corps he had recruited in 1778. Later George Dabney testified that General Nelson had raised and equipped the cavalry at his own expense and had furnished horses from his estate for the corps. The plantation manager further affirmed that forage and provisions required along the march toward Philadelphia were paid for by the Gen-eral.[49]

During the desperate period of invasion in 1780, Thomas Nelson had literally begged people to lend money to the state by pledging his own funds and property as a guaranty for the government. In the exigency of the mo-ment when money was needed promptly to expedite the war effort, the gen-erous patriot had paid for products. Tobacco had also been borrowed from the citizens to bolster the credit of the Commonwealth. Slaves were taken as payment for the bonds. In innumerable transactions, exact expenditures were not always recorded correctly. Compensation for food and forage, arti-cles and animals, became complicated.

After Lucy gave birth to Judith, the couple celebrated their twentieth wedding anniversary the last of July. Thirteen children had been born to the union, two stillborn, but the remaining eleven lived to maturity, a remark-able record for the era. Lucy deserved the compliments of the colonials who praised mothers who produced the most progeny.

The sixth baby and last little daughter had been born to the Jeffersons in May. Unlike Lucy, Martha Jefferson recovered slowly from pregnancies. De-clining steadily through the summer, she died in September. Thomas Jeffer-son was so saddened that he stayed in his mountaintop residence as almost a recluse for many months.[50]

As General Nelson attempted to straighten out obligations, he deter-mined to collect a definite debt owed him by his cousin Carter Braxton. After Carter had reached Philadelphia in 1776 as a representative to the Congress to relieve Thomas, he had asked Thomas to secure a loan of £2,000. The debt had dragged on for years. Since Nelson was desperately in debt, he notified the York County clerk to commence legal proceedings to recover the money. Braxton was commanded to appear in chancery court on August 3, 1782, to answer for the account under penalty of £100. Provision was made that Nelson would receive 1,500 acres of property in York County provided Braxton had not paid the loan by April 1, 1783. He did not fulfill the terms. In December 1784, General Nelson told authorities to foreclose the mortgage on the land.[51] No satisfactory settlement was ever made to Thomas Nelson.

Once again the constituents of the community elected their foremost citizen as representative to the House of Delegates convening at Richmond. Arriving late in the autumn of 1782 for the Assembly, Nelson was not active at the session. He missed his friend Patrick Henry. The delegates complained about the high cost of food and rent charged in the capital. Landlords were loath to take paper bills for lodging, but few members had any hard money.[52]

As General Nelson conversed with his colleagues in the cold chambers of the frame Capitol on Cary Street, they inquired about his indisposition and could see that the frequent spells of sickness had taken toll of his strength. Colonel Innes had suffered a severe stomach disorder and had an attack of jaundice that turned his complexion a yellowish color. He was representing the citizens of Williamsburg at the Convention. The statesmen spoke of John Page with sympathy as the Gloucester legislator had lost his second son, victim of a drowning accident.[53]

Across the Atlantic the British ministers who had managed the war had resigned and were rewarded with pensions and peerages. George III was disillusioned at the division of his people. Englishmen were disgruntled at the expense the conflict had cost, and the revenue lost by the revolt of the American colonies. Although the King relied on Lord North, finally the Prime Minister persuaded the monarch it was past time for him to relinquish the post so he resigned in March 1782.

News of the peace negotiations in Paris reached the representatives at Richmond. On the last day of November, the negotiators had signed a temporary treaty. The Continental Congress received a report before Christmas of 1782 that a British commission had been authorized to talk with the commissioners from the United States of America concerning complete independence.[54]

The members of the Virginia Assembly were aware that the royal regiments had abandoned Charleston by the middle of December, a development that did not surprise General Nelson. He had declared that the blow dealt the British troops at York Town had been so decisive that it was out of their power to replace so many soldiers or to raise another army.

By the spring of 1783, the official text of the Treaty of Paris was brought by Captain Joshua Barney of the ship *Washington* to the Congress at Philadelphia. It confirmed the formal cessation of hostilities between Great Britain and the United States of America.[55]

The tenuous power and prestige of the Continental Congress crumbled as the delegates wrestled with the problems of the postwar period. Inflation intensified their attempts at solutions. A pair of shoes cost $100, a barrel of flour, $1,500.[56] Discontinuing the issuance of paper currency had not solved the economic problem. Neither had the bank of North America authorized by the Congress. Robert Morris, as superintendent of finance, had recommended its founding in 1781. By 1782, it was incorporated and its funds secured by specie, so the notes issued were sound, yet Congress was still destitute of cash and credit. Funds from France and loans from other countries had been exhausted. The central government needed sterling to guarantee a stable monetary system. Requisitions for raising sound revenue from the states had failed. The republic was facing collapse though Continental troops had triumphed. Cash, credit, and collections formed a three-fold predicament for the Assemblymen trying to pay off the soldiers' claims, struggling to meet an enormous public debt, and wanting to regain the respect of their countrymen.

An impost on imports had been proposed several months previously allowing Congress to collect a five per cent customs duty on goods purchased abroad. Fearing central authority, the Founding Fathers had stipulated in the Articles of Confederation that all the states must approve the acts. The representatives of twelve states ratified the revenue tax with reservations, but Rhode Island rejected it.

Among the delegates in the Congress disappointed at the defeat of the duty measure was James Madison of Virginia. The thirty-two-year-old scholarly statesman was well aware of the weakness of the Continental Congress functioning under the Articles of Confederation. Through his writings and speaking, Madison had steadfastly supported a strong federal system of government. While a commission was sent from the Congress to reason with contrary Rhode Island, a second blow was struck to the bill when Virginia repealed its ratification of the revenue act. The nationalists, however, did not surrender their fight to secure funds for the Continental treasury. Madison and his friend and mentor Thomas Jefferson continued a spirited correspondence in code about public and private matters, particularly in the spring of 1783. It was anticipated that the impost act would be presented again for consideration at the May meeting of the Virginia Assembly. Jefferson emerged from his mountaintop retreat mourning his wife's death to ride to Richmond to lobby for the legislation. On May 7, he wrote Madison from Tuckahoe that he had been in the neighborhood a fortnight associating and conversing with the representatives regarding their stand on the revenue plan. His cousin Attorney Edmund Randolph would co-operate, but Jefferson predicted that Arthur Lee, his brother Richard Henry Lee, and Mann

Page would be against the act. Then Jefferson affirmed, "In their favour will probably be Tyler, Tazewell, Genl. Nelson, William Nelson, Nicholas, & a Mr. Stuart, a young man from the westward." Still irritated over the part Patrick Henry had played in investigating his wartime administration, Jefferson commented critically in cipher, "Henry as usual is involved in mystery; Should the popular tide run strongly in either direction, he will fall in with it." He also stated Henry would have a struggle with his hatred of the Lees on the matter.[57] A controversy did develop between the two factions as soon as the Assemblymen arrived in the capital for the Convention May 12. Patrick Henry promptly nominated John Tyler for Speaker of the House of Delegates, and George Nicholas seconded the motion. Richard Henry Lee was nominated for the post, but Tyler won by an overwhelming majority.[58]

When General Nelson arrived at the Assembly, he noticed many newcomers from the upper region among the representatives, yet there were familiar faces of friends among the Assemblymen as he presented his youngest brother William to the parliamentarians with pride. Looking at twenty-two-year-old Billy, the forty-four-year-old Thomas recalled that he had embarked on his own political career at the same age when first elected a Burgess from York County after returning from Britain in 1761. Billy had been born in 1760 while his eldest brother was still in England acquiring his education. Now William was a mature man, married, admitted to the bar as an attorney, and attending the Assembly as a delegate from James City County.[59]

The revenue measure met with difficulty in the session, so the final vote was postponed until the fall meeting.

On May 19, 1783, General Nelson was appointed chairman of the committee on trade. Soon he was banging his gavel for order as controversial opinions arose. Heated debates resounded through the hall when Patrick Henry proposed reopening trade with England. Eloquently, he offered a resolution to repeal the acts that prohibited commercial relations with the English. The legislators were aroused over his liberal attitude. Representatives remembered vividly the ravages of the British throughout the Virginia region. Speaker Tyler's blue eyes snapped as he voiced his opposition to the measure.[60]

Serving as chairman of defense for the state, General Nelson attempted to alert the Assemblymen to maintain adequate militia troops throughout Virginia. Indifference rather than interest was the reaction since the war was won. Nevertheless, the representatives recommended internal improvements and resolved to construct roads to the western section of the state and to connect the waterways by building canals.[61]

Some members had their minds on celebrations to commemorate the peace treaty. Representatives from the Tidewater region were anxious to attend the grand parade planned in Williamsburg on Thursday, May 1. In

April Governor Harrison had issued a proclamation with the order of the procession for the great day. Appointed attendants were to lead the assemblage, "Supporting the staffs decorated with Ribbons, etc. The Herald mounted on a Gelding neatly Caparisoned." Following with other attendants, the sergeant bearing the mace, the mayor, and other officials were to continue in formation, two by two, walking together down Duke of Gloucester Street. Citizens would convene at the Court House at one o'clock summoned by a bell. After the proclamation announcing the peace treaty was read, "Bells at the Church, College, & Capitol are to ring in peal," and then the parade would proceed to the College where the proclamation would be repeated. The observers of the joyous occasion were to return to the Capitol and "make proclamation there and from thence to the Raleigh & pass the rest of the Day." [62]

Groups of gentlemen gathered at Gault's Tavern at Richmond in the dusk of June nights. Talk of trade and taxes, claims and cessions echoed from the ordinary as the officials drank their beer and brandy. As Thomas strolled toward the tavern with his brother William, he noted numerous changes in the capital. Shops lined the thoroughfare of the growing town. Signs announcing the services of tailors, tanners, saddlers, shoemakers, attorneys, physicians, and apothecaries flapped in front of the buildings. The high prices charged for food caused constant complaints. Sprawling Richmond had become a crowded city with no sanitation system, so the stench of refuse pervaded the atmosphere, and flies swarmed like a plague over the place.

If the Nelson clan called on their cousin Benjamin Harrison who lived in the large plank house on Shockoe Hill provided for the Governor, they found the executive mansion did not compare to the elegant Palace at Williamsburg. Governor Henry and Governor Jefferson had also lived there during their terms of office, but Governor Nelson had not. That grand dwelling had burned to the ground in 1781.

Before the Assembly adjourned, the representatives of the Tidewater region sponsored a resolution to remove the capital from Richmond back to Williamsburg. General Nelson and his brother William supported the proposal, but it failed to pass. Although he was disappointed at the defeat of the measure, General Nelson decided to move his family back to Williamsburg. His brick home at York was still unsuitable to live in. It had been damaged during the siege, and the French soldiers who used it as headquarters after the surrender had abused the ancestral home.

Through the fair weather, workmen had been repairing and improving the closets, stairway, fireplaces and nursery of the large rectangular frame residence on Francis Street in Williamsburg. Humphrey Harwood listed in his ledger that repairs were made to the kitchen, smokehouse, dairy, and laundry. There was a little lodging back of the big house on Lot 26 and four small structures on Lot 27. General Nelson purchased a piece of property on the south side of Capitol Square from his friend John Blair September 1, 1783.[63]

In addition to the Nelson's immediate family of eleven children ranging from twenty-year-old William down to infant Judith, there were slaves and servants in the cavalcade returning to the old capital. Records of 1783 listed Bob, Cooper, George, Pompey, and George Dean as tithables and reported that General Nelson had three slaves baptized at Williamsburg.[64] While Lucy supervised the servants, Thomas talked with the townspeople about the opportunities of trade since the Treaty of Peace had become official. Only optimistic young men were eager to take a chance on commerce. Experienced businessmen still felt that the uncertain economy with its scarcity of sterling made an enterprise too risky.

Merchant John Greenhow had not moved from his location across from Market Square close to Chowning's Tavern. Customers had always complained about the cost he charged for his merchandise, and during the war people had raved even more over the high prices. The Carter brothers were still in business in the big brick building next to Raleigh Tavern. John operated a store selling saucepans, shoe soles, and soap; James and William, both doctors, ran the apothecary shop.[65]

When General Nelson needed papers notarized, he walked through his back yard to the law office of his friend James Innes, across the street from the Raleigh Tavern. The "Fat Knight" found his legal duties laborious and was often discontented, yet he prospered.[66]

The advantages of learning were better for the boys at Williamsburg, the Nelsons thought, and the city provided more interests and cultural improvements for their growing girls. The five oldest sons, still in their teens except William, could enter the College of William and Mary to continue their education. Since Elizabeth would turn thirteen in December, Lucy wanted her eldest daughter to have dancing lessons and musical instruction just as she had studied twenty-five years previously with the versatile Peter Pelham.

Although the Nelsons noted many changes in the old capital wrought by the war, the couple still had family and friends living in the town. The Reverend John Bracken still served as rector of Bruton Parish Church, and he was pleased to see the pews fill up with numerous Nelsons. In 1776, the minister had married Sally Burwell, Tom's first cousin. Four-year-old John and two-year-old Julia Carter Bracken, made fine playmates for five-year-old Robert and three-year-old Susanna Nelson. The Brackens lived in a handsome brick house on Francis Street once owned by William Byrd, III.[67]

If the couple visited the College in the shimmering fall days and returned along Duke of Gloucester Street, they might have stopped by the Blair dwelling. William Nelson and John Blair, Sr., had been Council colleagues and their sons had followed in their footsteps to serve the state. The two men shared many memories; both were also members of the hospital board.

General Nelson also had a common interest with James Galt, who had been a lieutenant in the Virginia militia during the Revolution. Galt had resumed his old position as superintendent of the institution for the insane. As a trustee for the asylum, Thomas often had occasion to talk with him about his unfortunate charges.[68]

Thomas Nelson had known some of the residents around Palace Green all their lives. Thomas Everard, still serving as clerk of York County, lived in his comfortable frame house on the east side of the double drive leading to the now burned Governor's dwelling. In his recommendation to the representatives on May 30, 1782, Governor Harrison had said:

> The Governor's house at Williamsburg is burnt Down and many of the walls have tumbled. The executive have given order for the Sale of the Bricks the only method by which they could be saved to the public: the outhouses are going fast to destruction and will soon be in ruins.[69]

The official then had proposed that the property and adjoining lands be sold by a lottery scheme. Sadly, Tom and Lucy recalled the elegant gatherings they had attended there before the Revolution.

The spacious Peyton Randolph home on Nicholson Street was another place that was not the same, as Elizabeth Harrison Randolph, Lucy's aunt by marriage and a cousin to Tom, had died. By her will, proved February 17, 1783, Aunt Betty had bequeathed £130 for a "monument in memory of her dear and blessed husband." In 1775 Lucy and Tom had enjoyed traveling to Philadelphia with the Randolphs for the Continental Congress. Edmund Randolph had received a collection of silver by the will as well as his uncle's seal that Betty stated, "I wear on my watch." Elizabeth Harrison, who had lived with her aunt, was bequeathed £500 as well as all the wearing apparel, silver, watch, and a "treasury bond of the United States for 90 pounds."[70]

During the fine fall weather, the Nelson couple might catch Attorney George Wythe strolling in his garden, a long rectangular plot parallel to Bruton Parish churchyard that was always filled with plants and flowers. Tom and Wythe had been associates in the Assembly for several years and in 1776 had served as delegates to the Congress as strong supporters for independence and had signed the Declaration of Independence.[71]

No doubt Lucy was delighted when her cousin William Lee forwarded a letter to Thomas from Green Spring in October concerning a gift of china:

> I have a box containing four dozen blue and White china plates; complete set of Nankeen China, a fine enammelled 6 quart China punch bowl, a box containing an elegant tea urn more a new construction, with beater

and key, etc., etc. These articles I would presume be agreeable to my cousin Nelson as well as yourself, and if you will give me leave will be sent to you by waggon.[72]

In the autumn of 1783 the General Assembly opened October 20, but as usual several legislators were late for the session. General Nelson and his military colleague Colonel Josiah Parker were among the tardy. On Monday, November 10, the clerk recorded that they were "admitted to seats without paying fees." Though Thomas had to take more time to travel from Williamsburg to the capital than was required to ride to Richmond from his Hanover plantation, no doubt his indisposition caused the delay rather than the distance. On November 15 an act was presented to amend the law that declared tobacco, hemp, flour, and deerskins be taken as payment of certain taxes. General Nelson and his brother William voted *no* on the proposal, but the bill passed. Congress had recommended that the states set up regulations relating to duties and imposts on imported goods. The Nelson brothers were assigned to the committee to establish these taxes for the Commonwealth; but before the legislators had settled the levies, General Nelson was granted a leave of absence from the Assembly for a week because his asthmatic attacks were aggravated by the damp chilly days.[73]

As a frigid wind whipped snow flurries through the winter at Williamsburg, the Nelson family stayed close to their crackling fire. Powdery flakes piled up on fence posts and created fascinating patterns against windowpanes. Young Susanna Nelson pulled baby Judith toward the windows to peer out at the world of white. Slaves struggled through drifts to feed the stock. Even in inclement weather the five oldest sons could step through the back yard to the Eagle Tavern. Formerly known as the King's Arms Tavern, the new name of the inn was more appropriate for the emerging American nation. Looking at the quintet, the parents realized the boys were grown up. Three of the children's birthdays were observed in December. Thomas turned nineteen; Elizabeth became thirteen, and Mary celebrated her ninth birthday. The house was also filled with preparations for the holiday season as the cook and her helpers baked hams, hens, and ducks, roasted apples, readied pies and cakes, counted jars of preserves and jellies, stirred toddies and punch.

On Christmas Day the Nelson clan would crowd into the coach to ride to Bruton Parish Church to receive the sacraments. Then Tom would shake hands with all the slaves, pressing shillings in their palms, as was the custom. Although General Nelson was in debt, he would not forego this gesture.

After the family dined on an abundant meal in mid-afternoon, guests would arrive and be greeted hospitably. An atmosphere of conviviality and cheer with family and friends marked the festive season. General Nelson and daughter Elizabeth shared a birthday the day after Christmas, yet holiday merrymaking might preclude a special ceremony although the forty-five-year-old father was certainly conscious that Elizabeth was evolving into a charming young lady as she entered her teens.

In addition to the numerous Nelson family, many Burwell kin doubtless visited during the holidays. Nathaniel Burwell's brood of five children from nearby Carter's Grove, ranging from ten-year-old Carter down to baby Billy, reminded him of the five Nelson boys and little Elizabeth a few years back. When Nathaniel had stayed with the Nelson family and, as a college youth, courted Susanna, Lucy's sister, it had seemed that the stairstep quintet of Nelson sons were always underfoot! Now these five strapping youngsters were old enough to plan a hunt on his plantation when the weather permitted.

Lucy and Susanna naturally compared notes about their children. The Burwells had lost baby Lewis, born in 1781 and died the following year, but Carter, Philip, Lucy, Nathaniel, and William seemed healthy. Nine-year-old Mary Nelson probably vied with her visiting cousin Carter Burwell in leading the younger cousins in games. Little Lucy Nelson became seven years old on January 2, 1784; Philip Burwell had already attained that age and his sister Lucy Burwell would become seven in the year. If the contingent of young cousins raised too much hubbub with their toys, servants were soon summoned to tuck them in bed.[74]

+   +   +

The institution for the insane at Williamsburg had been neglected through the war. Manager James Galt and board member Thomas Nelson, Jr., had answered the call of their country, but individual inhabitants of the town had cared for some of the inmates. After York Town, the victorious French forces had used the hospital building for barracks. Dr. de Siqueyra had prescribed remedies for the unfortunate patients, but receiving no salary for his services had petitioned Governor Harrison for reimbursement. Now concerned citizens contacted the authorities about the condition of the asylum. On January 15, 1784, former trustees of the institution met together and made plans to restore the function of the hospital. General Nelson, Dudley Digges, and James Madison from the College attended the first session and were joined a few days later in another meeting by John Blair, Nathaniel Burwell, and Joseph Prentis who were appointed to ask the Governor for £300 for the hospital. Keeper James Galt was to receive the funds needed immediately for the "relief of the lunatics now in town," the solicitors stated.[75]

Citizens all over the Commonwealth were confronted with money matters. Typical was the situation of tradesman George Flowerdewe Norton who expressed in his petition to the House of Delegates that he was "reduced to greatest extremes," because of regulations that prohibited recovery of English debts.[76] Bankruptcies in Britain had also complicated collections. Receiving funds for debts in the depreciated paper currency created problems, so the merchants still had no real money.

Through the spring, General Nelson continued to straighten out his own indebtedness. Collections from some customers to the once prosperous family firm at York Town seemed impossible. Loss was often noted in the ledgers. Despite the act abrogating British accounts, Thomas was a man of integrity and intended to pay his huge debt to the Hunts in London. Proceeds from the sale of the Penrith property abroad were paid to the English merchants.

As the soldier and statesman struggled to reduce his remittances, he recalled that the representatives of the General Assembly had not fulfilled the conditions regarding repayment of funds he had solicited for the state. In the special loan drive during the desperate days of 1780, Nelson had pledged his own property as a guaranty for the government. He had also accepted the command of the militia forces of the Commonwealth without compensation.

On Tuesday, June 8, 1784, the memorial of Thomas Nelson, Jr., was mentioned in the *Journal of the House of Delegates* and declared in part:

> He had obtained considerable loans of money and tobacco for the use of the State, for which they made themselves liable, relying upon the assurances of that body, that the same should be repaid; but no provision has yet been made for the payment of the same, and praying that his said expenses may be reimbursed him; and that the Assembly will adopt such measures for the relief of those who thus advanced their money and tobacco, as it appears just and right.[77]

The Committee of Claims considered the memorial and on Tuesday, June 17, 1784, the record read that the "Senate agreed resolution paying a sum of money to Thomas Nelson, Jr." A special committee was appointed to study the settlement. Business often became bogged down before a bill was prepared, read three times, and passed or rejected by the delegates. That became the case with General Nelson's claim.[78]

Debts and claims were not the only matters that occupied the officials. The clergymen of the Established Church held a convention at Richmond in June and appealed to the Assembly for incorporation. Patrick Henry, becoming more conservative in his viewpoint, swung his support to the cause of the ministry, but Madison and the liberal legislators were able to defeat the acts at the autumn Assembly. The Lee forces also opposed the policies of Mr. Henry.[79]

In March, William Lee had written General Nelson a letter from Green Spring asking for some cash before he set off "as the sailors say, wind and weather permitting" for the upcountry. Besides money, Lee had considered the election of the members of the House of Delegates and noted to Nelson:

> Therefore let me now entreat you to exert yourself in having sound men & true, sent to the Assembly not only from this but the neighbouring Counties, for believe me there is much Mischief in Contemplation & on you depends more than any other man I know to save the lower part, indeed the whole Country from Confusion and Ruin. A dark mischievous Character is plotting to get into the next Assembly, for no good purpose we may be assured, therefore, I trust that your Patriotism will prevent you from retiring this year at least.[80]

Probably General Nelson pondered these words and remembered that he had played the role of mediator between conservative and progressive members in the past. He was not present, however, at the spring and summer sessions and relied on news of the proceedings from Nathaniel and William, as both brothers were serving in the General Assembly.

On Monday, October 18, 1784, the autumn Assembly was scheduled to start, but the legislators were late so little administrative action transpired until the second week. The few members on hand again heard the memorial of Thomas Nelson, Jr., requesting repayment of sums lent the state. The committee had considered the petition and recommended that a bill should be prepared to reimburse payment of over £10,000 to General Nelson. Thomas was not present in the House of Delegates in the fall so he would be informed again of the seemingly favorable resolution by his brothers. Yet he never received the compensation from the Commonwealth of Virginia.[81]

Patrick Henry was elected Governor again November 17. Probably General Nelson soon heard the rumors that the representatives opposed to the statutes Henry had sponsored in the previous session had helped to elect him, so now he could not sway the delegates from the floor to favor his projects.[82]

When illness or bad weather confined General Nelson at home during the damp weeks of winter, there were no dull moments for him as master of that crowded household. It was regrettable that proceeds from the Penrith property in England near the Scottish border could not be distributed to his sons, but indebtedness had destroyed that dream. William, already twenty-two years, and Thomas, twenty-one, were visiting plantation tracts near York Town—Cheesecake, Dowsings, or Terrapin Point, and also making the rounds of land in Hanover County, Mallory's, Long Row, Offley Hoo, Bridge Quarter, and Mont Air. Thus, they could relieve their father of much correspondence relating to the crops. Manager George Dabney no doubt discussed the prospects of the tobacco market with the two young men. Coachman James Rideout was still serving the family as was Negro blacksmith Harry. William had already been granted various properties from the vast Hanover plantations and also had slaves and stock at work on the land. After Thomas reached his majority, he was entrusted with a tract on New-found River and would eventually inherit 2,500 acres in the region as well as the houses and tenements in Williamsburg and all the land owned by General Nelson in James City County.[83]

Fine firewood was secured from Hobby's and the timber tracts in Warwick County. Wagons could haul from the York Town house mahogany tables, green Windsor chairs, Queen china dishes, decanters, dessert bowls, ivory-handled knives and forks, soup tureens, and butter boats if Lucy felt the need of more furnishings for the Francis Street home.[84]

Lucy often gathered her girls around her in the cozy sitting room on Francis Street in the late afternoon as candles spread a golden glow and the hearth fire blazed in scarlet streaks. Elizabeth, at fourteen, was adept at pouring tea and Mary, ten, helped with the cups. They had learned from Lucy just how long to steep the leaves. Seven-year-old Lucy helped four-year-old Susanna and Judith, not three until May. Judith could not join her sisters yet in sewing, but she enjoyed watching them make samplers and embroider fanciful scrolls on petticoats. Even Susanna was being taught how to stitch and to recognize colors from the strands of crewel yarn.

Manners for children at the table were strict: sit still, sing not, hum not, wriggle not, bite not your bread nor break it. Since Lucy was a firm disciplinarian, social courtesies and civilities were observed. Robert, who came between two older sisters and two younger ones in age, had learned his letters rapidly and could read with facility so his father had already predicted the little boy would want to enter a profession in the future.[85]

The parents had always been interested in education for their family and notwithstanding the interruptions of schooling caused by the conflict, General Nelson had contrived to increase his library collection. Speeches of Greek orators had been ordered and letters of Latin scholars filled the shelves. The sons could study the works of Tacitus, Pliny, Polybius, and Cicero, or read poems or plays. A five-volume set by Alexander Pope was on hand as well as Milton's "Paradise Lost." The complete works of Montesquieu had been purchased as well as six volumes of the *Memoirs of Sully*. Lighter reading could be found in the stories of the Turkish spy and eight volumes of this type of intriguing tale had been bought. General Nelson would later purchase more philosophic works, such as *Wisdom's Voice to the Rising Generation*, sermons and lectures by Hugh Blair, and the six-volume set of Gibbon's *The History of the Decline and Fall of the Roman Empire*.[86]

Although Tom and Lucy's home on Francis Street was filled to capacity, Thomas's mother, Elizabeth Burwell Nelson, wanted to be close to the family but not necessarily a member of their crowded household. Son Hugh and his wife Judy and their children, Jane Byrd, Lucy, Thomas, and Nathaniel were living in York Town looking after Nathaniel's three motherless children: little Elizabeth (called Betsey), another William, and an infant boy. (Jane Page Nelson had died in February 1782 at nineteen. She had married Nathaniel Nelson in June 1778 and had borne a baby every year.) In the spring of 1785, the senior Mrs. Nelson settled in Williamsburg at the William Royle residence on Nicholson Street. It was a familiar site to her as she and her husband had sold four lots to Joseph Royle, printer, twenty-two years before. The publisher had died in 1766, but the newspaper continued publication. Molly Davenport, sister to Royle, evidently cared for old Mrs. Nelson to extreme satisfaction, since later in her will Elizabeth left the lady twelve pounds and gave her the slaves Hannah, Nancy, and Phillis.[87]

◆　　◆　　◆

On Tuesday, October 18, 1785, the autumn Assembly opened its official session at Richmond. The name of Nelson appeared only briefly on the records since General Nelson did not attend the meetings as a member, and his brother William soon resigned as a representative. Nathaniel Nelson, however, was present for a few weeks and was assigned to the committees relating to commerce and the regulation of trade. On Tuesday, December 13, his affirmative vote was recorded to amend the act concerning the courts. The delegates discontinued their duties on Christmas Day but reconvened on Monday, December 26, 1786.[88] Nathaniel had suffered from sick spells and on Monday, January 2, 1786, the clerk recorded in the official *Journal of the House of Delegates*, "Ordered that Mr. Nelson have leave to be absent from the service of this House for the remainder of the session."[89]

Sensing that his illness was serious, Nathaniel Nelson "set his hand and seal" on his will in York County on March 15, 1786. He died later in the spring, leaving three small children without mother or father. Family and friends lamented the loss of this young man in his thirty-first year. His four remaining brothers were appointed guardians of his three children. If they deemed it necessary, property in Hanover County was to be sold for their maintenance and education; two stalled beeves, 20 barrels of corn, and 1,000 pounds of pork were to be provided from the estate for the minors. Thomas received the Hanover lands, and the York County and Dismal Swamp tracts were designated for Hugh, Robert, and William. Slaves were distributed to the brothers; Thomas received Sukey and her heirs as well as slave Dick.

Nathaniel Nelson left his brothers-in-law William Page and Matthew Page one hundred pounds each and remembered some servants with money: brother Hugh's man was to receive five pounds and "my man Dick 5 pounds." His daughter Betsey was bequeathed "twelve hundred pounds Specie [by] age twenty-one or twelve months after day of marriage." She also received the gold sleeve buttons of her father. William would be the heir of the "real and personal property" when he became of age.[90]

To his mother, Elizabeth Burwell Nelson, Nathaniel gave his large gold seal; but her heart was too heavy with grief to prize the possession. Five years later the grandmother bequeathed two rings to these grandchildren in her will: "To Elizabeth daughter of son Nathaniel died diamond hoop ring. . . . To William son diamond ring with single stone."[91]

♦   ♦   ♦

Despite his grief over Nathaniel's death, General Nelson remained attentive to his duties. He had attended a meeting of the hospital trustees on April 26 when members Dudley Digges, Nathaniel Burwell, James Madison, John Blair, Dr. Sequera, and Joseph Prentis were present, as recorded by the clerk, William Reynolds. The board unanimously elected Mr. Digges president. Then the officials ordered that the hospital, other houses, and outhouses included within the property of the institution for the insane should be repaired. On that day the administrators of the asylum appointed five new members to replace Robert Carter Nicholas, John Randolph, the Reverend John Camm, Lewis Burwell, and John Tazewell, deceased: Joseph Hornsby, John Bracken, Robert Andrews, James Innes, and Henry Tazewell. This necessary bit of business brought sober recollections to General Nelson and the other old-time trustees since they could remember their close association with these departed colleagues.[92]

Thomas Nelson, Jr., ran for representative to the House of Delegates from York County in the spring of 1786 and was elected easily. During the summer the forty-seven-year-old legislator had time to think about starting another legislative term, after serving twenty-four years as a statesman. Thomas would not pretend that family prestige and a powerful fortune had not been potent factors for his entry on the political path, however, through the years, he had proved his value to the voters so that his public service had extended from a Burgess under royal rule through the transitional period of the Crown Colony to the Commonwealth of Virginia.

When he arrived at Richmond in the autumn, he was glad to greet Governor Henry.[93] The friends could talk about many common experiences, public activities or private affairs, and the executive doubtless confided in Nelson that he did not choose to be a candidate that fall for the gubernatorial post after having served five terms. In fact, Henry was contemplating moving back to Hanover County and considered purchasing some property from General Nelson. This transaction did not take place at the time, but Nelson was selling tracts from his plantations to pay off his obligations. In September 1785, a parcel of land from Bullfield near the Pamunkey branch amounting to 593 acres had been sold to the Walker family.[94]

The official record of the opening session for the House of Delegates told the same old story about the tardy statesmen. On Monday, October 16, the clerk recorded that the Assembly adjourned, and it was not until a week later on Monday, October 23, that a quorum was present. Joseph Prentis from York County was elected Speaker of the House with the support of his county colleague.[95]

Beginning on Wednesday, November 1, General Nelson's name appeared almost every day on the official record, as the active representative proposed bills and read reports. On Friday, October 24, he had been placed on the committee to consider the finances of the Commonwealth. Nelson was associated on the assignments with James Madison, Archibald Stuart, Theodorick Bland, James Innes, and his cousins George Nicholas, John Page, and Mann Page. As chairman again of the Propositions and Grievances Committee, Nelson had to scrutinize claims, petitions, and protests, and make recommendations to the representatives. Money matters were of prime importance. Treasurer Jacquelin Ambler was anxious for the Assemblymen to set up a sound monetary system.[96]

A petition from John Pierce, who had been appointed commissary by Governor Nelson in 1781, alleged that "considerable sums of Money" had been distributed to the county deputies to "procure necessities for the army," but even to date some of the officials had failed to account for the receipts. Therefore, Pierce insisted that the legislature intervene in the matter.[97]

Major John Nelson was successful in obtaining settlement for a claim relating to supplies furnished his cavalry corps. On Wednesday, November 15, the request for reimbursement was read, and on Thursday, December 21, the record noted, "found petition John Nelson reasonable auditor ought to grant warrant for 4,537½ lbs. tobacco." The crop was recognized as currency. General Nelson was one of the seventy-two members voting affirmatively for an act to enable "citizens of the Commonwealth to discharge taxes in payment tobacco." It was read the third time on Friday, November 24, according to regulation, and passed by a majority vote.[98]

The delegate from York County and his committee colleagues were given one week to provide a bill concerning the appointment of Congressmen from the Commonwealth. On November 7, they recommended William Grayson, James Madison, Richard Henry Lee, Joseph Jones, and Edward Carrington.[99]

General Nelson reported on Thursday, November 2, that the committee considering the state of the Commonwealth had made some progress. Additionally he was in the process of preparing a bill to incorporate the town of York, checking requisitions of the Congress to raise troops and cavalry, and contemplating means to expedite the "slow and tedious methods" of the courts of justice since "innocent persons involved" were suffering great distress.[100]

The statesmen seeking to solve economic ills through a strong currency defeated the constituents of Brunswick and Campbell counties favoring the issue of paper money. The delegates declared that the emission would be "unjust, impolitic, and distrustful of public and private interests." There were eighty-five affirmative votes favoring the sound fiscal stand and seventeen negative votes. General Nelson advocated hard money and moved that the names of the members voting *aye* and *no* be inserted in the *Journal of the House of Delegates*.

Edmund Randolph was elected Governor for one year and thirty days, and General Nelson represented the committee on Thursday, November 9, to notify the acting Attorney General of his new appointment.[101]

An embarrassing bit of business occurred on Saturday, November 18, when the legislators, following the letter of the law, proceeded to "take into custody John Robinson, Sheriff York County, for not making in due time a return to the delegates elected to represent the said county in the present General Assembly."[102]

General Nelson was moving back and forth between the House of Delegates and the Senate during the autumn convention to acquaint the upper body with the bills and resolutions proposed and passed by the lower branch. It was his duty to notify the delegates that voting for an Attorney General was in order, since Edmund Randolph had been elected the new Governor. On November 23, the Assemblymen chose James Innes to become Attorney General for the Commonwealth.[103]

Taxes, trade, and the treasury occupied the officials throughout the fall. General Nelson was chairman of a special committee on taxes that proposed a plan to expedite tax collections. Working closely with his colleague James Madison on committees to stabilize the treasury system and to set up trade restrictions, Nelson learned that Madison felt deeply the need to strengthen the Congress.

The controversy over shipping charges between Virginia and Maryland for the ships sailing on the Potomac River and in Chesapeake Bay had been settled so successfully at a convention in Alexandria that another commercial conference had been called for September 1786. Madison suggested that all states should send commissioners to the Annapolis convention with the purpose of agreeing on a single currency system and authorizing the Congress to control trade. Only five states sent representatives to consider these reforms, but these delegates realized the situation of the states was critical with a powerless central government. The executives at Annapolis had asserted that adjustments to the Articles of Confederation were necessary to meet the needs of the union. The conference recommended that all thirteen states should appoint delegates to another convention to meet on the second Monday of May 1787 at Philadelphia.[104]

General Nelson served on the committee to select the delegates from the

Commonwealth of Virginia to attend the Constitutional Convention. On Monday, December 4, the names of seven representatives were recorded in the *Journal* according to the number of votes: George Washington, Patrick Henry, Edmund Randolph, John Blair, James Madison, George Mason, and George Wythe.[105]

When formal notification reached Henry at his residence in Prince Edward County, he refused the appointment. Henry was infuriated with the intrigue of the Spanish ambassador to surrender the navigation of the Mississippi River to the Americans. The Assemblymen of Virginia had been aware that John Jay had agreed to the demands of the diplomat from Spain. The representatives had resolved on November 29 that navigation of the river should be a common right. Sectional interests were focused by the issue since the New England states had received commercial concessions. The southern states were thwarted by the treaty in settling the western lands.

Thomas Nelson was also offered the position of being a representative to the Constitutional Convention, but he declined the post because of his health.

On January 3, 1787, Nelson presented for the third time the bill to incorporate the town of York. It passed the House, and the sponsor carried it to the Senate for concurrence. On that same day the Assembly agreed to alter court days in certain counties. Nelson proposed an act to assist the citizens who were partners with British firms that they be enabled "to recover their proportion debts due to the partnership under certain restrictions." Negative votes were recorded against amending certain laws relating to naval officers and allowing the admiralty to hold courts, but on Monday, January 8, 1787, Nelson voted affirmatively to "pay the directors further sum 5,000 £ applied toward completion Capitol."[106] Some of the gentlemen had questioned the cost of construction, but in reality the representatives were proud of the big building rising on the slope overlooking the James River. The Assemblymen had appealed to Ambassador Thomas Jefferson in Paris upon his arrival in the spring of 1785 to assist the state with the artistic assignments. He was asked to secure a sculptor to carve a lifelike statue of George Washington and contacted Jean Antoine Houdon for the commission. The artist was so overjoyed about the opportunity that he shut up his shop and sailed for America.

Interested in architecture, Thomas Jefferson was pleased to pore over plans with French architect Charles Louis Clarisseau to fashion a plaster model for the Capitol at Richmond. Copied after the classic Maison Carrée at Nimes, France, the elegant temple with its Ionic columns set a pattern of neo-classical architecture for countless other civic structures.[107]

CHAPTER TWENTY-FIVE

Last of Life: 1787–1789

Dunning for Debts ✦ *Constitutional Convention* ✦ *Death of Secretary Nelson* ✦ *Deterioration and Despondency* ✦ *Virginia Assembly Adopts Constitution* ✦ *Elizabeth Nelson Marries Mann Page, Jr.* ✦ *General Nelson Makes Final Will* ✦ *Passing of the Patriot*

General Nelson was still in Richmond when a raging fire swept through the city. It started January 11 at Hartshorn's store and spread to Anderson's Tavern, with forty to fifty dwellings destroyed by the blaze. Byrd's warehouse on the waterfront burned with a loss of seventeen hogsheads of tobacco. In its issue of Wednesday, January 31, 1787, the *Virginia Independent Chronicler* attested that in three hours the townspeople were "reduced to distress and ruin." Governor Randolph called a conference of leading citizens and appointed a committee to start a subscription for victims of the fire. Thomas Nelson, Esquire, of York County was listed among the contributors donating funds to those who had lost their homes.[1]

The name of Nelson appeared on other lists as Thomas and Hugh began selling several hundred acres from the Hanover County lands. Parting with property was a means of obtaining money to pay obligations. On February 19, 1787, General Nelson and his wife, Lucy, sold 105 acres from the county plantations to John Stanley. Hugh and his wife, Judy, signed deeds to 884 acres during the war, selling 584 in May from the north side of the South Anna River region at the mouth of Taylor's Creek. In October, the couple sold 300 acres to their kinsman Nathaniel Page, Jr.[2]

General Nelson had presented the bill at the past Assembly to incorporate York Town. He and his brother Billy attended the special meetings at the Court House March 5 and March 6, 1787, to set up the new system of government for the once thriving seaport town. At the second session the voters elected Thomas Nelson, Jr., as mayor and chose William Nelson as the recording clerk. Four aldermen were selected to assist the chief official: Dr. Corbin Griffin, William Reynolds, William Goosley, and Dr. Matthew Pope—all leading citizens with close connections to the Nelson family.[3]

Through the spring and summer weeks, General Nelson continued writing to family and friends to collect funds. Dunning was a disagreeable task. In his message of May 15 to his cousin Edmund Berkeley, he wrote:

I am unfortunately reduced to the necessity of dunning, or parting with more property than I can spare for my numerous family. . . . You are on my father's books for the bill of £50 which leaves me with a small balance in your power. If I do not raise a sum of money in the course of this week, some of my Negroes will be sold on Monday next.[4]

Unable to secure sufficient reimbursements for services rendered to the state or for commodities sold to customers to clear his indebtedness, General Nelson was compelled to put up 120 slaves from the Prince William County plantation for sale.[5]

While General Nelson struggled through the summer to straighten out his accounts, the delegates to the Constitutional Congress in Philadelphia were debating the defects of the Articles of Confederation. Vigorous arguments were advanced on whether to alter the Articles or create a new constitution. The session began Monday, May 14, 1787, but only Virginia and Pennsylvania were represented by a quorum of members. General Washington had arrived the afternoon before in clear weather and promptly paid a visit to venerable Benjamin Franklin. The fifty-five-year-old commander of the Continental forces and the eighty-one-year-old philosopher were the foremost delegates at the Convention. Both men had lived through troubled times, taken bold risks for their country, triumphed, and were now ready to accept again the responsibility of setting up a strong republic.

Delegates drifted in during the first few days of the month. James Madison was the first out-of-town representative to ride to Philadelphia from New York where he had served his state in the Congress. After his arrival on May 3, he greeted several Virginia colleagues, including John Blair and George Wythe. Governor Randolph reached the Convention May 7, and Dr. James McClurg and George Mason arrived by the seventeenth. The punctuality and planning of the Virginia delegates cast them as leading legislators. With the exception of Dr. McClurg, appointed after the refusal of Patrick Henry and General Nelson to be representatives, the members were all experienced in political matters. They met through the first few days in May to draw up a draft for union.[6]

On Friday, May 25, the Constitutional Convention officially opened its session since nine states had sufficient representation. George Washington was unanimously chosen chairman, and the delegates agreed to have secret proceedings. Before differences of outlook were presented in debate and opposition arose on various resolutions, General Washington commented:

It is too probable that no plan we propose will be adopted. Perhaps another dreadful conflict is to be sustained. If to please the people, we offer what we ourselves disapprove, how can we afterwards defend our work? Let us raise a standard to which the wise and honest can repair. The event is in the hand of God.[7]

Governor Edmund Randolph presented the Virginia plan that proposed the establishment of legislative, judicial, and executive branches. His premise emphasized that a strong central government would provide national security and general benefits and prevent foreign invasion and sedition by the states. He contrasted the power of a superior system of administration to the lack of authority under the Articles of Confederation. The resolutions were referred to a Committee of the Whole the next day, and on Wednesday the delegates voted to create a national government that consisted of legislative, judicial, and executive departments.[8]

James Madison sat near the front of the room and recorded the day's events, not missing a single day, but George Wythe returned to Richmond leaving six Virginia representatives at Philadelphia who were divided on the issues. Before leaving in June, Wythe had cast a favorable vote for a single executive, as did Washington, Madison, and Dr. McClurg. Blair, Mason, and Randolph opposed the election of one executive. Both Madison and Mason defended popular suffrage, but they disagreed on methods of raising revenue and on the central government's taxing exports. Sectional interest was involved, as the agricultural states were against taxing tobacco, rice, and indigo shipped to foreign ports. The southern states had succeeded in getting three-fifths of the slaves counted in the population, and the smaller states had scored a victory in July when the Convention voted for equal representation in the Senate. Though this compromise agreement passed, the delegates still had to deliberate on problems of trade, taxes, and treaties, and to make provisions about admitting new states. The representatives resolved that only nine states would be required for ratification, rather than all thirteen that had been the rule under the Articles of Confederation.[9]

By September, Governor Randolph was shifting from the stand of Madison to the side of Mason, who thought the Convention had been precipitate in passing the proposals and objected to the omission of a bill of rights. Randolph moved September 15 that the Constitution should be submitted to the states for study and suggestions, and proposed that a second Constitutional Convention should be called for final approval. Mason seconded the motion, but the delegates voted against the proposition. Over the week end the Constitution was penned on four parchment sheets and five hundred copies were printed. As the representatives reached the State House on Monday, September 17, 1787, many members still had reservations about the Constitution. George Washington assessed the action of the day in his diary:

> Met in Convention when the Constitution received the unanimous vote of 11 States and Colonel Hamilton's from New York (the only delegate from thence in Convention), and was subscribed to by every member present except Governor Randolph and Colonel Mason from Virginia, and Mr. Gerry from Massachusetts.[10]

A letter from General Nelson to his son Tom revealed that he had suffered from recurrent attacks in the summer. He wrote from York Town on August 12:

> Dear Tom—I was all packt up to set out for Hanover this morning but my disorder attackt me last night as violently as ever. I have written Major Minor to show and put you in possession of your plantation. Whatever the hands may fall short of 15 now, I will bring up in the fall. Do not omit calling on the Secretary on your way down. He will take it much amiss if you do.
>
> I hope you have succeeded with Lilly who I hear is at Warwick where he is loading his vessel. My compl'ts to the Airwell family.[11]

◆ ◆ ◆

Thomas Nelson, Sr., was in his seventy-first year and suffered from the infirmities of age. In a few months he passed away, but the exact date of his death and of his burial place are not established, and a legal document disposing of his property is not in existence. He had served as Secretary of the Colony over thirty years, had witnessed the changes of government from the Crown to the Commonwealth of Virginia, and had watched war wreck his home at York Town during the siege. His three surviving sons had served in the colonial forces in the fight for freedom.

◆ ◆ ◆

The activities of General Nelson in the autumn were affected by his continuing attacks. Since he did not improve from his illness, he could not become a candidate again from York County and consequently, did not attend the Assembly called at Richmond in October 1787, yet he was most aware of the important issues confronting the officials. The representatives' principal task would be the ratification of the Constitution. Through private contacts, personal correspondence, pamphlets, and newspapers, the well-organized Federalists had been active in advocating the adoption of the Constitution. The anti-Federalists, presenting arguments for amendments to the document before acceptance, had strong supporters in the state.

James Madison, relaying detailed accounts of developments to Ambassador Thomas Jefferson in France, October 24, 1787, revealed the division among the statesmen in Virginia:

> You will herewith receive the result of the Convention, which continued its session till the 17th of September. . . . It will not escape you that three names only from Virginia are subscribed to the Act. Mr. Wythe did not return after the death of his lady. Docr. McClurg left the Convention some time before the adjournment. The Governor and Colonel Mason refused to be parties to it. Mr. Gerry was the only other member who refused.[12]

Criticizing the conduct of his colleague Colonel Mason, Madison continued:

> A number of little circumstances arising in part from the impatience which prevailed toward the close of the business, conspired to whet his acrimony. He returned to Virginia with a fixed disposition to prevent the adoption of the plan if possible.[13]

He included his assessment of the stand of the different Virginians:

> I have a letter from General Washington which speaks favorably of the impression within a circle of some extent, and other from Chancellor Pendleton which expresses his full acceptance of the plan, and the popularity of it in his district. I am told that Innis and Marshall are patrons of it. In the opposite scale are Mr. James Mercer, Mr. R. H. Lee, Docr. Lee and their connections of course, Mr. M. Page according to a report, and most of the Judges and Bar of the general Court. The part Mr. Henry will take is unknown here. Much will depend on it. I had taken it for granted from a variety of circumstances that he would be in the opposition, and still think that will be the case.[14]

The prediction proved to be correct. Patrick Henry had definite objections to the "defects" of the document, yet he and other opponents were not as successful in winning adherents to oppose the adoption as were the Federalists in converting citizens to support the Constitution.[15]

Depressed by debts and weakened by his physical disorder, General Nelson was not able to campaign actively against approval. On December 9, Madison again wrote to Jefferson about prospects for adoption of the Constitution:

> It appears however that individuals of great weight both within and without the legislature are opposed to it . . . Mr. Henry, General Nelson, William Nelson, the family of Cabells, St. George Tucker, John Taylor, and the judges of the General Court except Paul Carrington.[16]

Conflicts arose over the ratification throughout the country with verbal abuse and violent attacks occurring among the opponents. Copies of the Constitution had been sent to influential legislators and important citizens in the several states. The average citizen, likewise, did not lack information about the document as pamphlets by the Federalists presented reasons for ratification while the anti-Federalists advocated in print resistance to adoption.

In his December 9 letter to Jefferson, Madison commented:

> The Constitution proposed by the late Convention engrosses almost the whole political attention of America. All the Legislatures except that of

Rhode Island, which have been assembled, have agreed in submitting it to the State Convention. Virginia has set the example by opening a door for amendments, if the Convention there should chuse to propose them.[17]

As far as he could ascertain, Madison said that the people of the upper and lower sections of Virginia and in the Northern Neck were disposed toward adoption, but those in the middle part and the south side of the James River were principally in opposition. A large majority of representatives would vote for ratification, he believed, but he also had reservations:

What change may be produced by the united influence of exertion of Mr. Henry, Mr. Mason, and the Governor with some pretty able auxiliaries, is uncertain.[18]

His information indicated that there were three viewpoints in Virginia. The first coincided with General Washington and the delegates who had signed the document at the Constitutional Convention. Pendleton, Marshall, Nicholas, and Colonel Innes were among other legislators who favored adoption without attempting amendments at the time. Second, Governor Randolph and Colonel Mason were members of the group who desired additional safeguards for the states and specific rights for individuals through amendments. Third, Patrick Henry headed the opposition to the adoption, including Benjamin Harrison and other officials, the courts, and members of the bar.
Madison continued:

Genl. Nelson, Mr. Jno. Page, Colonel Bland, & c are also opponents, but on what principle and to what extent, I am equally at a loss to say. In general I must note, that I speak with respect to many of these names, from information that may not be accurate, and merely as I should do in a free and confidential conversation with you. I have not yet heard Mr. Wythe's sentiments on the subject. Docr. McClurg, the other absolute deputy, is a very strenuous defender of the new Government. Mr. Henry is the great adversary who will render the event precarious.[19]

The delegates from Delaware approved the adoption of the Constitution December 7; representatives of Pennsylvania and New Jersey also ratified the document in December. In the early part of January 1788, the conventions of Georgia and Connecticut voted confirmation. On February 6, the members of Massachusetts authorized adoption by a close margin. Maryland assented in April by strong acceptance and South Carolina sanctioned adoption with a double majority. With the ratification of New Hampshire June 1, 1788, the necessary ninth state had been secured yet the victory vote was slim. Uneasiness was still current about a consolidated union. For the new government to be effective, the Federalist party felt it needed the support of the largest state, with its power and prestige. Victory in Virginia stimulated the advocates of the Constitution to work feverishly for its adoption.[20]

The Constitutional Convention of the Commonwealth started its session on June 2, 1788, by electing veteran lawmaker Edmund Pendleton as president. He was allowed to stay seated because of his crippled condition. The statesmen were more comfortable in the adequate quarters of the New Academy that had been constructed on Shockoe Hill in Richmond. Curious citizens and interested inhabitants from all across Virginia crowded into the capital that summer.[21]

Several familiar faces were absent from the Assembly. General Washington remained at his plantation on the Potomac, but he aided adoption of the Constitution by contacts and letters.

Ambassador Jefferson in Paris was kept abreast of dramatic developments. Upon receiving a copy of the document, he had expressed disappointment that particular rights to protect the people had not been included but closer study of the draft gained his good will.

Richard Henry Lee had not been elected a delegate.

Because of his deteriorating health, Thomas Nelson did not place his name in nomination. His family and friends realized that only pronounced physical disability had forced him to decline serving his state again.

Attorneys George Wythe and John Blair were chosen by the constituents of York County as the delegates, placing two more members in the Federalist camp at the convention.

The weeks of wrangling got under way almost immediately as 170 representatives had arrived at Richmond by Wednesday, June 4. "Light Horse" Harry Lee suggested speeding up the discussion on the draft, which the Federalists favored, but the Assemblymen adjourned until the next day when delegates convened as a Committee of the Whole.

A visitor to the Virginia Assembly could soon evaluate the stands of leading legislators. Scholarly James Madison was the real creator of the draft so he came to be called the "Father of the Constitution." He recommended a strong republic with central control but reiterated that the people had power through their representatives. Short of stature and sallow-skinned, Madison was not a good orator and when he stood to speak with his notes in his hat, he spoke so low that the shorthand reporter could not record his full remarks; nevertheless, his arguments were cogent.

Though Governor Randolph had not signed the Constitution at Philadelphia, he switched sides to support adoption. This change so disgusted anti-Federalist George Mason that he called his colleague an apostate and branded him "Young Benedict Arnold."[22] Patrick Henry also thundered "turncoat." Randolph reciprocated with bitter remarks so that the feud reached the duel point but fortunately was prevented.

The Federalists had strong support from two veteran lawyer-legislators, Edmund Pendleton and George Wythe. In the past they had been opponents, but on the cause of the Constitution they stood side by side.

Former Tory sympathizer Francis Corbin, who had returned to his native land after spending the war years in Britain, cast his lot with the Federalists. He concentrated his attack on the inflationary currency and inadequate credit conditions that existed under the Articles of Confederation.

George Nicholas was a strong Constitutionalist. His balding head, beaked nose, and bulging neck contrasted sharply with the commanding appearance of his brother-in-law Edmund Randolph, but Nicholas was a skillful speaker and defended the draft convincingly.

"Light Horse" Harry Lee, with bold assurance, had no qualms about countering denunciations of Patrick Henry. He criticized the out-of-doors, on-the-street campaign of the popular leader.

Thirty-two-year-old John Marshall presented logically the strong protection to be served under the general government.

As the foremost leader of the anti-Federalist faction, Patrick Henry first attacked the Constitutional Convention for not amending the Articles of Confederation, then criticized the Constitution for its ambiguity pertaining to privileges for the people. He took the floor frequently to thunder about the tyranny of rulers and loss of personal liberty and taunted the representatives with fiery tirades who favored ratification.[23]

Though both opposed adoption, George Mason and Patrick Henry did not cooperate well on strategy to thwart the Federalists. The sixty-two-year-old Mason attracted attention with his flowing white hair as he asserted that a complete investigation was indispensable. He objected to a continuance of the slave traffic and declared direct taxation by the general government would be detrimental to the states. As author of the Virginia Bill of Rights, Mason favored amendments to incorporate those privileges of a free people.

Benjamin Harrison and John Tyler were also anti-Federalists, and thirty-year-old James Monroe was apprehensive about authority for the president, fearing his powers would foster a monarchial form of government.

While Wythe presided, Pendleton struggled to stand with the support of his crutches to sustain the Constitution. He listed the limitations of the Articles of Confederation and asserted that powers of a national government would fulfill the general purposes for union. Pendleton pointed out that the people would delegate power through their representatives and states would still have special rights. The frail legislator affirmed that a strong system of administration would remedy the political ills.[24]

The anti-Federalists had an advantage over the Federalists relating to the touchy Mississippi River treaty. Henry forced the officials present who had served in the Congress to explain the concessions made to Spain concerning free navigation. Madison attempted to assure the alarmed Southerners wanting to push westward that they should not be apprehensive. Monroe, on the other hand, traced step-by-step the situation of the surrender to Spain. Henry seized the moment to paint a panorama of commercial prosperity with free navigation, then entranced his hearers by picturing the desolation without trade because of Spanish domination of the river.

The Federalists were stunned. Madison mumbled a feeble reply. With his gray eyes flashing, George Nicholas rose to refute the effect of the incident that had occurred under the authority of the Confederation. A system of checks and balances under the Constitution would control such situations, he stated. A sudden hailstorm prevented other speakers from being heard and the House adjourned.

On Saturday, June 14, Pendleton was absent because of the effects of the dampness the day before. The Federalists were apprehensive, as the controversy over the courts was pending, and they were depending on him to debate the case and hold Patrick Henry in line. Pendleton was back on Monday and began to present a detailed discussion of the federal jurisdiction. He reiterated his confidence in Congress to confine cases since every state had equal concern in justice.[25]

Mason criticized the overall powers of a supreme court and offered restrictions. Emotionally, Henry cried that the purse and sword had been relinquished and under the system being considered the courts would be ruined.

Both sides could count on a strong nucleus of support so strenuous efforts were made to influence the few individuals that had not committed themselves. As the long debates were concluding Monday, June 23, the tempers of the principal players flared. The Constitutionalists had a concerted plan to push through ratification on Tuesday, and Wythe moved for adoption. Arriving with a long list of amendments, Patrick Henry passionately protested the faults of the document as a sudden storm seemed to emphasize his points. On Wednesday, he made his last stand for amendments on individual rights and proposed reference to other states before ratification. By a margin of 80 to 88, the postponement was defeated. The Virginia Convention was then ready to consider ratification. It passed Wednesday, 89 to 79.[26]

✦   ✦   ✦

While the representatives at Richmond were debating ratification, the Nelson and Page families crowded into the homes of relatives at York Town and Williamsburg for the first wedding between the two families. The marriage of Elizabeth Nelson to Mann Page, Jr., on Thursday, June 5, 1788, started a trend of successive ceremonies between the sons and daughters of the two households. Since General Nelson and Frances Burwell Page were double first cousins and Thomas and John were also related, the marriages of their children compounded the close kinship. Elizabeth was seventeen years old, the eldest daughter of the Nelson family, and Mann Page, Jr., of Rosewell was the first son of his parents.[27]

Despite declining health and indebtedness, General Nelson, the indulgent father, spared no expense for his daughter's wedding. He ordered for her six pairs of black Calamanca pumps, two pairs of green leather, two pairs purple ones, one pair white, one pink satin, and one white embroidered satin pair as well as one dozen pairs of the best woolen stockings and two pairs of white silk ones. Another order listed fabrics appropriate for her trousseau: cambric cloth, fine corded dimity, pieces of dark brown cotton, purple and white linen. Perhaps Grandmother Nelson admired the dozen fine French gloves and mitts, exquisite lace, and "six fine lawn handkerchiefs with striped borders," while thirteen-year-old Mary would be impressed with the set of combs, the wax necklace and earrings. Ten-year-old Lucy must have longed to handle the two ivory stick fans while seven-year-old Susan, and Judith, who had turned six in May, were fascinated by an array of pins, colored thread, gauze, and blond lace caps. Included in the inventory of trousseau articles were:

> A fashionable Lushing Sacque and Coat, A rose white Satin Sacque and Coat, A fine suit of Mechlin lace, A fashionable Lushing gown, A white Sattin Capuchin and bonnet, A white sattin quilted petticoat.[28]

A pink satin quilted petticoat, fashionable stomacher and knot, sprigged lawn aprons, and one pair of tanned stays were also among the articles obtained for the special occasion.[29]

Lucy, Tom and all the wedding guests were rewarded by the bride's radiant appearance at the enjoyable event. No prophecy could warn the father that this wedding would be the only one of his offspring that he would witness.

William Nelson wed his cousin Sally Burwell, the eldest daughter of the Page clan in 1790. The second Nelson son, Thomas, worked for President Washington after the death of General Nelson. In 1795, he was thirty years old when he married Frances, the third Page daughter. Robert Nelson fulfilled his father's scholarly predictions and became a law professor and chancellor of the College of William and Mary. In 1803, he married his cousin Judith Carter Page. Robert died at age forty. Susan continued the custom of marrying the cousins in 1806 when she wed Francis Page, fifth son of the Gloucester group.[30]

Throughout her long life, Lucy would have time to recall the one joyous occasion of 1788 was the June wedding of Elizabeth and Mann Page, Jr., soon overshadowed by the death of sister Susanna at thirty-six years of age and Tom's prolonged illness. Just six weeks after the wedding, word came that Susanna Grymes Burwell had died at Carter's Grove on July 24.[31] Nathaniel was grief-stricken and mourned for his motherless children, Carter,

Philip, Lucy, Nathaniel, William, and Robert. Lucy felt handicapped in helping out with the Burwell boys and her namesake Lucy because her husband's asthmatic condition had become so acute. Through the last weeks of summer, General Nelson began to experience more suffocating spells, and doctors at the time were unaware of the part allergies and emotions played in that complex ailment. Dust, mold, feather pillows, certain foods, or pollen could have caused General Nelson to choke, cough, and gasp for breath as his bronchial tubes constricted.

An increasing sensitivity to situations was shown by Thomas, as revealed in his abnormal reaction to a report from General Washington who had mailed him a copy of the proceedings of the Virginia Convention's adoption of the Constitution. General Nelson interpreted the news as a personal thrust since he was opposed to ratification. On August 3, 1788, General Washington answered apologetically Nelson's letter of July 17:

> Far, very far indeed was it for my intention to embarrass you by the letter which enclosed the proceedings of the General Convention, and still farther was it from my wish that the communication should be received in any other light than as an instance of my attention and Friendship. I was well aware that the adoption or rejection of the Constitution should, as it ought to be, decided upon according to its merit and agreeably to the circumstances to which our public affairs had arriven.

His former Commander-in-Chief affirmed that important questions could be viewed in various ways and he closed with gentle advice and cordial wishes:

> Charity, mutual forbearance, and acquience in the Genl. choice; which, though it may be wrong is presumably right. Mrs. Washington unites with me in every good wish for Mrs. Nelson, yourself and family, and with sentiments of the highest esteem.[32]

In the cold, damp days of autumn, General Nelson became more despondent because of his illness and the debts that eroded the financial security he desired for his family. During his intermittent sick spells through the winter, Lucy stayed close to his bedside. Thomas still found his wife to be a source of strength. The couple had been married twenty-six years the last of July.

Thomas Nelson, Jr., drew up his last will and testament on his fiftieth birthday, December 26, 1788.[33] The document followed the traditional form. His beloved wife Lucy was bequeathed her wearing apparel, jewels, and chariot with four horses. During her lifetime, she was to hold the plantations of Mont Air, Mallorys, Long Row, and Smiths with the stocks, slaves, and equipment, as well as the farm near York with the same terms. She had the choice of the ten best house servants. Houses and lots in York Town not listed otherwise, with the household and kitchen furnishings, were granted Lucy.

From the profits of the estate, his mother was to be paid £100 sterling annually and furnished with beeves and hogs for food. His sons were also to provide stock for her household.

All the younger Nelson children were to be educated from the estate until they reached twenty-one or were married.

The houses and tenements in Williamsburg, James City County lands, and 2,500 acres in Hanover County, added to previous possessions, were transmitted to Thomas, the second son. The slaves, stocks, and utensils, with Negro Aggy and her future increase, except her oldest son Charles, were also granted to the twenty-four-year-old young man.

Philip was given Offley Hoo and surrounding tracts, stocks, slaves, utensils, and Negro Malinda then living at Bull Run.

Francis received lands "in the County of Hanover lying on the North Side of Little River and known by the name of Bridge Quarter," as well as other parcels of property.

Hugh inherited the holdings in Hanover County and also one hundred acres in York County, fifty in Charles Parish, a tract occupied by Mrs. Lucy Moore, and a water grist mill. He and Francis were each given slaves hoping to be increased to make up "ten hoe hands and five Plow boys."

Ten-year-old Robert would receive Mont Air after the death of his mother, plus slaves, equipment, stocks, but Francis was also granted an option on the plantation with provisions.

After the payments of debts, Elizabeth Nelson Page was to be given £1,000 sterling. Nancy, a slave in the possession of old Mrs. Nelson, was to be sent to Elizabeth. The other four daughters, Mary, Lucy, Susanna, and Judith were bequeathed £100 each after settlement of accounts and a Negro servant.

William, as the eldest son, was granted all the lands he presently possessed and "all the Rest and Residue" of the estate. After the death of his mother, he would have the choice of other property and slaves. The "trusty and faithful servant James Rideout" became William's possession as well as the fine amethyst seal that had belonged to his grandfather William.

General Nelson directed that Harry, the Negro blacksmith, should be discharged from all service and the freed man furnished a good house, clothes, three hundred weight of pork, and five barrels of corn during the rest of his life.

As a generous benefactor to his physician friend, Thomas stipulated:

> It is my will and desire that Dr. Augustine Smith shall not be charged with or called on to repay one shilling that I have expended on his mainte-

nance and education, and that he have credit in full for all sums which he may be charged on my books.[34]

Nathaniel Burwell of Carter's Grove, Francis Willis of Gloucester, and the two oldest sons, William and Thomas, were named as executors of the estate. As guardians of the younger children, they were to train Robert for "some profession, such as they shall think will best suit his genius."

To debts that totaled more than £13,000, Thomas Nelson, Jr., instructed the trustees to sell 1,568 acres, more or less, from the Bullfield tract in Hanover County, all the lands in Prince William and Loudon counties, and two surveys on the Elizabeth River.

The Nelson family, with the numerous kin and close friends, faced the fact that death was imminent for General Nelson. Lucy confronted the inevitable with courageous endurance. Even the servants spoke with admiration of the calm control of the mistress as she ministered to her husband. With strength and spirit, she attempted to alleviate Thomas's mental anguish as he lay ill and tortured by his accumulated debts.

Dr. Augustine Smith, just returned from Edinburgh, later expressed his emotions about his "Friend and Father" in a letter to a friend in Edinburgh, "To his care and attention I owe my entire education; and my support for near twenty years past."[35] The physician regretted that he could not show his gratitude to General Nelson "for the parental care of me—but Providence prevented it."

Attending his benefactor in his last illness at Mont Air in Hanover County, the doctor closed the eyes of Thomas Nelson, Jr., when he died on January 4, 1789, just past fifty years of age.

As the news spread, other friends lamented the loss of this statesman and soldier. On January 15, 1789, the newspaper published the obituary with black borders around the columns:

> The illustrious General THOMAS NELSON, is no more! He paid the last great debt to nature, on Sunday the 4th day of the present month, at his state in Hanover.
> He who undertakes barely to recite the exalted virtues, which adorned this good and great man will unavoidably pronounce a panegyric on human nature. As a man, a citizen, a Legislator, and a Patriot—he exhibited a conduct unvarnished, and undebased . . . by selfish interests.[36]

The paper proclaimed that the moral excellence of his life was expressed through true religion, benevolence, and liberality. With his ardent love of liberty, he was applauded for his zealous activities:

> As a soldier, he was indefatigably active, and cooly intrepid. Resolute and undejected in misfortune, he towered above distress,—and struggled with

the manifold difficulties, to which his situation exposed him with constancy and courage.[37]

Commending General Nelson for accepting the helm of government in 1781 when the British army invaded the state, the account concluded:

He did not avail himself of this opportunity to retire into the rear of danger—but on the contrary to the field, at the head of his countrymen— and at the hazard of his life, his fame and individual fortune—by his decision and magnanimity he served not only this Country, but all America, from disgrace—if not total ruin. . . . If after contemplating the splendid and he-roic parts of his character—we shall enquire for the milder virtues of human-ity, and seek for the man—we shall find the refined, beneficent, and social qualities of private life more thorough in all its forms, and combinations so happily modified, and united in him—that in the words of the darling poet of nature it may be said,

> "His life was gentle, and the elements,
> so mixed in him, that nature might stand up,
> And say to all the world, this was a man."[38]

NOTES

Works frequently cited have been identified by the following abbreviations:

DAB	*Dictionary of American Biography*
DNB	*Dictionary of National Biography*
JCC	*Journal of the Continental Congress*
JCS	*Journals of the Council of the State of Virginia*
JHB	*Journal of the House of Burgesses*
JHD	*Journal of the House of Delegates*
LC	Library of Congress
NFB	*Nelson Family Bible*
NLB	*Nelson Letter Book*
OL	Official Letters of the Governors of Virginia
VG	*Virginia Gazette*
VHS	Virginia Historical Society
VMHB	*Virginia Magazine of History and Biography*
VQ	*Virginia Quarterly*
VSL	Virginia State Library
WMQ	*William and Mary Quarterly*

Chapter ONE

1. Edward Miles Riley, "The Founding and Development of Yorktown, Virginia, 1691–1781" (dissertation, Univ. of Southern Ca., 1942), p. 149; *VMHB*, 51 (4), pp. 347–53; William Meade, *Old Churches, Ministers and Families of Virginia* (Philadelphia: J. B. Lippincott and Co., 1857), pp. 202–15.

2. *VMHB*, 51 (4), pp. 347–53.

3. Charles S. Sydnor, *Gentlemen Freeholders: Political Practices in Washington's Virginia* (Westport, Conn.: Greenwood Press, 1984), pp. 1–10.

4. Matthew Page Andrews, *Virginia, The Old Dominion* (Garden City, N.Y.: Doubleday, Doran and Co., Inc., 1937), pp. 195–23; Alf J. Mapp, Jr., *The Virginia Experiment: The Old Dominion's Role in the Making of America, 1607–1781* (Richmond: Dietz Press, 1957), pp. 223–81.

5. "George III," *DNB*; *DAB*, vol. 7, p. 472.

6. John Nicholls, *Recollections and Reflections Personal and Political as Connected with Public Affairs During the Reign of George III* (London: John Ridgeway, 1820), p. 11.

7. *VMHB*, 51 (4), pp. 347–53.

8. Meade, pp. 202–15, 284.

9. *WMQ*, 1 (2), p. 20; 6 (1), pp. 4, 28, 175; Louise Pecquet du Bellet, *Some Prominent Virginia Families* (Lynchburg: J. B. Bell Co., 1909), vol. 2, pp. 596–98; *VMHB* 28 (1), pp. 90-95, 187, 193, 228.

10. *WMQ*, 2 (1), p. 37.

11. Louis B. Wright, *The First Gentlemen of Virginia: Intellectual Qualities of the*

Early Colonial Ruling Class (San Marino, Ca.: Huntington Library, 1940).

12. *Colonial Williamsburg Guidebook* (Williamsburg, 1985), pp. 51, 52, 79.

13. Emory Gibbons Evans, "The Nelsons: A Biographical Study of a Virginia Family in the Eighteenth Century" (dissertation, Univ. of Va., 1957); *VMHB*, 21 (1), pp. 98, 196–98, 433.

14. *WMQ*, 2 (1), pp. 17, 18, 118.

15. Ibid.

16. Evans dissertation.

17. William and Mary Newton Stanard, *Colonial Virginia Register* (Albany: Joel Munsell's Sons, 1902), p. 21.

18. Ibid., p. 20.

19. Evans dissertation.

20. Meade, vol. 1, p. 207; *NLB*, Robert Carter Nicholas to John Norton, Nov. 30, 1772; Frances Norton Mason, *John Norton & Sons, Merchants of London and Virginia, 1750–1795* (Richmond: Dietz Press, 1937), p. 285.

21. Meade, vol. 1, p. 207.

22. *Another Secret Diary of William Byrd of Westover, 1739–1741*, ed. Maude H. Woodfin (Richmond: Dietz Press, 1942), pp. 417–43.

23. Meade, vol. 1, p. 207.

24. Description of Thomas Nelson, Jr., based on Mason Chamberlain's portrait, the only one ever painted. The work was done in London, 1754, when Thomas was 16. Original, Virginia Museum, Richmond.

25. *WMQ*, 9 (2), p. 162.

26. Ibid., 18 (1), p. 51.

27. du Bellet, pp. 596–98; Evans dissertation, pp. 100-01.

28. *Colonial Williamsburg Guidebook*, pp. 26, 47, 65, 73.

29. The social life and customs concerning women and children in the colonial period pertaining to fashion, culinary arts, courtships, pastimes were drawn from readings in the following: Charles M. Andrews, *Colonial Folkways: A Chronicle of American Life in the Reign of the Georges* (New Haven: Yale Univ. Press, 1920); Carl Holliday, *Women's Life in Colonial Days* (Boston: Corbill Publishing Co., 1922); James J. MacDonald, *Life in Old Virginia* (Norfolk: Old Va. Publishing Co., 1907); Edmund S. Morgan, *Virginians at Home: Family Life in the Eighteenth Century* (Colonial Williamsburg, 1952); George and Virginia C. Schaun, *Everyday Life in Colonial Virginia* (Annapolis: Greenberry Publishing Co., 1960); Julia Cherry Spruill, *Women's Life and Work in the Southern Colonies* (Chapel Hill: Univ. of N.C. Press, 1938).

30. See Note 29.

31. Spruill, pp. 136–62.

32. Byrd, pp. 382–83.

33. Spruill, p. 30.

34. J. A. Osborne, *Williamsburg in Colonial Times* (Richmond: Dietz Press, 1935), p. 62.

35. Ibid., p. 47.

36. Ibid., p. 50.

37. The privileges and powers of the gentry as members of His Majesty's Council and as leaders in the church and community discussed in Carl Bridenbaugh's *Myths and Realities* (Baton Rouge: Univ. of La. Press, 1952), Sydnor; Wright; R. C. M. Page, *Genealogy of the Page Family* (New York: Jenkins and

Thomas), p. 91. Sydnor testifies that only fifty-seven names, related by blood or marriage, appear in the Council list from 1690 to the American Revolution.

38. Hamilton J. Eckenrode, *The Randolphs: The Story of a Virginia Family* (Indianapolis: Bobbs-Merrill Co., 1946), pp. 3–30.

39. Clifford Dowdey, *The Virginia Dynasties* (Boston: Little, Brown and Co., 1969), pp. 147–72; Louis Morton, *Robert Carter of Nomini Hall: A Virginia Tobacco Planter in the Eighteenth Century* (Charlottesville: Univ. of Va. Press, 1941), pp. 41–51; Mary A. Stephenson, *Carter's Grove Plantation* (Colonial Williamsburg, 1964).

40. Stanard, p. 20; *Colonial Williamsburg Guidebook*, pp. 61, 62.

41. *WMQ*, 8 (1), pp. 7, 5, 10.

42. William Henry Foote, *Sketches of Virginia Historical and Biographical* (Richmond: John Knox Press, 1850), vol. 6, p. 45.

43. Thomas Tileston Waterman, *The Mansions of Virginia, 1706–1776* (Chapel Hill: Univ. of N.C. Press, 1946), pp. 110–23.

44. Wright, p. 91; Spruill, pp. 208–31.

45. *NFB*; Evans dissertation, pp. 20, 21; G. MacLaren Brydon, *Virginia's Mother Church and the Political Conditions Under Which It Grew* (Richmond: VHS, 1947), vol. 2, p. 336; Edward Lewis Goodwin, *Colonial Church in Virginia* (Milwaukee: Morehouse Publishing Co., 1927), p. 319; Meade, vol. 1, pp. 138, 168, 183.

46. Lucy Nelson's brocade gown is displayed at the Custom House, Yorktown, Va.; Thomas Nelson Page, *The Old South* (New York: Charles Scribner's Sons, 1905), p. 129.

47. Riley dissertation, p. 149; *Executive Journals, Council of Virginia*, eds. H. R. McIlwaine and Wilmer Hall (Richmond: VSL, 1690), pp. 60–71.

48. Meade, vol. 1, p. 206.

49. Douglas Southall Freeman, *George Washington* (New York: Charles Scribner's Sons, 1966), vol. 3, p. 210.

50. Wyndham Blanton, *Medicine in Virginia in the Eighteenth Century* (Richmond: Garrett and Massie, 1931), pp. 280–81, 346–47.

51. Ibid.

52. Ibid., p. 36.

53. Riley dissertation, chapters 5, 7.

54. Ibid., pp. 149, 153–56.

55. Ibid.

56. Clyde F. Trudell, *Colonial Yorktown* (Old Greenwich, Conn.: Chatham Press, Inc., 1938), pp. 95–105.

57. Ibid.

58. Osborne, p. 77.

59. Ibid., p. 67.

60. Ibid., pp. 28, 29.

61. Ibid., p. 61.

62. Ibid.

63. Ibid., pp. 92, 93, 94.

64. Ibid., p. 62.

65. Ibid.

66. *NLB*, William Nelson to William Cookson, July 2, 1766.

67. Trudell, p. 103.

68. York County Deeds and Bonds (No. 3, 1713–1729), pp. 178, 179, 394–95; *VMHB*, 33 (2), pp. 181–82, 188–93.

69. *NLB*, William Nelson to Samuel Athawes, Feb. 27, 1768.

70. *JHB*, 1761–1765, pp. 158, 160.

71. Stanard, pp. 20, 119, 187.

72. Mapp, p. 212.

73. *NLB*, William Nelson to Capel and Osgood Hansbury, Aug. 14, 1767.

74. Sydnor, pp. 112–19.

Chapter TWO

1. Matthew Page Andrews, *Virginia the Old Dominion* (Garden City, N.Y.: Doubleday, Doran and Co., Inc., 1937), pp. 170–74.

2. John Esten Cooke, *Virginia: A History of the People* (Cambridge: Houghton Mifflin and Co., 1883), p. 327.

3. Alf J. Mapp, Jr., *The Virginia Experiment: The Old Dominion's Role in the Making of America, 1607–1781* (Richmond: Dietz Press, 1957), p. 203.

4. Ibid., pp. 184–90.

5. *The Statutes at Large,* ed. William Waller Hening (Richmond, 1819), vol. 6, p. 197; *JHB*, pp. 294–328.

6. *VMHB*, 33 (2), p. 188; 13 (4), pp. 402, 403; *WMQ*, 3 (2), p. 166; 6 (1), pp. 143–45. Evans cites York Deeds 1702–1706, pp. 423, 8, 10, 125, 119; York Records and Wills 1713–1729, pp. 558–59; York Deeds, 1729–1740, pp. 33, 34, 101–02; York Orders and Wills, pp. 32–40, 478–79.

7. Edward Miles Riley, "The Founding and Development of Yorktown, Virginia, 1691–1781" (dissertation, Univ. of Southern Ca., 1942), pp. 66, 67, 77, 81, 83, 84. "The importance of the Nelson family in the history of Yorktown cannot be overestimated," p. 58.

8. Clyde F. Trudell, *Colonial Yorktown* (Old Greenwich, Conn.: Chatham Press, Inc., 1938), p. 58.

9. "Queen Anne," Imperial Encyclopedia.

10. Emory Gibbons Evans, "The Nelsons: A Biographical Study of a Virginia Family in the Eighteenth Century" (dissertation, Univ. of Va., 1957).

11. *The Journal and Letters of Philip Vickers Fithian, A Plantation Tutor of the Old Dominion, 1773–1774,* ed. Hunter Dickinson Farish (Colonial Williamsburg, 1957), p. 130.

12. Ibid.

13. *VMHB*, 32 (2), pp. 118, 132–33.

14. Hening, vol. 3, p. 285.

15. Philip Alexander Bruce, *The Virginia Plutarch* (Chapel Hill: Univ. of N.C. Press, 1929), vol. 1, p. 121.

16. Cooke, pp. 311–22; Mapp, pp. 190–220.

17. Louis B. Wright, *The Cultural Life of the American Colonies, 1607–1763* (New York: Harper Bros., 1957), p. 9.

18. Edward Eggleston, *Beginners of a Nation* (New York: D. Appleton and Co., 1900), p. 82.

19. J. A. C. Chandler and T. B. Thomas, *Colonial Virginia* (Richmond: Times Dispatch Co., 1907), pp. 256, 259; Eggleston, p. 82.

20. Leonidas Dodson, *Colonial Governors of Virginia* (Philadelphia: Univ. of Pa. Press, 1932), p. 34.

21. *Journal of John Fontaine: An Irish Huguenot Son in Spain and Virginia,* ed. Edward P. Alexander (Colonial Williamsburg, n.d.), p 102.

22. Cooke, p. 312.

23. York County Deeds and Bonds, 1713–1725, pp. 178–79, 374–95.

24. Ibid.

25. Evans dissertation.

26. Ibid.

27. *Memoirs of a Huguenot Family: John Fontaine's Diary,* ed. Ann Maury (New York: Putnam, 1853), p. 281.

28. Mapp, pp. 175–220.

29. Ibid., 223–81.

30. Cooke, p. 329.

31. Hening, vol. 6, pp. 196–97.

32. *Another Secret Diary of William Byrd of Westover, 1739–1741,* ed. Maude H. Woodfin (Richmond: Dietz Press, 1942), p. 136.

33. Ibid., p. 139. Byrd was speaking of Elizabeth (Betty) and Anne Harrison, daughters of Benjamin Harrison and Anne Carter Harrison of Berkeley. Elizabeth, who married Peyton Randolph, was Elizabeth Burwell Nelson's first cousin.

34. Ibid., p. 154.

35. Ibid., pp. 155–56.

36. Parks VG, Oct. 10, 1745.

37. Charles S. Sydnor, *Gentlemen Freeholders: Political Practices in Washington's Virginia* (Westport, Conn.: Greenwood Press, 1984), pp. 20, 29–31.

38. Andrews, p. 192; Philip Alexander Bruce, *Social Life of Virginia in the Seventeenth Century* (Richmond: Whittet and Shepperson, 1907), p. 218; Hugh Jones, *The Present State of Virginia* (Chapel Hill: Univ. of N.C. Press, 1956), p. 96; VMHB, 27 (1), p. 96; 28 (1), pp. 91–95, 187, 375; 31 (1), pp. 39–69.

39. Jones, p. 96.

40. VMHB, 22 (4), pp. 381–82; 31 (1), pp. 39–69.

41. VMHB, 31 (1), p. 47.

42. NLB, William Nelson to John Norton, Nov. 14, 1768.

43. VMHB, 31 (1), p. 46.

44. Ibid., 28 (1), p. 91–95.

45. Bruce, p. 218.

46. Romans 2:7, 10.

Chapter THREE

1. Matthew Page Andrews, *Virginia the Old Dominion* (Garden City, N.Y.: Doubleday, Doran and Co., Inc. 1937), pp. 22, 223. Nelson and Washington were both great-great-great grandsons of Nicholas Martiau.

2. Ibid., p. 230.

3. Jared C. Sparks, *The Writings of George Washington* (Boston: Russell, Odorne and Metcalf and Hilliard, Gray, and Co., 1834), vol. 2, p. 87.

4. David Mays, *Edmund Pendleton, 1721–1803: A Biography* (Cambridge: Harvard Univ. Press, 1952), vol. 1, p. 93.

5. JHB, 1761–1765, pp. 171, 172, 173.

6. Mary A. Stephenson, "Nelson-Galt House at Williamsburg," Colonial Research Library, Williamsburg.

7. *JHB*, 1761–1765, p. 171.

8. Ibid., p. 172.

9. *NLB*, William Nelson to Capel and Osgood Hansbury, Feb. 27, 1768.

10. Ibid., to Samuel Waterman; to James Buchanan, July 25, 1766.

11. Ibid., to Edward Hunt and Son, May 12, 1767.

12. Mays, vol. 1, p. 345.

13. *NLB*, William Nelson to James Gildart, Nov. 25, 1767.

14. *JHB*, 1761–1765, p. 173.

15. Claude G. Bowers, *The Young Jefferson, 1743–1789* (Boston: Houghton Mifflin, 1945), pp. 36, 38; Dumas Malone, *Jefferson the Virginian* (Boston: Little, Brown and Co., 1948), vol. 1, pp. 81–83; Nathan Schachner, *Thomas Jefferson* (New York: Thomas Yoseloff, 1951), pp. 40, 46, 79, 200, 216. Rebecca Burwell's mother had died at the time of Rebecca's birth, thus leaving the child's rearing to her father.

16. Stella Pickett Hardy, *Colonial Families of the Southern States of America* (New York: Tobias A. Wright, 1911), pp. 15–21.

17. Mays, vol. 1, p. 71.

18. *VMHB*, 10 (1), pp. 74, 218, 241–42.

19. Colonial Virginia Land Patent Bill, No. 31, p. 526–27, VSL.

20. Kenneth P. Bailey, *The Ohio Company of Virginia and the Westward Movement* (Glendale, Ca.: Arthur H. Clark Co., 1937), pp. 35, 44, 66, 67, 242–45, 298, 302, 306, 320–21; *WMQ*, 5 (1), pp. 129, 131, 175–80, 241–42.

21. Andrews, pp. 208, 210, 231, 234; Mapp, p. 286–88.

22. Thomas Perkins Abernethy, *Three Virginia Frontiers: Western Lands and the American Revolution* (Baton Rouge: La. State Univ. Press, 1940), pp. 8, 12, 45, 50, 68, 74, 77, 134, 158, 222, 236.

23. Ibid., p. 11.

24. Ibid., p. 12.

25. Douglas Southall Freeman, *George Washington* (New York: Charles Scribner's Sons, 1966), vol. 3, pp. 269–85; *VMHB*, 37 (1), pp. 64–65.

26. Proverbs 31:10.

27. York County Judgments and Orders, 1759–1763, p. 12; 1763–1765, pp. 307, 320.

28. Psalms 95:3–4.

29. Alf J. Mapp, Jr., *The Virginia Experiment: The Old Dominion's Role in the Making of America, 1607–1781* (Richmond: Dietz Press, 1957), pp. 52–53.

30. *NFB*.

31. Julia Cherry Spruill, *Women's Life and Work in the Southern Colonies* (Chapel Hill: Univ. of N.C. Press, 1938), p. 275.

32. Lucy Calthorpe Smith manuscript, Colonial Williamsburg Archives. Smith was the daughter of Dr. Augustine Smith whom Thomas Nelson, Jr., had educated.

33. *NFB*.

34. Louis B. Wright, *American Heritage History of the Thirteen Colonies* (New York: American Heritage Society, 1967), p. 342.

35. Andrews, pp. 186–87.

36. "John Camm," *DAB*; *The Statutes at Large*, ed. William Waller Hening (Richmond, 1822), vol. 10, p. 353–56; *VMHB*, 10 (4), p. 340; *WMQ*, 1 (3), pp. 70–73; 19 (1), pp. 28–30.

37. Jacob Axelrad, *The Voice of Freedom* (New York: Random House, 1947), p. 19; Julia M. H. Carson, *Son of Thunder: Patrick Henry* (New York: Longmans, Green and Co., Inc., 1945), p. 48; Freeman, vol. 3, pp. 104–05; Robert Douthat Meade, *Patrick Henry: Patriot in the Making* (Philadelphia: J. B. Lippincott Co., 1957), pp. 3–19.

38. Mapp, p. 299; *VMHB*, 18 (2), p. 215; *WMQ*, 10 (2), p. 210; 19 (1), pp. 21–23.

39. J. A. C. Chandler and T. B. Thomas, *Colonial Virgina* (Richmond: Times Dispatch Co., 1907), p. 256.

40. Edward Eggleston, *Beginners of a Nation* (New York: D. Appleton and Co., 1900), pp. 76–79, 81–82.

41. Hening, vol. 2, p. 242.

42. Lewis Cecil Gray, *History of Agriculture in the Southern United States to 1860* (Washington, D.C.: Carnegie Institution, 1933), vol. 1, pp. 184–85, 188–89.

43. Chandler, p. 160.

44. Ibid.

45. Ibid., p. 161.

46. Eggleston, pp. 81–82.

47. Ibid.

48. Hening, vol. 7, pp. 288, 563–64.

49. Ibid., vol. 8, p. 568.

Chapter FOUR

1. Alf J. Mapp, Jr., *The Virginia Experiment: The Old Dominion's Role in the Making of America, 1607–1781* (Richmond: Dietz Press, 1957), p. 225.

2. *The Statutes at Large*, ed. William Waller Hening (Richmond, 1823), vol. 1, p. 124.

3. Ibid., p. 223.

4. Thomas Nelson Page, *The Old South* (New York: Charles Scribner's Sons, 1905), p. 16.

5. Elizabeth Stansbury Kirkland, Short History of England for Young People (Chicago: A. C. McClurg & Co., 1892), pp. 257–73; Mapp, pp. 83–115.

6. "Robert Walpole," *DAB*; Mapp, p. 294.

7. "George Grenville," *DAB*; Mapp, pp. 294–97.

8. Andrew Burnaby, *Travels Through the Middle Settlements in North America in the Years 1759–1760* (New York: Wessels and Bissell, 1904), p. 34; *WMQ*, 28 (1), p. 151.

9. *WMQ*, 20 (4), p. 227; David Mays, *Edmund Pendleton, 1721–1803: A Biography* (Cambridge: Harvard Univ. Press, 1952), vol. 2, p. 93.

10. Matthew Page Andrews, *Virginia, The Old Dominion* (Garden City, N.Y.: Doubleday, Doran and Co., Inc., 1937), pp. 238–39.

11. *JHB*, 1761–1765, p. 348; Mapp, pp. 296–97.

12. *JHB*, 1761–1765, pp. 302–03; 314, 348.

13. *VMHB*, 12 (1), pp. 1–14.

14. Ibid., pp. 1–19.

15. *VMHB*, 22 (1), pp. 3–4.

16. Ibid., 12 (1), p. 156.

17. *JHB*, 1766–1769, pp. 165–71.

18. Frances Norton Mason, *John Norton & Sons, Merchants of London and Virginia, 1750–1795* (Richmond: Dietz Press, 1937), pp. 3, 6–7.

19. Mason, pp. 11–12.

20. *VMHB*, 22 (1), pp. 7–9.

21. *JHB*, 1761–1765, pp. 293, 302–03.

22. Douglas Southall Freeman, *George Washington* (New York: Charles Scribner's Sons, 1966), vol. 3, pp. 169–71; Mays, vol. 1, pp. 171-72

23. *WMQ*, 28 (1), p. 151.

24. *NFB*.

25. *JHB*, 1761–1765, p. 315.

26. John Esten Cooke, *Virginia: A History of the People* (Cambridge: Houghton-Mifflin and Co., 1883), p. 328.

27. Mays, vol. 1, p. 143.

28. Freeman, vol. 3, pp. 112, 180, 193, 207, 229, 327.

29. Mays, vol. 1, pp. 144, 146.

30. Richard Corbin, *Letter Book*, Colonial Williamsburg Archives, pp. 65–107.

31. Charles S. Sydnor, *Gentlemen Freeholders: Political Practices in Washington's Virginia* (Westport, Conn.: Greenwood Press, 1984), pp. 98–101.

32. *JHB*, 1761–1765, p. 230.

33. Ibid., p. 324.

34. Ibid.

35. Hamilton J. Eckenrode, *The Randolphs: The Story of a Virginia Family* (Indianapolis: Bobbs-Merrill Co., 1946), pp. 77–107. Descriptions of all patriots and signers of the Declaration of Independence from *DAB*.

36. Biographies of Patrick Henry cited: Jacob Alexrad, Julia Carson, William Wirt Henry, Robert Douthat Meade, Moses Coit Tyler, George Findlay Willison, William Wirt.

37. *JHB*, 1761–1765, p. 305.

38. Andrews, pp. 340, 353.

39. Freeman, vol. 3, p. 117; *NLB*, William Nelson to Robert Cary, Nov. 26, 1767.

40. Mays, vol. 1, pp. 144–46, 156, 173.

41. Charles Campbell, *History of the Colony and Ancient Dominion of Virginia* (Richmond: B. B. Minor, 1847), p. 523; Cooke, pp. 384–85.

42. *JHB*, 1761–1765, p. 305.

43. Edmund Randolph, *History of Virginia: 1753–1813* (Charlottesville: Univ. Press of Va., 1970), pp. 110–11.

44. *JHB*, 1761–1765, p. 356.

45. William Wirt Henry, *Patrick Henry: Life, Correspondence and Speeches* (New York: Charles Scribner's Sons, 1891), vol. 1, p. 71.

46. *JHB*, 1761–1765, p. 350.

47. Mapp, p. 297.

48. *JHB*, 1761–1765, p. 348.

49. Mays, vol. 1, pp. 144, 146, 156, 173.

50. Robert Douthat Meade, *Patrick Henry: Patriot in the Making* (Philadelphia: J. B. Lippincott, 1957), vol. 2, pp. 158–82.

51. *WMQ*, 18 (1), p. 23.

52. *JHB*, 1761–1765, Frontispiece; Freeman, vol. 3, p. 135.

53. Claude G. Bowers, *The Young Jefferson 1743–1789* (Boston: Houghton-Mifflin, 1945), pp. 40–41; Dumas Malone, *Jefferson, the Virginian* (Boston: Little, Brown and Co., 1948), vol. 1, pp. 92–93.

54. Freeman, vol. 3, pp. 135–37.

55. Ibid., p. 136.

56. Henry, p. 83.

57. *JHB*, 1761–1765, p. lxx.

58. Malone, vol. 1, p. 93.

59. *JHB*, 1761–1765, Governor Fauquier to Board of Trade, June 5, 1765, pp. lviii–lxvi.

60. Freeman, vol. 3, p. 138; Mapp, p. 304.

61. Corbin, p. 176.

62. Freeman, vol. 3, p. 138; Mapp, p. 304.

63. Purdie-Dixon VG, Apr. 11, 1766.

64. Freeman, vol. 3, p. 157.

65. Purdie-Dixon VG, Mar. 4, 1766.

66. Ibid., Mar. 21, 1766.

67. Freeman, vol. 3, p. 158.

68. Mapp, pp. 308–09.

69. *VMHB*, 9 (4), p. 359.

70. Mays, vol. 1, pp. 174–86; Mapp, pp. 310–16.

71. Mapp, p. 310.

72. *JHB*, 1761–1765, p. lxix.

73. Ibid.

74. Ibid., p. lxx.

75. Hunter VG, Nov. 3, 1752.

76. *NLB*, William Nelson to Edward and Samuel Athawes, Sept. 13, 1766.

77. Ibid.

78. Ibid. to John Backhouse, Nov. 26, 1767.

Chapter FIVE

1. *WMQ*, 20 (1), p. 173.

2. *NFB*.

3. Stella Pickett Hardy, *Colonial Families of the Southern States of America* (New York: Tobias A. Wright, 1911), pp. 15–21; William Meade, *Old Churches, Ministers and Families of Virginia* (Philadelphia: J. B. Lippincott and Co., 1857), vol. 1, pp. 106–08.

4. Alf J. Mapp, Jr., *The Virginia Experiment: The Old Dominion's Role in the Making of America, 1607–1781* (Richmond: Dietz Press, 1957), pp. 318–21.

5. Ibid.

6. Douglas Southall Freeman, *George Washington* (New York: Charles Scribner's Sons, 1966), vol. 3, pp. 153–56.

7. Purdie-Dixon VG, Apr. 11, 1766.

8. Ibid., Mar. 30, 1766.

9. Ibid., Mar. 21, 1766.

10. Ibid., Jan. 8, 1766.

11. Ibid., Apr. 18, 1766.

12. Ibid., Feb. 14, 1766.

13. Ibid., Mar. 4, 1776.

14. Ibid., Apr. 26, 1766.

15. Ibid., May 2, 1766.

16. Freeman, vol. 3, pp. 165–67.

17. *JHB*, 1761–1765, p. 305.

18. David Mays, *Edmund Pendleton, 1721–1803: A Biography* (Cambridge: Harvard Univ. Press, 1952), vol. 1, pp. 358–75. In a complete list of debtors to the Robinson estate, the Nelson name is conspicuously absent.

19. *NLB*, William Nelson to Samuel Athawes, Nov. 13, 1776.

20. Mays, vol. 1, p. 213.

21. Ibid.

22. Mays, vol. 1, pp. 358–75.

23. Lewis Burwell's land sale ad appeared in the Purdie-Dixon VG, Jan. 7, 1768; Benjamin Grymes advertised in the Rind VG, Feb. 2, 1769.

24. Purdie-Dixon *VG*, Apr. 25, 1766.

25. *NLB*, William Nelson to the Athawes, Nov. 13, 1766.

26. Emory Gibbons Evans, "The Nelsons: A Biographical Study of a Virginia Family in the Eighteenth Century" (dissertation, Univ. of Va., 1957); York Judgments and Orders, pp. 52–53.

27. Evans dissertation, p. 102.

28. *NLB*, William Nelson to John Norton, July 25, 1766.

29. Ibid.

30. *WMQ*, 6 (1), p. 143.

31. Ibid., pp. 143–45.

32. Frances Norton Mason, *John Norton & Sons, Merchants of London and Virginia, 1750–1795* (Richmond: Dietz Press, 1937), pp. 127–28.

33. Various sources supply construction dates ranging from 1711 to 1740 for "Scotch" Tom Nelson's Yorktown home now operated by the National Park Service. Emmie Ferguson Farrar, *Old Virginia Houses Along the James* (New York: Bonanza Books, 1907), pp. 216–19; Clyde F. Trudell, *Colonial Yorktown* (Old Greenwich, Conn.: Chatham Press, Inc., 1938), pp. 106–10; Thomas Tileston Waterman, *The Mansions of Virginia, 1706–1776* (Chapel Hill: Univ. of N.C. Press, 1946), pp. 419–20.

34. *NLB*, William Nelson to William Cookson, Nov. 26, 1767.

35. Ibid.

36. Wyndham Blanton, *Medicine in Virginia in the Eighteenth Century* (Richmond: Garrett and Massie, 1931), pp. 20, 36, 106, 204, 280–81, 346–48.

37. *NLB*, Nov. 26, 1767.

38. *Tyler's Quarterly*, 10, p. 289; VMHB, 4 (3), p. 359; 8 (3), p. 249–52; 16 (2), p. 206; WMQ, 2 (4), 238–39.

39. Purdie-Dixon *VG*, July 5, 1766.

40. *WMQ*, 7 (1), p. 15.

41. *NLB*, William Nelson to John Norton, Sept. 6, 1766.

42. *WMQ*, 9 (4), p. 265.

43. Ibid., 27 (4), p. 301. *NLB* contains other letters expressing William Nelson's relief at the Stamp Act repeal: James Buchanan, July 25, 1766; Samuel Waterman, July 25, 1766; John Backhouse, July 26, 1766.

44. *NLB*, William Nelson to John Norton, July 25, 1766.

45. Rind *VG*, Aug. 8, 1766.

46. The custom house is still standing at Yorktown. Construction dates vary from 1706 to 1721. Mason, p. 13; Meade, vol. 1, pp. 104, 109.

47. Charles S. Sydnor, *American Revolutionaries in the Making: Political Practice in Washington's Virginia* (N.Y.: Collier Books, 1962), p. 65; *NLB*, William Nelson to John Norton, Mar. 11, 1769; to John Norton, Mar. 11, 1769.

48. Mary A. Stephenson, "Nelson-Galt House at Williamsburg," Colonial Research Library, Williamsburg.

49. *Colonial Williamsburg Guidebook* (Williamsburg, 1985), pp. vi, vii, viii.

50. Jane Carson, *Colonial Virginians at Play* (Colonial Williamsburg Research Studies, 1958), pp. 27–34.

51. *Colonial Williamsburg Guidebook*, p. xii, 9, 14, 21, 25.

52. Carson, p. 27–34.

53. Ibid.

54. Philip Alexander Bruce, *Social Life of Virginia in the Seventeenth Century* (Richmond: Whittet and Shepperson, 1907), pp. 185–86; Louis B. Wright, *The Cultural Life of the American Colonies, 1607–1763* (New York: Harper Bros., 1957), p. 88; *Virginia Cavalcade*, Spring 1960, pp. 311–16.

55. Marshall W. Fishwick, *Virginia, a New Look at the Old Dominion* (New York: Harper and Bros., 1959), pp. 197, 303.

56. Hugh Jones, *The Present State of Virginia* (Chapel Hill: Univ. of N.C. Press, 1956), p. 48.

57. *The Statutes at Large*, ed. William Waller Hening (Richmond, 1819), vol. 6, p. 119.

58. Purdie-Dixon *VG*, June 4, 1767.

59. *VMHB*, 37 (1), pp. 55, 65, 86, 140, 177, 213, 214, 280–81, 245–73.

60. Ibid., 35 (4), pp. 308–09, 329–70.

61. Ibid.

62. Carson, p. 258; *VMHB*, 2 (3), pp. 292–05.

63. *VMHB*, 2 (3), p. 299.

64. Ibid., 35 (4), pp. 308–09, 329–70.

65. Ibid.

66. *VMHB*, 2 (2), p. 299.

67. Ibid., pp. 188–301.

68. Ibid.

69. Fishwick, p. 197; *VMHB*, 2 (3), p. 294; 35 (4), pp. 231–45.

70. Trudell, p. 50.

71. *NLB*, William Nelson to Samuel Athawes, Jan. 10, 1769.

72. Ibid., to Samuel Athawes, July 5, 1769.

73. Ibid., to John Norton, Nov. 14, 1768.

74. *VQ*, 23, pp. 91–92.

75. Purdie-Dixon *VG*, Oct. 10, 1766.

76. Julia Cherry Spruill, *Women's Life and Work in the Southern Colonies* (Chapel Hill: Univ. of N.C. Press, 1938), pp. 113–35.

77. Sydney George Fisher, *Men, Women and Manners in Colonial Times* (Philadelphia: J. B. Lippincott Co., 1900), preface; *NLB*, William Nelson to George Maynard, Feb. 27, 1768.

78. *Colonial Williamsburg Guidebook*, pp. 76–78.

79. Ibid., p. 87.

80. *Virginia Cavalcade*, Winter 1953, pp. 4–7.

81. *Colonial Williamsburg Guidebook*, pp. v–viii, xvi, xvii, 3, 14, 44, 61, 84–87; Waterman, p. 416.

82. Evans dissertation; *Colonial Williamsburg Guidebook*, p. 87.

83. *Colonial Williamsburg Guidebook*, pp. xvii, 5, 8, 81.

84. Hunter VG, Nov. 17, 1752; *WMQ*, 5 (3), pp. 359–74.

85. *JHB*, 1761–1765, pp. 11, 245–46.

Chapter SIX

1. Matthew Page Andrews, *Virginia, The Old Dominion* (Garden City, N.Y.: Doubleday, Doran and Co., Inc. 1937, 1937), p. 69.

2. Ibid., pp. 88–89, 190–91.

3. Ibid., pp. 190, 420, 429.

4. Lewis Cecil Gray, *History of Agriculture in the Southern United States to 1880* (Washington, D.C.: Carnegie Institute, 1933), vol. 1, chapter 10.

5. Emory Gibbons Evans, "The Nelsons: A Biographical Study of a Virginia Family in the Eighteenth Century" (dissertation, Univ. of Va., 1957); *WMQ*, 6 (1), pp. 143–45.

6. *VMHB*, 5 (2), pp. 175–80.

7. Kenneth P. Bailey, *The Ohio Company of Virginia and the Westward Movement* (Glendale, Ca.: Arthur H. Clark Co., 1937), pp. 35, 44, 66, 242–45, 298, 302, 306; Alf J. Mapp, Jr., *The Virginia Experiment: The Old Dominion's Role in the Making of America, 1607–1781* (Richmond: Dietz Press, 1957), pp. 226–27, 232, 235, 240, 246, 286, 288, 289.

8. Douglas Southall Freeman, *George Washington* (New York: Charles Scribner's Sons, 1966), vol. 3, pp. 94–95, 101–02, 109–10, 162–63, 168, 174–75, 180–81, 208.

9. Ibid., p. 94.

10. Gray, pp. 139–60.

11. Ibid.

12. Ibid.

13. *NLB*, William Nelson to John Norton, July 25, 1766.

14. *The Statutes at Large*, ed. William Waller Hening (Richmond, 1821), vol. 8, pp. 69–88.

15. Ibid., p. 69.

16. *Tyler's Quarterly*, 3, pp. 151, 193, 249.

17. "John Camm," *DAB*; William Meade, *Old Churches, Ministers and Families of Virginia* (Philadelphia: J. B. Lippincott and Co., 1857), vol. 1, pp. 216–28; *VMHB*, 10 (1), pp. 340, 352, 355.

18. *JHB*, 1761–1765; pp. xii, 58–61.

19. *Tyler's Quarterly*, 1, pp. 69, 73; *WMQ*, 1 (1), p. 28.

20. *VMHB*, 10 (1), p. 340.

21. Ibid., 37 (4), pp. 360–64.

22. Ibid., 10 (1), p. 351.

23. Thomas Tileston Waterman, *The Mansions of Virginia, 1706–1776* (Chapel Hill: Univ. of N.C. Press, 1946), pp. 25, 103.

24. Ibid., pp. 110, 111–12, 115.

25. John Esten Cooke, *Virginia: A History of the People* (Cambridge: Houghton-Mifflin and Co., 1883), pp. 21, 32.

26. Ibid., pp. 33–35.

27. Emmie Ferguson Farrar, *Old Virginia Houses Along the James* (New York: Bonanza Books, 1907), pp. 201–03; Freeman, vol. 3, pp. 1–2.

28. Freeman, vol. 3, p. 79.

29. Ibid., p. 227n.

30. Waterman, p. 200. Mary, fourth daughter of "King" Carter married George Braxton making their son Carter a second cousin to Thomas Nelson, Jr.; Louis Morton, *Robert Carter of Nomini Hall: A Virginia Tobacco Planter in the Eighteenth Century* (Charlottesville: Univ. of Va. Press, 1941), pp. 3–30.

31. *VMHB*, 33 (2), pp. 190–92; York County Records, Wills and Inventories, xxii, pp. 132–36.

32. Ibid.

33. Clifford Dowdey, *The Virginia Dynasties* (Boston: Little, Brown and Co., 1969), pp. 333–377. Characteristics of the era and aristocrats are found in Louis B. Wright, *The Cultural Life of the American Colonies, 1607–1763* and *The First Gentlemen of Virginia: Intellectual Qualities of the Early Colonial Ruling Class.*

34. Andrews, pp. 188, 199, 202; Dowdey, pp. 147–72.

35. Waterman, pp. 123, 130.

36. Ibid., pp. 146–63.

37. *Another Secret Diary of William Byrd of Westover, 1739–1741*, ed. Maude H. Woodfin (Richmond: Dietz Press, 1942), p. 31.

38. Waterman, pp. 132–35.

39. Morton, p. 26; *VMHB*, 31 (1), p. 44.

40. Waterman, pp. 178–86, 190–92, 414.

41. Ibid., pp. 163–68, 394–08.

42. Ibid., pp. 173–78, 346–58, 422.

43. *NLB*, William Nelson to John Norton, July 25, 1766.

44. Ibid., to Samuel Waterman, July 25, 1766.

45. Ibid., to James Buchanan, July 25, 1766.

46. Ibid., to John Backhouse, July 26, 1766.

47. Ibid., to James Gildart, July 26, 1766.

Chapter SEVEN

1. Frances Norton Mason, *John Norton & Sons, Merchants of London and Virginia, 1750–1795* (Richmond: Dietz Press, 1937), p. 22.

2. Ibid.

3. *NLB*, William Nelson to John Norton, Dec. 23, 1766.

4. Mason, p. 22.

5. Charles S. Sydnor, *Gentlemen Freeholders: Political Practices in Washington's Virginia* (Westport, Conn.: Greenwood Press, 1984), pp. 96–97; *NLB*, William Nelson to Edward and Samuel Athawes, Nov. 13, 1766.

6. *NLB*, William Nelson to Capel and Osgood Hansbury, Aug, 14, 1767.

7. Ibid., to John Norton, Nov. 12, 1766.

8. William Meade, *Old Churches, Ministers and Families of Virginia* (Philadelphia: J. B. Lippincott and Co., 1857), vol. 1, p. 207; Lucy Calthorpe Smith manuscript, Colonial Williamsburg Archives.

9. Edmund S. Morgan, *Virginians at Home: Family Life in the Eighteenth Century* (Colonial Williamsburg, 1952), chapter 3; Mary Newton Stanard, *Colonial*

Virginia: Its People and Customs (Philadelphia: J. B. Lippincott and Co., 1917); Louis B. Wright, *The Cultural Life of the American Colonies, 1607–1763* (New York: Harper Bros., 1957), pp. 6, 8, 14, 39, 43, 49.

10. Jean Francois Chastellux, *Travels in North America in the Years 1780, 1781, 1782* (New York: White, Gillespie and White, 1787), vol. 1, p. 219.

11. Julia Cherry Spruill, *Women's Life and Work in the Southern Colonies* (Chapel Hill: Univ. of N.C. Press, 1938) pp. 20–42, 64–84.

12. Meade, vol. 1, pp. 202–15.

13. *JHB*, 1766, pp. 105, 110, 118.

14. Ibid., p. 126.

15. *NLB*, William Nelson to Capel and Osgood Hansbury, Aug. 14, 1767.

16. *JHB*, 1766, p. 118.

17. Ibid.

18. Ibid.

19. Ibid., pp. 10–11.

20. Ibid.

21. William Oliver Stevens, *Old Williamsburg and Her Neighbors* (New York: Dodd, Mead and Co., 1938), p. 140.

22. Mason, pp. 21, 25.

23. *NLB*, William Nelson to John Norton, July 9, 1768.

24. *NFB*.

25. *NLB*, William Nelson to William Fauquier, June 13, 1767.

26. Purdie-Dixon VG, July 16, 1767.

27. Ibid.

28. *NLB*, William Nelson to William Fauquier, June 13, 1767.

29. Mason, pp. 25–26.

30. Ibid.

31. J. A. Osborne, *Williamsburg in Colonial Times* (Richmond: Dietz Press, 1935), p. 27.

32. "William Pitt, Earl of Chatham," *Imperial Encyclopedia*. Pitt's wife was Grenville's sister. "George Grenville," *DAB*; John C. Miller, *Origins of the American Revolution* (Boston: Little, Brown and Co., 1943), p. 242; *Triumph of Freedom, 1775–1783* (Boston: Little, Brown and Co., 1948), pp. 23, 35.

33. Alf J. Mapp, Jr., *The Virginia Experiment: The Old Dominion's Role in the Making of America, 1607–1781* (Richmond: Dietz Press, 1957), pp. 324, 327–30.

34. *NLB*, William Nelson to Charles Grove, Nov. 25, 1767.

35. Purdie-Dixon VG, July 16, 1767.

36. Ibid., Mar. 16, 1767.

37. Ibid.

38. *NLB*, William Nelson to John Norton, Sept. 12, 1766.

39. Mason, p. 22.

40. *NLB*, William Nelson to John Norton, Aug. 14, 1767.

41. Ibid., to Edward and Samuel Athawes, Sept. 12, 1767.

42. Ibid., to Edward Hunt and Son, Nov. 28, 1767.

43. Ibid., to Charles Grove, Nov. 25, 1767.

44. Ibid., to Edward Hunt and Son, Nov. 20, 1767.

45. Mason, p. 22.

46. *NLB*, William Nelson to Edward Hunt and Son, May 12, 1767.

47. Ibid., to Edward and Samuel Athawes, May 12, 1767.

48. Ibid., to Edward Hunt and Son, Oct. 13, 1767.

49. Ibid., to Edward Hunt and Son, Nov. 20, 1767.

50. Mason, p. 29.

51. Ibid., p. 33.

52. Ibid., p. 32–33.

53. Ibid., p. 510.

54. *NLB*, William Nelson to Edward and Samuel Athawes, Aug. 12, 1767.

55. The gold snuff box is exhibited at the VHS in Richmond.

56. *NLB*, William Nelson to Cousin William Cookson, Sept. 10, 1766.

57. Ibid., to John Dunbar, Nov. 24, 1767.

58. Ibid., to John Norton, July 9, 1768.

59. Ibid., to James Buchanan, Nov. 24, 1767.

Chapter EIGHT

1. Lucy Calthorpe Smith manuscript, Colonial Williamsburg Archives.

2. Hamilton J. Eckenrode, *The Randolphs: The Story of a Virginia Family* (Indianapolis: Bobbs-Merrill Co., 1946), pp. 42, 81–82, 87, 93, 109, 111.

3. Wyndham Blanton, *Medicine in Virginia in the Eighteenth Century* (Richmond: Garrett and Massie, 1931), p. 338.

4. Frances Norton Mason, *John Norton & Sons, Merchants of London and Virginia, 1750–1795* (Richmond: Dietz Press, 1937), pp. 127–28, 136.

5. Purdie-Dixon VG, Jan. 21, 1768.

6. *NLB*, William Nelson to Samuel Athawes, Feb. 27, 1768.

7. Rind VG, Mar. 3, 1768.

8. *WMQ*, 8 (1), pp. 173–77.

9. Ibid.

10. Ibid.

11. Purdie-Dixon VG, Mar. 3, 1768; Apr. 7, 1768.

12. David Mays, *Edmund Pendleton, 1721–1803: A Biography* (Cambridge: Harvard Univ. Press, 1952), vol. 1, p. 149.

13. *NLB*, William Nelson to Capel and Osgood Hansbury, Feb. 27, 1768.

14. Robert E. and Katherine Brown, *Virginia 1705–1786: Democracy or Aristocracy?* (East Lansing: Mich. State Univ. Press, 1964), p. 97; the Browns list two hundred Virginia debtors. Mays, vol. 1, pp. 358–75.

15. "Alexander Spotswood," *DAB*, p. 383.

16. *JHB*, 1767–1768, pp. 147, 156, 159, 164.

17. "Francis Lightfoot Lee," *DAB*.

18. Douglas Southall Freeman, *George Washington* (New York: Charles Scribner's Sons, 1966), vol. 3, p. 201; *JHB*, 1767–1768, pp. 135–36.

19. *The Letters of Richard Henry Lee*, ed. James Curtis Ballagh (New York: The Macmillan Co., 1911), vol. 1, pp. 26, 28.

20. Ibid.

21. Ibid.

22. *JHB*, 1767–1768, pp. 165–66, 169, 171.

23. "Sam Adams," *DAB*.

24. *NLB*, William Nelson to John Norton, July 9, 1768.

25. Mason, p. 63.

26. *NLB*, William Nelson to Robert Cary, Feb. 27, 1768.

27. Mason, pp. 44–45.

28. Ibid.

29. Purdie-Dixon VG, Mar. 10, 1768.

30. Ibid., Feb. 4, 1768.

31. Blanton, pp. 60, 62–63. Blanton states that smallpox killed, crippled, or disfigured every tenth person in Virginia as late as 1754. It was unknown in the New World before the coming of Spanish ships.

32. NLB, William Nelson to John Norton, Aug. 14, 1767.

33. Ibid., Feb. 27, 1768.

34. Purdie-Dixon VG, Apr. 17, 1768.

35. NLB, William Nelson to Samuel Athawes, Aug. 16, 1768.

36. Ibid., to Edward Hunt, Sept. 13, 1768.

37. Ibid., July 9, 1768.

38. Ibid., to John Norton, Aug. 27, 1768.

39. Mason, pp. 59–60.

40. Ibid., p. 65.

41. NFB.

42. NLB, William Nelson to Samuel Athawes, Nov. 15, 1768.

43. Ibid., to John Norton, Nov. 14, 1768; Mason, pp. 144–45.

44. Mason, pp. 144–45.

45. NLB, William Nelson to William Cookson, Nov. 19, 1768; Nov. 26, 1767.

46. WMQ, 14 (1), p. 128.

47. Ibid., 16 (1), pp. 1–65.

48. VMHB, 63 (4), pp. 379–409.

49. Purdie-Dixon VG, Oct. 27, 1768.

50. NLB, William Nelson to Samuel Athawes, Nov. 15, 1768.

51. VMHB, 63 (4), pp. 379–09.

52. WMQ, 5 (3), pp. 165–71.

53. Rutherfoord Goodwin, *A Brief and True Report Concerning Williamsburg, Virginia* (Richmond: Dietz Press, 1941), pp. 214, 239.

54. NLB, William Nelson to William Fauquier, Aug. 16, 1768.

55. Goodwin, pp. 214, 239.

56. Ibid., p. 239.

57. Colonial Williamsburg Guidebook (Williamsburg, 1985), pp. 14–16.

58. Ibid., pp. 20–22.

59. Goodwin, p. 56.

60. NLB, William Nelson to John Norton, Nov. 14, 1768.

61. Mason, p. 76.

62. Goodwin, p. 239.

63. Ibid.

64. Emory Gibbons Evans, "The Nelsons: A Biographical Study of a Virginia Family in the Eighteenth Century" (dissertation, Univ. of Va., 1957).

65. Rind VG, Jan. 10, 1771.

66. Mason, pp. 93–95.

67. Freeman, vol. 3, pp. 183–86.

68. Purdie-Dixon VG, Oct. 18, 1768.

69. Ibid., Apr. 25, 1766; Oct. 13, 1766.

70. Ibid., Oct. 14, 1768.

71. Ibid., Oct. 18, 1768.

72. *NLB*, William Nelson to William Cookson, Sept. 2, 1769.

73. Ibid., to Samuel Waterman, Sept. 6, 1768.

74. *NLB*, William Nelson to Samuel Waterman, Sept. 6, 1768; to Edward Hunt, July 9, 1768; Sept. 6, 1768; Sept. 13, 1768; to Robert Cary, July 28, 1768; to Hansburys, July 9, 1768; to Bosworth Griffith, July 28, 1768; to John Norton, Nov. 14, 1768; to Samuel Athawes, Aug. 16, 1768; Nov. 15, 1768.

75. *NLB*, William Nelson to Samuel Athawes, Nov. 15, 1768.

76. Ibid., to William Cookson, Nov. 19, 1768.

77. *The Statutes at Large*, ed. William Waller Hening, (Richmond, 1812, 1820), vol. 3, p. 243; vol. 7, p. 306. An excellent discussion pertaining to elections appears in Charles Sydnor's *Gentlemen Freeholders: Political Practices in Washington's Virginia*.

78. *JHB*, 1752–1758, p. 335; Charles Sydnor, *Gentlemen Freeholders: Political Practices in Washington's Virginia* (Westport, Conn.: Greenwood Press, 1984), pp. 11–12.

79. Sydnor, pp. 11–12.

80. Ibid.

81. Freeman, vol. 2, pp. 32, 320; Sydnor, p. 19.

82. Sydnor, pp. 53–54.

Chapter NINE

1. Jean Francois Chastellux, *Travels in North America in the Years 1780, 1781, 1782* (New York: White, Gillespie and White, 1787), vol. 1, p. 219; William Meade, *Old Churches, Ministers and Families of Virginia* (Philadelphia: J. B. Lippincott and Co., 1857), vol. 1, pp. 212–13.

2. Walnut secretary of General Nelson at Custom House, Yorktown, Va.

3. *Colonial Williamsburg Guidebook* (Williamsburg, 1985) pp. 76–78.

4. Jane Carson, *Colonial Virginians at Play* (Colonial Williamsburg Research Studies, 1958).

5. Nathan Schachner, *Thomas Jefferson* (New York: Thomas Yoseloff, 1951), p. 69.

6. *WMQ*, 13 (1), p. 20–21.

7. Ibid., 12 (1), pp. 13, 22, 133, 134.

8. Ibid., 12 (1), p. 133.

9. Ibid., 12 (1), p. 134.

10. Ibid., 4 (2), pp. 118, 121, 132, 134.

11. Ibid., p. 20.

12. *The Statutes at Large*, ed. William Waller Hening (Richmond, 1821), vol. 8, p. 314.

13. Douglas Southall Freeman, *George Washington* (New York: Charles Scribner's Sons, 1966), vol. 3, pp. 214, 215, 591.

14. "John Wilkes," *Imperial Encyclopedia*.

15. "Arthur Lee," *DAB*.

16. Rind's *VG* ran the accounts from the end of February through April 1768.

17. *NLB*, William Nelson to John Norton, Aug. 27, 1768.

18. *JHB*, 1766–1769, pp. xi, xiii, xl–xliii, 187–90, 211, 214, 215, 218, 412.

19. Ibid., p. 187.

20. Alf J. Mapp, Jr., *The Virginia Experiment: The Old Dominion's Role in the*

Making of America, 1607–1781 (Richmond: Dietz Press, 1957), pp. 331–38; David Mays, *Edmund Pendleton, 1721–1803: A Biography* (Cambridge: Harvard Univ. Press, 1952), vol. 1, pp. 249–57, 321, 344.

21. Purdie-Dixon VG, May 11, 1769.

22. JHB, 1766–1769, pp. 187–89.

23. Charles S. Sydnor, *Gentlemen Freeholders: Political Practices in Washington's Virginia* (Westport, Conn.: Greenwood Press, 1984), p. 64; Louis B. Wright, *The First Gentlemen of Virginia: Intellectual Qualities of the Early Colonial Ruling Class* (San Marino, Ca.: Huntington Library, 1940), p. 54.

24. "John Blair," *DAB*; Matthew Page Andrews, *Virginia, The Old Dominion* (Garden City, N.Y.: Doubleday, Doran and Co., Inc., 1937), pp. 231, 236n., 249, 328, 351; Freeman, vol. 3, pp. 197–98, 220, 225, 240, 308, 331, 334.

25. Andrews, pp. 270, 284; Freeman, vol. 3, pp. 174, 422; Mapp, pp. 293, 306, 421; Thomas Tileston Waterman, *The Mansions of Virginia, 1706–1776* (Chapel Hill: Univ. of N.C. Press, 1946), pp. 384, 387, 420; *Colonial Williamsburg Guidebook*, p. 76.

26. Andrews, pp. 208–09; Freeman, p. 396.

27. "Francis Lightfoot Lee," *DAB*.

28. Carson, p. 20.

29. VMHB, 63 (4), pp. 377–409.

30. Andrews, pp. 189, 205; *Another Secret Diary of William Byrd of Westover, 1739–1741*, ed. Maude H. Woodfin (Richmond: Dietz Press, 1942); Freeman, vol. 3, pp. 37, 50–51, 59, 99; Mapp, pp. 200–01; Waterman, pp. 107, 146, 149–50, 160, 423; *A Memorial Volume of Virginia Historical Portrature, 1585-1830*, ed. Alexander Wilbourne Weddell (Richmond, 1930).

31. Andrews, pp. 188, 199, 202; Mapp, pp. 203–04, 229, 390, 411, 424, 447; Louis Morton, *Robert Carter of Nomini Hall: A Virginia Tobacco Planter in the Eighteenth Century* (Charlottesville: Univ. of Va. Press, 1941), pp. 33, 43, 145, 202, 215; Waterman, pp. 73, 136, 139–45.

32. Freeman, vol. 3, pp. 15, 103; JHB, 1761–1765, p. 359; WMQ, 2 (1), p. 37; 27 (1), p. 210.

33. NLB, William Nelson to Samuel Athawes, Aug. 12, 1767.

34. Andrews, pp. 167, 187, 209, 269; Freeman, vol. 1, pp. 127, 230; vol. 3, pp. 13, 15, 27, 204, 293, 306; Mapp, pp. 204, 233, 240, 244.

35. Agnes Rothery, *Houses Virginians Have Loved* (New York: Rinehart and Co., Inc., 1954), pp. 34, 37, 45; Waterman, pp. 330–31.

36. JHB, 1766–1769, pp. 187–88.

37. Ibid., pp. 188–89.

38. Ibid.; Purdie-Dixon VG, May 11, 1769.

39. JHB, 1766–1769, p. 190.

40. Ibid., p. 211.

41. JHB, 1766–1769, p. 146.

42. NLB, William Nelson to Farrell J. Jones, Nov. 19, 1768.

43. Mapp, pp. 328–29.

44. Andrews, pp. 233, 245, 280, 287; Freeman, vol. 3, pp. 3–5.

45. "Peyton Randolph," *DAB*; Hamilton J. Eckenrode, *The Randolphs: The Story of a Virginia Family* (Indianapolis: Bobbs-Merrill Co., 1946), pp. 77–107. Edmund Randolph married Elizabeth ("Betsy") Nicholas, daughter of Robert Carter Nicholas.

46. Andrews, pp. 242, 250, 281, 283, 288, 323, 328; Freeman, vol. 3, pp. 5, 33, 134, 166, 224–27, 350–52; *JHB*, 1766–1769, p. 141; *WMQ*, 16 (1), p. 29; Mapp, pp. 301, 308, 327, 329.

47. Morton, pp. 3–19; *Diary of Colonel Landon Carter of Sabine Hall, 1752–1778*, ed. Jack P. Green (Charlottesville: Univ. of Va. Press, 1965).

48. Andrews, pp. 242, 250, 280; Freeman, vol. 3, pp. 389–90.

49. "Richard Henry Lee," *DAB*. Biographies by Ethel Armes, James Curtis Ballagh, Oliver Perry Chitwood, Burton J. Hendrick.

50. Freeman, vol. 3, pp. 3–5.

51. *JHB*, 1766–1769, p. 188.

52. Ibid.

53. Ibid., pp. xi, xli–xliii.

54. Ibid., p. xlii.

55. Ibid., pp. xl, xli.

56. Freeman, vol. 3, p. 212–27.

57. Purdie-Dixon VG, May 25, 1769.

58. Ibid.

59. Freeman, vol. 3, p. 225.

60. Rind VG, May 25, 1769.

61. *Colonial Williamsburg Guidebook*, pp. 29–31, 97; Archibald Bolling Shepperson, *John Paradise and Lucy Ludwell of London and Williamsburg* (Richmond: Dietz Press, 1942).

62. Frances Norton Mason, *John Norton & Sons, Merchants of London and Virginia, 1750–1795* (Richmond: Dietz Press, 1937), p. 63.

63. Ibid., p. 99.

64. Ibid., p. 98.

65. Romance of John Hatley Norton and Sarah Nicholas, daughter of Robert Carter Nicholas, traced through many letters in Frances Norton Mason's *John Norton & Sons, Merchants of London and Virginia, 1750–1795.*

66. *Tyler's Quarterly*, 7, pp. 181–84, 200, 213, 279–82; *WMQ*, 2 (1), pp. 50, 54, 123–24, 200, 235–37; 5 (1), pp. 15, 17, 83–89, 153, 168, 203; 13 (1), pp. 133–37.

67. Mason, p. 102.

68. *NLB*, William Nelson to Samuel Athawes, July 5, 1769.

69. Ibid., to William Cookson, Sept. 2, 1769.

70. Ibid., to Lamar, Hill and Bispet, Sept. 16, 1769.

71. Rind VG, Sept. 14, 1769.

72. *NLB*, William Nelson to Samuel Athawes, Sept. 16, 1769; to Samuel Waterman, Oct. 30, 1769; to Dobson Daltena J. Walker, Dec. 23, 1769.

73. *NLB*, William Nelson to Samuel Athawes, Nov. 7, 1769.

74. Ibid., to Samuel Waterman, Oct. 30, 1769.

75. Emory Gibbons Evans, "The Nelsons: A Biographical Study of a Virginia Family in the Eighteenth Century," (dissertation, Univ. of Va., 1957).

76. Berkeley Papers (Bill 204, Manuscript Dept., Univ. of Va. Library, No. 4028); *NLB*, William Nelson to John Norton, July 19, 1770.

77. *NLB*, William Nelson to Edward Hunt, Nov. 17, 1769.

78. *JHB*, 1766–1769, p. xliii.

79. *NLB*, William Nelson to John Norton, Jan. 29, 1770.

80. Purdie-Dixon VG, Dec. 14, 1769.

Chapter TEN

1. Edward Lewis Goodwin, *Colonial Church in Virginia* (Milwaukee: Morehouse Publishing Co., 1927); George Carrington Mason, *Colonial Churches in Tidewater Virginia* (Richmond: Whittet and Shepperson, 1945), pp. 217–22; William Meade, *Old Churches, Ministers and Families of Virginia* (Philadelphia: J. B. Lippincott and Co., 1857), vol. 1, pp. 202–15; vol. 2, pp. 216–28.

2. Mason, chapter 12; Louis Morton, *Robert Carter of Nomini Hall: A Virginia Tobacco Planter in the Eighteenth Century* (Charlottesville: Univ. of Va. Press, 1941), pp. 7, 20–21; Thomas Tileston Waterman, *The Mansions of Virginia, 1706–1776* (Chapel Hill: Univ. of N.C. Press, 1946), pp. 103, 123, 130, 218.

3. *Vestry Book, Christ Church Parish, Middlesex County, Va., 1663–1767*, ed. Churchill G. Chamberlayne (Richmond: Old Dominion Press, 1927), pp. 270, 273, 312–31; Mason, pp. 275–82.

4. Louis B. Wright, *The Cultural Life of the American Colonies, 1607–1763* (New York: Harper Bros., 1957), p. 74.

5. Clyde F. Trudell, *Colonial Yorktown* (Old Greenwich, Conn.: Chatham Press, Inc., 1938), pp. 57–62.

6. Goodwin, pp. 217–22; Mason, p. 223; William S. Perry, *Historical Collections Related to American Colonial Churches* (Hartford, Conn.: Church Press Corp., 1967), pp. 281–83.

7. Perry, p. 281.

8. Hugh Jones, *The Present State of Virginia* (Chapel Hill: Univ. of N.C. Press, 1956), p. 62.

9. Jones, p. 62; Meade, pp. 216–18.

10. G. MacLaren Brydon, *Virginia's Mother Church and the Political Conditions Under Which It Grew* (Richmond: VHS, 1947), vol. 2, pp. 238–55.

11. Henry Cabot Lodge, *A Short History of the English Colonies in America* (New York: Harper and Bros., 1899), vol. 2, pp. 60–61, 65.

12. Philip Alexander Bruce, *Social Life of Virginia in the Seventeenth Century* (Richard: Whittet and Shepperson, 1907), pp. 208–11.

13. *The Secret Diary of William Byrd of Westover, 1709–1712*, eds. Louis B. Wright and Marion Tinling (Richmond: Dietz Press, 1941), p. 98.

14. *JHB*, 1758–1761, pp. 16–18; *WMQ*, 9 (3), pp. 152–64.

15. Perry, p. 269–87; Brydon, p. 269–87.

16. Perry, p. 283.

17. Marshall W. Fishwick, *Virginia, a New Look at the Old Dominion* (New York: Harper and Bros., 1959), p. 203.

18. Meade, vol. 1, p. 18; Brydon, vol. 2, p. 324.

19. Brydon, vol. 2, p. 324.

20. *JHB*, 1758–1761, pp. 16–18.

21. Ibid., p. 17–18.

22. *JHB*, 1758–1761, p. 18.

23. Brydon, vol. 2, pp. 139–53, 238–55.

24. Matthew Page Andrews, *Virginia, The Old Dominion* (Garden City, N.Y.: Doubleday, Doran and Co., Inc., 1937), pp. 49–50, 175, 346, 350; *The Journal and Letters of Philip Vickers Fithian, A Plantation Tutor of the Old Dominion, 1773–1774*, ed. Hunter Dickinson Farish (Colonial Williamsburg, 1957), pp. 72, 211; Alf J. Mapp, Jr., *The Virginia Experiment: The Old Dominion's Role in the Making of Amer-*

ica, 1607–1781 (Richmond: Dietz Press, 1957), pp. 447–48; Wright, pp. 59, 84, 88, 90, 184, 194.

25. Brydon, vol. 1, p. 185.

26. Agnes Rothery, *Houses Virginians Have Loved* (New York: Rinehart and Co., Inc., 1954), pp. 218–21; Ethel Armes, *Stratford Hall, The Great House of the Lees* (Richmond: Garrett and Massie, 1936).

27. Morton, pp. 231–50. Carter embraced deism, became a Baptist, allied with Arminianism, and later turned to the teachings of Swedenborg.

28. Wright, pp. 91, 93, 115, 121, 163, 183; Andrews, pp. 349, 353; Mapp, p. 449.

29. Andrews, pp. 188–89, 343, 349; Richard Beale Davis, *Intellectual Life in Jefferson's Virginia, 1790–1830* (Chapel Hill: Univ. of N.C. Press, 1964), pp. 48, 80, 108, 134–35, 371, 374; Fithian, pp. 61, 90, 97, 105, 126, 146; Mapp, pp. 184, 407; Wright, pp. 16, 43, 72, 75, 88–89, 92–93, 97, 108–09, 120–21, 180, 184–85, 193.

30. Davis, pp. 48, 80, 108, 134–35, 371, 374.

31. Henry Howe, *Historical Collections* (Charleston: W. R. Babcock, 1847), p. 294.

32. Julia M. H. Carson, *Son of Thunder: Patrick Henry* (New York: Longmans, Green and Co., Inc., 1945), pp. 21–22; Meade, vol. 1, p. 70.

33. Andrews, p. 228.

34. Hamilton J. Eckenrode, *The Randolphs: The Story of a Virginia Family* (Indianapolis: Bobbs-Merrill Co., 1946), p. 50; Claude G. Bowers, *The Young Jefferson, 1743–1789* (Boston: Houghton-Mifflin, 1945), pp. 32–35.

35. Meade, vol. 1, p. 183; William Henry Foote, *Sketches of Virginia Historical and Biographical* (Richmond: John Knox Press, 1850), chapters 8–13.

36. William Nelson was president of the council from October 15, 1770 to September 25, 1771.

37. *NLB*, William Nelson to Samuel Athawes, Nov. 15, 1768.

38. Brydon, vol. 2, pp. 288–30.

39. Ibid., pp. 334, 336–37, 339, 341–60, 362; Goodwin, p. 245.

40. Douglas Southall Freeman, *George Washington* (New York: Charles Scribner's Sons, 1966), vol. 3, pp. 202–03; *JHB*, 1770–1772, p. xxxii, President William Nelson to Lord Hillsborough, Nov. 15, 1770 and Apr. 14, 1771.

41. Wesley H. Gewehr, *The Great Awakening in Virginia, 1740–1790* (Durham: Duke Univ. Press, 1930).

42. *NLB*, William Nelson to Edward Hunt, May 16, 1771.

43. Ibid.

44. Ibid.

45. Freeman, vol. 2, pp. 202–03.

46. *JHB*, 1770–1772, p. xxxii.

47. Ibid., p. xx–xxi, President William Nelson to Lord Hillsborough, Nov. 15, 1770; Apr. 14, 117.

48. Brydon, vol. 2, p. 332. A writer to the VG suggested Horrocks probably went so suddenly to England hoping to be the first bishop—perhaps a logical assumption since Horrocks left in the middle of a fight.

49. Ibid., p. 330.

50. Mason, p. 187.

51. Brydon, vol. 2, p. 330.

52. Ibid., p. 326.
53. Ibid., p. 330.
54. *VMHB*, 6 (3), pp. 351, 357; 20 (4), pp. 372–80; 35 (4), pp. 375–78; Mapp, pp. 195, 205.
55. Freeman, vol. 2, pp. 276–302; Meade, vol. 1, pp. 180–81.
56. *VMHB*, 35 (4), p. 377; *WMQ*, 3 (1), p. 258.
57. *VMHB*, 35 (1), p. 379.
58. Freeman, vol. 3, pp. 225–27, 281–82; *VMHB*, 35 (4), pp. 372–80.
59. *VMHB*, 36 (1), p. 37n.
60. Ibid.
61. Ibid., 35 (4), p. 377; 20 (4), pp. 375, 377.
62. Fishwick, p. 29.
63. Freeman, vol. 2, p. 298.
64. Ibid., pp. 225–27, 282, 287, 335.
65. Ibid., p. 225.
66. Freeman states that the letters of William Nelson are a good source for tracing the Dunbar-Custis case.
67. *NLB*, William Nelson to John Dunbar, Sept. 11, 1766.
68. Ibid., to Samuel Athawes, Nov. 15, 1768.
69. Ibid., to John Dunbar, June 12, 1769.
70. Ibid.

Chapter ELEVEN

1. Edward Miles Riley, "The Founding and Development of Yorktown, Virginia, 1691-1781" (dissertation, Univ. of Southern Ca., 1942), p. 149.
2. Frances Norton Mason, *John Norton & Sons, Merchants of London and Virginia, 1750–1795* (Richmond: Dietz Press, 1937), p. 2; Clyde F. Trudell, *Colonial Yorktown* (Old Greenwich, Conn.: Chatham Press, Inc., 1938), p. 91; *WMQ*, 19 (3), pp. 331–33.
3. Purdie-Dixon VG, Feb. 9, 1769; Jan. 18, 1770; Sept. 13, 1770.
4. Rind VG, Jan. 25, 1770.
5. "Lord North," *DNB*.
6. Gold snuffbox now on display at the VHS.
7. Dumas Malone, *Jefferson the Virginian* (Boston: Little, Brown and Co., 1948), vol. 1, p. 125.
8. Ibid., p. 126.
9. Julian P. Boyd, *The Papers of Thomas Jefferson* (Princeton: Princeton Univ. Press, 1951), pp. 7, 37.
10. *NLB*, William Nelson to Samuel Athawes, Jan. 30, 1771.
11. Ibid., to Robert Cary, July 20, 1770.
12. Ibid., to John Norton, July 19, 1770.
13. Douglas Southall Freeman, *George Washington* (New York: Charles Scribner's Sons, 1966), vol. 3, p. 250; *JHB*, 1766–1769, pp. xi, xiii.
14. Freeman, vol. 3, p. 251; *Virginia Historical Register*, ed. William Maxwell (Richmond: MacFarland and Fergusson, 1850), vol. 3, p. 22.
15. *NLB*, William Nelson to Dobson, Dalthena, and Walker, July 21, 1770.
16. Ibid., to Samuel Athawes, July 26, 1770.
17. Ibid., Sept. 3, 1770.

18. Ibid., to William Cookson, Nov. 26, 1770.
19. Ibid., to Samuel Athawes, Jan. 10, 1769.
20. Robert E. and Katherine Brown, *Virginia 1705–1786: Democracy or Aristocracy?* (East Lansing: Mich. State Univ. Press, 1964), p. 97.
21. Mason, pp. 127–28.
22. Ibid., p. 127.
23. Rind VG, Mar. 8, 1770; Mason, pp. 144–45.
24. Mason, pp. 144–45.
25. Mary A. Stephenson, *Carter's Grove Plantation* (Colonial Williamsburg, 1964).
26. *NLB*, William Nelson to Samuel Athawes, Dec. 18, 1770.
27. Stephenson, *Carter's Grove Plantation.*
28. Rind VG, Nov. 30, 1769.
29. *NLB*, William Nelson to Farrell J. Jones, Jan. 11, 1769.
30. Ibid., to Francis Farley, Feb. 22, 1770.
31. *WMQ*, 16 (1), p. 33.
32. Ibid.
33. Purdie-Dixon VG, Oct. 18, 1770.
34. Ibid.
35. *NLB*, William Nelson to Samuel Athawes, Dec. 6, 1770.
36. Ibid., to Frances Farley, Feb. 22, 1770.
37. *Tyler's Quarterly*, 3, p. 107; *WMQ*, 3 (1), p. 144, 270.
38. *Tyler's Quarterly*, 3, pp. 106–26.
39. Ibid.
40. Ibid.
41. *NLB*, William Nelson to Samuel Athawes, Dec. 6, 1770.
42. Ibid., May 10, 1771.
43. Ibid., Dec. 6, 1770.
44. *JHB*, 1770–1772, pp. xxii–xxv.
45. Freeman, vol. 1, p. 268.
46. Ibid., vol. 3, pp. 237, 244, 252–53, 256–57.
47. Matthew Page Andrews, *Virginia, the Old Dominion* (Garden City, N.Y.: Doubleday, Doran and Co., Inc. 1937), p. 235; Alf. J. Mapp, Jr., *The Virginia Experiment: The Old Dominion's Role in the Making of America, 1607–1781* (Richmond: Dietz Press, 1957), p. 287.
48. *JHB*, 1770–1772, pp. xx, xxi.
49. Ibid., p. xxi.
50. Freeman, vol. 1, p. 268.
51. *NFB.*
52. Purdie-Dixon VG, Nov. 29, 1770.
53. Ibid., Jan. 17, 1771.
54. Thomas Nelson Page, *The Old Dominion, Her Making and Her Manners* (New York: Jenkins and Thomas, 1883), pp. 368–69.
55. *WMQ*, 13 (1), p. 163.
56. William Meade, *Old Churches, Ministers and Families of Virginia* (Philadelphia: J. B. Lippincott and Co., 1857), vol. 1, p. 36.
57. Page, pp. 378–79.
58. Meade, vol. 1, p. 206.
59. Mason, pp. 138–39.

60. *NLB*, William Nelson to Samuel Athawes, Jan. 30, 1771.

61. Ibid., to John Norton, May 17, 1771.

62. References to the plans and personnel of the hospital for the insane taken from Eastern State Hospital Court of Directors' Minutes, Virginia State Library. (With permission from the Virginia Department of Mental Health, Mental Retardation and Substance Abuse Services, Eastern State Hospital, Williamsburg, Virginia.)

63. *The Statutes at Large*, ed. William Waller Hening (Richmond, 1821), vol. 8, p. 378.

64. *NLB*, William Nelson to Robert Cary, Jan. 21, 1771.

65. Ibid., Aug. 7, 1771.

66. Ibid., Mar. 25, 1771.

67. Ibid., to Edward Hunt, May 16, 1771.

68. *Virginia Cavalcade*, Autumn 1951, pp. 20–22. Many of William Nelson's letters mentioned the flood: to the Hunts, June 5, 1771; to Samuel Athawes, July 8, 1771; to Robert Cary, Aug. 7, 1771.

69. *JHB*, 1770–1772, pp. xxii–xxv, 119–22, President William Nelson to Lord Hillsborough, June 14, 1771.

70. Ibid., Rind *VG*, May 30, 1771; Purdie-Dixon *VG*, June 6, 1771; June 13, 1771.

71. Thomas Tileston Waterman, *The Mansions of Virginia, 1706–1776* (Chapel Hill: Univ. of N.C. Press, 1946), pp. 112, 163–68, 173–76, 343–45, 360–73, 413–14, 422–23.

72. Ibid., pp. 173, 176, 346–48.

73. Jane Carson, *Colonial Virginians at Play* (Colonial Williamsburg Research Studies, 1958), p. 7.

74. Waterman, pp. 180, 186, 192, 414–15.

75. *NLB*, William Nelson to Samuel Athawes, Jan. 30, 1771.

76. Ibid., to Rowland Hunt, May 16, 1771.

77. *WMQ*, 1 (1), pp. 36, 124.

78. *NLB*, William Nelson to Rowland Hunt, July 25, 1771.

79. Purdie-Dixon *VG*, Dec. 15, 1771.

80. Mason, p. 169.

81. Ibid., p. 153–54.

82. *NLB*, William Nelson to Samuel Athawes, Aug. 12, 1771.

83. Ibid., July 8, 1771.

84. Ibid., Aug. 20, 1771.

85. Mason, p. 174.

86. Ibid., p. 198.

87. Ibid., p. 174.

88. *NLB*, William Nelson to Samuel Waterman, Aug. 12, 1772.

89. Ibid., to Samuel Athawes, Nov. 19, 1771.

90. Mason, p. 186.

91. Ibid., p. 201.

92. Ibid., p. 238.

93. Ibid., p. 177.

94. Ibid., p. 202.

95. Ibid., pp. 187–88.

96. Ibid., p. 200.

97. Ibid.
98. *NLB*, William Nelson to John Norton, May 17, 1771.
99. Mason, p. 186.
100. Ibid.
101. Ibid.
102. Ibid., p. 208.
103. Purdie-Dixon VG, Jan. 26, 1772.
104. Mason, p. 225.
105. Ibid.
106. *JHB*, 1770–1772, p. 119.
107. Ibid., p. 123.
108. Ibid., p. 129; Hening, vol. 8, p. 497.
109. *JHB*, 1770–1772, p. 138; Purdie-Dixon VG, July 25, 1771.
110. Mason, p. 224.
111. Ibid., pp. 267–68.
112. *JHB*, 1770–1772, p. xxi.
113. Purdie-Dixon VG, June 4, 1770; Oct, 4, 1770; Rind VG, Aug. 2, 1770.
114. Andrews, pp. 235, 253, 272; Mapp, pp. 342–46; Purdie-Dixon VG, Sept. 26, 1771.
115. Mason, p. 202.
116. Description of Lord Dunmore from his portrait by Sir Joshua Reynolds. A copy hangs at the VHS, Richmond.
117. *NLB*, William Nelson to Samuel Athawes, Nov. 19, 1771.
118. Purdie-Dixon VG, Sept. 26, 1771.
119. Ibid., Nov. 7, 1771.
120. *VMHB*, 6 (2), pp. 128–34.
121. Freeman, vol. 3, p. 282.
122. *JHB*, 1770–1771, p. 145; *The Diaries of George Washington*, ed. John C. Fitzpatrick (Boston: Houghton Mifflin, 1925), vol. 2, pp. 49–51.
123. *JHB*, 1770–1771, p. 153.
124. Freeman, vol. 3, p. 289n.
125. *JHB*, 1770–1772, p. 154.
126. Ibid., pp. 157, 172, 191, 261, 282, 288, 294, 304–05, 307.
127. Ibid., pp. 261, 288, 294.
128. Andrews, pp. 170–74; *Colonial Williamsburg Guidebook* (Williamsburg, 1985), pp. 51, 56–58, 79; Mapp, pp. 185–190. *WMQ*, 16 (1), pp. 188–99.
129. Marshall W. Fishwick, *Virginia, a New Look at the Old Dominion* (New York: Harper and Bros., 1959), p. 203.
130. *Colonial Williamsburg Guidebook*, p. 51.
131. Carl Bridenbaugh, *Myths and Realities* (Baton Rouge: Univ. of La. Press, 1952), p. 37.
132. Malone, pp. 51–53, 64–65, 68, 69.
133. *Virginia Historical Register*, vol. 3, pp. 194–98.
134. *WMQ*, 13 (1), p. 47.
135. *The Journal and Letters of Philip Vickers Fithian, A Plantation Tutor of the Old Dominion, 1773–1774*, ed. Hunter Dickinson Farish (Colonial Williamsburg, 1957), p. 19.
136. *WMQ*, 20 (1), p. 265.

137. *NLB*, William Nelson to Samuel Athawes, Jan. 30, 1771; July 8, 1771; to Samuel Martin, July 2, 1772.

138. *WMQ*, 13 (1), p. 232.

139. Hamilton J. Eckenrode, *The Randolphs: The Story of a Virginia Family* (Indianapolis: Bobbs-Merrill Co., 1946), pp. 45, 51, 77–107, 112.

140. *Tyler's Quarterly*, 3, p. 102; *WMQ*, 17 (1), pp. 235–36.

141. *NLB*, William Nelson to Samuel Athawes, July 8, 1771.

142. Ibid.

143. *WMQ*, 1 (1), pp. 124–25.

144. Ibid., pp. 57, 59, 61.

145. Ibid., pp. 124–25.

146. Purdie-Dixon VG, Aug. 20, 1772; *WMQ*, 17 (1), pp. 235–36.

147. Purdie-Dixon VG, July 30, 1772.

148. Ibid., Aug. 30, 1772.

Chapter TWELVE

1. *NLB*, William Nelson to Samuel Athawes, Nov. 19, 1771.

2. Ibid., to Hunts, July 5, 1772.

3. Ibid., to Samuel Athawes, Nov. 19, 1771.

4. Ibid., to Hunts, July 5, 1772.

5. Ibid., to Samuel Waterman, Mar. 25, 1771.

6. Ibid., to Hyndman and Lancaster, Aug. 12, 1772.

7. Ibid., to Samuel Athawes, June 18, 1772.

8. Ibid.

9. Frances Norton Mason, *John Norton & Sons, Merchants of London and Virginia, 1750–1795* (Richmond: Dietz Press, 1937), p. 210.

10. Ibid., pp. 219–21.

11. *NLB*, William Nelson to Hyndman and Lancaster, Aug. 20, 1771.

12. Ibid., Feb. 21, 1772.

13. Mason, pp. 226–27.

14. Ibid., p. 251.

15. *NLB*, William Nelson to Hyndman and Lancaster, Aug. 12, 1772.

16. Ibid., to Edward Hunt, Apr. 4, 1771.

17. *NLB*, to Samuel Martin, July 3, 1772.

18. Ibid., to Rowland Hunt, Sept. 14, 1772.

19. York County Records, Wills and Inventories, xxii, pp. 132–36.

20. Correspondence from the *NLB* reveals a steady decline: "A late Indisposition I contracted . . ." (to the Hunts, July 3, 1772); ". . . not being well enough to answer . . ." (to John Norton, Aug. 12, 1772); "I have had for the past two months a Disorder in my Stomach and Bowell . . ." (to Samuel Athawes, Aug. 14, 1772); "On account of a bad illness I have deferred answering your letter . . ." (a September letter to Samuel Athawes).

21. Mason, p. 280.

22. Ibid., p. 282.

23. *WMQ*, 14 (1), p. 38.

24. *VMHB*, 17 (4), p. 374.

25. Ibid., 23 (2), pp. 190–92; *WMQ*, 12 (1), p. 163.

26. *The Statutes at Large,* ed. William Waller Hening (Richmond, 1820, 1821), vol. 7, pp. 288, 290, 513; vol. 8, p. 365.

27. Rind VG, Nov. 19, 1772.

28. Hamilton J. Eckenrode, *The Randolphs: The Story of a Virginia Family* (Indianapolis: Bobbs-Merrill Co., 1946), pp. 77–107; Louis Morton, *Robert Carter of Nomini Hall: A Virginia Tobacco Planter in the Eighteenth Century* (Charlottesville: Univ. of Va. Press, 1941), 3–30.

29. Clyde F. Trudell, *Colonial Yorktown* (Old Greenwich, Conn.: Chatham Press, Inc., 1938), pp. 9, 24–25, 84–88; VMHB, 17 (1), p. 381.

30. Trudell, p. 75, 112–14.

31. Wyndham Blanton, *Medicine in Virginia in the Eighteenth Century* (Richmond: Garrett and Massie, 1931), p. 117; Edward Miles Riley, "The Founding and Development of Yorktown, Virginia, 1691–1781" (dissertation, Univ. of Southern Ca., 1942), p. 116; Trudell, p. 117, 125–27.

32. Mason, p. 281.

33. "Funerals in Eighteenth Century Virginia," manuscript, Colonial Williamsburg Library; VMHB, 31 (1), pp. 39–61.

34. York County Records, Wills and Inventories, xxii, pp. 132–36.

35. Mason, p. 285.

36. William Meade, *Old Churches, Ministers and Families of Virginia* (Philadelphia: J. B. Lippincott and Co., 1857), vol. 1, p. 208.

37. Rind VG, Nov. 26, 1772.

38. WMQ, 7 (3), p. 193.

39. Louise Pecquet du Bellet, *Some Prominent Virginia Families* (Lynchburg; J. B. Bell Co., 1909), pp. 545–46; Stella Pickett Hardy, *Colonial Families of the Southern States of America* (New York: Tobias A. Wright, 1911), pp. 94–103, 113–14, 151, 284, 289.

40. York County Records, Wills and Inventories, xxii, pp. 132–36; VMHB, 33 (2), pp. 190–92.

41. Ibid.

42. Ibid.

43. *NLB,* Thomas Nelson, Jr., to Samuel Martin, Jan. 27, 1773.

44. Ibid., to William Cookson, Jan. 27, 1773.

45. Ibid., to the Hunts, Jan. 21, 1773.

46. Ibid., Feb. 16, 1773.

47. Ibid.

48. Purdie-Dixon VG, Dec. 16, 1772.

49. *NLB,* Thomas Nelson, Jr., to the Hunts, Feb. 16, 1773.

50. Mason, p. 297.

51. *Tyler's Quarterly,* 7, p. 113.

52. *NLB,* Thomas Nelson, Jr., to John Norton, Jan. 20, 1773.

53. Mason, pp. 308–14.

54. *NLB,* Thomas Nelson, Jr., to John Norton, Jan. 20, 1773; WMQ, 17 (1), p. 133.

55. Mason, p. 285.

56. Ibid., p. 313.

57. York County Records, Judgments and Orders, No. 3 (1772–1774), p. 209.

58. Purdie-Dixon VG, Jan. 29, 1773; Feb. 4, 1773.

59. JHB, 1773–1776, p. ix.

60. Ibid., p. 22.
61. Ibid.
62. Ibid., p. xi.
63. Ibid., pp. 10, 17, 21.
64. Purdie-Dixon VG, Nov. 19, 1772.
65. Mason, pp. 338–39.
66.*JHB*, 1773–1776, p. 35.
67. Ibid.; Hening, vol. 8, pp. 647–50.
68. *JHB*, 1773–1776, p. 28.
69. Ibid.
70. Ibid., pp. ix, x.
71. Ibid., p. 36.
72. *Colonial Williamsburg Guidebook*, (Williamsburg, 1985), pp. 34–36, 61–62, 65, 67–68.
73. Eastern State Hospital Court of Directors' Minutes, May 7, 1773, p. 20. With permission from the Virginia Dept. of Mental Health, Mental Retardation and Substance Abuse Services, Eastern State Hospital, Williamsburg, Va.
74. *Colonial Williamsburg Guidebook*, pp. 53–58.
75. *WMQ*, 1 (1), pp. 24, 124; 1 (2), pp. 36, 124; 8 (2), p. 243; 19 (1), p. 26.
76. Ibid., 2 (2), p. 124.
77. Ibid.
78. Mason, p. 326.
79. David Mays, *Edmund Pendleton, 1721–1803: A Biography* (Cambridge: Harvard Univ. Press, 1952), vol. 1, p. 269.
80. *NLB*, Thomas Nelson to Robert Cary, May 15, 1773.
81. Ibid.
82. Ibid., to the Hunts, May 20, 1773; Dec. 7, 1773.
83. Ibid., Dec. 7, 1773.
84. Mason, p. 355.
85. Ibid., pp. 225–26.
86. *NLB*, Thomas Nelson to John Backhouse, Aug. 4, 1773.
87. Mason, p. 345.
88. Ibid., p. 332.
89. *NLB*, Thomas Nelson to John Backhouse, Aug. 4, 1773.
90. Ibid., Nov. 7, 1773.
91. Ibid., to Samuel Athawes, July 21, 1773.
92. Ibid., to Robert Cary, July 21, 1773.
93. Ibid., Aug. 19, 1773.
94. Ibid.
95. Ibid., to Thomas and Rowland Hunt, July 29, 1773.
96. Ibid., to John Norton, Aug. 7, 1773.
97. Douglas Southall Freeman, *George Washington* (New York: Charles Scribner's Sons, 1966), vol. 3, p. 368.
98. *NLB*, Thomas Nelson to Samuel Athawes, Dec. 7, 1773.
99. Ibid., to Samuel Waterman, Sept. 14, 1773.
100. Ibid.
101. Blanton, pp. 291–94; Eastern State Hospital Court of Directors' Minutes, pp. 21, 23–24, 26. "Jeremiah Cassidy" is a fictitious name.
102. Mason, p. 356.

103. Ibid., pp. 295, 354.

104. *NLB*, Thomas Nelson to Samuel Waterman, Sept. 14, 1773.

105. Ibid., to Robert Cary, Dec. 7, 1773.

106. *Colonial Williamsburg Guidebook*, p. 88.

107. *NLB*, Thomas Nelson to John Norton, Jan. 1, 1774.

108. Mason, pp. 281, 289, 340.

109. Ibid., p. 329.

110. Ibid., p. 310.

111. Ibid., p. 330.

112. *NLB*, Thomas Nelson to Samuel Athawes, May 1774.

113. Julia Cherry Spruill, *Women's Life and Work in the Southern Colonies* (Chapel Hill: Univ. of N.C. Press, 1938), pp. 361–64.

114. Purdie-Dixon VG, Nov. 19, 1772.

115. Spruill, pp. 43–63.

116. Purdie-Dixon VG, June 3, 1773.

117. Mason, p. 341.

118. *NLB*, Thomas Nelson to the Hunts, Dec. 7, 1773.

119. Ibid., to Robert Cary, Dec. 7, 1773.

120. York County Records, June 2, 1789, provide an appraisement of the estate of General Thomas Nelson.

121. *NLB*, William Nelson to John Norton, Sept. 4, 1769.

122. Purdie-Dixon VG, Oct. 14, 1773.

123. Ibid., Nov. 11, 1773.

124. Ibid., Oct. 14, 1773.

125. *WMQ*, 14 (1), p. 42.

126. Ibid., 21 (3), p. 364.

127. Freeman, vol. 3, pp. 318–32, 344.

128. *NLB*, Thomas Nelson to Samuel Athawes, Oct. 8, 1774.

129. *WMQ*, 3 (2), p. 176.

130. Purdie-Dixon VG, Sept. 2, 1773.

131. Mays, vol. 1, p. 144; vol. 2, pp. 358–75; Purdie-Dixon VG, Mar. 7, 1769.

132. Trudell, pp. 30–32.

133. Evans dissertation; Purdie-Dixon VG, Sept. 9, 1774.

134. Mason, p. 337.

135. Matthew Page Andrews, *Virginia, The Old Dominion* (Garden City, N.Y.: Doubleday, Doran and Co., Inc., 1937), pp. 275–77; *WMQ*, 19 (1), p. 234.

136. Rind VG, Dec. 30, 1773.

Chapter THIRTEEN

1. Frances Norton Mason, *John Norton & Sons, Merchants of London and Virginia, 1750–1795* (Richmond: Dietz Press, 1937), pp. 178, 250–51.

2. Mason, p. 188.

3. Eastern State Hospital Court of Directors' Minutes, pp. 28, 29, 34. (With permission from the Virginia Department of Mental Health, Mental Retardation and Substance Abuse Services, Eastern State Hospital, Williamsburg, Va.)

4. *NLB*, Thomas Nelson to the Hunts, May 3, 1774.

5. Douglas Southall Freeman, *George Washington* (New York: Charles Scribner's Sons, 1966), vol. 3, p. 348.

6. *WMQ*, 14 (1), p. 43.

7. Purdie-Dixon VG, May 5, 1774.

8. Ibid., Apr. 21, 1774.

9. *JHB*, 1773–1776, pp. xiii–xv; *Virginia Historical Register*, ed. William Maxwell (Richmond: MacFarland and Fergusson, 1850), vol. 3, p. 148.

10. Claude G. Bowers, *The Young Jefferson, 1743–1789* (Boston: Houghton-Mifflin, 1945), pp. 78–79.

11. Walter Ray Wineman, *Landon Carter Papers* (Charlottesville: Univ. of Va. Press, 1962), pp. 189–90.

12. *JHB*, 1773–1776, pp. 77, 125.

13. Ibid., pp. 81, 89, 109, 117.

14. Ibid., p. 88.

15. Purdie-Dixon VG, May 19, 1774.

16. *JHB*, 1773–1776, p. 124.

17. Matthew Page Andrews, *Virginia, The Old Dominion* (Garden City, N.Y.: Doubleday, Doran and Co., Inc., 1937), p. 275; Alf J. Mapp, Jr., *The Virginia Experiment: The Old Dominion's Role in the Making of America, 1607–1781* (Richmond: Dietz Press, 1957), pp. 346, 351.

18. "John Adams" and "Sam Adams," *Family Encyclopedia of American History*.

19. *JHB*, 1773–1776, p. xv.

20. *NLB*, Thomas Nelson to Rowland Hunt, Aug. 7, 1774.

21. Freeman, vol. 3, p. 350n.

22. Edmund Randolph, *History of Virginia, 1753–1813*, ed. Arthur H. Shaffer (Charlottesville: Univ. of Va. Press, 1970), pp. 236–49.

23. David Mays, *Edmund Pendleton, 1721–1803: A Biography* (Cambridge: Harvard Univ. Press, 1952), vol. 2, pp. 270–71.

24. Dumas Malone, *Jefferson the Virginian* (Boston: Little, Brown and Co., 1948), vol. 1, pp. 171–72.

25. Mapp, pp. 347–48.

26. Ibid.

27. Kate Mason Rowland, *Life of George Mason, 1725–1792* (New York: G. P. Putnam's and Son, 1892), vol. 1, p. 169.

28. *JHB*, 1773–1776, pp. xiii–iv.

29. Ibid., p. 124.

30. Ibid., p. 130.

31. *WMQ*, 14 (1), p. 184.

32. Freeman, vol. 3, p. 354.

33. *JHB*, 1773–1776, p. 132.

34. Purdie-Dixon VG, May 26, 1774; Rind VG, May 26, 1774.

35. Ibid.

36. Ibid.

37. Many histories state Lady Dunmore arrived in April. The Purdie-Dixon VG announced her arrival Mar. 3, 1774.

38. John Esten Cooke, *Virginia: A History of the People* (Cambridge: Houghton-Mifflin and Co., 1883), p. 417.

39. Purdie-Dixon VG, May 12, 1774.

40. Ibid., May 26, 1774.

41. John D. Burk, *History of Virginia from Its First Settlement to the Present Day* (Petersburg, Va.: Dixon and Pescud, 1804–1816), vol. 3, p. 376.

42. John Esten Cooke, *Stories of the Old Dominion* (New York: Harper and Bros., 1967), pp. 193–204.

43. Ibid., chapter 9.

44. Ethel Armes, *Stratford Hall, The Great House of the Lees* (Richmond: Garrett and Massie, 1936), pp. 111, 113; Stella Pickett Hardy, *Colonial Families of the Southern States of America* (New York: Tobias A. Wright, 1911), p. 322.

45. Armes, p. 113.

46. *The Journal and Letters of Philip Vickers Fithian, A Plantation Tutor of the Old Dominion, 1773–1774*, ed. Hunter Dickinson Farish (Colonial Williamsburg, 1957), p. 40; Louis Morton, *Robert Carter of Nomini Hall: A Virginia Tobacco Planter in the Eighteenth Century* (Charlottesville: Univ. of Va. Press, 1941), p. 52.

47. *JHB*, 1773–1776, p. xii, xiv.

48. Freeman, vol. 3, pp. 356–57; John Sanderson, *Biography of the Signers of the Declaration of Independence* (Philadelphia: W. Brown and C. Peters, 1828), vol. 7, pp. 282–85.

49. *JHB*, 1773–1776, p. 124.

50. Ibid., p. 139.

51. Ibid., p. 126.

52. Ibid.

53. *WMQ*, 14 (1), p. 184.

54. Rowland, vol. 1, p. 169.

55. Fithian, pp. 110–11.

56. Randolph, p. 25.

57. *NLB*, Thomas Nelson to the Hunts, May 31, 1774.

58. Ibid., Thomas Nelson to John Norton, Mar. 30, 1774.

59. Purdie-Dixon *VG*, July 21, 1774.

60. Rind *VG*, July 21, 1774.

61. Ibid.

62. Ibid.

63. Malone, vol. 1, pp. 180–83.

64. Purdie-Dixon *VG*, Aug. 11, 1774.

65. Freeman, p. 373; *VMHB*, 43 (3), pp. 216–17.

66. Randolph, p. 26.

67. Ibid.

68. *NLB*, Thomas Nelson to Samuel Athawes, Aug. 7, 1774.

69. Ibid., to the Hunts, Aug. 7, 1774. Douglas Southall Freeman cites Nelson's letters as a valuable source for events of this period (vol. 3, p. 350n).

70. Emory Gibbons Evans, "The Nelsons: A Biographical Study of a Virginia Family in the Eighteenth Century" (dissertation, Univ. of Va., 1957).

71. *NLB*, Thomas Nelson to Thomas and Rowland Hunt, Oct. 10, 1774; to Frank and Beckerton, Oct. 10, 1774.

72. Julian P. Boyd, *The Papers of Thomas Jefferson* (Princeton: Princeton Univ. Press, 1951), vol. 1, pp. 156–68.

73. Purdie-Dixon *VG*, Aug. 11, 1774.

74. Richard Channing Moore Page, *Genealogy of the Page Family in Virginia* (New York: Jenkins and Thomas, 1883).

75. *NLB*, Thomas Nelson to John Norton, Oct. 8, 1774.

76. Ibid., to Samuel Athawes, Oct. 8, 1774.

77. Purdie-Dixon VG, Sept. 8, 1774; Oct. 10, 1774.

78. Freeman, vol. 3, p. 372.

79. *WMQ*, 1 (1), p. 50.

80. Mary Haldane Coleman, *St. George Tucker, Citizen of No Mean City* (Richmond: Dietz Press, 1938), p. 32.

81. Freeman, vol. 3, p. 372.

82. Purdie-Dixon VG, Nov. 10, 1774.

83. Ibid.

84. Purdie-Dixon VG, Nov. 8, 1774.

85. Mason, p. 368.

86. Purdie-Dixon VG, Nov. 24, 1774.

87. Ibid.

88. Ibid.

89. Mason, p. 368.

90. Purdie-Dixon VG, Nov. 24, 1774.

91. *NFB.* Lucy Calthorpe Smith's manuscript states that Lucy Grymes Nelson bore two stillborn children.

92. Dixon VG, Jan. 7, 1775.

93. Pinckney VG, Jan. 5, 1775.

94. Bowers, pp. 100–02; "William Pitt," Imperial Encyclopedia.

95. Bowers, p. 93.

96. "Edmund Burke," Imperial Encyclopedia.

97. Dixon VG, Jan. 28, 1775.

98. Purdie-Dixon VG, Feb. 24, 1775.

99. Dixon VG, Feb. 25, 1775.

100. John Esten Cooke, *Virginia: A History of the People* (Cambridge: Houghton-Mifflin and Co., 1883), pp. 329–330.

101. Robert Douthat Meade, *Patrick Henry* (Philadelphia: J. B. Lippincott Co., 1969), vol. 2, pp. 18–20.

102. Freeman, vol. 3, pp. 401–02; Malone, vol. 1, pp. 194–95; Meade, vol. 2, pp. 194–95.

103. Robert Lecky, Jr., ed., *The Proceedings of the Virginia Convention in the Town of Richmond on the 23rd of March 1775*, original publication copyrighted 1927 (Richmond, Va., 1938), p. 251. All delegates listed in and proceedings published in Dixon-Hunter VG, Apr. 1, 1775.

104. Ibid., p. 7.

105. Ibid., p. 8.

106. Ibid.

107. Ibid.

108. Ibid., p. 9.

109. Ibid.

110. Ibid.

111. Ibid., p. 10.

112. Ibid., p. 10–11.

113. Ibid.

114. Ibid.

115. Meade, p. 35.

116. Ibid.

117. Meade, vol. 2, p. 35. Philip Ludwell Lee, member of the Council, Feb. 28, 1774. "The day following his death his Lady was lately delivered of a son, and on Friday his remains were attended to the place of interment by a very numerous company of relatives and friends." (Dixon-Hunter VG, Mar. 11, 1775); Bernard Mayo, *Myths and Men: Patrick Henry, George Washington and Thomas Jefferson* (Athens, Ga.: Univ. of Ga. Press, 1959), p. 1.

Chapter FOURTEEN

1. Charles R. Lingley, *The Transition in Virginia from Colony to Commonweath* (New York: Columbia Univ. Press, 1910), pp. 385–99; Dixon-Hunter VG, Apr. 6; Apr. 13, 1775.

2. Douglas Southall Freeman, *George Washington* (New York: Charles Scribner's Sons, 1966), vol. 3, p. 408.

3. Charles Campbell, *History of the Colony and Ancient Dominion of Virginia* (Richmond: B. B. Minor, 1847), p. 607; Hamilton J. Eckenrode, *The Randolphs: The Story of a Virginia Family* (Indianapolis: Bobbs–Merrill Co., 1946), p. 50; Alf. J. Mapp, Jr., *The Virginia Experiment: The Old Dominion's Role in the Making of America, 1607–1781* (Richmond: Dietz Press, 1957), pp. 393–94; Edmund Randolph, *History of Virginia, 1753–1813*, ed. Arthur H. Shaffer (Charlottesville: Univ. of Va. Press, 1970), p. 37; Robert Douthat Meade, *Patrick Henry* (Philadelphia: J. B. Lippincott Co., 1969), vol. 2, pp. 44–56.

4. Dixon-Hunter VG, Apr. 21, 1775.

5. Jane Carson, *James Innes and His Brothers of the Flat Hat Club* (Colonial Williamsburg Research Studies, 1965), p. 84.

6. *JHB*, 1773–1776, p. xviii; Mapp, p. 394.

7. Freeman, vol. 3, p. 410.

8. Dixon-Hunter VG, Apr. 21, 1775.

9. Mapp, p. 395.

10. *American Archives*, II (4), p. 443.

11. Meade, pp. 50–51.

12. Ivor Noel Hume, *1775: Another Part of the Field* (New York: Knopf, 1966), p. 205; *JHB*, 1773–1776, p. 173. Both accounts list John Page as a member of the council, but he had died.

13. Pinckney VG, May 4, 1775.

14. Meade, pp. 51–52.

15. Purdie VG, May 12, 1775.

16. Dixon-Hunter VG,, Apr. 13, 1775.

17. Meade, p. 55.

18. Campbell, p. 623; Mapp, p. 396; Meade, p. 65.

19. Hume, pp. 201–05.

20. *JHB*, pp. xxi, 193.

21. Dixon-Hunter VG, May 4, 1775.

22. Ibid., May 6, 1775.

23. Ibid.

24. *The Bland Papers of Colonel Theodorick Bland, Jr.*, ed. Charles Campbell (Petersburg: Edmund and Julian C. Ruffin, 1840–1843), June 24, 1775.

25. Dixon-Hunter VG, May 27, 1775.

26. *JHB*, 1773–1776, p. 241.

27. Dixon-Hunter VG, June 3, 1775.

28. Ibid.

29. Claude G. Bowers, *The Young Jefferson, 1743–1789* (Boston: Houghton-Mifflin, 1945), pp. 103–04; Dumas Malone, *Jefferson the Virginian* (Boston: Little, Brown and Co., 1948), vol. 1, p. 198.

30. JHB, 1773–1776, pp. 241, 250, 257.

31. Ibid., p. 193.

32. Ibid., pp. 176–77, 179, 188–89, 196, 217.

33. Ibid., p. 188.

34. Ibid., p. 179.

35. Ibid., pp. 193, 241.

36. Dixon-Hunter VG, June 10, 1775.

37. JHB, 1773–1776, pp. 189, 193.

38. John Tackett Goolrick, *Life of General Hugh Mercer* (New York: Neale Publishing Co., 1906); "Hugh Mercer," *DAB*.

39. JHB, 1773–1776, pp. 193, 223.

40. Ibid., p. 247.

41. Ibid.

42. *Maryland Historical Magazine*, 8 (3), pp. 217–35; WMQ, 22 (1), pp. 158–59; 23 (1), pp. 46–47.

43. *The Journal and Letters of Philip Vickers Fithian, A Plantation Tutor of the Old Dominion, 1773–1774*, ed. Hunter Dickinson Farish (Colonial Williamsburg, 1957), pp. 6, 7, 20.

44. *Letters of the Members of the Continental Congress*, ed. Edmund C. Burnett (Washington, D.C.: Carnegie Institution, 1921–1936), vol. 1, pp. 89–90.

45. JCC, II, pp. 24–25.

46. Freeman, vol. 3, p. 421; JCC, II, p. 53.

47. Charles Francis Adams, *The Works of John Adams* (Boston: Little, Brown and Co., 1850), pp. 145–46; JCC, II, pp. 52, 56, 67; David Mays, *Edmund Pendleton, 1721–1803: A Biography* (Cambridge: Harvard Univ. Press, 1952), vol. 2, p. 24; Lynn Montross, *The Reluctant Rebels: The Story of the Continental Congress, 1774–1789* (New York: Harper and Bros., 1950), pp. 71, 72, 75.

48. *American Archives*, III (4), pp. 365–91; *Journal of the Virginia Convention*, pp. 461–81; Mapp, p. 409.

49. Mays, vol. 2, pp. 22, 32–34; Matthew Page Andrews, *Virginia, The Old Dominion* (Garden City, N.Y.: Doubleday, Doran and Co., Inc., 1937), p. 285n.

50. Purdie-Dixon VG,, June 30, 1775; JHB, 1773–1776, p. 176.

51. Andrews, p. 285n.

52. Mays, p. 22.

53. Dixon-Hunter VG,, Aug. 5, 1775.

54. *American Archives*, III (4), pp. 365–91.

55. Mapp, p. 410; "Hugh Mercer," *DAB*; Meade, vol. 2, pp. 73–80.

56. Meade, p. 75.

57. Mays, vol. 2, pp. 32–34.

58. Ibid., p. 78.

59. JCC, II, pp. 128–29; Malone, vol. 1, pp. 204–08.

60. Mays, vol. 2, pp. 22, 35.

61. *American Archives*, III (4), p. 379; Malone, vol. 1, p. 209.

62. Malone, vol. 1, p. 209.

63. Frances Norton Mason, *John Norton & Sons, Merchants of London and Virginia, 1750–1795* (Richmond: Dietz Press, 1937), p. 378.

64. *American Archives*, III (4), pp. 365–91; JCC, II.

65. *American Archives*, III (4), p. 391; Mays, vol. 2, pp. 35–36; Mapp, pp. 410–12.

66. Pinckney VG,, Nov. 7, 1775; Robert Lecky, Jr., *The Proceedings of the Virginia Convention*.

67. *Ibid.*, *Nov.* 16, 1775; *Purdie VG*,, Nov. 17, 1775.

68. Montross, pp. 56–58; Mason, pp. 380, 382.

69. Eckenrode, pp. 100–01.

70. Purdie-Dixon VG, July 12, 1775.

71. Ibid.

72. Eckenrode, p. 106.

73. Hugh Blair Grigsby, *The Virginia Convention of 1775* (Richmond: J. W. Randolph, 1865), p. 73.

74. Freeman, vol. 3, p. 591.

75. Malone, vol. 1, p. 211.

Chapter FIFTEEN

1. Lynn Montross, *The Reluctant Rebels: The Story of the Continental Congress, 1774–1789* (New York: Harper and Bros., 1950), pp. 32–33.

2. Ibid., p. 89.

3. *Diary and Autobiography of John Adams*, ed. L. H. Butterfield (Cambridge: Harvard Univ. Press, 1961), vol. 2, p. 103.

4. Montross, pp. 24–26.

5. Ibid., pp. 59–61.

6. Cornel Adam Lengyel, *Four Days in July: The Story Behind the Declaration of Independence* (Garden City, N.Y.: Doubleday, 1958), p. 70.

7. Montross, pp. 33, 36, 55.

8. Lengyel, p. 240.

9. Ibid., p. 208.

10. Ibid., p. 169; Adams *Diary*, vol. 2, p. 156.

11. Adams *Diary*, vol. 2, p. 172.

12. Ibid., p. 121; Montross, p. 92.

13. Adams *Diary*, vol. 2, p. 121.

14. Ibid., vol. 3, p. 367.

15. Ibid., vol. 2, p. 120.

16. Ibid., p. 126.

17. Ibid., pp. 136, 370.

18. Edmund Cody Burnett, *The Continental Congress* (New York: W. W. Norton and Co., Inc., 1941), p. 156.

19. Montross, p. 9.

20. JCC, III, p. lxv; II, pp. 117, 125, 157.

21. Montross, pp. 28–42.

22. "John Hancock," DAB; Esther Forbes, *Paul Revere and the World He Lived In* (Boston: Houghton-Mifflin Co., 1942), pp. 80–81; Montross, p. 91.

23. Montross, pp. 34–35, 38.

24. JCC, III, pp. 262–63.

25. Ibid., pp. 221, 472.

26. Burnett, p. 60.

27. Montross, p. 78. Virginia's population: 496,278.

28. Ibid., pp. 85–86; JCC, II, p. 187.

29. JCC, III, *p. 472*.

30. *Montross, p. 32.*

31. *Adams Diary,* vol. 2, p. 180.

32. Ibid., p. 179.

33. Ibid., p. 181.

34. Ibid.; Burnett, p. 27; Montross, pp. 34, 73.

35. Louis B. Wright, *The Cultural Life of the American Colonies, 1607–1763* (New York: Harper Bros., 1957), p. 235–36.

36. Adams *Diary,* vol. 2, p. 185.

37. JCC, III, p. 475.

38. Burnett, p. 60; Montross, p. 33.

39. Charles Francis Adams, *The Works of John Adams* (Boston: Little, Brown and Co., 1850), vol. 2, p. 455; JCC, III, p. 328.

40. Montross, pp. 16, 48.

41. Montross, p. 51.

42. Adams, vol. 2, p. 452; Montross, pp. 31, 51–52.

43. Adams *Diary,* vol. 2, p. 185; Adams, vol. 2, p. 451.

44. JCC, III, pp. 476–77.

45. Ibid., p. 259.

46. Ibid., pp. 476–77.

47. Adams, vol. 2, p. 458.

48. Ibid., p. 460.

49. David Mays, *Edmund Pendleton, 1721–1803: A Biography* (Cambridge: Harvard Univ. Press, 1952), vol. 2, pp. 35–36.

50. North Callahan, *Royal Raiders, The Tories of the American Revolution* (Indianapolis: Bobbs-Merrill, 1963), pp. 58–80.

51. JCC, III, p. 319.

52. Adams, vol. 2, p. 121.

53. Ibid.

54. Ibid., p. 401.

55. Ibid., p. 121.

56. JCC, III, pp. 273, 277, 293–94.

57. Adams, vol. 3, p. 7.

58. Montross, pp. 96–98.

59. JCC, III, p. 348.

60. Adams *Diary,* vol. 2, pp. 378–87.

61. Montross, p. 40.

62. Ibid., pp. 3, 9, 14, 16, 26, 32–33, 66; Lengyel, pp. 205–06.

63. WMQ, 5 (3), pp. 359–74; Wright, pp. 179, 182–83.

64. Wright, p. 193; WMQ, 8 (1), p. 33; Lucy Calthorpe Smith manuscript, Colonial Williamsburg Archives.

65. Wright, pp. 42–43, 205, 214, 235–36.

66. Montross, p. 38.

67. Adams *Diary,* p. 365.

68. Ibid., p. 72.

69. JCC, III, p. 334; Douglas Southall Freeman, *George Washington* (New York: Charles Scribner's Sons, 1966), vol. 3, pp. 474–75, 547, 554.

70. Montross, pp. 98–99, 101.

71. Adams, vol. 2, p. 218; JCC, III, pp. 259, 265, 296, 302–03; Burnett, p. 240.

72. JCC, III, pp. 302, 265.

73. Purdie-Dixon VG,, Nov. 3, 1775; Nov. 10, 1775.

74. Adams, vol. 2, p. 468; Burnett, pp. 106–07; Montross, p. 93; JCC, III, pp. 321–22.

75. JCC, III, p. 428.

76. Burnett, p. 107.

77. Lengyel, pp. 40, 160; Montross, p. 110.

78. JCC, III, p. 348.

79. Ibid., pp. 378–387.

80. Burnett, p. 125; Lengyel, pp. 160–61; Montross, pp. 33, 35, 150.

81. Montross, p. 100.

82. Burnett, p. 125.

83. Mays, vol. 2, pp. 32, 35, 43, 86–102.

84. Ibid., pp. 43–44.

85. Ibid., pp. 44, 45, 48.

86. Alf J. Mapp, Jr., *The Virginia Experiment: The Old Dominion's Role in the Making of America, 1607–1781* (Richmond: Dietz Press, 1957), p. 351; Frances Norton Mason, *John Norton & Sons, Merchants of London and Virginia, 1750–1795* (Richmond: Dietz Press, 1937), pp. 81, 378; Montross, pp. 61, 117.

87. Christopher Ward, *The War of the Revolution* (New York: Macmillan, 1952), pp. 845–49.

88. Robert Douthat Meade, *Patrick Henry* (Philadelphia: J. B. Lippincott Co., 1969), vol. 2, pp. 82–84.

89. Matthew Page Andrews, *Virginia, The Old Dominion* (Garden City, N.Y.: Doubleday, Doran and Co., Inc., 1937), p. 288; Mapp, p. 414.

90. Mapp, p. 413.

91. Mays, vol. 2, p. 57.

92. JCC, III, p. 343; IV, pp. 365, 529; VI, p. 1067.

93. JCC, II, p. 110; Montross, pp. 83, 107.

94. *American Heritage Book of the Revolution*, ed. Richard M. Ketchum (New York: The American Heritage Publishing Co., 1958); George F. Scheer and Hugh Rankin, *Rebels and Redcoats* (Cleveland: World Publishing Co., 1957), pp. 111–129; Willard M. Wallace, *Appeal to Arms: A Military History of the American Revolution* (New York: Harper and Bros., 1951), pp. 67–75.

95. JCC, III, p. 328; IV, p. 23; Burnett, p. 112.

96. Lengyel, p. 78; Montross, pp. 70, 94.

97. Freeman, vol. 3, pp. 557–58.

98. Mays, vol. 2, p. 30; Mapp, pp. 416–19.

99. Mays, vol. 2, pp. 68–85; Meade, pp. 88, 90–92.

100. Mapp, pp. 412–19.

101. Ibid.

102. *American Archives*, IV (4), p. 224.

103. *Southern Literary Messenger*, XXVII, p. 325.

104. Mays, vol. 2, pp. 66–85.

105. Ibid.

106. Mapp, pp. 418–19.

107. "Jacob Duche," *DAB*; Montross, pp. 47–48, JCC, IV, p. 23.

108. JCC, IV, p. 23.

109. Burnett, p. 476.

110. Ibid., p. 49.

111. John Sanderson, *Biography of the Signers of the Declaration of Independence* (Philadelphia: W. Brown and C. Peters, 1828), vol. 7, pp. 277–78.

112. Ibid.

113. Ibid.

114. Montross, p. 123.

115. JCC, IV, pp. 19-21.

116. Ibid., p. 70; Montross, pp. 122–25.

117. JCC, IV, p. 301.

118. Julian P. Boyd, *The Papers of Thomas Jefferson* (Princeton: Princeton Univ. Press, 1951), vol. 1, pp. 285–86.

119. North Callahan, *Henry Knox, General Washington's General* (New York: Holt, Rinehart and Winston, 1958), pp. 33–60.

120. John C. Miller, *Origins of the American Revolution* (Boston: Little, Brown and Co., 1943), pp. 114–15.

121. Boyd, pp. 285–86.

122. Ibid.

123. Adams, vol. 2, p. 423.

124. Boyd, pp. 285–86.

125. John Dos Passos, *The Men Who Made the Nation* (Garden City. N.Y.: Doubleday, 1957), pp. 203–06; Montross, pp. 112–15.

126. *The American Tradition in Literature*, eds. Sculley Bradley, Richmond Croom Beatty, E. Hudson Long (New York: Grosset & Dunlap, Inc., 1967), p. 284.

127. Ibid., p. 285.

128. Ibid., pp. 288, 296.

129. Dos Passos, p. 203.

130. Montross, pp. 116–17, 123–24.

131. JCC, IV, pp. 157, 167.

132. William Wirt Henry, *Patrick Henry: Life, Correspondence and Speeches* (New York: Charles Scribner's Sons, 1891), vol. 1, pp. 412–13, 421; Richard Channing Moore Page, *Genealogy of the Page Family in Virginia* (New York: Jenkins and Thomas, 1883). Braxton's debt to Nelson dragged on for years.

133. Mary A. Stephenson, *Carter's Grove Plantation* (Colonial Williamsburg, 1964).

134. JCC, IV, p. 349.

135. WMQ, 16 (1), p. 154.

136. *Virginia Historical Register*, ed. William Maxwell (Richmond: MacFarland and Fergusson, 1850), vol. 4, p. 196.

137. Edward Miles Riley, "The Founding and Development of Yorktown, Virginia, 1691–1781" (dissertation, Univ. of Southern Ca., 1942).

138. *Calendar of Virginia State Papers, 1652–1781* (Richmond, 1875), p. 235.

139. Ibid., pp. 80, 103, 110, 135, 231, 294; Francis B. Heitman, *Historical*

Register of Officers of the Continental Army During the War of the Revolution, April 1775–December 1783 (Baltimore: Genealogical Publishing Co., 1967), p. 307; Dixon-Hunter VG, July 6, 1776.

140. Purdie VG,, Apr. 1776.

141. WMQ, 16 (1), p. 155.

142. Purdie-Dixon VG, May 7, 1772; Dec. 9, 1773.

143. Mapp, p. 421; Mays, vol. 2, pp. 76–102; WMQ, 16 (1), p. 259.

144. American Archives, V (4), p. 1392.

145. Ibid., IV (4), pp. 403–08; Freeman, vol. 4, pp. 78–80; Scheer and Rankin, p. 133.

146. Freeman, p. 80.

147. American Archives, VI (4), pp. 403–08.

148. Ivor Noel Hume, 1775: Another Part of the Field (New York: Knopf, 1966), pp. 204–05.

149. WMQ, 16 (1), p. 259.

150. Hume, p. 205.

151. Hamilton J. Eckenrode, The Randolphs: The Story of a Virginia Family (Indianapolis: Bobbs-Merrill Co., 1946), pp. 144–45.

152. Purdie VG, Apr. 26, 1776.

153. Eckenrode, pp. 144–45; Mays, vol. 2, p. 118.

Chapter SIXTEEN

1. Hugh Blair Grigsby, The Virginia Convention of 1776 (Richmond: J. W. Randolph, 1865), pp. 12–60.

2. Robert Douthat Meade, Patrick Henry (Philadelphia: J. B. Lippincott Co., 1957), vol. 2, pp. 73–95.

3. Charles R. Lingley, The Transition in Virginia from Colony to Commonwealth (New York: Columbia Univ. Press, 1910), pp. 482–511; David Mays, Edmund Pendleton, 1721–1803: A Biography (Cambridge: Harvard Univ. Press, 1952), vol. 2, pp. 103–05.

4. Grigsby, pp. 12–17, 34, 36, 45, 56, 57, 60; William Hirt Henry, Patrick Henry: Life, Correspondence and Speeches (New York: Charles Scribner's Sons, 1891), vol. 1, pp. 211–23, 307–443.

5. Grigsby, p. 13.

6. Ibid.

7. Ibid.; Hamilton J. Eckenrode, The Randolphs: The Story of a Virginia Family (Indianapolis: Bobbs-Merrill Co., 1946), pp. 144–45.

8. Purdie-Dixon VG, Apr. 22, 1776.

9. American Archives, VI (4), p. 1585.

10. Meade, vol. 2, p. 104.

11. Charles Campbell, History of the Colony and Ancient Dominion of Virginia (Richmond: B. B. Minor, 1847), p. 650.

12. Ibid., p. 645.

13. Henry, vol. 1, p. 395.

14. Campbell, p. 645.

15. Meade, vol. 2, p. 100.

16. Campbell, p. 645.

17. *American Archives*, VI (4), pp. 1512, 1514, 1522; Dixon-Hunter VG, May 18, 1776.

18. *American Archives*, VI (4), pp. 403–09.

19. Grigsby, p. 13.

20. *American Archives*, VI (4), p. 403.

21. Meade, vol. 2, p. 106.

22. "Meriwether Smith," *DAB*; Meade, vol. 2, p. 106.

23. Mays, vol. 2, p. 107.

24. Henry, vol. 1, pp. 394–95; Meade, vol. 2, pp. 107–08.

25. Henry, p. 349. William Wirt Henry states Patrick Henry selected Nelson to move for independence (p. 349); Edmund Randolph's history indicates the same.

26. Grigsby, pp. 54, 65; Alf J. Mapp, Jr., *The Virginia Experiment: The Old Dominion's Role in the Making of America, 1607–1781* (Richmond: Dietz Press, 1957), p. 426; Mays, vol. 2, p. 106.

27. Grigsby, p. 17.

28. Ibid.

29. Henry, p. 395.

30. Julian P. Boyd, *The Papers of Thomas Jefferson* (Princeton: Princeton Univ. Press, 1951), vol. 1, p. 292.

31. Ibid.

32. Kate Mason Rowland, *Life of George Mason, 1725–1792* (New York: G. P. Putnam's and Son, 1892), vol. 2, p. 226.

33. Boyd, vol. 1, pp. 296–97.

34. William Wirt, *Life of Patrick Henry* (Hartford: S. Andrews and Son, 1846), vol. 1, pp. 410–11.

35. Ibid., p. 412.

36. Meade, vol. 2, p. 118.

37. Wirt, p. 412.

38. *The Letters of Richard Henry Lee*, ed. James Curtis Ballagh (New York: The MacMillan Co., 1911), pp. 190–92.

39. Ibid.

40. Ibid., pp. 196–97.

41. Henry, vol. 1, p. 400.

42. Ibid., p. 395.

43. Rowland, vol. 1, pp. 230–67.

44. Edmund Randolph, *History of Virginia: 1753–1813*, ed. Arthur H. Shaffer (Charlottesville: Univ. Press of Va., 1970), p. 255.

45. Rowland, vol. 1, p. 440; Mapp, pp. 426–29.

46. Rowland, vol. 1, p. 240–41.

47. Boyd, vol. 1, p. 292.

48. Dumas Malone, *Jefferson the Virginian* (Boston: Little, Brown and Co., 1948), vol. 1, pp. 235–37; Mapp, p. 431; *American Archives*, VI (4), p. 1599.

49. Mays, vol. 2, p. 124. Richard Henry Lee proposed the idea to Edmund Pendleton in a letter dated May 12, 1776.

50. Meade, vol. 2, p. 127.

51. *WMQ*, 20 (1), pp. 179–80.

52. Meade, vol. 2, p. 128.

53. *American Archives*, VI (4), p. 1599.

54. Meade, vol. 2, p. 128.

55. Rowland, vol. 2, p. 213.

56. Campbell, pp. 664–69; Mapp, pp. 427–28; *Virginia Cavalcade*, Spring 1953, p. 41.

57. Henry, vol. 1, p. 400; *American Archives*, VI (4), pp. 101–07.

58. Douglas Southall Freeman, *George Washington* (New York: Charles Scribner's Sons, 1966), vol. 4, pp. 101–07.

59. John Richard Alden, *The American Revolution* (New York: Harper and Row, 1954), pp. 42–58.

60. Cornel Adam Lengyel, *Four Days in July: The Story Behind the Declaration of Independence* (Garden City, N.Y.: Doubleday, 1958), pp. 23, 67, 73, 96; Freeman, vol. 4, p. 104.

61. John C. Miller, *Triumph of Freedom* (Boston: Little, Brown and Co., 1948), p. 44; Lynn Montross, *The Reluctant Rebels: The Story of the Continental Congress, 1774–1789* (New York: Harper and Bros., 1950), p. 140–41; Alden, pp. 66–68.

62. Lengyel, pp. 23, 67, 73, 96.

63. *Letters of the Members of the Continental Congress*, ed. Edmund C. Burnett (Washington, D.C.: Carnegie Institution, 1921–1936), vol. 1, p. 156.

64. Montross, pp. 120, 130, 145.

65. JCC, V, pp. 424–25; Montross, pp. 143–44.

66. Charles Francis Adams, *The Works of John Adams* (Boston: Little, Brown and Co., 1850), vol. 2, p. 360; *Diary and Autobiography of John Adams*, ed. L. H. Butterfield (Cambridge: Harvard Univ. Press, 1961), p. 117; Montross, p. 120.

67. Lengyel, pp. 22, 36, 38, 66; Montross, pp. 130, 136, 154, 163, 171, 198. *DAB* supplies information on all the delegates.

68. Lengyel, p. 91; Montross, pp. 130, 145.

69. Lengyel, pp. 20, 23; Montross, pp. 130, 145; Burnett *Letters*, vol. 1, p. 476.

70. Lengyel, pp. 17–19, 48–50, 57, 75, 105–06, 175, 217, 265, 267, 312; Mongross, pp. 17–22, 24–27, 30, 34, 48, 128–29.

71. Lengyel, pp. 41, 77, 182, 272; Montross, pp. 143–44.

72. Lengyel, pp. 41, 77, 254; Montross, pp. 100, 119.

73. Adams, vol. 2, p. 514; JCC, V, p. 431; Montross, pp. 145–46, 194.

74. JCC, V, p. 433.

75. Montross, pp. 146–47.

76. Lengyel, p. 160; Montross, p. 150.

77. Burnett *Letters*, vol. 1, p. 497.

78. Ibid., p. 401.

79. Edmund Cody Burnett, *The Continental Congress* (New York: W. W. Norton and Co., Inc., 1941), pp. 180–81.

80. Adams, vol. 2, p. 422.

81. Freeman, vol. 4, pp. 143–49; Montross, p. 147.

82. Burnett *Letters*, vol. 1, p. 147.

83. Claude G. Bowers, *The Young Jefferson, 1743–1789* (Boston: Houghton-Mifflin, 1945), pp. 109–39, 140–46; Lengyel, p. 22; Malone, vol. 1, pp. 219–31; Montross, pp. 145–46, 154, 157.

84. Lengyel, p. 17.

85. Ibid., p. 23.

86. Ibid.; Montross, p. 154.

87. Burnett *Letters*, vol. 2, p. 420; Montross, p. 146.

88. Montross, p. 153.

89. Burnett *Letters*, vol. 1, p. 455.

90. Lengyel, pp. 42–45; Montross, pp. 152–53.

91. Lengyel, p. 41; Malone, p. 240.

92. Lengyel, p. 103.

93. Ibid., p. 46.

94. Catherine Brinker Bowen, *John Adams and the American Revolution* (Boston: Little, Brown and Co., 1949), p. 596; Lengyel, pp. 49–50.

95. Lengyel, p. 50; Montross, p. 153; Adams *Works*, vol. 4, p. 8.

96. Montross, p. 153.

97. Lengyel, pp. 18, 83; Malone, vol. 1, p. 240.

98. Bowen, p. 596; Lengyel, p. 77.

99. Ibid., p. 97.

100. Ibid., pp. 91–92, 99.

101. Bowen, pp. 598–99.

102. Lengyel, pp. 163–65.

103. Ibid., pp. 159, 241.

104. Freeman, vol. 4, p. 111.

105. Lengyel, pp. 233–95; Montross, pp. 154–56. *DAB* details all the Signers.

106. Robert Lecky, Jr., ed., *Proceedings of the Virginia Convention in the Town of Richmond on the 23rd of March 1775* (Richmond, Va., 1938).

107. Lengyel, pp. 245–46; Montross, pp. 154–56; Malone, p. 222.

108. Burnett *Letters*, vol. 2, p. 2; Freeman, vol. 4, p. 131.

109. Freeman, vol. 4, p. 131.

110. Lengyel, pp. 263–66; Montross, pp. 162–63.

111. Ibid.

112. Montross, p. 119.

113. Ibid., p. 163, 174.

114. JCC, V, pp. 342, 351, 357.

115. Ibid., VI, pp. 425, 427–28, 431; Montross, pp. 171, 175.

116. Lengyel, pp. 341–42. Note: The majority of the members signed the Declaration August 2, 1776; others signed in the fall after returning to Congress.

Chapter SEVENTEEN

1. JCC, VI, p. 1068.

2. Dixon-Hunter VG, July 29, 1776.

3. Purdie-Dixon VG, July 26, 1776. Both papers published the Declaration of Independence.

4. Robert Douthat Meade, *Patrick Henry* (Philadelphia: J. B. Lippincott Co., 1969), vol. 2, p. 130.

5. WMQ, 20 (1), p. 184.

6. JCS, I, pp. 154, 163, 168.

7. Ibid., p. 6, 8.

8. Ibid., p. 163.

9. JCS, I, pp. 86, 100, 135, 191.

10. Ibid., p. 181.

11. *VMHB*, 18 (4), pp. 373–75.

12. Ibid., 30 (4), pp. 368–75.

13. Ibid.

14. Purdie-Dixon *VG*, Aug. 30, 1776. In 1776 Williamsburg citizens could choose from three newspapers edited by Alexander Purdie, John Pinckney, or John Dixon and William Hunter.

15. Dixon-Hunter *VG*, Aug. 31, 1776.

16. Purdie *VG*, Aug. 30, 1776.

17. Pinckney *VG*, Aug. 30, 1776.

18. Ibid.

19. Purdie *VG*, Aug. 16, 1776.

20. *The Letters of Richard Henry Lee*, ed. James Curtis Ballagh (New York: The MacMillan Co., 1911), vol. 1, p. 201.

21. Ibid., pp. 208–09.

22. Ibid., pp. 207–08.

23. *Letters of the Members of the Continental Congress*, ed. Edmund C. Burnett (Washington, D.C.: Carnegie Institution, 1921–1936), vol. 1, p. 519.

24. Cornel Lengyel, *Four Days in July: The Story Behind the Declaration of Independence* (Garden City, N.Y.: Doubleday, 1958), pp. 19, 33, 67.

25. Julian P. Boyd, *The Papers of Thomas Jefferson* (Princeton: Princeton Univ. Press, 1951), vol. 1, pp. 482–83.

26. *Autobiography of Benjamin Rush*, ed. George W. Corner (Princeton: Princeton Univ. Press for the American Philosophical Society, 1948), pp. 151–52.

27. Lynn Montross, *The Reluctant Rebels: The Story of the Continental Congress, 1774–1789* (New York: Harper and Bros., 1950), p. 140; JCC, V, p. 640.

28. Ballagh, pp. 203–04.

29. JCC, V, p. 649.

30. Boyd, vol. 1, pp. 454–55.

31. Ibid., pp. 461–62.

32. Ibid., pp. 468–70.

33. Ibid., pp. 454–55.

34. Ibid., pp. 471–72.

35. *Biography of the Signers of the Declaration of Independence*, ed. John Sanderson (Philadelphia: W. Brown and C. Peters, 1828), vol. 7, pp. 277–78.

36. Ibid.

37. *The Writings of Thomas Jefferson*, ed. Paul Leicester Ford (New York: G. P. Putnam's Sons, 1892–1899), vol. 1, p. 61; JCC, VI, p. 1068.

38. Lengyel, p. 103.

39. JCC, V, pp. 117. This volume charts Nelson's service on the following pages: 125, 156, 433, 544, 696, 709, 712, 733, 751, 754, 756, 762, 979, 982, 992, 1008, 1038.

40. Ibid., p. 751.

41. Ibid., p. 762.

42. Ibid., p. 763.

43. Burnett *Letters*, vol. 2, p. 28; Montross, p. 247.

44. Burnett *Letters*, vol. 2, p. 97.

45. *Diary and Autobiography of John Adams*, ed. L. H. Butterfield (Cambridge: Harvard Univ. Press, 1961), vol. 2, pp. 250–51.

46. JCC, VI, p. 1068; Burnett *Letters*, vol. 2, p. 62–64.

47. *Tyler's Quarterly,* 12, p. 91.

48. Authors Henry B. Carrington, Douglas Southall Freeman, Willard M. Wallace and Christopher Ward provide fine descriptions of the New York battle.

49. *EJCCV,* I, p. 243.

50. JCC, VI (Nov. 10, 1776–Jan. 30, 1777), cites Nelson's service on the following pages: pp. 18, 28, 32, 35, 40, 61, 314, 335.

51. Edmund Cody Burnett, *The Continental Congress* (New York: W. W. Norton and Co., Inc., 1941), pp. 230–47.

52. Burnett *Letters,* vol. 2, pp. 146–47.

53. Boyd, vol. 2, pp. 3–4.

54. JCC, VI, pp. 917, 979–80, 982, 1008.

55. Ibid., p. 992.

56. Boyd, vol. 1, pp. 296–97; Dixon-Hunter VG, Nov. 6, 1776; Nov. 29, 1776.

57. Montross, pp. 188–92.

58. *American Archives,* III (5), p. 1035.

59. Howard Fast, *Citizen Tom Paine* (Cleveland: World Publishing Co., 1945), p. 145. Freeman's study of Washington reveals the general wrote on Nov. 30, 1776, "I will not, however, despair."

60. JCC, VI, p. 1042. Several congressmen wrote about conditions and the move to Baltimore: Samuel Adams to his wife, Dec. 19, 1776 (Burnett *Letters,* vol. 2, p. 179); Francis Lee to Landon Carter, Jan. 14, 1777 (Burnett *Letters,* vol. 2, p. 217); Richard Henry Lee to William Shippen, Jan. 1, 1777 (Ballagh, vol. 1, p. 166); Benjamin Harrison to Robert Morris, Jan. 8, 1777 (Burnett *Letters,* vol. 2, p. 208).

61. Boyd, vol. 2, pp. 3–4.

62. Henry B. Carrington, *Battles of the American Revolution* (New York: A. S. Barnes and Co., 1877), pp. 284–94; Douglas Southall Freeman, *George Washington* (New York: Charles Scribner's Sons, 1966), vol. 4, pp. 303–24; Willard M. Wallace, *Appeal to Arms: A Military History of the American Revolution* (New York: Harper and Bros., 1951), pp. 124–33.

63. Boyd, vol. 2, pp. 3–4.

64. Ibid.

65. Charles Francis Adams, *The Works of John Adams* (Boston: Little, Brown and Co., 1850), vol. 2, pp. 433–34; Burnett *Letters,* vol. 2, p. 196.

66. JCC, VI, p. 1038.

67. Adams, vol. 2, pp. 433–34.

68. JCC, VI, p. 1042.

69. Ibid., pp. 1045–46; Freeman, vol. 4, pp. 336–37.

70. JCC, VI, p. 544.

71. Burnett *Letters,* vol. 2, p. 199.

72. Carrington, p. 24; Freeman, vol. 4, pp. 303–59; Wallace, pp. 124–33.

73. Purdie VG, Jan. 3, 1777.

74. Burnett *Letters,* vol. 2, p. 225.

75. Ibid.

76. Ibid., p. 232n. Burnett also quotes a letter about fevers and illness from Hooper to Joseph Hewes, p. 256.

77. JCC, VII, pp. 169, 335. Burnett notes that President Hancock informed Robert Morris to send wagons to convey the public papers back to Philadelphia, Feb. 18, 1777, p. 260.

78. Dixon-Hunter *VG*, Jan. 17, 1777; Jan. 24, 1777. The Dixon-Hunter *VG*, Jan. 19, 1777, stated, "Since our last, two troops Lt. Horse from Virginia commanded by Captain Nelson and Jameson arrived in town on their way to General Washington's army in Jersey."

79. Ibid., Jan. 31, 1777; Mar. 7, 1777; *VMHB*, 20 (1), p. 193.

80. Ibid., Jan. 31, 1777.

81. Ibid., Mar. 7, 1777; Francis B. Heitman, *Historical Register of the Officers of the Continental Army During the War of the Revolution, April 1775 to December 1783* (Baltimore: Genealogical Publishing Co., 1967), p. 387.

82. Dixon-Hunter *VG*, Apr. 11, 1777.

83. JCC, VII, p. 169.

84. Ibid., pp. 122, 133; Burnett, pp. 248–58.

85. JCC, VII, pp. 174, 180, 211; Montross, pp. 181–85.

86. JCC, VII, p. 174.

87. Ibid., p. 211.

88. Ibid., pp. 79, 242, 258.

89. *Tyler's Quarterly*, 12, p. 122.

90. JCC, VII, pp. 314–15.

91. Montross, p. 147.

92. Burnett *Letters*, vol. 2, p. 363; Ballagh, vol. 1, p. 290. Burnett cites Nelson's illness, "Nelson by advice of a physician goes tomorrow. He is in a bad state of health," vol. 2, p. 232n.

93. *JHD*, May 19, 1777, p. 20; Ballagh, vol. 1, p. 290; Burnett, vol. 2, p. 232n.; JCC, VII, p. 335.

Chapter EIGHTEEN

1. Dixon-Hunter *VG*, Apr. 11, 1777; Robert Douthat Meade, *Patrick Henry* (Philadelphia: J. B. Lippincott Co., 1969), vol. 2, p. 155.

2. Louis Morton, *Robert Carter of Nomini Hall: A Virginia Tobacco Planter in the Eighteenth Century* (Charlottesville: Univ. of Va. Press, 1941), p. 215.

3. Dixon-Hunter *VG*, May 17, 1777.

4. *Journal of Nicholas Cresswell, 1774–1777*, ed. Lincoln MacVeagh (New York: Dial Press, 1924), pp. 206–09.

5. Ibid.

6. Purdie *VG*, May 2, 1777.

7. *JHD*, p. 40; Purdie *VG*, May 9, 1777.

8. Kate Mason Rowland, *Life of George Mason, 1725–1792* (New York: G. P. Putnam's and Son, 1892), vol. 1, pp. 228–66; Emily J. Salmon, *A Hornbook of Virginia History* (Richmond: VSL, 1983), p. 25.

9. Rowland, vol. 1, pp. 228–66.

10. *JHD*, p. 40.

11. Ibid.

12. Meade, vol. 2, pp. 162–65.

13. Dixon-Hunter *VG*, Aug. 8, 1777.

14. Ibid.

15. Dixon-Hunter *VG*, July 11, 1777.

16. JCS, I, p. 470.

17. Purdie-Dixon *VG*, Apr. 4, 1777; Dixon-Hunter *VG*, Sept. 5, 1777.

18. Purdie *VG*, May 31, 1777.

19. General Nelson to General Washington, Aug. 15, 1777, LC.

20. Ibid.

21. JCS, I, p. 470.

22. General Nelson to General Washington, Aug. 23, 1777, LC.

23. *Writings of Washington*, ed. John C. Fitzpatrick (Washington, D.C.: U.S. Government Printing Office, 1927), vol. 9, pp. 163–64.

24. Dixon-Hunter *VG*, Aug. 22, 1777.

25. *VMHB*, 6 (1), p. 279. Frances Norton Mason notes that at John Page's recommendation, John Norton had shown Robert Andrews "every courtesy" when Andrews was in London to be ordained, Sept. 18, 1772 (*John Norton & Sons, Merchants of London and Virginia, 1750–1795* [Richmond: Dietz Press, 1937] p. 271).

26. JCS, I, p. 476.

27. Cresswell, pp. 206–09.

28. Letter of resignation dated Aug. 7, 1777, among Washington's papers at the Library of Congress.

29. Fitzpatrick, vol. 9, p. 93.

30. Meade, vol. 2, pp. 162–63; Lincoln Lorenz, *John Paul Jones, Fighter for Freedom and Glory* (Annapolis: United States Naval Institute, 1953), pp. 38-39, 359.

31. Douglas Southall Freeman, *George Washington* (New York: Charles Scribner's Sons, 1966), vol. 4, pp. 462–63.

32. John C. Miller, *Triumph of Freedom, 1775–1783* (Boston: Little, Brown and Co., 1948), pp. 202–04; Lynn Montross, *The Reluctant Rebels: The Story of the Continental Congress, 1774–1789* (New York: Harper and Bros., 1950), p. 208.

33. Fitzpatrick, vol. 9, pp. 271–73. Richard Henry Lee informed Gov. Patrick Henry of the Brandywine defeat, Sept. 13, 1777 (*The Letters of Richard Henry Lee*, ed. James Curtis Ballagh [New York: The MacMillan Co., 1911], vol. 1, p. 322). Captain Chilton, who kept a diary of army conditions, lost his life in the battle (*Tyler's Quarterly*, XII, pp. 283–89).

34. Fitzpatrick, vol. 10, p. 27. General Francis Nash was killed at Germantown, Oct. 9, 1777. Fitzpatrick notes his funeral orders (vol. 9, pp. 307–09). Ballagh, vol. 1, pp. 305–26.

35. *American Heritage Book of the Revolution*, ed. Richard M. Ketchum (New York: The American Heritage Publishing Co., 1958), pp. 230–55; Willard M. Wallace, *Appeal to Arms: A Military History of the American Revolution* (New York: Harper and Bros., 1951), pp. 146–68.

36. JCC, XI, p. 448. King Louis XVI notified Benjamin Franklin of the Treaty of Alliance. Edmund Cody Burnett, *The Continental Congress* (New York: W. W. Norton and Co., Inc., 1941), pp. 330–55.

37. Dixon-Hunter *VG*, Oct. 31, 1771.

38. Ibid.

39. JCS, I, p. 499.

40. General Nelson to General Washington, Sept. 12, 1777, LC.

41. Ibid.

42. Fitzpatrick, vol. 9, pp. 271–73.

43. Emory Gibbons Evans, "The Nelsons: A Biographical Study of a Virginia

Family in the Eighteenth Century" (dissertation, Univ. of Va., 1957). Evans states Secretary Nelson lent several hundred pounds.

44. General Nelson to General Washington, Oct. 24, 1777, LC.

45. Ibid.

46. *JHD*, p. 499.

47. Purdie *VG*, Nov. 14, 1777.

48. Dixon-Hunter *VG*, Oct. 17, 1777; Oct. 31, 1777; Purdie *VG*, Nov. 14, 1777.

49. Fitzpatrick, vol. 9, pp. 280–82.

50. Meade, vol. 2, p. 223.

51. Colonel William Nelson to General Washington, Oct. 13, 1777, Pennsylvania Historical Society.

52. Julian P. Boyd, *The Papers of Thomas Jefferson* (Princeton: Princeton Univ. Press, 1951), vol. 2, p. 33.

53. Ibid., p. 36.

54. Fitzpatrick, vol. 10, pp. 271–73.

55. Ibid., p. 27.

56. *OL*, I, p. 211.

57. Sanderson, p. 291.

58. Fitzpatrick, vol. 10, p. 27.

59. Purdie *VG*, Oct. 31, 1777; Dixon-Hunter *VG*, Dec. 19, 1777.

60. General Washington to General Nelson, Nov. 8, 1777, LC.

61. Fitzpatrick, vol. 10, pp. 431–32.

62. Ibid.

63. Ibid. Washington expressed the same sentiment to other Virginia friends concerning their return to Congress. Fitzpatrick (vol. 10, pp. 466–67) notes a letter to Benjamin Harrison dated Dec. 18, 1778.

64. Freeman, vol. 4, pp. 564–611; JCC (X, p. 399) reveals Congress accepted Conway's resignation Apr. 28, 1778; Meade, vol. 2, pp. 185–92; Miller, pp. 233–61; George F. Scheer and Hugh Rankin, *Rebels and Redcoats* (Cleveland: World Publishing Co., 1957), pp. 288–302.

65. "'Light Horse' Harry Lee," *DAB*; Freeman, vol. 4, p. 627.

Chapter NINETEEN

1. *JHD*, pp. 4, 9, 119, 121, 125.

2. *JCS*, II, p. 53; *OL*, I, p. 221.

3. *Diary of Robert Honeyman*, pp. 343–44, 388, LC.

4. *JHD*, p. 13.

5. Stuart E. Brown, Jr., in his *Virginia Baron: The Story of Thomas, Sixth Lord of Fairfax* (Berryville, Va.: Chesapeake Bay Book Co., 1965), and other historians note that Lord Fairfax remained undisturbed.

6. *JHD*, p. 113; The act was first read Jan. 17, 1778, and again on Jan. 21. Julian P. Boyd, *The Papers of Thomas Jefferson* (Princeton: Princeton Univ. Press, 1951), vo. 2, pp. 168–71.

7. *Biography of the Signers of the Declaration of Independence*, ed. John Sanderson (Philadelphia: W. Brown and C. Peters, 1828), vol. 7, p. 282.

8. Matthew Page Andrews, *Virginia, The Old Dominion* (Garden City, N.Y.: Doubleday, Doran and Co., Inc., 1937), p. 289; *EJCCV*, II, p. 73; *OL*, I, p. 234.

9. Dumas Malone in his biography of Jefferson details the assemblyman's at-

tendance: Oct. 20, 1777–Jan. 24, 1778 (*Jefferson the Virginian* [Boston: Little, Brown and Co., 1948], vol. 1).

10. Purdie-Dixon *VG*, Jan. 13, 1776.

11. JCC, X, pp. 214, 766; JHD, pp. 9–10.

12. EJCCV, II, p. 144.

13. General Nelson to General Washington, May 5, 1778, LC.

14. *Writings of Washington*, ed. John C. Fitzpatrick (Washington, D.C.: U.S. Government Printing Office, 1927), vol. 11, pp. 392–94.

15. Pinckney *VG*, May 1, 1778; VMHB, 12 (2), p. 154.

16. Robert Douthat Meade, *Patrick Henry* (: J. B. Lippincott Co., 1969), vol. 2, pp. 218–19.

17. General Nelson to General Washington, June 30, 1778, LC.

18. Fitzpatrick, vol. 12, pp. 203–04.

19. "Casimir Pulaski," *DAB*; JCC, X, pp. 291, 631, 673, 687–88, 711, 745; Fitzpatrick, vol. 9, p. 244.

20. *Letters of the Members of the Continental Congress*, ed. Edmund C. Burnett (Washington, D.C.: Carnegie Institution, 1921–1936), vol. 3, p. 373n; Lynn Montross, *The Reluctant Rebels: The Story of the Continental Congress, 1774–1789* (New York: Harper and Bros., 1950), pp. 239–40.

21. JCC, X, pp. 671, 766, 767.

22. Sanderson, vol. 7, p. 286.

23. General Nelson to General Washington, Aug. 11, 1778, LC.

24. General Washington to General Nelson, Aug. 20, 1778, LC.

25. WMQ, 13 (1), pp. 45, 51, 53.

26. Meade, vol. 2, p. 202.

27. NFB.

28. Riley, p. 153; Frances Norton Mason, *John Norton & Sons, Merchants of London and Virginia, 1750–1795* (Richmond: Dietz Press, 1937), p. 413.

29. Mason, pp. 399, 411, 413, 418–19.

30. "William Pitt," Imperial Encyclopedia.

31. JCS, II, p. 10.

32. Meade, vol. 2, pp. 196–98; OL, I, pp. 285–87.

33. Fitzpatrick, vol. 12, p. 343.

34. Douglas Southall Freeman, *George Washington* (New York: Charles Scribner's Sons, 1966), vol. 4, pp. 290–92; JCC, X, pp. 295, 303; Fitzpatrick, vol. 9, pp. 623–24n.

35. George F. Scheer and Hugh Rankin, *Rebels and Redcoats* (Cleveland: World Publishing Co., 1957), p. 226.

36. JHD, pp. 5–6, 9–10, 13, 20, 22, 24, 31, 43, 65, 71, 75, 79–83, 91, 101–02, 104–05, 107, 111, 122; JCS, II, pp. 152, 165, 191.

37. JHD, p. 6, 80, 104.

38. Ibid., pp. 71, 111.

39. Ibid., p. 13.

40. Ibid., p. 9–10.

41. Meade, vol. 2, pp. 134, 206–08.

42. Alf J. Mapp, Jr., *The Virginia Experiment: The Old Dominion's Role in the Making of America, 1607–1781* (Richmond: Dietz Press, 1957), pp. 472–74.

43. *The Letters of Richard Henry Lee*, ed. James Curtis Ballagh (New York: The MacMillan Co., 1911), vol. 1, p. 451.

44. Fitzpatrick, vol. 13, pp. 462–68.

45. *JHD*, pp. 102, 105, 107; Meade, vol. 2, p. 215.

46. Evans dissertation states Nelson sold 600 acres in York County, December 1778, for £1,200 to William Trebell at "unquestionable sacrifice but had to provide for his family." There were nine children under the Nelson roof in addition to Lucy's sister, the servants, and slaves.

47. JCC, XIII, p. 195. Nelson's service cited: pp. 245, 292, 336, 436; votes, pp. 208, 237, 246, 250, 254–55, 258, 262, 298, 309, 314–15, 333–34, 347, 350–52, 361–62, 370–71, 373, 375, 377, 379–83, 390, 398–401, 405, 410, 415, 417–18, 424, 458, 471, 477–80, 482–87, 489, 499–500.

48. Ibid., pp. 209, 256; XIV, p. 626; Montross, pp. 281–82.

49. General Nelson to General Washington, Mar. 23, 1779, LC.

50. Fitzpatrick, vol. 13, pp. 462–68.

51. JCC, XIII, p. 108. Washington had recommended several times that an act should be passed to pay officers half pay for life, but his proposal was not passed until October 1780.

52. James Thomas Flexner, *The Traitor and the Spy: Benedict Arnold and John Andre* (New York: Harcourt, Brace and Co., 1953), p. 187–201.

53. John C. Miller, *Triumph of Freedom, 1775–1783* (Boston: Little, Brown and Co., 1948), pp. 357–77; Montross, pp. 253, 257–61, 264, 267–71, 279, 286, 288; Burnett, vol. 4, pp. 168–71, 245.

54. JCC, XIII, pp. 306, 336, 436.

55. Fitzpatrick, vol. 14, pp. 246–49.

56. Freeman, vol. 5, pp. 87–107; Scheer and Rankin, pp. 355–69.

57. *Magazine of American History*, XX, Sept. 1888, p. 325.

58. JCC, XIII, pp. 363–68; *JHD, pp. 4, 9.*

59. OL, I, pp. 365–68; Meade, vol. 2, p. 218.

60. Dixon-Hunter VG, May 15, 1779.

61. Sanderson, vol. 7, pp. 286–89.

62. Dixon-Hunter VG, May 26, 1779.

63. *JHD*, pp. 29, 33, 35, 53, 56, 64; Meade, vol. 2, p. 219.

64. *JHD*, pp. 27–29; Malone, pp. 301–08.

65. Malone, pp. 301–08.

66. Ibid., pp. 4, 29, 77, 80.

67. Friederike Charlotte Luise von Massow Riedesel, *Letters and Journals Relating to the War of the American Revolution and the Capture of the German Troops at Saratoga*, tr. William L. Stone (Albany: J. Munsell, 1867); Claude G. Bowers, *The Young Jefferson, 1743–1789* (Boston: Houghton-Mifflin, 1945), pp. 231–38; Malone, pp. 293–97.

68. *VMHB*, 2 (3), p. 303; 5 (1), p. 82; 10 (1), p. 107.

69. Jane Carson, *James Innes and His Brothers of the Flat Hatt Club* (Colonial Williamsburg Research Studies, 1965), pp. 102–09. Carson states the Mar. 20, 1779, VG is no longer extant.

70. Meade, vol. 2, p. 209.

71. Ibid.; *WMQ*, 20 (1), pp. 146–47; 21 (1), pp. 134–36; 25 (1), pp. 161–64.

72. Honeyman, pp. 343, 388.

73. Montross, p. 283.

74. Ibid.

75. *JHD*, pp. 3–5, 53, 56, 67.

76. Ibid., pp. 6, 9–15, 17, 30, 34–36, 38, 47, 50, 52, 57, 65–73, 75, 79–81, 83, 85, 87–89, 94.

77. Bowers, pp. 244–50; *The Writings of Thomas Jefferson,* ed. Paul Leicester Ford (New York: G. P. Putnam's Sons, 1892–1899), vol. 2, pp. 250, 258, 260–61, 279.

78. Burnett *Letters,* vol. 4, pp. 464, 470, 512; *JHD,* p. 24.

79. *JHD,* p. 15.

80. Ibid., p. 17.

81. Ibid., p. 15.

82. Ibid., p. 47.

83. Ibid., p. 35.

84. Ibid., p. 71.

85. Ibid., p. 74.

86. Boyd, vol. 2, pp. 168–71; *The Statutes at Large,* ed. William Waller Hening (Richmond, 1819), vol. 9, pp. 377–80; *JHD,* p. 83.

87. *Colonial Williamsburg Guidebook* (Williamsburg, 1985), p. 97.

88. Hamilton J. Eckenrode, *The Randolphs: The Story of a Virginia Family* (Indianapolis: Bobbs-Merrill Co., 1946), pp. 42, 104.

89. Mason, p. 427, 429–32, 436, 514–15. John Norton's wife, Courtenay Norton, died in Barbados at the home of John Tucker in 1780.

90. *JHD,* p. 83.

91. Ibid., p. 94.

92. Ibid.

93. General Nelson to General Washington, Nov. 29, 1779, LC. Honeyman states Virginia had £26,000 debt (p. 376).

94. Dixon-Hunter VG, Jan. 15, 1780; May 23, 1780; May 31, 1780; June 14, 1780; June 19, 1780.

95. Ibid., Jan. 22, 1780.

96. Boyd, vol. 3, p. 283; Carson, pp. 108–09; Clarkson VG, Dec. 11, 1779.

97. Fitzpatrick, vol. 17, p. 246.

98. General Nelson to General Washington, Nov. 29, 1779, LC.

Chapter TWENTY

1. *JHD,* pp. 31, 32, 35, 36; *Biography of the Signers of the Declaration of Independence,* ed. John Sanderson (Philadelphia: W. Brown and C. Peters, 1828), vol. 7, p. 290.

2. Julian P. Boyd, *The Papers of Thomas Jefferson* (Princeton: Princeton Univ. Press, 1951), vol. 3, James Madison to Governor Jefferson, Mar. 27, 1780, pp. 335–36.

3. *Letters of the Members of the Continental Congress,* ed. Edmund C. Burnett (Washington, D.C.: Carnegie Institution, 1921–1936), vol. 4, p. 512.

4. James Thomas Flexner, *The Traitor and the Spy: Benedict Arnold and John Andre* (New York: Harcourt, Brace and Co., 1953), pp. 275–306.

5. JCC, XIV, p. 626.

6. Ibid., XV, p. 1377.

7. Lynn Montross, *The Reluctant Rebels: The Story of the Continental Congress, 1774–1789* (New York: Harper and Bros., 1950), pp. 294, 316.

8. Ibid., p. 295.

9. JCC, XVI, p. 326.

10. North Callahan, *Daniel Morgan, Ranger of the Revolution* (New York: Holt, Rinehart and Winston, 1961), pp. 189–90.

11. Charles Campbell, *History of the Colony and Ancient Dominion of Virginia* (Richmond: B. B. Minor, 1847), p. xxii; JCC, XV, p. 1367; XVI, p. 154.

12. Boyd, vol. 5, pp. 269–70; 283; *JHD*, May 12, 1779, p. 7.

13. Boyd, vol. 3, p. 349.

14. JCS, II, Oct. 6, 1777—Nov. 10, 1781.

15. *JHD*, p. 75. Jefferson was absent Feb. 20 to Mar. 14, 1780.

16. JCC, XVI, p. 150.

17. Boyd, vol. 3, pp. 346–47, 364–65.

18. Ibid., pp. 333–34, 430–31; Jane Carson, *James Innes and His Brothers of the Flat Hat Club* (Colonial Williamsburg Research Studies, 1965), pp. 117–18.

19. *JHD*, p. 4; service: pp. 5–8, 10–11, 14–15, 18–20, 22–23, 34, 50, 55–56, 59, 62.

20. Ibid., p. 5.

21. Ibid., p. 21.

22. Ibid., p. 7.

23. Ibid., pp. 10, 14.

24. Boyd, vol. 3, pp. 346–47.

25. Ibid., pp. 364–65.

26. *JHD*, p. 14.

27. Ibid., pp. 20–21.

28. Ibid.

29. Ibid., p. 23.

30. Boyd, vol. 3, pp. 378–80; JCC, XVII, pp. 473–79. President Samuel Huntington informed Governor Jefferson May 19, 1780, men were needed.

31. Boyd, vol. 3, p. 423.

32. *JHD*, pp. 36, 55.

33. Ibid., pp. 1–8.

34. Henry B. Carrington, *Battles of the American Revolution* (New York: A. S. Barnes and Co., 1877), pp. 439–502; Douglas Southall Freeman, *George Washington* (New York: Charles Scribner's Sons, 1975), vol. 5, pp. 132–67; Willard M. Wallace, *Appeal to Arms: A Military History of the American Revolution* (New York: Harper and Bros., 1951), pp. 204–15; Christopher Ward, *The War of the Revolution* (New York: Macmillan, 1952), pp. 695–703.

35. Boyd, vol. 3, p. 388. Nathaniel Pendleton an officer in the Eleventh Virginia Regiment had been held captive forty-seven months. When exchanged in November 1780, Pendleton joined General Greene in the South.

36. Governor Jefferson to President Samuel Huntington, June 9, 1780, OL, II, pp. 125–27.

37. Burnett *Letters*, vol. 5, p. 181.

38. Boyd, vol. 3, p. 403. The Dixon-Hunter VG of June 7, 1780, published the Articles of Capitulation of the Charleston battle.

39. Governor Jefferson to General Washington, June 11, 1780, OL, II, pp. 127–28.

40. James Monroe to Governor Jefferson, June 16, 1780, Boyd, vol. 3, pp. 451–52; "James Monroe," DAB; *JHD*, p. 50.

41. Julian P. Boyd and W. Edwin Hemphill, *The Murder of George Wythe* (Wil-

liamsburg, Va.; Institute of Early American History and Culture, 1955), p. 5. Wythe professorship of Law and Police established at the College of William and Mary on Dec. 4, 1779.

42. "Hugh Nelson," *DAB*.

43. Boyd, vol. 3, pp. 451–52.

44. Sanderson, vol. 7, p. 290.

45. Boyd, vol. 3, pp. 471–72.

46. Sanderson, vol. 7, pp. 289.

47. Governor Jefferson to General Washington, June 11, 1780, OL, II, pp. 125–27.

48. Sanderson, vol. 7, p. 291.

49. Freeman, vol. 5, pp. 164–65.

50. OL, II, pp. 170–74, 187–95; Dumas Malone, *Jefferson the Virginian* (Boston: Little, Brown and Co., 1948), vol. 1, pp. 314, 319; Nathan Schachner, *Thomas Jefferson* (New York: Thomas Yoseloff, 1951), pp. 196–213.

51. Carrington, pp. 513–52; Wallace, pp. 204–15; Ward, pp. 722–30.

52. George F. Scheer and Hugh Rankin, *Rebels and Redcoats* (Cleveland: World Publishing Co., 1957), pp. 401–11.

53. Dixon-Hunter VG, Nov. 4, 1780.

54. OL, II, Sept. 13, 1780, p. 205; *VMHB*, 8 (1), p. 116, letter thought to be written to Richard Henry Lee. John Page to Governor Jefferson, Dec. 9, 1780, Boyd, vol. 4, pp. 191–92.

55. David Mays, *Edmund Pendleton, 1721–1803: A Biography* (Cambridge: Harvard Univ. Press, 1952), vol. 2, p. 170.

56. Dixon-Hunter VG, Sept. 13, 1780.

57. Boyd, vol. 3, pp. 617–18.

58. Ibid.

59. Freeman, vol. 4, pp. 534, 536, 570–71; vol. 5, p. 141; *JHD*, p. 29, 184; Robert Douthat Meade, *Patrick Henry* (Philadelphia: J. B. Lippincott Co., 1969), vol. 2, pp. 219–20.

60. JCC, X, p. 269.

61. Dixon-Hunter VG, Sept. 6, 1780.

62. Callahan, pp. 189–90.

63. Boyd, vol. 4, p. 54; Dixon-Hunter VG, Oct. 25, 1780.

64. General Nelson to General Weedon, Nov. 3, 1780, American Philosophical Society, Philadelphia.

65. Ibid.

66. Ibid.

67. Sanderson, vol. 7, p. 290.

68. NFB. Lucy Elizabeth Jefferson died Apr. 15, 1781. Malone, p. 434.

69. JHD, Tuesday, Oct. 24, 1780, p. 3; Meade, vol. 2, p. 230.

70. General Nelson to General Weedon, Nov. 22, 1780, American Philosophical Society.

71. Dixon-Hunter VG, Nov. 18, 1780.

72. General Nelson to General Weedon, Nov. 4, 1780, American Philosophical Society.

73. The sword, sash, and field glasses of Major Patrick Ferguson were captured by Colonel John Sevier and donated by a grandson to the Tennessee Historical Society and are exhibited at the Tennessee State Museum, Nashville. Governor

Jefferson was excited over capturing the emissary and sent detailed descriptions to General Gates, Nov. 10, 1780, Boyd, vol. 4, p. 109; *The Writings of Thomas Jefferson*, ed. Paul Leicester Ford (New York: G. P. Putnam's Sons, 1892–1899), to President Samuel Huntington at Congress, vol. 2, pp. 271–72.

Chapter TWENTY-ONE

1. Julian P. Boyd, *The Papers of Thomas Jefferson* (Princeton: Princeton Univ. Press, 1951), vol. 4, pp. 256–78; JCS, II, pp. 268–72; OL, II, pp. 260–61; Dumas Malone, *Jefferson the Virginian* (Boston: Little, Brown and Co., 1948), vol. 1, pp. 230–31.

2. Boyd, vol. 4, p. 297.

3. Ibid., pp. 273–74; Nathan Schachner, *Thomas Jefferson* (New York: Thomas Yoseloff, 1951), p. 199; WMQ, 25 (1), pp. 83–86.

4. Boyd, vol. 4, p. 251.

5. OL, II, pp. 254–56, 270–71.

6. Boyd, vol. 4, p. 294.

7. JCS, II, pp. 260–72; Malone, vol. 1, pp. 330–51.

8. Boyd, vol. 4, p. 307.

9. Ibid., *Virginia Historical Register*, ed. William Maxwell (Richmond: MacFarland and Fergusson, 1850), vol. 4, pp. 195–99.

10. Jane Carson, *James Innes and His Brothers of the Flat Hat Club* (Colonial Williamsburg Research Studies, 1965), pp. 123–24; *Virginia Historical Register*, vol. 4, pp. 195–99, John Page to Col. Theodorick Bland.

11. Malone, vol. 1, p. 338.

12. Boyd, vol. 4, p. 307.

13. Malone, vol. 1, pp. 338–39.

14. Boyd, vol. 4, p. 307.

15. Ibid.

16. John McAuley Palmer, *General von Steuben* (New Haven: Yale Univ. Press, 1937), pp. 245–55.

17. Boyd, vol. 4, pp. 256–75.

18. Ibid.

19. Malone, vol. 1, pp. 339–40.

20. Boyd, vol. 4, p. 351. This letter also recommended that General Weedon return to Fredericksburg to protect the forge. Dixon-Hunter VG, Jan. 13, 1781. "On the 3rd Dec., a letter from a private Gentleman to General Nelson reached this place notify 27 Sail."

21. Boyd, vol. 4, pp. 675–76; Boyd, vol. 5, pp. 671–705; Carson, pp. 126–31.

22. Hamilton J. Eckenrode, *The Revolution in Virginia* (Cambridge: Houghton Mifflin, 1916), pp. 195–231; Malone, vol. 1, pp. 340–41; Schachner, p. 201; George F. Scheer and Hugh Rankin, *Rebels and Redcoats* (Cleveland: World Publishing Co., 1957), pp. 467–74.

23. WMQ, 25 (1), pp. 83–86.

24. Carson, pp. 122–23.

25. OL, II, pp. 272.

26. Ibid.

27. Ibid.

28. Boyd, vol. 4, p. 372.

29. Ibid.

30. Ibid., p. 351.

31. Ibid.

32. Ibid., pp. 312, 316–18.

33. Ibid., p. 312.

34. Ibid., p. 316.

35. Ibid., p. 371.

36. Ibid., pp. 373, 382.

37. Ibid., p. 344.

38. Ibid.

39. Ibid., pp. 256–78; Dixon and Nicholson VG, Jan. 13, 1781. (Only one copy survived.)

40. Boyd, vol. 4, pp. 422–23.

41. General Steuben to Governor Jefferson, Feb. 11, 1781, Boyd, vol. 4, pp. 584; Governor Jefferson to General Steuben, Feb. 11, 1781, Boyd, vol. 4, pp. 592–94; OL, II, pp. 333–34, 346–57.

42. Palmer, pp. 252–53.

43. Boyd, vol. 4, pp. 466–68.

44. Ibid., pp. 589–90.

45. *The Statutes at Large*, ed. William Waller Hening (Richmond, 1822), vol. 10, p. 473.

46. Boyd, vol. 4, pp. 655–657.

47. Ibid., pp. 426–27.

48. Ibid.

49. Ibid.

50. Ibid., p. 407.

51. Ibid., pp. 427–28.

52. Ibid., pp. 449–51.

53. Ibid., p. 520.

54. Ibid., pp. 553–54.

55. Ibid., pp. 569–70; 608–09.

56. Ibid., p. 612.

57. Ibid., pp. 553–54.

58. A complete account of the mutiny of Wayne's Pennsylvanians can be found in John Bakeless's *Turncoats, Traitors and Heroes* (Philadelphia: J. B. Lippincott, 1959), pp. 318–27; Douglas Southall Freeman, *George Washington* (New York: Charles Scribner's Sons, 1966), vol. 5, pp. 236–50.

59. North Callahan, *Daniel Morgan, Ranger of the Revolution* (New York: Holt, Rinehart and Winston, 1961), pp. 194–225; Donald Barr Chidsey, *The War in the South* (New York: Crown Publishers, Inc., 1969); Scheer and Rankin, pp. 423–33.

60. General Greene to Governor Jefferson, Feb. 15, 1781, Boyd, vol. 4, pp. 615–16; General Morgan to Governor Jefferson, Feb. 1, 1781, Boyd, vol. 4, pp. 495–96; General Robert Lawson to Governor Jefferson, Feb. 15, 1781, Boyd, vol. 4, pp. 616–18.

61. Governor Jefferson to General Steuben, Feb. 15, 1781, Boyd, vol. 4, pp. 621–22.

62. Ibid., p. 638.

63. Ibid., p. 687.

64. General Nelson to Governor Jefferson, Feb. 18, 1781, Boyd, vol. 4,

pp. 650–51; Governor Jefferson to General Nelson, Feb. 21, 1781, Boyd, vol. 4, pp. 677–78; Governor Jefferson to General Muhlenberg, Jan. 31, 1781, Boyd, vol. 4, p. 487; OL, II, pp. 312–13.

65. Boyd, vol. 4, p. 651.

66. Ibid.

67. Ibid., pp. 650–51.

68. Ibid., pp. 658–59.

69. Ibid.

70. Ibid., p. 659.

71. Ibid., pp. 650–51.

72. Colonel Innes to General Steuben, Feb. 27, 1781, Boyd, vol. 5, pp. 694, 696; Colonel Innes to Governor Jefferson, Boyd, vol. 5, pp. 671–705.

73. Carson, pp. 126, 131.

74. Boyd, vol. 4, pp. 675–76.

75. Ibid.

76. Ibid., p. 687.

77. Ibid., pp. 683–84.

78. Ibid., p. 631.

79. Governor Jefferson to General Steuben, Mar. 7, 1781, Boyd, vol. 5, p. 89.

80. General Steuben to Governor Jefferson, Mar. 7, 1781, Boyd, vol. 5, p. 90; Governor Jefferson to Governor Lafayette, Mar. 14, 1781, Boyd, vol. 5, p. 144.

81. General Lafayette to Governor Jefferson, Mar. 16, 1781, Boyd, vol. 5, p. 159.

82. Boyd, vol. 5, pp. 166, 187, 193.

83. Ibid., p. 203. Details relating to military matters in Virginia, p. 250.

84. General Lafayette to Governor Jefferson, Mar. 27, 1781, Boyd, vol. 5, p. 261.

85. Ibid., p. 217.

86. Richard Henry Lee to Governor Jefferson, Mar. 27, 1781, *The Letters of Richard Henry Lee*, ed. James Curtis Ballagh (New York: The Macmillan Co., 1911), vol. 2, p. 217; JHD, pp. 6–7; Boyd, vol. 5, pp. 276–77.

87. Boyd, vol. 5, p. 218.

88. Louis R. Gottschalk, *Lafayette and the Close of the American Revolution* (Chicago: Univ. of Chicago, 1942), pp. 160–68; Robert Douthat Meade, *Patrick Henry* (Philadelphia: J. B. Lippincott Co., 1969), vol. 2, p. 226; VMHB, 9 (1), p. 421. Colonel Theodorick Bland had attended a party in Philadelphia and talked with Lafayette appealing to the ardent Frenchman to assist Virginia in the war crisis. John C. Miller, *Triumph of Freedom, 1775–1783* (Boston: Little, Brown and Co., 1948), pp. 425–77.

89. Gottschalk, pp. 160–88.

90. *Journal of Nicholas Cresswell, 1774–1777*, ed. Lincoln MacVeagh (New York: Dial Press, 1924), p. 251. His entry was dated July 13, 1777.

91. *JCS, II, p. 302.*

92. *Scheer and Rankin, pp. 443–52.*

Chapter TWENTY-TWO

1. Dumas Malone, *Jefferson the Virginian* (Boston: Little, Brown and Co., 1948), vol. 1, p. 348; Robert Douthat Meade, *Patrick Henry* (Philadelphia: J. B. Lippincott Co., 1969), vol. 2, p. 234.

2. Emory Gibbons Evans, "The Nelsons: A Biographical Study of a Virginia Family in the Eighteenth Century" (dissertation, Univ. of Va., 1957).

3. Malone, vol. 1, p. 346; Nathan Schachner, *Thomas Jefferson* (New York: Thomas Yoseloff, 1951), pp. 179–85; Julian P. Boyd, *The Papers of Thomas Jefferson* (Princeton: Princeton Univ. Press, 1951), vol. 5, pp. 23–24.

4. *Writings of Washington*, ed. John C. Fitzpatrick (Washington, D.C.: U.S. Government Printing Office, 1927), vol. 21, p. 415.

5. Gilbert Chinard, *Lafayette in Virginia* (Baltimore: John Hopkins Press, 1928), p. 13.

6. Louis B. Gottschalk, *Lafayette and the Close of the American Revolution* (Chicago: Univ. of Chicago, 1942), pp. 189–208.

7. Ibid., p. 187, 209–45.

8. Fitzpatrick, vol. 22, pp. 14–15; Douglas Southall Freeman, *George Washington* (New York: Charles Scribner's Sons, 1966), vol. 5, pp. 282–83. Freeman states Lund is a remote cousin. Other sources, unfortunately, list Lund as a brother or a nephew of Washington.

9. Freeman, vol. 5, pp. 281–82. Harrison letter, Feb. 25, 1781, appears among the Washington Papers, LC.

10. John McAuley Palmer, *General von Steuben* (New Haven: Yale Univ. Press, 1937), pp. 256–61.

11. Malone, vol. 1, pp. 330–51; George F. Scheer and Hugh Rankin, *Rebels and Redcoats* (Cleveland: World Publishing Co., 1957), pp. 467–74; Christopher Ward, *The War of the Revolution* (New York: Macmillan, 1952), pp. 866–78.

12. Charles Campbell, *History of the Colony and Ancient Dominion of Virginia* (Richmond: B. B. Minor, 1847), p. 306.

13. Palmer, pp. 261, 267–72.

14. Colonel John Banister to Colonel Theodorick Bland, May 16, 1781, *The Bland Papers of Colonel Theodorick Bland, Jr.*, ed. Charles Campbell (Petersburg: Edmund and Julian C. Ruffin, 1840–1843).

15. Ibid.

16. Boyd, vol. 5, pp. 499–592.

17. Governor Jefferson to General Steuben, Apr. 24, 1781, Boyd, vol. 5, pp. 549–50.

18. Gottschalk, pp. 188–89.

19. Malone, vol. 1, pp. 350–51.

20. Gottschalk, pp. 209–245, 352–53.

21. Matthew Page Andrews, *Virginia, The Old Dominion* (Garden City, N.Y.: Doubleday, Doran and Co., Inc., 1937), p. 304; Malone, vol. 1, pp. 351–52. Governor Jefferson to General Lafayette, OL, II, p. 515.

22. Scheer and Rankin, pp. 467–74.

23. Gottschalk, pp. 209–45; Malone, vol. 1, pp. 352–53; Palmer, pp. 267–72.

24. General Nelson to General Lafayette, *Calendar of Virginia State Papers, 1652–1781* (Richmond, 1875), II, p. 92.

25. Gottschalk, pp. 209–45. Major John Nelson's corps "fatigued to death."

26. *Calendar*, II, p. 92; North Callahan, *Daniel Morgan, Ranger of the Revolution* (New York: Holt, Rinehart and Winston, 1961), p. 248.

27. General Nelson to Governor Jefferson, May 10, 1781, Boyd, vol. 5, p. 631.

28. Major John Nelson to Governor Jefferson, May 25, 1781, *Calendar*, II, p. 118.

29. Ibid.

30. Ibid.

31. Gottschalk, p. 469; Scheer and Rankin, p. 470.

32. Malone, vol. 1, p. 353.

33. Gottschalk, pp. 209–45; Scheer and Rankin, pp. 469–70.

34. Thomas Nelson Page, *The Old South* (New York: Charles Scribner's Sons, 1905), pp. 201–02. "Jimmy Rideout, the carriage driver, in emulation of Cacus, had his horses shod at night with the shoes reversed so that if they were followed the pursuers would be misled."

35. Gottschalk, p. 15.

36. Callahan, pp. 249–50.

37. *WMQ*, 27 (1), pp. 167–68.

38. *JHD*, pp. 10, 15, 17, 21–22.

39. Claude G. Bowers, *The Young Jefferson, 1743–1789* (Boston: Houghton Mifflin, 1945), pp. 275–76; Malone, vol. 1, pp. 354–55; Meade, vol. 2, pp. 237–38.

40. Boyd, vol. 6, Memoirs, pp. 78–79.

41. Ibid.

42. Malone, vol. 1, pp. 355–58; Scheer and Rankin, pp. 468–74; Ward, pp. 866–78; Gail E. Haley, *Jack Jouett's Ride* (New York: Viking, 1973); *VMHB*, 64 (4), pp. 452–61.

43. Malone, vol. 1, pp. 356–59; Meade, vol. 2, pp. 236–38; *VMHB*, 74 (4), pp. 452–61. Letters of Newman Brockenbrough and Peter Lyons. Hays was released by Cornwallis.

44. Ibid.; *VMHB*, 74 (4), pp. 452–61.

45. Malone, vol. 1, pp. 356–58.

46. Meade, vol. 2, p. 238.

47. *The Letters of Richard Henry Lee*, ed. James Curtis Ballagh (New York: The Macmillan Co., 1911), vol. 2, pp. 233–35.

48. Ibid.

49. Boyd, vol. 6, pp. 74–108.

50. Bowers, pp. 275–76; William Wirt Henry, *Patrick Henry: Life, Correspondence and Speeches* (New York: Charles Scribner's Sons, 1891), vol. 2, pp. 128–29; Malone, vol. 1, p. 359; Meade, vol. 2, pp. 237–38.

51. Albert J. Beveridge, *The Life of John Marshall, 1755–1788* (Boston: Houghton Mifflin, 1916–1919), vol. 1, p. 144.

52. Malone, vol. 1, pp. 358–59.

53. Gottschalk, pp. 246–72; Palmer, pp. 273–82.

54. Gottschalk, pp. 246–72.

55. Scheer and Rankin, pp. 453–66; Ward, pp. 802–34.

56. "General Anthony Wayne," *DAB*; *Pennsylvania Magazine of History*, V, pp. 290–305; Gottschalk, pp. 189–208; Scheer and Rankin, pp. 469–70.

57. *Pennsylvania Magazine of History*, V, pp. 290–305; *Journal of Lt. William Feltman of the First Pennsylvania Regiment 1781–1782 Including the March into Virginia and the Siege of Yorktown*, ed. Peter Decher (Salem, NH: Ayer Co. Pubs. Inc., 1969), p. 4.

58. Malone, vol. 1, p. 390.

59. *JHD*, p. 15; *JCS*, p. 348.
60. Fitzpatrick, vol. 22, p. 415.
61. *JHD*, pp. 21–23.
62. *JCS*, pp. 84–86, 89; Meade, vol. 2, pp. 240–42.
63. Henry, vol. 1, p. 506; Meade, vol. 2, p. 148.
64. *The Statutes at Large*, ed. William Waller Hening (Richmond, 1822), vol. 10, pp. 413–16; *JCS*, p. 348; *OL*, III, p. 23. These historians praised the selection of Thomas Nelson, Jr., as governor of Virginia. Hamilton J. Eckenrode (*The Revolution in Virginia* [Cambridge: Houghton-Mifflin, 1916]) states, "Strange the logic of history. Thomas Nelson, Jr.'s, succession proved to be the man for the crisis. He was a commonplace planter of some military knowledge, much energy, and great devotion to duty, and further was not handicapped by any special veneration for the Constitution."

Meade writes, "On June 1, General Thomas Nelson was elected Governor by a majority vote. It was an excellent appointment, for the forty-two-year-old General, 'alert and active for his weight,' brought to the gubernatorial office not only the remaining wealth and influence of a leading Tidewater family but considerable civil and military experience. Happily, Nelson was not deterred by the difficulties of his task, including the vulnerability of his lower Tidewater estate to enemy raids."

Palmer remarks, "Jefferson's renunciation too late to do much good—military resources dissipated and exhausted beyond recovery. Nelson labored with intelligence and industry but even the best administration cannot recall lost opportunity."

65. Boyd, vol. 6, p. 96; Malone, vol. 1, pp. 361–62.
66. Hening, vol. 10, pp. 413–16; *JHD*, pp. 20–21. The delegates agreed that a sword and pistols be presented to Captain Jack Jouett (p. 17).
67. *JHD*, p. 22.
68. *OL*, III, p. 41.
69. *JCS*, II, pp. 348–49; 351–53.
70. Governor Nelson to General Weedon, July 2, 1781, American Philosophical Society, Philadelphia.
71. Colonel William Nelson to General Weedon, June 18, 1781, American Philosophical Society.
72. Colonel William Nelson to General Weedon, June 19, 1781, American Philosophical Society.
73. Colonel William Nelson to General Weedon, June 18, 1781, American Philosophical Society.
74. *JCS*, II, July 10, 1781, p. 354.
75. Gottschalk, pp. 246–72; Chinard, pp. 16–17; "Lafayette's Virginia Campaign," *Magazine of American History*, VI, 1881, pp. 341–52.
76. Chinard, p. 24.
77. *Pennsylvania Magazine of History*, V, p. 293.
78. Feltman, p. 5.
79. *Pennsylvania Magazine of History*, V, p. 294.
80. Gottschalk, pp. 246–72.
81. Ibid., pp. 16–17.
82. Henry P. Johnston, *Yorktown Campaign and the Surrender of Cornwallis* (New York: Harper and Bros., 1881), p. 51.

83. St. George Tucker to Fanny Randolph Rucker, July 11, 1781, Tucker–Coleman Papers, College of William and Mary.

84. Ibid., *WMQ*, 16 (1), p. 57.

85. *WMQ*, 16 (1), p. 57.

86. Chinard, p. 31.

87. Gottschalk, pp. 246–82.

88. *Pennsylvania Magazine of History*, V, p. 294.

89. Ibid., July 4, 1781, pp. 294–95.

90. Gottschalk, pp. 246–72; Scheer and Rankin, pp. 470–71.

91. Scheer and Rankin, pp. 470–71; Johnston, p. 190; Palmer, pp. 283–87; Frank Moore, *Diary of the American Revolution from Newspapers and Original Documents* (New York: Charles Scribner's Sons, 1860), letter from an unknown soldier, Holt's Forge, Kent County, July 11, 1781. *New Jersey Gazette*, Aug. 8, 1781, stated action obstinate. Americans lost two field pieces. American wounded were treated more humanely than usual.

92. General Lafayette to Governor Nelson, July 10, 1781, Chinard, p. 25.

93. Ibid., p. 26.

94. Ibid., pp. 26–27.

95. Ibid.

96. OL, III, pp. 5–6; JCS, II, July 16, 1781, p. 356.

97. David Ross to Governor Nelson, Executive Papers, VSL.

98. Charles Dick to Governor Nelson, Executive Papers; Hening, vol. 10, p. 473.

99. Boyd, vol. 6, pp. 72–73.

100. Colonel Preston to Governor Nelson, July 26, 1781, Executive Papers.

101. Colonel Davies to Governor Nelson, July 26, 1781, Executive Papers.

102. General Lawson to Governor Nelson, July 26, 1781, Executive Papers.

103. Colonel Lewis Burwell to Governor Nelson, July 30, 1781, Executive Papers.

104. Commodore Barron to Governor Nelson, July 30, 1781, Executive Papers.

105. Colonel James Innes to Governor Nelson, July 24, 1781, *Calendar*, II, p. 268.

106. Governor Nelson to Colonel Innes, July 30, 1781, *Calendar*, II, p. 268.

107. Jane Carson, *James Innes and His Brothers of the Flat Hat Club* (Colonial Williamsburg Research Studies, 1965), p. 102.

108. John Bakeless, *Turncoats, Traitors and Heroes* (Philadelphia: J. B. Lippincott, 1959), pp. 324–44; Carson, pp. 150–53.

109. Colonel Innes to Sir John Peyton, Aug. 6, 1781, *Calendar*, II, p. 296.

110. Chinard, pp. 48–49.

111. Chinard, pp. 42–43.

112. Freeman, vol. 5, pp. 305–06, 309.

113. Scheer and Rankin, pp. 471–74.

114. Governor Nelson to General Lafayette, Aug. 15, 1781, *Letters of Thomas Nelson, Jr., Governor of Virginia* (Richmond: VHS, 1874).

115. Chinard, p. 50.

116. Ibid., p. 52.

117. Major John Nelson to Governor Nelson, Aug. 3, 1781, Executive Papers.

118. James McHenry to Governor Nelson, Aug. 8, 1781, Executive Papers.

119. Colonel Matthews to Governor Nelson, July 23, 1781, Executive Papers.

120. David Garland to Governor Nelson, July 23, 1781, Executive Papers.

121. Mr. Maxwell to Governor Nelson, July 24, 1781, Executive Papers.

122. Governor Nelson to Colonel Josiah Parker, July 26, 1781, *OL*, III, pp. 13–14.

123. Ibid.

124. Governor Nelson to General Washington, July 27, 1781, *OL*, III, pp. 13–14.

125. Ibid.

126. Ibid.

127. Fitzpatrick, vol. 22, pp. 472–73.

128. Governor Nelson's Circular Letter to County Lieutenants, July 30, 1781, *OL*, III, p. 17. General Lafayette had asked the legislature and Governor Jefferson for carriages but had been turned down.

129. Governor Nelson to Colonel Davies, July 31, 1781, *OL*, III, p. 17.

130. Governor Nelson to Commodore Barron, Aug. 1, 1781, *OL*, III, p. 18.

131. Governor Nelson to Colonel Sir John Peyton, Aug. 1, 1781, *OL*, III, p. 18.

132. Governor Nelson to Governor Thomas Sim Lee, Aug. 1, 1781, *OL*, III, p. 19.

133. Lieutenant George North, Q.M.B., July 24, 1781, Chinard, p. 32.

134. Governor Nelson to General Lafayette, Aug. 3, 1781, Nelson *Letters*.

135. General Wayne to Governor Nelson, Aug. 19, 1781, Executive Papers.

136. Governor Nelson to Congressional Delegates, Aug. 3, 1781, Nelson *Letters*.

137. Ibid.

138. Governor Nelson to Governor Burke, Aug. 10, 1781, Nelson *Letters*.

139. General Greene to Governor Nelson, Aug. 10, 1781, Clements Library, Ann Arbor, MI.

140. Major I. Burnett to General Greene, Aug. 20, 1781, Clements Library.

141. Lt. Governor Jameson to Governor Nelson, Aug. 24, 1781, *OL*, III, pp. 26–27. "Hear you were prevented in intended trip to camp last week by an indisposition."

142. Fitzpatrick, vol. 23, p. 33.

143. *Calendar*, II, p. 380; Gottschalk, p. 297.

144. Fitzpatrick, vol. 23, p. 55.

145. Governor Nelson to Commissary John Brown, Sept. 2, 1781, Nelson *Letters*.

146. Governor Nelson to Captain Pierce, Sept. 2, 1781, Nelson *Letters*.

147. Governor Nelson to Comte de Grasse, Sept. 2, 1781, Nelson *Letters*.

148. Governor Nelson to Governor Thomas Sim Lee, Sept. 2, 1781, Nelson *Letters*.

149. Governor Nelson to Governor Thomas Burke, Sept. 3, 1781, Nelson *Letters*.

150. Governor Nelson to President of Congress, Sept. 2, 1781, Nelson *Letters*.

151. Governor Nelson to Governor Greene, Sept. 5, 1781, Nelson *Letters*.

152. Ibid.

153. Governor Nelson to Robert Morris, Sept. 5, 1781, Nelson *Letters*.

154. *OL*, III, p. 35.

155. Colonel Lewis Burwell to Governor Nelson, Sept. 9, 1781, Executive Papers.

156. Colonel Burwell to Colonel Davies, Sept. 11, 1781, Executive Papers.

157. General Lafayette to Governor Nelson, Sept. 11, 1781, Chinard, p. 59.

158. Governor Nelson to Commissary Pierce, Sept. 12, 1781, Nelson *Letters*.

159. Governor Nelson to Council, Sept. 5, 1781, *OL*, III, p. 36.

160. Governor Nelson to Governor Burke, Sept. 11, 1781, Nelson *Letters*.

161. Freeman, vol. 5, pp. 325–28. General Washington and one aide rode sixty miles on September 9 to reach Mount Vernon.

162. Ibid.

163. *OL*, III.

164. Governor Nelson to Colonel Wills, Sept. 12, 1781, Nelson *Letters*.

165. Governor Nelson to Commissary Pierce, Sept. 12, 1781, Nelson *Letters*.

166. Governor Nelson to David Ross, Sept. 12, 1781, Nelson *Letters*.

167. Letters sent to Col. Davies, Lt. Gov. Jameson, Gov. Burke, North Carolina, Col. Innes, Sept. 13, 1781, Nelson *Letters*.

168. Governor Nelson to General Lawson, Sept. 13, 1781, Nelson *Letters*.

169. Letters to county lieutenants of Fairfax, Prince William, Stafford, Spotsylvania, Caroline, Hanover, New Kent, *OL*, III, pp. 43–44, 47–48.

170. Governor Nelson to Governor Burke, Sept. 13, 1781, Nelson *Letters*.

171. Petition of Tories, Sept. 8, 1781, Executive Papers; *Calendar*, II, p. 181.

172. Governor Nelson to Ralph Wormeley, Jr., Sept. 14, 1781, Nelson *Letters*.

173. Governor Nelson to Major Boyce, Sept. 13, 1781, *OL*, III, p. 41.

174. Governor Nelson to Lord Cornwallis, Sept. 18, 1781, *OL*, III.

175. Governor Nelson to Colonel Davies, Sept. 19, 1781, Nelson *Letters*.

176. Governor Nelson to Colonel Barbour, Sept. 19, 1781, *OL*, III, pp. 60–61.

177. Ibid.

178. Governor Nelson to Colonel Blount, Sept. 12, 1781, Nelson *Letters*.

179. W. Edmunds, Sept. 18, 1781, Executive Papers, VSL.

180. Lt. Gov. Jameson to Governor Nelson, Sept. 13, 1781, *OL*, III, p. 44.

181. Governor Nelson to John Penn, Oct. 6, 1781, *OL*, III, pp. 80–81.

182. Lt. George Corbin to Governor Nelson, Sept. 30, 1781, Executive Papers.

183. Governor Nelson to George Webb, Oct. 17, 1781, *OL*, III. Webb had notified Governor Nelson he did not know what to do with the Reverend Mr. Lyon.

184. Governor Nelson to Colonel Innes, Sept. 18, 1781, *OL*, III, pp. 55–56. Colonel George Nicholas was writing for Governor Nelson, *OL*, III, p. 48.

185. Freeman, vol. 5, pp. 329–30.

186. *WMQ*, 16 (1), pp. 58–59.

187. Governor Nelson to Lt. Governor Jameson, Sept. 14, 1781, *OL*, III, p. 51.

188. Governor Nelson to Colonel William Davies, Sept. 14, 1781, *OL*, III, pp. 49–50.

189. Governor Nelson to Commissary John Pierce, Sept. 14, 1781, *OL*, III, pp. 49–50; to Lt. Governor Jameson, Sept. 18, 1781, *OL*, III, p. 58: forage, 5,000 horses; 35,000 food rations per day.

190. Governor Nelson to Colonel Davies, Sept. 16, 1781, *OL*, III, p. 54.

191. Governor Nelson to Lt. Governor Jameson, Sept. 16, 1781, Nelson *Letters.*

192. Mary Haldane Coleman, *St. George Tucker, Citizen of No Mean City* (Richmond: Dietz Press, 1938), p. 71.

193. Lt. Governor Jameson to Governor Nelson, Sept. 15, 1781, Executive Papers.

194. Ibid.

195. Lt. Governor Jameson to Governor Nelson, Sept. 26, 1781, Executive Papers. On Sept. 21, 1781, James Hendricks, Alexandria, mentions the difficulties of competing with the French agents. On September 30, Richard Young, Fredericksburg, states several men were employed as French agents purchasing corn, flour, etc., paying a generous price in hard money for the products.

196. Governor Nelson to Lt. Governor Jameson, Sept. 21, 1781, OL, III, p. 65.

197. Ibid.

198. Governor Nelson to Lt. Governor Jameson, Sept. 27, 1781, OL, III, p. 70.

199. Governor Nelson to Lt. Governor Jameson, Oct. 1, 1781, OL, III, pp. 74–75.

200. Governor Nelson to Mann Page, Sept. 21, 1781, OL, III, p. 62; *Calendar,* II, p. 474.

201. Robert Andrews to Richard Henry Lee, Sept. 26, 1781, OL, III, p. 68; Richard Henry Lee to Governor Nelson, July 25, 1781, Executive Papers, VSL

202. Governor Nelson to Buller Claiborne, Sept. 25, 1781, OL, III, p. 67; *Calendar,* II, p. 491.

203. Governor Nelson to Sir Peyton Skipwith, Sept. 26, 1781, and Sept. 27, 1781; Robert Andrews to Sir Peyton Skipwith, Oct. 5, 1781, OL, III, p. 77.

204. Colonel Lewis Burwell to Governor Nelson, Sept. 30, 1781, Executive Papers.

205. General Lawson to Governor Nelson, Sept. 25, 1781, Executive Papers.

206. General Morgan to Governor Nelson, Sept. 20, 1781, Executive Papers.

207. North Carolina news that Governor Burke captured from Mr. Burton, Sept. 22, 1781, Executive Papers.

Chapter TWENTY-THREE

1. Colonel Davies to Governor Nelson, Sept. 28, 1781, Executive Papers, VSL.

2. Governor Nelson to Colonel Davies, Sept. 27, 1781, Executive Papers; OL, III, p. 72–73.

3. Colonel Davies to Governor Nelson, Oct. 6, 1781, Executive Papers.

4. Governor Thomas Sim Lee to Governor Nelson, Sept. 21, 1781, Executive Papers.

5. Lt. Governor Jameson to Governor Nelson, Sept. 15, 1781, Executive Papers.

6. *Writings of Washington*, ed. John C. Fitzpatrick (Washington, D.C.: U.S. Government Printing Office, 1927), vol. 23, p. 220.

7. Governor Nelson to Major Benjamin Day, Sept. 30, 1781, OL, III, p. 74.

8. Fitzpatrick, vol. 23, p. 161; Douglas Southall Freeman, *George Washington* (New York: Charles Scribner's Sons, 1966), vol. 5, pp. 334–39.

9. Freeman, vol. 5, pp. 334–39.

10. Governor Nelson to Lt. Governor Jameson, Sept. 21, 1781, OL, III, p. 65.

11. Freeman, vol. 5, p. 338.

12. Henry B. Carrington, *Battles of the American Revolution* (New York: A. S. Barnes and Co., 1877), pp. 631–46; Donald Barr Chidsey, *Victory at Yorktown* (New York: Crown Publishers, Inc., 1962); Freeman, vol. 5, pp. 297–321, 322–44, 345–60, 361–77, 378–93; Louis R. Gottschalk, *Lafayette and the Close of the American Revolution* (Chicago: Univ. of Chicago, 1942), chap. 13; Henry P. Johnston, *Yorktown Campaign and the Surrender of Cornwallis* (New York: Harper and Bros., 1881); John McAuley Palmer, *General von Steuben* (New Haven: Yale Univ. Press, 1937), pp. 288–96; George F. Scheer and Hugh Rankin, *Rebels and Redcoats* (Cleveland: World Publishing Co., 1957), pp. 475–95; James Thacher, *Military Journal of the American Revolution* (Hartford: Hurlbut, Williams and Co., 1862); Williard M. Wallace, *Appeal to Arms: A Military History of the American Revolution* (New York: Harper and Bros., 1951), pp. 246–62; Christopher Ward, *The War of the Revolution* (New York: Macmillan, 1952), pp. 886–96.

13. Baron Ludwig von Closen, *Revolutionary Journal, 1780–1783,* tr. and ed. Evelyn M. Acomb (Chapel Hill: Univ. of N.C. Press for the Institute of Early American History and Culture at Williamsburg, 1958), p. 153.

14. Benjamin F. Stevens, *The Campaigns in Virginia, 1781* (London: 1888), vol. 1, pp. 131–36, 176–77, 188.

15. *Tyler's Quarterly,* 2, p. 457.

16. Governor Nelson to General Weedon, Sept. 19, 1781, OL, III, p. 60.

17. Governor Nelson to Lt. Governor Jameston, Oct. 1, 1781, OL, III, pp. 74–75.

18. Fitzpatrick, vol. 23, p. 171.

19. Governor Nelson to General Choisy, Oct. 6, 1781, OL, III, p. 80.

20. *Pennsylvania Magazine of History,* V, pp. 290–311.

21. Ibid., p. 303.

22. *Historical Magazine,* VIII, (March 1864).

23. Governor Nelson to Virginia Delegates in Congress, Oct. 5, 1781, OL, III, pp. 78–79.

24. Ibid.

25. Ibid.

26. Governor Nelson to Lt. Governor Jameson, Oct. 8, 1781, OL, III, p. 81.

27. Thacher, pp. 283–84.

28. WMQ, 22 (2), pp. 229–74.

29. *Pennsylvania Magazine of History,* XXVI, pp. 25–41.

30. Charles Stedman, *The History of the Origin, Organization, and Termination of the American War* (London, n.p., 1794), vol. 2, pp. 409–10.

31. WMQ, 5 (3), pp. 375–85; *Biography of the Signers of the Declaration of Independence,* ed. John Sanderson (Philadelphia: W. Brown and C. Peters, 1828), vol. 7, pp. 296–98. Chastellux states he witnessed the cruel anxiety of the Secretary's sons as their father walked under a flag with his eyes fixed on the town.

32. Henry Howe, *Historical Collections* (Charleston: W. R. Babcock, 1847–1849), p. 295; Johnston, pp. 139–40; Sanderson, vol. 7, p. 295. General Nelson's

house is still standing at Yorktown. The Secretary's house was demolished in the siege and a plaque marks the site of the residence.

33. Thacher, p. 283.

34. Freeman, vol. 5, p. 364.

35. *Journal of Lt. William Feltman of the First Pennsylvania Regiment 1781–1782 Including the March into Virginia and the Siege of Yorktown*, ed. Peter Decher (Salem, NH: Ayer Co. Pubs. Inc., 1969), p. 16.

36. Ibid., p. 18.

37. Stevens, pp. 176–66; Johnston, pp. 105–111; Scheer & Rankin, p. 487.

38. Feltman, p. 20; *WMQ*, 5 (3), p. 390.

39. Johnston, p. 114; Freeman, vol. 5, p. 369.

40. Scheer and Rankin, p. 487. The authors quote many times from Joseph Plumb Martin's *A Narrative of Some of the Adventures, Dangers and Sufferings of a Revolutionary Soldier* (Hallowell, Me., 1830). Martin entered patriot forces at 16.

41. Johnston, p. 144.

42. Ibid.

43. Feltman, p. 20.

44. Stevens, vol. 2, p. 188.

45. Gov. Nelson to Col. Godfrey, Oct. 16, 1781, *OL*, III, p. 85.

46. Gov. Nelson to county lieutenants, *OL*, III, p. 85.

47. Gov. Nelson Proclamation, Oct. 16, 1781, *OL*, III, p. 86.

48. Ibid.

49. Johnston, pp. 53–54. Ibid. Historian Johnston quotes part of Nelson's letter in describing events.

50. Freeman, vol. 5, p. 377.

51. Ibid., p. 378.

52. *WMQ*, 5 (3), p. 281.

53. von Closen, p. 155.

54. Fitzpatrick, vol. 23, pp. 244–47; Freeman, vol. 5, p. 385.

55. Fitzpatrick, vol. 23, pp. 244–47.

56. Governor Nelson to Virginia delegates in Congress, Oct. 20, 1781, *OL*, III, pp. 88–89.

57. Governor Nelson to Lord Cornwallis, Oct. 21, 1781, *OL*, III, p. 90.

58. Governor Nelson to Lord Cornwallis, Oct. 22, 1781, *OL*, III, p. 90; *VMHB*, 18 (1), p. 323.

59. *OL*, III, p. 90.

60. Governor Nelson to General Weedon, Oct. 21, 1781, *OL*, III, p. 90.

61. Ibid.

62. Governor Nelson to General Lawson, Oct. 20, 1781, *OL*, III, p. 88. Chidsey speaks of Governor Nelson as a man of great energy and action (p. 96). Johnston gives a breakdown of troop strength and information on commanders. He states, "Nelson's patriotism was conspicuous all through the campaign" (p. 140).

Chapter TWENTY-FOUR

1. *Writings of Washington*, ed. John C. Fitzpatrick (Washington, D.C.: U.S. Government Printing Office, 1927), vol. 23, pp. 271–72.

2. North Callahan, *Henry Knox, General Washington's General* (New York: Holt, Rinehart and Winston, 1958), pp. 189–90.

3. *Journal of Lt. William Feltman of the First Pennsylvania Regiment 1781–1782 Including the March into Virginia and the Siege of Yorktown,* ed. Peter Decher (Salem, NH: Ayer Co. Pubs. Inc., 1969), p. 28–31.

4. Ibid.

5. Ibid.

6. Gilbert Chinard, *Lafayette in Virginia* (Baltimore: John Hopkins Press, 1928), p. 60.

7. Governor Nelson to Governor Thomas Sim Lee, Oct. 21, 1781, OL, III, p. 89.

8. Governor Nelson to County Lieutenant of Gloucester, Oct. 22, 1781, OL, III, p. 91.

9. Fitzpatrick, vol. 23, pp. 324–25.

10. Ibid., pp. 332–34.

11. OL, III, p. 436; Jacquelin Ambler to Captain Henry Young, OL, III, p. 92; to Thomas Nicholson, printer, OL, III, p. 44.

12. George Webb to Lt. Governor Jameson, OL, III, p. 46.

13. Ibid.

14. Major John Nelson to Governor Nelson, Nov. 3, 1781, Executive Papers, VSL; Robert Andrews to Major John Nelson, Nov. 4, 1781, Executive Papers.

15. Ibid.

16. Governor Nelson to David Ross, Nov. 3, 1781, OL, III, p. 92.

17. Robert Andrews to General Lawson, Colonel Richard Henry Lee, and Colonel Barbour, OL, III, p. 94. If a record had remained of the recipients of this letter, it would have created an honor roll of patriots.

18. Captain Nathaniel Terry to Governor Nelson, Nov. 4, 1781, Executive Papers.

19. Colonel Timothy Pickering to Governor Nelson, Nov. 8, 1781, Executive Papers. On Nov. 9, 1781, Andrews wrote the Virginia delegates in Congress of Governor Nelson's illness; see their reply, Nov. 20, 1781, *Calendar of Virginia State Papers, 1652–1781* (Richmond, 1875), II, p. 614.

20. Colonel Thomas Newton to Governor Nelson, Nov. 2, 1781, Executive Papers.

21. Colonel Thomas Newton to Governor Nelson, Nov. 10, 1781, Executive Papers.

22. Ibid.

23. General Rochambeau to Governor Nelson, Nov. 6, 1781, Executive Papers.

24. Ibid.

25. Ibid.

26. Ibid.

27. Douglas Southall Freeman, *George Washington* (New York: Charles Scribner's Sons, 1966), vol. 5, pp. 401–02.

28. WMQ, 20 (2), p. 246.

29. William Reynolds to Governor Nelson, Nov. 16, 1781, Executive Papers.

30. Ibid.

31. JHD, pp. 17, 21–23, 53–54, 58–59; *Biography of the Signers of the Declaration of Independence,* ed. John Sanderson (Philadelphia: W. Brown and C. Peters, 1828), vol. 5, pp. 41–76; vol. 7, p. 298.

32. *JHD*, p. 22.

33. Ibid., pp. 53, 58–59.

34. Ibid.

35. Baron Ludwig von Closen, *Revolutionary Journal, 1780–1783,* tr. and ed. Evelyn M. Acomb (Chapel Hill: Univ. of N.C. Press for the Institute of Early American History and Culture at Williamsburg, 1958), pp. 179–81, 186.

36. Ibid.

37. Ibid., pp. 208–09.

38. Ibid. The diarist makes no mention of mourning in the household. Jane Byrd Nelson, wife of Nathaniel, died at Offley Hoo in Hanover County, Feb. 2, 1782.

39. Plantation names from General Nelson's will.

40. Jean Francois Chastellux, *Travels in North America in the Years 1780, 1781, 1782* (New York: White, Gillespie and White, 1787), vol. 2, pp. 217–19.

41. Ibid.

42. Ibid.

43. Ibid.

44. Ibid.

45. Ibid.

46. *NFB*.

47. *JHD*, pp. 8, 11, 12–14, 18.

48. Ibid., p. 11.

49. Ibid., pp. 1–10, Document 9, Item 13. Dabney was the principal manager of one of General Nelson's plantations. Although General Nelson's heirs petitioned the delegates, the family was never repaid.

50. Dumas Malone, *Jefferson the Virginian* (Boston: Little, Brown and Co., 1948), vol. 1, p. 396.

51. York County Papers.

52. Robert Douthat Meade, *Patrick Henry* (Philadelphia: J. B. Lippincott Co., 1969), vol. 2, p. 253.

53. Jane Carson, *James Innes and His Brothers of the Flat Hat Club* (Colonial Williamsburg Research Studies, 1965), p. 154.

54. John C. Miller, *Triumph of Freedom, 1775–1783* (Boston: Little, Brown and Co., 1948), pp. 616–49.

55. Ibid.

56. *Diary of Robert Honeyman,* pp. 387, 388, LC.

57. Julian P. Boyd, *The Papers of Thomas Jefferson* (Princeton: Princeton Univ. Press, 1951), vol. 6, p. 266.

58. *JHD*, pp. 4, 8, 11, 13, 18, 47, 53, 59, 66, 82, 92, 97; Meade, vol. 2, p. 261.

59. Ibid.

60. Ibid.

61. *JHD*, pp. 82, 92; *VMHB*, 18 (1), p. 323.

62. *WMQ*, 14 (1), pp. 278–79.

63. Mary A. Stephenson, "Nelson-Galt House at Williamsburg," Colonial Research Library, Williamsburg; *WMQ*, 5 (1), pp. 166–67, 170; 11 (1), p. 114.

64. *WMQ*, 23 (1), p. 136.

65. *Colonial Williamsburg Guidebook* (Williamsburg, 1985).

66. Carson, p. 155.

67. Rutherfoord Goodwin, "Historical Magazine of the Protestant Episcopal Church," December 1941, pp. 354–89.

68. Eastern State Hospital Court of Directors' Minutes, p. 9. Galt served from 1773 until his death in 1800. (With permission from the Virginia Department of Mental Health, Mental Retardation and Substance Abuse Services, Eastern State Hospital, Williamsburg, Va., VSL.)

69. *Tyler's Quarterly*, 4, p. 422.

70. York County Records, Wills and Inventories, 1783–1811, No. 23; VMHB, 37, portrait p. 214; WMQ, 12 (1), p. 66.

71. *Colonial Williamsburg Guidebook*, pp. 89–91.

72. William Lee to General Nelson, *Lee Letter Book*, 1783–1787, VHS, p. 16; VMHB, 38 (1), p. 43.

73. *JHD*, pp. 13, 18, 24.

74. Mary A. Stephenson, *Carter's Grove Plantation* (Colonial Williamsburg, 1964).

75. Eastern State Hospital Court of Directors' Minutes, p. 11; Lyon Gardiner Tyler, *Williamsburg, The Old Colonial Capital* (Richmond: Whittet and Shepperson, 1907), p. 244.

76. Frances Norton Mason, *John Norton & Sons, Merchants of London and Virginia, 1750–1795* (Richmond: Dietz Press, 1937), p. 459.

77. *JHD*, pp. 44, 46, 60.

78. Ibid., pp. 86–87, 90; Emory Gibbons Evans gives the sum as £10,525. ("The Nelsons: A Biographical Study of a Virginia Family in the Eighteenth Century" [dissertation, Univ. of Va., 1957]).

79. Meade, vol. 2, pp. 276–77.

80. William Lee to General Nelson, March 1784, *Lee Letter Book*, p. 83.

81. *JHD*, pp. 86–87.

82. *JHD*, p. 33; Meade, vol. 2, p. 280.

83. Plantations and workers from General Nelson's will, York County Records, Wills and Inventories, 1783–1811, No. 23, pp. 171–75.

84. Ibid.

85. Alice Morse Earle, *Child Life in Colonial Days* (New York: Macmillan, 1932), p. 215.

86. An accession list and some of General Nelson's books appear in the Custom House at Yorktown.

87. York County Records, Wills and Inventories, 1783–1811, No. 23, pp. 504–05; WMQ, 5 (1), pp. 166–67, 170.

88. *JHD*, pp. 1, 6, 12, 65, 66, 67, 81, 123.

89. Ibid., p. 125.

90. York County Records, Wills and Inventories, 1783–1811, No. 23.

91. See Note 87.

92. Eastern State Hospital Court of Directors' Minutes, p. 70.

93. *JHD*, pp. 3–4; Meade, vol. 2, p. 319.

94. WMQ, 23 (1), p. 123.

95. *JHD*, p. 16.

96. Ibid., p. 15.

97. Ibid., pp. 44, 58–59.

98. Ibid., pp. 18, 24, 27.

99. Ibid., pp. 12, 19.
100. Ibid.
101. Ibid., pp. 27, 30.
102. Ibid., p. 51.
103. Ibid., p. 36; Calendar of Virginia State Papers, IV, p. 184; Carson, pp. 155–56.
104. *JHD*, p. 86.
105. Ibid.
106. Ibid., pp. 133–35, 137–39, 141, 147, 149.
107. Claude G. Bowers, *The Young Jefferson, 1743–1789* (Boston: Houghton Mifflin, 1945), pp. 370–72. Jefferson arrived at Portsmouth, England, July 29, 1784, and Le Havre, France, July 31, 1784; *Virginia: A Guide to the Old Dominion*, compiled by the Writers Program of the Work Projects Administration in the state of Virginia (New York: Oxford Univ. Press, 1940), p. 289.

Chapter TWENTY-FIVE

1. *Virginia Independent Chronicler*, Jan. 31, 1787; *Tyler's Quarterly*, 8, p. 67.
2. *WMQ*, 22 (1), p. 128.
3. *Tyler's Quarterly*, 9, pp. 95–96.
4. General Nelson to Edmund Berkeley, May 15, 1787, Berkeley Papers, Univ. of Va. Library (used by permission of the owner).
5. Emory Gibbons Evans, "The Nelsons: A Biographical Study of a Virginia Family in the Eighteenth Century" (dissertation, Univ. of Va., 1957).
6. Carl Van Doren, *The Great Rehearsal, The Story of the Making and Ratifying of the Constitution of the United States* (New York: Viking Press, 1948), pp. 1–22.
7. Ibid., p. 9, 15.
8. Van Doren, pp. 51–82.
9. Ibid.
10. *The Diaries of George Washington*, ed. John C. Fitzpatrick (Boston: Houghton Mifflin, 1925), vol. 3, p. 236.
11. General Nelson to son Thomas, Oct. 24, 1787, VHS ms. (2N 3774a1).
12. Julian P. Boyd, *The Papers of Thomas Jefferson* (Princeton: Princeton Univ. Press, 1951), vol. 3, p. 279.
13. Ibid., p. 280.
14. Ibid., p. 281.
15. Robert Douthat Meade, *Patrick Henry* (Philadelphia: J. B. Lippincott Co., 1969), vol. 2, pp. 322–24, 342–67.
16. Boyd, vol. 12, pp. 409–13.
17. Ibid.
18. Ibid.
19. Ibid.
20. Van Doren, pp. 216–25.
21. David Mays, *Edmund Pendleton, 1721–1803: A Biography* (Cambridge: Harvard Univ. Press, 1952), vol. 2, pp. 217–41; Meade, vol. 2, pp. 342–67.
22. Kate Mason Rowland, *Life of George Mason, 1725–1792* (New York: G. P. Putnam's and Son, 1892), vol. 2, p. 308.
23. Meade, vol. 2, pp. 368–97.
24. Mays, vol. 2, pp. 228–41.

25. Ibid., pp. 242–72.

26. Meade, vol. 2, pp. 371–72.

27. Richard Channing Moore, *Genealogy of the Page Family in Virginia* (New York: Jenkins and Thomas, 1883), p. 149.

28. Thomas Nelson Page, *The Old South* (New York: Charles Scribner's Sons, 1905), pp. 129–30.

29. Ibid.

30. Jane Carson, *Colonial Virginians at Play* (Colonial Williamsburg Research Studies, 1958), p. 7; Page, *Genealogy of the Page Family in Virginia*, p. 149.

31. Mary A. Stephenson, *Carter's Grove Plantation* (Colonial Williamsburg, 1964).

32. General Washington to General Nelson, Aug. 3, 1788, *Writings of Washington*, ed. John C. Fitzpatrick (Washington, D.C.: U.S. Government Printing Office, 1927), vol. 30, pp. 33–34.

33. York County Records, Wills and Inventories, 1783–1811, No. 23, pp. 171–75.

34. Ibid.

35. Augustine Smith to W. W. Erskine at Edinburgh from York, May 16, 1787, Augustine Smith *Letter Book*, Colonial Williamsburg Archives.

36. *Richmond Weekly Advertiser*, Jan. 15, 1789.

37. Ibid.

38. Ibid.

GLOSSARY

abatis—(military) defense formed of felled trees

calamanco—glossy woolen fabric striped or checked on one side

camelot (camlet)—name originally applied to a fabric of silk and camel's hair

Capuchen—woman's hooded cloak

carronade—short iron cannon

clairvoyee—screen of ironwork in a wall

curtain—a plain wall of any fortified structure

demibastion—(military) fortification that has only one face and one flank

embrasure—(military) a hole with flaring sides from which cannon protrude

fascine—(military) a bundle of sticks tied together used to strengthen ramparts, fill ditches or retaining walls on a river bank

flip—spiced sweet drink

flummery—custard

fudejoy—party

fustian—cotton and linen cloth

gabion—(military) cylinder filled with earth

horn work—(military) outwork composed of two demibastions joined by a curtain

lucerne—alfalfa

modillion—ornamental bracket

pistole—quarter doubloon or any old gold coin

puccoon—bloodroot

rundlet—small barrel varying in capacity, about sixty-eight liters

sapper—(military) engineer who specialized in digging trenches

sennight—one week

shalloon—woolen fabric woven as twill

stomacher—ornamental covering for the front of the body

superfine—descriptive of a fabric's quality which might be middling, fine, or superfine

water table—(architecture) the sloping top of a plinth or a moulding set along a wall to throw off rainfall

BIBLIOGRAPHY

Principal Unpublished Sources

Berkeley Papers. University of Virginia Library.

Burnett, I. Letter to Gen. Nathanael Greene. Clements Library. University of Michigan, Ann Arbor.

Corbin, Richard. *Letter Book*. Colonial Williamsburg Archives.

Evans, Emory Gibbons. "The Nelsons: A Biographical Study of a Virginia Family in the Eighteenth Century." Dissertation, University of Virginia, 1957.

Executive Papers, Virginia State Library.

Greene, General Nathanael. Letter to Governor Thomas Nelson. Clements Library, University of Michigan, Ann Arbor.

Hanover County Land Book, 1782. Virginia State Library.

Honeyman, Robert. *Diary of Robert Honeyman*. Library of Congress.

Jerdone Account Book. Colonial Williamsburg Archives.

Journal of Delegates, Document 9, Item 13. Virginia State Library.

Lee Richard Henry. Letter to his brother. Colonial Williamsburg Archives.

Lee, William. *Letter Book*, 1783–1787. Virginia Historical Society.

Nelson Family Bible. Virginia Historical Society.

Nelson Letter Book, 1766–1775. Virginia State Library.

Nelson, Thomas, Jr. Letter to Edmund Berkeley, May 15, 1787. University of Virginia.

Nelson, Thomas, Jr. Letter to Nathaniel Burwell, July 30, 1785. State Historical Society of Wisconsin.

Nelson, Thomas, Jr. Letters to son Thomas, August 12 and October 24, 1787. Virginia Historical Society.

Nelson, Thomas, Jr. Letter to John Page, August 13, 1776. Colonial Williamsburg.

Nelson, Thomas, Jr. Letters to General George Washington. Library of Congress.

Nelson, Thomas, Jr. Letter to General George Weedon. American Philosophical Society, Philadelphia.

Nelson, William. Letter to General George Washington, October 13, 1777. Pennsylvania Historical Society, Philadelphia.

Pringle, J. J. Letter to Arthur Lee, August 18, 1779. University of Virginia, Charlottesville.

Reynolds, Sir Joshua. Portrait of Lord Dunmore. Richmond: Virginia Historical Society.

Riley, Edward Miles. "The Founding and Development of Yorktown, Virginia, 1691–1781." Dissertation, University of Southern California, 1942.

Smith, Augustine. *Letter Book*. Colonial Williamsburg Archives.

Smith, Lucy Calthorpe. Manuscript on Lucy Grymes Nelson. Colonial Williamsburg Archives.

Stephenson, Mary A. "Nelson-Galt House at Williamsburg." Colonial Research Library, Williamsburg.

Tucker-Coleman Papers, St. George Tucker Letter. College of William and Mary. Williamsburg, Virginia.

Untitled manuscript on funerals in colonial Virginia. Colonial Williamsburg Archives.

Washington Papers. Library of Congress.

York County Records.

Newspapers and Periodicals

Bulletin of Virginia State Library.
The Historical Magazine.
Historical Magazine of the Protestant Episcopal Church.
Magazine of American History.
Maryland Historical Magazine.
Pennsylvania Magazine of History.
Richmond Weekly Advertiser.
Southern History Association Publications.
Southern Literary Messenger.
Tyler's Quarterly.
Virginia Cavalcade.
Virginia Gazette.
The Virginia Gazette & Weekly Advertiser.
Virginia Independent Chronicler.
Virginia Magazine of History and Biography.
Virginia Quarterly.
William and Mary Quarterly.

Published Sources

Abernethy, Thomas Perkins. *Three Virginia Frontiers: Western Lands and the American Revolution*. Baton Rouge: Louisiana State University Press, 1940.

_____. *Western Lands and the American Revolution*. New York: D. Appleton and Co., 1937.

Adams, Charles Francis. *The Works of John Adams*. Vols. 1, 2. Boston: Little, Brown and Co., 1850.

Adams, John. *Diary and Autobiography of John Adams*. Edited by L. H. Butterfield. Vols. 2, 3. Cambridge: Harvard University Press, 1961.

Alden, John Richard. *The American Revolution*. New York: Harper and Row, 1954.

_____. *A History of the American Revolution*. New York: Knopf, 1969.

Alderman, Clifford Lindsey. *Retreat to Victory: The Life of Nathanael Greene*. Philadelphia: Chilton Book Co., 1967.

_____. *The Royal Opposition: The History of the British Generals in the American Revolution*. London: Collier Macmillan Limited, n.d.

Alexander, Edward P., ed. *Journal of John Fontaine: An Irish Huguenot Son in Spain and Virginia*. Colonial Williamsburg, n.d.

Alexander, Holmes. *Aaron Burr: The Proud Pretender*. New York: Harper, 1937.

American Archives. 4th and 5th Series. Edited by Peter Force. Vols. 1–6. Washington, D.C.: M. St. Clair Clark and Peter Force, 1837–1853.

American Heritage Book of the Revolution. New York: American Heritage Publishing Co., Inc. 1958.

Anburey, Thomas. *Travels Through the Interior Parts of America*. Boston: Houghton Mifflin, 1923.

Andrews, Charles M. *Colonial Folkways: A Chronicle of American Life in the Reign of the Georges*. New Haven: Yale University Press, 1920.

————. *Colonial Period of American History*. New Haven: Yale University Press, 1938.

Andrews, Matthew Page. *Virginia, The Old Dominion*. Garden City, N.Y.: Doubleday, Doran and Co., Inc., 1937.

Armes, Ethel. *Stratford Hall, The Great House of the Lees*. Richmond: Garrett and Massie, 1936.

Axelrad, Jacob. *The Voice of Freedom*. New York: Random House, 1947.

Bailey, Kenneth P. *The Ohio Company of Virginia and the Westward Movement*. Glendale, Ca.: Arthur H. Clark Co., 1937.

Bakeless, John. *Turncoats, Traitors and Heroes*. Philadelphia: J. B. Lippincott, 1959.

Ballagh, James Curtis, ed. *The Letters of Richard Henry Lee*. Vols. 1, 2. New York: The Macmillan Co., 1911.

Bass, Robert D. *The Green Dragon: The Lives of Banastre Tarleton and Mary Robinson*. New York: Henry Holt and Co., 1957.

Becker, Carl. *Declaration of Independence: A Study in the History of Political Ideas*. New York: Vintage, 1922.

————. *The Eve of the Revolution*. New Haven: Yale University Press, 1921.

Beveridge, Albert J. *The Life of John Marshall, 1755–1788*. Vol. 1. Boston: Houghton Mifflin, 1916–1919.

Beverley, Robert. *The History and Present State of Virginia*. Chapel Hill: University of North Carolina Press for the Institute of Early American History and Culture, 1947.

Bland, Theodorick, Jr. *The Bland Papers of Colonel Theodorick Bland, Jr*. Edited by Charles Campbell. Petersburg, Va.: Edmund and Julian C. Ruffin, 1840–1843.

Blanton, Wyndham. *Medicine in Virginia in the Eighteenth Century*. Richmond: Garrett and Massie, 1931.

Bonsal, Stephen. *When the French Were Here: A Narrative of the Yorktown Campaign*. Garden City, N.Y.: Doubleday, Doran, 1945.

Boogher, William Fletcher. *Gleanings of Virginia History*. Baltimore: Genealogical Publishing Co., 1903, 1965.

Boorstin, Daniel J. *The Americans: The Colonial Experience*. New York: Random House, 1958.

Bowen, Catherine Drinker. *John Adams and the American Revolution*. Boston: Little, Brown and Co., 1950.

Bowers, Claude G. *The Young Jefferson, 1743–1789*. Boston: Houghton Mifflin, 1945.

Boyd, Julian P. *The Papers of Thomas Jefferson*. Vols. 1–5, 7. Princeton: Princeton University Press, 1951.

Boyd, Julian P., and W. Edwin Hemphill. *The Murder of George Wythe.* Williamsburg, Va.: Institute of Early American History and Culture, 1955.

Bradley, A. G. *Colonial Americans in Exile.* New York: E. P. Dutton and Co., 1932.

Bradley, Sculley, Richmond Croom Beatty, and E. Hudson Long, eds. *The American Tradition in Literature.* New York: Grosset & Dunlap, Inc., 1967.

Brant, Irving. *James Madison, the Virginia Revolutionist.* Indianapolis: Bobbs-Merrill, 1941.

Bridenbaugh, Carl. *Myths and Realities.* Baton Rouge: University of Louisiana Press, 1952.

_____. *Seat of Empire.* Colonial Williamsburg, 1950.

Brock, Henry Irving. *Colonial Churches in Virginia.* Richmond: Dale Press, 1930.

Brown, Robert E., and Katherine Brown. *Virginia 1705–1786: Democracy or Aristocracy?* East Lansing: Michigan State University Press, 1964.

Brown, Stuart E., Jr. *Virginia Baron: The Story of Thomas, Sixth Lord of Fairfax.* Berryville, Va.: Chesapeake Bay Book Co., 1965.

Bruce, Philip Alexander. *Social Life of Virginia in the Seventeenth Century.* Richmond: Whittet and Shepperson, 1907.

_____. *The Virginia Plutarch.* Vol. 1. Chapel Hill: University of North Carolina Press, 1929.

Brumbaugh, Gaius Marcus. *Revolutionary War Records of Virginia.* Washington. D.C., 1936.

Brydon, G. MacLaren. *Virginia's Mother Church and the Political Conditions Under Which It Grew.* Vols. 1, 2. Richmond: Virginia Historical Society, 1947.

Burgess, Louis A. *Virginia Soldiers of 1776.* Richmond: Dietz Press, 1929.

Burk, John D. *History of Virginia from Its First Settlement to the Present Day.* Vol. 3. Petersburg, Va.: Dixon and Pescud, 1804–1816.

Burnaby, Andrew. *Travels Through the Middle Settlements in North America in the Years 1759–1760.* New York: Wessels and Bissell, 1904.

Burnett, Edmund C., ed. *Letters of the Members of the Continental Congress.* Vols. 1–5. Washington, D.C.: Carnegie Institution, 1921–1936.

_____. *The Continental Congress.* New York: W. W. Norton Co., Inc., 1941.

Butler, Richard. "Journal of the Siege of Yorktown." *The Historical Magazine,* XIII (March 1864).

Byrd, William. *Another Secret Diary of William Byrd of Westover, 1739–1741.* Edited by Maude H. Woodfin. Richmond: Dietz Press, 1942.

_____. *The Secret Diary of William Byrd of Westover, 1709–1712.* Edited by Louis B. Wright and Marion Tinling. Richmond: Dietz Press, 1941.

Calendar of Virginia State Papers, 1652–1781. Richmond, 1875.

Callahan, North. *Daniel Morgan, Ranger of the Revolution.* New York: Holt, Rinehart, and Winston, 1961.

_____. *Henry Knox, General Washington's General.* New York: Holt, Rinehart and Winston, 1958.

_____. *Royal Raiders, The Tories of the American Revolution.* Indianapolis: Bobbs-Merrill, 1963.

Campbell, Charles. *History of the Colony and Ancient Dominion of Virginia.* Richmond: B. B. Minor, 1847.

Carrington, Henry B. *Battles of the American Revolution*. New York: A. S. Barnes and Co., 1877.

Carson, Jane. *Colonial Virginians at Play*. Colonial Williamsburg Research Studies, 1958.

_____. *James Innes and His Brothers of the Flat Hat Club*. Colonial Williamsburg Research Studies, 1965.

Carson, Julia M. H. *Son of Thunder: Patrick Henry*. New York: Longmans, Green and Co., Inc., 1945.

Carter, Landon. *Diary of Colonel Landon Carter of Sabine Hall, 1752–1778*. 2 vols. Edited by Jack P. Green. Charlottesville: University of Virginia Press, 1965.

_____. *See also* Wineman, Walter Ray.

Chamberlain, Mason. Portrait of Thomas Nelson, Jr. Richmond: Virginia Museum.

Chamberlayne, Churchill G., ed. *Vestry Book, Christ Church Parish, Middlesex County, Va., 1663–1767*. Richmond: Old Dominion Press, 1927.

_____. *Vestry Book of St. Paul's Parish*. Hanover County, Virginia, 1706–1786. Richmond: Public Library Board, 1940.

Chandler, J. A. C., and T. B. Thames. *Colonial Virginia*. Richmond: Times Dispatch Co., 1907.

Chastellux, Jean Francois. *Travels in North America in the Years 1780, 1781, and 1782*. Vol. 1. New York: White, Gillespie and White, 1787.

Chidsey, Donald Barr. *Victory at Yorktown*. New York: Crown Publishers, Inc., 1962.

_____. *The War in the South*. New York: Crown Publishers, Inc., 1969.

Chinard, Gilbert. *Lafayette in Virginia*. Baltimore: John Hopkins Press, 1928.

Chitwood, Oliver Perry. *Richard Henry Lee: Statesman of the Revolution*. Morgantown: West Virginia University, 1967.

Clos, Jean Henri. *The Glory of Yorktown*. Yorktown Historical Society, 1924.

Coleman, Mary Haldane. *St. George Tucker, Citizen of No Mean City*. Richmond: Dietz Press, 1938.

Colonial Williamsburg Guidebook. Williamsburg, 1985.

Commager, Henry Steele, and Richard B. Morris. *The Spirit of "Seventy-Six": The Story of the American Revolution as Told by Participants*. Vols. 1, 2. Indianapolis: Bobbs-Merrill, 1958.

Conrad, Robert T., ed. *Sanderson's Biography of the Signers of the Declaration of Independence*. Philadelphia: Thomas Cowperthait & Co., 1846.

Cook, Fred J. *What Manner of Men: Forgotten Heroes of the American Revolution*. New York: William Morrow and Co., 1959.

Cooke, Jacob E. *Alexander Hamilton: A Profile*. New York: Hill and Wang, 1967.

Cooke, John Esten. *Stories of the Old Dominion*. New York: Harper and Bros., 1967.

_____. *Virginia: A History of the People*. Cambridge: Houghton Mifflin and Co., 1883.

Cox, William E., and Olivia Cox McCormac. *Our Family Genealogy*. Southern Pines, N.C.: Mary Nelson Smith family, 1938.

Cresswell, Nicholas. *Journal of Nicholas Cresswell, 1774–1777*. Edited by Lincoln MacVeagh. New York: Dial Press, 1924.

Davis, John. "Journal of Captain John Davis." *Pennsylvania Magazine of History and Biography,* V (1881).

Davis, Richard Beale. *Intellectual Life in Jefferson's Virginia, 1790–1830.* Chapel Hill: University of North Carolina Press, 1964.

Dictionary of American Biography. New York: Charles Scribner's Sons, 1938.

Dictionary of National Biography. London: Smith and Elder, 1885–1901.

Dodson, Leonidas. *Colonial Governors of Virginia.* Philadelphia: University of Pennsylvania Press, 1932.

Doehla, Johann C. "An Exaggerated Account." *William and Mary Quarterly,* 22 (2).

Donovan, Frank. *Mr. Jefferson's Declaration: The Story Behind the Declaration of Independence.* New York: Dodd, Mead and Co., 1968.

Dos Passos, John. *The Men Who Made the Nation.* Garden City, N.Y.: Doubleday, 1957.

Dowdey, Clifford. *The Virginia Dynasties.* Boston: Little, Brown and Co., 1969.

Downey, Fairfax. *Our Lusty Forefathers.* New York: Charles Scribner's Sons, 1947.

Draper, Lyman C. *King's Mountain and Its Heroes.* Edited by J. D. Bailey. New York: Dauber and Pine Bookshops, 1881, 1929.

Dumbauld, Edward. *The Declaration of Independence and What It Means Today.* Norman: University of Oklahoma Press, 1950.

Duncan, James. "Diary of James Duncan of Colonel Moses Hazen's Regiment in the Yorktown Campaign, 1781." *Pennsylvania Archives,* XV (2).

Dwight, Timothy. *Sketches of the Lives of the Signers of the Declaration of Independence.* New York: Harper, 1830.

Earle, Alice Morse. *Child Life in Colonial Days.* New York: Macmillan, 1932.

————. *Colonial Dames and Goodwives.* Boston: Houghton-Mifflin, 1900.

————. *Curious Punishments of Bygone Days.* New York: Macmillan, 1932.

————. *Stage Coach and Tavern Days.* New York: Macmillan, 1912.

Early, R. H. *By-Ways of Virginia History.* Richmond: Everett Waddy Co., 1907.

Eastern State Hospital Court of Directors' Minutes. Eastern State Hospital, Virginia Department of Mental Health, Mental Retardation and Substance Abuse Services. Williamsburg, Va. Virginia State Library.

Eckenrode, Hamilton J. *The Randolphs: The Story of a Virginia Family.* Indianapolis: Bobbs-Merrill Co., 1946.

————. *The Revolution in Virginia.* Boston: Houghton Mifflin, 1916.

————. *The Story of the Campaign and the Siege of Yorktown.* Washington, D.C.: U.S. Government Printing Office, 1931.

Eggleston, Edward. *Beginners of a Nation.* New York: D. Appleton and Co., 1900.

Eggleston, George Cary. *Life in the Eighteenth Century.* New York: U. S. Barnes and Co., 1905.

Einstein, Lewis. *Divided Loyalties: Americans in England During the War of Independence.* New York: Russell and Russell, 1970.

————. *Thomas Nelson and the Revolution in Virginia.* Williamsburg: Virginia Independence Bicentennial Commission, 1978.

_____. *Thomas Nelson of Yorktown, Revolutionary Virginian*. Williamsburg in America Series, No. 10. Colonial Williamsburg Foundation, 1975.

Encyclopedia of Virginia Biography. New York: Lewis Historical Publishing Co., 1915.

Executive Journals of the Council of Colonial Virginia. Edited by H. R. McIlwaine. Richmond: Virginia State Library, 1925–1966.

Family Encyclopedia of American History. Pleasantville, N.Y.: Readers Digest Association, 1975.

Farrar, Emmie Ferguson. *Old Virginia Houses Along the James*. New York: Bonanza Books, 1907.

Fast, Howard. *Citizen Tom Paine*. Cleveland: World Publishing Co., 1945.

Fay, Bernard. *George Washington, Republican Aristocrat*. Boston: Houghton Mifflin, 1931.

Fehrenbach, T. R. *Greatness to Spare: The Heroic Sacrifices of the Men Who Signed the Declaration of Independence*. Princeton: D. Van Nostrand Co., Inc., 1968.

Feltman, William. *Journal of Lt. William Feltman of the First Pennsylvania Regiment 1781–1782 Including the March into Virginia and the Siege of Yorktown*. Edited by Peter Decher. Salem, NH: Ayer Company Publishers, Inc., 1969.

Ferguson, Elmer James. *The Power of the Purse: A History of American Public Finance, 1776–1790*. Chapel Hill: University of North Carolina Press for the Institute of Early American History and Culture, 1961.

Fisher, Sydney George. *Men, Women and Manners in Colonial Times*. Philadelphia: J. B. Lippincott Co., 1900.

Fishwick, Marshall W. *Gentlemen of Virginia*. New York: Dodd, Mead, 1961.

_____. *Virginia, a New Look at the Old Dominion*. New York: Harper and Bros., 1959.

_____. *The Virginia Tradition*. Washington. D.C.: Public Affairs Printing, 1956.

Fiske, John. *The American Revolution*. 2 vols. Boston: Houghton Mifflin, 1902.

_____. *Old Virginia and Her Neighbors*. Boston: Houghton Mifflin, 1897.

Fithian, Philip Vickers. *The Journal and Letters of Philip Vickers Fithian, A Plantation Tutor of the Old Dominion, 1773–1774*. Edited by Hunter Dickinson Farish. Colonial Williamsburg, 1957.

Fitzpatrick, John C., ed. *The Diaries of George Washington*. 4 vols. Boston: Houghton Mifflin, 1925.

_____. *George Washington: Colonial Traveller, 1732–1775*. Indianapolis: Bobbs-Merrill, 1927.

_____. *The Writings of George Washington from the Original Manuscript Sources, 1949–1799*. Vols. 9–13, 17. Washington, D.C.: U.S. Government Printing Office, 1931–1944.

Fleming, Thomas. *The Man from Monticello: An Intimate Life of Thomas Jefferson*. New York: William Morrow and Co., Inc., 1969.

Flexner, James Thomas. *The Traitor and the Spy: Benedict Arnold and John Andre*. New York: Harcourt, Brace and Co., 1953.

Flippen, Percy Scott. *The Royal Government in Virginia, 1624–1775*. New York: Columbia University Press, 1919.

Fontaine, John. *Memoirs of a Huguenot Family: John Fontaine's Diary*. Edited by Ann Maury. New York: Putnam, 1853.

Foote, William Henry. *Sketches of Virginia Historical and Biographical*. Vol. 6. Richmond: John Knox Press, 1850.

Forbes, Esther. *Paul Revere and the World He Lived In*. Boston: Houghton Mifflin Co., 1942.

Ford, Paul Leicester, ed. *The Writings of Thomas Jefferson*. Vols. 1, 2. New York: G. P. Putnam's Sons, 1892–1899.

Freeman, Douglas Southall. *George Washington*. Vols. 1–5. New York: Charles Scribner's Sons, 1948–1975.

Friedenwald, Herbert. *The Declaration of Independence: An Interpretation and An Analysis*. New York: Macmillan, 1904.

Frothingham, Richard. *Rise of the Republic of the United States*. Boston: Little, Brown and Co., 1872.

Gewehr, Wesley H. *The Great Awakening in Virginia, 1740–1790*. Durham: Duke University Press, 1930.

Glenn, Thomas Allen. *Some Colonial Mansions and Those Who Lived in Them*. Philadelphia: Henry Holt and Co., 1937.

Goodrich, Charles A. *Lives of the Signers of the Declaration of Independence*. New York: William Reed and Co., 1829.

Goodwin, Edward Lewis. *Colonial Church in Virginia*. Milwaukee: Morehouse Publishing Co., 1927.

Goodwin, Maud Wilder. *The Colonial Cavalier*. Boston: Little, Brown and Co., 1895.

Goodwin, Rutherfoord. *A Brief and True Report Concerning Williamsburg, Virginia*. Richmond: Dietz Press, 1941.

Goolrick, John Tackett. *Life of General Hugh Mercer*. New York: Neale Publishing Co., 1906.

Gottmann, Jean. *Virginia at Mid-Century*. New York: Henry Holt and Co., 1955.

Gottschalk, Louis R. *Lafayette and the Close of the American Revolution*. Chicago: University of Chicago, 1942.

Gray, Lewis Cecil. *History of Agriculture in the Southern United States to 1860*. Vol. 1. Washington, D.C.: Carnegie Institution, 1933.

Grigsby, Hugh Blair. *The Virginia Convention of 1776*. Richmond: J. W. Randolph, 1865.

Guilford Courthouse, National Military Park, North Carolina. Historical handbook, series no. 30. Washington, D.C.: U.S. National Park Service, 1959.

Gwathmey, John H. *Historical Register of Virginians in the Revolution, 1775–1783*. Richmond: Dietz Press, 1938.

————. *Twelve Virginia Counties*. Richmond: Dietz Press, 1937.

Haley, Gail E. *Jack Jouett's Ride*. New York: Viking, 1973.

Hardy, Stella Pickett. *Colonial Families of the Southern States of America*. New York: Tobias A. Wright, 1911.

Harrell, Isaac Samuel. *Loyalism in Virginia*. Durham: Duke University Press, 1926.

Harris, Malcolm H. *A History of Louisa County, Virginia*. Richmond: Dietz Press, 1936.

Hart, Albert Bushnell. *Colonial Children*. New York: Macmillan, 1925.

Hartwell, Henry James Blair, and Edward Chilton. *The Present State of Virginia and the College*. Edited by Hunter Dickinson Farish. Charlottesville: University of Virginia, 1940.

Hawke, David. *A Transaction of Free Men: The Birth and Course of the Declaration of Independence*. New York: Charles Scribner's Sons, 1964.

Hawthorne, Hildegarde. *Williamsburg, Old and New*. New York: D. Appleton and Co., 1941.

Hazleton, John H. *The Declaration of Independence: Its History*. New York: Dodd, Mead, 1906.

Heitman, Francis B. *Historical Register and Dictionary of the United States Army, 1838–1926*. Washington, D.C.: Government Printing Office, 1903.

_____. *Historical Register of the Officers of the Continental Army During the War of the Revolution, April 1775 to December 1783*. Baltimore: Genealogical Publishing Co., 1967.

Hemphill, William Edwin, Marvin Wilson, and S. E. E. Schlegel. *Cavalier Commonwealth*. Dallas: McGraw-Hill, 1957, 1963.

Hendrick, Burton J. *The Lees of Virginia*. Boston: Little, Brown and Co., 1935.

Hening, William Waller, ed. *The Statutes at Large*. Vols. 1–3, 6–10. Richmond: Thomas Jefferson Library, 1819–1822.

Henry, William Wirt. *Patrick Henry: Life, Correspondence and Speeches*. Vols. 1–3. New York: Charles Scribner's Sons, 1891.

Hill, Helen. *George Mason, Constitutionalist*. Cambridge: Harvard University Press, 1938.

Hilldrup, Robert Leroy. *Life and Times of Edmund Pendleton*. Chapel Hill: University of North Carolina Press, 1939.

Holliday, Carl. *Women's Life in Colonial Days*. Boston: Corbill Publishing Co., 1922.

Howe, Henry. *Historical Collections*. Charleston: W. R. Babcock, 1847–1849.

Howison, Robert R. *A History of Virginia*. New York: Drinker and Morris, 1848.

Hume, Ivor Noel. *1775: Another Part of the Field*. New York: Knopf, 1966.

Imperial Encyclopedia. New York: Henry G. Allen and Co., 1890–1893, 1897, 1903.

Jefferson, Thomas. *Memoir, Correspondence, and Miscellanies from the Papers of Thomas Jefferson*. Edited by T. J. Randolph. Charlottesville: F. Carr, 1824.

_____. *See* Boyd, Julian P. and Ford, Paul Leicester.

Johnston, Henry P. *Yorktown Campaign and the Surrender of Cornwallis*. New York: Harper and Bros., 1881.

Jones, Hugh. *The Present State of Virginia*. Chapel Hill: University of North Carolina Press, 1956.

Journal of the House of Burgesses. Edited by H. R. McIlwaine. Richmond, 1912.

Journal of the House of Delegates. Williamsburg: Alexander Purdie, 1778.

Journal of the Virginia Convention.

Journals of the Continental Congress, 1774–1789. Washington, D.C.: 1904–1937.

Journals of the Council of the State of Virginia. Vols. 1–3, 1776–1781. Edited by H. R. McIlwaine. Richmond: 1931.

Ketchum, Richard M., ed. *American Heritage Book of the Revolution.* New York: The American Heritage Publishing Co., 1958.

Kibler, J. Luther. *Colonial Virginia Shrines: A Complete Guide to Jamestown, Williamsburg, and Yorktown.* Richmond: Garrett and Massie. 1936.

Kimball, Fiske. *The Restoration of Colonial Williamsburg in Virginia.* New York: F. W. Dodge Corp., 1935.

Kirkland, Elizabeth Stansbury. *Short History of England for Young People.* Chicago: A. C. McClurg & Co., 1892.

Knollenberg, Bernard. *Washington and the Revolution: A Reappraisal of Gates, Conway, and the Continental Congress.* New York: Macmillan, 1940.

Lancaster, Bruce. *From Lexington to Liberty: The Story of the American Revolution.* Garden City, N.Y.: Doubleday and Co., Inc., 1955.

Lancaster, Robert A. *Historic Virginia Homes and Churches.* Philadelphia: J. B. Lippincott Co., 1915.

Lecky, Robert, Jr., ed. *Proceedings of the Virginia Convention in the Town of Richmond on the 23rd of March 1775.* Richmond, 1938.

Lee, Cazenone Gardiner, Jr. *Lee Chronicle: Studies of the Early Generations of the Lees.* Compiled and edited by Dorothy Mills Parker. New York University Press, 1957.

Lee, Richard Henry. *See* Ballagh, James Curtis.

Lengyel, Cornel Adam. *Four Days in July: The Story Behind the Declaration of Independence.* Garden City, N.Y.: Doubleday, 1958.

Lingley, Charles R. *The Transition in Virginia from Colony to Commonwealth.* New York: Columbia University Press, 1910.

Lodge, Henry Cabot. *A Short History of the English Colonies in America.* Vol. 2. New York: Harper and Bros., 1899.

Lossing, Benson J. *Biographical Sketches of the Signers of the Declaration of Independence.* New York: George F. Cooledge and Best, 1848. G. G. Evans, 1860.

———. *The Pictorial Field Book of the Revolution.* Vols. 1, 2. New York: Harper, 1851.

MacDonald, James J. *Life in Old Virginia.* Norfolk: Old Virginia Publishing Co., 1907.

MacKenzie, Frederick. "Diary of Frederick MacKenzie." *Tyler's Quarterly,* 2.

MacKenzie, George N. *Colonial Families of the United States of America.* Vol. 3. Baltimore: Genealogical Publishing Co., 1966.

Macmillan, Margaret B. *The War Governors of the American Revolution.* New York: Columbia University Press, 1943.

Malone, Dumas. *Jefferson, the Virginian.* Vol. 1. Boston: Little, Brown and Co., 1948.

———. *The Story of the Declaration of Independence.* New York: Oxford University Press, 1954.

Mapp, Alf J., Jr. *The Virginia Experiment: The Old Dominion's Role in the Making of America, 1607–1781*. Richmond: Dietz Press, 1957.

Mason, Frances Norton. *John Norton & Sons, Merchants of London and Virginia, 1750–1795*. Richmond: Dietz Press, 1937.

Mason, George Carrington. *Colonial Churches in Tidewater Virginia*. Richmond: Whittet and Shepperson, 1945.

Mayo, Bernard. *Jefferson Himself*. Boston: Houghton Mifflin, 1942.

———. *Myths and Men: Patrick Henry, George Washington and Thomas Jefferson*. Athens, Ga.: University of Georgia Press, 1959.

Mays, David. *Edmund Pendleton, 1721–1803: A Biography*. Vols. 1, 2. Cambridge: Harvard University Press, 1952.

McGee, Dorothy Horton. *Famous Signers of the Declaration of Independence*. New York: Dodd, Mead, 1959.

McMurray, Charles A. *The Virginia Plantation*. Nashville: George Peabody College for Teachers, 1921.

Meade, Robert Douthat. *Patrick Henry*. Vol. 1. Philadelphia: J. B. Lippincott Co., 1957.

———. *Patrick Henry*. Vol. 2. Philadelphia: J. B. Lippincott Co., 1969.

Meade, William. *Old Churches, Ministers and Families of Virginia*. Vols. 1, 2. Philadelphia: J. B. Lippincott and Co., 1857.

Meigs, Cornelia. *The Violent Men: A Study of Human Relations in the First Continental Congress*. New York: Macmillan, 1949.

Michael, William H. *Story of the Declaration of Independence*. Washington, D.C.: Government Printing Office, 1904.

Miller, John C. *Origins of the American Revolution*. Boston: Little, Brown and Co., 1943.

———. *Triumph of Freedom, 1775–1783*. Boston: Little, Brown and Co., 1948.

Montross, Lynn. *Rag, Tag and Bobtail: The Story of the Continental Army, 1775–1783*. Harper and Bros., 1952.

———. *The Reluctant Rebels: The Story of the Continental Congress, 1774–1789*. New York: Harper and Bros., 1950.

Moore, Frank. *Diary of the American Revolution from Newspapers and Original Documents*. New York: Charles Scribner's Sons, 1860.

Moore, Virginia. *Virginia Is a State of Mind*. New York: E. P. Dutton and Co., Inc., 1942.

Morgan, Edmund S. *The American Revolution: Two Centuries of Interpretation*. Englewood Cliffs: Prentice-Hall, 1965.

———. *The Birth of the Republic, 1763–1789*. University of Chicago Press, 1956.

———. *Virginians at Home: Family Life in the Eighteenth Century*. Colonial Williamsburg, 1952.

Morrison, A. J. *Travels in Virginia in Revolutionary Times*. Lynchburg: J. B. Bell Co., 1922.

Morton, Louis. *Robert Carter of Nomini Hall: A Virginia Tobacco Planter in the Eighteenth Century*. Charlottesville: University of Virginia Press, 1941.

Nelson, Thomas, Jr. *Letters of Thomas Nelson, Jr., Governor of Virginia*. Richmond: Virginia Historical Society, 1864.

Nelson, William H. *The American Tory*. Oxford: Clarendon Press, 1961.

Nevins, Allan. *The American States During and After the Revolution, 1775–1789*. New York: Macmillan, 1924.

Newman, Eric P. *Coinage for Colonial Virginia*. American Numismatic Society, 1956.

Nicholls, John. *Recollections and Reflections Personal and Political as Connected with Public Affairs During the Reign of George III*. London: James Ridgeway, 1820.

Official Letters of the Governors of the State of Virginia. Edited by H. R. McIlwaine. Vol. 1, The Letters of Patrick Henry; Vol. 2, The Letters of Thomas Jefferson; Vol. 3, The Letters of Thomas Nelson and Benjamin Harrison. Richmond: 1926–1929.

Osborne, J. A. *Williamsburg in Colonial Times*. Richmond: Dietz Press, 1935.

Page, Richard Channing Moore. *Genealogy of the Page Family in Virginia*. New York: Jenkins and Thomas, 1883.

Page, Rosewell. *Hanover County: Its History and Legends*. Richmond: 1926.

Page, Thomas Nelson. *The Old Dominion, Her Making and Her Manners*. New York: Jenkins and Thomas, 1883.

————. *The Old South*. New York: Charles Scribner's Sons, 1905.

Palmer, John McAuley. *General von Steuben*. New Haven: Yale University Press, 1937.

Parton, Thomas. *Andrew Jackson*. Boston: Houghton Mifflin, 1860.

Pecquet, Louise du Bellet. *Some Prominent Virginia Families*. Vol. 2. Lynchburg: J. B. Bell Co., 1909.

Peixotto, Ernest. *A Revolutionary Pilgrimage*. New York: Charles Scribner's Sons, 1917.

Perry, William S. *Historical Collections Related to American Colonial Churches*. Hartford, Conn.: Church Press Corp., 1967.

Pleasants, J. Hall. "Jacob Hall, Surgeon and Editor, 1747–1812." *Maryland Historical Magazine*, 8 (3), Sept. 1913.

Popp, Stephen. "Journal, 1777–1783." *Pennsylvania Magazine of History and Biography*, XXVI (1912).

Preston, John Hyde. *Revolution in Virginia*. New York: Harcourt, Brace, 1933.

Randall, Henry S. *Life of Thomas Jefferson*. Vols. 1–3. New York: Derby and Jackson, 1858.

Randolph, Edmund. *History of Virginia: 1753–1813*. Edited by Arthur H. Shaffer. Charlottesville: University Press of Virginia, 1970.

Rankin, Hugh F. *The American Revolution*. New York: G. P. Putnam's Sons, 1964.

Riedesel, Friederike Charlotte Luise von Massow. *Letters and Journals Relating to the War of the American Revolution and the Capture of the German Troops at Saratoga*. Translated by William L. Stone. Albany: J. Munsell, 1867.

Roche, John F., and the editors of Silver Burdett Co. *Alexander Hamilton*. Morristown, N.J.: Silver Burdett Co., 1967.

Rose, Grace Norton. *Williamsburg, Today and Yesterday*. New York: G. P. Putnam's Sons, 1930.

Rothery, Agnes. *Houses Virginians Have Loved*. New York: Rinehart and Co., Inc., 1954.

———. *Manors of Virginia in Colonial Times*. Philadelphia: J. B. Lippincott, 1909.

———. *Virginia, The New Dominion*. New York: D. Appleton Century Co., 1940.

Rowland, Kate Mason. *Life of George Mason, 1725–1792*. Vols. 1, 2. New York: G. P. Putnam's and Son., 1892.

Rush, Benjamin. *Autobiography of Benjamin Rush*. Edited by George W. Corner. Princeton: Princeton University Press for the American Philosophical Society, 1948.

Sabine, Lorenzo. *Biographical Sketches of Loyalists of the American Revolution*. Vols. 1, 2. Boston: Little, Brown and Co., 1864.

Salmon, Emily J. *A Hornbook of Virginia History*. Richmond: Virginia State Library, 1983.

Sanderson, John, ed. *Biography of the Signers of the Declaration of Independence*. Vols. 1–7. Philadelphia: W. Brown and C. Peters, 1828.

Schachner, Nathan. *Thomas Jefferson*. New York: Thomas Yoseloff, 1951.

Schaun, George, and Virginia C. Schaun. *Everyday Life in Colonial Virginia*. Annapolis: Greenberry Publishing Co., 1960.

Scheer, George F., and Hugh Rankin. *Rebels and Redcoats*. Cleveland: World Publishing Co., 1957.

Schlesinger, Arthur M. *Colonial Merchants and the American Revolution*. New York: Columbia University Press, 1918.

Schouler, James. *Americans of 1776*. New York: Dodd, Mead and Co., 1906.

Scribner, Robert L. "Nemesis at Gwynn's Island." *Virginia Cavalcade*. Spring 1953.

Seaver, J. Montgomery. *Nelson Family Records*. Philadelphia: American Historical Genealogical Society, 1929.

Shepperson, Archibald Bolling. *John Paradise and Lucy Ludwell of London and Williamsburg*. Richmond: Dietz Press, 1942.

Smith, Margaret V. *Virginia, 1492–1892: A History of the Executives*. Washington, D.C.: W. H. Loudermilk and Co., 1893.

Sparks, Jared C. *Correspondence of the American Revolution*. Boston: Little, Brown and Co., 1853.

———. *The Writings of George Washington*. Vol. 2. Boston: Russell, Odorne and Metcalf and Hilliard, Gray, and Co., 1834.

Spruill, Julia Cherry. *Women's Life and Work in the Southern Colonies*. Chapel Hill: University of North Carolina Press, 1938.

Stanard, Mary Newton. *Colonial Virginia: Its People and Customs*. Philadelphia: J. B. Lippincott and Co., 1917.

Stanard, William, and Mary Newton Stanard. *Colonial Virginia Register*. Albany: Joel Munsell's Sons, 1902.

Stedman, Charles. *The History of the Origin, Organization, and Termination of the American War*. Vols. 1, 2. London, n.p., 1794.

Stephenson, Mary A. *Carter's Grove Plantation*. Prepared for Sealantic Fund, Inc., Colonial Williamsburg Research Department, 1964.

Stephenson, Nathaniel, and Waldo Hilary Dunn. *George Washington*. Vols. 1, 2. New York: Oxford University Press, 1910.

Stevens, Benjamin F. *The Campaigns in Virginia, 1781*. London: 1888.

Stevens, William Oliver. *Old Williamsburg and Her Neighbors*. New York: Dodd, Mead and Co., 1938.

Stoudt, John Baer. *Nicholas Martiau: The Adventurous Huguenot*. Norristown, Pa.: Norristown Press, 1932.

Swem, Earl Gregg, and J. W. Williams. *Register of the General Assembly of Virginia, 1776–1918, and of the Constitutional Convention*. Richmond: Davis Bottom, 1918.

Swiggett, Howard. *The Forgotten Leaders of the American Revolution*. Garden City, N.Y.: Doubleday and Co., Inc., 1955.

_____. *Virginia Historical Index*. 2 vols. Roanoke, Va., 1934–36.

Sydnor, Charles S. *American Revolutionaries in the Making: Political Practice in Washington's Virginia*. New York: Collier Books, 1962.

_____. *Gentlemen Freeholders: Political Practices in Washington's Virginia*. Westport, Conn.: Greenwood Press, 1984.

Tarleton, Lt. Col. Banastre. *A History of the Campaigns of 1780 and 1781 in the Southern Provinces of North America*. London: T. Cadell, 1787.

Taylor, Raymond L. *Plants of Colonial Days*. Williamsburg: Colonial Williamsburg Foundation, 1969.

Thacher, James. *Military Journal of the American Revolution*. Hartford: Hurlbut, Williams and Co., 1862.

Thane, Elswyth. *The Family Quarrel: A Journey Through the Years of the Revolution*. New York: Duell, Sloan and Pearce, 1959.

Thayer, Theodore. *Nathanael Greene: Strategist of the American Revolution*. New York: Twayne Publishers, 1960.

They Gave Us Freedom—The American Struggle for Life, Liberty, and the Pursuit of Happiness as seen in Portraits, Sculptures, Historical Paintings and Documents of the Period, 1761–1789. Colonial Williamsburg and the College of William and Mary, 1951.

Treacy, M. F. *Prelude to Yorktown: The Southern Campaign of Nathanael Greene, 1780–1781*. Chapel Hill: University of North Carolina Press, 1963.

Trevelyan, George Otto. *The American Revolution*. Vols. 1–4. New York: Longmans, Green and Co., 1908, 1914.

Trudell, Clyde F. *Colonial Yorktown*. Old Greenwich, Conn.: Chatham Press, Inc., 1938.

Tucker, St. George. "Journal of the Siege of Yorktown, 1781." *William and Mary Quarterly*, 5 (3).

Tyler, Lyon Gardiner. *History of Virginia*. Chicago: American Historical Society, 1924.

_____. *Williamsburg, The Old Colonial Capital*. Richmond: Whittet and Shepperson, 1907.

Tyler, Moses Coit. *Patrick Henry, American Statesman*. Boston: Houghton Mifflin, 1857.

Van Doren, Carl. *The Great Rehearsal, The Story of the Making and Ratifying of the Constitution of the United States*. New York: Viking Press, 1948.

_____. *Mutiny in January*. New York: Viking, 1943.

_____. *Secret History of the American Revolution*. New York: Viking, 1941.

Virginia Historical Register. Edited by William Maxwell. Vols. 3, 4. Richmond: MacFarland and Fergusson, 1850.

von Closen, Baron Ludwig. *Revolutionary Journal, 1780–1783*. Translated and edited by Evelyn M. Acomb. Chapel Hill: University of North Carolina Press for the Institute of Early American History and Culture at Williamsburg, 1958.

Wallace, David Duncan. *South Carolina: A Short History, 1520–1948*. Columbia: University of South Carolina Press, 1966.

Wallace, Willard M. *Appeal to Arms: A Military History of the American Revolution*. New York: Harper and Bros., 1951.

Ward, Christopher. *The War of the Revolution*. New York: Macmillan, 1952.

Wardlow, Georgia Dickinson. *The Old and the Quaint in Virginia*. Richmond: Dietz Press, 1939.

Warner, Charles Willard Hoskins. *Road to Revolution: Virginia's Rebels from Bacon to Jefferson, 1676–1776*. Richmond: Garrett and Massie, 1961.

Washington, George. *See* Fitzpatrick, John C. and Sparks, Jared C.

Waterman, Thomas Tileston. *The Mansions of Virginia, 1706–1776*. Chapel Hill: University of North Carolina Press, 1946.

Weddell, Alexander Wilbourne, ed. *A Memorial Volume of Virginia Historical Portraiture, 1585–1830*. Richmond: The William Byrd Press, 1930.

Weedon, General George. *Orderly Book*. New York: Dodd, Mead, 1902.

Werstein, Irving. *1776: The Adventure of the American Revolution Told with Pictures*. Totowa, N.J.: Cooper Square Publishers, Inc., 1962.

Willison, George Findlay. *Patrick Henry and His World*. Garden City, N.Y.: Doubleday, 1969.

Wilstach, Paul. *Tidewater Virginia*. Indianapolis: Bobbs-Merrill, 1929.

Wineman, Walter Ray. *Landon Carter Papers*. Charlottesville: University of Virginia Press, 1962.

Wirt, William. *Life of Patrick Henry*. Hartford: S. Andrews and Son, 1847.

Wright, Louis B. *American Heritage History of the Thirteen Colonies*. New York: American Heritage Society, 1967.

_____. *The Cultural Life of the American Colonies, 1607–1763*. New York: Harper Bros., 1957.

_____. *The First Gentlemen of Virginia: Intellectual Qualities of the Early Colonial Ruling Class*. San Marino, Ca.: Huntington Library, 1940.

Index

(Page numbers set in bold indicate quotations.)

brigades, 417, 420

regiments, Anspacher battalions, 419; Eighty-second Light Infantry, 417; Fourth Regiment, 277; Jagers, 431; Queen's Rangers, 431; Royal Welsh Fusiliers, 465; Seventeenth British Dragoons, 329; Seventy-first Highlanders, 417; Thirty-third West Ridings Guard, 417; Twenty-second Guards, 417; Twenty-third Watch, 417

smallpox, 431

strength, 330, 383, 390

surrender at Yorktown, 490

in Virginia, 415–16

Brockenbrough, Newman, 422

Brock's Bridge, 424

Brown, Dr. Robert, 103

Brunswick County, Va., 516

Bruton Parish Church, 26, 152, 184, 227, 506–08; Fast Day, 292

Buckingham County, Va., 427

Buckner, William, 445

Bullfield, 514

Bullocke, James, 83

Bull Run, 529

Bunker Hill, 265, 267, 424

Bunting, Solomon, 454

Burgoyne, Gen. John, 347, 481

Burke, Edmund, 237, 247

Burke, Gov. Thomas, 445, 447–49, 451, 460

Burnaby, Rev. Andrew, **56, 59,** 92

Burnett, Maj., 446

Burwell, 67

Burwell, Armistead, 236

Burwell, Carter, 97, 110, 164, 184

Burwell, Carter (son of Carter), 175, 186, 189, 204, 284

Burwell, Carter (son of Nathaniel), 509, 527

Burwell, Elizabeth. *See* Nelson, Elizabeth Burwell (Mrs. William)

Burwell, Frances, 23

Burwell, James, 5

Burwell, Judith (Mrs. Samuel), 370

Burwell, Maj. Lewis (of Fairfield), 57, 93

Burwell, Lewis (Nathaniel Burwell's son), 509

Burwell, Lewis (son of Lewis of Mecklenberg County), 202, 232; death 370

Burwell, Lewis, Mecklenberg County (uncle of Thomas Nelson, Jr.), 46, 60, 63, 74, 82, 134, 202, 232, 514; cavalry, 357; death, 370; House of Burgesses, 136, 172

Burwell, Lucy. *See* Lilly, Lucy Burwell (Mrs. Thomas)

Burwell, Lucy Grymes (Mrs. Carter), 97, 196

Burwell, Lucy (Nathaniel Burwell's daughter), 509, 528

Burwell, Martha "Patty" Digges (Mrs. Nathaniel), 379–80

Burwell, Mary. *See* Berkeley, Mary "Molly" Burwell (Mrs. Edmund)

Burwell, Mary Blair Braxton (Mrs. Robert Carter), 236

Burwell, Nathaniel, 93, 130, 135, 164, 228, 251, 355, 372, 379–80, 394; Botetourt Medal,

187; College, 174–75, 185; executor, Gen. Nelson's estate, 530; marriage, 196; robbed, 392; trustee hospital, 204, 509, 514, 527

Burwell, Nathaniel (Nathaniel Burwell's son), 509, 528

Burwell, Philip (Nathaniel Burwell's son), 509, 528

Burwell, Rebecca. *See* Ambler, Rebecca Burwell (Mrs. Jacquelin)

Burwell, Robert (Nathaniel Burwell's son), 528

Burwell, Robert Carter, 23, 63, 74, 135, 194, 225, 236, 385; Assembly, 234; Council, 103, 115, 133, 183, 245; death, 335; executor, William Byrd's estate, 339, 350; takes oath of allegiance, 287

Burwell's Ferry, 390, 395, 399

Burwell, Susanna Grymes (Mrs. Nathaniel), 84, 112–13, 196, 212, 508; courtship, 165, 175, 177, 185; death, 527

Burwell, William (Nathaniel Burwell's son), 509, 528

Butler, Col. Richard, 425, 431, 468, 478, 483

Byrd, Evelyn, 20

Byrd, Lucy Parke (Mrs. William, II), 157

Byrd, Mary Willing (Mrs. William, III), 226, 339, 398

Byrd, Otway, 255, 287

Byrd, Thomas, 130–31

Byrd's Tavern, 396, 399, 432, 462

Byrd's Warehouse, 180, 518

Byrd, William II, 11, 20, 21, 78, 115, 131, 149, 157, 232, **238;** diary, 39–40; expansionist, 39; ideas on medicine, 20; Westover, **96**

Byrd, William III, 74, 103, 134, 221, 225, 234, 255, 287, 319, 506; council, 133, 183, 244; death, 333, 339; debts, 125; gambling, 60, 82, 169, 214–15; Ohio Company, 48; Westover, **96**

Cabell, William, 426; Constitution, 522

Cabin's Point, Va., 400

Call, Col., 418

Cambridge, England, 273

Cambridge, Mass., 253, 260, 271

Camden, S.C., 387, 424

Camm, Betsey Hansford (Mrs. John), 141, 204; death, 370

Camm, Rev. John, 17, 78, 121, 130, 141, 154, 186–87, 228; Council, 234, 245; death, 369–70; evicted presidency College, 342; marries Betsey Hansford, 141, 204; Tory, 287; Two Penny Act, 51; at William Nelson's funeral, **196**

Campbell, Maj. (British), surrenders Redoubt No. 10, 476–77

Campbell, Dr. Archibald, 452

Campbell County, militia, 464; paper currency, 516

Campbell, Col. William, death at Eutaw Springs, N.C., 460; Patrick Henry's brother-in-law, 386–87; riflemen, 429, 432; Virginia Convention, 1781, 426

Camp Newcastle, 444